Ford Mondeo Diesel
Service and Repair Manual

James Robertson

Models covered

(3465-288)

All Ford Mondeo models with 1753 cc (1.8 litre) Diesel engine, including special/limited editions,

Does not cover petrol engine or four-wheel-drive models

© Haynes Publishing 1998

A book in the **Haynes Service and Repair Manual Series**

ISBN **1 85960 465 X**

British Library Cataloguing in Publication Data
A catalogue record for this book is available from the British Library.

ABCDE
FGHIJ
KLMNO
PQRST

Printed by **J H Haynes & Co. Ltd, Sparkford, Nr Yeovil,**
Somerset BA22 7JJ

Haynes Publishing
Sparkford, Nr Yeovil, Somerset BA22 7JJ, England

Haynes North America, Inc
861 Lawrence Drive, Newbury Park, California 91320, USA

Editions Haynes S.A.
147/149, rue Saint Honoré, 75001 PARIS, France

Haynes Publishing Nordiska AB
Box 1504, 751 45 UPPSALA, Sverige

Contents

LIVING WITH YOUR FORD MONDEO DIESEL

Roadside Repairs

Weekly Checks

MAINTENANCE

Routine Maintenance and Servicing

Contents

Ford Mondeo Diesel

Introduced in March 1993, the Ford Mondeo models are available in four-door Saloon, five-door Hatchback and five-door Estate configurations. All feature a high standard of equipment, with driver/passenger safety in accidents being a particularly high design priority; all models are fitted with features such as side impact bars in all doors, "anti-submarine" seats combined with "seat belt grabbers" and pre-tensioners, and an airbag fitted to the steering wheel. Vehicle security is enhanced, with an in-built alarm system and engine immobiliser being fitted as standard, as well as double-locking doors with shielded locks, and security-coded audio equipment.

The transversely-mounted engine drives the front roadwheels through a five-speed manual]transmission.

The fully-independent suspension is by MacPherson strut on all four roadwheels, located by transverse lower arms at the front, and by transverse and trailing arms at the rear; anti-roll bars are fitted at front and rear. The Estate rear suspension is of a different design, to give maximum loadspace inside the vehicle, with self-levelling suspension units available as an option.

The steering is power-assisted, the pump being belt-driven from the engine, and the rack-and-pinion steering gear mounted behind the engine.

The vacuum servo-assisted brakes are disc at the front, with drums at the rear, an electronically-controlled Anti-lock Braking System (ABS) is available on some models.

References to the 'left' or 'right' of the vheicle are in the sense of a person in the driver's seat facing forwards.

Ford Mondeo 1.8 TD Saloon

Ford Mondeo 1.8 TD Estate

Acknowledgements

Thanks are due to Champion Spark Plug who supplied the illustrations showing glow plug conditions and to Duckhams Oils, who provided lubrication data. Thanks are also due to Sykes-Pickavant Limited, who supplied some of the workshop tools, and to all those people at Sparkford who helped in the production of this Manual. Technical authors who contributed to this project include Jeremy Churchill, Andy Legg, Matthew Minter and Christopher Rogers.

We take great pride in the accuracy of information given in this manual, but vehicle manufacturers make alterations and design changes during the production run of a particular vehicle of which they do not inform us. No liability can be accepted by the authors or publishers for loss, damage or injury caused by any errors in, or omissions from the information given.

Working on your car can be dangerous. This page shows just some of the potential risks and hazards, with the aim of creating a safety-conscious attitude.

General hazards

Scalding

• Don't remove the radiator or expansion tank cap while the engine is hot.
• Engine oil, automatic transmission fluid or power steering fluid may also be dangerously hot if the engine has recently been running.

Burning

• Beware of burns from the exhaust system and from any part of the engine. Brake discs and drums can also be extremely hot immediately after use.

Crushing

• When working under or near a raised vehicle, always supplement the jack with axle stands, or use drive-on ramps. *Never venture under a car which is only supported by a jack.*
• Take care if loosening or tightening high-torque nuts when the vehicle is on stands. Initial loosening and final tightening should be done with the wheels on the ground.

Fire

• Fuel is highly flammable; fuel vapour is explosive.
• Don't let fuel spill onto a hot engine.
• Do not smoke or allow naked lights (including pilot lights) anywhere near a vehicle being worked on. Also beware of creating sparks (electrically or by use of tools).
• Fuel vapour is heavier than air, so don't work on the fuel system with the vehicle over an inspection pit.
• Another cause of fire is an electrical overload or short-circuit. Take care when repairing or modifying the vehicle wiring.
• Keep a fire extinguisher handy, of a type suitable for use on fuel and electrical fires.

Electric shock

• Ignition HT voltage can be dangerous, especially to people with heart problems or a pacemaker. Don't work on or near the ignition system with the engine running or the ignition switched on.

• Mains voltage is also dangerous. Make sure that any mains-operated equipment is correctly earthed. Mains power points should be protected by a residual current device (RCD) circuit breaker.

Fume or gas intoxication

• Exhaust fumes are poisonous; they often contain carbon monoxide, which is rapidly fatal if inhaled. Never run the engine in a confined space such as a garage with the doors shut.
• Fuel vapour is also poisonous, as are the vapours from some cleaning solvents and paint thinners.

Poisonous or irritant substances

• Avoid skin contact with battery acid and with any fuel, fluid or lubricant, especially antifreeze, brake hydraulic fluid and Diesel fuel. Don't syphon them by mouth. If such a substance is swallowed or gets into the eyes, seek medical advice.
• Prolonged contact with used engine oil can cause skin cancer. Wear gloves or use a barrier cream if necessary. Change out of oil-soaked clothes and do not keep oily rags in your pocket.
• Air conditioning refrigerant forms a poisonous gas if exposed to a naked flame (including a cigarette). It can also cause skin burns on contact.

Asbestos

• Asbestos dust can cause cancer if inhaled or swallowed. Asbestos may be found in gaskets and in brake and clutch linings. When dealing with such components it is safest to assume that they contain asbestos.

Special hazards

Hydrofluoric acid

• This extremely corrosive acid is formed when certain types of synthetic rubber, found in some O-rings, oil seals, fuel hoses etc, are exposed to temperatures above 400°C. The rubber changes into a charred or sticky substance containing the acid. *Once formed, the acid remains dangerous for years. If it gets onto the skin, it may be necessary to amputate the limb concerned.*
• When dealing with a vehicle which has suffered a fire, or with components salvaged from such a vehicle, wear protective gloves and discard them after use.

The battery

• Batteries contain sulphuric acid, which attacks clothing, eyes and skin. Take care when topping-up or carrying the battery.
• The hydrogen gas given off by the battery is highly explosive. Never cause a spark or allow a naked light nearby. Be careful when connecting and disconnecting battery chargers or jump leads.

Air bags

• Air bags can cause injury if they go off accidentally. Take care when removing the steering wheel and/or facia. Special storage instructions may apply.

Diesel injection equipment

• Diesel injection pumps supply fuel at very high pressure. Take care when working on the fuel injectors and fuel pipes.

⚠ *Warning: Never expose the hands, face or any other part of the body to injector spray; the fuel can penetrate the skin with potentially fatal results.*

Remember...

DO

• Do use eye protection when using power tools, and when working under the vehicle.

• Do wear gloves or use barrier cream to protect your hands when necessary.

• Do get someone to check periodically that all is well when working alone on the vehicle.

• Do keep loose clothing and long hair well out of the way of moving mechanical parts.

• Do remove rings, wristwatch etc, before working on the vehicle – especially the electrical system.

• Do ensure that any lifting or jacking equipment has a safe working load rating adequate for the job.

DON'T

• Don't attempt to lift a heavy component which may be beyond your capability – get assistance.

• Don't rush to finish a job, or take unverified short cuts.

• Don't use ill-fitting tools which may slip and cause injury.

• Don't leave tools or parts lying around where someone can trip over them. Mop up oil and fuel spills at once.

• Don't allow children or pets to play in or near a vehicle being worked on.

The following pages are intended to help in dealing with common roadside emergencies and breakdowns. You will find more detailed fault finding information at the back of the manual, and repair information in the main chapters.

If your car won't start and the starter motor doesn't turn

☐ Open the bonnet and make sure that the battery terminals are clean and tight.
☐ Switch on the headlights and try to start the engine. If the headlights go very dim when you're trying to start, the battery is probably flat. Get out of trouble by jump starting (see next page) using a friend's car.

If your car won't start even though the starter motor turns as normal

☐ Is there fuel in the tank?
☐ Does the glow plug warning light come on and then go out when the ignition is switched on? If the light does not come on, check the wiring to the glow plugs. If there is moisture on the wiring, spray a water-repellent aerosol product (such as WD-40) or equivalent) on the wiring terminals shown in the photos.
☐ Is there air in the fuel system? If so, bleed the system as described in Chapter 4.

A Check the security and condition of the battery connections.

B The stop solenoid wiring terminal may cause problems if not connected securely.

C Check the wiring to the glow plugs

D If there is air in the fuel system, the system can be bled as described in Chapter 4.

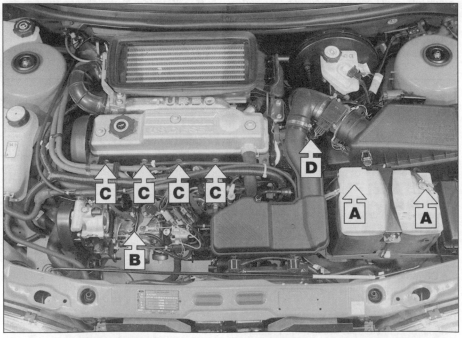

Check that electrical connections are secure (with the ignition off) and spray them with a water-dispersing spray like WD40 if you suspect a problem due to damp.

Jump starting

HAYNES HiNT

Jump starting will get you out of trouble, but you must correct whatever made the battery go flat in the first place. There are three possibilities:

1 *The battery has been drained by repeated attempts to start, or by leaving the lights on.*

2 *The charging system is not working properly (alternator drivebelt slack or broken, alternator wiring fault or alternator itself faulty).*

3 *The battery itself is at fault (electrolyte low, or battery worn out).*

When jump-starting a car using a booster battery, observe the following precautions:

✔ Before connecting the booster battery, make sure that the ignition is switched off.

✔ Ensure that all electrical equipment (lights, heater, wipers, etc) is switched off.

✔ Take note of any special precautions printed on the battery case.

✔ Make sure that the booster battery is the same voltage as the discharged one in the vehicle.

✔ If the battery is being jump-started from the battery in another vehicle, the two vehicles MUST NOT TOUCH each other.

✔ Make sure that the transmission is in neutral (or PARK, in the case of automatic transmission).

1 Connect one end of the red jump lead to the positive (+) terminal of the flat battery

2 Connect the other end of the red lead to the positive (+) terminal of the booster battery.

3 Connect one end of the black jump lead to the negative (-) terminal of the booster battery

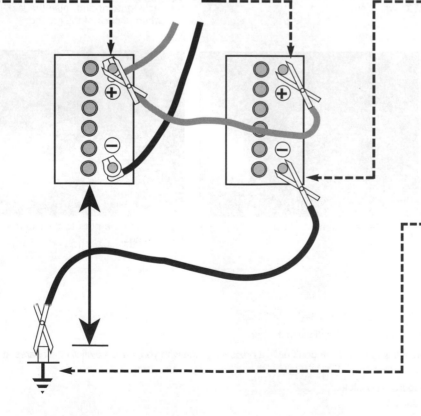

4 Connect the other end of the black jump lead to a bolt or bracket on the engine block, well away from the battery, on the vehicle to be started.

5 Make sure that the jump leads will not come into contact with the fan, drive-belts or other moving parts of the engine.

6 Start the engine using the booster battery and run it at idle speed. Switch on the lights, rear window demister and heater blower motor, then disconnect the jump leads in the reverse order of connection. Turn off the lights etc.

Wheel changing

- ☐ When a puncture occurs, stop as soon as it is safe to do so.
- ☐ Park on firm level ground, if possible, and well out of the way of other traffic.
- ☐ Use hazard warning lights if necessary.
- ☐ If you have one, use a warning triangle to alert other drivers of your presence.
- ☐ Apply the handbrake and engage first or reverse gear .
- ☐ Chock the wheel diagonally opposite the one being removed – a couple of large stones will do for this.
- ☐ If the ground is soft, use a flat piece of wood to spread the load under the jack.

1 The spare wheel and tools are located in the boot.

2 Unscrew the retaining bolt and remove the spare wheel, then remove the jack and wheelbrace, also secured by a retaining bolt

3 Remove the trim from the wheel to be changed to expose the wheel nuts.

4 Use the wheel brace to slightly loosen the wheel nuts.

5 Locate the jack head in the correct jacking point and raise the jack until the wheel is clear of the ground

6 Remove the wheel nuts and lift off the wheel.

7 Fit the replacement wheel

8 Tighten the nuts to their correct torque settings.

Finally...

- ☐ Remove the wheel chocks.

- ☐ Stow the damaged tyre or wheel, jack and tools in the correct locations in the car.

- ☐ Check the tyre pressure on the wheel just fitted. If it is low, or if you don't have a pressure gauge with you, drive slowly to the nearest garage and inflate the tyre to the right pressure.

- ☐ Have the damaged tyre or wheel repaired as soon as possible.

Identifying leaks

Puddles on the garage floor or drive, or obvious wetness under the bonnet or underneath the car, suggest a leak that needs investigating. It can sometimes be difficult to decide where the leak is coming from, especially if the engine bay is very dirty already. Leaking oil or fluid can also be blown rearwards by the passage of air under the car, giving a false impression of where the problem lies.

⚠️ **Warning: Most automotive oils and fluids are poisonous. Wash them off skin, and change out of contaminated clothing, without delay.**

 HAYNES HiNT *The smell of a fluid leaking from the car may provide a clue to what's leaking. Some fluids are distinctively coloured. It may help to clean the car and to park it over some clean paper as an aid to locating the source of the leak. Remember that some leaks may only occur while the engine is running.*

Sump oil

Engine oil may leak from the drain plug...

Oil from filter

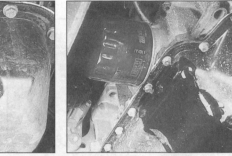

...or from the base of the oil filter.

Gearbox oil

Gearbox oil can leak from the seals at the inboard ends of the driveshafts.

Antifreeze

Leaking antifreeze often leaves a crystalline deposit like this.

Brake fluid

A leak occurring at a wheel is almost certainly brake fluid.

Power steering fluid

Power steering fluid may leak from the pipe connectors on the steering rack.

Towing

When all else fails, you may find yourself having to get a tow home – or of course you may be helping somebody else. Long-distance recovery should only be done by a garage or breakdown service. For shorter distances, DIY towing using another car is easy enough, but observe the following points:

☐ Use a proper tow-rope – they are not expensive. The vehicle being towed must display an 'ON TOW' sign in its rear window.
☐ Always turn the ignition key to the 'on' position when the vehicle is being towed, so that the steering lock is released, and that

the direction indicator and brake lights will work.
☐ Towing eyes are provided at the front and rear of the vehicle, on the right-hand side. Do not attach the tow-rope to anything else.
☐ Before being towed, release the handbrake and select neutral on the transmission.
☐ Note that greater-than-usual pedal pressure will be required to operate the brakes, since the vacuum servo unit is only operational with the engine running.
☐ On models with power steering, greater-than-usual steering effort will also be required.

☐ The driver of the car being towed must keep the tow-rope taut at all times to avoid snatching.
☐ Make sure that both drivers know the route before setting off.
☐ Only drive at moderate speeds and keep the distance towed to a minimum. Drive smoothly and allow plenty of time for slowing down at junctions.
☐ On models with automatic transmission, special precautions apply. If in doubt, do not tow, or transmission damage may result.

Introduction

There are some very simple checks which need only take a few minutes to carry out, but which could save you a lot of inconvenience and expense.

These "Weekly checks" require no great skill or special tools, and the small amount of time they take to perform could prove to be very well spent, for example;

☐ Keeping an eye on tyre condition and pressures, will not only help to stop them wearing out prematurely, but could also save your life.

☐ Many breakdowns are caused by electrical problems. Battery-related faults are particularly common, and a quick check on a regular basis will often prevent the majority of these.

☐ If your car develops a brake fluid leak, the first time you might know about it is when your brakes don't work properly. Checking the level regularly will give advance warning of this kind of problem.

☐ If the oil or coolant levels run low, the cost of repairing any engine damage will be far greater than fixing the leak, for example.

Underbonnet check points

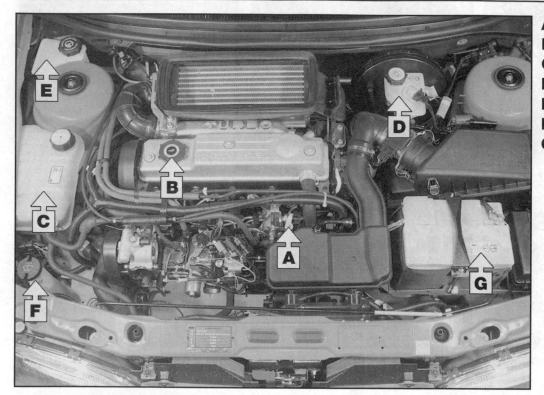

A Engine oil level dipstick

B Engine oil filler cap

C Coolant expansion tank

D Brake fluid reservoir

E Power steering fluid reservoir

F Screen washer fluid reservoir

G Battery

Engine oil level

Before you start

✔ Make sure that your car is on level ground.
✔ Check the oil level before the car is driven, or at least 5 minutes after the engine has been switched off.

 HAYNES HINT *If the oil level is checked immediately after driving the vehicle, some of the oil will remain in the upper engine components, resulting in an inaccurate reading on the dipstick!*

The correct oil

Modern engines place great demands on their oil. It is very important that the correct oil for your car is used (See "Lubricants and fluids").

Car care

● If you have to add oil frequently, you should check whether you have any oil leaks. Place some clean paper under the car overnight, and check for stains in the morning. If there are no leaks, the engine may be burning oil *(see "Fault finding").*

● Always maintain the level between the upper and lower dipstick marks (see photo 3). If the level is too low severe engine damage may occur. Oil seal failure may result if the engine is overfilled by adding too much oil.

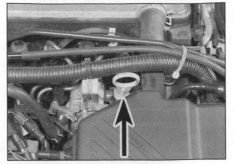

1 The dipstick is located at the front of the engine (arrowed). Withdraw the dipstick.

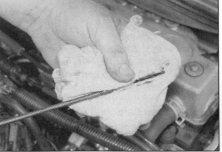

2 Using a clean rag or paper towel, wipe all the oil from the dipstick. Insert the clean dipstick into the tube as far as it will go, then withdraw it again.

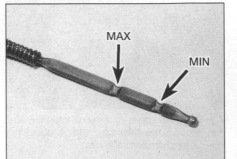

MAX MIN

3 Note the oil level on the end of the dipstick, which should be between the upper MAX mark and the lower MIN mark

4 Oil is added through the filler cap. A funnel may help to reduce spillage. Add oil slowly, checking the level on the dipstick often. Do not overfill.

Power steering fluid level

Before you start:

✔ Park the vehicle on level ground.
✔ Set the steering wheel straight-ahead.
✔ The engine should be turned off.

HAYNES HINT *For the check to be accurate, the steering must not be turned once the engine has been stopped.*

Safety first!

● The need for frequent topping-up indicates a leak, which should be investigated immediately.

1 The power steering fluid reservoir is located on the right-hand rear corner of the engine compartment, MAX and MIN level marks are indicated on the side of the reservoir and the fluid level should be maintained between these marks at all times.

2 If topping-up is necessary, first wipe the area around the filler cap with a clean rag before removing the cap.

3 When adding fluid, pour it carefully into the reservoir to avoid spillage. Be sure to use only the specified fluid. After filling the reservoir to the proper level, make sure that the cap is refitted securely to avoid leaks and the entry of foreign matter into the reservoir.

Brake fluid level

Warning:
- **Brake fluid can harm your eyes and will damage painted surfaces, so use extreme caution when handling and pouring it.**
- **Do not use fluid that has been standing open for some time, as it absorbs moisture from the air, which can cause a dangerous loss of braking effectiveness.**

- *Make sure that your car is on level ground.*
- *The fluid level in the reservoir will drop slightly as the brake pads wear down, but the fluid level must never be allowed to drop below the "MIN" mark.*

Safety first!
- If the reservoir requires repeated topping-up this is an indication of a fluid leak somewhere in the system, which should be investigated immediately.
- If a leak is suspected, the car should not be driven until the braking system has been checked. Never take any risks where brakes are concerned.

1 The brake fluid reservoir is located on the top of the brake master cylinder, which is attached to the frontof the vacuum servo unit. The MAX and MIN level marks are indicated on the side of the translucent reservoir and the fluid level should be maintained between these marks at all times.

2 If topping-up is necessary, wipe the area around the filler cap with a clean rag before removing the cap.

3 When adding fluid, pour it carefully into the reservoir to avoid spilling it on surrounding painted surfaces. It is also a good idea to inspect the reservoir for contamination. The system should be drained and refilled if deposits, dirt particles or contamination are seen in the fluid. After filling the reservoir to the proper level, make sure that the cap is refitted securely to avoid leaks and the entry of foreign matter.

Screen washer fluid level

Screenwash additives not only keep the winscreen clean during foul weather, they also prevent the washer system freezing in cold weather - which is when you are likely to need it most. Don't top up using plain water as the screenwash will become too diluted, and will freeze during cold weather. *On no account use coolant antifreeze in the washer system - this could discolour or damage paintwork.*

1 The reservoir for the windscreen/tailgate washer system (and, where applicable, headlight washer) is located in the right front corner of the engine compartment, rearwards of the suspension turret.

2 When topping-up the reservoir(s) a screenwash additive should be added in the quantities recommended on the bottle.

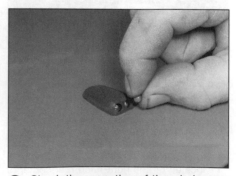

3 Check the operation of the windscreen and rear window washers. Adjust the nozzles using a pin if necessary, aiming the spray to a point slightly above the centre of the swept area.

Coolant level

 Warning: DO NOT attempt to remove the expansion tank pressure cap when the engine is hot, as there is a very great risk of scalding. Do not leave open containers of coolant about, as it is poisonous.

Car care

● Adding coolant should not be necessary on a regular basis. If frequent topping-up is required, it is likely there is a leak. Check the radiator, all hoses and joint faces for signs of staining or wetness, and rectify as necessary.

● It is important that antifreeze is used in the cooling system all year round, not just during the winter months. Don't top-up with water alone, as the antifreeze will become too diluted.

1 The coolant level varies with the temperature of the engine. When the engine is cold, the coolant level should be between the MAX and MIN marks on the side of the expansion tank, which is located on the right-hand side of the engine compartment. When the engine is hot, the level may rise slightly.

2 If topping-up is necessary, wait until the engine is cold, then cover the expansion tank with a thick layer of rag and unscrew the filler cap anti-clockwise until a hissing sound is heard. Wait until the hissing ceases, indicating that all pressure is released, then slowly unscrew the filler cap until it can be removed. If more hissing sounds are heard, wait until they have stopped before unscrewing the cap completely. At all times keep well away from the filler opening.

3 Add a mixture of water and antifreeze through the expansion tank filler neck, until the coolant is up to the MAX level mark. Refit the cap, turning it clockwise as far as it will go until it is secure.

Wiper blades

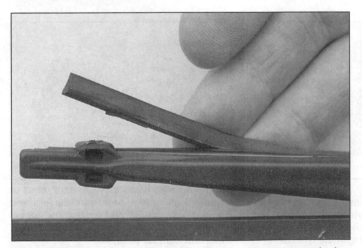

1 Check the condition of the wiper blades. If they are cracked or show any signs of deterioration, or if the glass swept area is smeared, renew them. For maximum clarity of vision, wiper blades should be renewed annually, as a matter of course.

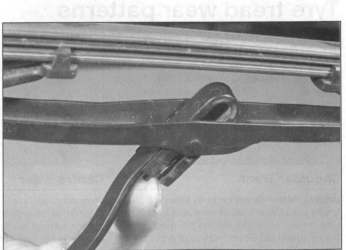

2 To remove a wiper blade, pull the arm fully away from the glass until it locks. Swivel the blade through 90°, press the locking tab with a finger nail and slide the blade out of the arm's hooked end. On refitting, ensure that the blade locks securely into the arm.

Tyre condition and pressure

It is very important that tyres are in good condition, and at the correct pressure - having a tyre failure at any speed is highly dangerous. Tyre wear is influenced by driving style - harsh braking and acceleration, or fast cornering, will all produce more rapid tyre wear. As a general rule, the front tyres wear out faster than the rears. Interchanging the tyres from front to rear ("rotating" the tyres) may result in more even wear. However, if this is completely effective, you may have the expense of replacing all four tyres at once!

Remove any nails or stones embedded in the tread before they penetrate the tyre to cause deflation. If removal of a nail does reveal that the tyre has been punctured, refit the nail so that its point of penetration is marked. Then immediately change the wheel, and have the tyre repaired by a tyre dealer.

Regularly check the tyres for damage in the form of cuts or bulges, especially in the sidewalls. Periodically remove the wheels, and clean any dirt or mud from the inside and outside surfaces. Examine the wheel rims for signs of rusting, corrosion or other damage. Light alloy wheels are easily damaged by "kerbing" whilst parking; steel wheels may also become dented or buckled. A new wheel is very often the only way to overcome severe damage.

New tyres should be balanced when they are fitted, but it may become necessary to re-balance them as they wear, or if the balance weights fitted to the wheel rim should fall off. Unbalanced tyres will wear more quickly, as will the steering and suspension components. Wheel imbalance is normally signified by vibration, particularly at a certain speed (typically around 50 mph). If this vibration is felt only through the steering, then it is likely that just the front wheels need balancing. If, however, the vibration is felt through the whole car, the rear wheels could be out of balance. Wheel balancing should be carried out by a tyre dealer or garage.

1 Tread Depth - visual check
The original tyres have tread wear safety bands (B), which will appear when the tread depth reaches approximately 1.6 mm. The band positions are indicated by a triangular mark on the tyre sidewall (A).

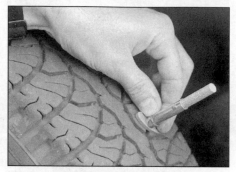

2 Tread Depth - manual check
Alternatively, tread wear can be monitored with a simple, inexpensive device known as a tread depth indicator gauge.

3 Tyre Pressure Check
Check the tyre pressures regularly with the tyres cold. Do not adjust the tyre pressures immediately after the vehicle has been used, or an inaccurate setting will result.

Tyre tread wear patterns

Shoulder Wear

Underinflation (wear on both sides)
Under-inflation will cause overheating of the tyre, because the tyre will flex too much, and the tread will not sit correctly on the road surface. This will cause a loss of grip and excessive wear, not to mention the danger of sudden tyre failure due to heat build-up.
Check and adjust pressures
Incorrect wheel camber (wear on one side)
Repair or renew suspension parts
Hard cornering
Reduce speed!

Centre Wear

Overinflation
Over-inflation will cause rapid wear of the centre part of the tyre tread, coupled with reduced grip, harsher ride, and the danger of shock damage occurring in the tyre casing.
Check and adjust pressures

If you sometimes have to inflate your car's tyres to the higher pressures specified for maximum load or sustained high speed, don't forget to reduce the pressures to normal afterwards.

Uneven Wear

Front tyres may wear unevenly as a result of wheel misalignment. Most tyre dealers and garages can check and adjust the wheel alignment (or "tracking") for a modest charge.
Incorrect camber or castor
Repair or renew suspension parts
Malfunctioning suspension
Repair or renew suspension parts
Unbalanced wheel
Balance tyres
Incorrect toe setting
Adjust front wheel alignment
Note: *The feathered edge of the tread which typifies toe wear is best checked by feel.*

Battery

Caution: *Before carrying out any work on the vehicle battery, read the precautions given in "Safety first" at the start of this manual.*

✔ Make sure that the battery tray is in good condition, and that the clamp is tight. Corrosion on the tray, retaining clamp and the battery itself can be removed with a solution of water and baking soda. Thoroughly rinse all cleaned areas with water. Any metal parts damaged by corrosion should be covered with a zinc-based primer, then painted.

✔ Periodically (approximately every three months), check the charge condition of the battery as described in Chapter 5A.

✔ If the battery is flat, and you need to jump start your vehicle, see *Roadside Repairs*.

HAYNES HiNT

Battery corrosion can be kept to a minimum by applying a layer of petroleum jelly to the clamps and terminals after they are reconnected.

1 The battery is located on the left-hand side of the engine compartment. The exterior of the battery should be inspected periodically for damage such as a cracked case or cover.

2 Check the tightness of the battery cable clamps to ensure good electrical connections. You should not be able to move them. Also check each cable for cracks and frayed conductors.

3 If corrosion (white fluffy deposits) is evident, remove the cables from the battery terminals, clean them with a small wire brush, then refit them. Automotive stores sell a useful tool for cleaning the battery post . . .

4 . . . as well as the battery cable clamps.

Electrical systems

✔ Check all external lights and the horn. Refer to the appropriate Sections of Chapter 12 for details if any of the circuits are found to be inoperative.

✔ Visually check all accessible wiring connectors, harnesses and retaining clips for security, and for signs of chafing or damage.

HAYNES HiNT *If you need to check your brake lights and indicators unaided, back up to a wall or garage door and operate the lights. The reflected light should show if they are working properly.*

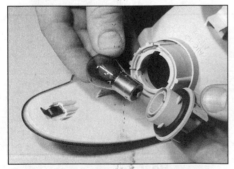

1 If a single indicator light, brake light or headlight has failed, it is likely that a bulb has blown and will need to be replaced. Refer to Chapter 12 for details. If both brake lights have failed, it is possible that the brake light switch operated by the brake pedal has failed. Refer to Chapter 9 for details.

2 If more than one indicator light or headlight has failed, it is likely that either a fuse has blown or that there is a fault in the circuit (see Chapter 12). Most fuses are located behind the cover in the right-hand lower facia panel. Other fuses are located in the fusebox on the right-hand side of the engine compartment.

3 To replace a blown fuse, simply prise it out. Fit a new fuse of the same rating. It is important that you find the reason for the fuse blowing.

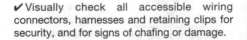

Lubricants and fluids

Component or system	Lubricant or fluid
Engine	Multigrade engine oil to specification API SG/CD and CCMC PD2 (Ford Super Oil 15W/40 or equivalent) *(Duckhams Diesel, QS, QXR, Hypergrade Plus or Hypergrade)*
Cooling system	Soft water, and antifreeze (ethylene glycol-based, suitable for use in mixed-metal cooling systems) to Ford specification ESD-M97B-49-A *(Duckhams Antifreeze & Summer Coolant)*
Transmission	Gear oil to Ford specification ESD-M2C-186-A *(Duckhams Hypoid)*
Brake system	Hydraulic fluid to Ford specification ESD-M6C-57-A, DOT 4 or equivalent *(Duckhams Universal Brake & Clutch Fluid)*
Power steering system	Transmission fluid to Ford specification ESP-M2C-166-H *(Duckhams Unimatic)*

Choosing your engine oil

Oils perform vital tasks in all engines. The higher the engine's performance, the greater the demand on lubricants to minimise wear as well as optimise power and economy. Duckhams tailors lubricants to the highest technical standards, meeting and exceeding the demands of all modern engines.

HOW ENGINE OIL WORKS

• Beating friction

Without oil, the surfaces inside your engine which rub together will heat, fuse and quickly cause engine seizure. Oil, and its special additives, forms a molecular barrier between moving parts, to stop wear and minimise heat build-up.

• Cooling hot spots

Oil cools parts that the engine's water-based coolant cannot reach, bathing the combustion chamber and pistons, where temperatures may exceed 1000°C. The oil assists in transferring the heat to the engine cooling system. Heat in the oil is also lost by air flow over the sump, and via any auxiliary oil cooler.

• Cleaning the inner engine

Oil washes away combustion by-products (mainly carbon) on pistons and cylinders, transporting them to the oil filter, and holding the smallest particles in suspension until they are flushed out by an oil change. Duckhams oils undergo extensive tests in the laboratory, and on the road.

Note: It is antisocial and illegal to dump oil down the drain. To find the location of your local oil recycling bank, call this number free.

OIL BANK LINE
0800 66 33 66

Capacities

Engine oil:	
With filter change	5.00 litres
Without filter change	4.50 litres
Fuel tank	61.5 litres
Cooling system	9.3 litres
Transmission	2.6 litres

Tyre pressures

Tyre pressures (tyres cold)	Front	Rear
Normal loading with up to 3 people	2.1 bar (31 psi)	2.1 bar (31 psi)
Fully laden with more than 3 people	2.4 bar (35 psi)	2.8 bar (41 psi)

Note: *Pressures apply only to original equipment tyres and may vary if any other make or type is fitted. Check with the tyre manufacturer or supplier for correct pressures if necessary.*

Chapter 1
Routine maintenance and servicing

Contents

Degrees of difficulty

Easy, suitable for novice with little experience	**Fairly easy,** suitable for beginner with some experience	**Fairly difficult,** suitable for competent DIY mechanic	**Difficult,** suitable for experienced DIY mechanic	**Very difficult,** suitable for expert DIY or professional

Engine

Oil filter	Champion C148

Valve clearances (cold):

Inlet	0.30 to 0.40 mm
Exhaust	0.45 to 0.55 mm

Cooling system

Coolant protection at 40% antifreeze/water mixture ratio:

Slush point	-25°C (-13°F)
Solidifying point	-30°C (-22°F)
Coolant specific gravity at 40% antifreeze/water mixture ratio and 15°C/59°F - with no other additives in coolant	1.061

Fuel system

Idle speed	850 rpm
Air filter element	Champion U654

Fuel filter:

Bosch	Champion L134
CAV RotoDiesel	Champion L131 or L137

Braking system

Note: *No minimum lining thicknesses are given by Ford - the following is given as a general recommendation. If the pad wear warning light comes on before the front brake pad linings reach the minimum thickness, the pads should nevertheless be renewed immediately.*

Minimum front or rear brake pad lining thickness	1.5 mm
Minimum rear brake shoe lining thickness	1.0 mm

Suspension and steering

Tyre pressures (cold):	Front	Rear
Normally laden*	2.1 bar (31 psi)	2.1 bar (31 psi)
Fully laden*	2.4 bar (35 psi)	2.8 bar (41 psi)

Normally laden means up to 3 persons.

Wiper blades

Windscreen:

Driver's side	Champion X 5303 (and SP 01 spoiler)
Passenger's side	Champion X 5103

Tailgate:

Hatchback	Champion X 5103
Estate	Champion X 33

Torque wrench settings

	Nm	lbf ft
Auxiliary drivebelt cover fasteners	5 to 10	4 to 7
Engine oil drain plug	25	18
Transmission filler/level plug	35	26
Radiator undershield screws	7	5
Roadwheel nuts	85	63
Seat belt mounting bolts	28	21

The manufacturer's recommended maintenance schedule for these vehicles is as described below - note that the schedule starts from the vehicle's date of registration. These are the minimum maintenance intervals recommended by the factory for Mondeos driven daily, but subjected only to "normal" use. If you wish to keep your vehicle in peak condition at all times, you may wish to perform some of these procedures even more often. Because frequent maintenance enhances the efficiency, performance and resale value of your vehicle, we encourage you to do so. If your usage is not "normal", shorter intervals are also recommended - particularly if you drive in dusty areas, tow a caravan or trailer, sit with the engine idling or drive at low speeds for extended periods (ie, in heavy traffic), or drive for short distances (less than four miles) in below-freezing temperatures.

When your vehicle is new, it should be serviced by a Ford dealer service department to protect the factory warranty. In many cases, the initial maintenance check is done at no cost to the owner. Note that this first free service (carried out by the selling dealer 1500 miles or 3 months after delivery), although an important check for a new vehicle, is not part of the regular maintenance schedule, and is therefore not mentioned here.

Every 250 miles, weekly or before a long journey
☐ See "Weekly checks"

Every 5000 miles or 6 months - whichever comes first
☐ Renew engine oil and filter (Section 3)
☐ Drain water from fuel filter (Section 4)
☐ Check idle speed and adjust if necessary (Section 5)
☐ Check for fluid leakage (Section 6)
☐ Check operation of brake vacuum pump (Section 7)

Every 10 000 miles or 12 months, whichever occurs first
☐ Check the electrical system (Section 8)
☐ Check the battery (Section 9)
☐ Check the seat belts (Section 10)
☐ Check the auxiliary drivebelt (Section 11)
☐ Check under the bonnet for fluid leaks and hose condition (Section 12)
☐ Check the condition of all engine compartment wiring (Section 13)
☐ Check the condition of all air conditioning system components (Section 14)
☐ Check the transmission oil level (Section 15)
☐ Check the adjustment of the clutch pedal (Section 16)
☐ Check the steering, suspension and roadwheels (Section 17)
☐ Check the driveshaft rubber gaiters and CV joints (Section 18)
☐ Check the exhaust system (Section 19)
☐ Check the underbody, and all fuel/brake lines (Section 20)

Every 10 000 miles or 12 months, whichever occurs first (continued)
☐ Check the brake system (Section 21)
☐ Check the doors and bonnet, and lubricate their hinges and locks (Section 22)
☐ Check the security of all roadwheel nuts (Section 23)
☐ Road test (Section 24).

Every 20 000 miles or 2 years, whichever occurs first
Carry out all operations listed above, plus the following:
☐ Renew the fuel filter element (Section 25)
☐ Renew the air cleaner element (Section 26)
☐ Renew the ventilation system pollen filter (Section 27)
☐ Renew the coolant (see "Weekly Checks" and Section 28)

Every 30 000 miles or 3 years, whichever occurs first
☐ Renew camshaft and injection pump drivebelts (Section 29)

Every 50 000 miles
☐ Check valve clearances (Section 30)

Every 3 years (regardless of mileage)
☐ Renew the brake fluid (Section 31)

1

Underbonnet view of a 1.8 litre turbocharged diesel

1 *Engine oil level dipstick*
2 *Fuel injection pump*
3 *Coolant expansion tank*
4 *Engine oil filler cap*
5 *Suspension strut turret*

6 *Charge air cooler*
7 *Turbocharger intake duct*
8 *Battery*
9 *Engine compartment relays and fuses*
10 *Brake and clutch fluid reservoir*

11 *Power steering fluid reservoir*
12 *Washer fluid reservoir cap*
13 *Air cleaner unit*
14 *Vacuum pump*
15 *Fuel pump and filter*

Front underview of a 1.8 litre turbocharged diesel

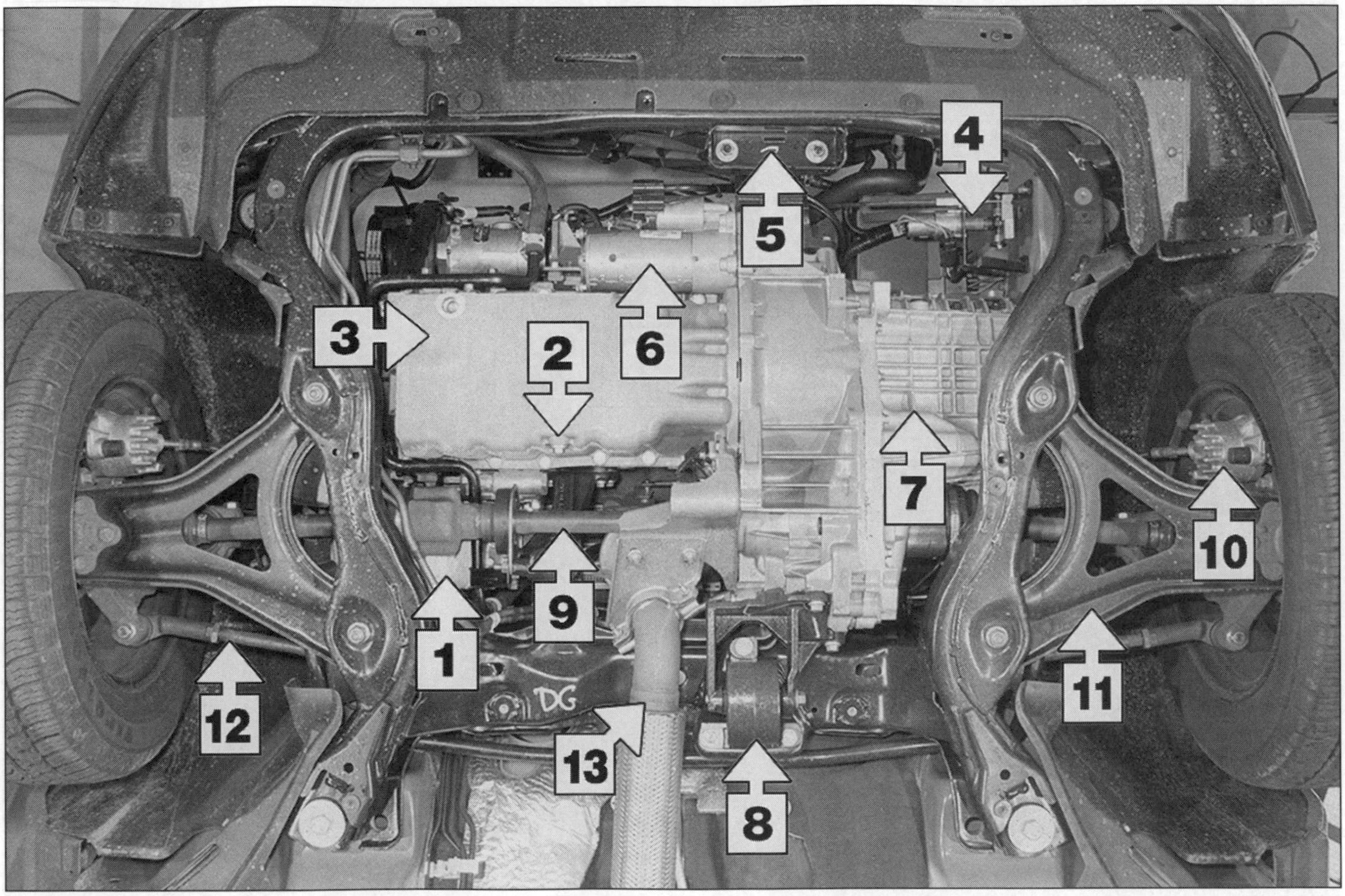

1 Engine oil filter
2 Engine oil drain plug
3 Engine oil sump
4 Engine up speed control unit
5 Engine/transmission unit front mounting
6 Starter motor
7 Gearbox
8 Engine/transmission unit rear mounting
9 Driveshaft
10 Front brake caliper
11 Suspension arm
12 Track rod
13 Exhaust system

Rear underview - Saloon and Hatchback models

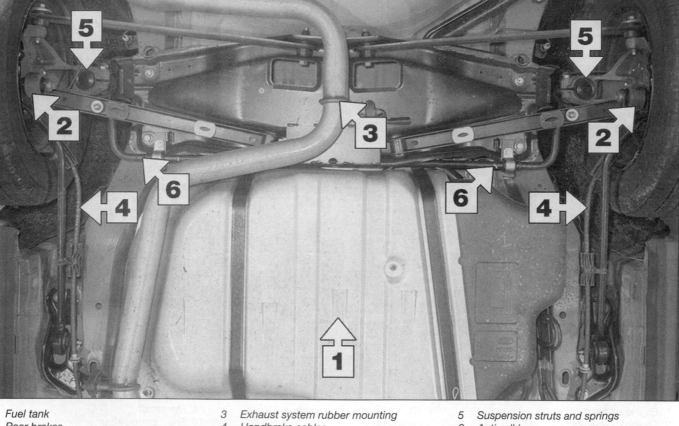

1   Fuel tank
2   Rear brakes

3   Exhaust system rubber mounting
4   Handbrake cables

5   Suspension struts and springs
6   Anti-roll bars

Rear underview - Estate models (petrol model shown, diesel similar)

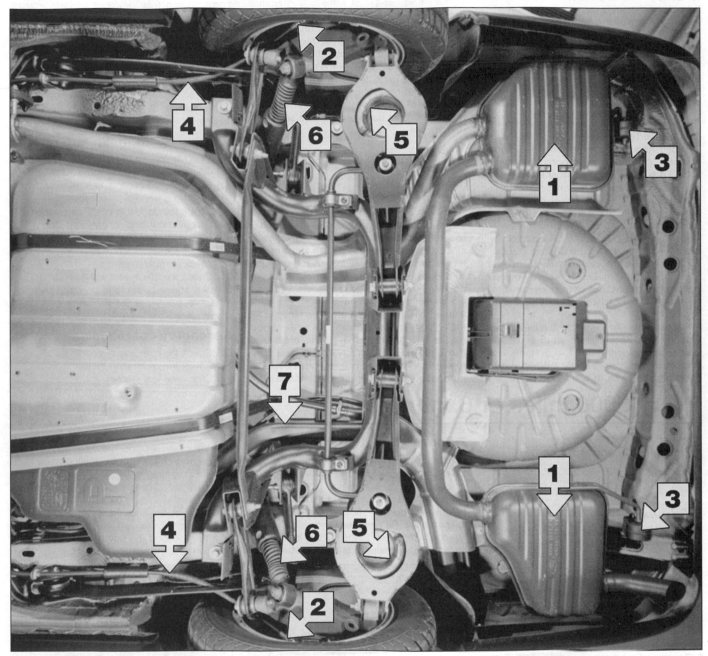

1	Silencers	4	Handbrake cables
2	Rear brakes	5	Suspension springs
3	Exhaust system rubber mountings		

6	Suspension shock absorbers
7	Fuel tank filler neck

1 Introduction

This Chapter is designed to help the home mechanic maintain the Ford Mondeo models for peak performance, economy, safety and long life.

On the following pages are Sections dealing specifically with each item on the maintenance schedule. Visual checks, adjustments, component replacement and other helpful items are included. Refer to the accompanying illustrations of the engine compartment and the underside of the vehicle for the location of various components.

Servicing your Mondeo in accordance with the mileage/time maintenance schedule and the following Sections will provide it with a planned maintenance programme, which should result in a long and reliable service life. This is a comprehensive plan, so maintaining some items but not others at the specified service intervals will not produce the same results.

As you service your Mondeo, you will discover that many of the procedures can - and should - be grouped together, because of the nature of the particular procedure you're performing, or because of the close proximity to one another of two otherwise-unrelated components.

For example, if the vehicle is raised for any reason, you should inspect the exhaust, suspension, steering and fuel systems while you're under the vehicle. When you're checking the tyres, it makes good sense to check the brakes and wheel bearings, especially if the roadwheels have already been removed.

Finally, let's suppose you have to borrow or hire a torque wrench. Even if you only need to tighten the spark plugs, you might as well check the torque of as many critical fasteners as time allows.

The first step of this maintenance programme is to prepare yourself before the actual work begins. Read through all the Sections which are relevant to the procedures you're planning to carry out, then make a list of, and gather together, all the parts and tools you will need to do the job. If it looks as if you might run into problems during a particular segment of some procedure, seek advice from your local parts man or dealer service department.

2 Intensive maintenance

1 If from the time the engine is new, the routine maintenance schedule is followed closely and frequent checks are made of fluid levels and high-wear items, then the engine will be kept in relatively good running condition, and the need for additional work will be minimised.

2 It is possible that there will be times when the engine is running poorly due to the lack of regular maintenance. This is even more likely if a used vehicle, which has not received regular and frequent maintenance checks, is purchased. In such cases, additional work may need to be carried out, outside of the regular maintenance intervals.

3 If engine wear is suspected, a compression test will provide valuable information regarding the overall performance of the main internal components. Such a test can be used as a basis to decide on the extent of the work to be carried out. If, for example, a compression test indicates serious internal engine wear, conventional maintenance as described in this Chapter will not greatly improve the performance of the engine, and may prove a waste of time and money, unless extensive overhaul work is carried out first.

4 The following series of operations are those most often required to improve the performance of a generally poor-running engine:

Primary operations

a) Clean, inspect and test the battery
b) Check all the engine-related fluids
c) Check the condition and tension of the auxiliary drivebelt
d) Check the condition of the air cleaner filter element, and renew if necessary
e) Renew the fuel filter
f) Check the condition of all hoses, and check for fluid leaks
g) Check the idle speed settings

5 If the above operations do not prove fully effective, carry out the following secondary operations:

Secondary operations

a) Check the charging system
b) Check the preheating system
c) Check the fuel system

Every 5000 miles or 6 months

3 Engine oil and filter renewal

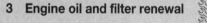

Oil draining

1 The engine oil should be drained just after a run, when the contaminants which it carries are still in suspension.

2 Park the vehicle on level ground. Position a drain pan of adequate capacity beneath the sump. Wipe clean around the sump drain plug, then unscrew and remove it **(see illustration)**. Be careful to avoid scalding if the oil is very hot. Do not lose the drain plug washer.

3 Remove the oil filler cap to speed up the draining process. Allow the oil to drain for at least 15 minutes. Inspect the drain plug washer and renew it if necessary.

4 When draining is complete, refit the drain plug with washer and tighten it to the specified torque. Before refilling the engine with oil, renew the oil filter as follows.

Filter renewal

5 Position the drain pan underneath the oil filter. Unscrew the filter and remove it. A chain or strap wrench will probably be needed to undo the filter. Failing this, a screwdriver can be driven through the filter and used as a lever to unscrew it. Be prepared for considerable oil spillage in this case. Some spillage is inevitable as the filter is withdrawn **(see illustration)**.

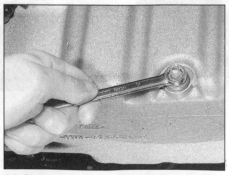

3.2 Clean around the sump drain plug, then remove it to drain the engine oil

6 Wipe clean around the filter seat on the engine and check that no sealing rings have been left behind. Smear the sealing ring on the new filter with clean engine oil or grease, then screw the filter into position. Unless instructed otherwise by the filter maker, tighten the filter by hand only. Usually, tightening by two-thirds of a turn beyond the point where the sealing ring contacts the seat is sufficient.

3.5 Using a chain wrench to unscrew the oil filter

Oil refilling and engine checks

7 Refill the engine with new oil of the specified type through the filler cap. A funnel may help to reduce spillage. Add the oil slowly, checking the level on the dipstick often. Do not overfill. Ensure that the oil level is at least up to the MIN mark on the dipstick.

8 Refit the filler cap, then start the engine. The oil pressure warning light will take a few seconds to go out as the filter fills with oil. Do not rev the engine until the light has gone out.

9 With the engine running, check for leaks around the filter base and the drain plug. Tighten further if necessary. Stop the engine and check again for leaks.

10 Allow a couple of minutes for the oil to return to the sump, then recheck the level on the dipstick and top-up if necessary to the MAX mark. The new filter will absorb approximately 0.5 litre of oil.

11 Put the old oil into a sealed container and dispose of it safely.

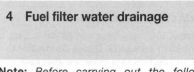

4 Fuel filter water drainage

Note: *Before carrying out the following procedure, read carefully the precautions listed in Chapter 4, Section 1.*

Bosch filter (spin-on cartridge)

1 Disconnect the battery earth lead.

2 In addition to taking the precautions noted in Chapter 4 to catch any fuel spillages, connect a tube to the drain spigot on the base of the fuel filter. Place the other end of the tube in a clean jar or can.

3 Open the drain cock by unscrewing the knurled wheel.

4 Allow the filter to drain until clean fuel, free of dirt or water, emerges from the tube (approximately 100 cc is usually sufficient). Close the drain cock and remove the tube, containers and rag, mopping up any spilt fuel.

5 If, as often happens, no fuel emerges on opening the drain cock, slacken the vent screw (the single, slotted, hexagon-headed screw) on the filter head to allow sufficient air into the filter for fuel to flow. If this does not

work, remove the filter cartridge and check it carefully until the reason for the lack of flow can be identified and is cured. It is unwise simply to probe the drain cock with a piece of wire in an attempt to clear the obstruction; the small seals in the drain cock may be damaged or dislodged. Note that the system may require bleeding if the vent screw is disturbed or the filter unscrewed.

6 On completion, dispose safely of the drained fuel and reconnect the battery earth lead. Check carefully all disturbed components to ensure that there are no leaks (of air or fuel) when the engine is restarted.

CAV RotoDiesel filter

7 Disconnect the battery earth lead.

8 Connect a tube to the drain spigot (where fitted) on the base of the fuel filter. Place the other end of the tube in a clean jar or can.

9 Open the drain cock either by unscrewing the knurled wheel/thumbscrew or by using a spanner, as appropriate **(see illustration)**.

10 Allow the filter to drain until clean fuel, free of dirt or water, emerges from the tube (approximately 100 cc is usually sufficient). Close the drain cock and remove the tube, containers and rag, mopping up any spilt fuel.

11 If, as often happens, no fuel emerges on opening the drain cock, either operate the hand-priming pump to get fuel flowing or slacken the bleed nipple on the filter outlet union to allow sufficient air into the filter for fuel to flow. If this does not work, remove the filter element and check the element and bowl carefully until the reason for the lack of flow can be identified and is cured. In some cases, it would appear that the drain cock passage in the bowl was never made on manufacture. In such cases, either the filter element must be removed at each draining interval so that any water or foreign matter can be tipped out of the filter bowl, or the necessary replacement parts must be obtained so that the drain cock can be used as described above. It is unwise simply to probe the drain cock with a piece of wire in an attempt to clear the obstruction as the small seals in the drain cock may be damaged or dislodged. Note that the system may require bleeding if the bleed nipple is disturbed or the filter dismantled.

12 On completion, refit the air cleaner duct (if removed), dispose safely of the drained fuel and reconnect the battery earth lead. Check carefully all disturbed components to ensure that there are no leaks (of air or fuel) when the engine is restarted.

5 Idle speed check and adjustment

1 The usual type of tachometer (rev counter), which works from ignition system pulses, cannot be used on diesel engines. If it is not felt that adjusting the idle speed "by ear" is satisfactory, one of the following alternatives must be used:

a) *Purchase or hire of an appropriate tachometer*

b) *Delegation of the job to a Ford dealer or other specialist*

c) *Timing light (strobe) operated by a petrol engine running at the desired speed. If the timing light is pointed at a chalk mark on the diesel engine crankshaft pulley, the mark will appear stationary when the two engines are running at the same speed (or multiples of that speed)*

d) *Calculating the mph/rpm relationship for a particular gear and running the engine, in that gear, with the front wheels free. The speedometer accuracy may not be adequate, especially at low speeds. Stringent safety precautions must be observed*

Note: *Pump adjustments should only be disturbed if the idle speed is unreliable, or significantly above or below the specified range. See Chapter 5 for details of the idle speed adjustment actuator.*

Stage 1 - Idle and residual fuel setting checks

2 Run the engine until it reaches normal operating temperature, that is until the cooling fan cuts in.

3 Check that there is 2.0 mm of play on the waxstat cable at the pump end. If necessary, use the cable adjuster to alter the amount of play **(see illustrations)**.

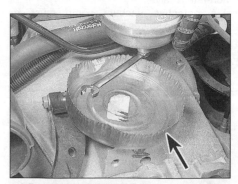

4.9 Draining water from CAV fuel filter using a container (arrowed) to prevent spillage

5.3a Check for play in the waxstat cable at the pump end . . .

5.3b . . . and, if necessary, use the cable adjuster to alter the amount of play

1

5.5 Insert a 4.0 mm gauge between the residual fuel screw and throttle lever

5.6 Rotate the stop lever in a clockwise direction and insert a 3.0 mm diameter "pin" through the idle lever

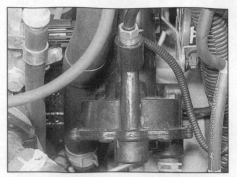

7.1 Inspect the vacuum pump hoses for leakage and security

4 Take a note of the idle speed.

5 Insert a 4.0 mm gauge (feeler blade, or twist drill), between the residual fuel screw and throttle lever **(see illustration)**.

6 Rotate the stop lever in a clockwise direction and insert a 3.0 mm diameter pin, or twist drill, through the idle lever **(see illustration)**.

7 Take a note of the residual idle speed.

8 If the idle and residual speeds are correct, then check that the engine deceleration time from maximum no load speed to idle is no more than 5 seconds without stalling or undershoot. If adjustment is required, proceed as follows:

Stage 2 - Idle resetting procedure

9 Insert a 4.0 mm feeler blade between the residual fuel screw and throttle lever.

10 Rotate the stop lever in a clockwise direction and insert a 3.0 mm diameter pin through the idle lever.

11 Adjust the residual fuel screw to give an engine speed of 900 ± 100 rpm.

12 Remove the feeler blade and pin.

13 Turning the idle speed adjuster screw, **see illustration 11.6**, set the idle speed to 850 ± 50 rpm.

14 Now check that the engine deceleration time from maximum no load speed to idle is no more than 5 seconds without stalling.

15 If the engine stalls, turn the residual fuel screw anti-clockwise (viewed from the rear of the pump) one quarter turn.

16 Recheck all operations from paragraph 9.

17 If the deceleration time exceeds 5 seconds, turn the residual fuel screw clockwise (viewed from the rear of the pump) one quarter turn.

18 Recheck all operations from paragraph 9.

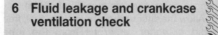

6 Fluid leakage and crankcase ventilation check

Fluid leakage

1 Visually inspect the engine joint faces, gaskets and seals for any signs of coolant or oil leaks. Pay particular attention to the areas around the cylinder head, oil filter and sump joint faces. Bear in mind that over a period of time some very slight seepage from these areas is to be expected but what you are really looking for is any indication of a serious leak. Should a leak be found, renew the offending gasket or oil seal by referring to the appropriate Chapter of this Manual.

2 Check the security and condition of all engine related pipes and hoses. Ensure that all cable-ties or securing clips are in place and in good condition. Clips which are broken or missing can lead to chafing of the hoses, pipes or wiring which could cause more serious problems in the future. If wire type hose clips are used, it may be a good idea to replace them with screw-type clips.

3 Renew any hose which is cracked, swollen or deteriorated. Cracks will show up better if the hose is squeezed.

4 If any damage or deterioration is discovered, do not drive the vehicle until the necessary repair work has been carried out.

HAYNES HiNT *Leaks in the cooling system will usually show up as white or rust-coloured deposits around the area adjoining the leak.*

Crankcase ventilation

5 Inspect the crankcase ventilation hoses as described in paragraph 3 **(see illustration)**.

6 Clean the hoses if they are blocked with sludge or "mayonnaise". Also clean the non-return valve on the camshaft cover.

7 Vacuum pump check

1 Inspect the vacuum pump for oil leaks, the security and condition of hoses and security of mountings **(see illustration)**.

2 Check the operation of the pump as follows.

3 With the engine stopped, operate the footbrake several times to destroy any residual vacuum in the servo. Keep the brake pedal depressed and start the engine. The pedal should be felt to move downwards as the vacuum pump operates on the servo. If not, there is a fault in the pump, the servo or their connecting pipe (not forgetting the non-return valve).

4 A defective vacuum pump must be renewed - no spares are available.

Every 10 000 miles or 12 months

8 Electrical system check

1 Check the operation of all external lights and indicators (front and rear).

2 Check for satisfactory operation of the instrument panel, its illumination and warning lights, the switches and their function lights.

3 Check the horn(s) for satisfactory operation.

4 Check all other electrical equipment for satisfactory operation.

5 Check all electrical wiring in the engine compartment for correct routing, and for any signs of physical or heat-damage or chafing.

9 Battery check, maintenance and charging

⚠ *Warning: Certain precautions must be followed when checking and servicing the*

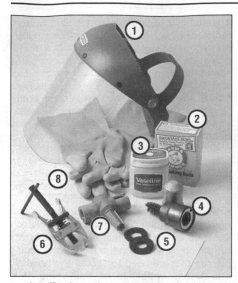

9.1 Tools and materials required for battery maintenance

1 **Face shield/safety goggles** - *When removing corrosion with a brush, the acidic particles can easily fly up into your eyes*
2 **Baking soda** - *A solution of baking soda and water can be used to neutralise corrosion*
3 **Petroleum jelly** - *A layer of this on the battery terminals will help prevent corrosion*
4 **Battery terminal/lead cleaner** - *This wire brush cleaning tool will remove all traces of corrosion from the battery terminals and lead clamps*
5 **Treated felt washers** - *Placing one of these on each terminal, directly under the lead clamps, will help prevent corrosion*
6 **Puller** - *Sometimes the lead clamps are very difficult to pull off the terminals, even after the nut has been completely slackened. This tool pulls the clamp straight up and off the terminal without damage*
7 **Battery terminal/lead cleaner** - *Here is another cleaning tool which is a slightly different version of number 4 above, but does the same thing*
8 **Rubber gloves** - *Another safety item to consider when servicing the battery; remember, that's acid inside the battery!*

battery. Hydrogen gas, which is highly flammable, is always present in the battery cells, so keep lighted tobacco and all other open flames and sparks away from the battery. The electrolyte inside the battery is actually dilute sulphuric acid, which will cause injury if splashed on your skin or in your eyes. It will also ruin clothes and painted surfaces. When disconnecting the battery, always detach the negative (earth) lead first and connect it last!
Note: *Before disconnecting the battery, refer to Section 1 of Chapter 5.*

9.6A Battery terminal corrosion usually appears as light, fluffy powder

9.7A When cleaning the lead clamps, all corrosion must be removed - the inside of the clamp is tapered to match the terminal, so don't remove too much material

General

1 A routine preventive maintenance programme for the battery in your vehicle is the only way to ensure quick and reliable starts. Before performing any battery maintenance, make sure that you have the proper equipment necessary to work safely around the battery **(see illustration)**.
2 There are also several precautions that should be taken whenever battery maintenance is performed. Before servicing the battery, always turn the engine and all accessories off, and disconnect the lead from the negative terminal of the battery - see Chapter 5, Section 1.
3 The battery produces hydrogen gas, which is both flammable and explosive. Never create a spark, smoke, or light a match around the battery. Always charge the battery in a well-ventilated area.
4 Electrolyte contains poisonous and corrosive sulphuric acid. Do not allow it to get in your eyes, on your skin, or on your clothes. Never ingest it. Wear protective safety glasses when working near the battery. Keep children away from the battery.
5 Note the external condition of the battery. If the positive terminal and lead clamp on your vehicle's battery is equipped with a plastic cover or rubber protector, make sure that it's not torn or damaged. It should completely

9.6B Removing a lead from the battery terminal - always remove the earth lead first, and connect it last!

9.7B Regardless of the method used to clean the terminals, a clean, shiny surface should result

cover the terminal. Look for any corroded or loose connections, cracks in the case or cover, or loose hold-down clamps. Also check the entire length of each lead for cracks and frayed conductors.
6 If corrosion, which looks like white, fluffy deposits **(see illustration)** is evident, particularly around the terminals, the battery should be removed for cleaning. Slacken the lead clamp nuts with a spanner, being careful to remove the negative (earth) lead first, and slide them off the terminals **(see illustration)**. Then unscrew the hold-down clamp nuts, remove the clamp, and lift the battery from the engine compartment.
7 Clean the lead clamps thoroughly, using a soft wire brush or a terminal cleaner, with a solution of warm water and baking soda. Wash the terminals and the top of the battery case with the same solution, but make sure that the solution doesn't get into the battery. When cleaning the leads, terminals and battery top, wear safety goggles and rubber gloves, to prevent any solution from coming in contact with your eyes or hands. Wear old clothes too - even when diluted, sulphuric acid splashed onto clothes will burn holes in them. If the terminals have been extensively corroded, clean them up with a terminal cleaner **(see illustrations)**. Thoroughly wash all cleaned areas with plain water.
8 Make sure that the battery tray is in good

1

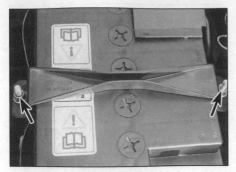

9.8 Make sure the battery hold-down nuts (arrowed) are tight

condition and the hold-down clamp nuts are tight **(see illustration)**. If the battery is removed from the tray, make sure no parts remain in the bottom of the tray when the battery is refitted. When refitting the hold-down clamp nuts, do not overtighten them.

9 Information on removing and installing the battery can be found in Chapter 5. Information on jump starting can be found at the front of this manual. For more detailed battery checking procedures, refer to the Haynes *Automobile Electrical and Electronic Systems Manual.*

Cleaning

10 Corrosion on the hold-down components, battery case and surrounding areas can be removed with a solution of water and baking soda. Thoroughly rinse all cleaned areas with plain water.

11 Any metal parts of the vehicle damaged by corrosion should be covered with a zinc-based primer, then painted.

Charging

 Warning: When batteries are being charged, hydrogen gas, which is very explosive and flammable, is produced. Do not smoke, or allow open flames, near a charging or a recently-charged battery. Wear eye protection when near the battery during charging. Also, make sure the charger is unplugged before connecting or disconnecting the battery from the charger.

12 Slow-rate charging is the best way to restore a battery that's discharged to the point where it will not start the engine. It's also a good way to maintain the battery charge in a vehicle that's only driven a few miles between starts. Maintaining the battery charge is particularly important in winter, when the battery must work harder to start the engine, and electrical accessories that drain the battery are in greater use.

13 It's best to use a one- or two-amp battery charger (sometimes called a "trickle" charger). They are the safest, and put the least strain on the battery. They are also the least expensive. For a faster charge, you can use a higher-

amperage charger, but don't use one rated more than 1/10th the amp/hour rating of the battery (ie no more than 5 amps, typically). Rapid boost charges that claim to restore the power of the battery in one to two hours are hardest on the battery, and can damage batteries not in good condition. This type of charging should only be used in emergency situations.

14 The average time necessary to charge a battery should be listed in the instructions that come with the charger. As a general rule, a trickle charger will charge a battery in 12 to 16 hours.

10 Seat belt check

1 Check the seat belts for satisfactory operation and condition. Inspect the webbing for fraying and cuts. Check that they retract smoothly and without binding into their reels.

2 Check that the seat belt mounting bolts are tight, and if necessary tighten them to the specified torque wrench setting.

11 Auxiliary drivebelt check

1 With each drivebelt fully accessible, rotate its drive pulley to inspect its full length. Check for signs of cracks, splitting and fraying, or for signs of wear or damage such as glazing (shiny patches) or separation on the belt plies. Renew the belt if worn or damaged and check the condition and security of the pulleys, the mounting brackets and the adjuster components and their fasteners.

2 If the belt is in good condition, check the tension and adjust as necessary.

3 For information on belt renewal and adjustment, refer to Chapter 2.

12 Underbonnet check for fluid leaks and hose condition

Caution: Renewal of air conditioning hoses must be left to a dealer service department or air conditioning specialist who has the equipment to depressurise the system safely. Never remove air conditioning components or hoses until the system has been depressurised.

General

1 High temperatures in the engine compartment can cause the deterioration of the rubber and plastic hoses used for engine, accessory and emission systems operation. Periodic inspection should be made for cracks, loose clamps, material hardening and leaks.

2 Carefully check the large top and bottom radiator hoses, along with the other smaller-diameter cooling system hoses and metal pipes; do not forget the heater hoses/pipes which run from the engine to the bulkhead, and those to the engine oil cooler (where fitted). Inspect each hose along its entire length, replacing any that is cracked, swollen or shows signs of deterioration. Cracks may become more apparent if the hose is squeezed **(see illustration)**. If you are using non-Ford specification antifreeze, and so have to renew the coolant every two years or so, it's a good idea to renew the hoses at that time, regardless of their apparent condition.

3 Make sure that all hose connections are tight. A leak in the cooling system will usually show up as white- or rust-coloured deposits on the areas adjoining the leak; if the spring clamps that are used to secure the hoses in this system appear to be slackening, they should be renewed to prevent the possibility of leaks.

4 Some other hoses are secured to their fittings with clamps. Where clamps are used, check to be sure they haven't lost their tension, allowing the hose to leak. If clamps aren't used, make sure the hose has not expanded and/or hardened where it slips over the fitting, allowing it to leak.

5 Check all fluid reservoirs, filler caps, drain plugs and fittings etc, looking for any signs of leakage of oil, transmission and/or brake hydraulic fluid, coolant and power steering fluid. If the vehicle is regularly parked in the same place, close inspection of the ground underneath it will soon show any leaks; ignore the puddle of water which will be left if the air conditioning system is in use. As soon as a leak is detected, its source must be traced

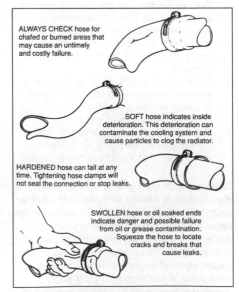

ALWAYS CHECK hose for chafed or burned areas that may cause an untimely and costly failure.

SOFT hose indicates inside deterioration. This deterioration can contaminate the cooling system and cause particles to clog the radiator.

HARDENED hose can fail at any time. Tightening hose clamps will not seal the connection or stop leaks.

SWOLLEN hose or oil soaked ends indicate danger and possible failure from oil or grease contamination. Squeeze the hose to locate cracks and breaks that cause leaks.

12.2 Hoses, like drivebelts, have a habit of failing at the worst possible time - to prevent the inconvenience of a blown radiator or heater hose, inspect them carefully as shown here

and rectified. Where oil has been leaking for some time, it is usually necessary to use a steam cleaner, pressure washer or similar, to clean away the accumulated dirt, so that the exact source of the leak can be identified.

Vacuum hoses

6 It's quite common for vacuum hoses, especially those in the emissions system, to be colour-coded, or to be identified by coloured stripes moulded into them. Various systems require hoses with different wall thicknesses, collapse resistance and temperature resistance. When renewing hoses, be sure the new ones are made of the same material.

7 Often the only effective way to check a hose is to remove it completely from the vehicle. If more than one hose is removed, be sure to label the hoses and fittings to ensure correct installation.

8 When checking vacuum hoses, be sure to include any plastic T-fittings in the check. Inspect the fittings for cracks, and check the hose where it fits over the fitting for distortion, which could cause leakage.

9 A small piece of vacuum hose (quarter-inch inside diameter) can be used as a stethoscope to detect vacuum leaks. Hold one end of the hose to your ear, and probe around vacuum hoses and fittings, listening for the "hissing" sound characteristic of a vacuum leak.

 Warning: When probing with the vacuum hose stethoscope, be very careful not to come into contact with moving engine components such as the auxiliary drivebelt, radiator electric cooling fan, etc.

Fuel hoses

 Warning: There are certain precautions which must be taken when inspecting or servicing fuel system components. Work in a well-ventilated area, and do not allow open flames (cigarettes, appliance pilot lights, etc.) or bare light bulbs near the work area. Mop up any spills immediately, and do not store fuel-soaked rags where they could ignite.

10 Check all fuel hoses for deterioration and chafing. Check especially for cracks in areas where the hose bends, and also just before fittings, such as where a hose attaches to the fuel filter.

11 High-quality fuel line, usually identified by the word "Fluoroelastomer" printed on the hose, should be used for fuel line renewal. Never, under any circumstances, use unreinforced vacuum line, clear plastic tubing or water hose for fuel lines.

12 Spring-type clamps are commonly used on fuel lines. These clamps often lose their tension over a period of time, and can be "sprung" during removal. Replace all spring-type clamps with screw clamps whenever a hose is replaced.

Metal lines

13 Sections of metal piping are often used for fuel line between the fuel tank and the engine. Check carefully to be sure the piping has not been bent or crimped, and that cracks have not started in the line.

14 If a section of metal fuel line must be renewed, only seamless steel piping should be used, since copper and aluminium piping don't have the strength necessary to withstand normal engine vibration.

15 Check the metal brake lines where they enter the master cylinder and ABS hydraulic unit (if used) for cracks in the lines or loose fittings. Any sign of brake fluid leakage calls for an immediate and thorough inspection of the brake system.

13 Engine compartment wiring check

1 With the vehicle parked on level ground, apply the handbrake firmly and open the bonnet. Using an inspection light or a small electric torch, check all visible wiring within and beneath the engine compartment.

2 What you are looking for is wiring that is obviously damaged by chafing against sharp edges, or against moving suspension/transmission components and/or the auxiliary drivebelt, by being trapped or crushed between carelessly-refitted components, or melted by being forced into contact with the hot engine castings, coolant pipes, etc. In almost all cases, damage of this sort is caused in the first instance by incorrect routing on reassembly after previous work has been carried out.

3 Depending on the extent of the problem, damaged wiring may be repaired by rejoining the break or splicing-in a new length of wire, using solder to ensure a good connection, and remaking the insulation with adhesive insulating tape or heat-shrink tubing, as appropriate. If the damage is extensive, given the implications for the vehicle's future reliability, the best long-term answer may well be to renew that entire section of the loom, however expensive this may appear.

4 When the actual damage has been repaired, ensure that the wiring loom is re-routed correctly, so that it is clear of other components, and not stretched or kinked, and is secured out of harm's way using the plastic clips, guides and ties provided.

5 Check all electrical connectors, ensuring that they are clean, securely fastened, and that each is locked by its plastic tabs or wire clip, as appropriate. If any connector shows external signs of corrosion (accumulations of white or green deposits, or streaks of "rust"), or if any is thought to be dirty, it must be unplugged and cleaned using electrical contact cleaner. If the connector pins are severely corroded, the connector must be renewed; note that this may mean the renewal of that entire section of the loom - see your local Ford dealer for details.

6 If the cleaner completely removes the corrosion to leave the connector in a satisfactory condition, it would be wise to pack the connector with a suitable material which will exclude dirt and moisture, preventing the corrosion from occurring again; a Ford dealer may be able to recommend a suitable product.

7 Check the condition of the battery connections - remake the connections or renew the leads if a fault is found (see Chapter 5). Use the same techniques to ensure that all earth points in the engine compartment provide good electrical contact through clean, metal-to-metal joints, and that all are securely fastened. (In addition to the earth connection at the engine lifting eye, and that from the transmission to the body/battery, there are one or two earth points behind each headlight assembly, and one below the power steering fluid reservoir.)

14 Air conditioning system check

 Warning: The air conditioning system is under high pressure. Do not loosen any fittings or remove any components until after the system has been discharged. Air conditioning refrigerant must be properly discharged into an approved type of container, at a dealer service department or an automotive air conditioning repair facility capable of handling R134a refrigerant. Always wear eye protection when disconnecting air conditioning system fittings.

1 The following maintenance checks should be performed on a regular basis, to ensure that the air conditioner continues to operate at peak efficiency:

(a) *Check the auxiliary drivebelt. If it's worn or deteriorated, renew it (see Section 11).*

(b) *Check the system hoses. Look for cracks, bubbles, hard spots and deterioration. Inspect the hoses and all fittings for oil bubbles and seepage. If there's any evidence of wear, damage or leaks, renew the hose(s).*

(c) *Inspect the condenser fins for leaves, insects and other debris. Use a "fin comb" or compressed air to clean the condenser.*

(d) *Check that the drain tube from the front of the evaporator is clear - note that it is normal to have clear fluid (water) dripping from this while the system is in operation, to the extent that quite a large puddle can be left under the vehicle when it is parked.*

Warning: Wear eye protection when using compressed air!

1

15.2 Topping-up the transmission oil

2 It's a good idea to operate the system for about 30 minutes at least once a month, particularly during the winter. Long term non-use can cause hardening, and subsequent failure, of the seals.

3 Because of the complexity of the air conditioning system and the special equipment necessary to service it, in-depth fault diagnosis and repairs are not included in this manual. For more complete information on the air conditioning system, refer to the Haynes *Automotive Heating and Air Conditioning Manual.*

4 The most common cause of poor cooling is simply a low system refrigerant charge. If a noticeable drop in cool air output occurs, the following quick check will help you determine if the refrigerant level is low.

5 Warm the engine up to normal operating temperature.

6 Place the air conditioning temperature selector at the coldest setting, and put the blower at the highest setting. Open the doors - to make sure the air conditioning system doesn't cycle off as soon as it cools the passenger compartment.

7 With the compressor engaged - the clutch will make an audible click, and the centre of the clutch will rotate - feel the inlet and outlet pipes at the compressor. One side should be cold, and one hot. If there's no perceptible difference between the two pipes, there's something wrong with the compressor or the system. It might be a low charge - it might be something else. Take the vehicle to a dealer service department or an automotive air conditioning specialist.

15 Transmission oil level check

1 The manual transmission does not have a dipstick. To check the oil level, raise the vehicle and support it securely on axle stands, making sure that the vehicle is level. On the lower front side of the transmission housing, you will see the filler/level plug. Unscrew and remove it. If the lubricant level is correct, the oil should be up to the lower edge of the hole.

2 If the transmission needs more lubricant (if

the oil level is not up to the hole), use a syringe, or a plastic bottle and tube, to add more **(see illustration)**. Stop filling the transmission when the lubricant begins to run out of the hole.

3 Refit the filler/level plug, and tighten it to the specified torque wrench setting. Drive the vehicle a short distance, then check for leaks.

4 A need for regular topping-up can only be due to a leak, which should be found and rectified without delay.

16 Clutch pedal adjustment

The procedure is described in Chapter 8, Section 3.

17 Steering, suspension and roadwheel check

Front suspension and steering check

1 Apply the handbrake, then raise the front of the vehicle and support it on axle stands.

2 Visually inspect the balljoint dust covers and the steering gear gaiters for splits, chafing or deterioration **(see illustrations)**. Any wear

of these components will cause loss of lubricant, together with dirt and water entry, resulting in rapid deterioration of the balljoints or steering gear.

3 Check the power-assisted steering fluid hoses for chafing or deterioration, and the pipe and hose unions for fluid leaks. Also check for signs of fluid leakage under pressure from the steering gear rubber gaiters, which would indicate failed fluid seals within the steering gear.

4 Grasp the roadwheel at the 12 o'clock and 6 o'clock positions, and try to rock it **(see illustration)**. Very slight free play may be felt, but if the movement is appreciable, further investigation is necessary to determine the source. Continue rocking the wheel while an assistant depresses the footbrake. If the movement is now eliminated or significantly reduced, it is likely that the hub bearings are at fault. If the free play is still evident with the footbrake depressed, then there is wear in the suspension joints or mountings.

5 Now grasp the wheel at the 9 o'clock and 3 o'clock positions, and try to rock it as before. Any movement felt now may again be caused by wear in the hub bearings or the steering track rod balljoints. If the outer track rod balljoint is worn, the visual movement will be obvious. If the inner joint is suspect, it can be felt by placing a hand over the rack-and-pinion rubber gaiter, and gripping the track rod. If the wheel is now rocked, movement will be felt at the inner joint if wear has taken place.

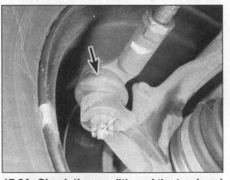

17.2A Check the condition of the track rod balljoint dust cover (arrowed)

17.2B Check the condition of the lower arm balljoint dust cover (arrowed)

17.2C Check the condition of the steering rack gaiters

17.4 Checking for wear in the front suspension and hub bearings

6 Using a large screwdriver or flat bar, check for wear in the suspension mounting bushes by levering between the relevant suspension component and its attachment point. Some movement is to be expected as the mountings are made of rubber, but excessive wear should be obvious. Also check the condition of any visible rubber bushes, looking for splits, cracks or contamination of the rubber.

7 With the vehicle standing on its wheels, have an assistant turn the steering wheel back-and-forth, about an eighth of a turn each way. There should be very little, if any, lost movement between the steering wheel and roadwheels. If this is not the case, closely observe the joints and mountings previously described, but in addition, check the steering column universal joints for wear, and also check the rack-and-pinion steering gear itself.

Rear suspension check

8 Chock the front wheels, then raise the rear of the vehicle and support it on axle stands.

9 Check the rear hub bearings for wear, using the method described for the front hub bearings (paragraph 4).

10 Using a large screwdriver or flat bar, check for wear in the suspension mounting bushes by levering between the relevant suspension component and its attachment point. Some movement is to be expected as the mountings are made of rubber, but excessive wear should be obvious.

Roadwheel check and balancing

11 Periodically remove the roadwheels, and clean any dirt or mud from the inside and outside surfaces. Examine the wheel rims for signs of rusting, corrosion or other damage. Light alloy wheels are easily damaged by "kerbing" whilst parking, and similarly, steel wheels may become dented or buckled. Renewal of the wheel is very often the only course of remedial action possible.

12 The balance of each wheel and tyre assembly should be maintained, not only to avoid excessive tyre wear, but also to avoid wear in the steering and suspension components. Wheel imbalance is normally signified by vibration through the vehicle's bodyshell, although in many cases it is particularly noticeable through the steering wheel. Conversely, it should be noted that wear or damage in suspension or steering components may cause excessive tyre wear. Out-of-round or out-of-true tyres, damaged wheels and wheel bearing wear/maladjustment also fall into this category. Balancing will not usually cure vibration caused by such wear.

13 Wheel balancing may be carried out with the wheel either on or off the vehicle. If balanced on the vehicle, ensure that the wheel-to-hub relationship is marked in some way prior to subsequent wheel removal, so that it may be refitted in its original position.

18.2 Check the driveshaft gaiters by hand for cracks and/or leaking grease

18 Driveshaft rubber gaiter and CV joint check

1 The driveshaft rubber gaiters are very important, because they prevent dirt, water and foreign material from entering and damaging the constant velocity (CV) joints. External contamination can cause the gaiter material to deteriorate prematurely, so it's a good idea to wash the gaiters with soap and water occasionally.

2 With the vehicle raised and securely supported on axle stands, turn the steering onto full-lock, then slowly rotate each front wheel in turn. Inspect the condition of the outer constant velocity (CV) joint rubber gaiters, squeezing the gaiters to open out the folds. Check for signs of cracking, splits, or deterioration of the rubber, which may allow the escape of grease, and lead to the ingress of water and grit into the joint **(see illustration)**. Also check the security and condition of the retaining clips. Repeat these checks on the inner CV joints. If any damage or deterioration is found, the gaiters should be renewed as described in Chapter 8.

3 At the same time, check the general condition of the outer CV joints themselves, by first holding the driveshaft and attempting to rotate the wheels. Repeat this check on the inner joints, by holding the inner joint yoke and attempting to rotate the driveshaft.

4 Any appreciable movement in the CV joint indicates wear in the joint, wear in the driveshaft splines, or a loose driveshaft retaining nut.

19 Exhaust system check

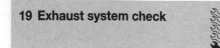

1 With the engine cold (at least three hours after the vehicle has been driven), check the complete exhaust system, from its starting point at the engine to the end of the tailpipe. Ideally, this should be done on a hoist, where unrestricted access is available; if a hoist is not available, raise and support the vehicle on axle stands.

2 Check the pipes and connections for evidence of leaks, severe corrosion, or damage. Make sure that all brackets and rubber mountings are in good condition, and tight; if any of the mountings are to be renewed, ensure that the replacements are of the correct type **(see illustration)**. Leakage at any of the joints or in other parts of the system will usually show up as a black sooty stain in the vicinity of the leak. **Note:** *Exhaust sealants should not be used on any part of the exhaust system upstream of the catalytic converter - even if the sealant does not contain additives harmful to the converter, pieces of it may break off and foul the element, causing local overheating.*

3 At the same time, inspect the underside of the body for holes, corrosion, open seams, etc. which may allow exhaust gases to enter the passenger compartment. Seal all body openings with silicone or body putty.

4 Rattles and other noises can often be traced to the exhaust system, especially the rubber mountings. Try to move the system, silencer(s) and catalytic converter. If any components can touch the body or suspension parts, secure the exhaust system with new mountings.

5 Check the running condition of the engine by inspecting inside the end of the tailpipe; the exhaust deposits here are an indication of the engine's state of tune. The inside of the tailpipe should be dry, and should vary in colour from dark grey to light grey/brown; if it is black and sooty, or coated with white deposits, the engine is in need of a thorough fuel system inspection.

20 Underbody and fuel/brake line check

1 With the vehicle raised and supported on axle stands or over an inspection pit, thoroughly inspect the underbody and wheel arches for signs of damage and corrosion. In particular, examine the bottom of the side

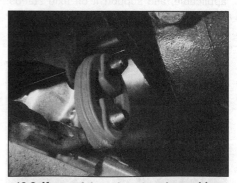

19.2 If any of the exhaust system rubber mountings are to be renewed, ensure that the replacements are of the correct type - their colour is a good guide. Those nearest to the catalytic converter are more heat-resistant than the others

1

sills, and any concealed areas where mud can collect. Where corrosion and rust is evident, press and tap firmly on the panel with a screwdriver, and check for any serious corrosion which would necessitate repairs. If the panel is not seriously corroded, clean away the rust, and apply a new coating of underseal. Refer to Chapter 11 for more details of body repairs.

2 At the same time, inspect the PVC-coated lower body panels for stone damage and general condition.

3 Inspect all of the fuel and brake lines on the underbody for damage, rust, corrosion and leakage. Also make sure that they are correctly supported in their clips. Where applicable, check the PVC coating on the lines for damage.

21 Brake check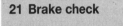

Note: *For detailed photographs of the brake system, refer to Chapter 9.*

1 The work described in this Section should be carried out at the specified intervals, or whenever a defect is suspected in the braking system. Any of the following symptoms could indicate a potential brake system defect:

(a) *The vehicle pulls to one side when the brake pedal is depressed.*
(b) *The brakes make scraping or dragging noises when applied.*
(c) *Brake pedal travel is excessive.*
(d) *The brake fluid requires repeated topping-up.*

2 A brake pad wear warning light is fitted, and it is illuminated when the thickness of the front (or rear) disc brake pad linings reach the minimum amount. However, a physical check should be made to confirm the thickness of the linings, as follows.

Disc brakes

3 Jack up the front or rear of the vehicle, as applicable, and support it on axle stands. Where rear brake pads are fitted, also jack up the rear of the vehicle and support on axle stands.

4 For better access to the brake calipers, remove the wheels.

5 Look through the inspection window in the caliper, and check that the thickness of the friction lining material on each of the pads is not less than the recommended minimum thickness given in the Specifications. **Note:** *Bear in mind that the lining material is normally bonded to a metal backing plate.*

6 If it is difficult to determine the exact thickness of the pad linings, or if you are at all concerned about the condition of the pads, then remove them from the calipers for further inspection (refer to Chapter 9).

7 Check the remaining brake caliper(s) in the same way.

8 If any one of the brake pads has worn down to, or below, the specified limit, *all four* pads at that end of the car must be renewed as a set (ie all the front pads or all the rear pads).

9 Measure the thickness of the discs with a micrometer, if available, to make sure that they still have service life remaining. If any disc is thinner than the specified minimum thickness, renew it (refer to Chapter 9). In any case, check the general condition of the discs. Look for excessive scoring and discolouration caused by overheating. If these conditions exist, remove the relevant disc and have it resurfaced or renewed (refer to Chapter 9).

10 Before refitting the wheels, check all brake lines and hoses (refer to Chapter 9). In particular, check the flexible hoses in the vicinity of the calipers, where they are subjected to most movement. Bend them between the fingers (but do not actually bend them double, or the casing may be damaged) and check that this does not reveal previously-hidden cracks, cuts or splits **(see illustration)**.

Rear drum brakes

11 Chock the front wheels, then jack up the rear of the vehicle and support on axle stands.

12 For better access, remove the rear wheels.

13 To check the brake shoe lining thickness without removing the brake drums, prise the rubber plugs from the backplates, and use an electric torch to inspect the linings of the leading brake shoes **(see illustration)**. Check that the thickness of the lining material on the brake shoes is not less than the recommendation given in the Specifications.

14 If it is difficult to determine the exact thickness of the brake shoe linings, or if you are at all concerned about the condition of the shoes, then remove the rear drums for a more comprehensive inspection (refer to Chapter 9) **(see illustration)**.

15 With the drum removed, check the shoe return and hold-down springs for correct installation, and check the wheel cylinders for leakage of brake fluid. Check the friction surface of the brake drums for scoring and discoloration. If excessive, the drum should be resurfaced or renewed.

16 Before refitting the wheels, check all brake lines and hoses (refer to Chapter 9). On completion, apply the handbrake and check that the rear wheels are locked. The handbrake is self-adjusting, and no manual adjustment is possible.

22 Door and bonnet check and lubrication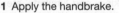

1 Check that the doors, bonnet and tailgate/boot lid close securely. Check that the bonnet safety catch operates correctly. Check the operation of the door check straps.

2 Lubricate the hinges, door check straps, the striker plates and the bonnet catch sparingly with a little oil or grease.

23 Roadwheel nut tightness check

1 Apply the handbrake.

2 Remove the wheel covers, using the flat end of the wheelbrace supplied in the tool kit (on models with the RS trim kit, it will be necessary to unscrew the retaining bolts with the special key).

3 Check that the roadwheel nuts are tightened to the specified torque wrench setting.

4 Refit the wheel covers.

21.10 Checking the condition of a flexible brake hose

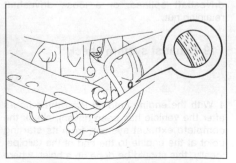

21.13 Prise the rubber plugs from the backplates to inspect the leading brake shoe linings

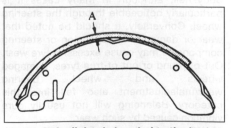

21.14 If the lining is bonded to the brake shoe, measure the lining thickness from the outer surface to the metal shoe, as shown here; if the lining is riveted to the shoe, measure from the lining outer surface to the rivet head

24 Road test

Check the operation and performance of the braking system

1 Make sure that the vehicle does not pull to one side when braking, and that the wheels do not lock prematurely when braking hard.
2 Check that there is no vibration through the steering when braking.
3 Check that the handbrake operates correctly, without excessive movement of the lever, and that it holds the vehicle stationary on a slope.
4 With the engine switched off, test the operation of the brake servo unit as follows. Depress the footbrake four or five times to exhaust the vacuum, then start the engine. As the engine starts, there should be a noticeable "give" in the brake pedal as vacuum builds up. Allow the engine to run for at least two minutes, and then switch it off. If the brake pedal is now depressed again, it should be possible to detect a hiss from the servo as the pedal is depressed. After about four or five applications, no further hissing should be heard, and the pedal should feel considerably harder.

Steering and suspension

5 Check for any abnormalities in the steering, suspension, handling or road "feel".
6 Drive the vehicle, and check that there are no unusual vibrations or noises.
7 Check that the steering feels positive, with no excessive sloppiness or roughness, and check for any suspension noises when cornering and driving over bumps.

Drivetrain

8 Check the performance of the engine, transmission and driveshafts.
9 Check that the engine starts correctly, both when cold and when hot.
10 Listen for any unusual noises from the engine and transmission.
11 Make sure that the engine runs smoothly when idling, and that there is no hesitation when accelerating.
12 On manual transmission models, check that all gears can be engaged smoothly without noise, and that the gear lever action is not abnormally vague or "notchy".
13 On automatic transmission models, make sure that all gearchanges occur smoothly without snatching, and without an increase in engine speed between changes. Check that all the gear positions can be selected with the vehicle at rest. If any problems are found, they should be referred to a Ford dealer.

14 Listen for a metallic clicking sound from the front of the vehicle as the vehicle is driven slowly in a circle with the steering on full-lock. Carry out this check in both directions. If a clicking noise is heard, this indicates wear in a driveshaft joint, in which case renew the joint if necessary.

Clutch

15 Check that the clutch pedal moves smoothly and easily through its full travel, and that the clutch itself functions correctly, with no trace of slip or drag. If the movement is uneven or stiff in places, check that the cable is routed correctly, with no sharp turns.
16 Inspect both ends of the clutch inner cable, both at the gearbox end and inside the car, for signs of wear and fraying.
17 Check the pedal stroke as described in Chapter 8, Section 3, and adjust if necessary.

Instruments and electrical equipment

18 Check the operation of all instruments and electrical equipment.
19 Make sure that all instruments read correctly, and switch on all electrical equipment in turn, to check that it functions properly.

Every 20 000 miles or 2 years

25 Fuel filter element renewal

Note: *Before carrying out the following procedure, read carefully the precautions listed in Chapter 4.*

Bosch clamp-fixing cartridge filter

1 Drain the filter completely.
2 Note carefully the orientation of the fuel inlet and outlet hoses and the filter vent screw **(see illustration)**. Clean them thoroughly and obtain new hose clamps and/or flexible hoses if the condition of those fitted is in any way suspect.
3 Releasing the clamps with pliers, disconnect the fuel inlet and outlet hoses from the filter stubs. Plug or cap hoses and unions to keep fuel in and dirt out.
4 Slacken the clamp screw and withdraw the filter from its bracket, taking care to spill as little as possible of any remaining fuel.
5 Fit the new filter to the clamp, aligning its stubs with the hoses as noted on removal and observing any directional markings on the

A   Fuel inlet hose
B   Fuel outlet hose
C   Vent screw
D   Drain cock
E   Clamp

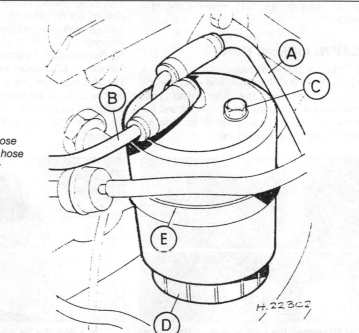

25.2 Bosch clamp-fixing cartridge filter

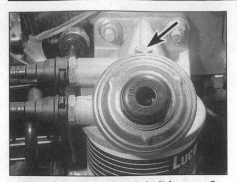

25.10 CAV filter through-bolt (arrowed)

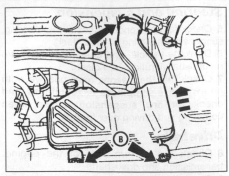

26.1 Loosen the hose retaining clip (A) and remove the air intake system resonator by pulling it from its two retainers (B)

26.2a Loosen the two retaining clips (arrowed) and detach the MAF sensor from the air cleaner cover

filter. Fit the new flexible hoses and/or clamps (if required), then connect the hoses to the filter and fasten them securely with the clamps.

6 Tighten the filter mounting clamp screw, but be careful not to overtighten it (nominal torque wrench setting of 1.5 to 2.5 Nm/1 to 2 lbf ft only), or the filter may be crushed. Check that the drain cock is closed.

7 Reconnect the battery earth lead and restart the engine. Considerable cranking may be required to bleed the air from the system. To spare the battery, this time may be reduced by filling the filter with clean fuel via its vent screw opening but it is essential that no dirt is introduced into the system and that no diesel fuel is poured over vulnerable components when doing this.

8 On completion, dispose safely of the old filter and the drained fuel. Check carefully all disturbed components to ensure that there are no leaks (or air or fuel) when the engine is restarted.

CAV RotoDiesel filter

9 Drain the filter completely.

10 Support the filter bowl and unscrew the through-bolt from the filter head **(see illustration)**. Withdraw the filter bowl and the element, taking care to spill as little as possible of any remaining fuel.

11 Using a small mirror and a torch if necessary, check that all seals are removed from above and below the filter element, from the through-bolt and from (the underside of) the filter head. Precise details of seal type and location will vary according to engine and model, as well as depending on the make of filter element used, but all these seals must be renewed as a matter of course before the filter is reassembled; usually they will be supplied with the new element.

12 Wipe clean the filter head and bowl. Check that the drain cock in the filter bowl is clean, that its seals are in good condition and correctly located, then tighten it securely closed.

13 Ensuring that all seals are renewed, fitted as noted on removal and are correctly located, refit the element to the filter head, followed by the filter bowl, then ensure that the seals above and below the element are not distorted or dislodged as the through-bolt is refitted and tightened securely.

14 Reconnect the battery earth lead, bleed the system, then restart the engine.

15 On completion, dispose safely of the old filter and the drained fuel. Check carefully all disturbed components to ensure that there are no leaks (of air or fuel) when the engine is restarted.

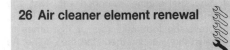

26 Air cleaner element renewal

1 On early models, loosen the hose retaining clip and remove the air inlet system resonator by pulling it from its two retainers **(see illustration)**.

2 On all models, loosen the two retaining clips and detach the mass airflow (MAF) sensor assembly from the air cleaner cover **(see illustration)**. This operation may prove difficult due to resistance from the rubber retaining ring. Unplug the vent pipe from the cover **(see illustration)**.

3 Release the air cleaner cover retaining clips. Some of these clips are not readily accessible and difficult to release because of adjoining components but it is possible to release them by pulling the air cleaner box clear of said components. Lift the cover to allow access to the air cleaner element **(see illustration)**.

4 Take out the air cleaner element and discard it **(see illustration)**.

5 Wipe out the casing and fit the new element into position.

6 Refit the cover and reconnect all disturbed components, lightly greasing the mating surface of the mass airflow (MAF) sensor rubber retaining ring.

26.2b Unplug the vent pipe from the cover

26.3 Release the air cleaner cover retaining clips and lift the cover to allow access to the air cleaner element

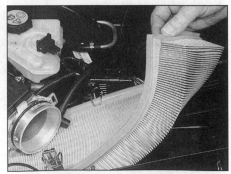

26.4 Remove the air cleaner element

27.3 Remove screws (arrowed) to release cowl grille panel . . .

27.5A . . . release clips to lift out pollen filter housing . . .

27.5B . . . then withdraw pollen filter element

27 Ventilation system pollen filter renewal

1 The air entering the vehicle's ventilation system is passed through a very fine pleated-paper air filter element, which removes particles of pollen, dust and other airborne foreign matter. To ensure its continued effectiveness, this filter's element must be renewed at regular intervals.

2 Remove the left-hand side windscreen wiper arm (Chapter 12).

3 Prise off their trim caps, then unscrew the two screws securing the windscreen edge of the cowl grille panel; open the bonnet and remove the remaining three retaining screws **(see illustration)**.

4 Peel back the rubber seal and withdraw the cowl grille panel.

5 Releasing the clip at each end, lift out the pollen filter housing, and withdraw the element **(see illustrations)**.

6 Wipe out the ventilation system intake and the filter housing, removing any leaves, dead insects etc.

7 If carrying out a routine service, the element must be renewed regardless of its apparent condition. If you are checking the element for any other reason, inspect its front surface; if it is very dirty, renew the element. If it is only moderately dusty, it can be re-used by blowing it clean from the rear to the front surface with compressed air.

  Warning: Wear eye protection when using compressed air! Because it is a pleated-paper type filter, it cannot be washed or re-oiled. If it cannot be cleaned satisfactorily with compressed air, discard and renew it.

8 Refitting is the reverse of the removal procedure; ensure that the element and housing are securely seated, so that unfiltered air cannot enter the passenger compartment.

28 Coolant renewal

Warning: Take care to avoid scalding when removing the expansion tank cap. Place a thick cloth over the cap before turning it anti-clockwise.
Caution: Never operate the vehicle with plain water in the cooling system, except in an emergency. Apart from the risk of freezing in winter weather, serious corrosion and rust and scale formation may occur.

Draining

1 Disconnect the battery earth lead.

2 Place a thick cloth over the expansion tank cap, see "Weekly checks". Turn the cap anti-clockwise as far as the first stop and wait for any pressure to be released, then depress

it and turn it further anti-clockwise to remove it. Take care to avoid scalding.

3 Position a drain tray beneath the radiator. Use a clean tray if the coolant is to be salvaged. Slacken the radiator drain plug until coolant flows out **(see illustration)**. Take care to avoid scalding if the coolant is hot.

4 When draining from the radiator is complete, move the tray under the engine and remove the block drain plug **(see illustration)**. Allow the coolant to drain from the block.

5 Close or refit the drain plugs now so that they are not lost or forgotten.

Flushing

6 Flushing should not be necessary if the specified coolant has been used and renewed at the correct intervals. When coolant renewal has been neglected, however, or if much running has been done using plain water or inferior coolant mixtures, rust and scale may clog the system and cause overheating. Flushing may then be beneficial and should be carried out as follows.

7 Drain the system.

8 Remove the thermostat.

9 Disconnect the bottom hose from the radiator. Insert a garden hose into the thermostat housing and run water through the engine in the reverse direction to normal flow, so that it goes in via the thermostat housing and out at the bottom hose. Continue until the water emerges clean.

10 Run the water through the radiator in the normal direction of flow, ie top to bottom. In severe cases of obstruction, reverse flushing may be helpful, but the radiator should be removed and inverted for this.

11 Chemical descalers or flushing agents should be used only as a last resort. Use such materials in accordance with their maker's instructions.

12 When flushing is complete, refit the thermostat and reconnect the disturbed hoses.

13 Refill the system.

Filling

14 Make sure that the drain plugs are secure, and that all hoses are in good condition and their clips tight.

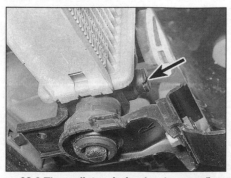

28.3 The radiator drain plug (arrowed)

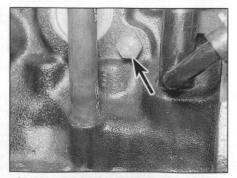

28.4 The engine block coolant drain plug (arrowed) next to dipstick tube

1

28.15 The coolant bleed screw (arrowed) is fitted in the radiator top hose

15 When a bleed screw is fitted in the radiator top hose, slacken it **(see illustration)**.
16 Fill with coolant via the expansion tank filler hole. If new antifreeze is being introduced, pour in the specified quantity of antifreeze first, followed by clean soft water.
17 Fill the system slowly, massaging the large coolant hoses to disperse airlocks.
18 When a bleed screw is fitted, close it when coolant begins to emerge.
19 Fill the system up to the MAX mark on the expansion tank, then refit the cap.
20 Reconnect the battery. Start the engine and run it up to operating temperature (indicated by the fan cutting in). Check for leaks.
21 Stop the engine and allow it to cool. Check the level in the expansion tank and top-up again to the MAX mark if necessary.
22 Recheck the level after the vehicle is next run.

Antifreeze mixture

23 Do not operate the vehicle with plain water in the system, except in an emergency. Apart from the risk of freezing in winter weather, serious corrosion and rust and scale formation may occur.
24 In climates where frost protection is not required, a corrosion inhibitor must be used in accordance with its maker's instructions.
25 Only use ethylene glycol based antifreeze to the maker's specification and soft water - rainwater is ideal. Do not use antifreeze containing methanol, which is inflammable and may evaporate.
26 The recommended concentration of antifreeze for the UK climate is given in *"Lubricants, fluids and capacities"*. Do not use widely different concentrations without first seeking expert advice.
27 Antifreeze must be renewed at the specified intervals to maintain the anti-corrosion properties.

Every 30 000 miles or 3 years

29 Camshaft and injection pump drivebelt renewal

 Warning: Never re-use or retension a camshaft drivebelt which has already been used. This could lead to the belt becoming over-tensioned, leading to its failure and resulting in serious engine damage.
Note: *Whenever the camshaft and fuel injection pump drivebelts are removed or if the belt tension is released for any reason, both belts must be discarded and new ones fitted. Do not re-use or retension a drivebelt which has already been used. This could lead to the belt becoming over-tensioned, leading to its failure which could result in serious engine damage*

Removal

1 Begin by carrying out the following preliminary dismantling procedures:

a) *Jack up the front right-hand side of the vehicle and support it on axle stands (see "Jacking and vehicle support")*
b) *Disconnect the battery earth (negative) lead*
c) *Detaching the shield(s) and/or cover(s) as necessary* **(see illustration)**, *remove the alternator/coolant pump drivebelt*
d) *With the engine still in the vehicle, it will probably be necessary to remove the alternator and, if fitted, the power-assisted steering pump to reach the TDC pin hole plug and to insert a timing pin*
e) *Where applicable, slacken the engine lifting eye retaining nut(s) or bolt(s) and swing it clear of the drivebelt cover. Where a throttle damper is fitted which will prevent the removal of the cover, this must first be removed*

2 Working under the vehicle, unscrew the front (vertical) retaining bolt and the rear (horizontal) pivot bolt, then withdraw the drivebelt lower cover from the crankshaft pulley/vibration damper **(see illustrations)**.
3 If not already removed, detach the plastic fuel deflector from the alternator mounting bracket **(see illustration)**.
4 Returning to the engine compartment, release the three camshaft drivebelt cover retaining clips and unscrew the single (central)

29.1 Detaching the alternator/coolant pump drivebelt cover

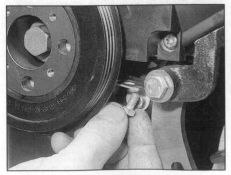

29.2a Remove the drivebelt lower cover retaining screw . . .

29.2b . . . and swivel the cover downwards

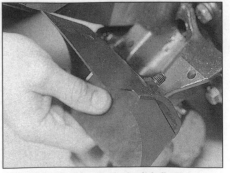

29.3 Detach the plastic fuel deflector from the alternator mounting bracket

29.4a Release the three camshaft drivebelt cover retaining clips . . .

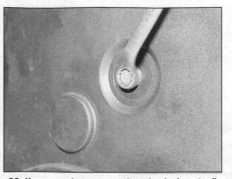

29.4b . . . and unscrew the single (central) cover retaining bolt

29.4c Manoeuvre the cover upwards and withdraw it . . .

29.4d . . . to provide access to the drivebelt

1 Camshaft sprocket
2 Idler sprocket
3 Fuel pump sprocket
4 Fuel pump belt tensioner
5 Crankshaft pulley vibration damper
6 Auxiliary shaft sprocket
7 Coolant pump sprocket
8 Camshaft belt tensioner

29.5a Toothed belt and sprocket identification (engine removed)

retaining bolt, then manoeuvre the cover upwards and withdraw it (see illustrations).

5 Using the bolt in the centre of the crankshaft pulley vibration damper, turn the crankshaft in the normal direction of rotation until the drilling in the injection pump flange (CAV) or the recess (Bosch) is aligned with the drilling in the pump housing. This gives the TDC position for pistons 1 and 4 (see illustrations).

6 Release the belt tensioner and then remove the camshaft drivebelt. If the injection pump drivebelt is to be renewed, then its tensioner should be removed and the belt withdrawn.

7 Align the camshaft sprocket and the injection pump sprocket, so that the drillings and the recess in the sprockets are aligned with the drillings in the cylinder head and the pump housing.

8 A special pin will now be required to time the camshaft sprocket and the injection pump sprocket. If a CAV pump is fitted, then pins number 23-019 will time both sprockets, but if a Bosch pump is fitted, pin number 23-029 will be required for the pump sprocket, and one pin 23-019 for the camshaft sprocket.

9 Twist drills will serve as substitute pins, but they must be in unworn condition, and be long enough to enter the holes in the pump or cylinder head. A drill of 9.5 mm diameter will be required for the Bosch type pump, plus one of 6.0 mm diameter for the camshaft sprocket.

10 Two drills of 6.0 mm diameter will be required for the CAV type pump (one for the camshaft sprocket and one for the pump).

11 Insert the appropriate timing pins (see illustrations).

12 Screw in the TDC setting pin referred to in

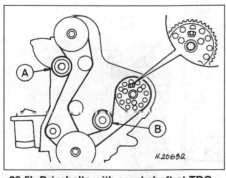

29.5b Drivebelts with crankshaft at TDC - Nos 1 and 4 pistons

A Camshaft drivebelt tensioner
B Fuel injection pump drivebelt tensioner

29.11a Fuel pump sprocket timing "pin"

29.11b Camshaft sprocket timing "pin"

1

29.12a TDC pin hole plug

29.12b Screwing in the TDC setting pin

Chapter 3. Make sure that the crankshaft is in contact with the timing pin **(see illustrations)**.

Fitting and tensioning

13 Fit the new injection pump drivebelt so that it is taut between the crankshaft and pump sprockets, and the directional arrows are pointing the correct way.

14 Slacken the injection pump sprocket bolts half a turn, and also slacken the belt tensioner bolts half a turn. Allow the belt tensioner to snap against the belt. Retighten all the slackened bolts, but make sure that the bolts are not at the ends of their slots, otherwise any further adjustment would be impossible.

15 Fit the new camshaft drivebelt, with the directional arrows correct for normal crankshaft rotational directional. The belt should be slack on the tensioner side and taut between sprockets.

16 Slacken the camshaft sprocket bolts and the tensioner bolts half a turn. Allow the tensioner to snap against the belt.

17 Retighten all slackened bolts. Remove all the timing pins and turn the crankshaft through two revolutions in the normal direction of rotation until the slot in the injection pump sprocket is at the highest point (12 o'clock).

18 Now turn the crankshaft anti-clockwise until the slot in the injection pump sprocket is at the 11 o'clock position.

19 Screw in the TDC setting pin.

20 Slowly turn the crankshaft clockwise until the crankshaft contacts the timing pin.

21 Insert the timing pins in the camshaft and the injection pump sprockets.

22 Slacken the bolts (through half a turn) that secure the camshaft and injection pump sprockets and the belt tensioners.

23 Depress both drivebelts on the taut side opposite to the tensioners, and then release them.

24 Retighten all slackened bolts.

25 Remove all timing pins and screw in the TDC pin hole plug.

26 Refit the belt covers.

27 Refit and tension the alternator drivebelt, then refit all components removed for better access.

28 Reconnect the battery.

Every 50 000 miles

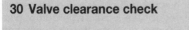

30 Valve clearance check

1 Release the breather hoses and remove the camshaft cover. It is secured by 3 bolts. When the camshaft cover is removed to reveal an oil baffle (**(see illustration)**, unscrew the retaining nuts and withdraw the baffle, then refit the nuts (which also secure the camshaft bearing caps), tightening them to the specified torque wrench setting. Recover the washers and the reinforcing strips, noting their locations. Remove the gasket, sealing strip and plug.

Obtain new ones for reassembly if necessary.

2 Turn the engine in the normal direction of rotation until two cam lobes for any one cylinder are pointing upwards (relative to the engine) at the same angle. It is permissible to "bounce" the engine round on the starter motor for this procedure, but disconnect the fuel shut-off solenoid first **(see illustration)**.

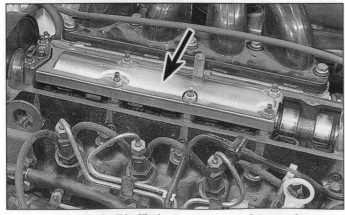

30.1 Camshaft oil baffle (arrowed) fitted to later engines

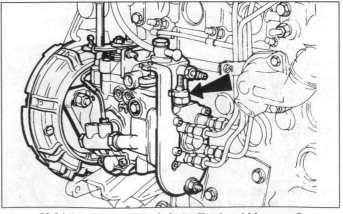

30.2 Injection pump fuel shut-off solenoid (arrowed)

30.3 Measuring a valve clearance

3 Measure the clearance between the bases of the two cam lobes and the underlying shims using feeler blades **(see illustration)**. Record the thickness of blade(s) required to give a firm sliding fit. The desired clearances are given in the Specifications. Note that the clearances for inlet and exhaust valves are different. From the pulley end of the engine, the valve sequence is:

I-E-I-E-I-E-I-E

4 Unscrew the retaining nuts, refit the baffle, then tighten all camshaft bearing cap nuts to the specified torque wrench setting and refit the camshaft cover

5 If adjustment is required, refer to Chapter 2.

Every 3 years (regardless of mileage)

31 Brake fluid renewal

The procedure is similar to that for the bleeding of the hydraulic system as described in Chapter 9, except that the brake fluid reservoir should be emptied by syphoning, and allowance should be made for the old fluid to be removed from the circuit when bleeding a section of the circuit.

1

Notes

Chapter 2
Engine

Contents

2

Degrees of difficulty

Easy, suitable for novice with little experience	**Fairly easy,** suitable for beginner with some experience	**Fairly difficult,** suitable for competent DIY mechanic	**Difficult,** suitable for experienced DIY mechanic	**Very difficult,** suitable for expert DIY or professional

Specifications

General

Engine type	Four-cylinder in-line, four-stroke, overhead camshaft, compression ignition, fitted with turbocharger (TCI)
Designation	RFM, RFN
Bore and stroke (nominal)	82.5 x 82.0 mm
Cubic capacity	1753 cc
Compression ratio	21.5 : 1
Compression pressure (at starter motor cranking speed)	28 to 34 bar (406 to 493 lbf/in²)
Maximum power (DIN):	
RFD, RFK	66 kW (90 PS) @ 4500 rpm
RFM, RFN	65 kW (88 PS) @ 4500 rpm
Maximum torque (DIN):	
RFD, RFK	180 Nm (132 lbf ft) @ 2000 rpm
RFM, RFN	178 Nm (130 lbf ft) @ 2000 rpm
Firing order	1 - 3 - 4 - 2 (No 1 at pulley end)

Note: RTG, RTH, RFK and RFN engines are fitted with catalytic converters

Cylinder block

Cylinder bore diameter:
Class A	82.500 to 82.515 mm
Class B	82.515 to 82.530 mm
Class C	82.660 to 82.675 mm
Class D	82.675 to 82.690 mm
Class E (first rebore)	83.000 to 83.015 mm
Class F (second rebore)	83.500 to 83.515 mm

Crankshaft

Main bearing journal diameter:
Standard	53.970 to 53.990 mm
Undersize (0.25 mm)	53.720 to 53.740 mm
Undersize (0.50 mm)	53.470 to 53.490 mm
Main bearing clearance	0.015 to 0.062 mm

Big-end bearing journal diameter:
Standard	48.970 to 48.990 mm
Undersize (0.25 mm)	48.720 to 48.740 mm
Undersize (0.50 mm)	48.470 to 48.490 mm
Big-end bearing clearance	0.016 to 0.074 mm
Crankshaft end float	0.14 to 0.37 mm
Connecting rod to crank web axial clearance	0.125 to 0.375 mm
Torque needed to rotate fitted crankshaft (without connecting rods or pistons)	10 Nm (7 lbf ft) max

Connecting rods

Big-end bore diameter	52.000 to 52.020 mm
Small-end bore diameter (with bush)	26.012 to 26.020 mm

Rod length:
Class A	129.880 to 129.940 mm
Class B	129.941 to 130.000 mm
Class C	130.001 to 130.060 mm
Class D	130.052 to 130.120 mm

Pistons

Diameter (measured at 90° to gudgeon pin bore):
Class A	82.461 to 82.479 mm
Class B	82.476 to 82.494 mm
Class C	82.621 to 82.639 mm
Class D	82.636 to 82.654 mm
Class E (first rebore)	82.961 to 82.979 mm
Class F (second rebore)	83.461 to 83.479 mm
Clearance in bore (new)	0.021 to 0.054 mm
Piston protrusion at TDC	0.500 to 0.840 mm
Gudgeon pin diameter	25.996 to 26.000 mm

Piston rings

Clearance in groove:
Top compression	0.090 to 0.122 mm
Second compression	0.070 to 0.102 mm
Oil control	0.050 to 0.082 mm

End gap (fitted):
Top compression	0.350 to 0.500 mm
Second compression	0.350 to 0.500 mm
Oil control	0.250 to 0.580 mm

Camshaft

Cam lift:
Inlet	9.0 mm
Exhaust	10.0 mm
Endfloat	0.100 to 0.240 mm
Bearing journal diameter	27.960 to 27.980 mm
Bearing clearance	0.016 to 0.075 mm

Valve timing

Inlet opens	6° BTDC
Inlet closes	32° ABDC
Exhaust opens	57° BTDC
Exhaust closes	7° ATDC

Valve clearances (cold) .... See Chapter 1 Specifications

Valves

Length:
Inlet .... 107.05 to 107.15 mm
Exhaust .... 109.15 to 109.25 mm
Head diameter:
Inlet .... 36.40 to 36.60 mm
Exhaust .... 31.90 to 32.10 mm
Stem diameter:
Standard:
Inlet .... 7.82 to 7.97 mm
Exhaust .... 7.81 to 7.96 mm
First oversize:
Inlet .... 8.02 to 8.17 mm
Exhaust .... 8.01 to 8.16 mm
Second oversize:
Inlet .... 8.22 to 8.37 mm
Exhaust .... 8.21 to 8.36 mm

Tappet diameter:

Standard .... 34.950 to 34.975 mm
Oversize .... 35.450 to 35.475 mm
Shim thicknesses available .... 3.00 to 4.75 mm in increments of 0.05 mm
Valve spring free length .... 43 mm approx.

Cylinder head gasket

Thickness identification:
Standard bores .... 2 to 4 teeth
Oversize bores .... 2 to 4 holes
Selection according to piston protrusion:
0.500 to 0.680 mm .... 2 teeth or holes
0.681 to 0.740 mm .... 3 teeth or holes
0.741 to 0.840 mm .... 4 teeth or holes

Cylinder head

Distortion limit .... 0.08 mm overall
Camshaft bearing bore diameter:
Standard .... 30.500 to 30.525 mm
Oversize .... 30.575 to 30.600 mm
Swirl chamber projection .... 0.000 to 0.061 mm
Swirl chamber seat dimensions:
Standard:
Diameter A .... 31.250 to 31.280 mm
Diameter B .... 27.530 to 27.660 mm
Depth C .... 4.938 to 5.034 mm
Oversize:
Diameter A .... 31.550 to 31.580 mm
Diameter B .... 27.830 to 27.960 mm
Depth C .... 5.233 to 5.284 mm
Valve seat dimensions:
Standard:
Diameter A (inlet) .... 38.000 to 38.003 mm
Depth B (inlet) .... 8.300 to 8.500 mm
Diameter A (exhaust) .... 33.000 to 33.030 mm
Depth B (exhaust) .... 8.800 to 9.000 mm
Class A (oversize):
Diameter A (inlet) .... 38.200 to 38.230 mm
Depth B (inlet) .... 8.600 to 8.800 mm
Diameter A (exhaust) .... 32.200 to 33.230 mm
Depth B (exhaust) .... 9.100 to 9.300 mm
Second oversize:
Diameter A inlet .... 38.400 to 38.430 mm
Depth B inlet .... 8.900 to 9.100 mm
Diameter A exhaust .... 33.400 to 33.430 mm
Depth B exhaust .... 9.400 to 9.600 mm
Valve tappet bore diameter:
Standard .... 35.000 to 35.030 mm
Oversize .... 35.500 to 35.530 mm

2

Cylinder head (continued)

Valve guide bore diameter:
Standard . . . . 8.000 to 8.025 mm
First oversize . . . . 8.263 to 8.288 mm
Second oversize . . . . 8.463 to 8.488 mm
Note: For details of above diameters, depths and dimensions A, B and C, see Chapter 3, Part A.

Lubrication system

Oil type/specification/capacity . . . . Refer to *"Lubricants, fluids and capacities"*
Oil pressure:
At 750 rpm . . . . 0.75 bar (11 lbf/in²)
At 2000 rpm . . . . 1.50 bar (22 lbf/in²)
Oil pressure relief valve setting . . . . 2.0 to 4.0 bar
Oil pump inner-to-outer rotor maximum clearance . . . . 0.174 mm

Coolant pump

Type . . . . Centrifugal
Drive . . . . From back of camshaft drivebelt

Thermostat

Type . . . . Wax
Opening commences . . . . 85° to 89° (185° to 192°F)
Fully open temperature . . . . 102°C (216°F)

Alternator drivebelt

Type . . . . Flat "polyvee" belt from crankshaft

	New	Used
Tension (deflection at centre of belt's longest run)	1 to 2 mm	2 to 4 mm

Power-assisted steering pump drivebelt

Type . . . . Flat "polyvee" belt from crankshaft

	New	Used
Tension (deflection at centre of belt's longest run)	1 to 2 mm	2 to 4 mm

Air conditioning compressor drivebelt

Type . . . . Flat "polyvee" belt from crankshaft

	New	Used
Tension (deflection at centre of belt's longest run)	1 to 2 mm	2 to 4 mm

Note - all engines: *A used drivebelt (V or "polyvee" type) is defined as one that has been run for at least 10 minutes.*

Torque wrench settings

	Nm	lbf ft
Cylinder head		
Cylinder head cover	5	4
Cylinder head bolts (Imperial thread and hexagonal head):		
Stage 1	30	22
Stage 2	92	68
Stage 3 (wait at least two minutes and then angle-tighten)	90°	90°
Cylinder head bolts (M12 and Torx T70 head):		
Stage 1	10	7
Stage 2	100	74
Stage 3 (after waiting 3 minutes):		
a)	Unscrew number 1 bolt 180°	
b)	Tighten number 1 bolt to 70 Nm (52 lbf ft)	
c)	Further tighten the number 1 bolt 120°	
Stage 4	Repeat stage three with each of the remaining bolts in sequence	
Camshaft		
Camshaft cover	4	3
Camshaft bearing cap bolts	23	17
Camshaft oil baffle	20	15
Camshaft sprocket bolts	9	7
Belt idler pulley	45	33
Tensioner to engine bolts	9	7
Tensioner clamp bolt	50	37
Belt cover spacer stud-to-coolant pump	6 to 8	4 to 6
Belt rear cover to cylinder block bolt	24	18
Belt front cover bolts	8	5

Torque wrench settings (continued)

	Nm	lbf ft
Connecting rods		
Big-end bearing cap bolts:		
Stage 1	25	18
Stage 2 (angle-tighten)	60°	60°
Stage 3 (angle-tighten)	20°	20°
Crankshaft		
Main bearing cap bolts:		
Stage 1	27	20
Stage 2 (angle-tighten)	75°	75°
Rear oil seal carrier	20	15
Crankshaft pulley vibration damper centre bolt		
a)	150	111
b)	Unscrew 90°	
c)	120	89
d)	Further tighten 60°	
Auxiliary shaft		
Thrustplate bolts	9	7
Oil seal carrier bolts	23	17
Sprocket bolt	45	33
Flywheel/Clutch		
Flywheel bolts:		
Stage 1	18	13
Stage 2 (angle-tighten)	45°	45°
Stage 3 (angle-tighten)	45°	45°
Clutch pressure plate to flywheel	25 to 34	18 to 25
Oil system components		
Oil pump	25	18
Oil pick-up pipe bracket	22	16
Oil dipstick tube	10	7
Sump pan bolts	11	8
Oil drain plug	25	18
Cooling system components		
Thermostat housing to cylinder head	22	16
Thermostat housing to vacuum line bracket	9	7
Coolant pump bolts	25	18
Coolant pipe to cylinder block	25	18
Radiator bracket to subframe bolt (air conditioning only)	10	7
Power steering components		
Steering gear to subframe	130	96
For pump settings refer to Chapter 10		
Air conditioning components		
Compressor mounting nuts	25	18
Condenser to radiator bolt	7	5
Dehydrator bolts	7	5
Other engine components		
Engine front plate	24	18
TDC timing pin plug	24	18
Main earth lead to transmission	40	30
Subframe to body	130	96
Left-hand engine mounting	83	62
Right-hand engine mounting bracket to engine	83	62
Engine mounting to bracket	83	62
Rear engine roll restrictor bracket	84	62
Front and rear engine roll restrictors to subframe	48	36
Front and rear engine roll restrictor centre bolts	120	89
Front axle driveshaft bracket bolts	48	36
Lifting eye to engine mounting/vacuum pump bracket	23	17
Gearchange rod stabiliser to engine roll restrictor	55	41
Lower suspension arm balljoint to spindle carrier	83	62
Track rod end balljoint nut	26	19
Stabiliser bar link rod to suspension strut	47	35

Torque wrench settings (continued)

	Nm	lbf ft
Gearchange linkage to body	44	33
Gearchange rod to transmission	23	17
Gearchange rod clamp bolt	16	12
Engine/transmission earth lead flange bolt	40	30
Hose/cable bracket to lifting eye	23	17
Driveshaft centre bearing bolts	27	20
Front exhaust pipe nuts	40	30
Alternator mounting bracket to engine bolts	42	31
Alternator bolts (front)	50	37
Alternator bolt (rear)	24	18
Oil cooler bracket to engine bolts	25	18

1 General information and modifications

General information

Although essentially an increased-capacity version of the 1.6 litre unit, the 1.8 litre engine has several major differences which are as follows:

a) Changed dimensions and tolerances - see Specifications.

b) The cylinder bore diameters are increased, and the undersides of the pistons are cooled by oil jets.

c) The oil pump is mounted externally, and is driven by an auxiliary shaft.

d) Two toothed drivebelts are used, one to drive the fuel injection pump and the other to drive the camshaft, the oil pump auxiliary shaft and the coolant pump.

e) The inlet manifold comprises an upper moulded plastic section bolted to a cast aluminium alloy lower section.

f) The engine mountings have been designed to reduce vibration and the air cleaner is remotely-sited from the engine.

Modifications

Some modifications have been made to the 1.8 litre engine since its introduction and these include the following:

a) The sump pan is now cast in aluminium and is bolted to the clutch housing at its transmission end

b) An oil baffle is now fitted above the camshaft to improve lubrication

c) Cylinder head bolts modified from Imperial thread with hexagonal head to metric thread with Torx head. The tightening sequence differs according to bolt type (see Specifications)

d) An Exhaust Gas Recirculation (EGR) system is fitted to later engines

e) Both the camshaft and the fuel injection pump drivebelts must be renewed as a matter of course at the specified intervals - see Chapter 1

f) Depending on the exact date of manufacture of the vehicle, a modified camshaft sprocket may be available to prevent premature wear (and perhaps breakage) of the camshaft drivebelt. Whenever the camshaft drivebelt cover is removed, check whether the sprocket has any red paint marks on it. If no marks are found it may be necessary to replace the sprocket with the modified item. Any Ford dealer will be able to identify exactly the vehicle's date of manufacture and to decide accordingly whether a modified sprocket is required

g) The dust shield at the bottom of the camshaft drivebelt cover has been modified to improve its dust-excluding properties so preventing premature wear (and perhaps breakage) of the camshaft drivebelt. Whenever the cover is removed check the dust shield with reference to the accompanying illustration (see illustration). If it is of the old type, measure and note the location of the retaining screws inside the slots, remove the shield and use a small saw to cut away the drivebelt cover as shown (see illustration). Obtain a new-type dust shield and fit it to the cover using the original screws at the points noted before removal.

h) If it is ever suspected that any of the pistons have contacted their respective valves (usually as a result of camshaft drivebelt slipping or breakage), be particularly careful to check the pistons for indentations on their crowns and for signs of scuffing or other damage to their lands or skirts, the piston rings and cylinder bores for signs of scuffing and the valves for signs of bending. Check carefully all these points and renew any component that is thought to have been damaged before the engine is reassembled, or poor engine performance, excessive smoke emission and oil consumption, higher than normal noise levels and eventual piston seizure may result. Note that the above procedure will require a full engine strip and, possibly, a full overhaul; this must be carried out to ensure that the engine's future reliability, economy and performance

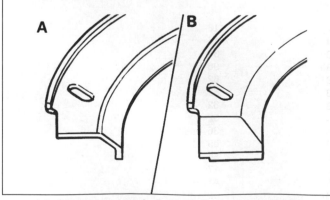

1.0a Identifying camshaft drivebelt cover dust shields

A Old type   B New type

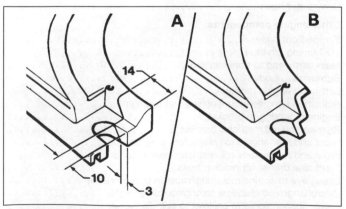

1.0b Modify camshaft drivebelt cover to accept new-type dust shield

A Area to be cut away - dimensions in mm   B The cover modified

2 Major operations possible with the engine in the vehicle

1 The cylinder head and sump can both be removed from the engine *in situ*; the pistons and connecting rods can therefore be removed also.

2 Any operation which involves slackening the crankshaft pulley bolt cannot be carried out with the engine in place unless the necessary special tools are purchased or made.

3 Subject to undoing the pulley bolt, the timing cover, timing case and oil pump can all be removed with the engine installed. It must be said that access is not good and the procedures are lengthy.

4 All the engine oil seals can be dealt with in situ; some are easier than others.

5 The engine must be removed for attention to the crankshaft, main bearings and cylinder block.

6 In practice it will probably be quicker and more satisfactory to remove the engine for most major tasks. Refer to following Sections 3 to 19 for those operations which can be carried out with the engine in the vehicle.

3 Engine oil and oil filter - renewal

Refer to Section 3, Chapter 1.

4 Auxiliary drivebelt - inspection, renewal and adjustment

Note: *The auxiliary drivebelts are somewhat inaccessible. If adjustment is necessary it will have to be done from beneath the vehicle, so start by driving the front of the car up onto ramps or over an inspection pit. Apply the handbrake and securely chock the rear wheels.*

General

1 The alternator is driven from the crankshaft pulley by a flat "polyvee" type of drivebelt.

2 Alternator drivebelt adjustment is by means of a tensioner pulley adjuster screw.

3 Pump drivebelt adjustment is by means of a screw adjuster.

4 On models with air conditioning, the compressor is mounted on a bracket that is bolted to the cylinder block and driven from the crankshaft pulley by a flat "polyvee" drivebelt. Drivebelt adjustment is by a tensioner pulley arrangement.

Inspection

5 Refer to Section 14, Chapter 1.

Preliminary operations

6 Before any drivebelt servicing operations can be undertaken, adequate access must first be gained by jacking up the front of the vehicle and supporting it on axle stands (see "*Jacking and vehicle support*"). Disconnect the battery earth (negative) lead.

7 The splash shield and/or cover protecting each drivebelt and its adjuster components must be removed. There should be either a cover immediately over the alternator pulley, or a splash shield fitted to the right-hand end of the engine or to the inner wing panel. On some models, both cover and shield(s) may be fitted

8 The method of drivebelt adjustment is easily identifiable from the accompanying illustrations.

Renewal

Alternator

9 Remove the belt shield and release the tensioner pulley adjuster screw until the drivebelt is slack enough to be slipped off the pulleys.

10 Fit the new drivebelt, ensuring that it is routed correctly and settled in the pulley grooves, then tension the drivebelt.

11 After adjustment, refit any disturbed covers.

Power-assisted steering pump

12 Remove the pump drivebelt cover and loosen the pump mounting bolt.

13 Loosen the pump clamp bolt and rotate the adjuster screw to detension the drivebelt until it can be slipped off the pulleys **(see illustration)**.

14 Fit the new drivebelt, ensuring that it is settled in the pulley grooves, then tension the drivebelt.

15 After adjustment, refit the belt cover.

Air conditioning compressor

16 With the appropriate shield removed, release the clamp bolt to detension the compressor drivebelt until it can be slipped off the pulleys **(see illustration)**.

17 Fit the new drivebelt, ensuring that it is settled in the pulley grooves, then tension the drivebelt the specified amount.

18 After adjustment, refit any disturbed shield.

Adjustment

Alternator

19 To tension the drivebelt, rotate the tensioner pulley adjuster screw until the following tension is obtained **(see illustration)**.
Used drivebelt - 2 to 4 mm deflection at centre of belt's longest run
New drivebelt - 1 to 2 mm deflection at centre of belt's longest run

20 On completion of tensioning, tighten the pulley securing screw to the specified torque setting.

Power-assisted steering pump

21 To tension the drivebelt, rotate the tensioner screw until the following tension is obtained - see illustration 4.13.
Used drivebelt - 2 to 4 mm deflection at centre of belt's longest run
New drivebelt - 1 to 2 mm deflection at centre of belt's longest run

22 On completion of tensioning, tighten the tensioner screw, clamp bolt and pump mounting bolt to the specified torque setting.

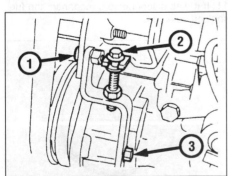

4.13 Power steering pump drivebelt adjuster components

1 Clamp bolt
2 Adjuster screw
3 Tensioner retaining bolt

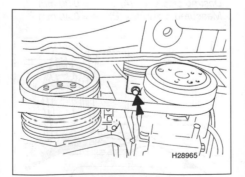

4.16 Detension the air conditioning compressor drivebelt by releasing the clamp bolt (arrowed)

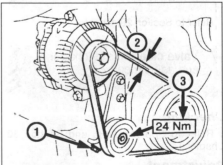

4.19 Tensioning the alternator drivebelt

1 Tensioner pulley adjuster screw
2 Drivebelt deflection
3 Tensioner pulley securing screw

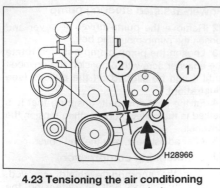

4.23 Tensioning the air conditioning compressor drivebelt

1 *Tensioner pulley*
2 *Drivebelt deflection*

Air conditioning compressor

23 To tension the drivebelt, rotate the tensioner pulley adjuster screw until the following tension is obtained **(see illustration)**.

Used drivebelt - 2 to 4 mm deflection at centre of belt's longest run
New drivebelt - 1 to 2 mm deflection at centre of belt's longest run

24 On completion of tensioning, tighten the pulley screw to the specified torque setting.

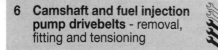

5 Camshaft and fuel injection pump drivebelts - inspection

Disconnect the battery earth (negative) lead.

With their covers removed, inspect each belt for cracks, fraying and damage to the teeth. Pay particular attention to the roots of the teeth. A belt which is damaged must be renewed. An oil-soaked belt must also be renewed, and the source of oil contamination dealt with. Similarly, a drivebelt must be renewed if flooded with diesel fuel.

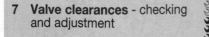

6 Camshaft and fuel injection pump drivebelts - removal, fitting and tensioning

Refer to Section 29, Chapter 1.

7 Valve clearances - checking and adjustment

Checking

1 Refer to *Specifications* and Section 30, Chapter 1.

Adjustment

2 If adjustment is required, turn the engine in the normal direction of rotation through approximately 90°, to bring the pistons to mid-stroke. If this is not done, the pistons at

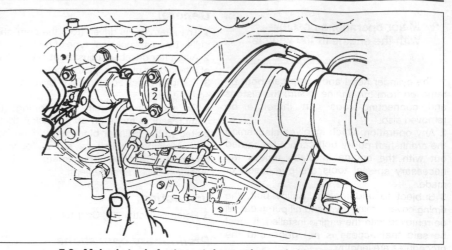

7.2a Maker's tools for tappet depression and shim extraction

TDC will prevent the tappets being depressed, and damage may result. Depress the tappets and then either shim can be withdrawn if the peak of the cam does not prevent access. The Ford tools for this operation are Nos 21-106 and 21-107, but with care and patience a C-spanner or screwdriver can be used to depress the tappet and the shim can be flicked out with a small screwdriver **(see illustrations)**.

3 If the valve clearance was too small, a thinner shim must be fitted. If the clearance was too large, a thicker shim must be fitted. The thickness of the shim (in mm) is engraved on the side facing away from the camshaft **(see illustration)**. If the marking is missing or illegible, a micrometer will be needed to establish shim thickness.

4 When the shim thickness and the valve clearance are known, the required thickness of the new shim can be calculated as follows:

Sample calculation - clearance too small

Desired clearance (A)   = 0.50 mm
Measured clearance (B)   = 0.35 mm
Shim thickness found (C)   = 3.95 mm
Shim thickness required (D) = C + B - A
= 3.80 mm

Sample calculation - clearance too large

Desired clearance (A)   = 0.30 mm
Measured clearance (B)   = 0.40 mm

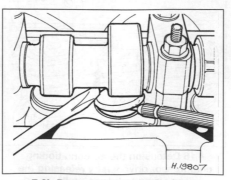

7.2b Depressing a tappet with a screwdriver and removing a shim

Shim thickness found (C)   = 4.05 mm
Shim thickness required (D) = C + B - A
= 4.15 mm

5 With the correct shim fitted, release the tappet depressing tool. Turn the engine back so that the cam lobes are again pointing upwards and check that the clearance is now correct.

6 Repeat the process for the remaining valves, turning the engine each time to bring a pair of cam lobes upwards.

7 It will be helpful for future adjustment if a record is kept of the thickness of shim fitted at each position. The shims required can be purchased in advance once the clearances and the existing shim thicknesses are known.

8 It is permissible to interchange shims between tappets to achieve the correct clearances but it is not advisable to turn the camshaft with any shims removed, since there is a risk that the cam lobe will jam in the empty tappet.

9 When all the clearances are correct, refit the camshaft cover, using a new gasket etc. if necessary. Fit the bolts with washers and reinforcing strips. Tighten the bolts progressively to the specified torque.

10 Secure the breather hoses.

11 If it was disconnected, reconnect the fuel shut-off solenoid.

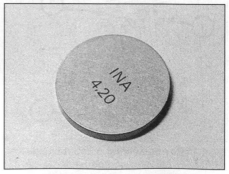

7.3 Shim thickness marking

8.2 Removing the camshaft sprocket bolt and washer

8.3a Undoing the drivebelt tensioner bolt

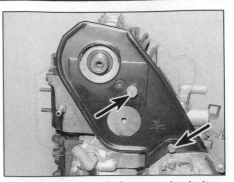

8.3b Drivebelt backplate securing bolts (arrowed)

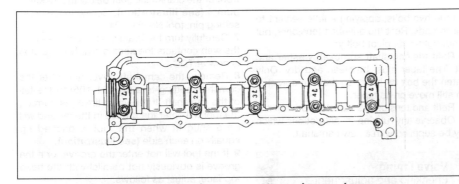

8.4 Camshaft bearing caps - note numbers and arrows

8.8 Fitting a camshaft lower bearing shell

8 Camshaft - removal and refitting

Removal

1 Remove the camshaft drivebelt.

2 Remove the camshaft sprocket bolt and washer **(see illustration)**. Release the sprocket from its taper by tapping it with a wooden or plastic mallet and remove it.

3 Remove the drivebelt tensioner (one Torx bolt) and the drivebelt backplate (secured by two hex head bolts) **(see illustrations)**.

4 Undo the nuts of bearing caps Nos 2 and 4. Remove these caps and their shells. Keep the

shells with their caps if they are to be re-used. Note that the caps are numbered and carry an arrow pointing to the pulley end of the engine **(see illustration)**.

5 Slacken the nuts of bearing caps Nos 1, 3 and 5 one turn at a time, working from end to end so that the camshaft is released gradually. Remove the bearing caps and shells, again keeping the shells with their caps if necessary.

6 Lift out the camshaft with its oil seal. Recover the lower half bearing shells, keeping them in order if necessary.

7 If purchasing new bearing shells, note that either standard or oversize outside diameter shells may have been fitted in production. Oversize shells are identified by a green mark.

Refitting

8 Commence refitting by placing the lower half bearing shells (the ones with the oil holes) in position **(see illustration)**. Lubricate the shells.

9 Make sure that all tappets, shims and the vacuum pump plunger are in place. Remove the old oil seal, if not already done, and place the camshaft on the lower half bearings **(see illustration)**. Position the camshaft with the groove in the tail parallel with the head top face and the larger semi-circular segment uppermost **(see illustration)**.

10 Clean any old sealant from No. 1 bearing cap. Fit the upper bearing shells to their caps and lubricate them **(see illustration)**. Coat the

2

8.9a Fitting the camshaft

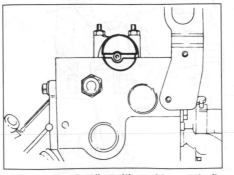

8.9b Camshaft tail position with camshaft correctly fitted

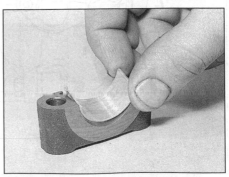

8.10a Fitting a camshaft upper bearing shell to its cap

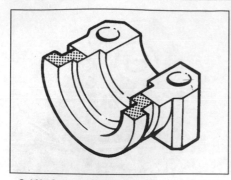

8.10b Camshaft No 1 bearing cap - coat shaded area with sealant

8.13 Tightening a camshaft bearing cap nut

mating surfaces of No. 1 cap with sealant (to Ford spec SPM-41G-9112 F/G) in the areas shown **(see illustration)**.

11 Fit bearing caps and shells Nos 1, 3 and 5, making sure that they are the right way round. Tighten the cap nuts, half a turn at a time, in the sequence No. 3 - No. 1 - No. 5. Carry on until the caps are seated.

12 Fit caps and shells Nos 2 and 4, tapping them down with a mallet if necessary to seat them. Fit their nuts.

13 Tighten all the bearing cap nuts to the specified torque **(see illustration)**.

14 Insert the camshaft setting tool into the groove on the tail so that it is a snug fit. See Section 9 for details.

15 Fit a new oil seal to the camshaft nose as described in Section 14. There is a temptation to fit this seal to the camshaft before it is installed, but to do so risks pinching or cocking the seal as the bearing cap is tightened.

16 Lubricate the cam lobes liberally with engine oil, or with special cam lube if supplied with a new camshaft.

17 Refit the drivebelt backplate. Secure it

with the two bolts, applying a little sealant to their threads. Refit the drivebelt tensioner, but do not tighten its pivot bolt yet.

18 Refit the camshaft sprocket, washer and bolt. The taper must be clean and dry. Only tighten the bolt by hand, so that the sprocket can still move on its taper.

19 Refit and tension the camshaft drivebelt.

20 Observe any running-in instructions which may be supplied with a new camshaft.

9 Valve timing - checking and adjustment

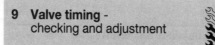

1 Valve timing is more complicated than on similar petrol engines because there are no camshaft or crankshaft timing marks. The camshaft sprocket is not keyed to the shaft so no permanent mark can be made there. Two special tools must therefore be made or bought.

2 Ensure that the injection pump timing is correct before the valve timing is checked. See Chapter 4.

3 There is one pair of timing marks on the injection pump sprocket and timing cover. When the pump timing is correct, these marks are aligned at 50° BTDC, No. 1 on compression.

4 If the valve timing has been lost, be careful when turning the crankshaft and camshaft in case piston/valve contact occurs.

Using Ford special tools

5 Remove the camshaft drivebelt cover. Turn the crankshaft until the injection pump sprocket timing mark is aligned with the pointer on the timing case.

6 Remove the TDC setting hole plug from the front of the crankcase (just below the injection pump) **(see illustration)**. Screw in the TDC setting pin, tool No. 21-104.

7 Carefully turn the crankshaft clockwise until the web contacts the setting pin. No. 1 piston is now at TDC.

8 Remove the camshaft cover and offer the camshaft setting tool (No. 21-105) to the tail of the camshaft. If the valve timing is correct, the tool will enter the groove in the tail and will be a snug fit when the tool is packed up equally on each side **(see illustration)**.

9 If the tool will not enter the groove, or if the groove is obviously not parallel with the head top face, adjust as follows.

10 Counterhold the camshaft sprocket and slacken the sprocket bolt. Tap the sprocket with a wooden or plastic mallet if necessary to break the taper, so that the camshaft can turn independently of the sprocket.

11 Turn the camshaft until the setting tool is a snug fit in the tail. Restrain the camshaft sprocket and tighten the sprocket bolt to the specified torque.

12 Remove the special tools and refit the disturbed components.

Using home-made tools

13 The camshaft setting tool is easily improvised from a piece of angle iron. The piece seen here has dimensions 25 x 25 x 100 mm approx. and is 5 mm thick. It fits very well, with no need for packing up and no

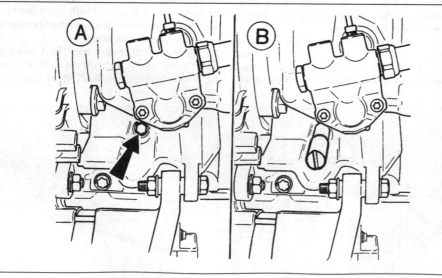

9.6 TDC setting hole plug (A - arrowed) and setting pin fitted (B)

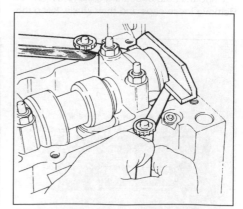

9.8 Making the camshaft setting tool fit by packing it up with feeler blades

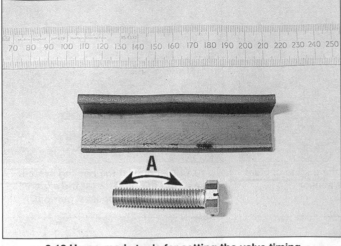

9.13 Home-made tools for setting the valve timing

A Highlighted portion of bolt may need grinding, to work (see text)

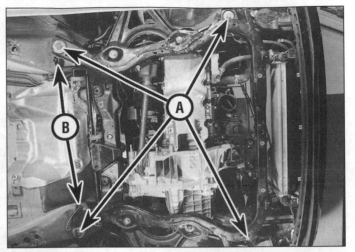

10.5a Tighten subframe mounting bolts (A) ensuring that alignment remains correct - Ford service tools (B) shown in use here . . .

perceptible play in the camshaft groove **(see illustration)**.

14 The TDC setting pin can be replaced by an M10 bolt, ground to a length (from the underside of the bolt head to the tip) of 47.5 mm. However, an ordinary bolt cannot be inserted without first removing the alternator bracket because there is insufficient clearance for the bolt head - therefore the bolt head must be ground down and a screw slot cut in it. Note that if difficulty is experienced in using the bolt, it may be necessary to grind down the first 36 mm of the threaded end of the bolt to a diameter of 6 mm.

15 Once the tools have been made, proceed as described in paragraphs 5 to 12.

10 Cylinder head -
removal and refitting

 Warning: Where a vehicle is fitted with an air conditioning system, do not disconnect the refrigerant hoses.

Removal

1 Disconnect the battery earth lead.

2 Raise the front of the vehicle and securely support it on axle stands (see *"Jacking and vehicle support"*).

3 Remove the engine undershield.

4 Refer to Chapter 1 and drain the engine coolant.

5 Ford recommend that the subframe is now checked for correct alignment on the underbody. Ford specify the use of service tool 15-097 (a pair of tapered guides with attachments to hold them in the subframe as it is refitted) for this task. However, since the working diameter of these tools is 20.40 mm, and since the corresponding aligning holes in the subframe and underbody are respectively 21 mm and 22 mm in diameter, there is a significant in-built tolerance possible in subframe alignment, even if the correct tools are used. If these tools are not available, you can align the subframe by eye, centring the subframe aligning holes on those of the underbody. Alternatively, you can align the subframe using a tapered drift (such as a clutch-aligning tool) or even a deep socket spanner of suitable size **(see illustrations)**.

6 With the subframe aligned, remove the centre bolt of the engine front roll restrictor

10.5b . . . but alternative methods using ordinary hand tools can achieve acceptable alignment, with care

and detach the restrictor from the subframe by removing its two securing bolts **(see illustration)**.

7 It is now necessary to replace the front roll restrictor with Ford tool 21 172, as shown **(see illustration)**. This tool must fit without having to apply undue force, otherwise recheck the subframe alignment.

8 Remove the vibration damper splash shield from the wheel arch **(see illustration)**.

9 Lower the vehicle to the ground.

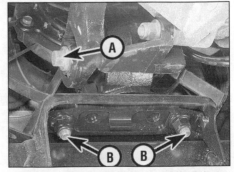

10.6 Remove the centre bolt (A) of the engine front roll restrictor, followed by the restrictor to subframe securing bolts (B)

10.7 Special tool required to hold engine/gearbox unit precisely, so that mountings can be tightened into correct position

10.8 Remove the vibration damper splash shield from the wheel arch - securing bolts (arrowed)

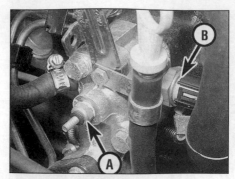

10.13a Disconnect the temperature gauge sender unit (A) and the cooling fan thermoswitch (B) . . .

10.13b . . . followed by the engine coolant temperature sensor

10.14 Disconnect the cooling system hoses from the radiator (A) the expansion tank (B) and the coolant pump (C)

10 Refer to Chapter 4, and remove the charge air cooler.

11 On early models, loosen the hose retaining clip and remove the air inlet system resonator by pulling it from its two retainers - see illustration, Section 17, Chapter 1.

12 On all models, disconnect the multiplug from the mass airflow (MAF) sensor. Loosen the two retaining clips and detach the sensor assembly. This operation may prove difficult due to resistance from the rubber retaining ring. Remove the air cleaner box by first releasing the rubber retaining band, releasing the box from the end bellows and pulling it from the base retaining spigots (see illustrations Chapters 1 and 4).

13 Disconnect the following electrical connectors **(see illustrations):**

a) *Temperature gauge sender unit plug*
b) *Cooling fan thermoswitch (CFS) multiplug*
c) *Engine coolant temperature (ECT) sensor multiplug*

14 Disconnect the cooling system hoses from the following components **(see illustration):**

a) *The radiator*
b) *The expansion tank*
c) *The coolant pump*

15 Release the hoses and cables from their retaining clip on the cylinder head and move them to one side. Remove the clip from the lifting eye and disconnect the fuel return line adjacent to it **(see illustration).**

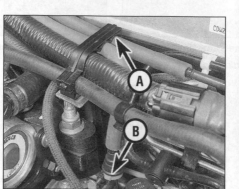

10.15 Release the hoses and cables from their retaining clip on the cylinder head (A) and disconnect the fuel return line adjacent to it (B)

16 Disconnect the fuel feed line to the injection pump (A) **(see illustration).**

17 Disconnect the fuel line to the fuel tank (B).

18 Disconnect the following electrical connectors to the cylinder head - **see illustration 9.16:**

a) *Oil pressure switch plug*
b) *Fuel heater multiplug*
c) *Glow plug feed*

19 Unscrew the vacuum pipe union from the vacuum pump and detach the pipe **(see illustration).**

20 Detach the oil return line from the vacuum pump.

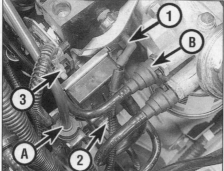

10.16 Disconnect the following fuel lines and electrical connectors

A *Fuel feed line to injection pump*
B *Fuel line to fuel tank*
1 *Oil pressure switch plug*
2 *Fuel heater multiplug*
3 *Glow plug feed*

21 Remove the oil dipstick tube bracket with cable bracket from the thermostat housing.

22 Unbolt and remove the thermostat housing - see Chapter 3.

23 Remove the crankcase ventilation system hoses from the camshaft cover **(see illustration).**

24 Disconnect the heater hose from the cylinder head (A) **(see illustration).**

25 Disconnect the vacuum hose from the EGR valve (B).

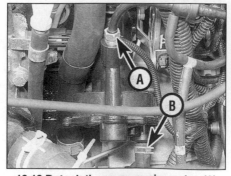

10.19 Detach the vacuum pipe union (A) and oil return line (B) from the vacuum pump

10.23 Remove the crankcase ventilation system hoses from the camshaft cover

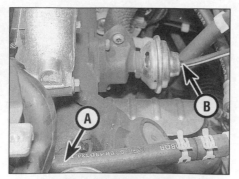

10.24 Disconnect the heater hose from the cylinder head (A) and the vacuum hose from the EGR valve (B)

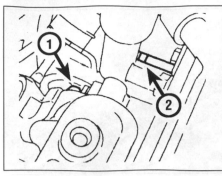

10.26 Disconnect the turbocharger oil feed hose (1) and vacuum hose (2)

10.28 Fit a lifting eye to the alternator retaining bolt (arrowed)

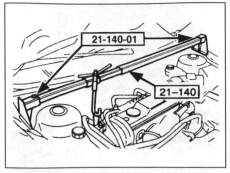

10.29 Fit the engine support bar and connect it to the lifting eye. Ensure the bar is placed under load by tightening down its lifting spindle

26 Disconnect the turbocharger oil feed hose and vacuum hose (see illustration).
27 Detach the cable bracket from the alternator and the expansion tank to cylinder head coolant hose.
28 To suspend the engine, first fit a lifting eye to the alternator retaining bolt shown (see illustration).
29 Fit the engine support bar and connect it to the lifting eye, ensuring that the bar is placed under load by tightening down its lifting spindle (see illustration).
30 Remove the two bolts retaining the cover of the power steering pump drivebelt. Remove the cover and loosen the pump mounting bolt (see illustration).

31 Loosen the power steering pump clamp bolt. Rotate the adjuster screw to de-tension the drivebelt and remove the tensioner from the front cover (see illustration).
32 Remove the pump drivebelt and the pump mounting bolt and lift the pump clear of the engine.
33 Remove the engine right-hand mounting bracket, noting that the self-locking nuts will have to be renewed (see illustration).
34 Where fitted, detach the lifting eye from the engine mounting/power steering pump bracket by removing its two retaining bolts (see illustration).
35 Disconnect the hose from the coolant pump to facilitate removal of the drivebelt

pulley from the fuel injection pump (see illustration).
36 Raise the front of the vehicle and securely support it on axle stands (see "Jacking and vehicle support").
37 Disconnect the exhaust pipe from the turbocharger.
38 Obtain a container in which to catch oil and position it beneath the turbocharger oil return line. Disconnect the oil line from the cylinder block (see illustration).
39 Detach the turbocharger to engine bracket.
40 Refer to Section 4 and remove the alternator drivebelt.

10.30 Remove the power steering pump drivebelt cover

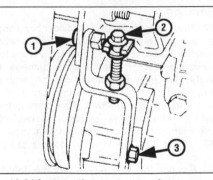

10.31 Loosen the power steering pump clamp bolt (1) rotate the adjuster screw to detension the drivebelt (2) and remove the tensioner from the front cover (3)

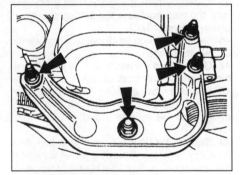

10.33 Remove the engine right-hand mounting bracket self-locking nuts (arrowed)

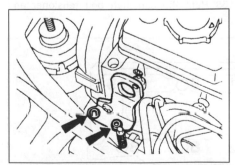

10.34 Detach the lifting eye from the engine mounting/power steering pump bracket by removing its two retaining bolts (arrowed)

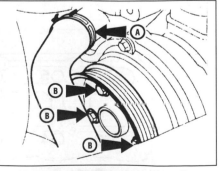

10.35 Disconnect the hose from the coolant pump (A) to facilitate removal of the drivebelt pulley bolts (B)

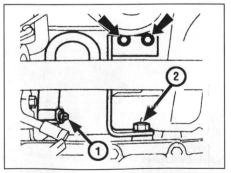

10.38 Disconnect the turbocharger oil return line (1) and detach the turbocharger to engine bracket (2)

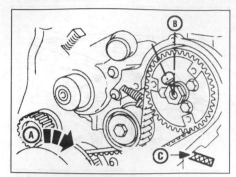

10.43 Turn the crankshaft in the direction of rotation until the injection pump sprocket timing mark is aligned with the pointer on the timing case (11 o'clock)

A *Crankshaft direction of rotation*
B *Injection pump sprocket timing mark*
C *TDC setting pin, tool No. 21-104.*

41 Remove the camshaft drivebelt lower cover.
42 Lower the vehicle and remove the camshaft drivebelt upper cover.
43 Turn the crankshaft in the direction of rotation until the injection pump sprocket timing mark is aligned with the pointer on the timing case (11 o'clock) **(see illustration)**.
44 Remove the TDC setting hole plug from the crankcase and screw in the TDC setting pin, tool No. 21-104.
45 Carefully turn the crankshaft clockwise until the web contacts the setting pin. No. 1 piston is now at TDC.
46 Release the belt tensioner and remove the camshaft drivebelt.
47 Unbolt and remove the camshaft belt tensioner and camshaft sprocket.
48 Remove the camshaft drivebelt idler sprocket and pull the drivebelt rear cover away from the cylinder head and camshaft end.
49 Detach the leak-off pipes and fuel lines from the injectors. Detach the fuel lines from the injection pump. Cap all openings to prevent the entry of dirt.
50 Remove the fuel injectors and heat shields from the cylinder head - see Chapter 4.
51 Refer to Chapter 5 and remove the glow plugs.

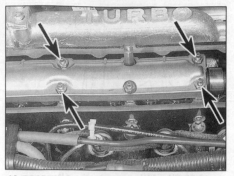

10.53 Unscrew the four nuts (arrowed) and remove the oil baffle

52 Unscrew the three bolts and take off the camshaft cover and gasket.
53 Unscrew the four nuts and remove the oil baffle **(see illustration)**.
54 Unscrew and remove the cylinder head bolts in the reverse sequence to tightening.
55 Remove the cylinder head assembly, either with the assistance of another person or by using lifting gear attached to the head lifting eyes.
56 Remove the cylinder head gasket which should be renewed. Note that three possible thicknesses of cylinder head gasket are available, depending on piston protrusion, the details of which are given in the *Specifications* of this Chapter.

Refitting

57 The mating faces of the cylinder head and block must be perfectly clean before the head is refitted. Also check the mating surfaces for nicks, deep scratches and other damage. If slight, they may be removed carefully with a file, but if excessive, machining may be the only alternative to renewal. If warpage of the cylinder head gasket surface is suspected, use a straight edge to check it for distortion.
58 Check that the locating dowels are in position in the cylinder block.
59 Position the new gasket over the dowels and onto the cylinder block surface so that the "TOP/OBEN" mark is uppermost and the identification teeth point to the front of the vehicle **(see illustrations)**.
60 Ensure that the pistons are not positioned

10.59a Head gasket fitted to block

at TDC and that all cylinder head bolt holes are free from oil.
61 Refit the cylinder head, locating it on the dowels and taking care not to damage the camshaft drivebelt rear cover.
62 Fit the cylinder head bolts dry (ie. do not oil their threads). Carefully enter each new bolt into its hole and screw it in by hand only, until finger-tight.
63 Working progressively and in the sequence shown **(see illustration)**, use first a torque wrench, then an ordinary socket extension bar and an angle gauge, to tighten the cylinder head bolts in the stages given in the *Specifications* Section of this Chapter. **Note:** *Once tightened correctly, following this procedure, the cylinder head bolts do not require check-tightening and must **not** be re-torqued.*
64 Refit the fuel injectors with new heat shields, tightening them to the specified torque wrench setting.
65 Reattach the leak-off pipes and fuel lines to the injectors and the fuel lines to the injection pump. Remember to remove all blanking material and tighten all connections to the specified torque wrench settings.
66 Refer to Chapter 5 and refit the glow plugs.
67 Position the drivebelt rear cover against the cylinder head. Refit the camshaft drivebelt idler sprocket, tightening its retaining bolt to the specified torque wrench setting.
68 Refit the camshaft belt tensioner and

10.59b Head gasket top marking

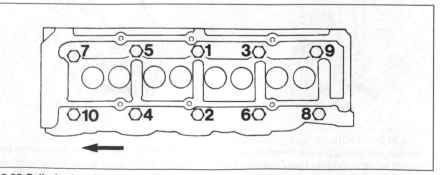

10.63 Cylinder head bolt tightening sequence. Arrow points to pulley end of engine

camshaft sprocket, tightening all fasteners to the specified torque wrench settings.

69 Refer to Section 9, Chapter 1. Align the camshaft and fuel injection pump sprockets and fit and tension the camshaft and pump drivebelts.

70 Referring to the appropriate Sections in Chapter 1 and this Chapter, check and adjust the valve clearances.

71 Refit the oil baffle, tightening its retaining nuts to the specified torque wrench setting.

72 Refit the camshaft cover with a new gasket and tighten its retaining bolts to the specified torque wrench setting.

73 Refit the camshaft drivebelt upper cover.

74 Raise the front of the vehicle and securely support it on axle stands (see "*Jacking and vehicle support*").

75 Refit the camshaft drivebelt lower cover.

76 Refer to Section 4 and refit and tension the alternator drivebelt.

77 Reattach the turbocharger to engine bracket, the turbocharger oil return line and the exhaust pipe to the turbocharger.

78 Lower the vehicle to the ground.

79 Refit the pulley to the fuel injection pump, tightening the bolts to the specified torque setting, and reconnect the hose to the coolant pump.

80 Refit the lifting eye to the engine mounting/power steering pump bracket, tightening the two bolts to the specified torque setting.

81 Refit the engine right-hand mounting bracket, tightening the four new self-locking nuts to the specified torque setting.

82 Refit the power steering pump tensioner to the front cover.

83 Refer to Chapter 10 and refit the power steering pump, tensioning its drivebelt and refitting its belt cover.

84 Remove the engine support bar and the lifting eye fitted to the alternator retaining bolt.

85 Reattach the cable bracket to the alternator.

86 Reconnect the following hoses:
a) *Expansion tank to cylinder head coolant hose*
b) *Turbocharger oil feed hose*
c) *Turbocharger vacuum hose*
d) *Vacuum hose to EGR valve*
e) *Heater hose to cylinder head*
f) *Crankcase ventilation system hoses to camshaft cover*

87 Refit the hose and cable retaining clip to the cylinder head lifting eye and reconnect the fuel return line adjacent to it.

88 Refit the thermostat housing to the cylinder head, using a new gasket and tightening its retaining bolts to the specified torque setting.

89 Refit the oil dipstick tube bracket with cable bracket, tightening the retaining bolt to the specified torque setting

90 Reattach the oil return line and vacuum pipe to the vacuum pump.

91 Reconnect the following electrical connectors to the cylinder head:
a) *Glow plug feed*
b) *Fuel heater multiplug*
c) *Oil pressure switch plug*

92 Reconnect the fuel line to the fuel tank and the fuel feed line to the injection pump.

93 Relocate the hoses and cables in their retaining clip on the cylinder head.

94 Reconnect the cooling system hoses to the following components:
a) *The coolant pump*
b) *The expansion tank*
c) *The radiator*

95 Reconnect the following electrical connectors:
a) *Engine coolant temperature (ECT) sensor multiplug*
b) *Cooling fan thermoswitch (CFS) multiplug*
c) *Temperature gauge sender unit multiplug*

96 Lightly grease the mating surface of the mass airflow (MAF) sensor rubber retaining ring and refit the sensor, reconnecting its multiplug.

97 Refit the air inlet system resonator.

98 Refer to Chapter 4, and refit the charge air cooler.

99 Raise the front of the vehicle and securely support it on axle stands (see "*Jacking and vehicle support*").

100 Remove Ford tool 21 172 and refit the engine front roll restrictor, securing it to the subframe first and then fitting the centre bolt. Tighten the retaining bolts to the specified torque settings.

101 Refit the vibration damper splash shield to the wheel arch.

102 Refit the engine coolant drain plug and the engine undershield.

103 Lower the vehicle to the ground.

104 Add coolant, engine oil and power steering fluid, as needed.

105 Reconnect the battery earth lead.

106 Carry out a final check to ensure that all cables and wiring looms are correctly routed, clear of any moving parts, and firmly secured.

107 Once the engine has been restarted and warmed-up to normal operating temperature, check all disturbed joints for signs of oil or coolant leakage.

108 Finally, a road test must be carried out to enable the EEC module to collect data.

11 Cylinder head - dismantling, overhaul and reassembly

Dismantling

1 With the head removed, remove the injectors and glow plugs (if not already done). Clean the accessible parts of the head, removing all oil and coolant. Take care not to damage the protruding valves.

2 Unbolt and remove the inlet and exhaust manifolds. Recover the gaskets.

3 Unbolt the vacuum pump. Slacken its bolts evenly until any tension is released. Recover the O-ring seal.

4 Remove camshaft bearing caps and shells Nos 2 and 4.

5 Slacken the nuts securing camshaft bearing caps Nos 1, 3 and 5 one turn at a time, working from end to end so that the camshaft is released gradually. Remove the caps and shells. Keep all the shells with their respective caps if they are to be re-used.

6 Lift out the camshaft with its oil seal. Recover the lower half bearing shells, keeping them in order too if they are to be re-used. Remove and discard the oil seal.

7 Remove the valve tappets and shims. Keep them in order in a segmented box or some similar arrangement.

8 Remove the vacuum pump operating plunger **(see illustration)**.

9 Unbolt and remove the lifting eyes.

10 Unscrew and remove the oil pressure switch **(see illustration)** and the coolant connector.

11 Using a valve spring compressor, depress one valve spring retainer to gain access to the collets. The valves are deeply recessed, so the end of the compressor may need to be extended with a tube or box section with a "window" for access. Remove the collets and release the compressor. Recover

11.8 Removing the vacuum pump operating plunger

11.10 Removing the oil pressure switch

11.11a Valve spring compressor in use - note extension tube (arrowed)

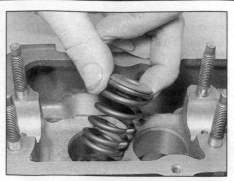

11.11b Removing a valve spring and retainer

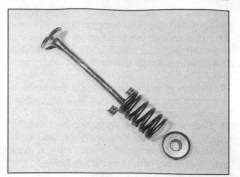

11.11c Valve, spring, retainer and collets

the valve, spring and retainer **(see illustrations)**.

12 Repeat the procedure to remove the other seven valves. Keep the valve components in order if they are to be re-used.

13 Remove the valve stem oil seals from the valve guides, using long-nosed pliers.

14 Dismantling of the cylinder head is now complete.

Overhaul

15 Clean all components and examine them for wear. Oil seals O-rings and gaskets should be renewed as a matter of course. Inspect the head for cracks or other damage.

16 Check the head gasket face for distortion using a straight-edge and feeler blades. Distortion in excess of the maximum specified

11.16 Measuring swirl chamber projection

means that the head must be renewed. No refinishing is permitted. Do not be deceived by the (permitted) projection of the swirl chambers **(see illustration)**.

17 Inspect the valve seats and swirl chambers for burning or cracks. Both can be renewed, and valve seats can sometimes be recut but again this is specialist work. Note that oversize seats and/or swirl chambers may have been fitted in production - see *Specifications* and illustrations **(see illustrations)**.

18 Check each valve for straightness, freedom from burning or cracks, and for an acceptable fit in its guide. Excessive play in the guide may be caused by wear in either component. Measure the valve stem with a micrometer, or try the fit of a new valve if available, to establish whether it is the valve or the guide which is worn.

19 Valve guides as such are not renewable. The guide bores must be reamed accurately to a specific oversize and valves with the appropriate oversize stems fitted. Consult a Ford dealer or other reputable specialist.

20 Slight marking of the sealing area on the valve head may be removed by grinding. Any more severe damage means that the valve must be refaced, if possible, or renewed. The amount of grinding needed to remove large burn marks, besides being tedious, may cause the valve to sit unacceptably deeply in its seat.

21 New or refaced valves and seats should be ground together as follows (the coarse paste may be omitted if the fit is already good).

22 Invert the head and support it securely. Smear a little coarse grinding paste round the sealing area of the valve head. Insert the valve in its guide and grind it to the seat with a to-and-fro motion. The customary tool for this operation is a stick with a rubber sucker on the end **(see illustration)**. Lift the valve occasionally to redistribute the grinding paste.

23 When an unbroken ring of grinding paste is present on the valve head and seat, wipe them clean, then repeat the operation with fine grinding paste.

24 When all the valves have been ground in, clean away all traces of grinding paste, first with a paraffin-soaked rag then with clean dry rags, finally with compressed air if available. Do not overlook the valve guides. It will be obvious that even a small quantity of grinding paste remaining in the engine could cause extremely rapid wear.

25 Examine the valve springs for distortion or signs of fatigue. Measure their free length and compare it with that given in the Specifications. It is worth renewing the springs as a precautionary measure if the old ones have seen much service, even if they appear to be in good condition.

26 Examine the tappets and their bores for

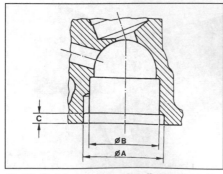

11.17a Swirl chamber seat dimensions. For A, B and C see *Specifications*

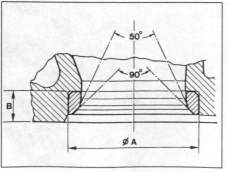

11.17b Valve seat dimensions. For A and B see *Specifications*

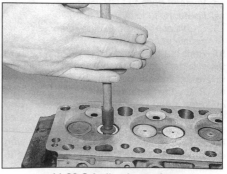

11.22 Grinding in a valve

11.31 Fitting a valve stem oil seal. The end of the stem is covered with plastic film

11.37a Fitting a tappet . . .

11.37b . . . and its shim

scoring or other damage. Oversize tappets may already have been fitted in production. If purchasing new tappets, measure the old ones or take them along for comparison to be sure of obtaining the right size.

27 Renew the camshaft bearing shells unless they are obviously in perfect condition. Two sizes of shell are fitted, one for standard bearing bores and the other for oversize bores. Oversize shells are identified by a green mark. Either size may have been fitted in production.

28 Examine the camshaft bearing journals and the cam lobes for scoring or other deterioration. If a micrometer is available, check the journal diameters. Bearing clearance can be measured using Plastigage. Renew the camshaft if it is badly worn or if the journals are out of round. Once wear has begun on the lobes it usually progresses rapidly as the surface hardening is penetrated.

29 Inspect the manifold and camshaft bearing cap studs. Renew any which are in poor condition, or transfer them to the new head if one is being fitted. To remove a stud either use a proprietary stud extractor, or lock two nuts together on the exposed thread and use them to unscrew it. Studs which have come out by mistake should be cleaned up and refitted using thread locking compound.

30 Overhaul of the cylinder head is now complete.

Reassembly

31 Begin reassembly by oiling a valve stem and inserting it into its guide. Fit the new valve stem oil seal. It is advisable to protect the seal by covering the grooves in the valve stem with a plastic sleeve (which may be provided with the new seals) or with plastic film **(see illustration)**. Lubricate the seal and press it into position with a tube or a small box spanner. Remove the protective sleeve or film.

32 Fit the valve spring (either way up) and the spring retainer. Apply the valve spring compressor and depress the spring retainer far enough to give access to fit the collets. A smear of grease on the collets will hold them in position on the grooves. When the collets

are properly located, carefully release the valve spring compressor. Tap the spring retainer smartly with a mallet and tube to settle the collets.

33 Repeat the operations on the remaining seven valves and associated components.

34 Refit the oil pressure switch and the coolant connector. Use a little sealant on their threads.

35 Oil and refit the vacuum pump plunger.

36 Refit and secure the lifting eyes.

37 Oil and insert the tappets and shims, observing their previously fitted sequence when applicable **(see illustrations)**. Make a note of the shim thickness fitted at each position, if not already done, for reference when checking the valve clearances. Remember to fit the shims with the size markings downwards.

38 Fit the camshaft and its bearings.

39 Fit a new camshaft oil seal.

40 Refit the inlet and exhaust manifolds, using new gaskets (even if one was not originally fitted). Also make sure that the plastic expansion sleeve is located on the upper right-hand end manifold stud. Note also that on later models, an oil baffle is fitted above the camshaft to improve lubrication.. Tighten the securing nuts and bolts progressively to the specified torque. For the exhaust manifold tightening sequence see Chapter 4.

41 Turn the camshaft so that the vacuum pump cam lobe is pointing away from the pump. Insert the vacuum pump lower bolt and screw it in a few turns. Fit a new O-ring seal to the vacuum pump and slide its slotted fixing hole onto the lower bolt. Fit the upper bolt, make sure that the O-ring is still correctly located, then tighten both bolts evenly.

42 The cylinder head is now ready for refitting.

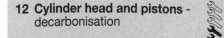

12 Cylinder head and pistons - decarbonisation

1 With the cylinder head removed, the carbon deposits should be removed from the combustion spaces using a scraper and a

wire brush fitted into an electric drill. Take care not to damage the valve heads, otherwise no special precautions need be taken as the cylinder head is of cast iron construction.

2 Where a more thorough job is to be carried out, the cylinder head should be dismantled so that the valves may be ground in and the ports and combustion spaces cleaned, brushed and blown out after the manifolds have been removed.

3 Before grinding-in a valve, remove the carbon and deposits completely from its head and stem. With an inlet valve, this is usually quite easy, simply scraping off the soft carbon with a blunt knife and finishing with a wire brush. With an exhaust valve the deposits are very much harder and those on the valve head may need a rub on coarse emery cloth to remove them. An old woodworking chisel is a useful tool to remove the worst of the valve head deposits.

4 An important part of the decarbonising operation is to remove the carbon deposits from the piston crowns. To do this, turn the crankshaft so that two pistons are at the top of their stroke and press some grease between these pistons and the cylinder walls. This will prevent carbon particles falling down into the piston ring grooves. Stuff rags into the other two bores.

5 Cover the oilways and coolant passages with masking tape and then using a blunt scraper remove all the carbon from the piston crowns. Take care not to score the soft alloy of the crown or the surface of the cylinder bore.

6 Rotate the crankshaft to bring the other two pistons to TDC and repeat the operations.

7 Wipe away the circle of grease and carbon from the cylinder bores.

8 Clean the top surface of the cylinder block by careful scraping.

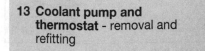

13 Coolant pump and thermostat - removal and refitting

See Chapter 3.

2

14.10a Fit the new oil seal to the camshaft nose . . .

14.10b . . . and seat it with a tube or socket

14.18a Fitting a new injection pump gear oil seal

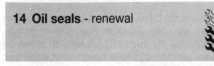

14 Oil seals - renewal

1 The procedures described here are for renewal with the engine in the vehicle. With the engine removed, the steps taken to gain access may be ignored. Read through the procedures first to see what is involved - some are quite lengthy.

Camshaft

2 Remove the camshaft drivebelt.

3 Unbolt and remove the camshaft sprocket. Tap the sprocket with a mallet if necessary to break the taper fit.

4 Unbolt and remove the drivebelt tensioner and the belt backplate.

5 Unbolt and remove No. 1 camshaft bearing cap. Do not lose the shell.

6 Extract the old oil seal, preferably using fingers only. Take care not to scratch the bearing journal or the sealing surface if tools are used.

7 Clean old sealant from the bearing cap. Apply fresh sealant (to Ford spec SPM-4G-9112-F/G) to the areas of the cap shown - see illustration, Section 8.

8 Refit No. 1 bearing shell and cap. Tighten the cap nuts to the specified torque.

9 Lubricate the new seal and make sure that its seat is clean. Also lubricate the taper on the camshaft nose.

10 Fit the new seal, lips inwards, and seat it with a piece of tube or a large socket **(see**

illustrations)**. The maker's tool uses a bolt and washers to draw the seal into position.

11 Refit the drivebelt backplate and the tensioner. Do not tighten the tensioner pivot bolt yet.

12 Refit the camshaft sprocket, making sure that the taper is clean and dry. Insert the sprocket bolt but do not tighten it.

13 Refit and tension the camshaft drivebelt.

Injection pump gear

14 Remove the camshaft and injection pump drivebelts.

15 Unbolt and remove the injection pump sprocket.

16 Remove the old seal using a suitable hooked tool. Alternatively, drill a small hole in the face of the seal, fit a self-tapping screw into the hole and lever or pull on the screw head to remove the seal. If all else fails, the timing cover will have to be removed.

17 Lubricate the new seal and make sure that its seat is clean.

18 Fit the new seal, lips inwards, and press it home. Ford tool 21-111 uses a couple of sprocket bolts to press the seal into position. An acceptable alternative is to use the old seal, a drilled metal bar and some bolts and spacers **(see illustrations)**. Care must be taken that the seal enters its seat squarely.

19 Refit the injection pump sprocket, making sure that the locating dowel engages correctly. Fit the sprocket bolts and tighten them to the specified torque.

20 Refit and tension the camshaft and injection pump drivebelts.

14.18b Pressing the new seal into position using the old seal, a bar, bolts and spacers

Crankshaft pulley

21 Remove the camshaft timing belt as described in Chapter 1.

22 Detach the crankshaft vibration damper from the flange, then detach the vibration flange from the crankshaft, holding the flange using Ford special tool no 15-030A to remove the centre bolt.

23 Remove the fuel injection pump drivebelt as described in Chapter 1.

24 Remove the crankshaft pulley bolt. This bolt is extremely tight. The makers call up two special tools (Nos. 21-108 and 21-109) **(see illustrations)**, one of which locks the pulley bolt while the other turns the crankshaft by meshing with the ring gear through the starter motor aperture.

25 Remove the crankshaft pulley. Note the locating pin **(see illustration)**.

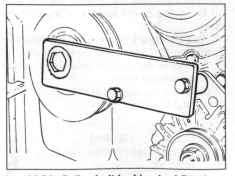

14.24a Pulley bolt locking tool fitted

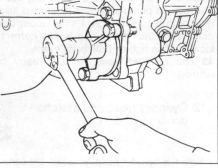

14.24b Crankshaft turning tool in use

14.25 Removing the crankshaft pulley. Note locating pin and hole (arrowed)

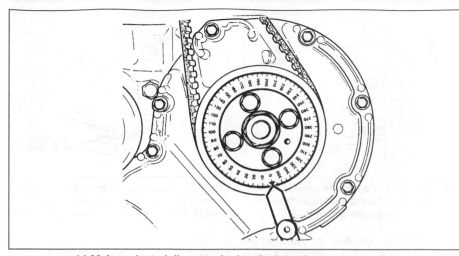

14.30 A graduated disc attached to the injection pump sprocket

15.5 Removing the flywheel cover plate

26 Remove the old seal using a suitable hooked tool. Alternatively, drill a small hole in the face of the seal, fit a self-tapping screw into the hole and lever or pull on the screw head to remove the seal. If all else fails, the timing cover will have to be removed.

27 Lubricate the new seal and clean its seat.

28 Fit the seal, lips inwards, and push it home as far as possible by hand. Seat the seal fully with the aid of a suitable tube or the old seal. It is possible to use the crankshaft pulley bolt and the pulley to apply pressure to the tube or seal.

29 Refit the crankshaft pulley, making sure that the O-ring in the timing belt pulley is in satisfactory condition. Oil the threads and the head contact face of the new bolt and insert it finger tight.

30 Tighten the crankshaft pulley bolt to the specified torque. If using the Ford special tools or equivalent, angular rotation for the second stage of tightening can be measured by attaching a graduated disc to the injection pump sprocket **(see illustration)**. Remember that the pump sprocket turns at half engine speed, so (for instance) 150° crankshaft movement will be read as 75° at the pump sprocket.

31 Refit the vibration damper flange to the crankshaft, noting that the lug and the notch must line up.

32 Refit the vibration damper to the flange.

33 Refit the fuel-injection pump and camshaft drivebelts, as described in Chapter 1.

15 Sump - removal and refitting

Steel type

Removal

1 Disconnect the battery earth (negative) lead.

2 Remove the starter motor.

3 Raise and securely support the front of the vehicle (see "*Jacking and vehicle support*").

4 Drain the engine oil by removing the sump drain plug. Refit the plug when draining is complete to avoid losing it.

5 Remove the flywheel cover plate, which is secured by two nuts **(see illustration)**.

6 Remove the 16 bolts which secure the sump. Access to the two bolts nearest the flywheel is tight so a socket spanner, extension and universal joint will be required.

7 Pull the sump off the engine block. If it is stuck, strike its sides with a wooden or plastic mallet. Avoid levering between the mating faces if possible, as distortion or other damage may result.

8 Remove the old gasket from the sump or block.

Refitting

9 Clean the sump both inside and out, dressing the sealing surface if it is distorted.

10 Clean the block mating face then apply non-setting jointing compound to the areas shown **(see illustration)**.

11 Position a new gasket on the sump, using a smear of grease to retain it in position.

12 Offer the sump to the block, making sure that the lug on the gasket (flywheel side) engages in the recess in the crankshaft oil seal retainer **(see illustrations)**. Insert the four corner bolts and tighten them finger tight.

13 Insert the remaining 12 bolts and tighten them to the specified torque.

14 Tighten the four corner bolts to the specified torque.

15 Refit the flywheel cover plate and the starter motor.

16 Make sure that the drain plug is fitted and tightened, then refill the engine with the specified quantity and grade of oil.

17 Reconnect the battery and lower the vehicle.

18 Check for leaks around the drain plug and sump gasket when the engine is next run.

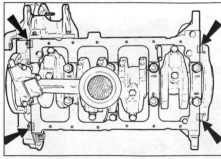

15.10 Apply jointing compound to the critical sealing areas (arrowed) of the sump mating face

15.12a Sump gasket in position

15.12b Sump gasket lug engaged in recess (arrowed)

Aluminium type

Removal

19 Note that when an aluminium sump pan is used, it bolts direct to the clutch housing at the transmission end and there is no bottom cover plate fitted. In order to remove the aluminium type sump pan, it is necessary to remove the transmission, clutch and flywheel to gain access to the rear seal housing lower securing bolts, which screw directly into the sump.

Refitting

20 Ensure all mating surfaces are clean.
21 Apply Ford approved sealant to the cylinder block/sump mating surfaces as shown **(see illustration)**.
22 Fit the sump and a new gasket, tightening the retaining bolts finger-tight only.
23 Refit and tighten the carrier retaining bolts to the specified torque loading.
24 Fully tighten the sump retaining bolts, in a diagonal sequence to the specified torque loading. Note that this must be done within 20 minutes of applying the sealant.

16 Oil pump - removal, inspection and refitting

Removal

1 Drain the engine oil.
2 Disconnect the battery negative lead.
3 Unscrew and discard the oil filter cartridge.
4 On turbocharged engines, disconnect the oil feed line to the turbocharger and remove the line to engine casing securing bolt **(see illustration)**.
5 Where fitted, the cylindrical oil cooler can also be removed by referring to Section 17.
6 Unscrew the four retaining bolts and withdraw the oil pump from the engine crankcase.

Inspection

7 Clean all parts and inspect them for wear or damage. Using a feeler blade, measure the inner to outer rotor clearance. If the clearance exceeds that specified then the pump must be renewed as pump components are not available individually. It is wise to renew the pump on a precautionary basis at time of major overhaul, especially if there is evidence of oil starvation elsewhere.
8 Clean the pick-up pipe and strainer in solvent and blow them dry. If fitted, inspect the oil cooler for damage and renew if necessary.

Refitting

9 A worn oil pump should be renewed complete.
10 Before refitting, pour engine oil into the pump to prime it, and use a new flange gasket **(see illustrations)**.

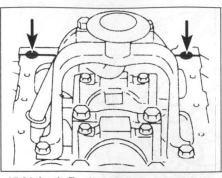

15.21 Apply Ford approved sealant to the cylinder block/sump mating surfaces at the points arrowed

11 Observe all specified torque settings when tightening disturbed fasteners **(see illustration)**.

17 Oil cooler - removal and refitting

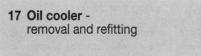

1 The oil cooler (where fitted) is part of the oil pump and filter assembly and does not normally require any maintenance **(see illustration)**. Should it however become damaged, renew it as follows.

Removal

2 Drain the cooling system and disconnect the coolant hoses from the cooler.
3 Unscrew the oil filter, catching any escaping oil in a drip tray.

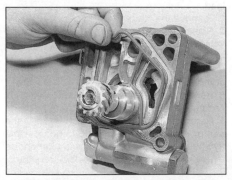

16.10a Fit the oil pump gasket . . .

16.11 . . . and tighten the oil pump bolts

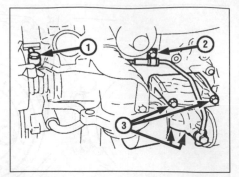

16.4 Disconnect the turbocharger oil feed line (1) the line to engine casing securing bolt (2) and the oil pump retaining bolts (3)

4 Unscrew the filter adapter from the oil pump and withdraw the oil cooler. Note how the unions are aligned and be prepared for oil loss from the cooler.

Refitting

5 Refitting is the reverse of the removal procedure, noting the following points:

a) Renew all O-rings and seals disturbed on removal.
b) Align the cooler unions as noted on removal.
c) Refill the cooling system.
d) Check the engine oil level and top-up as necessary.
e) Check for signs of oil or coolant leaks once the engine has been restarted and warmed-up to normal operating temperature.

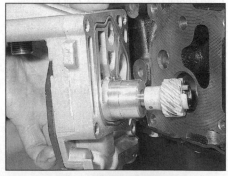

16.10b . . . fit the oil pump . . .

17.1 Oil cooler location (arrowed)

18.13a Fitting a bearing shell to the connecting rod . . .

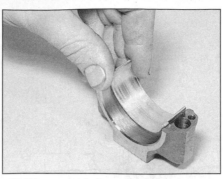

18.13b . . . and to the connecting rod cap

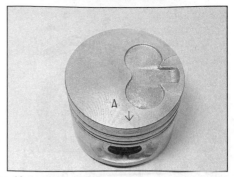

18.14 Arrow on piston crown points to oil pump end of engine

18 Pistons and connecting rods - removal and refitting

Removal

1 Remove the cylinder head.

2 Remove the sump.

3 To improve access, it is preferable to remove the oil pump pick-up pipe, bracket and strainer.

4 If there is a pronounced wear ridge at the top of any bore, it may be necessary to remove it with a scraper or ridge reamer to avoid piston damage during removal. Such a ridge may indicate that reboring is necessary, which will entail new pistons in any case.

5 Turn the crankshaft to bring two pistons to BDC. Check that the connecting rods and their caps are numbered on one side - make paint or punch identifying marks if necessary.

6 Remove the bolts from the two accessible connecting rod caps. Take off the caps and recover the bottom half bearing shells. Keep the shells with their caps if they are to be re-used.

7 Push the two pistons up through the bores. Gentle persuasion (eg with a hammer handle) may be needed to make the piston rings clear the wear ridge.

8 Remove the pistons, complete with rings and connecting rods. Keep the upper half bearing shells with their pistons and rods if they are to be re-used.

9 Turn the crankshaft 180° to bring the other two pistons to BDC. Repeat the removal process.

10 The examination and renovation of pistons is considered in Section 27.

Refitting

11 If new piston rings are to be fitted to old bores, the bores must be deglazed to allow the new rings to bed-in properly. Protect the big-end journals by wrapping them in masking tape, then use a piece of coarse emery paper to produce a cross-hatch pattern in each

bore. A flap wheel in an electric drill may also be used, but beware of spreading abrasive dust. When deglazing is complete, unwrap the big-end journals and wash away all abrasive particles.

12 Commence refitting by laying out the assembled pistons and rods in order, with the bearing shells, connecting rod caps and new bolts. Stagger the ring gaps evenly.

13 Wipe any protective grease off the new bearing shells (if used). Make sure that the shell seats are clean, then press the shells into the rods and caps so that the locating tangs engage in the grooves **(see illustrations)**.

14 Lubricate the bores, pistons, crankpins and shells. Fit a piston ring compressor to the first piston to be fitted. Offer the piston to its bore, making sure that it is the correct bore, and that the arrow on the piston crown and the F mark on the connecting rod are both facing the oil pump end of the engine **(see illustration)**.

15 Tap the piston through the ring compressor and into the bore, using a hammer handle or similar "soft" tool. Release the ring compressor as the piston enters the bore.

16 Guide the connecting rod onto the crankpin, taking care not to scratch the bearing surface. Check also that the bearing shell is not displaced. Fit the connecting rod cap with shell, making sure it is the right way round.

17 Oil the threads of two new connecting rod

19.6 Tightening a flywheel bolt

cap bolts. Fit the bolts and tighten them in stages to the specified torque.

18 Repeat these operations to fit the other three pistons. Turn the crankshaft as necessary to bring the crankpins into positions convenient for fitting.

19 If new components have been fitted, check the piston protrusion as described in Section 29.

20 Refit the oil pump pick-up pipe, bracket and strainer, if removed, using a new gasket. Tighten the bolts to the specified torque.

21 Refit the sump and cylinder head.

19 Flywheel - removal and refitting

Removal

1 Either remove the engine and transmission and separate them, or remove the transmission alone.

2 Make alignment marks then slacken the clutch pressure plate bolts evenly. Remove the bolts, the pressure plate and the driven plate.

3 Make alignment marks between the flywheel and the crankshaft tail, then unbolt and remove the flywheel. Do not drop it, it is heavy. Obtain new bolts for reassembly.

4 Examination and overhaul of the flywheel is considered in Section 27.

Refitting

5 Commence refitting by placing the flywheel on the end of the crankshaft. Observe the alignment marks if refitting the original components.

6 Insert the new securing bolts. Tighten them in stages to the specified torque **(see illustration)**.

7 Refit and secure the clutch driven and pressure plates. Take the opportunity to renew any worn clutch components. Make sure that the driven plate is centred.

8 Refit the transmission, or mate and refit the engine/transmission assembly, as appropriate.

2

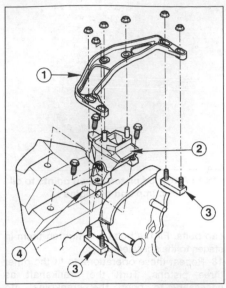

20.6a Engine/transmission right-hand mounting - standard type

1 Bracket
2 Mounting
3 Brackets bolted to cylinder block/crankcase
4 Vehicle body

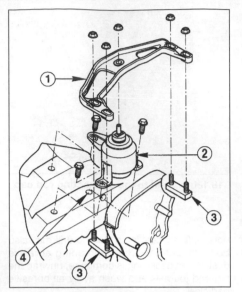

20.6b Engine/transmission right-hand mounting - hydraulic type

1 Bracket
2 Hydraulic mounting
3 Brackets bolted to cylinder block/crankcase
4 Vehicle body

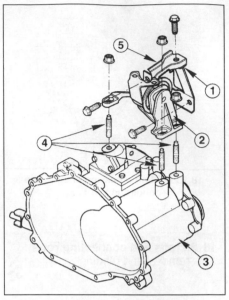

20.7 Engine/transmission left-hand mounting

1 Mounting bracket	4 Studs
2 Mounting	5 Fastening plate -
3 Transmission	where fitted

20 Engine/transmission mountings - inspection, removal and refitting

Inspection

1 During inspection, the engine/transmission must be raised slightly, to remove its weight from the mountings.
2 Raise the front of the vehicle, and support it securely on axle stands. Position a jack under the sump, with a large block of wood between the jack head and the sump, then carefully raise the engine/transmission just enough to take the weight off the mountings.
3 Check the mountings to see if the rubber is cracked, hardened or separated from the metal components. Sometimes the rubber will split right down the centre.
4 Check for relative movement between each mounting's brackets and the engine/transmission or body (use a large screwdriver or lever to attempt to move the mountings). If movement is noted, lower the engine and check/tighten the mounting fasteners.

Removal

5 Before removing any mounting, support the engine/transmission with a hoist or a suitably padded jack.

Right-hand mounting

6 Unscrew the retaining nuts and withdraw the mounting bracket. Note that these nuts are self-locking and must therefore be renewed whenever they are disturbed. Unbolt the mounting from the body **(see illustrations)**.

Left-hand mounting

7 Unscrew the three nuts to release the mounting from the transmission, then unbolt it from the body **(see illustration)**. Note that the nuts are self-locking, and must therefore be renewed whenever they are disturbed.

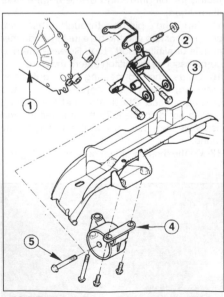

20.8 Engine/transmission rear mounting

1 Transmission
2 Mounting bracket
3 Front suspension subframe
4 Mounting
5 Mounting centre bolt

Rear mounting

8 Remove the rear mounting by first removing its centre bolt and then the three bolts which secure it to the subframe **(see illustration)**.
9 If necessary, remove the two bolts and one nut and detach the bracket of the mounting from the gearbox, along with the gearchange stay bracket **(see illustration)**.

Front mounting

10 Remove the bolts and nuts securing the mounting to the subframe, unscrew the centre bolt and withdraw the mounting **(see illustration)**. The mounting's bracket can be unbolted from the transmission if required.

Refitting

11 On reassembly, the weight of the engine/transmission must not be taken by the mountings until all are correctly fitted.

Right-hand mounting

12 Renew the self-locking nuts and tighten

20.9 The gearchange stay bracket (arrowed)

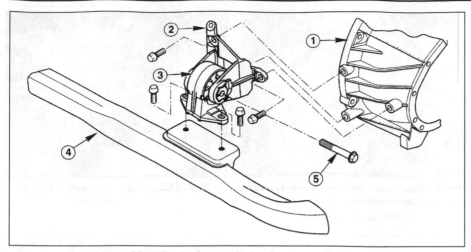

20.10 Engine/transmission front mounting

1 Transmission	3 Mounting	5 Mounting centre bolt
2 Mounting bracket	4 Front suspension subframe	

all fasteners to the torque wrench settings specified. When tightening the nuts, tighten first the four bracket-to-engine nuts, then release the hoist or jack to allow the engine/transmission's weight to rest on the mounting. Do not allow the mounting to twist as the last two of the nuts are tightened.

Left-hand mounting

13 On refitting, renew the self-locking nuts and do not allow the mounting to twist as the nuts are tightened. Tighten all fasteners to the specified torque wrench settings.

Rear mounting

14 On refitting, ensure that the mounting-to-transmission bolts are securely tightened, then refit the mounting. Tighten first the mounting-to-subframe bolts to the specified torque wrench setting. Finally tighten the mounting's centre bolt, again to the specified torque wrench setting.

Front mounting

15 On refitting, ensure that the mounting-to-transmission bolts are securely tightened, then refit the mounting. Tighten first the mounting-to-subframe bolts and nuts to the specified torque wrench setting. Finally tighten the mounting's centre bolt, again to the specified torque wrench setting.

All mountings

16 When the hoist or jack is lowered, check again that the mountings are not under excessive tension, causing twisting or deformation of the rubbers. Slacken and retighten the fastenings if necessary.

21 Engine/transmission - methods of removal

1 The engine is removed together with the transmission in a downward direction and withdrawn from underneath the vehicle.

2 Ensure that the vehicle can be raised sufficiently to allow the engine/transmission to be withdrawn from underneath. Axle stands will be required to ensure that the vehicle is suitably supported when raised. Ensure that these stands are correctly positioned according to model type.

3 The ideal piece of equipment on which to lower the engine/transmission is a low and strongly made trolley which is capable of taking the weight whilst being easily manoeuvrable when beneath the vehicle.

22 Engine/transmission - removal

Note illustrations: *For the following text relating to removal of components associated with the cylinder head, refer to the illustrations given in Section 10 of this Chapter.*

⚠ *Warning: Where a vehicle is fitted with an air conditioning system, do not disconnect the refrigerant hoses.*

1 Disconnect the battery earth lead.
2 Although not essential, removal of the bonnet will provide additional access during subsequent operations.
3 Raise the front of the vehicle, securely support it on axle stands (see "Jacking and vehicle support") and remove the engine undershield.
4 Disconnect the multiplug from the crankshaft position sensor, see Chapter 5.
5 Disconnect the speedometer drive cable at the engine end (close to the crankshaft position sensor).
6 Drain the cooling system and disconnect the lower cooling system hose from the radiator and connector pipe. If the engine is to be dismantled, drain the engine oil and remove the oil filter.

7 Lower the front of the vehicle and slacken the nuts securing both front roadwheels.
8 Loosen the hose retaining clip and remove the air inlet system resonator by pulling it from its two retainers - see illustration, Section 17, Chapter 1.
9 Disconnect the multiplug from the mass airflow (MAF) sensor. Loosen the sensor retaining clips and remove the sensor. This operation may prove difficult due to resistance from the rubber retaining ring (see illustrations Chapters 1 and 4).
10 Refer to Chapter 1 and remove the air cleaner element.
11 Loosen the retaining clip and disconnect the air inlet hose from the turbocharger. Blank off the turbocharger inlet to prevent the ingress of dirt.
12 Refer to Chapter 4, and remove the charge air cooler.
13 Release the hoses and cables from their retaining clip on the cylinder head and move them to one side.
14 Remove the hose/cable retaining clip from the engine lifting eye.
15 Disconnect the fuel return line from the fuel injection pump.
16 Disconnect the cooling system hoses from the following components:
  a) The expansion tank
  b) The inlet manifold
  c) The thermostat housing
17 Move to the front of the fuel heater (Chapter 4) and separate the quick-release coupling of the fuel feed pipe.
18 Disconnect the heater hoses to the oil cooler and cylinder head by releasing their retaining clips at the points shown.
19 Disconnect the vacuum hose from the EGR valve.
20 Release the throttle cable from the injection pump, remove the cable retaining clip from the mounting bracket, pull the cable out of the bracket and move it to one side - refer to illustrations, Section 12, Chapter 4.
21 Unscrew the vacuum pipe union from the vacuum pump and detach the pipe.
22 Disconnect the following electrical connectors:
  a) Glow plug feed
  b) EDC module multiplug (see illustration)
  c) Alternator multiplug and cable

2

22.22a Disconnect the EDC module multiplug (arrowed)

22.22b Disconnect the self test and service connectors (arrowed)

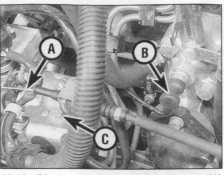

22.22c Disconnect the fuel shut-off valve (A) and the temperature gauge sender unit (B)

C is the throttle cable bracket retaining bolt

22.22d Disconnect the vehicle speed sensor multiplug

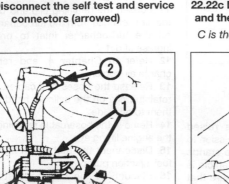

22.22e Disconnect the main engine wiring loom multiplugs (1) and the CVT sensor multiplug (2)

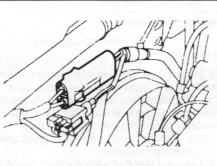

22.22f Disconnect the lighting wire loom multiplug (air conditioned models only)

22.25a Unhook the clutch cable from the clutch release lever . . .

d) *Fuel injection pump multiplugs (3)*
e) *Self test and service connectors (at bulkhead)* **(see illustration)**
f) *Fuel shut-off valve* **(see illustration)**
g) *Temperature gauge sender unit plug*
h) *Engine coolant temperature (ECT) sensor multiplug*
i) *Cooling fan thermoswitch (CFS) multiplug*
j) *Oil pressure switch plug*
k) *Fuel heater multiplug*
l) *Vehicle speed sensor multiplug (and release loom from bracket)* **(see illustration)**
m) *Starter motor (2 nuts) (Chapter 5)*
n) *Main engine wiring loom multiplugs (2)* **(see illustration)**
o) *CVT sensor multiplug*

p) *Earth strap to transmission*
q) *Lighting wire loom multiplug (air conditioned models only)* **(see illustration)**

23 Cut the main engine wiring loom cable-ties and remove the complete loom from the vehicle.
24 Remove the throttle cable bracket retaining bolt and detach the bracket.
25 On models equipped with cable-operated clutch, unhook the clutch cable from the clutch release lever, disconnect the cable from its retaining bracket and move it to one side **(see illustrations)**.
26 On models equipped with hydraulically-operated clutch, disconnect the hydraulic pipe and move it to one side.
27 Remove the two bolts retaining the cover of the power steering pump drivebelt. Remove the cover and loosen the pump mounting bolt.

28 Loosen the power steering pump clamp bolt. Rotate the adjuster screw to de-tension the drivebelt and remove the tensioner from the front cover. Remove the pump drivebelt and the pump mounting bolt and lift the pump clear of the engine.
29 Fit a lifting eye to the alternator retaining bolt. Fit the engine support bar and connect it to the lifting eye, ensuring that the bar is placed under load by tightening down its lifting spindle.
30 Raise the front of the vehicle and securely support it on axle stands (see "*Jacking and vehicle support*").
31 From beneath the vehicle, disconnect the following electrical connectors **(see illustration)**:
a) *Left and right-hand fan motor multiplugs (air conditioned models only)*

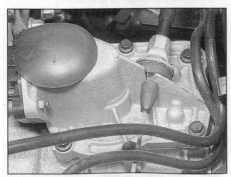

22.25b . . . and disconnect the cable from its retaining bracket

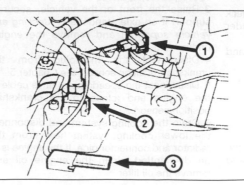

22.31 From beneath the vehicle, disconnect the following electrical connectors (air conditioned models only)

1 *Left and right-hand fan motor multiplugs*
2 *Ballast resistor multiplug*
3 *Diode*

22.32 Use split pins to secure radiator in its raised position . . .

22.33 . . . while unbolting the bottom mountings (arrowed). Note that the mountings are handed and do not lose the mounting rubbers

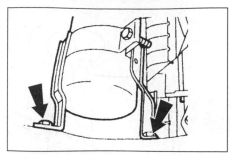

22.34 Remove the conditioning dehydrator to subframe bolts (arrowed)

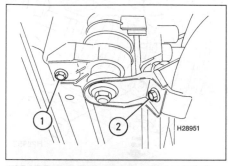

22.35 Remove the condenser to radiator bolt (1) and the radiator bracket to subframe bolt (2)

b) *Ballast resistor multiplug (air conditioned models only)*

c) *Diode (unclip - air conditioned models only)*

32 On vehicles without air conditioning, secure the radiator at the top as shown **(see illustration)**.

33 Detach the two lower radiator brackets **(see illustration)**.

34 On vehicles equipped with air conditioning, detach the conditioning dehydrator from the subframe and secure it clear of the engine with a length of wire **(see illustration)**.

35 On vehicles equipped with air conditioning, release each condenser by removing the condenser to radiator bolt and the radiator bracket to subframe bolt. Secure each condenser clear of the engine with a length of wire **(see illustration)**.

36 Remove the radiator and fan assembly from beneath the vehicle.

37 Unscrew the nuts retaining the front exhaust pipe to the exhaust manifold flange, remove the retaining pins and remove the stud/spring assembly. Remove the front exhaust pipe rear securing nuts and lower the pipe from the vehicle.

38 Disconnect the selector rod from the selector shaft by loosening the clamp bolt and unscrewing the selector rod bolt **(see illustrations)**.

39 Detach the gearchange stabiliser from the engine mounting by removing its retaining bolt **(see illustration)**.

40 Remove the gearchange linkage heat shield **(see illustration)**.

41 Remove the gearchange lever guide

mounting retaining bolts and swivel the gearchange linkage rearwards, securing it with a length of wire **(see illustrations)**.

22.38a Remove the selector rod bolt . . .

22.38b . . . and disconnect the selector rod from the selector shaft (clamp bolt arrowed)

22.39 Remove the gearchange stabiliser to engine mounting retaining bolt

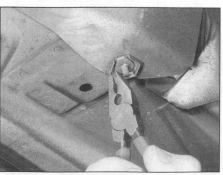

22.40 Remove the gearchange linkage heat shield

22.41a Remove the gearchange lever guide mounting bolts (arrowed) . . .

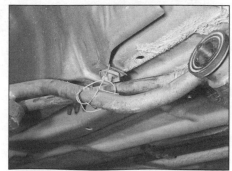

22.41b . . . and swivel the gearchange linkage rearwards, securing it with a length of wire

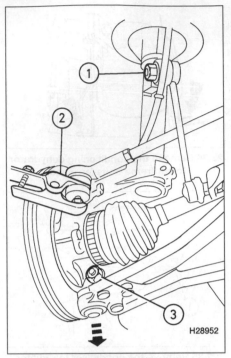

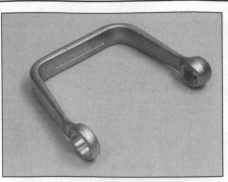
22.46a U-shaped Ford service tool for removing the steering gear securing bolts

22.46b Removing the steering gear to subframe securing bolts from underneath the vehicle

22.42 Detach each stabiliser link rod from the suspension strut (1) disconnect each track rod end balljoint by using a balljoint separator (2) and release each lower suspension arm balljoint from the spindle carrier (3)

42 Remove both front wheels and detach each stabiliser link rod from its respective suspension strut **(see illustration)**.

43 Disconnect each track rod end balljoint from its respective steering arm by unscrewing the retaining nut and using a balljoint separator to release the tapered joint.

44 Release each lower suspension arm balljoint from its respective spindle carrier by removing the retaining bolt and withdraw each brake hose from its bracket. Remove each ABS wiring loom bracket from the suspension strut.

45 Remove the engine rear roll restrictor by first removing its centre bolt and then the

remaining three securing bolts - see Section 20.

46 Detach the steering gear assembly from the subframe by removing its two securing bolts. If the bolts are not accessible from above, a Ford service tool will be required to reach them from underneath the vehicle **(see illustrations)**.

47 Remove the two bolts and one nut and detach the bracket of the engine rear roll restrictor from the gearbox.

48 Remove the centre bolt of the engine front roll restrictor.

49 Remove the four subframe securing bolts and lower the subframe away from the vehicle.

50 Position a suitable container under the gearbox and drain the gearbox of oil.

51 Remove the two bolts securing the right-hand driveshaft centre bearing. Pull the shaft clear of the gearbox and tie it up to the suspension member to support it and to prevent the tripode joint from being strained. The joint must not be angled more than 18° **(see illustrations)**.

52 Using Ford tool 16-057 as shown **(see illustration)** drive the left-hand driveshaft from its seat. Pull the shaft clear of the gearbox and tie it up to the suspension member to support it and to prevent the tripode joint from being strained. The joint must not be angled more than 18°.

53 When each shaft is removed, plug the

gearbox aperture to prevent the ingress of dirt.

54 On vehicles equipped with air conditioning, release the clamp bolt and remove the compressor drivebelt. Disconnect the multiplug from the magnetic clutch of the compressor, remove the three compressor retaining bolts and tie the compressor clear of the engine with a length of wire - see Chapter 3.

55 The engine/transmission should now be hanging on the right and left-hand mountings only, with all components which connect it to the rest of the vehicle disconnected or removed and secured well clear of the unit. Make a final check that this is the case.

56 Position a low bench trolley beneath the engine/transmission and lower the vehicle until the unit rests securely on the trolley.

57 Release the engine support bar.

58 Unscrew the nuts securing the engine right-hand mounting bracket, then the nuts securing the left-hand bracket - see Section 20.

59 Raise the vehicle and ensure that it is securely supported, high enough to permit the withdrawal of the engine/transmission and bench trolley from underneath.

60 If the vehicle is to be moved whilst the engine is out, temporarily reconnect the front suspension components and ensure that the driveshafts are suitably supported so that they can rotate without being damaged.

22.51a Removing the heat shield from the right-hand driveshaft centre bearing

22.51b Pulling the right-hand driveshaft clear of the gearbox

22.52 Using Ford tool 16-057 to drive the left-hand driveshaft from its seat

23 Engine/transmission - separation

1 Unbolt and remove the starter motor, noting that the starter motor and its support bracket are secured by four bolts and the engine bracket by three bolts

2 Remove the flywheel cover plate, which, on steel sump models, is secured by three bolts. The aluminium sump used on later models is secured to the base of the crankcase by 14 or 16 bolts (dependent on model type) and to the clutch bell housing by two bolts.

3 Remove the remaining engine-to-transmission bolts.

4 Withdraw the transmission from the engine. Once it is clear of the locating dowels, do not allow the transmission to hang on the input shaft.

5 Recover the split backplate from behind the flywheel.

6 Store the transmission as nearly as possible in its fitted position. Be prepared for oil to seep out of the driveshaft apertures in storage.

24 Engine dismantling - general information

1 Clean the engine thoroughly using a coolant-soluble grease solvent or similar product. Keep dirt and coolant out of vulnerable components such as the fuel injection pump and the alternator.

2 Although there is no reason why only partial dismantling should not be carried out to renew some specific component, if the engine has seen much service it is probably worth dismantling it completely to assess the degree of wear in all areas.

3 When possible, the engine should be dismantled on a workbench or stout table. If an engine dismantling stand is available, so much the better. Avoid working directly on a concrete floor as grit presents a serious problem. If there is no alternative to working on the floor, cover it with an old piece of lino or carpet.

25.6 Remove the turbocharger mounting bracket bolts (arrowed)

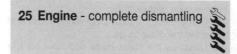

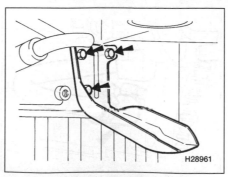

25.7 Remove the front axle driveshaft bracket to cylinder block securing bolts (arrowed)

4 As well as the usual selection of tools, have available some wooden blocks for propping up the engine. A notebook and pencil will be needed, as will a couple of segmented boxes or a good supply of plastic bags and labels.

5 A coolant proof marker pen is useful for making alignment marks without recourse to punches or chisels. Take care that the marks are not erased during cleaning, however.

6 Whenever possible, refit nuts, washers etc. to the components from which they were removed. This makes reassembly much simpler. Do not rely on memory.

7 Spills of oil, fuel and coolant are bound to occur during dismantling. Have rags and newspapers handy to mop up the mess.

8 Do not throw away old gaskets immediately, but save them for comparison with new ones or for use as patterns if new gaskets have to be constructed.

25 Engine - complete dismantling

1 Unbolt and remove the exhaust manifold. If this is the first time that the engine has been dismantled, then no exhaust manifold gasket

25.4 Disconnect the oil cooler feed hose (1) and remove the bracket bolts (2)

will be found, but one will be required at reassembly.

2 Unbolt and remove the clutch assembly from the flywheel.

3 Unbolt and remove the flywheel followed by the crankshaft rear radial oil seal carrier.

4 Disconnect the oil cooler feed hose and remove the bracket bolts shown (see illustration).

5 Remove the complete oil pump assembly, referring to the appropriate Section of this Chapter.

6 With the turbocharger removed, detach its mounting bracket from the cylinder block by removing the three securing bolts (see illustration).

7 Detach the front axle driveshaft bracket from the cylinder block by removing its three securing bolts (see illustration).

8 Remove the alternator and belt tensioner assembly by first loosening the tensioner pulley clamp bolt and rotating the pulley adjuster screw to slacken the drivebelt and allow its removal. Remove the tensioner pulley bracket by releasing its two securing bolts and then the alternator by releasing its three securing bolts (see illustration).

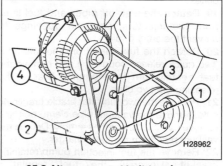

25.8 Alternator and belt tensioner assembly

1 Tensioner pulley clamp bolt
2 Tensioner pulley adjuster screw
3 Tensioner pulley bracket securing bolts
4 Alternator securing bolts

2

25.14 Method of locking crankshaft

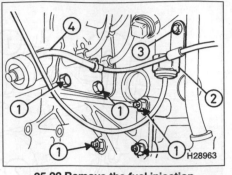

25.22 Remove the fuel injection pump/retaining bracket bolts and nuts (1) the fuel regulating thermostat (2) the vacuum pipe retaining bracket (3) and disconnect the vacuum pipe from the pump (4)

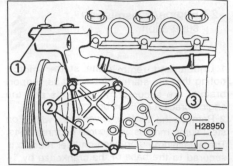

25.24 Remove the engine mounting/vacuum pump bracket to engine lifting eye bolts (1) the bracket to cylinder block bolts (2) and detach the coolant hose from the pump and thermostat housing (3)

9 Detach the alternator mounting bracket from the cylinder block by removing its four securing bolts.

10 Disconnect the coolant hose adjacent to the fuel injection pump pulley. Unscrew the three fuel injection pump pulley retaining bolts and remove the pulley from the pump.

11 Unscrew the bolts, release the clips, and take off the upper and lower camshaft toothed belt covers.

12 Using a spanner on the crankshaft pulley bolt, turn the crankshaft in the normal direction of rotation until the drilling in the injection pump flange (CAV) or the recess (Bosch) is aligned with the drilling in the pump housing. This indicates TDC on Nos 1 and 4 pistons.

13 Remove the camshaft belt tensioner and spring. A Torx bit will be required for the spring bolt. Take off the camshaft drivebelt.

14 Unbolt and remove the crankshaft pulley vibration damper. To prevent rotation of the crankshaft while unscrewing the bolt, screw two bolts into the flywheel mounting flange, and place a long lever between them **(see illustration)**.

15 Remove the injection pump belt tensioner and its spring, and then take off the drivebelt.

16 Using a Torx bit, remove the camshaft belt idler pulley.

17 Unbolt and remove the camshaft belt sprocket, but only unscrew the outer bolts.

18 Unbolt and remove the belt cover backing plates.

19 Detach the leak-off pipes and fuel lines from the injectors. Cap the openings to prevent the entry of dirt.

20 Detach the fuel lines from the fuel filter (two quick release couplings) and remove the fuel heater from its mounting bracket by releasing the two clips.

21 Remove the two fuel filter bracket retaining nuts, remove the vacuum pipe clamp bolt and remove the filter/bracket assembly. Detach the vacuum pipe from the turbocharger.

22 Remove the fuel injection pump/retaining bracket. Unscrew the fuel regulating thermostat from the thermostat housing. Release the vacuum pipe retaining bracket and disconnect the pipe from the pump **(see illustration)**.

23 Extract the Torx screws and remove the fuel injection pump.

24 Remove the engine mounting/vacuum pump bracket to engine lifting eye bolts and then the bracket to cylinder block bolts. Remove the bracket **(see illustration)**.

25 Detach the coolant hose from the coolant pump and thermostat housing.

26 Pull off the crankcase ventilation system hoses from the camshaft cover, cylinder block and turbocharger.

27 Remove the oil dipstick bracket retaining bolt and remove the dipstick/bracket assembly.

28 Disconnect the vacuum pump oil return hose from the cylinder block. Unscrew the two pump securing bolts and remove the vacuum pump from the cylinder head, noting the fitted position of the glow plug wiring retaining bracket beneath one of the bolt heads - see Chapter 9.

29 Unbolt and remove the thermostat housing.

30 Unscrew the fuel injectors, using a deep socket - see Chapter 4.

31 Extract the heat shields. These should be renewed on reassembly.

32 Disconnect the glow plug wiring loom and unscrew the glow plugs.

33 Unscrew the three bolts and take off the camshaft cover and gasket.

34 Unscrew the four nuts and remove the oil baffle.

35 Remove the turbocharger oil return hose by loosening its retaining clips and pulling it from the cylinder block connection **(see illustration)**.

36 Unscrew and remove the cylinder head bolts in the reverse sequence to tightening.

37 Remove the cylinder head and gasket.

38 Refer to Chapter 5 and remove the crankshaft position sensor.

39 Unscrew the bolt and remove the auxiliary shaft sprocket.

40 Remove the three bolts and take off the auxiliary shaft oil seal carrier with seal.

41 Unscrew the auxiliary shaft thrustplate bolts, and withdraw the shaft with thrustplate.

42 Unbolt and remove the coolant pump.

43 Unscrew the sump pan bolts, and remove the pan.

44 Remove the belt sprocket from the crankshaft, using a puller if necessary.

45 Using a Torx bit, remove the engine front plate screws and withdraw the plate.

46 Invert the engine, and unbolt and remove the oil pick-up pipe and bracket.

47 Check that the big-end bearing caps and connecting rods are marked 1 to 4, from the camshaft belt end of the engine. Using an internally-splined Torx socket, unscrew the big-end bearing cap bolts and remove them **(see illustration)**.

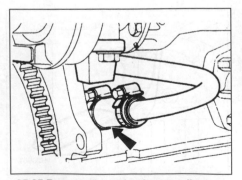

25.35 Remove the turbocharger oil return hose by loosening its retaining clips and pulling it from the cylinder block

25.47 No 12 Torx socket and big-end bearing cap bolt

48 Withdraw the piston/rod assemblies out of the top of the cylinder block.

49 If the original shells are to be used again, keep them with their respective caps or rods.

50 Unbolt the main bearing caps (numbered 1 to 5 from the camshaft belt end of the engine) and remove them. If the original shells are to be used again, keep them taped to their respective caps. Remove the crankshaft.

51 The piston-cooling oil jets are inserted into the cylinder block, projecting upwards from Nos 1 to 4 main bearings. These must be removed if the lubricating system is to be effectively and thoroughly cleaned at overhaul. See your local Ford dealer or engine reconditioning specialist for details.

26 Examination and renovation - general information

1 With the engine completely dismantled, all components should be cleaned and examined as detailed in the appropriate Sections of this Chapter.

2 Most components can be cleaned with rags, a soft brush (eg. an old toothbrush) and paraffin or some other solvent. Do not immerse parts with oilways in solvent, since it can be very difficult to remove and if left may contaminate the oil. Probe oilways with a pipe cleaner or similar item, and blow through with compressed air if available.

3 When faced with a borderline decision as to whether to renew a particular part, take into consideration the expected future life of the engine and the degree of trouble or expense which will be caused if the part fails before the next overhaul.

4 If extensive overhauling is required, estimate the likely cost and compare it with the cost of a complete reconditioned engine. The difference may not be great, and the reconditioned engine will have a guarantee.

27 Engine components - examination and renovation

Cylinder block and bores

1 Clean out the nooks and crannies inside the block.

2 Remove plugs and covers and clean their seats and threads. Expansion type plugs should be renewed whenever they are disturbed, so it is in order to remove them by destructive means - eg. by drilling a hole in the middle of the plug, inserting a self-tapping screw and using the screw to pull out the plug.

3 Oil gallery plugs should be removed and the galleries blown through with compressed air. Coat the plug threads with sealant (to Ford spec SM 4G 4644 AA/AB) when refitting.

4 Smear sealant on expansion plug seating areas when fitting them. Tap the plug into position with the flat face of a hammer, then spread it by striking the centre a couple of times with a ball face hammer.

5 If cracks in the block are suspected, it may be necessary to have it crack tested professionally. There are various ways of doing this, some involving special dyes and chemicals, some using ultrasonic or electromagnetic radiation.

6 Bore wear is indicated by a wear ridge at the top, as previously mentioned. For accurate assessment a bore micrometer is required. A rougher measurement can be made by inserting feeler blades between a piston (without rings) and the bore wall. Compare the clearance at the bottom of the bore, which should be unworn, with that just below the wear ridge. No wear limits are specified, but out-of-round or taper in excess of 0.1 mm would normally be considered grounds for a rebore. Scuffs, scores and scratches should also be attended to.

7 If reboring is undertaken, it is normal practice for the machine shop to obtain the oversize pistons and rings at the same time.

8 Where the degree of wear does not justify a rebore, the fitting of proprietary oil control rings may be considered. Any improvement brought about by such rings may not last long, however.

Crankshaft and bearings

9 The crankshaft is another item which may need to be crack tested. Normally an uncracked crankshaft will "ring" clearly if suspended from a cord and struck, while a cracked shaft will sound dull. This test is not infallible.

10 Examine the bearing shells for wear and scratches on the working surfaces. New shells should be fitted in any case, unless the old ones are obviously in perfect condition and are known to have covered only a nominal mileage. Refitting used shells is false economy.

11 Examine the bearing journals on the crankshaft for scoring or other damage, which

if present will probably mean that regrinding or renewal is necessary. If a micrometer is available, measure the journals in several places to check for out-of-round and taper. No limits are specified, but typically 0.025 mm is the maximum acceptable.

12 Note that the crankshaft may already have been reground, and that the makers only specify one stage of regrinding. Factory-reground crankshafts are indicated by green paint marks on No. 1 crank web. A green line shows that the main bearing journals have been reground, a green spot shows the same for the big-end journals. The corresponding undersize bearing shells also carry a green mark **(see illustration)**.

13 Bearing running clearances can be measured by using Plastigage, which is a calibrated plastic filament. If several measurements are taken, out-of-round and taper can also be determined as an alternative to using a micrometer. Proceed as follows.

14 Fit the top half main bearing shells, clean and dry, to their seats in the block. Place the crankshaft on the shells. Put a thread of Plastigage along the journal to be measured. Fit the main bearing cap with its shell, again clean and dry, and secure it with the (old) bolts. Do not turn the crankshaft.

15 Tighten the main bearing cap bolts to the specified torque, then remove them. Carefully lift off the cap and bearing shell. The Plastigage will have been squashed more or less flat. By reading the width of the squashed strip against a calibrated scale, the clearance can be known **(see illustration)**.

16 Scrape off the remains of the Plastigage and repeat the process on the other main bearings. Only one bearing cap should be fitted at a time when performing this check.

17 Big-end bearing clearances can be measured in the same way. They should be measured at the TDC position for the piston concerned, as this is where the most wear occurs.

18 As with the bearing shells, the thrustwashers should normally be renewed as a matter of course. A crankshaft which has been factory machined to accept oversize thrustwashers carries yellow lines on the

27.12 Crankshaft undersize markings

1 *Main bearing undersize mark (line)*
2 *Big-end bearing undersize mark (spot)*

27.15 Reading the width of a squashed Plastigage strip

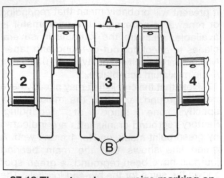

27.18 Thrustwasher oversize marking on crankshaft

A *Centre main bearing width*
B *Oversize marks (yellow lines)*

27.19 Using a feeler blade for piston ring removal

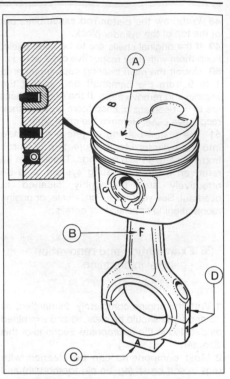

27.20 Piston and connecting rod. Inset shows ring profiles

A *Arrow*   C *Length class mark*
B *Front mark*   D *Cylinder number*

centre webs. Oversize thrustwashers also carry a yellow mark **(see illustration)**.

Pistons, piston rings and connecting rods

19 Remove the piston rings from a piston with the aid of some old feeler blades or similar thin metal strips **(see illustration)**. Carefully spread the top ring just far enough to slide the blades in between the ring and the piston, then remove the ring and blades together. Be careful not to scratch the piston with the ends of the ring.

20 Repeat the process to remove the second and third rings, using the blades to stop the rings falling into the empty grooves.

27.21 Measuring a piston ring end gap

Always remove rings from the top of the piston. Keep each set of rings with its piston if the old rings are to be re-used **(see illustration)**.

21 Measure the end gaps of the rings by fitting them, one at a time, to their bores. Push the ring to the bottom (unworn) section of the bore with a piston to keep it square. Measure the end gap with feeler blades **(see illustration)** and compare it with that given in the Specifications. If the gap is too big, the ring is worn and should be renewed.

22 If renewing the rings, note that two sizes of "standard" rings are available. The first size fits pistons of classes A and B, the second classes C and D (see Specifications and below). Deglaze the bores if new rings are fitted. Check the end gaps of the new rings before fitting, in case they are too tight. Careful filing or grinding of the ends of the ring will correct this.

23 Clean the pistons and inspect them for damage. Look for holes or dents in the crown, and for scores or other signs of picking-up on the sides. Scorch marks on the skirt show that blow-by has been occurring.

24 If the pistons pass this preliminary inspection, clean all the carbon out of the ring grooves using a piece of old piston ring. Protect your fingers as piston rings are sharp. Do not remove any metal from the ring grooves or lands.

25 Roll each ring around its groove to check for tight spots, and check the vertical clearance of the rings in their grooves **(see illustration)**. Excessive clearance which is not due to worn rings must be due to piston wear. Unless the pistons can be machined to accept special rings, renewal is required.

26 If renewing the pistons without reboring, ensure that pistons of the correct production class are obtained. The piston grade mark is stamped into the piston crown and a corresponding code mark on the cylinder block denotes the bore class **(see illustrations)**.

27 To separate a piston from its connecting rod, prise out the circlips and push out the

27.25 Checking the vertical clearance of a piston ring

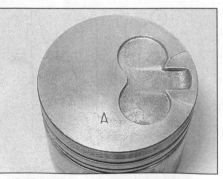

27.26a Letter on crown denotes piston class . . .

27.26b . . . corresponding with bore class letters on block (at flywheel end)

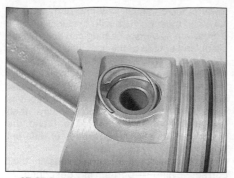

27.27 Removing a gudgeon pin circlip

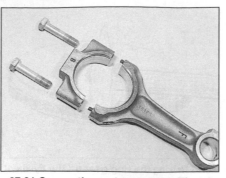

27.31 Connecting rod front mark (F) and length class letter (B)

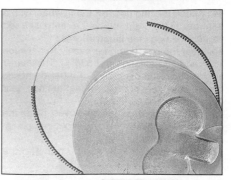

27.33a Oil control ring wire and spring

gudgeon pin **(see illustration)**. Hand pressure should be sufficient to remove the pin. Identify the piston so that it can be refitted to the correct rod.

28 Wear between the gudgeon pin and the connecting rod small-end bush can be cured by renewing both pin and bush. Bush renewal is a specialist job, however, because press facilities are required and because the new bush must be reamed accurately to fit the pin.

29 New gudgeon pins and circlips are supplied when purchasing new pistons of Ford manufacture. It is wise to renew the circlips in any case. If renewing the gudgeon pins separately from the pistons, note that they are graded by weight. Punch marks on the front of the pin denote the weight class, one mark being the lightest and six the heaviest. Only the lightest three grades are available as spares, and they must be fitted with the appropriate pistons as follows:

Piston Class	Gudgeon pin marks
A and B	3
C and D	2
E and F	1

30 The connecting rods themselves should not be in need of renewal unless seizure or some other major mechanical failure has occurred. Damage to the cap and bearing shell seats is possible if bearing failure was allowed to proceed to an advanced stage.

31 Four different lengths of connecting rod are supplied in production in order to equalise piston protrusion between the four cylinders.

The length class is denoted by a letter stamped on the front (oil pump side) of the connecting rod cap **(see illustration)**. The letter A denotes the shortest rod, D the longest. Unless there are good reasons for selecting a different length, and a supply of different length rods for experimentation, new rods should be of the same length class as those they replace.

32 Reassemble the pistons and rods. Make sure that the pistons are fitted the right way round - the arrow on the piston crown and the F (front) mark on the connecting rod must be on the same side. Oil and insert the gudgeon pins and secure with new circlips. The circlip gaps should be upwards. When assembled, the piston should pivot freely on the rod.

33 Fit the piston rings using the same technique as for removal. If the oil control ring was dismantled, reassemble it by inserting the wire into the spring; cover the spring join with the outer segment **(see illustrations)**. Observe the TOP markings on the two compression rings. Stagger the ring gaps evenly.

Oil pump

34 Refer to Section 16.

Camshaft drivebelt and sprockets

35 Inspect the drivebelt for cracks, fraying, broken teeth (especially at the roots) and contamination. It is as well to renew the belt in any case at time of major overhaul.

36 Spin the drivebelt tensioner wheel on its

bearing to check for roughness. Renew the tensioner complete if the bearing is in poor condition.

37 Inspect the sprockets for any signs of damage, paying particular attention to the teeth. Clean off any oil or other contamination. Renew damaged sprockets.

Cylinder head and camshaft

38 Refer to Section 10 for examination and renovation procedures.

39 If it is wished to remove the oil gallery plugs, of which there are many, refer to paragraph 3 of this Section. For expansion plugs see paragraphs 2 and 4.

40 Check that the lubrication jet for the vacuum pump plunger and cam is clear. Remove the plug and blow through the jet if necessary **(see illustration)**.

Flywheel

41 Examine the clutch mating surface of the flywheel for scoring or cracks. Light grooving or scoring may be ignored. Surface cracks or deep grooving can sometimes be removed by specialist machining, provided not too much metal is taken off; otherwise the flywheel must be renewed.

42 Inspect the starter ring gear for damaged or missing teeth. A damaged ring gear can be renewed separately. The average DIY mechanic may prefer to leave the job to a Ford dealer or other competent workshop; for the enthusiast the procedure is as follows.

43 Drill two adjacent holes, 7 or 8 mm in diameter, through the ring gear as shown **(see illustration)**. Take care not to drill into the flywheel.

2

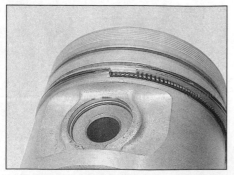

27.33b Fitting the oil control ring outer segment

27.40 Lubrication jet (arrowed) for vacuum pump plunger and cam

27.43 Drilling holes in the ring gear

44 Knock the ring gear off the flywheel with a hammer. Use light blows, evenly spaced around the ring **(see illustration)**.

45 Heat the new ring gear evenly to between 260° and 280°C (500° and 536°F). This is just about within the capability of most domestic ovens. Take care not to overheat the ring gear or its temper will be lost.

46 Using tongs or asbestos gloves, place the ring gear on the flywheel and tap it into place. Allow it to cool naturally.

47 If renewing the flywheel, transfer the clutch locating dowels.

Miscellaneous

48 The makers recommend that the following bolts be renewed whenever they have been slackened:

a) Flywheel securing
b) Main bearing cap
c) Connecting rod cap
d) Crankshaft pulley
e) Cylinder head

49 Renew the driveshaft circlips.

28 Engine reassembly - general information

1 Before commencing reassembly, make sure that all parts are clean and that the new components required have been obtained. A full set of oil seals and gaskets must be purchased.

2 Besides the critical area bolts listed in the

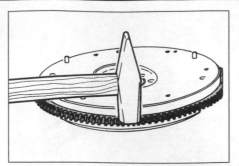

29.44 Driving the ring gear off the flywheel

previous Section, renew any nuts, bolts or studs with damaged threads.

3 A full set of hand tools will be needed, including a dial test indicator and stand. A squirt type oil can filled with clean engine oil should be used to lubricate working parts.

4 Small quantities of grease, thread locking compound, anti-seize compound and various types of sealant will be called for.

5 Have available a good quantity of clean lint-free rags for wiping excess oil off hands and engine parts.

6 If not already done, obtain or construct the tools needed for setting the valve timing.

29 Engine - complete reassembly

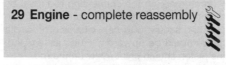

1 Position the block so that access to the bottom end is clear, and then wipe clean the main bearing shell seats in the block. Do not forget to check that the oil jets are clear and securely refitted **(see illustration)**.

2 Fit the bearing shells to the crankcase, noting that No. 1 is of twin-shell type, with a lubrication groove in each shell. All the other main bearings incorporate a lubrication groove in the crankcase shell only.

3 Fit the plain shells into the bearing caps.

4 Fit the thrustwashers on both sides of No. 3 main bearing, so that the oil grooves are visible.

5 Lower the crankshaft into place and oil the journals. Locate the main bearing caps with their shells, so that their numbered position is correct, and the triangular mark has its apex

towards the camshaft belt end of the engine. No 1 cap must be flush with the block.

6 Screw in new main bearing cap bolts (lightly oiled), and tighten to the specified torque **(see illustration)**.

7 Measure the crankshaft endfloat by levering the crankshaft back and forth and using feeler blades or a dial gauge. If the endfloat is not within the specified limits, then dismantling must be carried out and the thrustwashers changed for ones of different thickness.

8 Fit the pistons/connecting rods in their correct cylinder bores, as described in Section 18. Tighten the big-end bearing cap bolts as specified.

9 Fit the oil pick-up pipe and bracket. Make sure that the O-ring is correctly seated **(see illustrations)**.

10 Using a new gasket and new oilway seals, fit the engine front plate, making sure that its edge is flush with the lower edge of the cylinder block (tolerance 0.10mm). Note that the vibration damper must be centred with the hole in the plate - Ford tool 21 148 is supplied for this purpose.

11 Draw a new crankshaft front oil seal into place, using a suitable piece of tubing and the vibration damper centre bolt as an installer.

12 Fit the drivebelt sprocket fully onto the front of the crankshaft, making sure that the positioning dowel engages correctly and that the O-ring is in good condition. Lessen the risk of damage to the O-ring by lubricating it with engine oil.

13 Fit the vibration damper/ pulley, engaging the vee in its cut-out. Tighten the fixing bolt to the specified torque.

14 Refer to Section 15 of this Chapter and apply Ford approved sealant to the cylinder block/sump mating surfaces.

15 Fit the sump pan and a new gasket, tightening the retaining bolts finger-tight only.

16 Refit the crankshaft rear radial oil seal carrier and its new gasket. The carrier is centred by means of locating lugs in the carrier recess. Fit and tighten the carrier retaining bolts, in a diagonal sequence to the specified torque loading.

17 Fully tighten the sump retaining bolts, in a diagonal sequence to the specified torque

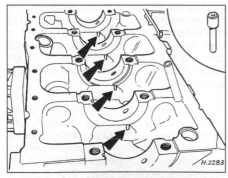

29.1 Location of piston-cooling oil jets

29.6 Angle-tightening a main bearing cap bolt

29.9a Pushing oil pick-up pipe into crankcase hole - note O-ring seal (arrowed)

29.9b Tightening oil pick-up pipe bracket bolt

29.22 Tightening a coolant pump bolt

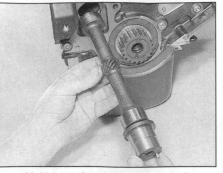

29.23 Inserting the auxiliary shaft

29.24 Auxiliary shaft thrustplate

29.25a Auxiliary shaft oil seal retainer with plastic installer

29.25b Tightening auxiliary shaft oil seal retainer bolts

29.25c Auxiliary shaft oil seal retainer with installer removed

loading. Note that this must be done within 20 minutes of applying the sealant.

18 Fit the new crankshaft rear radial oil seal into the carrier as far as the shoulder by using Ford tool 21 011F in conjunction with two flywheel bolts, as shown - see Section 14.

19 Using new bolts, refit the flywheel. Tighten the bolts to the specified torque through the stages stated.

20 Fit the clutch assembly, remembering to centralise the driven plate. Tighten the bolts to the specified torque in a diagonal sequence.

21 Refer to Chapter 5 and refit the crankshaft position sensor.

22 Using a new gasket and noting the torque setting for the retaining bolts, fit the coolant pump **(see illustration)**.

23 Oil the bearings, and fit the auxiliary shaft **(see illustration)**.

24 Fit the auxiliary shaft thrustplate so that the oil grooves are visible **(see**

illustration). Tighten the plate bolts to the specified torque.

25 Fit a new auxiliary shaft/oil seal assembly, which is supplied complete with a retainer. A plastic installer is provided to prevent damage to the oil seal lips as it is pushed over the step on the shaft, but insulating tape will serve as an alternative. Grease the seal lips before fitting the retainer plate **(see illustrations)**.

26 Check each piston protrusion at TDC. Select a cylinder head gasket from those specified and fit the cylinder head, referring to the appropriate Section of this Chapter. Remember that no subsequent retightening of the cylinder head bolts is required.

27 Screw in the glow plugs and connect the wiring, with the black coiled end towards flywheel.

28 Fit the fuel injectors, using new heat shields. Tighten the injectors to the specified torque.

29 Using a new gasket, fit the thermostat housing, and assemble its component parts. Fit the dipstick guide tube, using a new O-ring **(see illustrations)**.

30 Reconnect the coolant hoses to the coolant pump and thermostat housing.

31 Refit the vacuum pump bracket

32 Refit the vacuum pump, using a new O-ring and fitting the lower bolt first. Reconnect the pump oil return hose to the cylinder block. The glow plug wiring retaining bracket should be located beneath one of the bolt heads, as noted during removal.

33 Refit the fuel injection pump and bracket, tightening the retaining screws to the specified torque.

34 Refit the fuel regulating thermostat to the thermostat housing. Reattach the vacuum pipe retaining bracket and reconnect the pipe to the pump.

35 Refit the fuel filter/bracket assembly,

2

29.29a Fitting the thermostat housing . . .

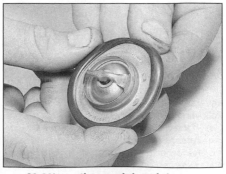

29.29b . . . thermostat seal ring . . .

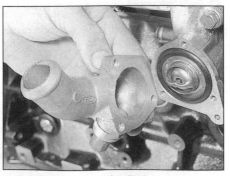

29.29c . . . and refit the cover

29.29d Lower end of the dipstick guide tube

29.29e Tightening dipstick guide tube upper bracket bolt

tightening the retaining nuts to the specified torque. Refit the vacuum pipe clamp bolt and reconnect the vacuum pipe to the turbocharger.

36 Reconnect the fuel heater to its mounting bracket by attaching the two clips and reconnect the fuel lines to the fuel filter by means of the two quick release couplings.

37 Remove any blanking material and reconnect the leak-off pipes and fuel lines to the injectors.

38 Refit the camshaft belt rear covers and idler sprocket.

39 Refit the camshaft sprocket, tightening its retaining bolt to the specified torque.

40 Refit the auxiliary shaft sprocket. The locating pin on the shaft must align with the hole in the pulley.

41 Refit the camshaft belt tensioner, compress the tensioner spring and secure it with the clamp bolt.

42 Refit the sprocket to the fuel injection pump. Centre the retaining bolts in the sprocket slots but do not tighten them until the drivebelt is tensioned.

43 Refit the injection pump belt tensioner, compress the tensioner spring and secure it with the bolt.

44 Lock the crankshaft in position by means of the flywheel ring gear and refit the crankshaft vibration damper whilst ensuring that the lug and notch are aligned. Tighten the damper retaining bolt to the specified torque through the stages stated.

45 Refer to the appropriate Section of this Chapter and check the valve timing adjustment.

46 Refer to Chapter 1 and fit and tension the fuel injection pump and camshaft drivebelts.

47 Refit the upper and lower camshaft belt covers.

48 Refit the pulley to the fuel injection pump, tightening the bolts to the specified torque setting.

49 Reconnect the coolant hose adjacent to the fuel injection pump pulley

50 Refit the alternator mounting bracket to the cylinder block, tightening the bolts to the specified torque setting.

51 Refit the alternator and belt tensioner assembly.

52 Refer to Section 4 and fit and tension the alternator drivebelt.

53 Refer to the appropriate Section of this

Chapter and check the valve clearances.

54 Fit the oil baffle and then the camshaft cover with a new gasket, tightening all disturbed fasteners to the specified torque setting.

55 Reconnect the crankcase ventilation system hoses to the camshaft cover, cylinder block and turbocharger.

56 Refit the front axle driveshaft bracket to the cylinder block, tightening the retaining bolts to the specified torque setting.

57 Refit the turbocharger mounting bracket to the cylinder block, tightening the retaining bolts to the specified torque setting.

58 Refit the complete oil pump assembly with a new filter and oil cooler, referring to the appropriate Section of this Chapter.

59 Reconnect the oil cooler feed hose and tighten the bracket bolts to the specified torque setting.

60 Refer to Chapter 4 and fit the exhaust manifold, with a new gasket.

61 Cover the inlet manifold ports to prevent the entry of dirt.

30 Engine - refitting to transmission

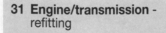

1 Offer the transmission to the engine, rocking it slightly until the locating dowels engage fully. Do not allow the weight of the transmission to hang upon the input shaft once it is engaged in the clutch.

2 Refit and tighten securely the engine-to-transmission bolts.

3 Bolt on the starter motor and bracket.

4 Bolt on the flywheel cover plate (where fitted) and the right-hand mounting, if removed.

31 Engine/transmission - refitting

1 Refitting the engine/transmission is the reverse of the removal procedure, noting the following points.

 a) Tighten all fasteners to the torque wrench settings specified.

 b) Renew all circlips and self-locking nuts disturbed on removal.

 c) Use new cable-ties to secure wiring,

etc. which had to be displaced on removal.

2 Manoeuvre the engine/transmission under the vehicle and carefully lower the vehicle into position until the right and left-hand mountings are in alignment.

3 Attach the engine support bar and use it to lift the engine/transmission until the right and left-hand mountings can be reassembled. Tighten the nuts only lightly at this stage.

4 Raise the front of the vehicle and securely support it on axle stands (see "Jacking and vehicle support").

5 Using a new circlip, refit the left-hand driveshaft. Ensure that the circlip is correctly engaged.

6 Refit the right-hand driveshaft and centre bearing, tightening the bearing bolts to the specified torque wrench setting.

7 Where the vehicle is fitted with air conditioning, refit the compressor, tightening the bolts to the specified torque wrench setting and plugging in its electrical connector.

8 Fit and tension the compressor drivebelt, see Section 4.

9 Refit the subframe and align it on the underbody. Ford specify the use of service tool 15-097 (a pair of tapered guides with attachments to hold them in the subframe as it is refitted) for this task. However, since the working diameter of these tools is 20.40 mm, and since the corresponding aligning holes in the subframe and underbody are respectively 21 mm and 22 mm in diameter, there is a significant in-built tolerance possible in subframe alignment, even if the correct tools are used. If these tools are not available, you can align the subframe by eye, centring the subframe aligning holes on those of the underbody. Alternatively, you can align the subframe using a tapered drift (such as a clutch-aligning tool) or even a deep socket spanner of suitable size - **see illustrations 10.5a and b.**

10 Once the subframe is aligned as precisely as possible with both the underbody and steering gear, refit the subframe bolts, ensuring that the washers are refitted correctly. Tighten the bolts in a diagonal sequence to the specified torque wrench setting without disturbing the subframe. Recheck alignment once all the bolts are securely tightened.

11 With the subframe aligned and securely fastened, the engine/transmission must now be positioned precisely to facilitate mounting reassembly. Ford specify the use of service tool 21-172. This is bolted to the subframe in place of the engine/transmission front mounting (roll restrictor), so that when the mounting's centre bolt is refitted, it is held 60 mm above the subframe's top surface, and offset 20 mm to the rear of the mounting's subframe bolt hole centres. DIY mechanics are advised to obtain the Ford tool as the only alternative is to have a copy fabricated - **see illustration 10.7.**

12 Fasten the tool to the subframe and lightly tighten the mounting's centre bolt. Lower the vehicle and refit the engine/transmission mountings in the following sequence, whilst referring to Section 20:

a) *Fit the left-hand mounting nuts and tighten to the specified torque wrench setting - do not allow the mounting to distort as the nuts are tightened.*

b) *Fit the right-hand mounting bracket-to-engine nuts and tighten to the specified torque wrench setting.*

c) *Slowly release and remove the engine support bar so that the weight of the engine/transmission is taken by the mountings.*

d) *Fit the right-hand mounting bracket-to-mounting nuts and tighten to the specified torque wrench setting - do not allow the mounting todistort as the nuts are tightened.*

e) *Reassemble the engine/transmission rear mounting (roll restrictor), tightening the fasteners to the specified torque wrench settings. Tighten the centre bolt last.*

f) *Refit the steering gear to the subframe. If the Ford service tool is used to tighten the bolts from underneath the vehicle, note that a torque wrench which can tighten in an anti-clockwise direction will be required.*

g) *Unbolt the special tool from the front mounting. Refit the mounting and tighten first the mounting's bolts/nuts, then its centre bolt, to their respective specified torque wrench settings.*

13 On vehicles without air conditioning, refit the radiator mounting brackets to the subframe, tightening the bolts to the torque wrench setting specified. Remove the top securing pins.

14 Swivel the gearchange linkage forwards and refit the mounting retaining bolts, tightening them to the specified torque setting. Refit the gearchange linkage heat shield.

15 Refit the gearchange stabiliser, tightening the Torx bolt to the specified torque setting.

16 Reconnect the selector shaft to the rod, tightening the fasteners to the specified torque setting.

17 Reconnect each lower suspension arm balljoint to its respective spindle carrier, inserting each brake hose in its bracket.

18 Reconnect each track rod end, using a new split-pin to lock the retaining nut in position.

19 Refit each stabiliser link rod to its respective suspension strut.

20 Refit each ABS wiring loom bracket to the suspension strut.

21 On vehicles equipped with air conditioning, refit the radiator and fan assembly, followed by each condenser and the conditioning dehydrator.

22 From beneath the vehicle, reconnect the following electrical connectors:

a) *Left and right-hand fan motor multiplugs (air conditioned models only)*

b) *Ballast resistor multiplug (air conditioned models only)*

c) *Diode (unclip - air conditioned models only)*

23 Lower the vehicle to allow easy access to the top of the engine.

24 Working in the reverse order to that given for engine removal, reconnect all electrical connectors.

25 Refit the power steering pump, its drivebelt and the belt tensioner.

26 Refer to Chapter 10 and tension the power steering pump drivebelt. On completion, refit the belt cover.

27 Reconnect all the electrical connectors disturbed during removal.

28 Reconnect the clutch cable to its retaining bracket. Reconnect the cable to the release lever and check it for correct adjustment

29 Reconnect the vacuum pipe union to the vacuum pump.

30 Refit the throttle cable mounting bracket. Reconnect the throttle cable to the bracket, retaining it with the clip, and reconnect the cable to the injection pump.

31 Reconnect the vacuum hose to the EGR valve.

32 Reconnect the heater hoses to the oil cooler and cylinder head, using new retaining clips where necessary.

33 Reconnect the quick-release coupling of the fuel feed pipe.

34 Reconnect the cooling system hoses to the following components:

a) *The thermostat housing*

b) *The inlet manifold*

c) *The expansion tank*

35 Refit the hose/cable retaining clip to the engine lifting eye and reconnect the fuel return line to the fuel injection pump.

36 Relocate all hoses and cables in the retaining clip on the cylinder head and fasten the clip.

37 Refer to Chapter 4, and refit the charge air cooler.

38 Remove the blank from the turbocharger inlet and reconnect the air inlet hose, using a new retaining clip where necessary.

39 Refer to Chapter 1 and refit the air cleaner element.

40 Lightly grease the mating surface of the mass airflow (MAF) sensor rubber retaining ring and refit the sensor, reconnecting its multiplug.

41 Refit the air inlet system resonator.

42 It is now necessary to adjust the gearchange linkage. Note that a special Ford tool 16-073 will be required in order to carry out the adjustment. This tool is simply a slotted ring which locks the gear lever in the neutral position during adjustment. If the tool is not available, adjustment is still possible by proceeding on a trial-and-error basis, preferably with the help of an assistant to hold the gear lever in the neutral position. Proceed as follows:

a) *Remove the gearchange lever gaiter and bellows.*

b) *Apply the handbrake, jack up the front of the vehicle and support it on axle stands. Move the gear lever to the neutral position.*

c) *Working beneath the vehicle, loosen the clamp bolt on the gearchange linkage.*

d) *With the gear lever still in neutral, fit the special Ford tool 16-073 over the gear lever, and locate it in the recess in the lever retaining housing on top of the transmission. Twist the tool clockwise to lock the lever in the neutral position. Take care during the adjustment not to move the gear lever or displace the adjustment tool (see illustration).*

e) *Check that the front part of the gearchange linkage from the transmission is in neutral. It will be necessary to move the linkage slightly forwards and backwards to determine that it is in the correct position.*

f) *Recheck that the adjustment tool is still correctly fitted to the gear lever, then tighten the clamp bolt on the gearchange linkage.*

g) *Remove the adjustment tool from the gear lever.*

43 Reconnect the lower cooling system hose to the radiator and connector pipe.

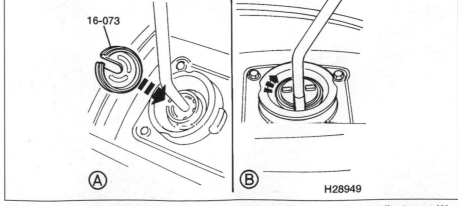

31.42 Ford tool 16-073 will be required to carry out gearchange linkage adjustment (A). This tool is a slotted ring which locks the gear lever in the neutral position (B)

44 Reconnect the front exhaust pipe to the exhaust manifold flange.

45 Reconnect the multiplug to the crankshaft position sensor.

46 Reconnect the speedometer drive cable at the engine end.

47 Refit the coolant drain plug, oil filter and oil drain plug. Refit the engine undershield.

48 Refit the front wheels and lower the vehicle to the ground.

49 Where removed, refit the bonnet.

50 Add coolant, engine oil, power steering fluid and gearbox oil as needed.

51 Reconnect the battery earth lead.

52 Carry out a final check to ensure that all cables and wiring looms are correctly routed, clear of any moving parts, and firmly secured.

53 Remember that, since the front suspension subframe and steering gear have been disturbed, the wheel alignment and steering angles must be checked fully and carefully as soon as possible, with any necessary adjustments being made. This operation is best carried out by an experienced mechanic, using proper checking equipment; the vehicle should therefore be taken to a Ford dealer or similarly-qualified person for attention.

54 Remember also that a road test must be carried out to enable the EEC module to collect data.

32 Engine -
initial start-up after overhaul

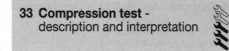

1 Check that oil, fuel and coolant have all been replenished and that the battery is well charged.

2 If a new injection pump has been fitted, the fuel system can be primed, and air bled out (as much as possible) as described in Chapter 4.

3 Start the engine in the usual way. Considerable cranking may be necessary to bleed the fuel system before the engine starts.

4 Once the engine starts, keep it running at a fast tickover. Check that the oil pressure light goes out, then check for leaks of oil, fuel and coolant.

5 If all is well, continue to run the engine until operating temperature is reached, denoted by the cooling fan cutting in.

6 Adjust the idle speed as described in Chapter 1.

7 Stop the engine and check for fluid leakage.

8 Tighten the exhaust system connection if necessary, being careful to avoid burns if the system is very hot.

9 Check oil and coolant levels and top-up if necessary.

10 If many new parts have been fitted, the engine should be treated as new and run in at reduced speeds and loads for the first 600 miles (1000 km) or so. After this mileage it is beneficial to change the engine oil and oil filter.

11 There is no need to tighten the cylinder head bolts further after the running-in period, but the valve clearances should be checked.

33 Compression test -
description and interpretation

1 A compression test involves measuring the pressure developed in each cylinder when the engine is being cranked by the starter motor. It can be a valuable aid in fault diagnosis. A special compression tester will be needed, with an adapter to connect it to a glow plug hole. Rather than buy such a tester it may be cheaper to let a Ford dealer or other specialist do the test.

2 The engine must be at normal operating temperature, the battery well charged and the valve clearances correct.

3 Disconnect the glow plug relay, then remove the glow plug bus bar and the glow plugs themselves.

4 Disconnect the fuel injection pump fuel shut-off solenoid.

5 Screw the compression tester adapter into one of the glow plug holes. Crank the engine on the starter and record the maximum pressure indicated on the tester.

6 Repeat the operations on the other three cylinders and record the pressures developed.

7 Compare the pressures with those given in the Specifications. Absolute values are not so significant as variation between cylinders.

8 A low reading in one cylinder may be due to burnt or poorly seating valves, to piston/bore wear, to a blown head gasket or a cracked head. With petrol engines it is normal to introduce a teaspoon of oil into a low-reading cylinder: if this improves the compression temporarily, worn pistons or bores are indicated. Be wary of using this diagnostic aid on a diesel engine, since there is much less combustion chamber space at TDC and a hydraulic lock may be caused.

9 A low reading obtained for two adjacent cylinders suggests strongly that the head gasket has blown between them.

10 Further tests (eg. leakdown and cooling system pressure tests) may be needed to determine the likely causes of poor compression.

11 When the tests are complete, refit and reconnect the glow plugs, glow plug relay and fuel shut-off solenoid.

Chapter 3
Cooling, heating, and air conditioning systems

Contents

Degrees of difficulty

Easy, suitable for novice with little experience	Fairly easy, suitable for beginner with some experience	Fairly difficult, suitable for competent DIY mechanic	Difficult, suitable for experienced DIY mechanic	Very difficult, suitable for expert DIY or professional

Specifications

Coolant
Mixture type .... See Chapter 1
Cooling system capacity .... See Chapter 1

System pressure
Pressure test .... 1.2 bar - should hold this pressure for at least 10 seconds

Expansion tank filler cap
Pressure rating .... 1.2 bar approximately - see cap for actual value

Thermostat
Starts to open .... 88°C

Radiator electric cooling fan
Switches on at:
    Single-speed fans, two-speed fans - first stage .... 100°C
    Two-speed fans - second stage .... 103°C
Switches off at:
    Single-speed fans, two-speed fans - first stage .... 93°C
    Two-speed fans - second stage .... 100°C

Coolant temperature sensor
Resistance:
    10°C .... 58 kOhms
    20°C .... 37 kOhms
    30°C .... 24 kOhms
    40°C .... 16 kOhms
    50°C .... 11 kOhms
    60°C .... 7 kOhms

Air conditioning system
Refrigerant R134a

Torque wrench settings

	Nm	lbf ft
Radiator mounting bracket-to-subframe bolts	23	17
Fluid cooler pipe unions - automatic transmission	23	17
Thermostat housing-to-cylinder head bolts	20	15
Water outlet-to-thermostat housing bolts	8 to 11	6 to 8
Coolant temperature sensor	23	17
Coolant temperature gauge sender	8	6
Water pump bolts	25	18
Water pump pulley bolts	7 to 10	5 to 7
Air conditioning compressor mounting bolts	25	18

1 General information

Engine cooling system

All vehicles covered by this manual employ a pressurised engine cooling system with thermostatically-controlled coolant circulation. A water pump mounted on the drivebelt end of the cylinder block/crankcase pumps coolant through the engine. The coolant flows around each cylinder and toward the transmission end of the engine. Cast-in coolant passages direct coolant around the inlet and exhaust ports, near the glow plug areas and close to the exhaust valve guides.

A wax pellet type thermostat is located in a housing bolted to the rear of the cylinder head. During warm-up, the closed thermostat prevents coolant from circulating through the radiator. Instead, it returns through the coolant metal pipe running across the front of the engine to the radiator bottom hose and the water pump. The supply to the heater is made from the rear of the thermostat housing. As the engine nears normal operating temperature, the thermostat opens and allows hot coolant to travel through the radiator, where it is cooled before returning to the engine.

The cooling system is sealed by a pressure-type filler cap in the expansion tank. The pressure in the system raises the boiling point of the coolant, and increases the cooling efficiency of the radiator. When the engine is at normal operating temperature, the coolant expands, and the surplus is displaced into the expansion tank. When the system cools, the surplus coolant is automatically drawn back from the tank into the radiator.

 Warning: DO NOT attempt to remove the expansion tank filler cap, or to disturb any part of the cooling system, while it or the engine is hot, as there is a very great risk of scalding. If the expansion tank filler cap must be removed before the engine and radiator have fully cooled down (even though this is not recommended) the pressure in the cooling system must first be released. Cover the cap with a thick layer of cloth, to avoid scalding, and slowly unscrew the filler cap until a hissing sound can be heard. When the hissing has stopped, showing that pressure is released, slowly unscrew the filler cap further until it can be removed; if more hissing sounds are heard, wait until they have stopped before unscrewing the cap completely. At all times, keep well away from the filler opening.

 Warning: Do not allow antifreeze to come in contact with your skin, or with the painted surfaces of the vehicle. Rinse off spills immediately with plenty of water. Never leave antifreeze lying around in an open container, or in a puddle in the driveway or on the garage floor. Children and pets are attracted by its sweet smell, but antifreeze is fatal if ingested.

Warning: If the engine is hot, the electric cooling fan may start rotating even if the engine is not running, so be careful to keep hands, hair and loose clothing well clear when working in the engine compartment.

Heating system

The heating system consists of a blower fan and heater matrix (radiator) located in the heater unit, with hoses connecting the heater matrix to the engine cooling system. Hot engine coolant is circulated through the heater matrix. When the heater temperature control on the facia is operated, a flap door opens to expose the heater box to the passenger compartment. When the blower control is operated, the blower fan forces air through the unit according to the setting selected.

Air conditioning system

See Section 10.

2 Antifreeze - general information

 Warning: Antifreeze is highly toxic if ingested. Read carefully the warnings given in Section 1 before proceeding.

The cooling system should be filled with a water/ethylene glycol-based antifreeze solution, of a strength which will prevent freezing down to at least -25°C, or lower if the local climate requires it. Antifreeze also provides protection against corrosion, and increases the coolant boiling point.

The cooling system should be maintained according to the schedule described in Chapter 1. If antifreeze is used that is not to Ford's specification, old or contaminated coolant mixtures are likely to cause damage, and encourage the formation of corrosion and scale in the system. Use distilled water with the antifreeze, if available - if not, be sure to use only soft water. Clean rainwater is suitable.

Before adding antifreeze, check all hoses and hose connections, because antifreeze tends to leak through very small openings. Engines don't normally consume coolant, so if the level goes down, find the cause and correct it.

The exact mixture of antifreeze-to-water which you should use depends on the relative weather conditions. The mixture should contain at least 40% antifreeze, but not more than 70%. Consult the mixture ratio chart on the antifreeze container before adding coolant. Hydrometers are available at most automotive accessory shops to test the coolant. Use antifreeze which meets the vehicle manufacturer's specifications.

3 Cooling system hoses - disconnection and renewal

Note: *Refer to the warnings given in Section 1 of this Chapter before starting work.*

1 If the checks described in Chapter 1 reveal a faulty hose, it must be renewed as follows **(see illustration)**.

2 First drain the cooling system (see Chapter 1); if the antifreeze is not due for renewal, the drained coolant may be re-used, if it is collected in a clean container.

3 To disconnect any hose, use a pair of pliers to release the spring clamps (or a screwdriver to slacken screw-type clamps), then move them along the hose clear of the union. Carefully work the hose off its stubs. The

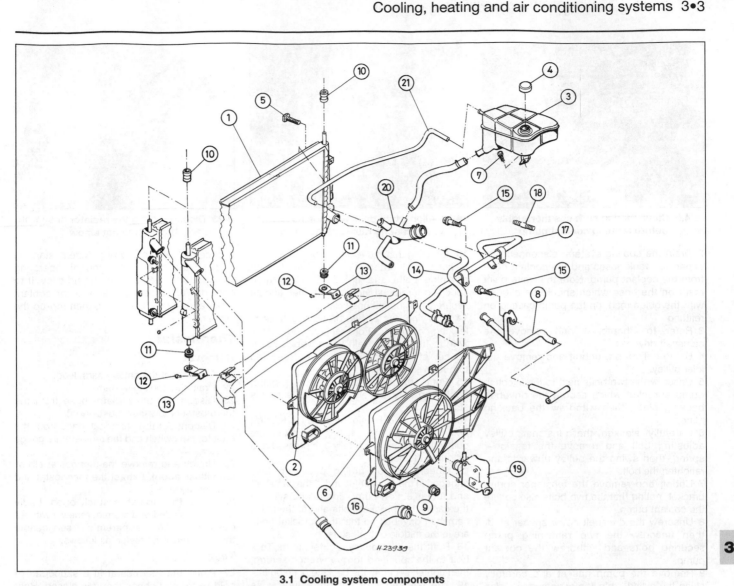

3.1 Cooling system components

1 Radiator	6 (Single) electric cooling fan	11 Bottom mounting rubber
2 (Twin) electric cooling fan	and shroud	12 Bolt
and shroud	7 Bolt	13 Radiator mounting bracket
3 Expansion tank	8 Coolant pipe	14 Coolant hose
4 Filler/pressure cap	9 Nut	15 Bolt
5 Bolt	10 Top mounting rubber	

16 Radiator top hose
17 Coolant pipe/hose
18 Stud
19 Thermostat housing
20 Radiator bottom hose

3

hoses can be removed with relative ease when new - on an older car, they may have stuck.

4 If a hose proves stubborn, try to release it by rotating it on its unions before attempting to work it off. Gently prise the end of the hose with a blunt instrument (such as a flat-bladed screwdriver), but do not apply too much force, and take care not to damage the pipe stubs or hoses. Note in particular that the radiator hose unions are fragile; do not use excessive force when attempting to remove the hoses. If all else fails, cut the hose with a sharp knife, then slit it so that it can be peeled off in two pieces. While expensive, this is preferable to buying a new radiator. Check first, however, that a new hose is readily available.

5 When refitting a hose, first slide the clamps onto the hose, then work the hose onto its unions. If the hose is stiff, use soap (or washing-up liquid) as a lubricant, or soften it by soaking it in boiling water, but take care to prevent scalding.

6 Work each hose end fully onto its union, then check that the hose is settled correctly and is properly routed. Slide each clip along the hose until it is behind the union flared end, before tightening it securely.

7 Refill the system with coolant (see Chapter 1).

8 Check carefully for leaks as soon as possible after disturbing any part of the cooling system.

4 Coolant pump and thermostat - removal and refitting

Note: *The coolant pump is driven from the back of the camshaft drivebelt. Ford recommend that the drivebelt is renewed whenever the coolant pump is renewed.*

Coolant pump

Removal

1 Start by carrying out the (applicable) preliminary dismantling procedures described in paragraphs 1 to 4 of Section 29, Chapter 1.

4.9 Clean mating surfaces thoroughly before refitting coolant pump

4.12 Align white paint mark on hose with pump casting raised rib as shown

4.23 Disconnecting the radiator hose from the thermostat elbow

2 Drain the cooling system, disconnect the expansion tank hoses and the coolant hose from the coolant pump. Note the white paint mark on the hose which should be aligned with the guide mark on the pump casting on refitting.

3 Refer to Chapter 1 and remove the camshaft drivebelt.

4 Using a Torx bit, unbolt and remove the idler pulley.

5 Unscrew the two bolts next to the injection pump sprocket which secure the drivebelt backing plate, then withdraw the backing plate.

6 Carefully slacken the tensioner pulley adjusting bolt and remove the tensioner spring, then swing the pulley upwards and retighten the bolt.

7 Unbolt and remove the tensioner spring bracket, noting that the two bolts also secure the coolant pump.

8 Unscrew the drivebelt cover spacer stud, then unscrew the two remaining pump securing bolts and withdraw the coolant pump.

9 Remove the pump gasket and carefully clean the cylinder block mating surface, also that of the pump, if it is to be refitted **(see illustration)**.

10 Note that a worn or damaged pump cannot be reconditioned, it must be renewed complete. Check the condition of the coolant hoses and clips, renewing them if there is any doubt about their condition.

11 Obtain a new camshaft drivebelt. This must be renewed as a matter of course whenever the coolant pump is renewed. Considering the amount of work required to renew the drivebelts, and the fact that they must be renewed anyway if liquids such as coolant, oil or diesel fuel are allowed to contaminate them, owners are advised to consider renewing both drivebelts on a precautionary basis whenever the pump is disturbed.

Refitting

12 On reassembly, fit the gasket to the pump mating surface and offer up the pump to the cylinder block. Engage the coolant hose on the pump union, ensuring that the hose's white paint mark aligns with the raised rib on the pump casting **(see illustration)**.

13 Ensuring that the tensioner spring bracket is correctly located, refit the pump's four retaining bolts and tighten them to their specified torque wrench setting, then tighten securely the coolant hose clip.

14 Applying one or two drops of a thread-locking compound (Ford recommend Loctite 242) to its threads, refit the drivebelt cover spacer stud, tightening it to its specified torque wrench setting.

15 Refit the drivebelt backing plate, tightening only loosely its two bolts at this stage.

16 Slacken the tensioner pulley adjusting bolt, refit the tensioner spring, then swing the pulley until the spring is fully compressed and retighten the bolt.

17 Check that all timing pegs are fully engaged in the crankshaft and in the camshaft and fuel injection pump sprockets, slacken the camshaft sprocket bolts and fit the (new) camshaft drivebelt so that the sprocket bolts are in the middle of their slots.

18 Refit the idler pulley, tightening its Torx bolt to the specified torque wrench setting, then tighten securely the backing plate bolts.

19 The remainder of the procedure is as described in Section 29 of Chapter 1, paragraph 16 onwards.

20 When all disturbed components have been correctly refitted and adjusted (where applicable), refill the cooling system, start the engine and run it to normal operating temperature, then switch off and allow it to cool down. Inspect the engine for coolant leaks and rectify if required, then top-up the system.

Thermostat

Removal

21 Disconnect the battery earth lead.

22 Drain the cooling system.

23 Disconnect the radiator hose from the thermostat elbow **(see illustration)**.

24 Disconnect the electrical leads from the radiator fan switch and the temperature gauge sender.

25 Unbolt and remove the thermostat elbow **(see illustration)**. Extract the thermostat and recover the O-ring.

26 If the thermostat is stuck open, badly scaled, corroded or distorted, renew it without question. An apparently serviceable thermostat can be tested as follows.

Testing

27 Place the thermostat in a saucepan of cold water and check that it is closed. Heat the water. The thermostat should commence to open as boiling point is approached, and be completely open when the water is boiling (actual temperatures are given in

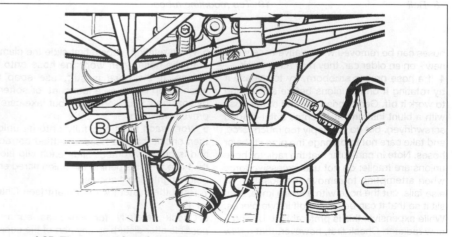

4.25 Thermostat housing-to-block bolts (A) and elbow retaining bolts (B)

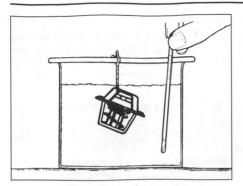

4.27 Testing a thermostat

4.28a Fitting the thermostat to the housing (housing removed)

4.28b Thermostat O-ring

Specifications). Allow the water to cool and check that the thermostat closes again **(see illustration)**. Discard it if it does not behave as described.

Refitting

28 Commence refitting by cleaning the thermostat housing and elbow mating faces.
28 Fit the thermostat, making sure it is the right way round, and a new O-ring **(see illustrations)**. Refit the elbow and secure it with the three bolts.
30 Reconnect the electrical leads to the temperature gauge sender and the radiator fan switch.
31 Reconnect the radiator hose to the thermostat elbow.
32 Refill the cooling system.
33 Reconnect the battery and run the engine up to operating temperature. Check for leaks around the disturbed components. Stop the engine, allow it to cool and top-up the coolant level if necessary.

5 Radiator electric cooling fan(s) - testing, removal and refitting

Note: *Refer to the warnings given in Section 1 of this Chapter before starting work.*

Testing

1 The radiator cooling fan is controlled by the engine management system's ECU, acting on

the information received from the coolant temperature sensor. Where twin fans or two-speed fans are fitted, control is through a resistor assembly, secured to the bottom left-hand corner of the fan shroud - this can be renewed separately if faulty.
2 First, check the relevant fuses and relays (see Chapter 12).
3 To test the fan motor, unplug the electrical connector, and use fused jumper wires to connect the fan directly to the battery. If the fan still does not work, renew the motor.
4 If the motor proved sound, the fault lies in the coolant temperature, in the wiring loom or in the engine management system.

Removal and refitting

5 Disconnect the battery negative (earth) lead (see Chapter 5, Section 1).
6 Drain the cooling system (see Chapter 1).
7 Remove the radiator top hose completely. Disconnect the metal coolant pipe/hose from the thermostat, and unbolt the coolant pipe from the exhaust manifold heat shield.
8 Unplug the cooling fan electrical connector(s), then release all wiring and hoses from the fan shroud.
9 Unscrew the two nuts securing the fan shroud, then lift the assembly to disengage it from its bottom mountings and from the radiator top edge **(see illustrations)**.
10 Withdraw the fan and shroud as an assembly **(see illustration)**.
11 At the time of writing, the fan, motor and

shroud are available only as a complete assembly, and must be renewed together if faulty.
12 Refitting is the reverse of the removal procedure. Ensure that the shroud is settled correctly at all four mounting points before refitting and tightening the nuts.

6 Cooling system electrical switches and sensors - testing, removal and refitting

Note: *Refer to the warnings given in Section 1 of this Chapter before starting work.*

Coolant temperature gauge sender

Testing

1 If the coolant temperature gauge is inoperative, check the fuses first (see Chapter 12).
2 If the gauge indicates Hot at any time, consult the *"Fault diagnosis"* section at the front of this manual, to assist in tracing possible cooling system faults.
3 If the gauge indicates Hot shortly after the engine is started from cold, unplug the coolant temperature sender's electrical connector. If the gauge reading now drops, renew the sender. If the reading remains high, the wire to the gauge may be shorted to earth, or the gauge is faulty.

3

5.9A Fan shroud is secured at top by mounting nut (A), at bottom by clip (B) . . .

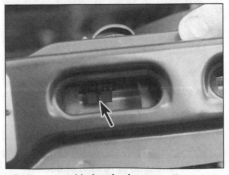

5.9B . . . and is hooked over radiator top edge (one point arrowed)

5.10 Removing radiator electric cooling fan and shroud assembly

4 If the gauge fails to indicate after the engine has been warmed up (approximately 10 minutes) and the fuses are known to be sound, switch off the engine. Unplug the sender's electrical connector, and use a jumper wire to connect the white/red wire to a clean earth point (bare metal) on the engine. Switch on the ignition without starting the engine. If the gauge now indicates Hot, renew the sender.

5 If the gauge still does not work, the circuit may be open, or the gauge may be faulty. See Chapter 12 for additional information.

Removal and refitting

6 See chapter 5, section 18

Coolant temperature sensor

Testing

7 Disconnect the battery negative (earth) lead (see Chapter 5, Section 1).

8 Unplug the electrical connector from the sensor **(see illustration)**.

9 Using an ohmmeter, measure the resistance between the sensor terminals. Depending on the temperature of the sensor tip, the resistance measured will vary, but should be within the broad limits given in the Specifications Section of this Chapter. If the sensor's temperature is varied - by removing it (see below) and placing it in a freezer for a while, or by warming it gently - its resistance should alter accordingly.

10 If the results obtained show the sensor to be faulty, renew it.

11 On completion, plug in the connector.

Removal

12 Disconnect the battery negative (earth) lead (see Chapter 5, Section 1).

13 With the engine *completely cool*, remove the expansion tank filler cap to release any pressure, then refit the cap. Provided you work swiftly and plug the opening as soon as the sensor is unscrewed, coolant loss will thus be minimised; this will avoid the draining of the complete cooling system which would otherwise be necessary (see Chapter 1).

14 Unplug the electrical connector from the sensor **(see illustration).**

15 Unscrew the sensor and withdraw it. If the cooling system has not been drained, plug the opening as quickly as possible.

Refitting

16 Clean as thoroughly as possible the opening in the thermostat housing, then apply a light coat of sealant to the sensor's threads. Remove the material used to plug the sensor hole (where applicable), and quickly install the sensor to prevent coolant loss. Tighten the sensor to the specified torque wrench setting, and plug in its electrical connector.

17 Top-up the cooling system (see Chapter 1) and run the engine, checking for leaks.

Coolant low level switch

Testing

18 The switch is a reed-type unit mounted in the bottom of the cooling system expansion tank, activated by a magnetic float. If the coolant level falls to the "MIN" level or less, the appropriate bulb lights in the warning display.

19 If the bulb fails to light during the 5-second bulb test, check the bulb, and renew if necessary as described in Chapter 12.

20 To check the switch itself, unplug its electrical connector, and use an ohmmeter to measure the resistance across the switch terminals. With the float up, a resistance of 90 ohms should be measured; when it is down, the resistance should increase to approximately 150 kilohms.

21 If the results obtained from the check are significantly different from those expected, the switch is faulty, and must be renewed.

22 If the switch and bulb are proven to be sound, the fault must be in the wiring or in the auxiliary warning control assembly (see Chapter 12).

Removal

23 Disconnect the battery negative (earth) lead (see Chapter 5, Section 1).

24 Remove the expansion tank (see Section 7).

25 Unplug the switch electrical connector.

26 Release the switch by twisting its retainer anti-clockwise, then withdraw it.

Refitting

27 Refitting is the reverse of the removal procedure. Refill the cooling system (see Chapter 1). Start the engine, and check for coolant leaks when it is fully warmed-up.

7 Radiator and expansion tank - removal, inspection and refitting

Note: *Refer to the warnings given in Section 1 of this Chapter before starting work.*

Radiator

Removal

Note: *If leakage is the reason for removing the radiator, bear in mind that minor leaks can often be cured using a radiator sealant with the radiator in situ.*

1 Remove the radiator fan and shroud assembly (see Section 5).

2 Disconnect the bottom hose from the radiator.

3 If the vehicle has air conditioning, unscrew the condenser mounting nuts or bolts, detach the condenser from the radiator, and tie it to the engine compartment front crossmember.

> ⚠ **Warning: Do not disconnect any of the refrigerant hoses.**

4 Unbolt the radiator mounting brackets from the subframe; note that they are handed, and are marked to ensure correct refitting **(see illustration)**.

5 Collect the bottom mounting rubbers, noting which way up they are fitted, and store them carefully.

6 Carefully lower the radiator from the vehicle, and withdraw it.

7 With the radiator removed, it can be inspected for leaks and damage. If it needs repair, have a radiator specialist or dealer service department perform the work, as special techniques are required.

8 Insects and dirt can be removed from the radiator with a garden hose or a soft brush. Don't bend the cooling fins as this is done.

6.8 Location (arrowed) of coolant temperature gauge sender

6.14 Location (arrowed) of coolant temperature sensor

7.4 Radiator mounting bracket-to-subframe bolts (A), air conditioning system condenser mounting bolt (B)

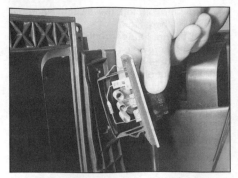

8.5 Heater blower motor control resistor can be prised out of heater unit

8.6 Ensure blower motor retaining lug (arrowed) engages securely in heater unit on reassembly

8.9a Coolant pipes to heater matrix must be disconnected . . .

Refitting

9 Refitting is the reverse of the removal procedure. Be sure the mounting rubbers are seated properly at the base of the radiator.
10 After refitting, refill the cooling system with the proper mixture of antifreeze and water (see Chapter 1).
11 Start the engine, and check for leaks. Allow the engine to reach normal operating temperature, indicated by the radiator top hose becoming hot.
12 Recheck the coolant level, and add more if required.

Expansion tank

13 With the engine *completely cool*, remove the expansion tank filler cap to release any pressure, then refit the cap.
14 Disconnect the hoses from the tank, upper hose first. As each hose is disconnected, drain the tank's contents into a clean container. If the antifreeze is not due for renewal, the drained coolant may be re-used, if it is kept clean.
15 Unscrew the tank's two mounting bolts and withdraw it, unplugging the coolant low level switch electrical connector (where fitted).
16 Wash out the tank, and inspect it for cracks and chafing - renew it if damaged.
17 Refitting is the reverse of the removal procedure. Refill the cooling system with the proper mixture of antifreeze and water (see Chapter 1), then start the engine and allow it

to reach normal operating temperature, indicated by the radiator top hose becoming hot. Recheck the coolant level and add more if required, then check for leaks.

8 Heater/ventilation components - removal and refitting

Heater blower motor

Removal

1 Disconnect the battery negative (earth) lead (see Chapter 5, Section 1).
2 Release the four clips (by pulling them out) securing the passenger side footwell upper trim panel, then withdraw the panel.
3 Unplug the motor's electrical connector.
4 Lift the motor's retaining lug slightly, twist the motor anti-clockwise (seen from beneath) through approximately 30°, then withdraw the assembly.
5 The motor's control resistor can be removed by sliding a slim screwdriver into the slot provided in one end. Press the screwdriver in approximately 5 mm against spring pressure, and prise the resistor out **(see illustration)**.

Refitting

6 Refitting is the reverse of the removal procedure. Refit the motor, and twist it

clockwise until the retaining lug engages securely **(see illustration)**.

Heater matrix

Removal

7 Disconnect the battery negative (earth) lead (see Chapter 5, Section 1).
8 Drain the cooling system (see Chapter 1).
9 Disconnect the coolant hoses from the heater matrix unions protruding through the engine compartment bulkhead **(see illustrations)**.
10 Working inside the passenger compartment, remove the trim panels from each footwell, just in front of the centre console. Each panel is secured by two screws. If additional clearance is required, the centre console can be removed as well (see Chapter 11), but this is not essential.
11 Remove the single screw to release the air duct in the base of the heater unit **(see illustration)**.
12 Remove the three Torx-type screws (size T20) securing the air distributor to the heater unit bottom cover, then release the clips. There is a single plastic clip on each side, and additional metal clips may be found. Push the duct up to retract it, and withdraw the air distributor **(see illustration)**.
13 Release the clips - there are two plastic clips on each side, and additional metal clips may be found - then withdraw the heater

8.9b . . . but can be reached best from beneath vehicle (arrowed)

8.11 Remove screw to allow air duct to be retracted into air distributor at base of heater unit . . .

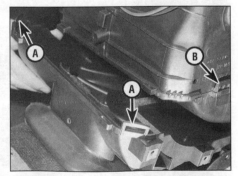

8.12 . . . release clips (A) to free air distributor from base of heater unit - note clips (B) securing . . .

8.13 . . . heater unit's bottom cover, complete with matrix

8.14 Remove clamp (one screw) to separate matrix from heater unit's bottom cover

unit's bottom cover, complete with the matrix **(see illustration)**.
14 Undo the screw and withdraw the clamp to separate the matrix from the bottom cover **(see illustration)**.

Refitting

15 Refitting is the reverse of the removal procedure. Additional metal clips may be required to secure the heater unit's bottom cover and the air distributor. Ensure that the duct is lowered from the air distributor and secured with its screw.
16 Refill the cooling system with the proper

mixture of antifreeze and water (see Chapter 1). Start the engine and allow it to reach normal operating temperature, indicated by the radiator top hose becoming hot. Recheck the coolant level and add more if required, then check for leaks. Check the operation of the heater.

Pollen filter

17 Refer to Chapter 1.

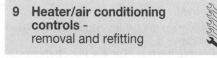

9 Heater/air conditioning controls - removal and refitting

Blower/air conditioning control

Removal

1 Disconnect the battery negative (earth) lead (see Chapter 5, Section 1).
2 Remove the ashtray. Referring to the relevant Sections of Chapter 11, undo the two upper screws from the centre console and pull out the cassette storage compartment, then remove the radio/cassette player.
3 Pull the heater control/radio bezel out of the three clips securing its top edge, pull it

forwards and unplug the switch electrical connector (where fitted).
4 Pull off the heater control knobs, and remove the screw securing each end of the heater control unit **(see illustration)**. Pull the control unit out of the facia.
5 Unplug the two electrical connectors from the blower/air conditioning control. Remove the retaining screw and withdraw the control, twisting it to release it from the panel.

Refitting

6 Refitting is the reverse of the removal procedure. Check the operation of the control on completion.

Temperature control

Removal

7 Remove the heater control unit as described in paragraphs 1 to 4 above.
8 On vehicles without air conditioning, unhook the operating cable from the temperature control **(see illustration)**; where air conditioning is fitted, unplug the control's electrical connector. Undo the retaining screw, and withdraw the control.

Refitting

9 Refitting is the reverse of the removal procedure; check the operation of the control on completion.

Air distribution control

Removal

10 Remove the heater control unit as described in paragraphs 1 to 4 above. Unplug the electrical connectors, and unhook the operating cable (where fitted) to withdraw the unit **(see illustration)**.
11 Use a pair of slim screwdrivers to release the clips on each side of the control, then withdraw the control from the unit.

Refitting

12 Refitting is the reverse of the removal procedure. Check the operation of the controls on completion.

9.4 Remove screws (arrowed) securing each end of heater control unit

9.8 Unhooking operating cable from temperature control - note retaining screw (arrowed)

9.10 Unplugging electrical connectors from rear of heater control unit

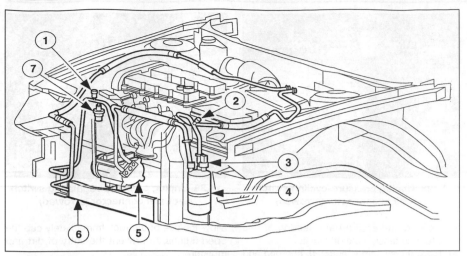

10.1 Air conditioning system components

1 Quick-release Schrader valve-type coupling - high-pressure side
2 Quick-release Schrader valve-type coupling - low-pressure side
3 Pressure-cycling switch - low-pressure side
4 Accumulator/dehydrator
5 Compressor
6 Condenser
7 Pressure-regulating switch - high-pressure side

10 Air conditioning system - general information and precautions

General information

The air conditioning system consists of a condenser mounted in front of the radiator, an evaporator mounted adjacent to the heater matrix, a compressor mounted on the engine, an accumulator/dehydrator, and the plumbing connecting all of the above components - this contains a choke (or "venturi") mounted in the inlet to the evaporator, which creates the drop in pressure required to produce the cooling effect **(see illustration)**.

A blower fan forces the warmer air of the passenger compartment through the evaporator core (rather like a radiator in reverse), transferring the heat from the air to the refrigerant. The liquid refrigerant boils off into low-pressure vapour, taking the heat with it when it leaves the evaporator.

Precautions

 Warning The air conditioning system is under high pressure. Do not loosen any fittings or remove any components until after the system has been discharged. Air conditioning refrigerant should be properly discharged into an approved type of container, at a dealer service department or an automotive air conditioning repair facility capable of handling the refrigerant safely. Always wear eye protection when disconnecting air conditioning system fittings.

When an air conditioning system is fitted, it is necessary to observe the following special precautions whenever dealing with any part of the system, its associated components, and any items which necessitate disconnection of the system:

a) While the refrigerant used on later models - R134a - is less damaging to the environment than the previously-used R12, both are very dangerous substances. They must not be allowed into contact with the skin or eyes, or there is a risk of frostbite. They must also not be discharged in an enclosed space, as there is a risk of suffocation. The refrigerant is heavier than air, and so must never be discharged over a pit.

b) The refrigerant must not be allowed to come in contact with a naked flame, otherwise a poisonous gas will be created - under certain circumstances, this can form an explosive mixture with air. For similar reasons, smoking in the presence of refrigerant is highly dangerous, particularly if the vapour is inhaled through a lighted cigarette.

c) Never discharge the system to the atmosphere - R134a is not an ozone-depleting ChloroFluoroCarbon (CFC) as is R12, but is instead a hydrofluorocarbon, which causes environmental damage by contributing to the "greenhouse effect" if released into the atmosphere.

d) R134a refrigerant must not be mixed with R12; the system uses different seals (now green-coloured, previously black) and has different fittings requiring different tools, so that there is no chance of the two types of refrigerant becoming mixed accidentally.

e) If for any reason the system must be disconnected, entrust this task to your Ford dealer or a refrigeration engineer.

f) It is essential that the system be professionally discharged prior to using any form of heat - welding, soldering, brazing, etc - in the vicinity of the system, before having the vehicle oven-dried at a temperature exceeding 70°C after repainting, and before disconnecting any part of the system.

11 Air conditioning system components - removal and refitting

 Warning: The air conditioning system is under high pressure. Do not loosen any fittings or remove any components until after the system has been discharged. Air conditioning refrigerant should be properly discharged into an approved type of container, at a dealer service department or an automotive air conditioning repair facility capable of handling R134a refrigerant. Cap or plug the pipe lines as soon as they are disconnected, to prevent the entry of moisture. Always wear eye protection when disconnecting air conditioning system fittings.

Note: This Section refers to the components of the air conditioning system itself - refer to Sections 9 and 10 for details of components common to the heating/ventilation system.

Condenser

1 Have the refrigerant discharged at a dealer service department or an automotive air conditioning repair facility.
2 Disconnect the battery negative (earth) lead (see Chapter 5, Section 1).
3 Remove the radiator undershield (see Chapter 1).
4 Using the Ford service tool 34-001, disconnect the refrigerant lines from the condenser. Immediately cap the open fittings, to prevent the entry of dirt and moisture.
5 Unbolt the condenser **(see illustration 7.4)** and lift it out of the vehicle. Store it upright, to prevent oil loss.
6 Refitting is the reverse of removal.
7 If a new condenser was installed, add 20 cc of refrigerant oil to the system.
8 Have the system evacuated, charged and leak-tested by the specialist who discharged it.

Evaporator

9 The evaporator is mounted with the heater matrix. Apart from the need to have the refrigerant discharged, and to use Ford service tools 34-001 and 34-003 to disconnect the lines, the procedure is as described in Section 8 of this Chapter.
10 On reassembly, if a new evaporator was installed, add 20 cc of refrigerant oil to the system.

3

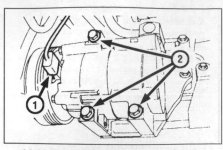

11.16 Removing the air conditioning compressor

1 *Wiring multiplug*
2 *Compressor retaining bolts*

11.23 Unplug pressure-cycling switch electrical connector (arrowed)

11.33 Unplug pressure-regulating switch electrical connector (arrowed)

11 Have the system evacuated, charged and leak-tested by the specialist who discharged it.

Compressor

Removal

12 Have the refrigerant discharged at a dealer service department or an automotive air conditioning repair facility.
13 Disconnect the battery negative (earth) lead. Apply the handbrake, then raise the front of the vehicle and securely support it on axle stands (see "*Jacking and vehicle support*").
14 Remove the auxiliary drivebelt.
15 Undo the six plastic screws, and remove the cover from under the condenser/radiator mounting bracket.
16 Disconnect the compressor clutch wiring multi-plug **(see illustration)**, then detach the compressor high and low-pressure pipes.
17 Undo the retaining bolts and remove the compressor from its mounting bracket. **Note:** *Keep the compressor level during handling and storage. If the compressor has seized, or if you find metal particles in the refrigerant lines, the system must be flushed out by an air conditioning technician, and the dehydrator must be renewed.*

Refitting

18 Refit the compressor in the reverse order of removal, renewing all disturbed seals.

19 Refer to the appropriate Section of this Chapter and tension the drivebelt.
20 Have the system evacuated, charged and leak-tested by the specialist that discharged it.

Accumulator/dehydrator

21 Have the refrigerant discharged at a dealer service department or an automotive air conditioning repair facility.
22 Disconnect the battery negative (earth) lead (see Chapter 5, Section 1).
23 The accumulator/dehydrator, which acts as a reservoir and filter for the refrigerant, is located in the left-hand front corner of the engine compartment. Using the Ford service tool 34-003, disconnect the refrigerant line next to the accumulator/dehydrator from the compressor. Immediately cap the open fittings, to prevent the entry of dirt and moisture, then unplug the pressure-cycling switch electrical connector **(see illustration)**.
24 Remove the radiator undershield (see Chapter 1).
25 Unbolt the accumulator/dehydrator from the front suspension subframe.
26 Using the Ford service tool 34-003, disconnect the lower refrigerant line from the accumulator/dehydrator. It may be necessary to unscrew the pressure-cycling switch to

allow the use of the tool. Immediately cap the open fittings, to prevent the entry of dirt and moisture.
27 Withdraw the accumulator/dehydrator.
28 Refit the accumulator/dehydrator in the reverse order of removal; renew all seals disturbed.
29 If you are installing a new accumulator/dehydrator, refer to the manufacturer's instructions for adding refrigerant oil to the system.
30 Have the system evacuated, charged and leak-tested by the specialist that discharged it.

Pressure-cycling and pressure-regulating switches

31 Have the refrigerant discharged at a dealer service department or an automotive air conditioning repair facility.
32 Disconnect the battery negative (earth) lead (see Chapter 5, Section 1).
33 Unplug the switch electrical connector, and unscrew it **(see illustration)**.
34 Refitting is the reverse of the removal procedure; there is no need to top-up the refrigerant oil.
35 Have the system evacuated, charged and leak-tested by the specialist that discharged it.

Chapter 4
Fuel and exhaust systems

Contents

Degrees of difficulty

Easy, suitable for novice with little experience	Fairly easy, suitable for beginner with some experience	Fairly difficult, suitable for competent DIY mechanic	Difficult, suitable for experienced DIY mechanic	Very difficult, suitable for expert DIY or professional

Specifications

General

System type	Rear mounted fuel tank, combined lift and injection pump, indirect injection
Firing order	1 - 3 - 4 - 2 (No. 1 at pulley end)
Glow plug type	Champion CH147
Air filter element type	Champion U654
Fuel filter types:	
Bosch	Champion L134
CAV RotoDiesel	Champion L131 or L137

Fuel

Fuel type	Commercial diesel fuel for road vehicles (DERV)
Fuel capacity	42 to 55 litres according to model

Injection pump

Make and type	Bosch VE or CAV RotoDiesel
Rotation (viewed from crankshaft pulley end)	Clockwise
Drive	By toothed belt from crankshaft

Injectors (Bosch)

Needle seat leakage/Injector dribble	Holds 125 bar (1813 lbf/in^2) for 10 seconds

Adjustment data

Idle speed	850 ± 50 rpm
Injection pump timing	By timing pegs, at TDC
Maximum engine speed:	
Continuous	4800 rpm
Intermittent	5200 ± 50 rpm

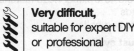

4

Torque wrench settings

	Nm	lbf ft
Fuel injection pump		
Pump-to-engine front plate	18 to 28	13 to 21
Pump-to-rear support bracket	18 to 22	13 to 16
Pump support bracket-to-cylinder block	18 to 27	13 to 20
Pump pulley bolts	20 to 25	15 to 18
Pump pulley to flange	23	17
Pump belt tensioner to cylinder block	45	33
Fuel injectors		
Injectors	70	52
Injector line to injector(s) and pump	25	18
Fuel filter		
Filter bracket-to-cylinder head/lifting eye	23	17
Other fuel system components		
Fuel pipe banjo union bolts	16 to 20	12 to 15
Fuel regulating thermostat to thermostat housing	23	17
Fuel shut-off solenoid - CAV RotoDiesel pump	16 to 20	12 to 15
Charge air cooler		
Cooler to bracket	18	13
Turbocharger		
Turbocharger oil return hose clip	5	4
Turbocharger to exhaust manifold nuts	38	28
Turbocharger to oil feed line	18	13
Turbocharger oil feed line bracket to cylinder block	48	35
Turbocharger/cylinder block bracket to turbocharger	23	17
Turbocharger/cylinder block bracket to cylinder block	47	35
Inlet manifold		
Manifold-to-cylinder head fasteners:		
Studs	10 to 14	7 to 10
Nuts and bolts	18 to 25	13 to 18
Exhaust system		
Manifold-to-cylinder head fasteners:		
Studs	10 to 14	7 to 10
Nuts and bolts	18 to 25	13 to 18
Manifold to turbocharger nuts	38	28
Front pipe to turbocharger	40	30

1 General information and precautions

General information

The fuel system comprises a rear-mounted fuel tank, a fuel filter, fuel injection pump, injectors and associated components.

Fuel is drawn from the tank by the transfer pump incorporated in the injection pump. En route it passes through the fuel filter, located in the engine bay, where foreign matter and water are removed. The injection pump is gear-driven from the crankshaft and supplies fuel under very high pressure to each injector in turn as it is needed. The amount of fuel delivered is determined by the pump governor, which reacts to throttle position and to engine speed. Injection timing is varied automatically to suit the prevailing speed and load.

Rigid pipes connect the pump and injectors. There are four injectors, situated where spark plugs would be found on a petrol engine. Each injector sprays fuel into a pre-combustion or "swirl" chamber as its piston approaches TDC on the compression stroke. This system is known as indirect injection. The injectors only open under very high pressure. Lubrication is provided by allowing a small quantity of fuel to leak back past the injector internal components. The leaked-back fuel is returned to the pump and then to the fuel tank.

Two systems, both automatic, assist cold starting. A cold start advance device on the injection pump alters the injection timing and causes fuel delivery to be increased during cold starts. It contains a heating element which is energised when the engine is running. Preheater or "glow" plugs are fitted to each swirl chamber: they are electrically heated before, during and immediately after a cold start. A warning light illuminates when the ignition is switched on, showing that the glow plugs are in operation. When the light goes out, preheating is complete and the engine can be started. The glow plugs are controlled by a special relay which incorporates a temperature sensor.

To stop the engine, a solenoid valve at the rear of the fuel pump is used. The valve is of the "fail safe" type, so it must be energised to allow the engine to run. When power is removed from the valve, its plunger moves under spring pressure and interrupts fuel delivery.

The fuel system on diesel engines is normally very reliable. Provided that clean fuel is used and the specified maintenance is conscientiously carried out, no problems should be experienced. The injection pump and injectors may require overhaul after a high mileage has been covered, but this cannot be done on a DIY basis.

On later models, the CAV RotoDiesel system is fitted to replace the Bosch version

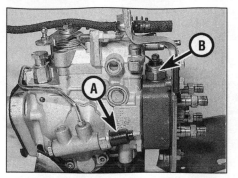

1.7a Side view of a Bosch fuel injection pump

A *Cold start element*
B *Fuel shut-off solenoid*

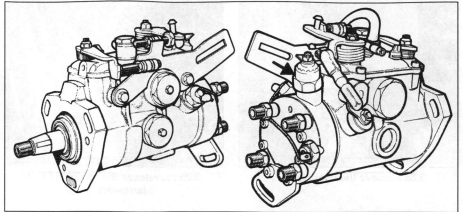

1.7b CAV RotoDiesel fuel injection pump. Fuel shut-off solenoid arrowed

used on earlier models. The components of the two systems are not interchangeable. Of the two pump types fitted, the CAV RotoDiesel fuel injection pump can be identified by the two large octagonal plugs on the side of the pump body **(see illustrations)**.

Precautions

Fuel - Warning

Many of the procedures given in this Chapter involve the disconnection of fuel pipes and system components which may result in some fuel spillage. Before carrying out any operation on the fuel system, refer to the precautions given in the *"Safety first"* Section at the beginning of this Manual and follow them implicitly.

Tamperproof adjustment screws - caution

Certain adjustment points in the fuel system are protected by "tamperproof" caps, plugs or seals. The purpose of such tamperproofing is to discourage adjustment by unqualified operators.

In some EEC countries (though not yet in the UK) it is an offence to drive a vehicle with missing or broken tamperproof seals. Before

disturbing a tamperproof seal, satisfy yourself that you will not be breaking local or national anti-pollution regulations by doing so. Fit a new seal when adjustment is complete when this is required by law.

Do not break tamperproof seals on a vehicle which is still under warranty.

Working procedures

When working on fuel system components, scrupulous cleanliness must be observed, and care must be taken not to introduce any foreign matter into fuel lines or components. Care should be taken not to disturb any components unnecessarily. Before attempting work, ensure that the relevant spares are available. If persistent problems are encountered, it is recommended that the advice of a Ford dealer or a Specialist is sought.

2 Air cleaner - element renewal

Refer to Section 26, Chapter 1.

3 Air cleaner casing - removal and refitting

Note: *It is not necessary to remove the air cleaner cover to facilitate removal of the cleaner casing.*

1 On early models, loosen the hose retaining clip and remove the air inlet system resonator by pulling it from its two retainers **(see illustration)**.

2 On all models, disconnect the multiplug from the mass airflow (MAF) sensor. Loosen the two retaining clips and detach the sensor assembly from the casing cover **(see illustration)**. This operation may prove difficult due to resistance from the rubber retaining ring.

3 Unplug the vent pipe from the casing cover. Remove the air cleaner casing by first releasing the rubber retaining band, releasing the casing from the end bellows and pulling it from the base retaining spigots **(see illustrations)**.

4 Refit in the reverse order of removal, lightly greasing the mating surface of the mass airflow (MAF) sensor rubber retaining ring.

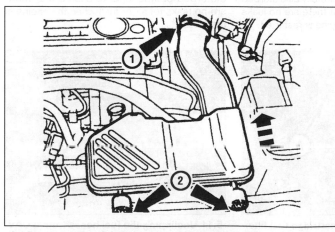

3.1 Removing the air intake system resonator - early model Mondeo

1 Hose clip   2 Retainers

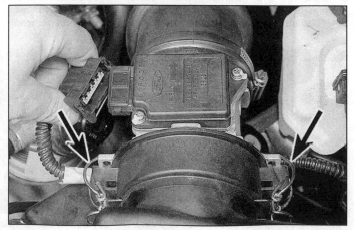

3.2 Disconnecting the MAF sensor multiplug. Sensor retaining clips arrowed

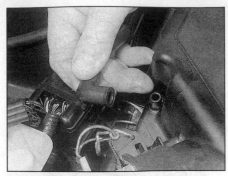

3.3a Remove the vent pipe . . .

3.3b . . . release the retaining band (arrowed) . . .

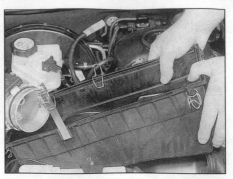

3.3c . . . and remove the air cleaner casing

4 Fuel filter - draining and element renewal

All filter types

Draining water

Refer to Section 4, Chapter 1.

Element renewal

Refer to Section 25, Chapter 1.

5 Fuel filter assembly - removal and refitting

Bosch clamp-fixing cartridge filter

Removal

1 Drain the filter completely.
2 Note carefully the orientation of the fuel inlet and outlet hoses and the filter vent screw. Clean them thoroughly and obtain new hose clamps and/or flexible hoses if the condition of those fitted is in any way suspect.
3 Releasing the clamps with pliers, disconnect the fuel inlet and outlet hoses from the filter stubs **(see illustration)**. Plug or

cap hoses and unions to keep fuel in and dirt out.
4 Slacken the clamp screw and withdraw the filter from its bracket, taking care to spill as little as possible of any remaining fuel **(see illustration)**.

Refitting

5 Fit the new filter to the clamp, aligning its stubs with the hoses as noted on removal and observing any directional markings on the filter. Fit the new flexible hoses and/or clamps (if required), then connect the hoses to the filter and fasten them securely with the clamps.
6 Tighten the filter mounting clamp screw, but be careful not to over tighten it (nominal torque wrench setting of 1.5 to 2.5 Nm only) or the filter may be crushed. Check that the drain cock is closed.
7 Reconnect the battery earth lead and restart the engine. Considerable cranking may be required to bleed the air from the system. To spare the battery, this time may be reduced by filling the filter with clean fuel via its vent screw opening but, as noted above, it is essential that no dirt is introduced into the system and that no diesel fuel is poured over vulnerable components when doing this.
8 On completion, check carefully all disturbed components to ensure that there are no leaks (or air or fuel) when the engine is restarted.

All other types

Removal

9 Drain the filter completely.
10 On early types, unscrew the fuel inlet and outlet hose banjo union bolts. Note carefully the location of the copper sealing washers at each union, check them meticulously for scratches or distortion and renew them if there is any doubt at all about their condition.
11 On later types, unclip the quick release fuel line connectors **(see illustration)**.
12 Plug or cap open connections to keep fuel in and dirt out.
13 Unscrew the mounting nuts and withdraw the filter assembly from the vehicle, taking care to spill as little as possible of any remaining fuel.

Refitting

14 On refitting, tighten the mounting nuts securely, to the specified torque wrench setting. Ensure that the copper sealing washers are located correctly on each side of each union and tighten securely the union banjo bolts; again, use the specified torque wrench setting.
15 Reconnect the battery earth lead, bleed the system, then restart the engine.
16 On completion, check carefully all disturbed components to ensure that there are no leaks (of air or fuel) when the engine is restarted.

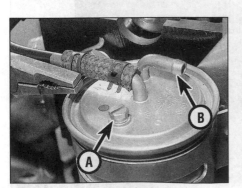

5.3 Connecting fuel outlet hose to Bosch filter

A Vent screw   B Fuel inlet hose

5.4 Bosch clamp-fixing cartridge fuel filter

A Clamp screw   B Drain cock

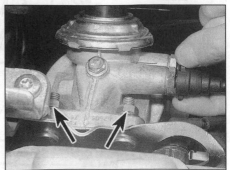

5.11 Unclipping the fuel hoses from a CAV fuel filter. Filter assembly retaining nuts arrowed

6 Fuel system - bleeding

Bosch system

1 As this system is intended to be "self-bleeding", no hand-priming pump or separate bleed screws/nipples are fitted.

2 When any part of the system has been disturbed therefore, air must be purged from the system by cranking the engine on the starter motor until it starts. When it has started, keep the engine running for approximately 5 minutes to ensure that all air has been removed from the system. To minimise the strain on the battery and starter motor when trying to start the engine, crank it in 10-second bursts, pausing for 30 seconds each time, until the engine starts.

3 Depending on the work that has been carried out, it may be possible partially to prime the system so as to spare the battery by reducing as much as possible the amount of cranking time required to start the engine. To spare the battery, fill the filter with clean fuel via its vent screw opening but it is essential that no dirt is introduced into the system and that no diesel fuel is poured over vulnerable components when doing this.

4 If a hand-operated vacuum pump is available, this can be connected to the pump's fuel return union and used to suck fuel through the supply lines and filter. This will obviously save the battery a good deal of work. If a long length of clear plastic tubing is used to connect the vacuum pump to the injection pump union, it will be easier to see when fuel emerges free from air bubbles. Do not forget to energise the fuel shut-off solenoid by switching on the ignition, to position "II" so that fuel can pass through the pump.

CAV RotoDiesel system

5 This system is fitted with a hand-priming pump, operated by depressing repeatedly the black button on the top of the filter assembly. If air has entered the system always purge it from the filter bleed nipple first, then (if required) from the pump union and the injector pipes. Ensure that rags are placed underneath the bleeding point to catch the spilt fuel. Diesel fuel must not be allowed to contaminate vulnerable components, especially the clutch, alternator and starter motor.

6 To bleed air from the system as far as the fuel filter, slacken the bleed nipple on the filter outlet union and operate the hand-priming pump until fuel emerges free from air bubbles. Tighten securely the bleed nipple, mop up any spilt fuel and operate the hand-priming pump until increased resistance is felt.

7 If air has reached the fuel injection pump, energise the fuel shut-off solenoid by switching on the ignition to position "II", slacken the pump's fuel return union and operate the hand-priming pump until fuel emerges free from air bubbles. Tighten securely the union banjo bolt, mop up any spilt fuel and operate the hand-priming pump until increased resistance is felt. Switch off the ignition.

8 Finally, start the engine and keep it running for approximately 5 minutes to ensure that all air is removed from the system.

Both systems

9 If air has entered the injector pipes, slacken each union at the injectors and crank the engine until fuel emerges, then tighten securely all unions and mop up the spilt fuel. Start the engine and keep it running for a few minutes to ensure that all air has been expelled.

Note: The valve fitted between the filter and the pump on later engines is used at the factory only to fill and bleed the system on production. Check regularly that it is tightly closed

7 Fuel system - contamination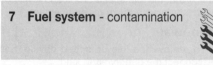

1 If, at any time, sudden fuel filter blockage, poor starting or otherwise unsatisfactory engine performance should be traced to the appearance of black sludge or slime within the fuel system, this may be due to corrosion caused by the presence of various micro-organisms in the fuel. These can live in the fuel tank if water is allowed to remain there in significant quantities, their waste products causing corrosion of steel and other metallic components of the fuel system.

2 If the fuel system is thought to be contaminated in this way, immediately seek the advice of a Ford dealer or diesel specialist. Thorough treatment is required to cure the problem and to prevent it from occurring again.

3 If you are considering treating the vehicle on a DIY basis proceed as follows. Do not re-use contaminated fuel.

4 First drain and remove the fuel tank, flush it thoroughly with clean diesel fuel and use a torch to examine as much as possible of its interior. If the contamination is severe, the tank must be steam-cleaned internally and then flushed again with clean diesel fuel.

5 Disconnect the fuel feed and return hoses from the injection pump, remove the fuel filter element and flush through the system's feed and return lines with clean diesel fuel.

6 Renew the filter element, refit the fuel tank and reconnect the fuel lines, then fill the tank with clean diesel fuel and bleed the system as described above. Watch carefully for signs of the problem occurring again.

7 While it is unlikely that such contamination will be found beyond the fuel filter, if it is thought to have reached the injection pump, the pump may require cleaning. This is a task only for the local Bosch or CAV RotoDiesel

agent. Do not attempt to disturb any part of the pump (other than the few adjustments detailed in this Manual) or to clean it yourself.

8 The most common cause of excessive quantities of water being in the fuel is condensation from the water vapour in the air. Diesel tanks (whether underground storage tanks or that in the vehicle) are more susceptible to this problem than petrol tanks because of petrol's higher vapour pressure. Water formation in the vehicle's tank can be minimised by keeping the tank as full as possible at all times and by using the vehicle regularly.

9 Note that proprietary additives are available to inhibit the growth of micro-organisms in vehicle fuel tanks or storage tanks.

10 If you buy all your fuel from the same source and suspect that to be the source of the contamination, the owner or operator should be advised. Otherwise, the risk of taking on contaminated fuel can be minimised by using only reputable filling stations which have a good turnover.

8 Idle speed - checking and adjustment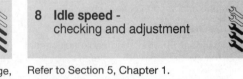

Refer to Section 5, Chapter 1.

9 Idle up speed control system - checking, adjustment and renewal

Checking

1 An idle up speed device may be fitted to automatically raise the engine speed and prevent stalling when reverse gear is selected. The unit is attached to a bracket on the left-hand inner wing panel in the engine compartment. The glow plug relay has been moved from its original position and is now secured to the up speed unit bracket (see illustrations).

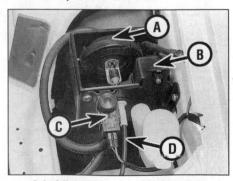

9.1a Idle up speed control system components - Escort with CAV fuel injection system

A Vacuum diaphragm
B Glow plug relay
C Reverse light switch circuit connector
D Up speed operating cable

4

9.1b Idle up speed device (viewed from beneath vehicle)

2 The control unit operates in conjunction with the reversing light circuit and the brake vacuum system. It differs according to the fuel injection type.

3 To check the idle up speed system for satisfactory operation, first check that the system wiring and vacuum hoses are in good condition and securely connected.

Adjustment

4 Check that the operating cable adjustment is as follows according to system:

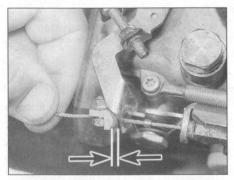

9.4a Adjust the up speed operating cable to allow the required clearance between clamp and lever

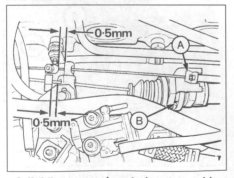

9.4b Idle up speed control system cable adjustment - Bosch injection system shown

A Up speed cable clip - on fast idle waxstat device cable bracket
B Slot in bracket for cable removal and refitting

CAV RotoDiesel - Ensure that the idle operating cable is fully released and there is no vacuum in the servo, then check that there is a clearance of 0.5 to 1.0 mm between the idle up speed operating cable clamp and the idle lever **(see illustration)**. If necessary, loosen off the adjuster clamp screw and move the clamp to set the clearance then retighten the screw.

Bosch - Fully extend the waxstat operating cable by switching on the ignition and leaving it in position "II" for a period of three minutes, then check that the clearance between the cable clamp and the idle lever is 0.5 mm **(see illustration)**.

5 If adjustment is required on either system, loosen off the cable clamp screw and set the clamp as required.

6 Start the engine and allow it to idle for a period of 5 minutes, then engage reverse gear. The idle speed should rise and then level off within three seconds of reverse gear being engaged. Now disengage reverse gear and check that the idle speed drops and levels off within three seconds of disengagement.

Renewal

7 To remove the idle up speed device, first disconnect the battery earth lead.

8 Unplug the electrical connector from the device.

9 Pull the lower vacuum pipe off the device.

10 Disconnect the cable from the fuel injection pump.

11 Remove the retaining bolts and withdraw the idle up speed device from the vehicle.

12 Refitting is the reverse of the removal procedure. Adjust the cable as described above.

10 Maximum speed - checking and adjustment

1 The maximum no load speed may be checked if wished, using one of the methods described in the first sub Section of Section 5, Chapter 1. Running the engine with the wheels free is not recommended, because of the risk of damage or injury if anything goes wrong.

11.4 Pump sprocket mark aligned with pointer on timing cover

2 The maximum speed adjusting screw is sealed in production. Adjustment should only be made by a Ford dealer or authorised fuel injection specialist. Unauthorised adjustment may invalidate the warranty.

3 When checking the maximum speed, do not hold the engine at this speed for more than five seconds. Keep well clear of the water pump/alternator drivebelt and pulleys.

4 The engine speed should drop from maximum to idle within the specified time when the throttle is released. If not, check that the throttle linkage is not binding or obstructed. If this is in order, seek specialist advice.

11 Fuel injection pump timing - checking and adjustment

Bosch

1 This is not a routine operation. It should only be necessary if the pump has been disturbed, after fitting a new pump, or if the crankshaft pulley bolt has been disturbed in the course of other work such as renewal of the crankshaft front oil seal. Whenever the crankshaft pulley bolt is slackened, it is possible for the drive gear to move very slightly in relation to the crankshaft - hence the need to check the injection pump timing.

2 Two special tools will be needed - a TDC setting pin and a dial test indicator with a suitable mounting or stand.

3 Slacken the pump mountings so that it is just free to be twisted back and forth within the limits of its slotted fixing holes.

4 Remove the camshaft drivebelt cover. Turn the engine until the pump sprocket timing mark is aligned with the pointer on the timing cover **(see illustration)**.

5 Remove the screw plug and insert the TDC setting pin. Carefully turn the engine in the normal direction of rotation until the crankshaft web contacts the setting pin, showing that No. 1 piston is at TDC.

6 Protect the alternator against fuel spillage, then unscrew and remove the central plug from the rear of the pump **(see illustration)**.

11.6 Removing the central plug (arrowed) from the rear of the pump

7 Mount the dial test indicator so that its probe enters the plug hole and bears on the plunger inside. It is preferable, though not essential, that the indicator be mounted on the pump rather than on the block. Depending on the length of the indicator probe, it may be necessary to remove the injection pipes.

8 Turn the engine slowly anti-clockwise, observing the dial test indicator. The reading will decrease and then become steady. Stop turning when the reading is steady and zero the indicator **(see illustration)**.

9 Turn the engine clockwise again until the setting pin is contacted. Read the dial test indicator. The value shown should correspond to that given for pump timing in the *Specifications*. If not, turn the pump one way or the other until it does.

10 Tighten the pump mountings. If the dial test indicator is mounted on the block, tightening the mountings may cause the reading to change. This does not matter provided that the indicator is reset to its new zero.

11 Repeat the operations from paragraph 8 onwards until the correct result is obtained with the pump mountings tightened.

12 Remove the dial test indicator and the TDC setting pin.

13 Refit the disturbed components, not forgetting the screw plug for the TDC pin hole.

14 Run the engine for a minute or two to bleed any air from the fuel

CAV RotoDiesel

15 For these operations a dial gauge, a TDC gauge pin and a dial gauge holding fixture will be required. The dial gauge fixture (Ford tool No 21-100) can probably be dispensed with if the radiator and cooling fan are removed to improve access.

16 Injection pump timing will only be required if the pump has been removed and refitted, or the crankshaft pulley vibration damper bolt has been disturbed. Whenever the sprocket bolt is slackened, it is possible for the sprocket to move very slightly in relation to the crankshaft, hence the need to check the injection pump timing.

17 If timing is being carried out for a reason other than pump removal or refitting, take off the camshaft drivebelt cover and alternator shield and remove the TDC gauge pin hole blanking plug - see illustrations, Chapter 2.

18 Turn the crankshaft in a clockwise direction until the injection pump sprocket and front cover timing marks are in alignment.

19 Remove the lower plug from the side of the pump body. Be prepared to catch any released fuel and prevent it from entering the alternator.

20 Fit the TDC gauge pin into its hole, then fit the dial gauge and its holding fixture to the fuel injection pump **(see illustration)**.

21 Turn the crankshaft clockwise until the dial gauge stops moving and then zero the gauge.

11.8 Dial test indicator with probe in plug hole

22 Continue turning the crankshaft until the crankshaft locks against the TDC pin. The dial gauge should register 1.40 ± 0.07 mm.

23 If the gauge reading is outside the specified range, release the pump mounting nuts and bolts and rotate the pump until the correct reading is indicated on the gauge.

24 Now turn the crankshaft anti-clockwise until the pump sprocket and front cover marks are in alignment. Tighten the pump nuts and bolts.

25 Repeat the operations described in paragraphs 21 and 22 to check the setting.

26 Remove the dial gauge, holding fixture and TDC pin. Refit the plug.

27 Fit the alternator plastic fuel deflector and camshaft drivebelt cover where applicable.

12 Fuel injection pump - removal and refitting

Removal

Note: *See Chapter 5 for details of the idle speed adjustment actuator.*

1 Disconnect the battery earth lead.

2 Remove the alternator and the air

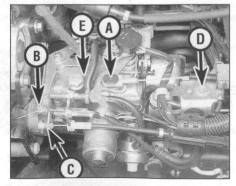

12.4 Fuel injection pump connections

A Throttle cable end fitting
B Idle up speed cable end clamp
C Waxstat cable grommet
D Throttle cable bracket screw
E Fuel supply connection

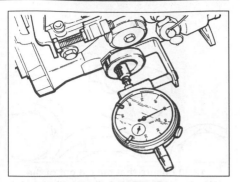

11.20 Checking CAV RotoDiesel fuel injection pump (static) timing

conditioning compressor (where fitted) drivebelts.

3 Disconnect the fuel pipes from the pump and the injectors. Blank off all open connections to prevent the ingress of dirt and moisture.

4 Detach the throttle cable from the pump **(see illustration)**.

5 Disconnect the waxstat and idle up speed cables from the pump.

6 Undo the throttle cable bracket retaining screw and detach the bracket from the pump.

7 Disconnect the pump electrical connections by separating the multiplugs.

8 Disconnect the fuel supply line and the remaining pipes from the pump.

9 With reference to Chapter 10, disconnect the hose and rigid pipe from the power steering pump, remove the pump drivebelt cover and loosen the locking bolt to slacken the drivebelt. Remove the drivebelt and the drive pulley.

10 Slowly release the coolant expansion tank cap and then drain the cooling system, see Chapter 1.

11 Referring to Chapter 2, support the engine and remove the right-hand engine mounting.

12 Detach the coolant hose to facilitate removal of the timing belt covers.

13 With the timing belt covers removed, remove the blanking plug and insert the TDC pin into the cylinder block - see Chapter 2.

14 Engage 4th gear, raise the right-hand front roadwheel and carefully turn it to rotate the engine clockwise until it is stopped by the pin.

15 Insert a 6.0 mm diameter pin into the pump timing slots.

16 Insert the camshaft timing pin.

17 Release the camshaft and fuel pump drivebelt tensioners and remove both bolts.

18 Remove the pump sprocket retaining bolts, remove the timing pin, followed by the sprocket and belt.

19 Support the weight of the pump, remove the three retaining bolts and remove the pump from the engine.

Refitting

20 Refitting the pump is a reversal of the

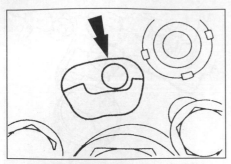

12.20 Ensure that the cut out of the injection pump flange aligns with the slot in its sprocket (arrowed)

removal procedure, noting the following points:

a) Before fitting a new pump, remove the blanking plugs and prime it with clean fuel, poured in through the return port
b) Align the peg cut-outs of the pump body and drive flange before fitting
c) Ensure that the mounting surfaces are clean before bolting the pump into position
d) Ensure that the cut out of the pump flange aligns with the sprocket slot when fitting the sprocket **(see illustration)**
e) Tighten the sprocket retaining bolts

finger-tight only, until the drivebelt is tensioned

f) With the pin reinserted through the sprocket and the belt refitted, tension the belt, see Chapter 1
g) Refer to Chapter 1 and fit and tension the camshaft drivebelt
h) With all the pins removed, rotate the engine two full turns clockwise. Reinsert the pins to confirm the timing. If the pins cannot be inserted, then repeat the timing procedure
i) Tighten all fasteners to the specified torque loading figures
j) Refer to Chapter 2, when refitting the top engine mounting.
k) Refer to Chapter 1 when refilling the cooling system
l) Clean all electrical connectors before reconnection
m) On completion, check for correct throttle cable operation and signs of fuel leakage

13 Injection pipes - removal and refitting

Removal

1 The injection pipes should be removed as a set. Individual pipes may then be renewed if necessary after slackening the anti-rattle clips.

2 Disconnect the battery earth lead. Clean around the pipe unions at the injectors and at the pump.

3 Protect the alternator against fuel spillage. Counterhold the pump adapters and unscrew the pipe union nuts **(see illustration)**.

4 Similarly unscrew the injector union nuts, counterholding the injector bodies as the nuts are slackened **(see illustration)**.

5 Remove the pipe assembly. Plug or cap open unions to keep fuel in and dirt out.

6 The pipes of the Bosch and CAV systems look similar but they have different bore sizes. To identify a pipe, insert a new twist drill of specified diameter into the pipe bore **(see illustration)**. The bore (internal diameter) sizes are as follows:

Bosch pipe - 2.0 mm
CAV RotoDiesel pipe - 2.5 mm

Refitting

7 When refitting, make sure that all the anti-rattle clips are in place **(see illustration)**. Do not bend or strain the pipes. Blow through the pipes with compressed air (from an air line or a foot pump) to expel any debris.

8 Counterhold the pump adapters and tighten the pump union nuts.

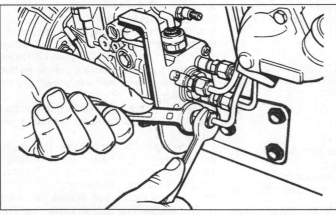

13.3 Counterhold the pump adapter when slackening or tightening a pipe union nut

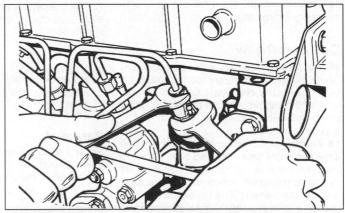

13.4 Counterhold the injector body when slackening a pipe union nut

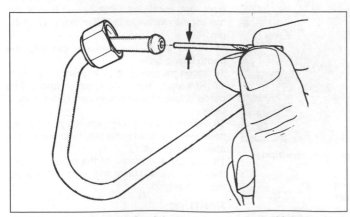

13.6 Using a drill bit to check bore diameter of a fuel injector pipe

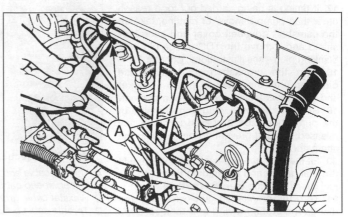

13.7 Injection pipe anti-rattle clips (A)

9 Reconnect the battery earth lead.
10 With the injector union nuts finger tight, have an assistant crank the engine on the starter in short bursts until fuel emerges from the unions. Tighten the injector unions - there is no need to counterhold the injectors.
11 Run the engine for a minute or two to purge any remaining air from the system. Check the disturbed unions for leaks.

14 Fuel injectors - removal, testing and refitting

14.2 Disconnecting a fuel return hose from an injector

14.4a Removing an injector, using a deep socket

⚠ *Warning: Exercise extreme caution when working on the fuel injectors. Never expose the hands or any part of the body to injector spray, as the high working pressure can cause the fuel to penetrate the skin, with possibly fatal results. You are strongly advised to have any work which involves testing the injectors under pressure carried out by a dealer or fuel injection specialist.*

Removal

1 Disconnect the battery earth lead. Clean around the injectors and the injection pipe unions.
2 Remove the fuel return hoses from the injectors **(see illustration)**.
3 Remove the injection pipes.
4 Unscrew and remove the injectors. A 27mm box spanner or deep socket will be required **(see illustrations)**.
5 Retrieve the heat protection washers from the injector bores **(see illustration)**. Obtain new washers for reassembly.
6 Take care not to drop the injectors, nor allow the needles at their tips to become damaged.

Testing

7 Testing of injectors is quite simple, but requires a special high pressure pump and gauge. Should such equipment be available, use it in accordance with its maker's instructions, referring to the Specifications for the desired values. Do not expose the skin to

14.4b Withdrawing an injector . . .

spray from the injectors - the pressure is high enough to penetrate the skin.
8 Defective injectors should be renewed or professionally repaired. DIY repair is not a practical proposition. To identify the injector type (Bosch or CAV), refer to the accompanying illustration **(see illustration)**.

Refitting

9 Commence refitting by inserting new heat protection washers, domed faces downwards, to the injector bores **(see illustration)**.
10 Insert the injectors and screw them in by hand, then tighten them to the specified torque. No outer sealing washer is used and the injectors are a taper fit in the head.
11 Reconnect the fuel return hoses. Make

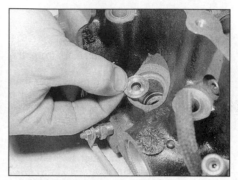

14.5 . . . followed by a heat protection washer

sure that a blanking cap is fitted to the unused connector on No 4 injector.
12 Refit the injection pipes.
13 Reconnect the battery and run the engine for a minute or two. Check for leaks around the disturbed components.

15 Fuel shut-off solenoid - removal and refitting

1 If the fuel shut-off solenoid is disconnected, the engine will not run. The same applies if the solenoid is defective. If the plunger jams in the raised position, the engine will not stop. A defective solenoid should be removed for inspection or renewal as follows:

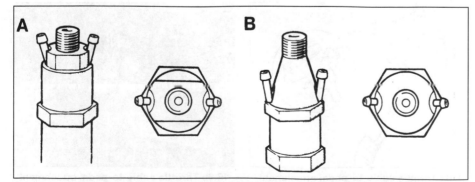

14.8 Difference between CAV RotoDiesel (A) and Bosch (B) fuel injectors

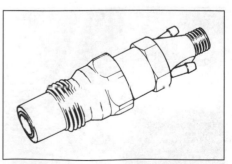

14.9 Fuel injector and heat protection washer. Observe correct fitted direction of washer (domed side downward)

15.3 Fuel shut-off solenoid electrical connector

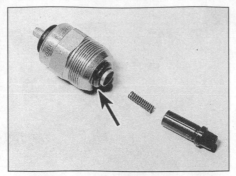

15.4 Solenoid, spring and plunger (O-ring is arrowed)

16.2a Removing the throttle cable inner retaining clip - early type

Bosch system

2 Disconnect the battery earth lead.
3 Disconnect the electrical lead from the solenoid **(see illustration)**.
4 Wipe clean around the solenoid, then unscrew it from the fuel injection pump using a deep socket or box spanner.
Caution: If the solenoid has recently been energised, it may be hot. Recover the spring and plunger (see illustration).
5 A defective solenoid must be renewed. Renew the O-ring in any case.
6 Refit the plunger, spring and solenoid to the pump. Tighten the solenoid body moderately.
7 Reconnect the solenoid lead and the battery earth lead. Run the engine to check for correct operation.

CAV RotoDiesel system

8 Disconnect the battery and check that the ignition key is in the "O" position, or removed from the ignition switch.
9 Disconnect the lead from the solenoid terminal then clean the exterior of the solenoid - see illustration 1.7b for solenoid location.
10 Using a deep socket or box spanner, unscrew and remove the solenoid from the injection pump.
11 Refitting is a reversal of removal, but use a new O-ring if the old one is in anything but perfect condition. Tighten the solenoid to its specified torque wrench setting.

16.2b Removing the throttle cable inner retaining clip - later type

16 Throttle cable - removal and refitting

Removal

1 Disconnect the battery earth lead.
2 Free the cable inner from the pump by prising off the retaining clip **(see illustrations)**. If this is done carefully, the clip can be re-used. Otherwise, obtain a new clip for reassembly.
3 Free the cable outer from the pump bracket by depressing the retaining tangs (early type) or pulling out the retaining clip (later type) **(see illustrations)**. If this proves difficult in situ,

16.3a Throttle cable outer retainer partly disengaged - early type

unbolt the bracket from the pump and remove it with the cable.
4 Where necessary, unclip the cable from the air cleaner cover.
5 Working inside the vehicle, remove any under-dash trim blocking access to the throttle pedal.
6 Disconnect the cable inner from the pedal by prising off the retaining clip (early type) or releasing the pedal collar and moving the cable inner through the slot in the pedal (later type) **(see illustrations)**.
7 Free the cable outer retainer from the bulkhead.
8 Withdraw the cable from the engine bay.
9 Transfer any hardware to the new cable, if applicable.

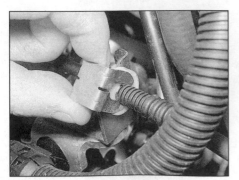

16.3b Releasing the throttle cable outer retaining clip - later type

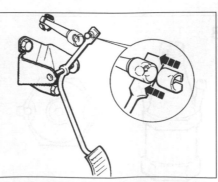

16.6a Throttle cable-to-pedal attachment - early type

16.6b Throttle cable-to-pedal attachment collar (arrowed) - later type

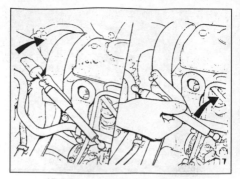

17.2 Throttle damper removal

18.2 Remove the rubber elbow from the compressor inlet

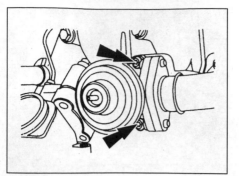

18.3 Remove the EGR valve retaining screws (arrowed)

Refitting

10 Commence refitting by passing the pedal end inner through the bulkhead. Press home the bulkhead retainer and reconnect the inner to the pedal.

11 Reconnect the cable inner and outer to the pump.

12 Adjust the cable if necessary, so that with the pedal released there is a small amount of slack in the inner. Have an assistant operate the throttle pedal and check that the throttle lever on the pump moves through its full range of travel (as limited by the idle and maximum speed adjusting screws). Adjust further if necessary.

13 Where necessary, clip the cable into place on the air cleaner cover.

14 Refit the under-dash trim, if applicable.

15 Reconnect the battery earth lead.

17 Throttle damper - removal and refitting

A revised throttle damper unit can be fitted to models equipped with the Bosch fuel injection system where the vehicle is regularly used under low speed and light throttle application, to help prevent vehicle shake and power "on/off" effect at low engine speeds.

The damper is detached by prising free the top balljoint and moving the damper up so that the lower joint disconnects from the throttle end **(see illustration)**. When refitting the damper, press it into position on the top and bottom end joints but ensure that the large diameter end joint is fitted to the top.

18 Turbocharger - removal and refitting

Removal

1 Disconnect the battery earth lead. Refer to the appropriate Sections of this Chapter and remove the air cleaner and charge air cooler assemblies.

2 Loosen the clip securing the rubber elbow

to the compressor inlet and remove the elbow with the mass airflow (MAF) sensor **(see illustration)**.

3 Remove the two EGR valve retaining screws and disconnect the valve **(see illustration)**.

4 Disconnect the breather hose from the turbocharger housing by loosening its retaining clip and pulling it from position **(see illustration)**.

5 Undo the oil feed pipe union bolt and detach the pipe from the turbocharger housing.

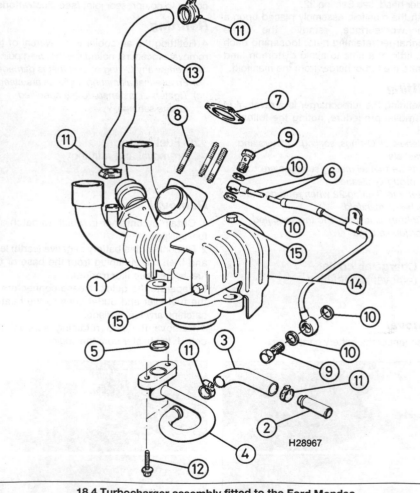

18.4 Turbocharger assembly fitted to the Ford Mondeo

1 Turbocharger	6 Oil feed pipe	11 Hose clamp
2 Oil drain pipe	7 Inlet gasket	12 Screw
3 Oil return hose	8 Stud	13 Vent hose
4 Oil drain	9 Union bolt	14 Heat shield
5 O-ring	10 Copper washer	15 Screw

4

19.2 Remove the elbow retaining clips

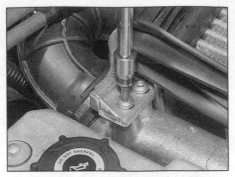

19.3a Remove the charge air cooler retaining screws from the right . . .

19.3b . . . and left-hand sides . . .

6 Loosen the oil drain pipe retaining clip and disconnect the pipe from the turbocharger housing.

7 Disconnect the exhaust system downpipe from the manifold.

8 It is now necessary to remove the exhaust manifold complete with turbocharger from the cylinder head, see Section 22.

9 With the manifold assembly placed upon a clean worksurface, remove the three turbocharger retaining nuts, loosening each one a little at a time to avoid distortion, and separate the turbocharger from the manifold.

Refitting

10 Refitting the turbocharger is a reversal of the removal procedure, noting the following points:

a) Renew all O-rings, sealing washers and gaskets

b) Ensure that all mating surfaces are thoroughly cleaned

c) Refer to Section 22 when refitting the exhaust manifold

d) Tighten all fasteners to the specified torque settings

19 Charge air cooler - removal and refitting

Removal

1 Disconnect the battery earth lead.

2 Loosen the two clips which hold the rubber elbow to the inlet manifold and charge air cooler assembly and remove the elbow (**see illustration**).

3 Remove the four air cooler retaining screws and lift the cooler clear of the engine, taking care to avoid damaging the O-rings on the cooler to compressor joint (**see illustrations**).

Refitting

4 Refitting the air cooler is a reversal of the removal procedure, noting the following points:

a) Renew any O-ring or seal that is damaged

b) Ensure that all mating surfaces are clean

c) Tighten all fasteners to the specified torque settings

20 Fuel heater - removal and refitting

Removal

1 Obtain a container in which to catch any fuel spillage.

2 Disconnect the battery negative (earth) lead and then the multiplug from the base of the fuel heater (**see illustration**).

3 Separate the quick release connectors of the fuel inlet and outlet lines to the heater, catching any fuel spillage.

4 Remove the two retaining screws and detach the heater from the engine.

Refitting

5 Refitting is the reverse of the removal procedure. On completion, prime the fuel system with the filter primer and carry out leak checks directly after the engine is first started.

21 Fuel tank - removal and refitting

> **Warning: Carry out removal of the fuel tank only when it is nearly empty. If not used, fuel can be syphoned or hand-pumped from the tank whilst observing normal fire precautions.**

Removal

2 Because a fuel tank drain plug is not provided, it is therefore preferable to carry out the removal operation when the tank is nearly empty.

3 Disconnect the battery negative (earth) lead.

4 Syphon or hand-pump any remaining fuel from the tank.

5 Unbolt or fold forwards (as appropriate) the rear seat base cushion. Withdraw from the vehicle floor the grommet covering the fuel sender unit. Unplug the fuel sender unit electrical connector (**see illustration**).

6 Raise the rear of the vehicle and support it securely on axle stands (see "*Jacking and*

19.3c . . . then remove the cooler, taking care to avoid damaging the O-rings (arrowed)

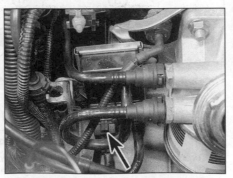

20.20 Location of fuel heater multiplug (arrowed)

21.5 Unplugging the sender unit electrical connector (arrowed)

vehicle support"). Familiarise yourself with the layout of the fuel tank assembly before proceeding **(see illustration)**.

7 Unhook the exhaust system rubber mountings. Lower the system onto a suitable support, so that the front downpipe-to-exhaust manifold joint is not strained, or remove it completely.

8 Unbolt the rear suspension anti-roll bar mounting clamps **(see illustration)**. Swing the bar down as far as possible. If clearance is very restricted, it is advisable to remove the bar completely.

9 Disconnect the flexible vent hose from the moulded plastic fuel tank filler neck as follows:

(a) *On Saloon and Hatchback models, reach up into the right-hand side aperture in the rear suspension crossmember, slacken the clamp, and work the hose off the filler neck stub. This is a job for someone with small hands, good tools and a lot of patience!* **(see illustration)**.

(b) *On Estate models, slacken the clamp immediately above the rear anti-roll bar, and work the hose off the filler neck stub* **(see illustration)**.

10 Unscrew the six retaining nuts, and withdraw the exhaust system's rear heat shield from the underbody **(see illustration)**.

11 Support the tank with a trolley jack or similar. Place a sturdy plank between the support and the tank, to protect the tank.

12 Unscrew the bolt at the front of each retaining strap and pivot the straps down until they are hanging out of the way. Note the earth lead under the left-hand strap bolt and clean its mating surfaces before the tank is refitted, so that clean, metal-to-metal contact is ensured.

13 Lower the tank enough to release the pipes from its top **(see illustration)**. If in doubt, clearly label all fuel lines and hoses and their respective unions. Plug the hoses, to prevent contamination of the fuel system.

14 Remove the tank from the vehicle, releasing it from the filler neck stub.

15 With the tank removed, unhook the retaining straps (twist them through 90° to do so) and check that they and their locations in the underbody are in good condition.

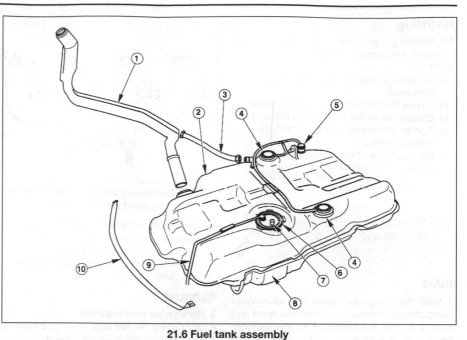

21.6 Fuel tank assembly

1 Fuel filler neck	6 Sender unit
2 Fuel tank	7 Fuel return pipe union
3 Flexible vent hose	8 Heat shield
4 Roll-over valves	9 Fuel pump-to-filter feed pipe
5 Anti-trickle fill valve	10 Fuel tank retaining strap - 2 off

21.8 Unbolt rear anti-roll bar mounting clamps (one arrowed) when preparing to remove the fuel tank

21.9a Fuel filler vent hose clamp (arrowed) is accessible through right-hand side aperture in rear suspension crossmember on Saloon and Hatchback models . . .

4

21.9b . . . on Estate models, it is immediately above rear suspension anti-roll bar

21.10 Exhaust system must be lowered and heat shield removed to enable fuel tank removal - arrows show location of retaining strap front bolts

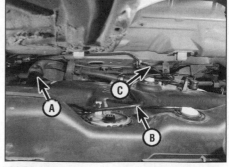

21.13 Lower fuel tank - do not distort filler neck stub (A) and unclip red-coded fuel return pipe (B) then disconnect charcoal canister vapour hose (C)

Refitting

16 Refitting is the reverse of the removal procedure, noting the following points:

a) *Renew any hose or pipeline that is damaged*

b) *Ensure that all mating surfaces are clean*

c) *Ensure that all hoses are correctly routed*

d) *Tighten all fasteners to the specified torque settings*

e) *Carry out leak checks directly after the engine is first started*

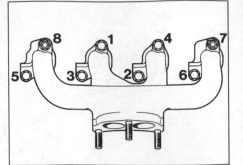

22.13 Tightening sequence for exhaust manifold nuts and bolts

(c) *Tighten the nuts/bolts in three or four equal steps to the torque listed in Specifications. Work from the centre outwards, to avoid warping the manifold.*

22 Manifolds -
removal and refitting

Inlet

1 With the charge air cooler and associated components removed, unscrew the bolts and nuts securing the manifold to the cylinder head and withdraw it. Take care not to damage vulnerable components such as the EGR pipe and valve as the manifold assembly is manoeuvred out of the engine compartment.

2 Refitting is the reverse of the removal procedure, noting the following points:

(a) *Provided the relevant mating surfaces are clean and flat, a new gasket will be sufficient to ensure that the joint is gas-tight. Do not use any kind of silicone-based sealant on the manifold.*

(b) *Fit a new gasket, then locate the manifold on the head and install the nuts and bolts, finger tight.*

Exhaust

3 Remove the inlet manifold.

4 Disconnect the exhaust downpipe from the manifold flange. Recover the gasket.

5 Unbolt the exhaust manifold from the cylinder head.

6 On models so equipped, note that the EGR valve must be unbolted from the manifolds before they can be removed.

7 Remove the manifold.

8 Note that the engine does not have a gasket fitted on production and that there is a plastic sleeve fitted around the stud.

9 When the manifold is first removed, a gasket must be obtained and fitted on reassembly. It must then be renewed as a matter of course whenever the manifold is disturbed after that.

10 The plastic sleeve is fitted to ensure that the correct clearance exists to allow for expansion when the manifold gets hot. Check it whenever the manifold is disturbed and renew it if there is any doubt about its condition..

11 Commence refitting by placing a new gasket over the studs.

12 Fit the manifold and secure it with the nuts and bolts. Only tighten them finger tight at this stage. It is a good idea to use anti-seize compound on the threads.

13 Tighten the nuts and bolts to the specified torque, following the sequence shown **(see illustration)**.

14 Refit and secure the exhaust downpipe, using a new gasket.

15 Refit the inlet manifold.

23 Exhaust system -
inspection

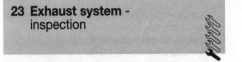

1 Inspect the system periodically for leaks, corrosion and other damage, and check the security and condition of the mountings. Small leaks are more easily detected if an assistant partly obstructs the tailpipe with a wad of cloth whilst the engine is idling.

2 Proprietary pastes and bandages are available for the repair of holes and splits. They work well in the short term, but renewal of the section concerned will probably prove more satisfactory in the long run.

3 The rubber mountings will crack and split eventually, and should then be renewed. It is sound practice to renew the mountings when renewing other parts of the system.

Chapter 5
Engine electrical systems

Contents

Degrees of difficulty

Easy, suitable for novice with little experience	Fairly easy, suitable for beginner with some experience	Fairly difficult, suitable for competent DIY mechanic	Difficult, suitable for experienced DIY mechanic	Very difficult, suitable for expert DIY or professional

Specifications

General
System type . . . . 12 V, negative earth

Battery
Rating - cold cranking/reserve capacity . . . . 500 A/75 RC, 590 A/90 RC, 600 A/110 RC or 650 A/130 RC, depending on year and model

Alternator

Type:	Model	Rated output
Bosch unit	NC 14V 60-90A	90A
Mitsubishi unit	A004T	90A

Minimum brush length - all types . . . . 5.0 mm
Regulated voltage @ 4000 (engine) rpm and 3 to 7 amp load - all types . . 13.5 to 14.6 volts

Starter motor
Make and type . . . . Bosch 1.7 kW short frame, Bosch DW (1.8 kW), Bosch EV (2.2 kW), or Lucas/Magneti Marelli M80R (1.8 kW)
Brush wear limit . . . . 8.0 mm length
Commutator refinishing limit . . . . 32.8 mm diameter
Armature endfloat . . . . 0.3 mm
Note: *Where a Magnetti Marelli M80R starter motor is fitted, note that these are simply renamed Lucas units. All procedures and specifications are exactly the same as those for Lucas M80R starter motors.*

Torque wrench settings

	Nm	lbf ft
Starter motor bracket to block	20	15
Starter motor to transmission	35 to 45	26 to 33
Crankshaft position sensor bolt	21	16
Glow plugs	28	21
Oil pressure switch	20	15
Alternator mounting bolts	50	37

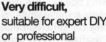

5

1 General information and precautions

General information

The engine electrical system follows conventional automobile practice, that is, 12 volt negative earth, with power being supplied by an alternator driven from the crankshaft pulley. A lead acid battery provides a reserve of power for starting the engine, and for situations where the demand on the system temporarily exceeds the alternator output.

Two types of starter motor are fitted. The first type is a larger version of that used on a petrol engine. The second type is unusual in having permanent magnets instead of field windings, and carries a planetary reduction gear set between the armature and the pinion.

Precautions

It is necessary to take extra care when working on the electrical system to avoid damage to any semi-conductor devices (diodes and transistors) and to avoid the risk of personal injury. In addition to the precautions given in the *Safety first!* Section at the beginning of this Manual, take note of the following points when working on the system.

Always remove rings, watches, etc. before working on the electrical system. Even with the battery disconnected, capacitive discharge could occur if a component live terminal is earthed through a metal object. This could cause a shock or nasty burn.

Do not reverse the battery connections. Components such as the alternator or any other having semi-conductor circuitry could be irreparably damaged.

If the engine is being started using jump leads and a slave battery, connect the batteries *positive to positive* and *negative to negative*. This also applies when connecting a battery charger.

Never disconnect the battery terminals, or alternator multi-plug connector, when the engine is running.

The battery leads and alternator multi-plug must be disconnected before carrying out any electric welding on the car.

Never use an ohmmeter of the type incorporating a hand cranked generator for circuit or continuity testing.

Battery disconnection

Several systems fitted to the vehicle require battery power to be available at all times, either to ensure their continued operation (such as the clock) or to maintain control unit memories (such as that in the engine management system's ECU) which would be wiped if the battery were to be disconnected. Whenever the battery is to be disconnected therefore, first note the following, to ensure that there are no unforeseen consequences of this action:

(a) First, on any vehicle with central locking, it is a wise precaution to remove the key from the ignition, and to keep it with you, so that it does not get locked in if the central locking should engage accidentally when the battery is reconnected!

(b) The engine management system's ECU will lose the information stored in its memory - referred to by Ford as the "KAM" (Keep-Alive Memory) - when the battery is disconnected. This includes idling and operating values, and any fault codes detected - in the case of the fault codes, if it is thought likely that the system has developed a fault for which the corresponding code has been logged, the vehicle must be taken to a Ford dealer for the codes to be read, using the special diagnostic equipment necessary for this (see Chapter 6). Whenever the battery is disconnected, the information relating to idle speed control and other operating values will have to be re-programmed into the unit's memory. The ECU does this by itself, but until then, there may be surging, hesitation, erratic idle and a generally inferior level of performance. To allow the ECU to relearn these values, start the engine and run it as close to idle speed as possible until it reaches its normal operating temperature, then run it for approximately two minutes at 1200 rpm. Next, drive the vehicle as far as necessary - approximately 5 miles of varied driving conditions is usually sufficient - to complete the relearning process.

(c) If the battery is disconnected while the alarm system is armed or activated, the alarm will remain in the same state when the battery is reconnected. The same applies to the engine immobiliser system (where fitted).

(d) If a trip computer is in use, any information stored in memory will be lost.

(e) If a Ford "Keycode" audio unit is fitted, and the unit and/or the battery is disconnected, the unit will not function again on reconnection until the correct security code is entered. Details of this procedure, which varies according to the unit and model year, are given in the "Ford Audio Systems Operating Guide" supplied with the vehicle when new, with the code itself being given in a "Radio Passport" and/or a "Keycode Label" at the same time. Ensure you have the correct code before you disconnect the battery. For obvious security reasons, the procedure is not given in this manual. If you do not have the code or details of the correct procedure, but can supply proof of ownership and a legitimate reason for wanting this information, the vehicle's selling dealer may be able to help.

Devices known as "memory-savers" (or "code-savers") can be used to avoid some of the above problems. Precise details vary according to the device used. Typically, it is plugged into the cigarette lighter, and is connected by its own wires to a spare battery; the vehicle's own battery is then disconnected from the electrical system, leaving the "memory-saver" to pass sufficient current to maintain audio unit security codes and ECU memory values, and also to run permanently-live circuits such as the clock, all the while isolating the battery in the event of a short-circuit occurring while work is carried out.

 Warning: Some of these devices allow a considerable amount of current to pass, which can mean that many of the vehicle's systems are still operational when the main battery is disconnected. If a "memory-saver" is used, ensure that the circuit concerned is actually "dead" before carrying out any work on it!

2 Battery - removal and refitting

Note: *See also the relevant Sections of Chapter 1.*

1 Disconnect the battery leads, negative (earth) lead first - see Section 1.

2 Remove the battery hold-down clamp **(see illustrations)**.

3 Lift out the battery. Be careful - it's heavy.

4 While the battery is out, inspect the tray for corrosion (see Chapter 1).

2.2a Unscrew hold-down nuts (one of two arrowed) . . .

2.2b . . . and withdraw hold-down clamp to release battery

5 If you are renewing the battery, make sure that you get one that's identical, with the same dimensions, amperage rating, cold cranking rating, etc. Dispose of the old battery in a responsible fashion. Most local authorities have facilities for the collection and disposal of such items - batteries contain sulphuric acid and lead, and should not be simply thrown out with the household rubbish!

6 Refitting is the reverse of the removal procedure.

3 Battery leads - check and renewal

Note: *See also the relevant Sections of Chapter 1.*

1 Periodically inspect the entire length of each battery lead for damage, cracked or burned insulation, and corrosion. Poor battery lead connections can cause starting problems and decreased engine performance.

2 Check the lead-to-terminal connections at the ends of the leads for cracks, loose wire strands and corrosion. The presence of white, fluffy deposits under the insulation at the lead terminal connection is a sign that the lead is corroded and should be renewed. Check the terminals for distortion, missing clamp bolts, and corrosion.

3 When removing the leads, always disconnect the negative lead first, and reconnect it last (see Section 1). Even if only the positive lead is being renewed, be sure to disconnect the negative lead from the battery first (see Chapter 1 for further information regarding battery lead removal).

4 Disconnect the old leads from the battery, then trace each of them to their opposite ends, and detach them from the starter solenoid and earth terminals. Note the routing of each lead, to ensure correct installation.

5 If you are renewing either or both of the old leads, take them with you when buying new leads. It is vitally important that you replace the leads with identical parts. Leads have characteristics that make them easy to identify: positive leads are usually red, larger in cross-section, and have a larger-diameter

battery post clamp; earth leads are usually black, smaller in cross-section and have a slightly smaller-diameter clamp for the negative post.

6 Clean the threads of the solenoid or earth connection with a wire brush to remove rust and corrosion.

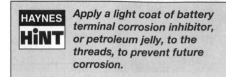

> **HAYNES HiNT** *Apply a light coat of battery terminal corrosion inhibitor, or petroleum jelly, to the threads, to prevent future corrosion.*

7 Attach the lead to the solenoid or earth connection, and tighten the mounting nut/bolt securely.

8 Before connecting a new lead to the battery, make sure that it reaches the battery post without having to be stretched.

9 Connect the positive lead first, followed by the negative lead.

4 Preheater system - description and testing
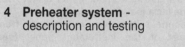

Description

1 Each swirl chamber has a preheater plug (commonly called a glow plug) screwed into it. The plugs are electrically operated before, during and immediately after starting the engine. The duration of the preheating and afterglow periods is determined by a special relay which incorporates a temperature sensor.

2 During the preheating phase, an instrument panel warning light is illuminated. No attempt should be made to start the engine until the light goes out.

3 If the system malfunctions, testing is ultimately by substitution of known good units, but some preliminary checks may be made as follows.

Testing

4 Connect a voltmeter (0 to 20 volt) or 12 volt test lamp between any glow plug terminal and

earth. Have an assistant switch on the ignition. The test lamp or voltmeter should give a positive indication for several seconds, corresponding to the preheating period, then give a zero reading or go out. If not, the relay (or associated wiring) is at fault. Switch off the ignition.

5 If an ammeter of suitable range (0 to 50 amp approx) is available, connect it between the glow plug feed wire and the bus bar. During the preheating period the ammeter should show a current draw of approximately 8 amps per working plug, ie. 32 amps if all four plugs are working.

6 If one or more plugs appear not to be drawing current, remove the bus bar and check each plug separately with a continuity tester or self-powered test lamp. Before condemning a plug, make sure that the problem is not simply a loose or dirty connection.

7 The whole preheater system is protected by a fusible link which will melt in the event of a short-circuit. Refer to Section 11 for further details.

5 Glow plugs, relay and fuse - removal and refitting
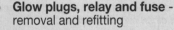

Glow plugs

1 Disconnect the battery earth lead and glow plug relay.

2 Disconnect the feed wire from the bus bar **(see illustration)**.

3 Unscrew the terminal nut from each plug to be removed **(see illustration)**. Remove the nuts, washers and bus bar.

4 Clean around the glow plug seats then unscrew and remove them **(see illustration)**.

5 When refitting, apply a little anti-seize compound to the glow plug threads. Screw the glow plugs into place and tighten them to the specified torque.

6 Refit the bus bar and washers and secure with the nuts. Make sure that the clamping areas are clean.

7 Reconnect the feed wire and the battery earth lead.

5.2 Glow plug feed wire connection

5.3 Unscrewing a glow plug terminal nut

5.4 Glow plug removed from cylinder head

5

Relay

8 The glow plug relay is located under the battery tray.

9 Disconnect and remove the battery (Section 2), raise the plastic base, then remove the relay securing screw **(see illustration)**.

10 Remove the relay and unplug the electrical connector **(see illustration)**.

11 Refit in the reverse order to removal.

Fuse

12 The glow plug circuit fuse is in the additional fuse block located in front of the battery.

5.9 **Glow plug relay location and securing screw (arrowed)**

5.10 **Unplugging electrical connector from the glow plug relay**

6 Glow plug warning light unit - renewal

Warning: Before disconnecting any instrument panel components, Disconnect the battery negative (earth) lead.

1 To facilitate removal of the instrument panel surround, remove the following components:

a) The clock, where fitted.
b) The trip computer module, where fitted.
c) The heated rear window switch.
d) The heated windscreen switch, where fitted.
e) The display assembly warning indicator for the foglights, where fitted.

f) Any blanking covers from the unused switch positions.

2 Remove the instrument panel surround by prising out the blanking covers, then unscrewing its retaining screws **(see illustrations)**.

3 Unscrew the mounting screws, and withdraw the instrument panel a little way from the facia **(see illustration)**.

4 Disconnect the two multi-plugs from the rear of the instrument panel **(see illustration)**.

5 Withdraw the instrument panel from the facia, at the same time releasing the speedometer intermediate cable.

6 Remove the warning light by twisting it anti-clockwise **(see illustration)**.

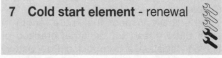

7 Cold start element - renewal

1 The electrically-operated cold start element is screwed into the advance device **(see illustration)**. No test data are available, but if the element is suspect it can be renewed as follows.

2 Disconnect the battery earth lead.

3 Disconnect the electrical lead from the cold start element.

4 Wipe clean around the element, then unscrew and remove it.

Caution: if it has just been energised, the element may be hot.

6.2a **With the blanking covers removed, unscrew the concealed screws . . .**

6.2b **. . . and the remaining screws . . .**

6.2c **. . . and lift out the instrument panel surround**

6.3 **Three of the instrument panel mounting screws (arrowed)**

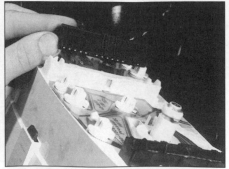

6.4 **Disconnecting the multi-plugs from the rear of the instrument panel**

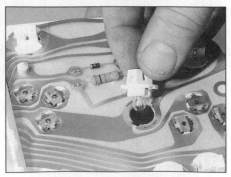

6.6 **Removing a bulb from the rear of the instrument panel**

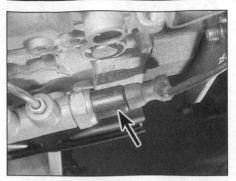

7.1 Cold start element (arrowed) on side of injector pump

5 Fit the new element, using a new sealing washer, and tighten it moderately.
6 Reconnect the electrical lead and the battery earth lead.
7 Run the engine to check for correct operation.

8 Charging system - general information and precautions

General information

The charging system includes the alternator, an internal voltage regulator, a no-charge (or "ignition") warning light, the battery, and the wiring between all the components. The charging system supplies electrical power for the ignition system, the lights, the radio, etc. The alternator is driven by the auxiliary drivebelt at the front (right-hand end) of the engine.

The purpose of the voltage regulator is to limit the alternator's voltage to a preset value. This prevents power surges, circuit overloads, etc., during peak voltage output.

The charging system doesn't ordinarily require periodic maintenance. However, the drivebelt, battery and wires and connections should be inspected at the intervals outlined in Chapter 1.

The dashboard warning light should come on when the ignition key is turned to positions "II" or "III", then should go off immediately the engine starts. If it remains on, or if it comes on while the engine is running, there is a malfunction in the charging system (see Section 9). If the light does not come on when the ignition key is turned, and the bulb is sound (see Chapter 12), there is a fault in the alternator.

Precautions

Be very careful when making electrical circuit connections to a vehicle equipped with an alternator, and note the following:
(a) When reconnecting wires to the alternator from the battery, be sure to note the polarity.
(b) Before using arc-welding equipment to repair any part of the vehicle, disconnect the wires from the alternator and the battery terminals.
(c) Never start the engine with a battery charger connected.
(d) Always disconnect both battery leads before using a battery charger.
(e) The alternator is driven by an engine drivebelt which could cause serious injury if your hand, hair or clothes become entangled in it with the engine running.
(f) Because the alternator is connected directly to the battery, it could arc or cause a fire if overloaded or shorted-out.
(g) Wrap a plastic bag over the alternator, and secure it with rubber bands, before steam-cleaning or pressure-washing the engine.
(h) Never disconnect the alternator terminals while the engine is running.

9 Charging system - testing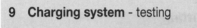

1 If a malfunction occurs in the charging circuit, don't automatically assume that the alternator is causing the problem. First check the following items:
(a) Check the tension and condition of the auxiliary drivebelt - renew it if it is worn or deteriorated (see Chapter 1).
(b) Ensure the alternator mounting bolts and nuts are tight.
(c) Inspect the alternator wiring harness and the electrical connections at the alternator; they must be in good condition, and tight.
(d) Check the large main fuses in the engine compartment (see Chapter 12). If any is blown, determine the cause, repair the circuit and renew the fuse (the vehicle won't start and/or the accessories won't work if the fuse is blown).
(e) Start the engine and check the alternator for abnormal noises - for example, a shrieking or squealing sound may indicate a badly-worn bearing or brush.
(f) Make sure that the battery is fully-charged - one bad cell in a battery can cause overcharging by the alternator.
(g) Disconnect the battery leads (negative first, then positive). Inspect the battery posts and the lead clamps for corrosion. Clean them thoroughly if necessary (see Section 3 and Chapter 1). Reconnect the lead to the negative terminal.
(h) With the ignition and all accessories switched off, insert a test light between the battery negative post and the disconnected negative lead clamp:
(1) If the test light does not come on, re-attach the clamp and proceed to the next step.
(2) If the test light comes on, there is a short in the electrical system of the vehicle. The short must be repaired before the charging system can be checked.

(3) To find the short, disconnect the alternator wiring harness:
(a) If the light goes out, the alternator is at fault.
(b) If the light stays on, remove each fuse until it goes out - this will tell you which component is short-circuited.
2 Using a voltmeter, check the battery voltage with the engine off. It should be approximately 12 volts.
3 Start the engine and check the battery voltage again. Increase engine speed until the voltmeter reading remains steady; it should now be approximately 13.5 to 14.6 volts.
4 Switch on as many electrical accessories (eg the headlights, heated rear window and heater blower) as possible, and check that the alternator maintains the regulated voltage at around 13 to 14 volts. The voltage may drop and then come back up; it may also be necessary to increase engine speed slightly, even if the charging system is working properly.
5 If the voltage reading is greater than the specified charging voltage, renew the voltage regulator (see Section 11).
6 If the voltmeter reading is less than that specified, the fault may be due to worn brushes, weak brush springs, a faulty voltage regulator, a faulty diode, a severed phase winding, or worn or damaged slip rings. The brushes and slip rings may be checked (see Section 11), but if the fault persists, the alternator should be renewed or taken to an auto-electrician for testing and repair.

10 Alternator - removal and refitting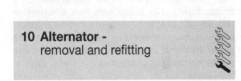

Removal

1 Disconnect the battery negative (earth) lead (Section 2).
2 Remove the charge air cooler (Chapter 4). Disconnect all wiring to the alternator **(see illustration)**.
3 Raise the vehicle front right-hand side and support on axle stands. Remove the roadwheel.

10.2 Disconnecting alternator wiring

5

10.4 Removing protective shield from wheelarch

10.5 Disconnecting anti-roll bar link rod top securing bolt (arrowed)

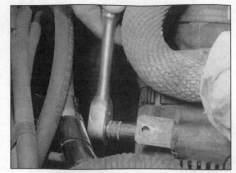

10.8a Removing alternator mounting bolts

4 Unbolt and remove the protective shield within the wheelarch **(see illustration)**.
5 Disconnect the top of the anti-roll bar link rod **(see illustration)**.
6 Slacken and remove the alternator drivebelt (Chapter 2)
7 Remove the engine oil filter (Chapter 1). Rather than refit a used filter, you are advised to drain the engine oil, and then to fit a new filter and refill the engine with clean oil on reassembly.
8 Undo and remove the three alternator mounting bolts **(see illustration)** and withdraw the alternator from the engine, manoeuvring it out through the wheel arch **(see illustration)**. Do not drop it, it is fragile.
9 If you are renewing the alternator, take the old one with you when purchasing a replacement unit. Make sure that the new or rebuilt unit is identical to the old alternator. Look at the terminals - they should be the same in number, size and location as the terminals on the old alternator. Finally, look at the identification markings - they will be stamped in the housing, or printed on a tag or plaque affixed to the housing. Make sure that these numbers are the same on both alternators.
10 Many new/rebuilt alternators do not have a pulley installed, so you may have to switch the pulley from the old unit to the new/rebuilt one. When buying an alternator, ask about the

installation of pulleys - some auto-electrical specialists will perform this service free of charge.

Refitting

11 Refitting is the reverse of the removal procedure, referring where necessary to the relevant Chapters of this manual. Tighten all fasteners to the specified torque wrench settings.
12 Check the charging voltage to verify proper operation of the alternator (see Chapter 11).

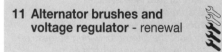

11 Alternator brushes and voltage regulator - renewal

Note: *This procedure assumes that replacement parts of the correct type have been obtained. At the time of writing, no individual alternator components were available as separate replacement Ford parts. An auto electrical specialist should be able to supply parts such as brushes.*

The following procedure is for the Bosch unit fitted to the project vehicle - details may vary for other alternator types.
1 Remove the alternator from the vehicle (see Section 10) and place it on a clean workbench.

2 Remove the three screws, and withdraw the plastic end cover **(see illustration)**.
3 Remove the two voltage regulator/brush holder mounting screws.
4 Remove the regulator/brush holder from the end frame **(see illustration)**. If you are renewing the assembly, proceed to paragraph 8, install the new unit, reassemble the alternator, and refit it to the engine (see Section 10). If you are going to check the brushes, proceed to the next paragraph.
5 Measure the exposed length of each brush, and compare it to the minimum length listed in this Chapter's Specifications. If the length of either brush is less than the specified minimum, renew the assembly.
6 Make sure that each brush moves smoothly in the brush holder.
7 Check that the slip rings - the ring of copper on which each brush bears - are clean. Wipe them with a solvent-moistened cloth; if either appears scored or blackened, take the alternator to a repair specialist for advice.
8 Refit the voltage regulator/brush holder, ensuring that the brushes bear correctly on the slip rings, and that they compress into their holders. Tighten the screws securely.
9 Install the rear cover, and tighten the screws securely.
10 Refit the alternator (see Section 10).

10.8b Withdrawing alternator through right-hand front wheel arch

11.2 Renew voltage regulator/brush holder - Bosch alternator. Remove three screws and withdraw end cover . . .

11.4 . . . then remove regulator/brush holder assembly (secured by two screws)

12 Starting system - general information and precautions

General information

The sole function of the starting system is to turn over the engine quickly enough to allow it to start.

The starting system consists of the battery, the starter motor, the starter solenoid, and the wires connecting them. The solenoid is mounted directly on the starter motor.

The solenoid/starter motor assembly is installed on the engine, next to the transmission bellhousing.

When the ignition key is turned to position "III", the starter solenoid is actuated through the starter control circuit. The starter solenoid then connects the battery to the starter. The battery supplies the electrical energy to the starter motor, which does the actual work of cranking the engine.

If the alarm system is armed or activated, the starter motor cannot be operated. The same applies with the engine immobiliser system (where fitted).

Precautions

Always observe the following precautions when working on the starting system:

(a) *Excessive cranking of the starter motor can overheat it, and cause serious damage. Never operate the starter motor for more than 15 seconds at a time without pausing to allow it to cool for at least two minutes. Excessive starter operation will also risk unburned fuel collecting in the catalytic converter's element, causing it to overheat when the engine does start (see Chapter 6).*

(b) *The starter is connected directly to the battery, and could arc or cause a fire if mishandled, overloaded or shorted-out.*

(c) *Always detach the lead from the negative terminal of the battery before working on the starting system (see Section 1).*

13 Starting system - testing

Note: *Before diagnosing starter problems, make sure that the battery is fully-charged, and ensure that the alarm/engine immobiliser system is not activated.*

1 If the starter motor does not turn at all when the switch is operated, make sure that the battery is fully-charged .

2 Make sure that all leads, both at the battery and starter solenoid terminals, are clean and secure.

3 If the starter motor spins but the engine is not cranking, the overrunning clutch or (when applicable) the reduction gears in the starter motor may be slipping, in which case the starter motor must be overhauled or renewed. (Other possibilities are that the starter motor mounting bolts are very loose, or that teeth are missing from the flywheel/driveplate ring gear.)

4 If, when the switch is actuated, the starter motor does not operate at all but the solenoid clicks, then the problem lies with either the battery, the main solenoid contacts, or the starter motor itself (or the engine is seized).

5 If the solenoid plunger cannot be heard to click when the switch is actuated, the battery is faulty, there is a fault in the circuit, or the solenoid itself is defective.

6 To check the solenoid, connect a fused jumper lead between the battery (+) and the ignition switch terminal (the small terminal) on the solenoid. If the starter motor now operates, the solenoid is OK, and the problem is in the ignition switch, selector lever position sensor (automatic transmission) or in the wiring.

7 If the starter motor still does not operate, remove it (see Section 14). The brushes and commutator may be checked (see Section 15), but if the fault persists, the motor should be renewed, or taken to an auto-electrician for testing and repair.

8 If the starter motor cranks the engine at an abnormally-slow speed, first make sure that the battery is charged, and that all terminal connections are tight. If the engine is partially seized, or has the wrong viscosity oil in it, it will crank slowly.

9 Run the engine until normal operating temperature is reached, then switch off and disconnect the fuel pump stop solenoid.

10 Connect a voltmeter positive lead to the battery positive terminal, and connect the negative lead to the negative terminal.

11 Crank the engine, and take the voltmeter readings as soon as a steady figure is indicated. Do not allow the starter motor to turn for more than 15 seconds at a time. A reading of 10.5 volts or more, with the starter motor turning at normal cranking speed, is normal. If the reading is 10.5 volts or more but the cranking speed is slow, the solenoid contacts are burned, the motor is faulty, or there is a bad connection. If the reading is less than 10.5 volts and the cranking speed is slow, the starter motor is faulty or there is a problem with the battery.

14 Starter motor - removal and refitting

Removal

1 The starter motor is removed from beneath the vehicle. Raise the vehicle on ramps, or drive it over a pit and apply the handbrake and securely chock the rear wheels.

2 Disconnect the battery earth (negative) lead.

3 Disconnect the main lead and the command lead from the starter motor solenoid **(see illustrations)**.

4 Remove the bolt which secures the tail bracket to the block **(see illustration)**. On some models there may be two such bolts.

5

14.3a Starter motor command lead (arrowed)

14.3b Starter motor main lead (arrowed)

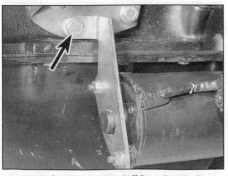

14.4 Starter motor tail bracket bolt (arrowed)

14.5 Removing a starter motor-to-gearbox bolt

15.1 Tail bracket securing nuts (arrowed). Note correct fitting of bracket as it can be fitted 180° out

15.2 Disconnecting the link lead from the solenoid terminal

5 Support the motor and remove the three bolts which secure it to the transmission **(see illustration)**. Remove the motor.

Refitting

6 When refitting, leave the tail bracket-to-motor nuts loose until the motor and bracket bolts have been fitted and tightened.
7 Tighten the motor-to-transmission bolts to the specified torque. Tighten the bracket-to-block bolts(s) next and finally tighten the bracket-to-motor nuts.
8 Reconnect the command and main leads to the solenoid.
9 Reconnect the battery and check for correct operation.

15 Starter motor - brush renewal

Bosch short frame

1 Remove the starter motor from the vehicle and detach its tail bracket **(see illustration)**.
2 Disconnect the link lead from the solenoid terminal **(see illustration)**.
3 Remove the two screws which secure the armature end cap. Remove the cap, the C-washer and plain washer(s) **(see illustration)**. Wipe away grease from the end of the armature shaft.
4 Remove the two through-bolts or studs. If

the stud nuts are inaccessible, lock two nuts onto the end of the stud and use them to unscrew it **(see illustrations)**.
5 Remove the commutator end cover to expose the brushgear **(see illustration)**.
6 Carefully withdraw the brushplate from the commutator. The brushes will be released with some force. To avoid damage, unclip them by pressing their holders towards the commutator as the brushplate is withdrawn.
7 Remove the old brushes and fit the new ones. On the reduction gear type of motor, the brushes are handled in pairs, each pair sharing a clip which fits over the brushplate **(see illustration)**. Otherwise, the brush leads must be removed from the stand-off connectors and the clips on the new leads soldered to the connectors **(see illustration)**.

15.3 Removing the C-washer (arrowed) from the end of the armature shaft

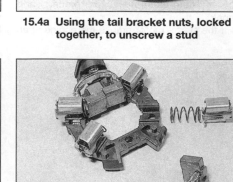

15.4a Using the tail bracket nuts, locked together, to unscrew a stud

15.4b Removing a stud - note cup washer (arrowed)

15.5 Starter motor with commutator end cover removed

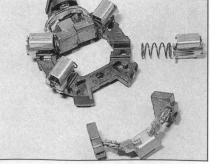

15.7a Brushgear fitted to reduction gear type motor

15.7b Brushplate and brushes - Bosch short frame starter motor

1 Stand-off connector   2 Clip

8 Clean the commutator with a rag moistened in petrol or other suitable solvent.

9 Fit the brushplate over the commutator. Either clip the brushes in place after locating the brushplate, or use a tube of suitable diameter to keep the brushes retracted during fitting **(see illustrations)**. Either way it is a fiddly business.

10 Refit the commutator end cover and secure it with the through-bolts or studs.

11 Refit the plain washer(s) to the end of the armature shafts and secure with the C-washer. Apply some grease to the shaft, then refit and secure the cap.

12 Reconnect the link lead to the solenoid. Refit the tail bracket, making sure that it is the right way round, but only tighten its nuts finger tight for now.

13 Refit the starter motor.

Bosch EV

14 Remove the starter motor from the vehicle and clean it thoroughly, then unscrew the nuts securing the tail bracket and withdraw it (if still fitted).

15 Undo the two retaining screws and remove the end cap **(see illustration)**.

16 Wipe clean the end of the armature shaft, then prise the C-washer from the groove in the shaft's end. Remove the plain washer(s).

17 Unscrew the two through-bolts, then remove the commutator end cover.

18 Unscrew the nut and disconnect the brush link lead from the solenoid's terminal stud.

19 Withdraw the thrustplate assembly (taking care to release the spring pressure from each brush before disturbing the assembly so as not to damage the brushes) then release the brushes from their holders in the brushplate.

20 Clean and inspect the brush assemblies. If any of the brushes have worn down to, or beyond, the specified minimum length they must be renewed as a set. To renew the brushes, their leads must be unsoldered from the brushplate terminals then the new brush leads soldered in their place.

21 Before refitting the brushes, check the condition of the commutator face on which they run. Wipe the commutator with a petrol-moistened cloth. If the commutator is dirty, it may be cleaned with fine glass paper, then wiped with the cloth.

22 Position the brushplate over the commutator **(see illustration)** and refit the brush holders, springs and brushes onto the brushplate, ensuring that the holders' securing lugs are positively located. Make sure that the brushes move freely in their holders.

23 Refit the commutator end cover and secure it with the throughbolts. Connect the brush link lead to the solenoid's terminal stud and secure it with the nut.

24 Refit the plain washer(s) to the end of the armature shaft and secure with the C-washer. Apply some grease to the shaft then refit and

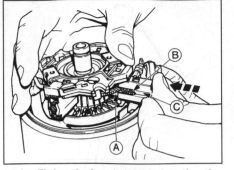

15.9a Fitting the brushes after locating the brushplate

A Brush   B Spring   C Holder

15.9b Using a socket to keep the brushes retracted

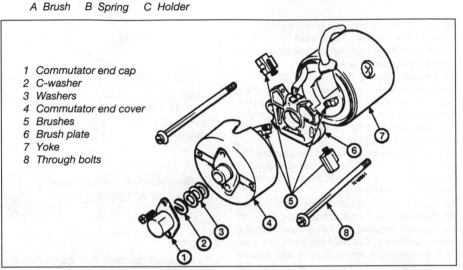

1 Commutator end cap
2 C-washer
3 Washers
4 Commutator end cover
5 Brushes
6 Brush plate
7 Yoke
8 Through bolts

15.15 Bosch EV starter motor brush assembly

secure the end cap. Finally, refit the tail bracket, tightening its retaining nuts only lightly at first.

Lucas/Magneti Marelli M80R

25 Remove the starter motor from the vehicle and clean it thoroughly, then unscrew the nuts securing the tail bracket and withdraw it (if still fitted).

26 Undo the two screws and remove the commutator end cover and the plastic insulator **(see illustration)**.

27 Unscrew the retaining nut and disconnect

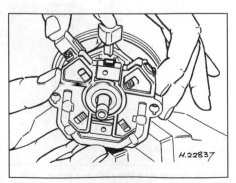

15.22 Refitting brushplate to commutator

the brush link lead from the solenoid's terminal stud.

28 Withdraw the brushplate assembly (taking care to release the spring pressure from each brush before disturbing the assembly so as not to damage the brushes) then release the brushes from their holders in the brushplate.

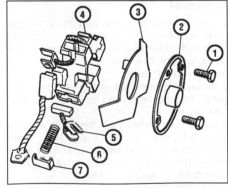

15.26 Lucas/Magneti Marelli (M80R) starter motor brush assembly

1 Screws
2 Commutator end cover
3 Insulator
4 Brushplate
5 Brush
6 Brush spring
7 Brush clip

5

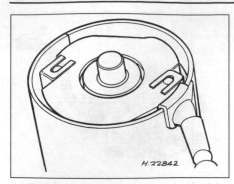

15.32 Correct location of insulator and brush connections

29 Clean and inspect the brush assemblies. If any of the brushes have worn down to or beyond the minimum length specified, they must be renewed as a set.

30 Before refitting the brushes, check the condition of the commutator face on which they run. Wipe the commutator with a petrol moistened cloth. If the commutator is dirty, it may be cleaned with fine glass paper then wiped with the cloth.

31 Fit the new brushes and reassemble the motor using a reversal of the dismantling procedure. Make sure that the brushes move freely in their holders.

32 Refit the plastic insulator **(see illustration)**, the commutator end cover and the support bracket, securing them with the screws and nuts. Connect the brush link lead to the solenoid's terminal stud and secure it with the nut. Finally, refit the tail bracket, tightening its retaining nuts only lightly at first.

16 Engine oil level sensor - removal and refitting

Removal

1 The oil level sensor is only fitted to high level models with the auxiliary warning system. It is located on the rear face of the block at the flywheel end, more or less opposite the dipstick.

2 Access to this side of the engine is not good. It may be improved by removing the air cleaner.

3 Unplug the sensor from the wiring harness and withdraw it from its tube **(see illustration)**. If a new sensor is not to be fitted immediately, fit a blanking plug - this is essential if the engine is to be run.

Refitting

4 Fit the new sensor and press it home in its tube. Connect the wiring harness plug.

5 Switch on the ignition and check for correct operation.

6 Refit any other disturbed components.

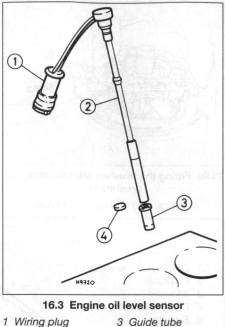

16.3 Engine oil level sensor

1 Wiring plug	3 Guide tube
2 Sensor	4 Blanking plug

17 Radiator fan switch - testing, removal and refitting

Testing

1 The radiator fan switch is located on the thermostat elbow. If it fails, the fan may run all the time (switch short-circuit) or not at all (open-circuit).

2 A short-circuit failure will be self-evident. To check for open-circuit failure, unplug the switch electrical connector and bridge the connector terminals with a screwdriver blade. With the ignition on, the fan should run - if not, the fan itself, or its wiring, must be at fault. If the fan runs now but did not when controlled by the switch, and overheating was occurring, the switch is almost certainly at fault.

3 The switch may be tested off the vehicle by using a low voltage test lamp across the switch contacts. The precise operating

17.5 Removing the radiator fan switch (thermostat housing removed)

temperature of the switch was not known at the time of writing. A defective switch must be renewed.

Removal

4 To remove the switch, first drain the cooling system.

5 Unplug the switch electrical connector. Unscrew the switch and remove it. Recover the fibre washer **(see illustration)**.

Refitting

6 Refit the switch using a new fibre washer and a little sealant on the threads. Plug in the electrical connector.

7 Refill the cooling system.

18 Temperature gauge sender - renewal

1 The temperature gauge sender is screwed into the thermostat housing. If it malfunctions it must be renewed.

2 Disconnect the battery earth lead.

3 Place a thick cloth over the expansion tank cap. Turn the cap anti-clockwise to the first stop, allow any pressure to escape, then remove and refit the cap. This will depressurise the system and minimise coolant loss.

4 Disconnect the wire from the temperature gauge sender **(see illustration)**.

5 Apply a little sealant to the threads of the new sender unit and have it ready for installation. Unscrew and remove the old sender and screw in and tighten the new one.

6 Connect the wire to the new sender unit.

7 Reconnect the battery earth lead.

8 Run the engine to operating temperature and check the gauge for correct operation.

9 Stop the engine and allow it to cool. Check the coolant level and top-up if necessary.

19 Crankshaft position sensor - renewal

1 The crankshaft position (engine speed) sensor is screwed into the flywheel housing. If it malfunctions it must be renewed.

18.4 Temperature gauge sender and connector

19.4 Unplug the electrical connector from the crankshaft position sensor

20.1 Oil pressure switch (arrowed)

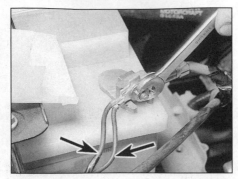

21.1 Fusible links (arrowed) are attached to the battery positive terminal

2 Disconnect the battery earth lead.
3 Raise the front of the vehicle and support it securely on axle stands (see *"Jacking and vehicle support"*).
4 Unplug the electrical connector from the sensor **(see illustration)**.
5 Undo the sensor retaining bolt and carefully withdraw the sensor.
6 Fitting is the reverse of the removal procedure. Tighten the retaining bolt to the specified torque setting.

20 Engine oil pressure switch - removal and refitting

Removal

1 The engine oil pressure switch is screwed into the left-hand side of the cylinder head **(see illustration)**. If it malfunctions it must be renewed.
2 Disconnect the battery earth lead.

3 Unplug the electrical connector from the switch.
4 Unscrew and remove the old sender.

Refitting

5 Clean the switch location in the head.
6 Apply a little sealant to the threads of the new switch and screw it into position, tightening to the specified torque loading.
7 Reconnect the electrical connector to the switch.
8 Reconnect the battery earth lead.
9 Start the engine and check the switch for correct operation.

21 Fusible links - description and renewal

Description

1 Apart from the starter motor feed lead (which also carries the alternator output), the

entire electrical system is protected by two fusible links. One link protects the preheater system, which is otherwise unfused, and the other protects the remaining circuits. Each link consists of a length of wire which is attached to the battery positive terminal at one end and soldered into the wiring harness at the other **(see illustration)**. If the current passing through the link exceeds a certain value, the link will melt and break the circuit.

Renewal

2 Should a link melt, this can only be due to a serious short-circuit. The short must be found and rectified before the link is renewed. The job should be entrusted to a Ford dealer or other competent specialist.
3 Do not attempt to repair a melted link using ordinary insulated wire. Although the electrical system will work, the protection afforded by the link will be missing. Should a short-circuit occur again, serious damage or even fire could result.

Notes

Chapter 6
Emissions control systems

Contents

Degrees of difficulty

Easy, suitable for novice with little experience	**Fairly easy,** suitable for beginner with some experience	**Fairly difficult,** suitable for competent DIY mechanic	**Difficult,** suitable for experienced DIY mechanic	**Very difficult,** suitable for expert DIY or professional

Specifications

Torque wrench settings	Nm	lbf ft
Catalytic converter flange joint nuts		
Front	48 to 64	35 to 47
Rear	35 to 40	26 to 30
EGR vacuum regulator valve-to-pump bolts	2 to 3	1 to 2
EGR valve-to-inlet manifold Allen bolts	17 to 22	12 to 16
EGR valve exhaust supply pipe bolts	20 to 25	15 to 18

1 Catalytic converters -
General information and precautions

General information

The exhaust gases of any internal combustion engine (however efficient or well-tuned) which burns hydrocarbon-based fuel consist largely (approximately 99%) of nitrogen (N_2), carbon dioxide (CO_2), oxygen (O_2) and other inert gases and water vapour (H_2O). The remaining 1% is made up of the noxious materials which are currently seen as the major polluters of the environment, ie. carbon monoxide (CO), unburned hydrocarbons (HC), oxides of nitrogen (NO_X) and some solid matter, including a small lead content.

Left to themselves, most of these pollutants are thought eventually to break down naturally (CO and NO_X, for example, break down in the upper atmosphere to release CO_2) having first caused ground-level environmental problems, but the massive increase world-wide in the use of motor vehicles and the current popular concern for the environment has caused the introduction in most countries of legislation, in varying stages of severity, to combat the problem.

The device most commonly used to clean up vehicle exhausts is the catalytic converter. It is fitted into the vehicle's exhaust system and consists of an element (or substrate) of ceramic honeycomb coated with a combination of precious metals in such a way as to produce a vast surface area over which the exhaust gases must flow; the whole being mounted in a stainless-steel box. The simple oxidation (or two-way) catalytic converter fitted to diesel engines uses platinum and palladium as catalysts to speed up the reaction between the pollutants and the oxygen in the vehicle's exhaust gases, CO and HC being oxidised to form H_2O and CO_2. Note that the catalytic converter is not a filter in the physical sense; its function is to promote a chemical reaction, but it is not itself affected by that reaction.

Precautions

The catalytic converter is a reliable and simple device which needs no maintenance in itself, but there are some facts of which an owner should be aware if the converter is to function properly for its full service life:

a) There is no need to worry about using leaded/unleaded fuel in a vehicle equipped with a catalytic converter and a diesel engine - no diesel fuel has added lead.

b) Always keep the fuel system well-maintained in accordance with the manufacturer's schedule. Ensure that the air cleaner filter element and the fuel filter are renewed at the correct intervals. If the inlet air/fuel mixture is allowed to become too rich due to neglect, the unburned surplus will enter and burn in the catalytic converter, overheating the element and eventually destroying the converter.

c) If the engine develops a misfire, do not drive the vehicle at all (or at least as little as possible) until the fault is cured. A misfire will allow unburned fuel to enter the converter, which will result in its overheating, as noted above. For the same reason do not persist if the engine ever refuses to start. Either trace the problem and cure it yourself or have the vehicle checked immediately by a qualified mechanic. Never allow the vehicle to run out of fuel.

d) DO NOT push-or tow-start the vehicle - this will soak the catalytic converter in unburned fuel, causing it to overheat when the engine does start.

e) Try to avoid repeated successive cold starts with short journeys. If the converter is never allowed to reach its proper working temperature it will gather unburned fuel, allowing some to pass into the atmosphere and the rest to soak the element with unburned fuel thereby causing it to overheat when the engine does start.

f) DO NOT use fuel or engine oil additives as these may contain substances harmful to the catalytic converter.

g) NEVER use silicon-based sealants on any part of the air inlet/inlet manifold, or any kind of sealant on exhaust system joints forward of the catalytic converter. If pieces of sealant (however small) should break off, they will be carried into the converter and cause it to overheat locally.

h) DO NOT continue to use the vehicle if the engine burns oil to the extent of leaving a visible trail of blue smoke. Unburned carbon deposits will clog the converter passages and reduce its efficiency; in severe cases the element will overheat.

i) Remember that the catalytic converter operates at very high temperatures (hence the heat shields on the vehicle's underbody) and the casing will become hot enough to ignite combustible materials which brush against it. DO NOT, therefore, park the vehicle in dry undergrowth, over long grass or piles of dead leaves.

j) Remember that the catalytic converter is FRAGILE - do not strike it with tools during servicing work, take great care when working on the exhaust system, ensure that the converter is well clear of any jacks or other lifting gear used to raise the vehicle and do not drive the vehicle over rough ground, roadhumps, etc., in such a way as to ground the exhaust system.

k) The catalytic converter, used on a well-maintained and well-driven vehicle, should last for between 50 000 and 100 000 miles. From this point on, careful checks should be made at all specified service intervals to ensure that the converter is still operating efficiently. If the converter is no longer effective it must be renewed.

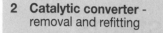

2 Catalytic converter - removal and refitting

1 The catalytic converter is located to the rear of the exhaust system downpipe lower end.

Removal

2 To remove the catalytic converter, undo the nuts securing its front and rear ends. Prise away the exhaust system centre section until the converter and downpipe can be swung down on the downpipe balljoints **(see illustration)**. Collect the gasket (where fitted). Carefully separate the converter from the downpipe.

3 When working on any other part of the system, note that the underbody of the vehicle is protected by heat shields from the very high operating temperatures of a catalytic converter These shields may have to be unbolted before the exhaust system itself can be removed from the vehicle.

Refitting

4 On refitting, clean carefully the mating surfaces, fit a new gasket (where applicable) and offer up the converter. Never use exhaust sealants upstream of the converter. On early models, ensure that the arrow on the converter's body points to the rear, in line with the exhaust gas flow. On later models, the converter will fit correctly only one way, as the front and rear flanges are either of different sizes or have offset studs to prevent incorrect installation. This fact must be remembered when renewing separately any of the affected parts of the system.

5 Tighten the nuts to their specified torque wrench settings.

6 If renewing the rubber mountings, ensure that the mounting nearest the converter is of the correct type. Due to the converter's high operating temperatures, this mounting must be of high-temperature resistant material.

3 Exhaust Gas Recirculation (EGR) system - Bosch injection only

1 This system is fitted to some models to ensure that the vehicle complies with the appropriate emission control legislation. Only vehicles with the Bosch fuel injection system are so equipped.

2 By recirculating a controlled amount of exhaust gases back through the inlet manifold to be burned in the combustion chamber, combustion chamber temperatures are reduced, also the amount of surplus oxygen in the inlet air, thus minimising the generation of oxides of nitrogen (NO_x).

3 The system consists of the following components:

a) The Thermal-Operated Vacuum Switch - fitted to the thermostat housing. This is closed until the coolant temperature reaches 60°C, thus preventing the system from operating while the engine is warming up

b) The Vacuum Regulator Valve - mounted on the top of the fuel injection pump. This regulates according to throttle opening the amount of vacuum applied to the EGR valve

c) The Vacuum Delay Valve - fitted in the vacuum line to control the rate at which vacuum is applied to the EGR valve

d) The Exhaust Gas Recirculation (EGR) Valve - bolted to the inlet manifold and connected by a supply pipe to the exhaust manifold. This opens under the control of the vacuum switch, regulator and delay valves, using the depression created by the vacuum pump which allows a proportion of the exhaust gases to flow up into the inlet manifold and into the combustion chamber

System checking

4 The system requires no maintenance except for the regular check of all hoses, pipes, etc.

5 Whenever the fuel injection pump is removed the vacuum regulator valve setting must be checked and, if necessary, adjusted.

6 To check the system's operation, warm the engine up to normal operating temperature and allow it to idle. Disconnect and reconnect several times the vacuum pipe from the top of the EGR valve **(see illustration)**. The valve should be heard to operate each time.

7 If the EGR valve does not operate and vacuum can be felt at the pipe end, first check the setting of the vacuum regulator valve.

8 If the vacuum regulator valve is functioning

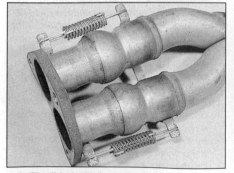

2.2 Flexible balljoint on exhaust downpipe permits removal of catalytic converter - joint removed for clarity

3.6 The EGR valve vacuum pipe (arrowed)

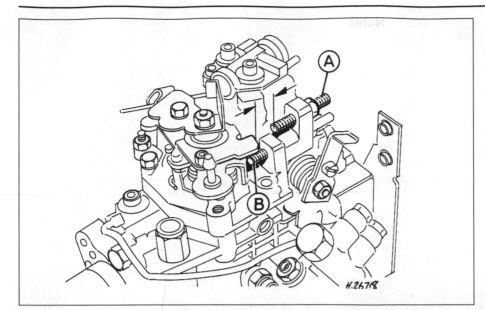

3.18 EGR system vacuum regulator valve adjustment

A Third stop screw - inset spacers in location shown   B Maximum speed adjusting screw

correctly, the fault must be in the EGR valve, which must then be renewed. If the valve is to be renewed, it is always worth first trying the effect of cleaning any carbon build-up from its passages to check whether this is the reason for the failure. If the valve's diaphragm has failed, on the other hand, there is no alternative to the renewal of the complete valve unit.

9 If no vacuum can be felt, check back through the system until the leak or blockage is found and rectified.

Thermal-operated vacuum switch - removal and refitting

10 This unit is screwed into the vacuum pump side of the thermostat housing and can be identified by the two vacuum pipes connected to it.

11 Drain the cooling system, either completely or down as far as the thermostat.

12 Disconnect the vacuum pipes and unscrew the switch.

13 On fitting the new switch, either ensure that a new sealing washer is used or apply a smear of suitable sealant to its threads, as applicable. Tighten the switch securely.

14 Refill the cooling system.

Vacuum regulator valve - adjustment

15 Checking and adjustment of the vacuum regulator valve is only possible if a hand-operated vacuum pump/gauge is available.

16 Connect the pump/gauge to the inlet port (the one nearest the engine) of the regulator valve.

17 Hold the throttle in the fully open position, and operate the hand pump continuously. Note the vacuum reading on the gauge, which should be around 0.6 bar (8.7 lbf/in2).

18 Fit an 11.8 mm thick spacer between the throttle lever and third stop screw (A) **(see illustration)**.

19 Push the throttle lever against the spacer and then operate the vacuum pump. The recorded vacuum pressure should be as previously noted.

20 Change the spacer for one 12.1 mm thick. This spacer should hold the regulator valve open, so that no vacuum reading can be obtained when the vacuum pump is operated.

21 If the regulator valve does not behave as indicated, remove the tamperproof cover (A) **(see illustration)**.

22 Hold the throttle lever hard against the maximum speed adjusting screw (B).

23 Using the vacuum pump, the vacuum should be between 0.6 and 0.7 bar (8.7 and 10.2 lbf/in2).

24 Fit a 12.0 mm thick spacer between the throttle lever and the third stop screw. Retain the throttle in this position, and operate the vacuum pump.

25 Turn the regulator adjuster screw to set the vacuum to 0.35 bar (5.1 lbf/in2).

26 Now recheck the vacuum readings using the 11.8 mm and 12.1 mm spacers as previously described.

27 Fit a new tamperproof cap, remove the pump and refit the original hose connections.

Vacuum regulator valve - removal and refitting

28 Note that the valve's inlet pipe (from the vacuum pump) is connected to the union nearest the engine. The valve's outlet union (to the EGR valve) is the union nearest the radiator. On later models this pipe will be marked with a yellow tracer.

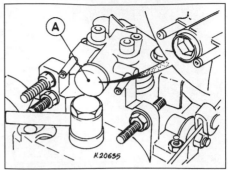

3.21 EGR system vacuum regulator valve adjustment screw under tamperproof cap (A)

29 If no identifying mark can be found, use paint to make your own before disconnecting either pipe.

30 Unbolt and remove the regulator valve.

31 Refitting is a reversal of removal but if a new valve is being fitted, it must be adjusted as described above.

Vacuum delay valve - removal and refitting

32 At the time of writing, no information was available concerning the precise location of this unit, or whether it is available separately from the vacuum pipes. See your local Ford dealer for details.

33 Note that valves of this type are usually clearly marked to show which way round they are to be fitted. Note any such markings or other identifying details of this unit before disturbing it. Ensure that the valve is fitted the correct way round, as noted on removal, and that the vacuum pipes are securely fastened to each end.

EGR valve - removal and refitting

34 Disconnect the battery earth (negative) terminal.

35 Disconnect the vacuum pipe from the top of the valve.

36 Unscrew the two bolts securing the supply pipe to the valve's underside. Withdraw and discard the gasket.

37 Unbolt the EGR valve from the inlet manifold and withdraw it. Withdraw and discard the gasket.

38 If the supply pipe is ever disturbed, always renew the gaskets at its upper and lower ends. Tighten the bolts to the torque wrench setting specified and ensure that the securing clamps are securely fastened on reassembly.

39 On refitting, always renew the gaskets and tighten the bolts to their specified torque wrench settings. Connect the vacuum pipe to the valve, start the engine and check that the system is operating correctly, as described above.

6

Notes

Chapter 7: Transmission

Contents

Degrees of difficulty

Easy, suitable for novice with little experience	**Fairly easy,** suitable for beginner with some experience	**Fairly difficult,** suitable for competent DIY mechanic	**Difficult,** suitable for experienced DIY mechanic	**Very difficult,** suitable for expert DIY or professional

Specifications

Manufacturer's code
Manual transmission MTX-75

Gear ratios
1st	3.666:1
2nd	2.047:1
3rd	1.258:1
4th	1.864:1
5th	0.674:1
Reverse	3.46:1

Final drive ratios 4.06:1

Torque wrench settings
	Nm	lbf ft
Transmission to engine	40	30
Gearchange support rod	55	41
Gearchange linkage clamp bolt	16	12
Gearchange assembly rear mounting	44	32
Gearchange linkage to selector shaft	23	17

1 General information

The vehicles covered by this manual are equipped with a 5-speed manual transmission.

The transmission is a compact, two-piece, lightweight aluminium alloy housing, containing both the transmission and differential assemblies. The transmission code name is MTX-75, MT standing for *Manual Transmission*, X for transa*X*le (front-wheel-drive), and 75 being the distance between the input and output shafts in mm.

Because of the complexity, possible unavailability of replacement parts and special tools necessary, internal repair procedures for the transmission are not recommended for the home mechanic. For readers who wish to tackle a transmission rebuild, exploded views and brief notes on overhaul are provided. The bulk of the information in this Chapter is devoted to removal and refitting procedures.

2 Gearchange linkage - adjustment

Note: *The special Ford tool 16-073 will be required in order to carry out the following adjustment. This tool is simply a slotted ring which locks the gear lever in the neutral position during adjustment. If the tool is not available, adjustment is still possible by proceeding on a trial-and-error basis, preferably with the help of an assistant to hold the gear lever in the neutral position.*

1 Remove the centre console as described in Chapter 11.

2 Apply the handbrake, jack up the front of the vehicle and support it on axle stands. Move the gear lever to the neutral position.

3 Working beneath the vehicle, loosen the clamp bolt on the gearchange linkage located behind the transmission.

4 With the gear lever still in neutral, fit the special Ford tool 16-073 over the gear lever, and locate it in the recess in the lever retaining

7

housing on top of the transmission. Twist the tool clockwise to lock the lever in the neutral position. Take care during the adjustment not to move the gear lever or displace the adjustment tool.

5 Check that the front part of the gearchange linkage from the transmission is in neutral. It will be necessary to move the linkage slightly forwards and backwards to determine that it is in the correct position.

6 Recheck that the adjustment tool is still correctly fitted to the gear lever, then tighten the clamp bolt on the gearchange linkage.

7 Remove the adjustment tool from the gear lever.

8 Lower the vehicle to the ground, then refit the centre console with reference to Chapter 11.

3 Gearchange linkage and gear lever - removal and refitting

Removal

1 Remove the centre console as described in Chapter 11 (see illustration).

2 Apply the handbrake, jack up the front of the vehicle and support it on axle stands. Move the gear lever to its neutral position.

3 Working beneath the vehicle, unscrew the bolt and disconnect the gearchange linkage from the selector shaft on the rear of the transmission.

4 Mark the position of the gearchange linkage front and rear sections in relation to each other. Loosen the clamp bolt and remove the front section.

5 Unscrew the bolt securing the gearchange support rod to the bracket on the rear of the transmission.

6 Remove the heat shield. Support the weight of the gearchange linkage assembly, unscrew the nuts from the rear mounting bracket, and lower the assembly from the underbody (see illustration).

7 Remove the insulator rubber from the rear of the assembly.

8 Examine the insulator rubber and the stabiliser bar mounting rubber for wear and deterioration, and if necessary obtain new ones.

3.1 View of the top of the gearchange assembly with the centre console removed

Refitting

9 Refitting is a reversal of the removal procedure, but adjust the linkage as described in Section 2.

4 Speedometer drive pinion - removal and refitting

Removal

1 Access to the speedometer drive pinion may be gained from the top of the engine (after removing air cleaner assembly - see Chapter 4), or from below by raising the front of the vehicle and reaching up over the top of the transmission. If the latter method is used, make sure that the vehicle is supported adequately on axle stands.

2 Unscrew the nut and disconnect the speedometer cable from the vehicle speed sensor on the transmission. Use two spanners to loosen the nut - one to counterhold the sensor, and the other to unscrew the cable nut.

3 Disconnect the wiring from the vehicle speed sensor, then unscrew the sensor from the top of the drive pinion.

4 Using a pair of grips, pull out the drive pinion retaining roll pin from the transmission casing.

5 Withdraw the speedometer drive pinion and bearing from the top of the transmission.

6 Using a small screwdriver, prise the O-ring from the groove in the bearing; obtain a new one for reassembly.

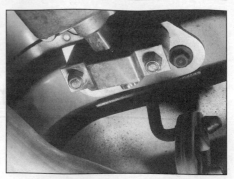

3.6 Gearchange linkage assembly rear mounting

7 Wipe clean the drive pinion and bearing, also the seating bore in the transmission casing.

Refitting

8 Refitting is a reversal of the removal procedure, but lightly oil the new O-ring before inserting the assembly in the transmission casing. Drive in the retaining roll pin using a hammer.

5 Oil seals - renewal

1 Oil leaks frequently occur due to wear or deterioration of the differential side gear seals and/or the gearchange selector shaft oil seal and speedometer drive pinion O-ring. Renewal of these seals is relatively easy, since the repairs can be performed without removing the transmission from the vehicle.

Differential side gear oil seals

2 The differential side gear oil seals are located at the sides of the transmission, where the driveshafts enter the transmission. If leakage at the seal is suspected, raise the vehicle and support it securely on axle stands. If the seal is leaking, oil will be found on the side of the transmission below the driveshaft.

3 Refer to Chapter 8 and remove the appropriate driveshaft. If removing the right-hand driveshaft, it will be necessary to remove the intermediate shaft as well.

4 Using a large screwdriver or lever, carefully prise the oil seal out of the transmission casing, taking care not to damage the transmission casing (see illustrations).

5.4a Prise out the oil seal with a suitable lever

5.4b Removing the oil seal from the transmission casing

> **HAYNES HINT** *If an oil seal is reluctant to move, it is sometimes helpful to carefully drive it into the transmission a little way, applying the force at one point only. This will have the effect of swivelling the seal out of the casing, and it can then be pulled out. If the oil seal is particularly difficult to remove, an oil seal removal tool may be obtained from a garage or accessory shop.*

5 Wipe clean the oil seal seating in the transmission casing.

6 Dip the new oil seal in clean oil, then press it a little way into the casing by hand, making sure that it is square to its seating.

7 Using suitable tubing or a large socket, carefully drive the oil seal fully into the casing until it contacts the seating.

8 Refit the driveshaft with reference to Chapter 8.

Gearchange selector shaft oil seal

9 Apply the handbrake, jack up the front of the vehicle and support it on axle stands.

10 Unscrew the bolt securing the gearchange linkage to the shaft on the rear of the transmission. Pull off the linkage and remove the rubber boot.

11 Using a suitable tool or grips, pull the oil seal out of the transmission casing. Ford technicians use a slide hammer, with an end fitting which locates over the oil seal extension. In the absence of this tool, if the oil seal is particularly tight, drill one or two small holes in the oil seal, and screw in self-tapping screws. The oil seal can then be removed from the casing by pulling on the screws.

12 Wipe clean the oil seal seating in the transmission.

13 Dip the new oil seal in clean oil, then press it a little way into the casing by hand, making sure that it is square to its seating.

14 Using suitable tubing or a large socket, carefully drive the oil seal fully into the casing.

15 Locate the rubber boot over the selector shaft.

16 Refit the gearchange linkage to the shaft on the rear of the transmission, and tighten the bolt.

17 If necessary, adjust the gearchange linkage as described in Section 2 of this Chapter.

Speedometer drive pinion oil seal

18 The procedure is covered in Section 4 of this Chapter.

7.3 Use split pins to hold the radiator in its raised position

6 Reversing light switch - removal and refitting

Removal

1 Remove the air cleaner as described in Chapter 4.

2 Disconnect the wiring leading to the reversing light switch on the top of the transmission.

3 Unscrew the mounting bolts, and remove the reversing light switch from the cover housing on the transmission.

Refitting

4 Refitting is a reversal of the removal procedure.

7 Transmission - removal and refitting

Note: Read through this procedure before starting work to see what is involved, particularly in terms of lifting equipment. Depending on the facilities available, the home mechanic may prefer to remove the engine and transmission together, then separate them on the bench, as described in Chapter 2.

Removal

1 Disconnect the battery negative (earth) lead

7.5 Disconnecting the wiring multi-plug from the reversing light switch

(Chapter 5). For better access, the battery may be removed completely.

2 If necessary, the bonnet may be removed as described in Chapter 11, Section 8 for better access, and for fitting the engine lifting hoist.

3 Hold the radiator in its raised position by inserting split pins through the holes in the upper mounting extensions **(see illustration)**. This is necessary to retain the radiator when the subframe is removed.

4 Remove the air cleaner assembly as described in Chapter 4.

5 Disconnect the wiring from the reversing light switch on the transmission **(see illustration)**.

6 Unscrew the bolt, and remove the wiring loom bracket from the top of the transmission **(see illustration)**.

7 Detach the earth cable located between the transmission and the body.

8 On models equipped with cable-operated clutch, disconnect the clutch cable from the release lever on the transmission. On models equipped with hyralically-operated clutch, disconnect the hydraulic pipe. (see Chapter 8).

9 Unscrew and remove the three upper bolts securing the transmission to the engine. Also unscrew the mounting bolt with the earth lead, located beneath the exhaust manifold **(see illustration)**.

10 Unscrew and remove the starter motor upper mounting bolt, noting that an earth cable is attached to it **(see illustration)**.

11 Apply the handbrake, jack up the front of the vehicle and support it on axle stands. Remove the front wheels.

7

7.6 Removing the wiring loom bracket from the top of the transmission

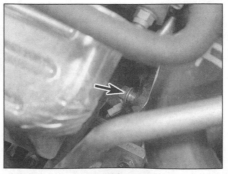

7.9 Mounting bolt with earth lead located beneath the exhaust manifold

7.10 Removing the starter motor bolt with the earth cable

7.12 Radiator front lower cover removal

7.20 Unscrew the bolt securing the gearchange linkage rod to the shaft on the rear of the transmission

7.21 Removing the gearchange linkage front section

12 Remove the front lower cover from under the radiator by prising out the side clips and unscrewing the retaining bolts **(see illustration)**.
13 Remove the wheel arch liner from the right-hand side of the vehicle as described in Chapter 11.
14 Unscrew the bolts and remove the auxiliary drivebelt cover.
15 Working on each side of the vehicle in turn, unscrew the nut and disconnect the anti-roll bar link from the strut, noting that the flexible brake hose bracket is attached to the link stud.
16 Extract the split pins, then unscrew the nuts securing the track rod ends to the steering knuckles on each side. Release the

balljoints from the steering knuckle arms, using a balljoint separator tool.
17 Working on each side in turn, note which way round the front suspension lower arm balljoint clamp bolt is fitted, then unscrew and remove it from the knuckle assembly. Lever the balljoint down from the knuckle - if it is tight, prise the joint open carefully using a large flat-bladed tool. Take care not to damage the balljoint seal during the separation procedure.
18 Disconnect the cooling fan multi-plug on the subframe behind the radiator, and unclip the plug from the bracket.
19 Remove the complete exhaust system as described in Chapter 4.

20 Unscrew the bolt securing the gearchange linkage to the selector shaft on the rear of the transmission **(see illustration)**.
21 Mark the position of the gearchange linkage front and rear sections, then unscrew the clamp bolt. Disconnect the linkage from the selector shaft on the rear of the transmission, and separate the front and rear sections of the linkage **(see illustration)**.
22 Unscrew the mounting bolt, and disconnect the gearchange support rod from the bracket on the rear of the transmission **(see illustration)**.
23 Remove the gear linkage heat shield from the underbody by unscrewing the nuts **(see illustration)**.
24 Unscrew and remove the gear linkage rear mounting bolts, swivel the linkage around to the rear, and tie it to the underbody **(see illustrations)**.
25 On models fitted with air conditioning, unscrew and remove the mounting bolts securing the dehydrator to the subframe, and tie it to one side.
26 Unscrew and remove the bolts securing the steering gear to the subframe. The bolts are difficult to reach using normal spanners; if possible, the special cranked Ford tool should be obtained (see Chapter 10).
27 Unscrew and remove the centre bolt from the engine/transmission rear mounting (roll restrictor), then unbolt the mounting from the subframe **(see illustrations)**.

7.22 Unscrewing the bolt securing the gearchange support rod to the bracket on the rear of the transmission

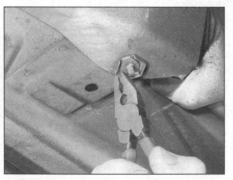

7.23 Removing the gear linkage heat shield

7.24a Unscrew the gear linkage rear mounting bolts (arrowed) . . .

7.24b . . . swivel the linkage around, and tie it to the underbody

7.27a Remove the centre bolt (arrowed) from the rear mounting . . .

7.27b ... then unbolt the mounting from the subframe and remove it

7.28a Unscrew the nut and bolt (arrowed) ...

7.28b ... and remove the transmission support rod bracket

28 Unscrew the nut and bolt, and remove the support rod bracket from the rear of the transmission **(see illustrations)**.

29 Unscrew the nuts and bolts, and remove the engine/transmission rear mounting bracket from the transmission **(see illustrations)**.

30 Unscrew and remove the centre bolt from the engine front mounting **(see illustration)**.

31 With the help of an assistant, support the weight of the subframe, using trolley jacks if possible. Unscrew the bolts securing the power steering fluid cooler pipes to the subframe, then unscrew the subframe mounting bolts, and lower the subframe to the ground **(see illustrations)**.

32 Position a suitable container beneath the transmission, then unscrew the drain plug and drain the oil **(see illustration)**. Refit and tighten the plug on completion.

33 Unscrew the bolts securing the right-hand driveshaft centre bearing to the cylinder block. Remove the heat shield, then pull out the right-hand strut so that the intermediate shaft is removed from the transmission differential gears. Be prepared for oil spillage.

34 Support the right-hand driveshaft on axle stands, making sure that the inner tripod joint is not turned through more than 18° (damage may occur if the joint is turned through too great an angle).

35 Insert a suitable lever between the left-hand driveshaft inner joint and the

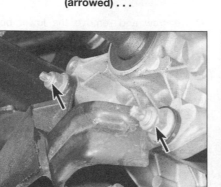

7.29a Nuts securing the rear mounting bracket to the transmission

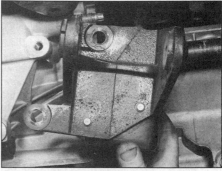

7.29b Removing the rear mounting bracket

7.30 Removing the bolt from the engine front mounting bracket

7.31a Removing the power steering fluid cooler pipes from the subframe

7.31b Unscrewing the subframe front ...

7.31c ... and rear mounting bolts

7.32 Unscrewing the transmission oil drain plug

7

7.40 Supporting the engine with a hoist

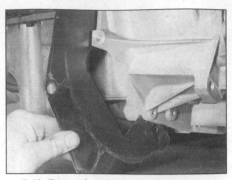

7.48 Removing the lower cover plate

transmission case (with a thin piece of wood against the case), then prise free the joint from the differential. If it proves reluctant to move, strike the lever firmly with the palm of the hand. Be careful not to damage the adjacent components, and be prepared for oil spillage. As the right-hand driveshaft has already been removed, it is possible to release the left-hand driveshaft by inserting a forked drift from the right-hand side, but care must be taken to prevent damage to the differential gears.

36 Support the left-hand driveshaft on axle stands, making sure that the inner tripod joint is not turned through more than 18° (damage may occur if the joint is turned through too great an angle).

37 Disconnect the multi-plug from the wiring leading to the vehicle speed sensor.

38 Unscrew the cable nut, and disconnect the speedometer cable from the top of the vehicle speed sensor. Hold the sensor with a spanner while the cable nut is loosened.

39 If necessary, the vehicle may be lowered to the ground at this stage, in order to connect an engine hoist. If an engine support bar which locates over the engine compartment is to be used, then the vehicle may be left in its raised position.

40 Attach the hoist to diagonally-opposite positions on the engine, and take the weight of the engine and transmission **(see illustration)**.

41 Unscrew the nuts from the engine right-hand mounting bracket. Note that, where a hydraulic mounting is fitted (see Chapter 2), the mounting must never be tilted by more than 5°.

42 Unscrew the retaining nuts, and remove the engine/transmission left-hand mounting from the transmission.

43 On models fitted with air conditioning, lower the engine until the compressor is below the right-hand side member.

44 On models without air conditioning, lower the transmission until it is opposite the aperture on the left-hand side of the engine compartment.

45 Support the weight of the transmission on a trolley jack. Use safety chains or a cradle to steady the transmission on the jack.

46 Remove the remaining starter motor mounting bolts.

47 Unscrew and remove the lower bolts securing the transmission to the engine. Also unscrew the bolts securing the lower cover plate to the transmission.

48 With the help of an assistant, withdraw the transmission squarely from the engine, taking care not to allow its weight to hang on the clutch friction disc. As the transmission is being withdrawn, remove the lower cover plate sandwiched between the transmission and engine **(see illustration)**. Lower the transmission to the ground.

49 The clutch components can now be inspected with reference to Chapter 8, and renewed if necessary. (Unless they are virtually new, it is worth renewing the clutch components as a matter of course, even if the transmission has been removed for some other reason.)

Refitting

50 If removed, refit the clutch components (see Chapter 8).

51 With the transmission secured to the trolley jack as on removal, raise it into position, and then carefully slide it onto the rear of the engine, at the same time engaging the input shaft with the clutch friction disc splines. Do not use excessive force to refit the transmission - if the input shaft does not slide into place easily, readjust the angle of the transmission so that it is level, and/or turn the input shaft so that the splines engage properly with the disc. If problems are still experienced, check that the clutch friction disc is correctly centred (Chapter 8).

52 Refit the lower bolts securing the transmission to the engine, and tighten moderately at this stage.

53 Insert and tighten the starter mounting bolts, noting that an earth cable is attached to one of them.

54 Raise the transmission to its normal position.

55 Refit the engine/transmission left-hand mounting, and tighten the nuts.

56 Refit the engine right-hand mounting bracket, and tighten the nuts.

57 If previously lowered, raise the front of the vehicle, and support on axle stands.

58 Refit the speedometer cable to the vehicle speed sensor, and tighten the cable nut.

59 Reconnect the wiring to the speed sensor.

60 Insert the left-hand driveshaft into the transmission, making sure that it is fully engaged with the internal circlip.

61 Refit the right-hand driveshaft and intermediate shaft, and tighten the bolts.

62 Refit and align the subframe, with reference to Chapter 2, Section 10. Tighten the mounting bolts to the specified torque.

63 Tighten the centre bolt in the engine front mounting.

64 Refit the engine rear mounting bracket, and tighten the bolts.

65 Refit the transmission support rod and bracket, and tighten the bolts and nut.

66 Refit the engine rear mounting to the subframe, and tighten the bolts.

67 Refit the steering gear to the subframe, and tighten the mounting bolts.

68 On models with air conditioning, refit the dehydrator to the subframe, and tighten the mounting bolts.

69 Refit the gear linkage and heat shield with reference to Section 3.

70 Refit the transmission gearchange support rod to the rear of the transmission, and tighten the bolt. Adjust the gear linkage if necessary, with reference to Section 2.

71 Refit the exhaust system, with reference to Chapter 4.

72 Reconnect and secure the cooling fan multi-plug.

73 Refit the front suspension lower arm balljoints to the knuckle assemblies, with reference to Chapter 10.

74 Refit the track rod ends to the steering knuckles on each side, with reference to Chapter 10.

75 Refit the anti-roll bar links to the struts, and tighten the nuts.

76 Refit the auxiliary drivebelt cover and the wheel arch liner.

77 Refit the front lower cover beneath the radiator.

78 Refit the wheels, and lower the vehicle to the ground.

79 Insert the upper bolts securing the transmission to the engine.

80 Reconnect the clutch cable with reference to Chapter 8.

81 Refit the earth cable between the transmission and the body.

82 Refit the wiring loom bracket to the top of the transmission.

83 Reconnect the wiring to the reversing light switch.

84 Tighten all transmission mounting bolts fully.

85 Refit the air cleaner assembly, air mass meter and air inlet duct, with reference to Chapter 4.

86 Remove the split pins holding the radiator in its raised position.

87 If removed, refit the bonnet with reference to Chapter 11.

88 If removed, refit the battery and reconnect the leads.

89 Fill the transmission with oil, and check the level as described in Chapter 1.
90 Make a final check that all connections have been made, and all bolts tightened fully.
91 Road test the vehicle to check for proper transmission operation, then check the transmission visually for leakage of oil.

8 Transmission mounting - checking and renewal

This procedure is covered in Chapter 2.

9 Transmission overhaul - general

1 Overhauling a transmission is a difficult job for the do-it-yourselfer. It involves the dismantling and reassembly of many small parts. Numerous clearances must be precisely measured and, if necessary, changed with selected spacers and circlips. As a result, if transmission problems arise, while the unit can be removed and refitted by a competent do-it-yourselfer, overhaul should be left to a transmission specialist. Rebuilt transmissions may be available - check with your dealer parts department, motor factors, or transmission specialists. At any rate, the time and money involved in an overhaul is almost sure to exceed the cost of a rebuilt unit.
2 Nevertheless, it's not impossible for an inexperienced mechanic to rebuild a transmission, providing the special tools are available, and the job is done in a deliberate step-by-step manner so nothing is overlooked.
3 The tools necessary for an overhaul include: internal and external circlip pliers, a bearing puller, a slide hammer, a set of pin punches, a dial test indicator, and possibly a hydraulic press. In addition, a large, sturdy workbench and a vice or transmission stand will be required.
4 During dismantling of the transmission, make careful notes of how each part comes off, where it fits in relation to other parts, and what holds it in place. Exploded views are included **(see illustrations)** to show where the parts go - but actually noting how they are fitted when you remove the parts will make it much easier to get the transmission back together.
5 Before taking the transmission apart for repair, it will help if you have some idea what area of the transmission is malfunctioning. Certain problems can be closely tied to specific areas in the transmission, which can make component examination and replacement easier. Refer to the *"Fault diagnosis"* section at the end of this manual for information regarding possible sources of trouble.

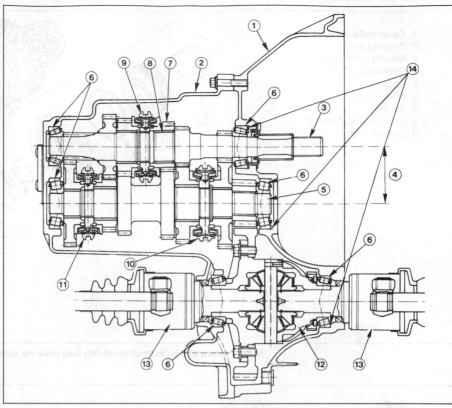

9.4a Sectional diagram of the manual transmission

1 Clutch housing	5 Output shaft	10 1st/2nd synchro
2 Transmission housing	6 Taper roller bearings	11 5th/reverse synchro
3 Input shaft	7 4th gear	12 Differential
4 Distance between shaft centres = 75 mm	8 Needle roller bearing	13 Driveshafts
	9 3rd/4th synchro	14 Shims

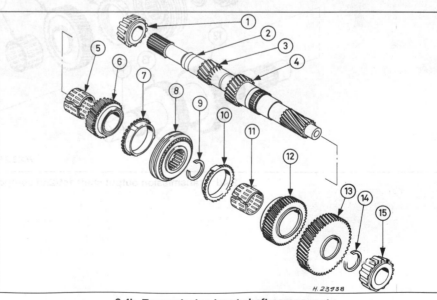

9.4b Transmission input shaft components

1 Taper roller bearing	6 3rd gear	11 Needle roller bearing
2 Input shaft	7 3rd/4th synchro ring	12 4th gear
3 1st gear	8 3rd/4th synchro hub	13 5th gear
4 2nd gear	9 Snap-ring	14 Snap-ring
5 Needle roller bearing	10 4th/5th synchro ring	15 Taper roller bearing

7

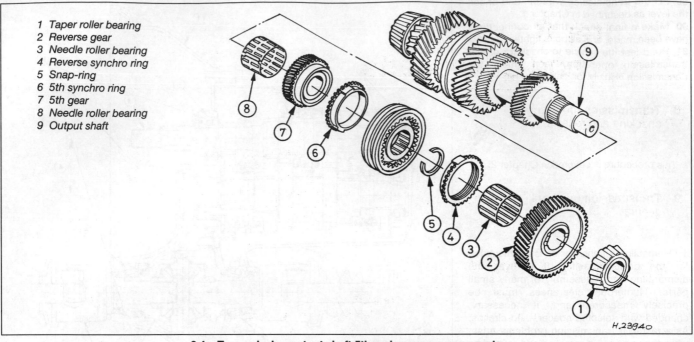

1 Taper roller bearing
2 Reverse gear
3 Needle roller bearing
4 Reverse synchro ring
5 Snap-ring
6 5th synchro ring
7 5th gear
8 Needle roller bearing
9 Output shaft

H.23940

9.4c Transmission output shaft 5th and reverse components

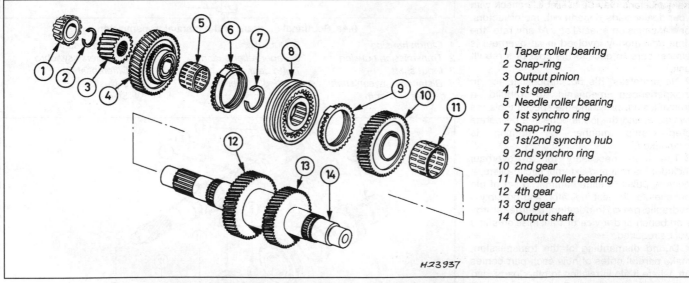

1 Taper roller bearing
2 Snap-ring
3 Output pinion
4 1st gear
5 Needle roller bearing
6 1st synchro ring
7 Snap-ring
8 1st/2nd synchro hub
9 2nd synchro ring
10 2nd gear
11 Needle roller bearing
12 4th gear
13 3rd gear
14 Output shaft

H.23937

9.4d Transmission output shaft 1st/2nd components

Chapter 8
Clutch and driveshafts

Contents

Degrees of difficulty

Easy, suitable for novice with little experience	**Fairly easy,** suitable for beginner with some experience	**Fairly difficult,** suitable for competent DIY mechanic

Difficult, suitable for experienced DIY mechanic	**Very difficult,** suitable for expert DIY or professional

Specifications

Clutch

Disc diameter	240 mm
Lining thickness (new)	8.84 mm
Pedal stroke:	
Hydraulically-operated clutch	130 ± 3.0 mm
Cable-operated clutch	
Right-hand-drive models	155 ± 5.0 mm
Left-hand-drive models	145 ± 5.0 mm

Torque wrench settings

	Nm	lbf ft
Clutch pressure plate to flywheel	25 to 34	18 to 25
Clutch release lever clamp bolt	21 to 27	15 to 20
Driveshaft support bearing bracket-to-cylinder block bolts	48	35
Driveshaft/hub retaining nut	340	251
Master cylinder securing bolts	10	8

1 General information

The information in this Chapter deals with the components from the engine flywheel to the front wheels, except for the transmission, which is dealt with in Chapter 7. For the purposes of this Chapter, these components are grouped into the two categories, clutch and driveshafts. Separate Sections within this Chapter offer general descriptions and checking procedures for each group.

Since many of the procedures covered in this Chapter involve working under the vehicle, make sure that it is securely supported on axle stands placed on a firm, level floor.

2 Clutch - description and check

1 All models are equipped with either cable or hydraulically-operated single dry plate diaphragm spring clutch assemblies. The cover assembly consists of a steel cover (dowelled and bolted to the rear face of the flywheel), the pressure plate, and a diaphragm spring.

2 The clutch disc is free to slide along the splines of the gearbox input shaft, and is held in position between the flywheel and the pressure plate by the pressure of the diaphragm spring. Friction lining material is riveted to the clutch disc (driven plate), which has a spring-cushioned hub, to absorb transmission shocks and help ensure a smooth take-up of the drive.

Cable-operated clutch

3 The clutch is actuated by a cable, controlled by the clutch pedal. The clutch release mechanism consists of a release arm, and a bearing which contacts the fingers of the diaphragm spring. Depressing the clutch pedal actuates the release arm by means of the cable. The arm pushes the release bearing against the diaphragm fingers, so moving the centre of the diaphragm spring inwards. As the centre of the spring is pushed inwards, the outside of the spring pivots outwards, so moving the pressure plate backwards and disengaging its grip on the clutch disc.

4 When the pedal is released, the diaphragm spring forces the pressure plate back into

8

contact with the friction linings on the clutch disc. The disc is now firmly held between the pressure plate and the flywheel, thus transmitting engine power to the gearbox.

5 Unlike some other models in the Ford range, the clutch pedal is not of the self-adjusting type, although it uses the same serrated segment fitted to models with a self-adjusting pedal. The normal self-adjusting spring-tensioned pawl is not fitted to the segment, although the pedal moves the segment when it contacts the end stops. This arrangement means that pedal adjustment must be carried out manually.

6 The following checks may be performed to diagnose a clutch problem.

(a) First check the entire length of the clutch release cable in the engine compartment for obvious damage. Check also that it is located correctly, without any sharp turns.

(b) To check "clutch spin down time", run the engine at normal idle speed with the transmission in Neutral (clutch pedal up). Disengage the clutch (pedal down), wait several seconds, then engage reverse. No grinding noise should be heard. A grinding noise would most likely indicate a problem in the pressure plate or the clutch disc. Remember, however, that the transmission reverse gear has synchromesh fitted to it, so the probable symptom of a clutch fault would be a slight rearwards movement (or attempted movement) of the vehicle. If the check is made on level ground with the handbrake released, the movement would be more noticeable.

(c) To check for complete clutch release, run the engine at idle, and hold the clutch pedal approximately half an inch from the floor. Shift between 1st gear and reverse several times. If the shift is not smooth, or if the vehicle attempts to move forwards or backwards, component failure is indicated. Check the clutch cable and the pedal adjustment.

(d) Check the clutch pedal for excessive wear of the bushes, and for any obstructions which may restrict the pedal movement.

Hydraulically-operated clutch

3 The clutch is actuated hydraulically by a master and slave cylinders. The clutch release mechanism consists of a release arm, and a bearing which contacts the fingers of the diaphragm spring. Depressing the clutch pedal actuates the release arm by means of the slave cylinder. The arm pushes the release bearing against the diaphragm fingers, so moving the centre of the diaphragm spring inwards. As the centre of the spring is pushed inwards, the outside of the spring pivots outwards, so moving the pressure plate backwards and disengaging its grip on the clutch disc.

4 When the pedal is released, the diaphragm spring forces the pressure plate back into contact with the friction linings on the clutch

disc. The disc is now firmly held between the pressure plate and the flywheel, thus transmitting engine power to the gearbox.

5 Unlike the cable-operated clutch, the clutch is automatically adjusted, although the pedal travel can be adjusted with the end stops.

6 The following checks may be performed to diagnose a clutch problem.

(a) First check the fluid level in the reservoir, then check the security and condition of the hydraulic pipes and connections.

(b) To check "clutch spin down time", run the engine at normal idle speed with the transmission in Neutral (clutch pedal up). Disengage the clutch (pedal down), wait several seconds, then engage reverse. No grinding noise should be heard. A grinding noise would most likely indicate a problem in the pressure plate or the clutch disc. Remember, however, that the transmission reverse gear has synchromesh fitted to it, so the probable symptom of a clutch fault would be a slight rearwards movement (or attempted movement) of the vehicle. If the check is made on level ground with the handbrake released, the movement would be more noticeable.

(c) To check for complete clutch release, run the engine at idle, and hold the clutch pedal approximately half an inch from the floor. Shift between 1st gear and reverse several times. If the shift is not smooth, or if the vehicle attempts to move forwards or backwards, component failure is indicated.

(d) Check the clutch pedal for excessive wear of the bushes, and for any obstructions which may restrict the pedal movement.

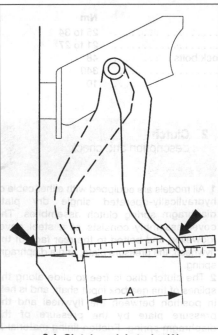

3.4 Clutch pedal stroke (A)

3 Clutch adjustment - check

Cable-operated clutch

1 If this check is being made after fitting a new clutch cable, the pedal should be depressed fully 10 times first.

2 Fully depress and hold down the clutch pedal, then place a steel rule against the bulkhead, and measure and record the distance to the middle of the rubber pad (dimension "C").

3 Release the pedal, and measure the distance from the bulkhead to the middle of the rubber pad again (dimension "B"). Do not lift the pedal when making the measurement.

4 Subtract dimension "C" from dimension "B" to determine the clutch pedal stroke (dimension "A") (see illustration).

"A" (stroke) = "B" (released dimension) minus "C" (depressed dimension)

5 Check that the dimension is within the tolerance given in the Specifications. If adjustment is required, proceed as follows.

6 Remove the air cleaner assembly as described in Chapter 4.

7 Loosen the locknut on the clutch cable adjuster sleeve near the release arm on the transmission. Turn the sleeve until the correct clutch pedal stroke is obtained (see illustration).

8 On completion, tighten the locknut.

Hydraulically-operated clutch

9 The procedure for measuring the pedal travel is the same as for the cable-operated clutch, noting the different stroke measurement given in the specifications section of this Chapter.

10 Adjustment is made using the stop bolt located under the clutch pedal.

4 Clutch cable - removal and refitting

Removal

1 Remove the air cleaner assembly as described in Chapter 4.

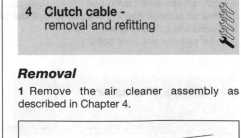
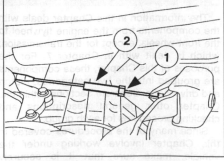

3.7 Locknut (1) and adjustment sleeve (2) for the clutch pedal stroke adjustment

4.3 Rubber cushion (arrowed) on the end of the outer cable

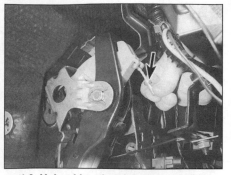

4.6 Unhooking the clutch inner cable (arrowed) from the pedal segment

4.7 Clutch cable support stay (arrowed) located next to the brake servo unit

2 Disengage the clutch cable from the release arm, by gripping the inner cable with pliers and pulling it forwards to disengage the cable nipple from the release arm. Take care not to damage the cable, if it is to be re-used.

3 Disengage the outer cable from the support lug on top of the gearbox bellhousing. Note the rubber cushion on the end of the outer cable **(see illustration)**.

4 Working inside the vehicle, remove the facia lower trim panel from beneath the steering column for access to the clutch pedal. Refer to Chapter 11 if necessary.

5 Disconnect the clutch pedal return spring from the pedal and bracket. Note where the spring is attached to the bracket, as the small hole is not easy to see.

6 Unhook the inner cable from the pedal segment **(see illustration)**.

7 Pull the cable through the aperture in the bulkhead. Detach the cable from the support stay near the brake servo unit, and withdraw it from the engine compartment **(see illustration)**.

Refitting

8 To refit the cable, thread it through the bulkhead from the engine compartment side. Fit the inner cable over the segment, engaging the end stop to secure it **(see illustration)**.

9 Reconnect the pedal return spring, making sure that it is correctly fitted in the small hole.

10 Reconnect the cable at the transmission end, passing it through the support lug on the top of the transmission, and engaging it with the release arm.

11 Locate the rubber grommet in the clutch cable support stay. Renew the grommet if necessary.

11 Adjust the pedal stroke as described in Section 3 of this Chapter.

12 Check the operation of the clutch.

13 Refit the trim panel under the steering column.

14 Refit the air cleaner assembly as described in Chapter 4.

5 Clutch pedal - removal and refitting

Removal

Cable-operated clutch

1 Remove the brake pedal as described in Chapter 9.

2 Remove the blue nylon spacer from the pedal pivot shaft.

3 Unhook and remove the clutch pedal return spring.

4 Remove the air cleaner assembly as described in Chapter 4.

5 Disconnect the clutch cable from the

release arm as described in the previous Section.

6 Working inside the vehicle, release the inner cable from the pedal segment on the clutch pedal.

7 Withdraw the pedal pivot shaft through the mounting bracket, and remove the pedal together with the blue nylon spacer. Note that this spacer is additional to the spacer located next to the brake pedal.

8 With the pedal removed, prise out the bushes from each side, and remove the segment **(see illustrations)**. Also remove the rubber pad. Renew the components as necessary.

Hydraulically-operated clutch

9 Proceed as described in paragraphs 1 to 3 in this section.

10 Disconnect the clip holding the master cylinder to the pedal.

11 Withdraw the pedal pivot through the mounting bracket and remove the pedal together with the spacers.

Refitting

12 Prior to refitting the pedal, apply a little grease to the pivot shaft and pedal bushes.

13 Refitting is a reversal of the removal procedure, making sure that the bushes and spacers are correctly located.

14 Adjust the clutch pedal stroke as described in Section 3.

4.8 Inner cable (arrowed) fitted to the pedal segment

5.8a Removing the clutch pedal bushes

5.8b Removing the segment from the clutch pedal

8

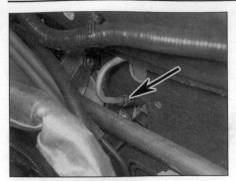

6.2 Hydraulic feed pipe and securing clamp (arrowed)

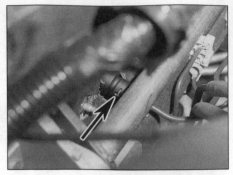

6.3 Hydraulic high pressure pipe and retaining clip (arrowed)

6.4 Removing the trim panel from the driver's footwell

6 Master cylinder - removal and refitting

⚠️ *Warning: Hydraulic fluid is poisonous; wash off immediately and thoroughly in the case of skin contact, and seek immediate medical advice if any fluid is swallowed or gets into the eyes. Certain types of hydraulic fluid are inflammable, and may ignite when allowed into contact with hot components; when servicing any hydraulic system, it is safest to assume that the fluid is inflammable, and to take precautions against the risk of fire as though it is petrol that is being handled. Hydraulic fluid is also an effective paint stripper, and will attack plastics; if any is spilt, it should be washed off immediately, usig coious quantities of fresh water. Finally, it is hygroscopic (it absorbs moisture from the air) - old fluid may be contaminated and unfit for further use. When topping-up or renewing the fluid, always use the recommended type, and ensure that it comes from a freshly-opened sealed container.*

Removal

1 Remove the charge air cooler as described in Chapter 4.
2 Disconnect the hose clamp and release the feed pipe **(see illustration)**.
3 Disconnect the retaining clip and withdraw the high pressure pipe **(see illustration)**.
4 Working inside the vehicle, remove the trim panel located above the pedals in the driver's seat **(see illustration)**.
5 Undo the two Torx retaining nuts **(see illustration)**.
6 Detach the clip holding the cylinder to the pedal and remove the master cylinder.

Refitting

7 Refitting is the reverse of the removal procedure, using a new hose clamp when refitting the feed pipe.
8 Bleed the clutch system as described in Section 8.

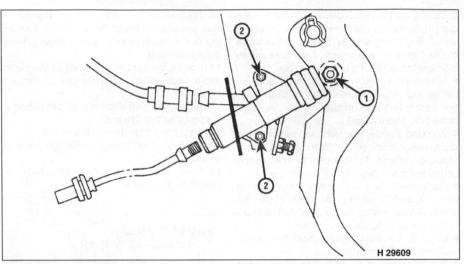

6.5 Master cylinder-to-bulkhead retaining bolts (2) and cylinder to pedal retaining clip (1)

7 Slave cylinder - removal and refitting

⚠️ *Warning: Hydraulic fluid is poisonous; wash off immediately and thoroughly in the case of skin contact, and seek immediate medical advice if any fluid is swallowed or gets into the eyes. Certain types of hydraulic fluid are inflammable, and may ignite when allowed into contact with hot components; when servicing any hydraulic system, it is safest to assume that the fluid is inflammable, and to take precautions against the risk of fire as though it is petrol that is being handled. Hydraulic fluid is also an effective paint stripper, and will attack plastics; if any is spilt, it should be washed off immediately, usig coious quantities of fresh water. Finally, it is hygroscopic (it absorbs moisture from the air) - old fluid may be contaminated and unfit for further use. When topping-up or renewing the fluid, always use the recommended type, and ensure that it comes from a freshly-opened sealed container.*

Removal

1 Remove the air cleaner assembly as described in Chapter 4.
2 The slave cylinder is located within the gearbox housing, with the bleed screw and high pressure pipe connection being located on top of the gearbox housing **(see illustration)**.
3 Remove the dust cover from the bleed screw.
4 Undo the quick release coupling and

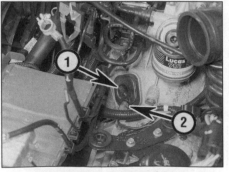

7.2 Location of bleed screw (1) and slave cylinder high pressure pipe (2)

7.4 Disconnecting the high pressure pipe connection

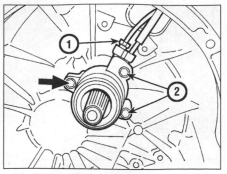

7.6 Slave cylinder high pressure pipe (1) and securing bolts (2)

disconnect the high-pressure pipe **(see illustration)**.

5 Separate the engine and transmission as described in Chapter 7. Note that the transmission need only be moved to the left of the engine compartment - it is not necessary to remove it completely.

6 From within the transmission, remove the high pressure pipe, unscrew the bolts and remove the slave cylinder complete with the release bearing **(see illustration)**.

Refitting

7 Refitting is the reverse of the removal procedure, using a new oil seal and sealer.
8 Bleed the clutch system as described in Section 8.

8 Hydraulic system - bleeding

Warning: Hydraulic fluid is poisonous; wash off immediately and thoroughly in the case of skin contact, and seek immediate medical advice if any fluid is swallowed or gets into the eyes. Certain types of hydraulic fluid are inflammable, and may ignite when allowed into contact with hot components; when servicing any hydraulic system, it is safest to assume that the fluid is inflammable, and to take precautions against the risk of fire as though it is petrol that is being handled. Hydraulic fluid is also an effective paint stripper, and will attack plastics; if any is spilt, it should be washed off immediately, usig coious quantities of fresh water. Finally, it is hygroscopic (it absorbs moisture from the air) - old fluid may be contaminated and unfit for further use. When topping-up or renewing the fluid, always use the recommended type, and ensure that it comes from a freshly-opened sealed container.

1 The correct operation of any hydraulic system is only possible after removing all air from the components and circuit; this is achieved by bleeding the system.
2 During the bleeding procedure, add only clean, unused hydraulic fluid of the recommended type; never re-use fluid that has already been bled from the system. Ensure that sufficient fluid is available before starting work.

3 If there is any possibility of incorrect fluid being already in the system, the brake and clutch components and circuit must be flushed completely with uncontaminated, correct fluid, and new seals should be fitted to the various components.

4 If hydraulic fluid has been lost from the system, or air has entered because of a leak, ensure that the fault is cured before proceeding further.

5 To improve access, remove the air cleaner assembly as described in Chapter 4.

6 Check that the clutch hydraulic pipe/hose is secure, that the unions are tight and that the bleed screw, is closed. Remove the dust cap **(see illustration)**, and clean any dirt from around the bleed screw.

7 Note that the brake fluid reservoir feeds both the brake and clutch hydraulic systems.

8 Collect a proprietary bleeding kit and suitable size ring spanner to fit the bleed screw

9 Fit the spanner and tube to the bleed screw **(see illustration)** and add fluid into the container.

10 Ensure that the brake/clutch fluid reservoir is maintained at the maximum level.

11 Loosen the bleed screw using the spanner and have an assistant depress the clutch pedal repeatedly until the emerging fluid is free of bubbles.

12 When bleeding is complete, tighten the bleed screw and disconnect the hose.

13 Wash off any spilt fluid, check once more that the bleed screw is tightened securely, and refit the dust cap.

14 Check the hydraulic fluid level in the reservoir and top-up if necessary (see *"Weekly checks"*).

15 Discard any hydraulic fluid that has been bled from the system; it will not be fit for re-use.

16 Check the feel of the clutch pedal. If it feels at all spongy, air must still be present in the system, and further bleeding is required. Failure to bleed satisfactorily after a procedure may be due to worn master or slave cylinder seals.

17 On complete, refit the air cleaner assembly.

9 Clutch components - removal, inspection and refitting

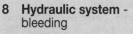

Warning: Dust created by clutch wear and deposited on the clutch components may contain asbestos, which is a health hazard. DO NOT blow it out with compressed air, and do not inhale any of it. DO NOT use petrol or petroleum-based solvents to clean off the dust. Brake system cleaner or methylated spirit should be used to flush the dust into a suitable receptacle. After the clutch components are wiped clean with rags, dispose of the contaminated rags and cleaner in a sealed, marked container.

Removal

1 Access to the clutch may be gained in one of two ways. The engine/transmission unit can be removed, as described in Chapter 2, and the transmission separated from the engine on the bench. Alternatively, the engine may be left in the vehicle and the transmission removed independently, as described in Chapter 7. If the latter course of action is

8.6 Removing the dust cap from the bleed screw

8.9 Fitting the spanner and bleed pipe to the bleed screw

8

9.1 Clutch is accessible with the transmission moved to one side

9.2 Marking the clutch cover and flywheel with a dab of paint (arrowed)

9.3 Unscrewing the clutch cover bolts

taken, note that the transmission need only be moved to the left of the engine compartment - it is not necessary to remove it completely **(see illustration)**.

2 Having separated the transmission from the engine, check if there are any marks identifying the relation of the clutch cover to the flywheel. If not, make your own marks using a dab of paint or a scriber **(see illustration)**. These marks will be used if the original cover is refitted, and will help to maintain the balance of the unit. A new cover may be fitted in any position allowed by the locating dowels.

3 Unscrew and remove the six clutch cover retaining bolts, working in a diagonal sequence, and slackening the bolts only a turn at a time **(see illustration)**. If necessary, the flywheel may be held stationary using a wide-bladed screwdriver, inserted in the teeth of the starter ring gear and resting against part of the cylinder block.

4 Ease the clutch cover off its locating dowels. Be prepared to catch the clutch disc, which will drop out as the cover is removed **(see illustration)**. Note which way round the disc is fitted.

Inspection

5 The most common problem which occurs in the clutch is wear of the clutch disc (driven plate). However, all the clutch components should be inspected at this time, particularly if the engine has covered a high mileage. Unless the clutch components are known to be virtually new, it is worth renewing them all as a set (disc, pressure plate and release bearing). Renewing a worn clutch disc by itself is not always satisfactory, especially if the old disc was slipping and causing the pressure plate to overheat.

6 Examine the linings of the clutch disc for wear and loose rivets, and the disc hub and rim for distortion, cracks, broken torsion springs, and worn splines. The surface of the friction linings may be highly glazed, but as long as the friction material pattern can be clearly seen, and the rivet heads are at least 1 mm below the lining surface, this is satisfactory. If there is any sign of oil contamination, indicated by shiny black

discoloration, the disc must be renewed, and the source of the contamination traced and rectified. This will be a leaking crankshaft oil seal or gearbox input shaft oil seal. The renewal procedure for the former is given in Chapter 2; renewal of the gearbox input shaft oil seal should be entrusted to a Ford dealer, as it involves dismantling the gearbox, and the renewal of the clutch release bearing guide tube, using a press. The disc must also be renewed if the lining thickness has worn down to, or just above, the level of the rivet heads.

7 Check the machined faces of the flywheel and pressure plate. If either is grooved, or heavily scored, renewal is necessary. The pressure plate must also be renewed if any cracks are apparent, or if the diaphragm spring is damaged or its pressure suspect. Pay particular attention to the tips of the spring fingers, where the release bearing acts upon them.

8 With the gearbox removed, it is also advisable to check the condition of the release bearing, as described in Section 7. Having got this far, it is almost certainly worth renewing it.

Refitting

9 It is important that no oil or grease is allowed to come into contact with the friction material of the clutch disc or the pressure plate and flywheel faces. To ensure this, it is advisable to refit the clutch assembly with

clean hands, and to wipe down the pressure plate and flywheel faces with a clean dry rag before assembly begins.

10 Ford technicians use a special tool for centralising the clutch disc at this stage. The tool holds the disc centrally on the pressure plate, and locates in the middle of the diaphragm spring fingers. If the tool is not available, it will be necessary to centralise the disc after assembling the cover loosely on the flywheel, as described in the following paragraphs.

11 Place the clutch disc against the flywheel, ensuring that it is the right way round. It should be marked "FLYWHEEL SIDE", but if not, position it so that the raised hub with the cushion springs is facing away from the flywheel **(see illustration)**.

12 Place the clutch cover over the dowels. Refit the retaining bolts, and tighten them finger-tight so that the clutch disc is gripped lightly, but can still be moved.

13 The clutch disc must now be centralised so that, when the engine and transmission are mated, the splines of the gearbox input shaft will pass through the splines in the centre of the clutch disc hub.

14 Centralisation can be carried out by inserting a round bar through the hole in the centre of the clutch disc, so that the end of the bar rests in the hole in the rear end of the crankshaft. Move the bar sideways or up and down, to move the clutch disc in whichever direction is necessary to achieve

9.4 Removing the clutch cover and disc

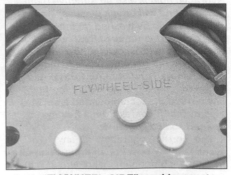

9.11 "FLYWHEEL-SIDE" marking on the clutch disc

9.15 Using a clutch-aligning tool to centralise the clutch disc

10.2a Clutch release bearing in place on the guide sleeve

10.2b Release bearing removed from the transmission

centralisation. Centralisation can then be checked by removing the bar and viewing the clutch disc hub in relation to the diaphragm spring fingers, or by viewing through the side apertures of the cover, and checking that the disc is central in relation to the outer edge of the pressure plate.

15 An alternative and more accurate method of centralisation is to use a commercially-available clutch-aligning tool, obtainable from most accessory shops (see *Tools and working facilities* at the beginning of this manual) **(see illustration)**.

16 Once the clutch is centralised, progressively tighten the cover bolts in a diagonal sequence to the torque setting given in the Specifications.

17 Ensure that the input shaft splines, clutch disc splines and release bearing guide sleeve are clean. Apply a thin smear of high melting-point grease to the input shaft splines and the release bearing guide sleeve.

18 Refit the transmission to the engine.

10 Clutch release bearing - removal, inspection and refitting

Removal

1 Separate the engine and transmission as described in the previous Section.

2 Withdraw the release bearing from its guide sleeve by turning the release arm **(see illustrations)**.

Inspection

3 Check the bearing for smoothness of operation, and renew it if there is any sign of harshness or roughness as the bearing is spun. Do not attempt to dismantle, clean or lubricate the bearing.

4 As mentioned earlier, it is worth renewing the release bearing as a matter of course, unless it is known to be in perfect condition.

Refitting

5 Refitting of the clutch release bearing is a reversal of the removal procedure, making

sure that it is correctly located on the release arm fork. It is helpful to slightly lift the release arm while locating the bearing on its guide sleeve. Keep the fork in contact with the plastic shoulders on the bearing as the bearing is being located.

11 Clutch release shaft and bush - removal and refitting

Removal

1 Remove the clutch release bearing as described in the previous Section.

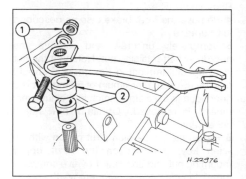

11.2a Clutch release arm removal

1 Clamp bolt
2 Protective cap and bearing bush

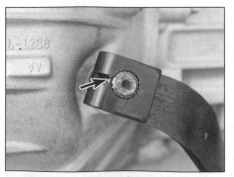

11.2c Master spline (arrowed) on the shaft

2 Unscrew the clamp bolt securing the release arm to the shaft. Mark the relative position of the shaft to the arm, then withdraw the arm from the shaft. The shaft has a master spline, to ensure that the arm is fitted correctly **(see illustrations)**.

3 Remove the protective cap from around the top of the release shaft splines, to allow access to the bush.

4 Extract the bush by gently levering it from the housing, using grips or a pair of screwdrivers, then lift it out over the splines of the shaft **(see illustration)**.

5 With the bush removed, the release shaft can be removed by lifting it from its lower bearing bore, manoeuvring it

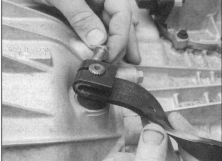

11.2b Removing the clamp bolt

11.4 Removing the bush using grips

8

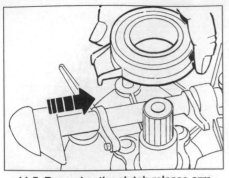

11.5 Removing the clutch release arm shaft

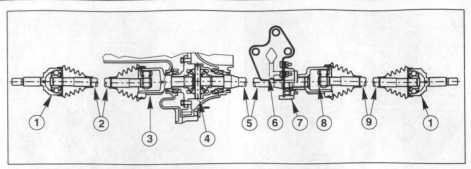

12.0 Cross-section of the driveshafts

1 Outer CV joint
2 Left-hand side driveshaft
3 Left-hand side inner tripod joint with external spline
4 Differential
5 Intermediate shaft
6 Intermediate shaft bearing support bracket
7 Intermediate shaft bearing
8 Right-hand side inner tripod joint with internal spline
9 Right-hand driveshaft

sideways and withdrawing it **(see illustration)**.

Refitting

6 Refitting is a reversal of the removal procedure. Apply a little grease to the bearing surfaces, both in the transmission and in the bush.

12 Driveshafts - description

Drive is transmitted from the transmission differential to the front wheels by means of two driveshafts. The right-hand driveshaft is in two sections, and incorporates a support bearing.

Each driveshaft consists of three main components: the sliding (tripod type) inner joint, the actual driveshaft, and the outer CV (constant velocity) joint. The inner (male) end of the left-hand tripod joint is secured in the differential side gear by the engagement of a circlip. The inner (female) end of the right-hand driveshaft is held on the intermediate shaft by the engagement of a circlip. The intermediate shaft is held in the transmission by the support bearing, which in turn is supported by a bracket bolted to the rear of the cylinder block. The outer CV joint on both driveshafts is of ball-bearing type, and is secured in the front hub by the hub nut **(see illustration)**.

13 Driveshafts - removal and refitting

Removal

1 Remove the wheel cover from the wheel, apply the handbrake, and engage 1st gear. Loosen the hub nut about half a turn. This nut is very tight.
2 Loosen the front wheel retaining nuts.
3 Apply the handbrake, jack up the front of the vehicle and support it on axle stands. Remove the wheel.
4 Remove the front brake disc as described in Chapter 9.
5 Completely unscrew and remove the hub/driveshaft retaining nut. Note that the nut is of special laminated design, and should only be re-used a maximum of 5 times. (It is a good idea to file a small notch in the nut every time it is removed.) Obtain a new nut if necessary.
6 Retain the suspension strut piston with an Allen key, then loosen the strut upper mounting nut and unscrew it by five complete turns. It is not necessary to remove the nut at this stage, but note that a new one will be required on refitting. Where necessary, detach the ABS wiring from the strut.

7 Unscrew the nut securing the anti-roll bar link to the front suspension strut, and position the link to one side.
8 Extract the split pin from the track rod end balljoint nut. Unscrew the nut, and detach the rod from the arm on the steering knuckle using a conventional balljoint removal tool. Take care not to damage the balljoint seal.
9 Note which way round the front suspension lower arm balljoint clamp bolt is fitted, then unscrew and remove it from the knuckle assembly. Lever the balljoint down from the knuckle; if it is tight, carefully prise the clamp open using a large flat-bladed tool. Take care not to damage the balljoint seal during the separation procedure.
10 Using a universal puller located on the hub flange, press the driveshaft through the front hub and steering knuckle by pulling the knuckle outwards **(see illustrations)**. When the driveshaft is free, support it on an axle stand, making sure that the inner tripod joint is not turned through more than 18° (damage may occur if the joint is turned through too great an angle).

Left-hand side

11 Insert a lever between the inner driveshaft joint and the transmission case, with a thin piece of wood against the case. Prise free the inner joint from the differential **(see illustration)**. If it proves reluctant to move, strike the lever

13.10a Using a puller on the hub flange ...

13.10b ... to press the driveshaft out of the front hub and steering knuckle

13.11 Removing the left-hand driveshaft from the transmission

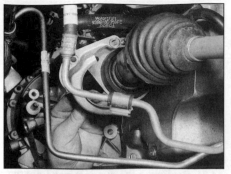

13.16 Removing the heat shield from the right-hand driveshaft support bearing

13.17 Removing the complete right-hand driveshaft

13.36 Torque-tightening the hub nut

firmly with the palm of the hand. Be careful not to damage the adjacent components, and be prepared for oil spillage. Note that if the right-hand driveshaft has already been removed, it is possible to release the left-hand driveshaft by inserting a forked drift from the right-hand side. However, care must be taken to prevent damage to the differential gears, particularly if the special Ford tool is not used.

12 Withdraw the driveshaft from under the vehicle.

13 Extract the circlip from the groove on the inner end of the driveshaft, and obtain a new one.

Right-hand side

14 The right-hand driveshaft may either be removed complete with the intermediate shaft from the transmission, or it may be disconnected from the outer end of the intermediate shaft. If the latter course of action is taken, use a soft-faced mallet to sharply tap the inner CV joint housing from the intermediate shaft. The internal circlip will be released, and the driveshaft may be withdrawn from the splines.

15 Extract the circlip from the groove on the outer end of the intermediate shaft. Obtain a new circlip for use when refitting.

16 If the complete driveshaft is to be removed, proceed as follows. Unscrew the bolts securing the driveshaft support bearing bracket to the rear of the cylinder block, and remove the heat shield **(see illustration)**.

17 Withdraw the complete driveshaft from the transmission and from the bearing bracket, and remove it from under the vehicle **(see illustration)**. Be prepared for oil spillage.

Both sides

18 Check the condition of the transmission oil seals, and if necessary renew them as described in Chapter 7. Check the support bearing, and if necessary renew it as described in Section 13 of this Chapter.

Refitting

Right-hand side

19 If the intermediate shaft has not been removed, proceed to paragraph 22. Otherwise, proceed as follows.

20 Carefully refit the complete driveshaft in the support bearing and into the transmission, taking care not to damage the oil seal. Turn the driveshaft until it engages the splines on the differential gears.

21 Tighten the bolts securing the support bearing to the bracket on the cylinder block to the specified torque. Proceed to paragraph 26.

22 Locate the new circlip in the groove on the outer end of the intermediate shaft, then smear 6 to 8 grams of grease (to Ford specification SQM1C-9004-A) over the entire circumference of the intermediate shaft splines. This grease prevents frictional corrosion.

23 Locate the right-hand driveshaft on the intermediate shaft splines, and push it on until the internal circlip is heard to engage with the groove in the shaft.

Left-hand side

24 Locate the new circlip in the groove on the inner end of the driveshaft.

25 Insert the driveshaft into the transmission, making sure that the circlip is fully engaged.

Both sides

26 Pull the knuckle outwards, and insert the outer end of the driveshaft through the hub. Turn the driveshaft to engage the splines in the hub, and fully push on the hub. Ford use a special tool to draw the driveshaft into the hub, but it is unlikely that the splines will be tight. However, if they are, it will be necessary to obtain the tool, or to use a similar home-made tool.

27 Screw on the hub nut finger-tight.

28 Locate the front suspension lower arm balljoint stub in the bottom of the knuckle. Insert the clamp bolt in the previously-noted position, screw on the nut, and tighten it to the specified torque.

29 Refit the track rod end balljoint to the steering knuckle, and screw on the nut. Tighten the nut to the specified torque.

30 Check that the balljoint nut split pin holes are aligned. If not, re-position the nut, but make sure that it is still tightened within the tolerance of the torque wrench setting. Insert a new split pin, and bend its legs back to secure it.

31 Locate the anti-roll bar link on the front suspension strut, and tighten the nut to the specified torque.

32 Remove the suspension strut upper mounting nut and fit the new nut, tightening it to the specified torque (Chapter 10). Where necessary, refit the ABS wiring to the strut bracket.

33 Refit the front brake disc with reference to Chapter 9.

34 Check the transmission oil level, and top-up if necessary as described in Chapter 1.

35 Refit the wheel, and lower the vehicle to the ground. Tighten the wheel retaining nuts to the specified torque.

36 Fully tighten the hub nut to the specified torque **(see illustration)**. Finally, refit the wheel cover.

14 Driveshaft inner CV joint gaiter - renewal

1 The inner CV joint gaiter is renewed by disconnecting the driveshaft from the inner CV joint housing at the transmission (left-hand side) or intermediate shaft (right-hand side). The work can be carried out either with the driveshaft removed from the vehicle, or with it *in situ*. If it is wished to fully remove the driveshaft, refer to Section 10 first. Note that if both the inner and outer gaiters are being renewed at the same time, the outer gaiter can be removed from the inner end of the driveshaft.

Renewal without removing the driveshaft

2 Loosen the front wheel nuts on the appropriate side. Apply the handbrake, jack up the front of the vehicle and support it on axle stands. Remove the wheel.

3 Unscrew the nut securing the anti-roll bar link to the front suspension strut, and position the link to one side.

4 Extract the split pin from the track rod end balljoint nut. Unscrew the nut, and detach the rod from the arm on the steering knuckle using a conventional balljoint removal tool. Take care not to damage the balljoint seal.

8

5 Note which way round the front suspension lower arm balljoint clamp bolt is fitted, then unscrew and remove it from the knuckle assembly. Lever the balljoint down from the knuckle; if it is tight, prise the clamp open carefully using a large flat-bladed tool. Take care not to damage the balljoint seal during the separation procedure.

6 Mark the driveshaft in relation to the joint housing, to ensure correct refitting.

7 Note the fitted location of both of the inner joint gaiter retaining clips. Release the clips from the gaiter, and slide the gaiter back along the driveshaft (away from the transmission) a little way.

8 Pull the front suspension strut outwards, while guiding the tripod joint out of the joint housing. As the joint tripod is being withdrawn from the housing, be prepared for some of the bearing rollers to fall out. Identify them for position with a dab of paint. Support the inner end of the driveshaft on an axle stand.

9 Remove the support ring from the joint housing.

10 Remove the remaining bearing rollers from the tripod, and identify them for position with a dab of paint.

11 Check that the inner end of the driveshaft is marked in relation to the splined tripod hub. If not, carefully centre-punch the two items, to ensure correct refitting. Alternatively, use dabs of paint on the driveshaft and one end of the tripod.

12 Extract the circlip retaining the tripod on the driveshaft.

13 Using a suitable puller, remove the tripod from the end of the driveshaft, and slide off the gaiter.

14 If the outer gaiter is also to be renewed, remove it with reference to Section 12.

15 Clean the driveshaft, and obtain a new tripod retaining circlip. The gaiter retaining clips and the steering track rod end split pin must also be renewed.

16 Slide the new gaiter on the driveshaft, together with new clips. Also locate the support ring on the joint housing.

17 Refit the tripod on the driveshaft splines, if necessary using a soft-faced mallet to drive it fully onto the splines. It must be fitted with the chamfered edge leading (towards the driveshaft), and with the previously-made

14.29 Removing the gaiter from the inner joint housing

marks aligned. Secure it in position using the new circlip. Ensure that the circlip is fully engaged in its groove.

18 Locate the bearing rollers on the tripod in their previously-noted positions, using grease to hold them in place.

19 With the front suspension strut pulled outwards, guide the tripod joint into the joint housing, making sure that the previously-made marks are aligned. Pack the joint with 180 grams of CV joint grease.

20 Slide the gaiter along the driveshaft, and locate it on the support ring located on the joint housing. The small-diameter end of the gaiter must be located in the groove on the driveshaft.

21 Ensure that the gaiter is not twisted or distorted, then insert a small screwdriver under the lip of the gaiter at the housing end. This will allow trapped air to escape during the next step.

22 Push the tripod fully into the housing, then pull it out by 20 mm. Remove the screwdriver, then fit the retaining clips and tighten them.

23 Reconnect the front suspension lower arm balljoint to the knuckle assembly. Refit and tighten the clamp nut and bolt.

24 Reconnect the track rod end balljoint to the steering knuckle, and tighten the nut to the specified torque. Check that the split pin holes are correctly aligned; if necessary, reposition the nut, making sure that it is still tightened within the torque tolerance. Insert a new split pin, and bend its legs back to secure it.

25 Refit the anti-roll bar link to the front

14.31 Removing the support ring from the joint housing

suspension strut, and tighten the nut to the specified torque.

26 Refit the wheel, and lower the vehicle to the ground. Tighten the wheel nuts.

Renewal with the driveshaft on the bench

27 Mount the driveshaft in a vice.

28 Mark the driveshaft in relation to the joint housing, to ensure correct refitting.

29 Note the fitted location of both of the inner joint gaiter retaining clips, then release the clips from the gaiter, and slide the gaiter back along the driveshaft a little way **(see illustration)**.

30 Remove the inner joint housing from the tripod. As the housing is being removed, be prepared for some of the bearing rollers to fall out. Identify them for position with a dab of paint.

31 Remove the support ring from the joint housing **(see illustration)**.

32 Remove the remaining bearing rollers from the tripod, and identify them for position with a dab of paint **(see illustration)**.

33 Check that the inner end of the driveshaft is marked in relation to the splined tripod hub. If not, carefully centre-punch the two items, to ensure correct refitting. Alternatively, use dabs of paint on the driveshaft and one end of the tripod.

34 Extract the circlip retaining the tripod on the driveshaft **(see illustration)**.

35 Using a puller, remove the tripod from the end of the driveshaft, and slide off the gaiter **(see illustration)**.

14.32 Removing the bearing rollers

14.34 Circlip (arrowed) retaining the tripod on the driveshaft

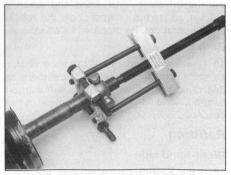

14.35 Using a puller to remove the tripod

14.38 Slide the gaiter and clips onto the driveshaft

14.40a Locate the tripod on the splines . . .

14.40b . . . and drive it fully onto the driveshaft

36 If the outer gaiter is also to be renewed, remove it with reference to Section 12.
37 Clean the driveshaft, and obtain a new joint retaining circlip. The gaiter retaining clips must also be renewed.
38 Slide the new gaiter on the driveshaft, together with new clips **(see illustration)**.
39 Locate the support ring on the CV joint housing.
40 Refit the tripod on the driveshaft splines, if necessary using a soft-faced mallet and a suitable socket to drive it fully onto the splines. It must be fitted with the chamfered edge leading (towards the driveshaft), and with the previously-made marks aligned. Secure it in position using a new circlip. Ensure that the circlip is fully engaged in its groove **(see illustrations)**.
41 Locate the bearing rollers on the tripod in their previously-noted positions, using grease to hold them in place.
42 Guide the joint housing onto the tripod joint, making sure that the previously-made marks are aligned. Scoop out all of the old grease, then pack the joint with 180 grams of new CV joint grease.
43 Slide the gaiter along the driveshaft, and locate it on the support ring on the CV joint housing. The small-diameter end of the gaiter must be located in the groove on the driveshaft.
44 Ensure that the gaiter is not twisted or distorted, then insert a small screwdriver under the lip of the gaiter at the housing end.

This will allow trapped air to escape during the next step.
45 Push the housing fully on the tripod, then pull it out by 20 mm. Remove the screwdriver, then fit the retaining clips and tighten them **(see illustration)**.

15 Driveshaft outer CV joint gaiter - renewal

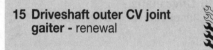

1 The outer CV joint gaiter can be renewed by removing the inner gaiter first as described in Section 11, or after removing the driveshaft complete as described in Section 10. If the driveshaft is removed, then the inner gaiter need not necessarily be removed. It is

impractical to renew the outer gaiter by dismantling the outer joint with the driveshaft in position in the vehicle. The following paragraphs describe renewal of the gaiter on the bench.
2 Mount the driveshaft in a vice.
3 Mark the driveshaft in relation to the CV joint housing, to ensure correct refitting.
4 Note the fitted location of both of the outer joint gaiter retaining clips, then release the clips from the gaiter, and slide the gaiter back along the driveshaft a little way **(see illustrations)**.
5 Using a brass drift or a copper mallet, carefully drive the outer CV joint hub from the splines on the driveshaft. Initial resistance will be felt until the internal circlips are released. Take care not to damage the bearing cage **(see illustrations)**.

14.45 Using pincers to tighten the retaining clips

15.4a Release the clips . . .

15.4b . . . and remove the gaiter

15.5a Drive off the outer CV joint hub . . .

15.5b . . . and remove the joint from the driveshaft

8

15.6 Circlips fitted on the outer end of the driveshaft

15.9 Fitting the new gaiter and clips on the driveshaft

15.11 Packing the outer CV joint with new grease

6 Extract the outer circlip from the end of the driveshaft **(see illustration)**.

7 Slide the gaiter over the remaining circlip, and remove it together with the clips.

8 Clean the driveshaft, and obtain new joint retaining circlips. The gaiter retaining clips must also be renewed.

9 Slide the new gaiter (together with new clips) onto the driveshaft and over the inner circlip **(see illustration)**.

10 Fit a new outer circlip to the groove in the driveshaft.

11 Scoop out all of the old grease, then pack the joint with 100 grams of new CV joint grease **(see illustration)**.

12 Locate the CV joint on the driveshaft so that the splines are aligned, then push the joint until the internal circlips are fully engaged.

13 Move the gaiter along the driveshaft, and locate it over the joint and onto the outer CV joint housing. The small-diameter end of the gaiter must be located in the groove on the driveshaft.

14 Ensure that the gaiter is not twisted or distorted, then insert a small screwdriver under the lip of the gaiter at the housing end, to allow any trapped air to escape.

15 Remove the screwdriver, fit the retaining clips in their previously-noted positions, and tighten them.

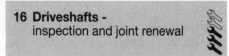

16 Driveshafts -
inspection and joint renewal

1 If any of the checks described in Chapter 1 reveal apparent excessive wear or play in any driveshaft joint, first remove the wheel cover, and check that the hub nut (driveshaft outer nut) is tightened to the specified torque. Repeat this check on the hub nut on the other side.

2 Road test the vehicle, and listen for a metallic clicking from the front, as the vehicle is driven slowly in a circle on full-lock. If a clicking noise is heard, this indicates wear in the outer constant velocity joint, which means that the joint must be renewed; reconditioning is not possible.

3 To renew an outer CV joint, remove the driveshaft as described in Section 10, then separate the joint from the driveshaft with reference to Section 12. In principle, the gaiter can be left on the driveshaft, provided that it is in good condition; in practice, it makes sense to renew the gaiter in any case, having got this far.

4 If vibration, consistent with road speed, is felt through the car when accelerating, there is a possibility of wear in the inner tripod joints.

5 To renew an inner joint, remove the driveshaft as described in Section 10, then separate the joint from the driveshaft with reference to Section 11.

6 Continual noise from the right-hand driveshaft, increasing with road speed, may indicate wear in the support bearing. To renew this bearing, the driveshaft and intermediate shaft must be removed, and the bearing extracted using a puller.

7 Remove the bearing dust cover, and obtain a new one.

8 Drive or press on the new bearing, applying the pressure to the inner race only. Similarly drive or press on the new dust cover.

Chapter 9 Braking system

Contents

Degrees of difficulty

Easy, suitable for novice with little experience	**Fairly easy,** suitable for beginner with some experience	**Fairly difficult,** suitable for competent DIY mechanic	**Difficult,** suitable for experienced DIY mechanic	**Very difficult,** suitable for expert DIY or professional

Specifications

Front brakes

Type	Ventilated disc, with single-piston floating caliper
Disc diameter	260.0 mm
Disc thickness:	
New	24.15 mm
Minimum	22.20 mm
Maximum disc run-out (fitted)	0.15 mm
Maximum disc thickness variation	0.015 mm
Front hub face maximum run-out	0.05 mm

Rear drum brakes

Type	Leading and trailing shoes, with automatic adjusters
Drum diameter:	
New	228.6 mm
Maximum diameter	229.6 mm

Torque wrench settings

	Nm	lbf ft
Front caliper bracket	120	89
Front caliper guide bolts	28	21
Rear drum brake backplate	50	37
Vacuum servo unit	40	30
Master cylinder	23	17
ABS hydraulic unit to bracket	20	15
Roadwheel nuts	85	63
Vacuum pump:		
Pump to cylinder head bolts	18 to 22	13 to 16
Pump to line	16	12
Vacuum line bracket to cylinder head	22	16
Bracket to cylinder block	47	35
Bracket to lifting eye	23	17

9

1 General information

The braking system is of diagonally-split, dual-circuit design, with ventilated discs at the front, and drum at the rear. The front calipers are of floating single-piston design, using asbestos-free pads. The rear drum brakes are of the leading and trailing shoe type. They are self-adjusting during footbrake operation. The rear brake shoe linings are of different thicknesses, in order to allow for the different proportional rates of wear.

Pressure-control relief (PCR) valves are fitted to the rear brakes, to prevent rear wheel lock-up under hard braking. The valves are sometimes referred to as pressure-conscious reducing valves. On non-ABS models, they are fitted in the master cylinder rear brake outlet ports; on ABS models, they are located on the ABS unit.

The handbrake is cable-operated, and acts on the rear brakes. The cables operate on the rear trailing brake shoe operating levers. The handbrake lever incorporates an automatic adjuster, which removes any slack from the cables when the lever is disengaged (see illustration). Handbrake lever movement remains consistent at all times, and no adjustment is necessary or possible.

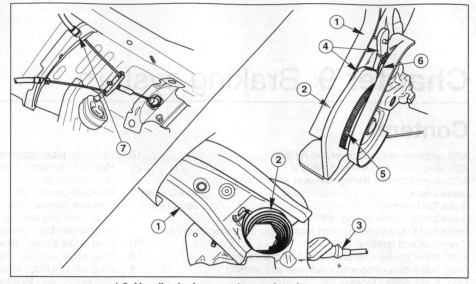

1.2 Handbrake lever and associated components

1 Handbrake lever
2 Clock spring
3 Handbrake cable
4 Toothed segment and pawl to lock the handbrake lever
5 Fine-toothed segment for the clock spring
6 Pawl for the clock spring
7 Underbody bracket

Where fitted, the anti-lock braking system (ABS) is of the four-channel low-pressure type (see illustration). It uses the basic conventional brake system, together with a

Bendix ABS hydraulic unit fitted between the master cylinder and the four wheel brakes. The hydraulic unit consists of a hydraulic actuator, an ABS brake pressure pump, an

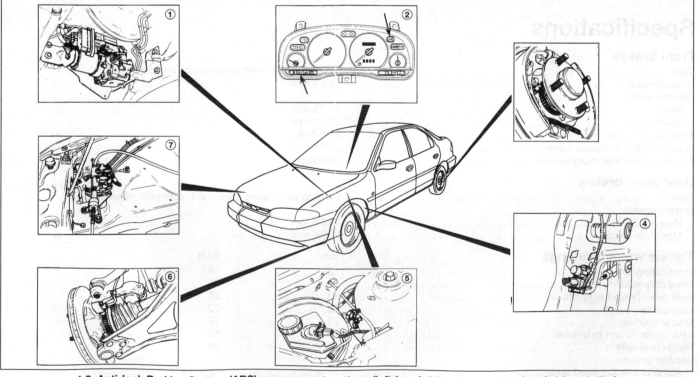

1.3 Anti-lock Braking System (ABS) component locations (left-hand-drive shown, right-hand-drive similar)

1 ABS unit
2 ABS warning lights
3 Rear wheel sensor ring location (drum brakes left, disc brakes right)
4 Stop-light switch
5 Self-test/diagnosis connectors
6 Front wheel sensor and ring
7 Throttle actuator

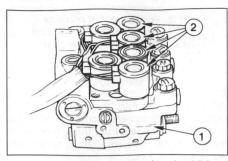

1.4 Solenoid valves fitted to the ABS hydraulic actuator

1 ABS actuator
2 ABS solenoid valves

ABS module with built-in relay box, and two pressure-control relief valves. Braking at each of the four wheels is controlled by separate solenoid valves in the hydraulic actuator. If wheel lock-up is detected on a wheel when the vehicle speed is above 3 mph, the valve opens, releasing pressure to the relevant brake, until the wheel regains a rotational speed corresponding to the speed of the vehicle. The cycle can be repeated many times a second. In the event of a fault in the ABS system, the conventional braking system is not affected. Diagnosis of a fault in the ABS system requires the use of special equipment,

and this work should therefore be left to a Ford dealer. Diagnostic connectors are located on the side of the left-hand front suspension turret.

2 Front brake pads - renewal

⚠ *Warning: Disc brake pads must be renewed on both front wheels at the same time - never renew the pads on only one wheel, as uneven braking may result. Although genuine Ford linings are asbestos-free, the dust created by wear of non-genuine pads may contain asbestos, which is a health hazard. Never blow it out with compressed air, and don't inhale any of it. DO NOT use petroleum-based solvents to clean brake parts; use brake cleaner or methylated spirit only. DO NOT allow any brake fluid, oil or grease to contact the brake pads or disc. Also refer to the warning at the start of Section 15 concerning brake fluid.*

1 Apply the handbrake. Loosen the front wheel nuts, jack up the front of the vehicle and support it on axle stands.
2 Remove the front wheels. Work on one

brake assembly at a time, using the assembled brake for reference if necessary.
3 Follow the accompanying photos, beginning with illustration 2.3A, for the pad removal procedure. Be sure to stay in order, and read the caption under each illustration.
4 Inspect the front brake disc for scoring and cracks. If a detailed inspection is necessary, refer to Section 4.
5 The piston must be pushed back into the caliper bore, to provide room for the new

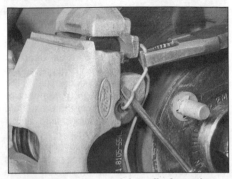

2.3a Prise the retaining clip from the caliper. Hold it with a pair of pliers, to avoid personal injury. On models fitted with pad wear sensors, it will be necessary to disconnect the wiring

2.3b Prise the plastic covers from the ends of the two guide pins

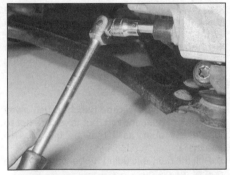

2.3c Using a 7 mm Allen key, unscrew . . .

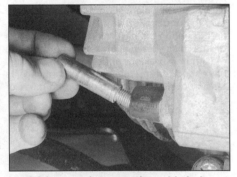

2.3d . . . and remove the guide bolts securing the caliper to the carrier bracket

2.3e Withdraw the caliper from the disc, and support it on an axle stand to avoid straining the hydraulic hose. The outer pad will normally remain in position against the disc, but the inner pad will stay attached to the piston in the caliper

2.3f Pull the inner pad from the piston in the caliper

2.3g Remove the outer pad from the caliper frame. Brush all dust and dirt from the caliper, pads and disc, but do not inhale it, as it may be harmful to health. Scrape any corrosion from the disc.

9

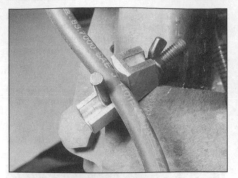

3.2 Brake hose clamp fitted to the front flexible brake hose

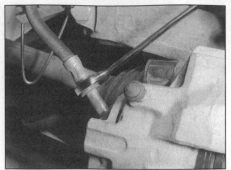

3.3 Loosening the flexible brake hose at the caliper

brake pads. A G-clamp can be used to accomplish this. As the piston is depressed to the bottom of the caliper bore, the fluid in the master cylinder will rise slightly. Make sure that there is sufficient space in the brake fluid reservoir to accept the displaced fluid, and if necessary, syphon some off first.

6 Fit the new pads using a reversal of the removal procedure, but tighten the guide bolts to the torque wrench setting given in the Specifications at the beginning of this Chapter.

7 On completion, firmly depress the brake pedal a few times, to bring the pads to their normal working position. Check the level of the brake fluid in the reservoir, and top-up if necessary.

8 Give the vehicle a short road test, to make sure that the brakes are functioning correctly, and to bed-in the new linings to the contours of the disc. New linings will not provide maximum braking efficiency until they have bedded-in; avoid heavy braking as far as possible for the first hundred miles or so.

3 Front brake caliper - removal, overhaul and refitting

Note: *Refer to the warning at the beginning of the previous Section before proceeding.*

Removal

1 Apply the handbrake. Loosen the front wheel nuts, jack up the front of the vehicle

and support it on axle stands. Remove the appropriate front wheel.

2 Fit a brake hose clamp to the flexible hose leading to the front brake caliper. This will minimise brake fluid loss during subsequent operations **(see illustration)**.

3 Loosen (but do not completely unscrew) the union on the caliper end of the flexible brake hose **(see illustration)**.

4 Remove the front brake pads as described in Section 2.

5 Support the caliper in one hand, and prevent the hydraulic hose from turning with the other hand. Unscrew the caliper from the hose, making sure that the hose is not twisted unduly or strained. Once the caliper is detached, plug the open hydraulic unions in the caliper and hose, to keep out dust and dirt.

6 If required, the caliper carrier bracket can be unbolted and removed from the steering knuckle **(see illustration)**.

Overhaul

7 With the caliper on the bench, brush away all traces of dust and dirt, but take care not to inhale any dust, as it may be injurious to health.

8 Pull the dust-excluding rubber seal from the end of the piston.

9 Apply low air pressure to the fluid inlet union, and eject the piston. Only low air pressure is required for this, such as is produced by a foot-operated tyre pump.

Caution: The piston may be ejected with some force.

10 Using a suitable blunt instrument (for instance a knitting needle or a crochet hook), prise the piston seal from the groove in the cylinder bore. Take care not to scratch the surface of the bore.

11 Clean the piston and caliper body with methylated spirit, and allow to dry. Examine the surfaces of the piston and cylinder bore for wear, damage and corrosion. If the piston alone is unserviceable, a new piston must be obtained, along with seals. If the cylinder bore is unserviceable, the complete caliper must be renewed. The seals must be renewed, regardless of the condition of the other components.

12 Coat the piston and seals with clean brake fluid, then manipulate the piston seal into the groove in the cylinder bore.

13 Push the piston squarely into its bore.

14 Fit the dust-excluding rubber seal onto the piston and caliper, then depress the piston fully.

Refitting

15 Refit the caliper, and where applicable the carrier bracket, by reversing the removal operations. Make sure that the flexible brake hose is not twisted. Tighten the mounting bolts and wheel nuts to the specified torque **(see illustration)**.

16 Bleed the brake circuit according to the procedure given in Section 15, remembering to remove the brake hose clamp from the flexible hose. Make sure there are no leaks from the hose connections. Test the brakes carefully before returning the vehicle to normal service.

4 Front brake disc - inspection, removal and refitting

Note: *To prevent uneven braking, BOTH front brake discs should be renewed or reground at the same time.*

Inspection

1 Apply the handbrake. Loosen the relevant wheel nuts, jack up the front of the vehicle and support it on axle stands. Remove the wheel.

2 Remove the front brake caliper and carrier bracket with reference to Section 3, but do not disconnect the flexible hose. Support the caliper on an axle stand, or suspend it out of the way with a piece of wire, taking care to avoid straining the flexible hose.

3 Temporarily refit two of the wheel nuts to diagonally-opposite studs, with the flat sides

3.6 Removing the caliper carrier bracket

3.15 Tightening the carrier bracket mounting bolts

4.4` Using a micrometer to measure the thickness of the front brake disc

4.4b Disc minimum thickness marking

4.5 Measuring the disc run-out with a dial gauge

4.10a Remove the special washers . . .

4.10b . . . and withdraw the disc

of the nuts against the disc. Tighten the nuts progressively, to hold the disc firmly.

4 Scrape any corrosion from the disc. Rotate the disc, and examine it for deep scoring, grooving or cracks. Using a micrometer, measure the thickness of the disc in several places. The minimum thickness is stamped on the disc hub (see illustrations). Light wear and scoring is normal, but if excessive, the disc should be removed, and either reground by a specialist, or renewed. If regrinding is undertaken, the minimum thickness must be maintained. Obviously, if the disc is cracked, it must be renewed.

5 Using a dial gauge or a flat metal block and feeler gauges, check that the disc run-out 10 mm from the outer edge does not exceed the limit given in the Specifications. To do this, fix the measuring equipment, and rotate the disc,

noting the variation in measurement as the disc is rotated (see illustration). The difference between the minimum and maximum measurements recorded is the disc run-out.

6 If the run-out is greater than the specified amount, check for variations of the disc thickness as follows. Mark the disc at eight positions 45° apart, then using a micrometer, measure the disc thickness at the eight positions, 15 mm in from the outer edge. If the variation between the minimum and maximum readings is greater than the specified amount, the disc should be renewed.

7 The hub face run-out can also be checked in a similar way. First remove the disc as described later in this Section, fix the measuring equipment, then slowly rotate the hub, and check that the run-out does not exceed the amount given in the Specifications. If the hub face run-out is excessive, this should be corrected (by renewing the hub bearings - see Chapter 10) before rechecking the disc run-out.

Removal

8 With the wheel and caliper removed, remove the wheel nuts which were temporarily refitted in paragraph 3.

9 Mark the disc in relation to the hub, if it is to be refitted.

10 Remove the two special washers (where fitted), and withdraw the disc over the wheel studs (see illustrations).

Refitting

11 Make sure that the disc and hub mating surfaces are clean, then locate the disc on the wheel studs. Align the previously-made marks if the original disc is being refitted.

12 Refit the two special washers, where fitted.

13 Refit the brake caliper and carrier bracket with reference to Section 3.

14 Refit the wheel, and lower the vehicle to the ground.

15 Test the brakes carefully before returning the vehicle to normal service.

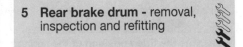

5 Rear brake drum - removal, inspection and refitting

Note: *To prevent uneven braking, BOTH rear brake drums should be renewed at the same time.*

Removal

1 Chock the front wheels, release the handbrake and engage 1st gear. Loosen the relevant wheel nuts, jack up the rear of the vehicle and support it on axle stands. Remove the wheel.

2 Remove the two special clips (where fitted), and withdraw the brake drum over the wheel studs. If the drum will not pass over the shoes, it is possible to release the automatic adjuster mechanism by prising out the small rubber grommet near the centre of the backplate, and inserting a screwdriver through the small hole. The self-adjusting ratchet can then be rotated, so that the brake shoes move to their lowest setting (see illustrations). Refit the rubber grommet before proceeding.

5.2a Releasing the automatic adjuster mechanism with a screwdriver inserted through the small hole in the backplate

5.2b Removing a rear brake drum

9

3 With the brake drum removed, clean the dust from the drum, brake shoes, wheel cylinder and backplate, using brake cleaner or methylated spirit. *Take care not to inhale the dust, as it may contain asbestos.*

Inspection

4 Clean the inside surfaces of the brake drum, then examine the internal friction surface for signs of scoring or cracks. If it is cracked, deeply scored, or has worn to a diameter greater than the maximum given in the Specifications, then it should be renewed, together with the drum on the other side.
5 Regrinding of the brake drum is not recommended.

Refitting

6 Locate the brake drum over the wheel studs, and (where fitted) refit the special clips. Make sure that the drum contacts the hub flange.
7 Refit the wheel, then check the remaining rear drum.
8 Lower the vehicle to the ground, and tighten the wheel nuts to the specified torque. Depress the brake pedal several times, in order to operate the self-adjusting mechanism

and set the shoes at their normal operating position.
9 Test the brakes carefully before returning the vehicle to normal service.

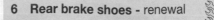

6 Rear brake shoes - renewal

⚠️ *Warning: Drum brake shoes must be renewed on both rear wheels at the same time - never renew the shoes on only one wheel, as uneven braking may result. Also, the dust created by wear of the shoes may contain asbestos, which is a health hazard. Never blow it out with compressed air, and don't inhale any of it. An approved filtering mask should be worn when working on the brakes. DO NOT use petroleum-based solvents to clean brake parts; use brake cleaner or methylated spirit only.*

1 Remove the rear brake drums as described in Section 5. Work on one brake assembly at a time, using the assembled brake for reference if necessary.
2 Follow the accompanying illustrations for the brake shoe renewal procedure (see illustrations

6.2A to 6.2O). Be sure to stay in order, and read the caption under each illustration.
3 If the wheel cylinder shows signs of fluid leakage, or if there is any reason to suspect it of being defective, inspect it now, as described in the next Section.
4 Fit the new brake shoes using a reversal of the removal procedure, but set the eccentric cam at its lowest position before assembling it to the trailing shoe.
5 Before refitting the brake drum, it should be checked as described in Section 5.
6 With the drum in position, refit the wheel, then carry out the renewal procedure on the remaining rear brake.
7 Lower the vehicle to the ground, and tighten the wheel nuts.
8 Depress the brake pedal several times, in order to operate the self-adjusting mechanism and set the shoes at their normal operating position.
9 Make several forward and reverse stops, and operate the handbrake fully two or three times. Give the vehicle a road test, to make sure that the brakes are functioning correctly, and to bed-in the new linings to the contours of the disc. Remember that the new linings will not give full braking efficiency until they have bedded-in.

6.2a Note the fitted position of the springs and the adjuster strut, then clean the components with brake cleaner, and allow to dry. Position a tray beneath the backplate, to catch the fluid and residue

6.2b Remove the two shoe hold-down springs, using a pair of pliers to depress the upper ends so that they can be withdrawn downwards off the pins

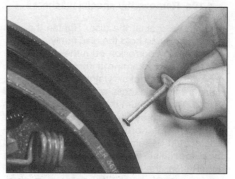

6.2c Remove the hold-down pins from the backplate

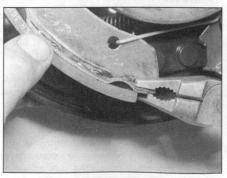

6.2d Pull the bottom end of the leading (front) brake shoe from the bottom anchor (use pliers or an adjustable spanner over the edge of the shoe to lever it away)

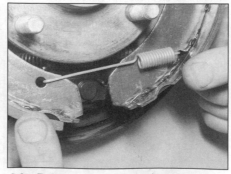

6.2e Release the trailing (rear) brake shoe from the anchor, then move the bottom ends of both shoes towards each other

6.2f Unhook the lower return spring from the shoes, noting the location holes

6.2g Move the bottom ends of the brake shoes together, and disconnect the top ends of the shoes from the wheel cylinder, taking care not to damage the rubber boots

6.2h Unhook the upper return spring from the shoes . . .

6.2i . . . and withdraw the leading shoe from the backplate

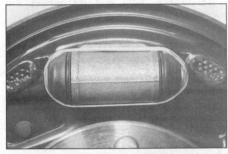

6.2j To prevent the wheel cylinder pistons from being accidentally ejected, fit a suitable elastic band or wire lengthwise over the cylinder/pistons. Don't press the brake pedal while the shoes are removed

6.2k Pull the handbrake cable spring back from the operating lever on the rear of the trailing shoe. Unhook the cable end from the cut-out in the lever, and remove the shoe

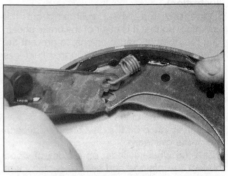

6.2l Unhook the automatic adjustment strut from the trailing brake shoe . . .

6.2m . . . and remove the small spring

6.2n Clean the backplate, and apply small amounts of high-melting-point brake grease to the brake shoe contact points. Be careful not to get grease on any friction surfaces

6.2o Lubricate the sliding components of the automatic adjuster with a little high-melting-point brake grease, but leave the serrations on the eccentric cam shown here clean

7 Rear wheel cylinder - removal, overhaul and refitting

Note: *Before starting work, check on the availability of parts (overhaul kit of seals). Also bear in mind that if the brake shoes have been contaminated by fluid leaking from the wheel cylinder, they must be renewed. In principle, the shoes on BOTH sides of the vehicle must be renewed, even if they are only contaminated on one side.*

Removal

1 Remove the brake drum as described in Section 5.

2 Minimise fluid loss either by removing the master cylinder reservoir cap, and then tightening it down onto a piece of polythene to obtain an airtight seal, or by using a brake hose clamp, a G-clamp, or similar tool, to clamp the flexible hose at the nearest convenient point to the wheel cylinder.

3 Pull the brake shoes apart at their top ends, so that they are just clear of the wheel cylinder. The automatic adjuster will hold the shoes in this position, so that the cylinder can be withdrawn.

4 Wipe away all traces of dirt around the hydraulic union at the rear of the wheel cylinder, then undo the union nut.

5 Unscrew the two bolts securing the

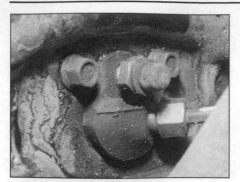

7.5 Bolts securing the wheel cylinder to the backplate. Hydraulic union nut and bleed screw cover are also visible

wheel cylinder to the backplate **(see illustration)**.

6 Withdraw the wheel cylinder from the backplate so that it is clear of the brake shoes. Plug the open hydraulic unions, to prevent the entry of dirt, and to minimise further fluid loss whilst the cylinder is detached.

Overhaul

7 Clean the external surfaces of the cylinder, and unscrew the bleed screw.

8 Carefully prise off the dust cover from each end of the cylinder.

9 Tap the wheel cylinder on a block of wood to eject the pistons and seals, keeping them identified for location. Finally remove the spring.

10 Clean the pistons and the cylinder by washing in methylated spirit or fresh hydraulic fluid. Do not use petrol, paraffin or any other mineral-based fluid. Remove and discard the old seals, noting which way round they are fitted.

11 Examine the surfaces of the pistons and the cylinder bores, and look for any signs of rust or scoring. If such damage is evident, the complete wheel cylinder must be renewed.

12 Reassemble by lubricating the first piston in clean hydraulic fluid, then manipulating a new seal into position, so that its raised lip faces away from the brake shoe bearing face of the piston.

13 Insert the piston into the cylinder. As the seal enters the bore, twist the piston back and forth so that the seal lip is not trapped.

8.1 Brake fluid reservoir and low level warning light multi-plug

14 Insert the spring, then refit the remaining piston and seal, again making sure that the seal lip is not trapped as it enters the bore.

15 Fit new dust covers to the grooves in the pistons and wheel cylinder body.

16 Refit the bleed screw.

Refitting

17 Wipe clean the backplate, and remove the plug from the end of the hydraulic pipe. Fit the cylinder onto the backplate, and screw in the hydraulic union nut by hand, being careful not to cross-thread it.

18 Tighten the mounting bolts, then fully tighten the hydraulic union nut.

19 Retract the automatic brake adjuster mechanism, so that the brake shoes engage with the pistons of the wheel cylinder. To do this, prise the shoes apart slightly, turn the automatic adjuster to its minimum position, and release the shoes.

20 Remove the clamp from the flexible brake hose, or the polythene from the master cylinder (as applicable).

21 Refit the brake drum with reference to Section 5.

22 Bleed the brake hydraulic system as described in Section 15. Providing suitable precautions were taken to minimise loss of fluid, it should only be necessary to bleed the relevant rear brake.

23 Test the brakes carefully before returning the vehicle to normal service.

---

8 Master cylinder - removal and refitting

Removal

1 Disconnect the low fluid level warning light multi-plug from the fluid reservoir filler cap **(see illustration)**. Unscrew and remove the

cap (note that the filler cap should not be inverted). Draw off the hydraulic fluid from the reservoir, using an old battery hydrometer or a poultry baster. *Do not* syphon the fluid by mouth; it is poisonous. Any brake fluid spilt on paintwork should be washed off with clean water, without delay - *brake fluid is also a highly-effective paint-stripper!*

2 Identify the locations of each brake pipe on the master cylinder. On non-ABS models, there are four pipes; the two rear brake pipes are attached to PCR (pressure-conscious relief) valves on the master cylinder. On ABS models, there are only two pipes, which lead to the ABS hydraulic unit **(see illustration)**.

3 Place rags beneath the master cylinder to catch spilt hydraulic fluid.

4 Clean around the hydraulic union nuts. Unscrew the nuts, and disconnect the hydraulic lines from the master cylinder.

5 Unscrew the mounting nuts, and withdraw the master cylinder from the studs on the front of the servo unit. If the nuts are tight, a split ring spanner should be used in preference to an open-ended spanner. Plug or cap open unions, to keep dust and dirt out.

6 Recover the gasket from the master cylinder.

7 If the master cylinder is faulty, it must be renewed. At the time of writing, no overhaul kits were available.

Refitting

8 Clean the contact surfaces of the master cylinder and servo.

9 Locate a new gasket on the master cylinder.

10 Position the master cylinder on the studs on the servo unit. Refit and tighten the nuts to the specified torque.

11 Carefully insert the hydraulic lines in the apertures in the master cylinder, then tighten the union nuts. Make sure that the nuts enter their threads correctly.

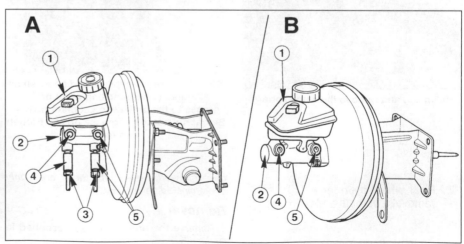

8.2 Master cylinder connections

A Non-ABS models
B ABS models
1 Brake fluid reservoir
2 Master cylinder
3 PCR valves for rear brakes
4 Primary brake hydraulic circuit (front right/rear left)
5 Secondary brake hydraulic circuit (front left/rear right)

12 Fill the reservoir with fresh brake fluid.
13 Bleed the hydraulic system as described in Section 15.
14 Refit the reservoir filler cap, and reconnect the multi-plug for the low fluid level warning light.
15 Test the brakes carefully before returning the vehicle to normal service.

9 Brake pedal -
removal and refitting

Removal

1 Working inside the vehicle, move the driver's seat fully to the rear, to allow maximum working area.
2 Remove the ashtray, then unscrew the screws and remove the lower facia panel.
3 Prise the hairpin clip from the right-hand end of the pedal pivot shaft, and remove the washer **(see illustration)**.
4 Unscrew the nut securing the pedal trunnion to the pushrod. The nut is located near the top of the pedal **(see illustrations)**.
5 Press the pedal pivot shaft to the left, through the mounting bracket, just far enough to allow the pedal to be withdrawn. Leave the blue nylon spacer (located between the clutch and brake pedals) on the pivot shaft **(see illustration)**.
6 With the pedal removed, prise out the bushes from each side. If necessary, also remove the pushrod trunnion and the rubber pad. Renew the components as necessary **(see illustrations)**.

Refitting

7 Prior to refitting the pedal, apply a little grease to the pivot shaft, pedal bushes and trunnion.
8 Refitting is a reversal of the removal procedure, but make sure that the pedal bushes are correctly located, and that the pedal shaft "D" section locates in the right-hand side of the pedal bracket. Also make sure that the hairpin clip is correctly located.

9.3 Removing the hairpin clip from the right-hand end of the brake pedal pivot shaft

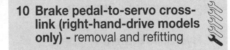

9.4b . . . and remove the tube from the pushrod

10 Brake pedal-to-servo cross-link (right-hand-drive models only) - removal and refitting

Removal

1 Disconnect the battery negative (earth) lead (Chapter 5, Section 1).
2 Remove the master cylinder and the vacuum servo unit as described in Sections 11 and 16. If wished, the master cylinder may be left attached to the servo unit.
3 Working inside the passenger compartment, fold down the covering from the front of both front footwells.
4 Have an assistant support the cross-link

9.4a Unscrew the nut securing the pedal trunnion to the pushrod . . .

9.5 Leave the nylon spacer (arrowed) in position on the pivot shaft (left-hand-drive model shown, right-hand-drive similar)

assembly from inside the engine compartment.
5 Unscrew and remove the nuts and bolts on each side of the bulkhead, and remove the link assembly from inside the engine compartment. If necessary, have the assistant hold the bolt heads from inside the engine compartment while the nuts are being loosened.
6 Clean the cross-link components, and examine the bushes for wear. Renew the bushes if necessary.

Refitting

7 Refitting is a reversal of the removal procedure. Refer to Sections 11 and 16 when refitting the master cylinder and vacuum servo unit.

9.6a Prise out the bushes . . .

9.6b . . . from each side of the pedal . . .

9.6c . . . and remove the pushrod trunnion

9

11 Hydraulic pipes and hoses - inspection, removal and refitting

Inspection

1 Jack up the front and rear of the vehicle, and support on axle stands.

2 Check for signs of leakage at the pipe unions, then examine the flexible hoses for signs of cracking, chafing and fraying.

3 The brake pipes should be examined carefully for signs of dents, corrosion or other damage. Corrosion should be scraped off, and if the depth of pitting is significant, the pipes renewed. This is particularly likely in those areas underneath the vehicle body where the pipes are exposed and unprotected.

4 Renew any defective brake pipes and/or hoses.

Removal

5 If a section of pipe or hose is to be removed, loss of brake fluid can be reduced by unscrewing the filler cap, and completely sealing the top of the reservoir with cling film or adhesive tape. Alternatively, the reservoir can be emptied (see Section 11).

> **HAYNES HINT**
> *If any brake fluid is spilt onto the bodywork, it must be washed off without delay - brake fluid is also a highly-effective paint-stripper!*

6 To remove a section of pipe, hold the adjoining hose union nut with a spanner to prevent it from turning, then unscrew the union nut at the end of the pipe, and release it. Repeat the procedure at the other end of the pipe, then release the pipe by pulling out the clips attaching it to the body **(see illustrations)**. Where the union nuts are exposed to the full force of the weather, they can sometimes be quite tight. If an open-ended spanner is used, burring of the flats on the nuts is not uncommon, and for this reason, it is preferable to use a split ring (brake) spanner, which will engage all the flats. If such a spanner is not available, self-

locking grips may be used as a last resort; these may well damage the nuts, but if the pipe is to be renewed, this does not matter.

7 To further minimise the loss of fluid when disconnecting a flexible brake line from a rigid pipe, clamp the hose as near as possible to the pipe to be detached, using a brake hose clamp or a pair of self-locking grips with protected jaws.

8 To remove a flexible hose, first clean the ends of the hose and the surrounding area, then unscrew the union nuts from the hose ends. Recover the spring clip, and withdraw the hose from the serrated mounting in the support bracket. Where applicable, unscrew the hose from the caliper.

9 Brake pipes supplied with flared ends and union nuts can be obtained individually or in sets from Ford dealers or accessory shops. The pipe is then bent to shape, using the old pipe as a guide, and is ready for fitting. Be careful not to kink or crimp the pipe when bending it; ideally, a proper pipe-bending tool should be used.

Refitting

10 Refitting of the pipes and hoses is a reversal of removal. Make sure that all brake pipes are securely supported in their clips, and ensure that the hoses are not kinked. Check also that the hoses are clear of all suspension components and underbody fittings, and will remain clear during movement of the suspension and steering.

11 On completion, bleed the brake hydraulic system as described in Section 15.

12 Hydraulic system - bleeding

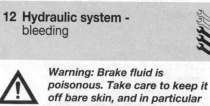

> ⚠ **Warning: Brake fluid is poisonous. Take care to keep it off bare skin, and in particular not to get splashes in your eyes. The fluid also attacks paintwork - wash off spillages immediately with cold water.**

1 If the master cylinder has been disconnected and reconnected, then the complete system (both circuits) must be bled of air. If a component of one circuit has been

disturbed, then only that particular circuit need be bled.

2 Bleeding should commence on one front brake, followed by the diagonally-opposite rear brake. The remaining front brake should then be bled, followed by its diagonally-opposite rear brake.

3 There are a variety of do-it-yourself "one-man" brake bleeding kits available from motor accessory shops, and it is recommended that one of these kits be used wherever possible, as they greatly simplify the brake bleeding operation. Follow the kit manufacturer's instructions in conjunction with the following procedure. If a pressure-bleeding kit is obtained, then it will not be necessary to depress the brake pedal in the following procedure.

4 During the bleeding operation, do not allow the brake fluid level in the reservoir to drop below the minimum mark. If the level is allowed to fall so far that air is drawn in, the whole procedure will have to be started again from scratch. Only use new fluid for topping-up, preferably from a freshly-opened container. *Never re-use fluid bled from the system.*

5 Before starting, check that all rigid pipes and flexible hoses are in good condition, and that all hydraulic unions are tight. Take great care not to allow hydraulic fluid to come into contact with the vehicle paintwork, otherwise the finish will be seriously damaged. Wash off any spilt fluid immediately with cold water.

6 If a brake bleeding kit is not being used, gather together a clean jar, a length of plastic or rubber tubing which is a tight fit over the bleed screw, and a new can of the specified brake fluid (see Chapter 1 Specifications). The help of an assistant will also be required.

7 Clean the area around the bleed screw on the front brake unit to be bled (it is important that no dirt be allowed to enter the hydraulic system), and remove the dust cap. Connect one end of the tubing to the bleed screw, and immerse the other end in the jar, which should be filled with sufficient brake fluid to keep the end of the tube submerged.

8 Open the bleed screw by one or two turns, and have the assistant depress the brake pedal to the floor. Tighten the bleed screw at the end of the downstroke, then have the assistant release the pedal. Continue this procedure until clean brake fluid, free from air bubbles, can be seen flowing into the jar. Finally tighten the bleed screw with the pedal in the fully-depressed position.

9 Remove the tube, and refit the dust cap. Top-up the master cylinder reservoir if necessary, then repeat the procedure on the diagonally-opposite rear brake.

10 Repeat the procedure on the remaining circuit, starting with the front brake, and followed by the diagonally-opposite rear brake.

11 Check the feel of the brake pedal - it should be firm. If it is spongy, there is still some air in the system, and the bleeding procedure should be repeated.

12 When bleeding is complete, top-up the master cylinder reservoir and refit the cap.

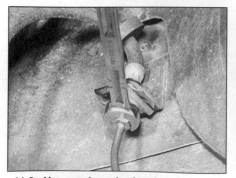

11.6a Unscrewing a brake pipe union nut using a split ring spanner

11.6b Pulling out a brake pipe mounting clip

13 Vacuum servo unit - testing, removal and refitting

Testing

1 To test the operation of the servo unit, depress the footbrake four or five times to dissipate the vacuum, then start the engine while keeping the footbrake depressed. As the engine starts, there should be a noticeable "give" in the brake pedal as vacuum builds up. Allow the engine to run for at least two minutes, and then switch it off. If the brake pedal is now depressed again, it should be possible to hear a hiss from the servo when the pedal is depressed. After four or five applications, no further hissing should be heard, and the pedal should feel harder.

2 Before assuming that a problem exists in the servo unit itself, inspect the non-return valve as described in the next Section.

Removal

3 Refer to Section 11 and remove the master cylinder.

4 Disconnect the vacuum hose adaptor at the servo unit by pulling it free from the rubber grommet. If it is reluctant to move, prise it free, using a screwdriver with its blade inserted under the flange.

5 Unscrew the four nuts securing the servo unit to the mounting brackets on the bulkhead in the engine compartment.

6 On right-hand drive models, withdraw the servo unit so that its studs are just clear of the brackets. Have an assistant hold the brake pedal depressed, then extract the spring clip and remove the clevis pin securing the servo unit pushrod to the pedal cross-link arm.

7 On left-hand drive models, unscrew the nut securing the pedal trunnion to the servo unit pushrod inside the passenger compartment. The nut is located near the top of the pedal, and is accessible through an access hole. For improved access, remove the lower facia panel first.

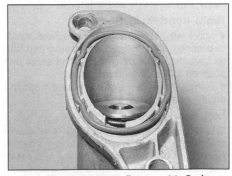

14.8 Vacuum pump flange with O-ring fitted

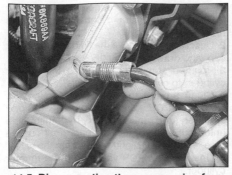

14.5 Disconnecting the vacuum pipe from the pump

8 Withdraw the servo unit from the bulkhead, and remove it from the engine compartment. On left-hand drive models, take care not to damage the bulkhead rubber grommet as the pushrod passes through it.

9 Note that the servo unit cannot be dismantled for repair or overhaul and, if faulty, must be renewed.

Refitting

10 Refitting is a reversal of the removal procedure. Refer to Section 11 for details of refitting the master cylinder.

14 Vacuum pump - location, removal and refitting

General

1 Because there is no throttling of the inlet manifold on a diesel engine, it is not a suitable source of vacuum for brake servo operation. Vacuum is therefore derived from a separate vacuum pump, driven by an eccentric on the tail of the camshaft.

Removal

2 Disconnect the battery earth lead.

3 Disconnect the breather hoses then unbolt and remove the camshaft cover. Note the

14.9 Fitting the pump over the lower bolt

14.6 Disconnecting the vacuum pump oil return hose

location of the reinforcing strips. Those bolts without reinforcing strips have washers.

4 Turn the engine until the vacuum pump cam lobe is pointing away from the pump.

5 Unscrew the vacuum pipe union from the pump **(see illustration)**. Plug the hole to keep dirt out.

6 Disconnect the pump oil return hose **(see illustration)**. Be prepared for oil spillage.

7 Remove the pump upper securing bolt. Slacken the lower bolt a few turns, tilt the pump and slide it upwards to remove it. Recover the sealing ring.

Refitting

8 Commence refitting by placing a new sealing ring in the groove on the pump flange **(see illustration)**.

9 Tilt the pump and engage its slotted lower mounting over the slackened lower bolt **(see illustration)**.

10 Insert the upper bolt. Tighten both bolts progressively to the specified torque.

11 Reconnect the pump oil return hose, using new clips if necessary.

12 Remove the blanking plug. Refit the vacuum pipe union and tighten it.

13 Refit the camshaft cover, using a new gasket if necessary. Tighten the bolts to the specified torque. Reconnect the breather hoses.

14 Reconnect the battery earth lead.

15 Start the engine and check for correct operation of the pump as described in Chapter 2.

15 Vacuum servo unit vacuum hose and non-return valve - removal, testing and refitting

Removal

1 Depress the brake pedal four or five times, to dissipate any remaining vacuum from the servo unit.

2 Disconnect the vacuum hose adaptor at the servo unit, by pulling it free from the rubber

15.2 Removing the plastic adaptor from the servo unit

grommet **(see illustration)**. If it is reluctant to move, prise it free, using a screwdriver with its blade inserted under the flange.

3 Detach the vacuum hose from the inlet manifold connection, pressing in the collar to disengage the tabs, then withdrawing the collar slowly.

4 If the hose or the fixings are damaged or in poor condition, they must be renewed.

Testing

5 Examine the non-return valve for damage and signs of deterioration, and renew it if necessary. The valve may be tested by blowing through its connecting hoses in both directions. It should only be possible to blow from the servo end towards the inlet manifold.

Refitting

6 Refitting is a reversal of the removal procedure. If fitting a new non-return valve, ensure that it is fitted the correct way round.

16 Pressure-control relief valve (non-ABS models) - removal and refitting

Removal

1 On non-ABS models, the two pressure-control relief valves (sometimes referred to as

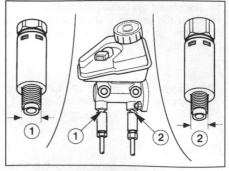

16.6 Pressure-control relief valve locations

1 Primary PCR valve (12 mm)
2 Secondary PCR valve (10 mm)

pressure-conscious reducing valves) are located on the master cylinder outlets to the rear brake line circuits.

2 Unscrew and remove the fluid reservoir filler cap, and draw off the fluid - see Section 11.

3 Position some rags beneath the master cylinder, to catch any spilled fluid.

4 Clean around the valve to be removed. Hold the PCR valve stationary with one spanner, and unscrew the hydraulic pipe union nut with another spanner. Pull out the pipe, and bend it slightly away from the valve.

5 Unscrew the PCR valve from the master cylinder.

6 Note that the primary and secondary PCR valves have different thread diameters, to prevent incorrect fitment. The primary valve has a 12 mm diameter thread, and the secondary valve has a 10 mm diameter thread **(see illustration)**.

Refitting

7 Refitting is a reversal of the removal procedure. On completion, bleed the hydraulic system as described in Section 15.

17 Pressure-control relief valve (ABS models) - removal and refitting

Removal

1 On ABS models, the pressure-control relief valves are located on the ABS hydraulic unit **(see illustration)**.

2 Disconnect the battery negative (earth) lead (Chapter 5, Section 1).

3 Remove the air cleaner assembly as described in Chapter 4.

4 Remove the engine air inlet duct and air plenum chamber.

5 Disconnect the low fluid level warning multi-plug from the brake fluid reservoir.

6 Unscrew and remove the brake fluid reservoir filler cap, and completely seal the

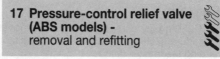
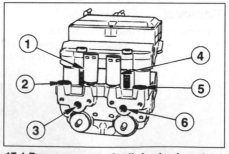

17.1 Pressure-control relief valve locations on the ABS hydraulic unit

1 PCR valve, rear right brake circuit
2 Outlet, front left brake circuit
3 Inlet, from brake master cylinder secondary circuit
4 PCR valve, rear left brake circuit
5 Outlet, front right brake circuit
6 Inlet, from brake master cylinder primary circuit

top of the reservoir using cling film or adhesive tape. This will reduce loss of fluid when the PCR valve is removed.

7 Unscrew the master cylinder mounting nuts, and carefully withdraw the cylinder from the servo unit, leaving the brake pipes still connected to it. Move the master cylinder over to the left-hand side of the engine compartment, to rest against the left-hand suspension turret. (Throughout this manual, left- and right-hand are as seen from the driver's seat.)

8 Unscrew the servo unit mounting nuts, and move the unit to one side.

9 Position some rags beneath the ABS unit, to catch spilled fluid.

10 Clean around the valve to be removed. Hold the PCR valve stationary with one spanner, and unscrew the hydraulic pipe union nut with another spanner. Pull out the pipe, and bend it slightly away from the valve.

11 Unscrew the PCR valve from the ABS unit.

Refitting

12 Refitting is a reversal of the removal procedure. On completion, bleed the hydraulic system as described in Section 15.

18 ABS hydraulic unit - removal and refitting

Note: *If any part of the ABS hydraulic unit is defective, it must be renewed as an assembly. Apart from the relay box (Section 22), individual spare parts are not available.*

Removal

1 Remove both pressure-control relief valves as described in Section 20.

2 Identify the location of the remaining brake hydraulic pipes on the ABS hydraulic unit, then unscrew the union nuts and pull out the pipes. Carefully bend the pipes away from the hydraulic unit, to allow the unit to be removed.

3 Disconnect the multi-plugs from the hydraulic unit. To disconnect the main 22-pin multi-plug, push the locktab, then swivel the multi-plug outwards and unhook it.

Right-hand drive models

4 Have an assistant hold the brake pedal depressed, then extract the spring clip and remove the clevis pin securing the servo unit pushrod to the pedal cross-link arm.

5 Remove the vacuum servo unit from the engine compartment.

Left-hand drive models

6 Unscrew the nut securing the pedal trunnion to the servo unit pushrod inside the passenger compartment. The nut is located near the top of the pedal, and is accessible through an access hole. For improved access, remove the lower facia panel first.

7 Remove the vacuum servo unit, together with the pushrod, from the engine compartment. Take care not to damage the rubber grommet in the bulkhead.

All models

8 Unscrew the pump mounting nut.
9 Raise the left-hand side of the ABS hydraulic unit, then swivel the unit out of the right-hand mounting. Take care not to lose the bracket studs and insulator ring.

Refitting

10 Locate the insulator ring on the pump end, and fit the stud cap to the insulator ring.
11 Lower the ABS hydraulic unit into position, right-hand end first.
12 Fit the right-hand bracket studs onto the insulators.
13 Lower the left-hand end of the ABS hydraulic unit onto the bracket, then fit and tighten the pump mounting nut.

Left-hand drive models

14 Locate the vacuum servo unit and pushrod on the bulkhead bracket, taking care not to damage the rubber grommet.
15 Insert the pushrod in the pedal trunnion, and tighten the nut.
16 Refit the lower facia panel if it was removed.

Right-hand drive models

17 Locate the vacuum servo unit and pushrod on the bulkhead bracket.
18 Refit the clevis pin and spring clip securing the servo unit pushrod to the pedal cross-link arm.

All models

19 Reconnect the multi-plugs to the hydraulic unit.
20 Reconnect the brake pipes to the hydraulic unit, and tighten the union nuts.
21 Refit both pressure-control relief valves, with reference to Section 21.

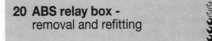

19 ABS wheel sensor - testing, removal and refitting

Testing

1 Checking of the sensors is done before removal, connecting a voltmeter to the disconnected sensor multi-plug. Using an analogue (moving coil) meter is not practical, since the meter does not respond quickly enough. A digital meter having an AC facility may be used to check that the sensor is operating correctly. To do this, raise the relevant wheel then disconnect the wiring to the ABS sensor and connect the meter to it. Spin the wheel and check that the output voltage is between 1.5 and 2.0 volts, depending on how fast the wheel is spun. Alternatively, an oscilloscope may be used to check the output of the sensor - an alternating current will be traced on the screen, of

19.4 Unscrew the mounting bolt and remove the ABS sensor

magnitude depending on the speed of the rotating wheel.
2 If the sensor output is low or zero, renew the sensor.

Removal

Front wheel sensor

3 Apply the handbrake, jack up the front of the vehicle and support it on axle stands. Remove the relevant wheel.
4 Unscrew the sensor mounting bolt located on the steering knuckle, and withdraw the sensor **(see illustration)**.
5 Remove the sensor wiring loom from the support brackets on the front suspension strut and wheel arch.
6 Prise out the stud clips, and remove the Torx screws and screw clips holding the wheel arch liner in position. Withdraw the liner.
7 Disconnect the multi-plug, and withdraw the sensor and wiring loom.

Rear wheel sensor

8 Chock the front wheels, and engage 1st gear. Jack up the rear of the vehicle and support it on axle stands. Remove the relevant wheel.
9 Unscrew the sensor mounting bolt, located on the brake backplate, and withdraw the sensor.
10 Disconnect the sensor wiring loom from the supports on the rear suspension strut (or knuckle) and wheel arch.

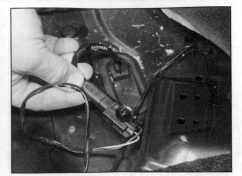

19.11 Rear ABS sensor wiring multi-plug located beneath the rear seat

11 Working inside the vehicle, lift the rear seat cushion, then disconnect the multi-plug for the sensor wiring loom **(see illustration)**.
12 Withdraw the sensor and wiring loom through the rubber grommet in the rear floor.

Refitting

Front and rear wheel sensors

13 Refitting is a reversal of the removal procedure.

20 ABS relay box - removal and refitting

Removal

1 Disconnect the battery negative (earth) lead (Chapter 5, Section 1).
2 Detach the vacuum hose from the inlet manifold connection, pressing in the collar to disengage the tabs, then withdrawing the collar slowly.
3 To improve access, free the heater hose from its retaining clips, and position it clear of the relay box.
4 Disconect the wiring connector(s) fron the relay box and, where necessary, the speed ssender unit.
5 Slacken and remove the four Torx retaining screws, and withdraw the relay box from the hydraulic unit **(see illustration)**.

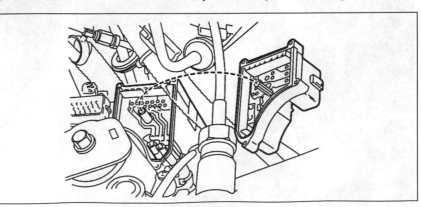

20.5 Removing the ABS relay box

21.4 Removing the stop-light switch

Refitting

6 Refitting is a reversal of the removal procedure. Do not overtighten the relay box retaining screws, as the plastic is easily cracked

21 Stop-light switch -
removal and refitting

Removal

1 Disconnect the battery negative (earth) lead (Chapter 5, Section 1).
2 Remove the lower facia panel, with reference to Chapter 11.
3 Disconnect the wiring multi-plug from the switch.
4 Rotate the switch anti-clockwise by a quarter-turn, and withdraw it from the pedal bracket (see illustration).

Refitting and adjustment

5 With the switch removed, reset it by fully extending its plunger.
6 Depress the brake pedal until the distance between the pedal and mounting bracket is as shown (see illustration).
7 Hold the pedal in this position, and refit the stop-light switch to the mounting bracket .
8 With the switch securely clipped in position,

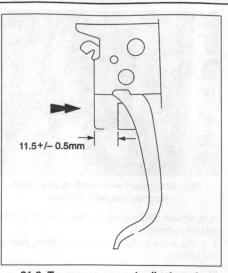

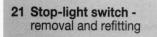

21.6 To ensure correct adjustment, position the brake pedal as shown prior to refitting the switch to its mounting bracket

release the brake pedal, and gently pull it fully back to the at-rest position. This will automatically set the adjustment of the stop-light switch.
9 reconnect the wiring connector and the battery, and check the operation of the switch prior to refitting the lower facia panel (Chapter 11).

22 Handbrake lever -
removal and refitting

Removal

1 Raise the front and rear of the vehicle, and support it on axle stands. Fully release the handbrake lever.
2 Remove the centre console as described in Chapter 11.
3 Working beneath the vehicle, release the exhaust system from the rubber mountings. Lower the exhaust system as far as possible,

supporting it on blocks or more axle stands.
4 Detach the exhaust heat shield from the underbody.
5 Unhook the secondary (rear) handbrake cables from the equaliser bar.
6 Working inside the vehicle, unscrew and remove the two mounting bolts securing the handbrake lever to the floor (see illustration).
7 Turn the handbrake lever upsidedown, then disconnect the primary cable end from the segment.
8 Withdraw the handbrake from inside the vehicle.

Refitting

9 Refitting is a reversal of the removal procedure, making sure that the primary cable is correctly located in the segment. Check the operation of the handbrake before returning the vehicle to normal service.

23 Handbrake cables -
removal and refitting

Removal

Primary (front)

1 Remove the handbrake lever as described in Section 22.
2 Prise the grommet from the underbody, and withdraw the cable from beneath the vehicle.

Secondary (rear)

3 Chock the front wheels, and engage 1st gear. Jack up the rear of the vehicle and support it on axle stands. Fully release the handbrake lever.
4 Remove the relevant rear wheel.
5 Working beneath the vehicle, release the exhaust system from the rubber mountings. Lower the exhaust system as far as possible, supporting it on blocks or more axle stands.
6 Unbolt the exhaust heat shield from the underbody.
7 Unhook the relevant cable from the equaliser bar.

22.6 Handbrake lever mounting bolts

23.8 Using a ring spanner to compress the retaining lugs securing the outer cable to the backplate

8 Remove the rear brake shoes on the relevant side as described in Section 6, then remove the outer cable from the backplate by compressing the three retaining lugs (use a suitable ring spanner) and pushing the cable through **(see illustration)**.

9 Release the lugs securing the outer cable to the underbody brackets, then release the cable from the clips, and withdraw it from under the vehicle **(see illustrations)**.

Refitting

All cables

10 Refitting is a reversal of the removal procedure, but make sure that the cable end fittings are correctly located. Check the operation of the handbrake before returning the vehicle to normal service.

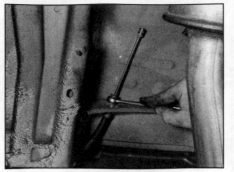

23.9a Release the lugs using a ring spanner . . .

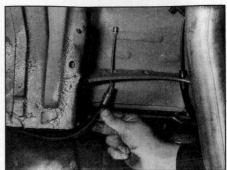

23.9b . . . and remove the outer cable from the underbody brackets

Notes

Chapter 10
Suspension and steering systems

Contents

Degrees of difficulty

Easy, suitable for novice with little experience	Fairly easy, suitable for beginner with some experience	Fairly difficult, suitable for competent DIY mechanic	Difficult, suitable for experienced DIY mechanic	Very difficult, suitable for expert DIY or professional

Specifications

Front wheel alignment

Toe setting:
  Tolerance allowed before resetting required .... 0.5 mm to 3.5 mm toe-out (0°05' to 0°35' toe-out)
  Adjustment setting (if required) .... 2.0 mm ± 1.0 mm toe-out (0°20' ± 0°10' toe-out)

Rear wheel alignment

Toe setting:
  Tolerance allowed before resetting required:
    Saloon/Hatchback .... 3.9 mm toe-in to 0.1 mm toe-out (0°38' toe-in to 0°02' toe-out)
    Estate .... 2.7 mm toe-in to 1.3 mm toe-out (0°27' toe-in to 0°13' toe-out)
  Adjustment setting (if required):
    Saloon/Hatchback .... 1.9 mm ± 1.2 mm toe-in (0°18' ± 0°12' toe-in)
    Estate .... 0.7 mm ± 1.2 mm toe-in (0°07' ± 0°12' toe-in)

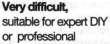

10

Roadwheels and tyres

Wheel sizes:

Steel	14 x 5 1/2
Alloy	14 x 5 1/2 or 15 x 6

Tyre sizes:

Wheel size 14 x 5 1/2	185/65/14 or 195/60VR/14
Wheel size 15 x 6	205/55VR/15
Tyre pressures	See Chapter 1 Specifications

Torque wrench settings

	Nm	lbf ft
Front suspension		
Front subframe	110 to 150	81 to 111
Lower arm balljoint to lower arm (service replacement, bolted on)	58	43
Lower arm balljoint-to-steering knuckle clamp bolt	48 to 60	35 to 44
Lower arm to subframe:		
Stage 1 (used components)	50	37
Stage 1 (new components)	70	52
Stage 2	Slacken completely	
Stage 3	50	37
Stage 4	Tighten through further 90°	
Anti-roll bar	24	18
Anti-roll bar link	41 to 58	30 to 43
Suspension strut-to-steering knuckle pinch-bolt	84	62
Suspension strut upper mounting nut	46	34
Suspension strut thrust bearing retaining nut	59	44
Driveshaft/hub retaining nut	340	251
Rear suspension (Saloon/Hatchback)		
Crossmember mounting bolts	102 to 138	75 to 102
Front lower arm to knuckle and to crossmember	70 to 98	52 to 72
Rear lower arm to knuckle	102 to 138	75 to 102
Rear lower arm to crossmember	70 to 98	52 to 72
Anti-roll bar	19 to 26	14 to 19
Anti-roll bar link	30 to 40	22 to 30
Suspension strut to knuckle	70 to 98	52 to 72
Drum brake backplate	45 to 54	33 to 40
Disc brake splash shield	90	66
Hub nut	290	214
Tie-bar and tie-bar bracket	102 to 138	75 to 102
Suspension strut upper mounting bolts	23 to 30	17 to 22
Suspension strut upper nut	41 to 58	30 to 43
Rear suspension (Estate)		
Same as for Saloon/Hatchback, except for the following.		
Crossmember mounting bolts	120	89
Front lower arm to knuckle and to crossmember	120	89
Upper arm to knuckle	120	89
Upper arm to crossmember	84	62
Rear lower arm to knuckle and to crossmember	84	62
Anti-roll bar	25	19
Anti-roll bar link	35	26
Hub assembly-to-knuckle retaining bolts	65	48
Tie-bar to bracket	120	89
Tie-bar bracket to underbody	120	89
Tie-bar to knuckle	84	62
Shock absorber upper mounting bolt	84	62
Shock absorber lower mounting bolt	120	89
Steering		
Steering gear mounting bolts	114 to 159	84 to 117
Track rod end to steering knuckle	25 to 30	18 to 22
Track rod end locknut	34 to 47	25 to 35
Steering wheel	45 to 55	33 to 41
Flexible coupling-to-pinion shaft clamp bolt	23 to 32	17 to 24
Power steering pipe unions to valve body	27 to 35	20 to 26
Steering column-to-coupling clamp bolt	20 to 27	14 to 20
Steering column mounting bolts	20 to 27	14 to 20
Steering pump mounting bolts	21 to 28	15 to 21
Steering pump pressure line	57 to 73	42 to 54
Roadwheel nuts	85	63

1 General information

The independent front suspension is of MacPherson strut type, incorporating coil springs, integral telescopic shock absorbers, and an anti-roll bar. The struts are attached to steering knuckles at their lower ends, and the knuckles are in turn attached to the lower suspension arm by balljoints. The anti-roll bar is bolted to the rear of the subframe, and is connected to the front suspension struts by links **(see illustration)**.

On Saloon/Hatchback models, the independent rear suspension is of "Quadralink" type, having four mounting points on each side of the vehicle. The two lower arms are attached to the rear suspension knuckle at their outer ends, and to the rear crossmember at their inner ends. A tie-bar, located between the bottom of the knuckle and the floor, counteracts braking and acceleration forces on each side **(see illustration)**.

On Estate models, the independent rear suspension is of "SLA" (Short and Long Arm) type. This allows a larger load area, since there are no suspension points projecting into

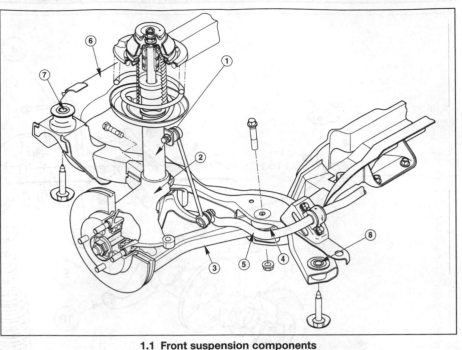

1.1 Front suspension components

1 MacPherson strut	4 Vertical silent bush on	6 Front subframe
2 Steering knuckle	lower arm	7 Front subframe rubber bush
3 Lower arm	5 Anti-roll bar	8 Rear subframe rubber bush

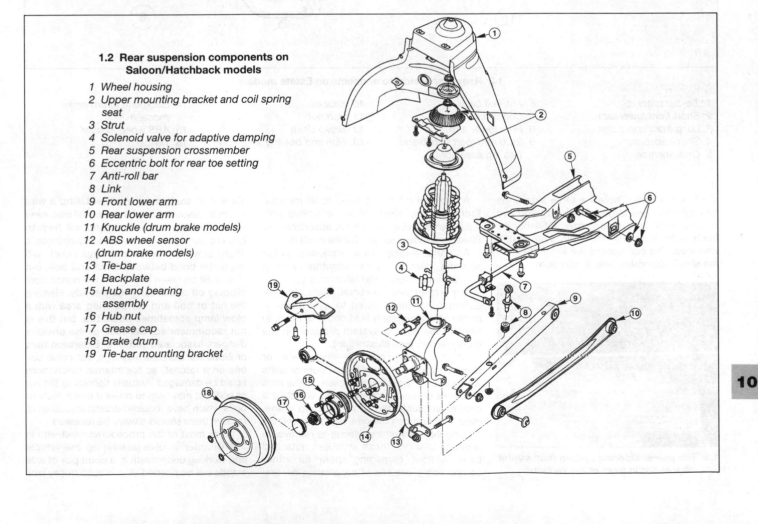

1.2 Rear suspension components on Saloon/Hatchback models

1. Wheel housing
2. Upper mounting bracket and coil spring seat
3. Strut
4. Solenoid valve for adaptive damping
5. Rear suspension crossmember
6. Eccentric bolt for rear toe setting
7. Anti-roll bar
8. Link
9. Front lower arm
10. Rear lower arm
11. Knuckle (drum brake models)
12. ABS wheel sensor (drum brake models)
13. Tie-bar
14. Backplate
15. Hub and bearing assembly
16. Hub nut
17. Grease cap
18. Brake drum
19. Tie-bar mounting bracket

10

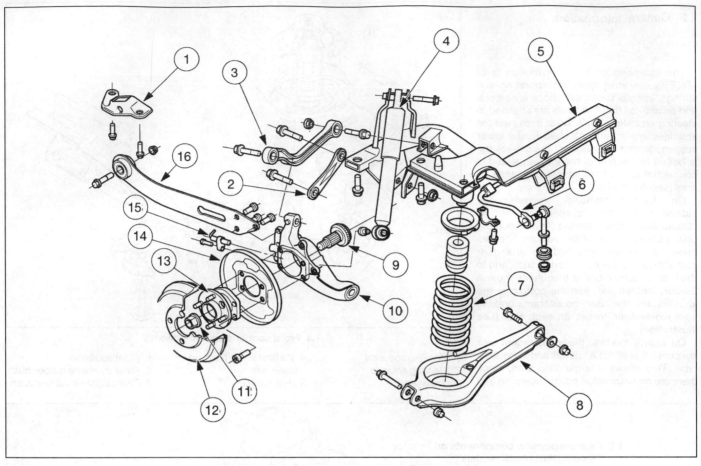

1.3 Rear suspension components on Estate models

1 Tie-bar bracket	6 Anti-roll bar	10 Knuckle	14 Backplate (drum brake
2 Short front lower arm	7 Coil spring	11 Hub nut	models)
3 Long front upper arm	8 Rear lower arm	12 Brake drum	15 ABS wheel sensor
4 Shock absorber	9 Stub axle (part of hub and	13 Hub and bearing assembly	16 Tie-bar
5 Crossmember	bearing assembly)		

the luggage area. There are three side arms on each side: one forged upper arm, and two pressed-steel lower side arms. A tie-bar on each side supports the rear suspension knuckles. The coil springs are separate from the shock absorbers **(see illustration)**.

1.5 The power steering system fluid cooler is located in front of the radiator

A rear anti-roll bar is fitted to all models. Front and rear shock absorbers filled with fluid. Self-levelling rear shock absorbers are fitted as standard to Ghia Estate models.

A variable-ratio type rack-and-pinion steering gear is fitted, together with a conventional column and telescopic coupling, incorporating two universal joints. Power-assisted steering is fitted to all models. A power steering system fluid cooler is fitted, in front of the cooling system radiator on the crossmember **(see illustration)**.

When working on the suspension or steering, you may come across nuts or bolts which seem impossible to loosen. These nuts and bolts on the underside of the vehicle are continually subjected to water, road grime, mud, etc, and can become rusted or seized, making them extremely difficult to remove. In order to unscrew these stubborn nuts and bolts without damaging them (or other components), use lots of penetrating oil, and

allow it to soak in for a while. Using a wire brush to clean exposed threads will also ease removal of the nut or bolt, and will help to prevent damage to the threads. Sometimes, a sharp blow with a hammer and punch will break the bond between a nut and bolt, but care must be taken to prevent the punch from slipping off and ruining the threads. Heating the nut or bolt and surrounding area with a blow lamp sometimes helps too, but this is not recommended, because of the obvious dangers associated with fire. Extension bars or pipes will increase leverage, but never use one on a ratchet, as the internal mechanism could be damaged. Actually *tightening* the nut or bolt first may help to break it loose. Nuts or bolts which have required drastic measures to remove them should always be renewed.

Since most of the procedures dealt with in this Chapter involve jacking up the vehicle and working underneath it, a good pair of axle stands will be needed. A hydraulic trolley jack is the preferred type of jack to lift the vehicle, and it can also be used to support certain components during removal and refitting operations.

 Warning: Never, under any circumstances, rely on a jack to support the vehicle while working beneath it. When jacking up the vehicle, do not lift or support it beneath the front or rear subframes.

2 Steering knuckle and hub assembly - removal and refitting

Removal

1 Apply the handbrake. Remove the wheel cover from the relevant front wheel, and loosen (but do not remove) the driveshaft/hub nut. This nut is very tight.

2 Loosen the front wheel nuts, jack up the front of the vehicle and support it on axle stands. Remove the front wheel.

3 Extract the split pin from the track rod end balljoint nut. Unscrew the nut, and detach the rod from the arm on the steering knuckle using a conventional balljoint removal tool. Take care not to damage the balljoint seal.

4 Remove the ABS sensor (when fitted) as described in Chapter 9.

5 Remove the brake caliper and brake disc as described in Chapter 9, but do not disconnect the flexible hose from the caliper. Suspend the caliper from a suitable point under the wheel arch, taking care not to strain the hose.

6 Unscrew and remove the driveshaft/hub nut. Note that the nut is of special laminated design, and should only be re-used a maximum of 5 times. (It is a good idea to file a small notch on the nut every time it is removed.) Obtain a new nut if necessary.

7 Note which way round the lower arm balljoint clamp bolt is fitted, then unscrew and remove it from the knuckle assembly. Lever the balljoint down from the knuckle; if it is tight, prise the clamp open using a large flat-bladed tool. Take care not to damage the balljoint seal during the separation procedure.

8 Unscrew and remove the pinch-bolt securing the steering knuckle assembly to the front suspension strut, noting which way round it is fitted. Prise open the clamp using a wedge-shaped tool, and release the knuckle from the strut. If necessary, tap the knuckle downwards with a soft-headed mallet to separate the two components. Support the knuckle on an axle stand.

9 Pull the steering knuckle and hub assembly from the driveshaft splines. If it is tight, connect a universal puller to the hub flange, and withdraw it from the driveshaft. When the driveshaft is free, support it on an axle stand, or suspend it from a suitable point under the

wheel arch, making sure that the inner constant velocity joint is not turned through more than 18°. (Damage may occur if the joint is turned through too great an angle.)

Refitting

10 Lift the steering knuckle and hub assembly onto the driveshaft splines, and support the assembly on an axle stand.

11 Locate the assembly on the front suspension strut. Insert the pinch-bolt with its head facing forwards. Fit the nut and tighten it to the specified torque.

12 Refit the lower arm balljoint to the knuckle assembly, and insert the clamp bolt with its head facing forwards. Refit the nut and tighten it to the specified torque.

13 Refit the driveshaft/hub nut, and tighten it moderately at this stage. Final tightening of the nut is made with the vehicle lowered to the ground.

14 Refit the brake caliper and brake disc as described in Chapter 9.

15 Where fitted, refit the ABS sensor as described in Chapter 9.

16 Reconnect the track rod end balljoint to the steering arm, and tighten the nut to the specified torque. Check that the split pin holes are aligned; if necessary, turn the nut to the nearest alignment, making sure that the torque wrench setting is still within the specified range. Insert a new split pin, and bend it back to secure.

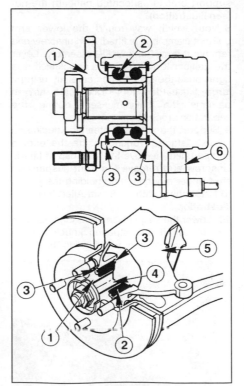

3.5 Front hub and bearing

1 Hub
2 Double-row ball-bearing
3 Circlips
4 Stub axle
5 Steering knuckle
6 ABS sensor

17 Refit the front wheel, and lower the vehicle to the ground. Tighten the wheel nuts to the specified torque.

18 Tighten the driveshaft/hub nut to the specified torque, and refit the wheel cover.

3 Front hub and bearings - inspection and renewal

Inspection

1 The front hub bearings are non-adjustable, and are supplied already greased.

2 To check the bearings for excessive wear, apply the handbrake, jack up the front of the vehicle and support it on axle stands.

3 Grip the front wheel at top and bottom, and attempt to rock it. If excessive movement is noted, it may be that the hub bearings are worn. Do not confuse wear in the driveshaft outer joint or front suspension lower arm balljoint with wear in the bearings. Hub bearing wear will show up as roughness or vibration when the wheel is spun; it will also be noticeable as a rumbling or growling noise when driving.

Renewal

4 Remove the steering knuckle and hub assembly as described in Section 2.

5 The hub must now be removed from the bearing inner races. It is preferable to use a press to do this, but it is possible to drive out the hub using a length of metal tube of suitable diameter (see illustration).

6 Part of the inner race will remain on the hub, and this should be removed using a puller.

7 Note that if this procedure is being used to renew the hub only (ie it is not intended to renew the bearings), then it is important to check the condition of the bearing balls and races, to see if they are fit for re-use. It is difficult to be sure that no damage has occurred, especially if makeshift methods have been used during removal; in practice, it is probably false economy not to renew the bearings in any case, having got this far.

8 Using circlip pliers, extract the inner and outer circlips securing the hub bearing in the steering knuckle (see illustration).

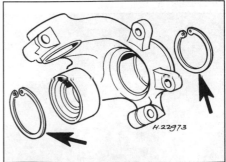

3.8 Front wheel bearing retaining circlips (arrowed)

10

4.2 Removing the brake hose support bracket from the front of the front suspension strut

4.7 Removing the anti-roll bar link and ABS sensor wiring bracket

4.9 Front suspension strut upper mounting nut

9 Press or drive out the bearing, using a length of metal tubing of diameter slightly less than the bearing outer race.

10 Clean the bearing seating faces in the steering knuckle.

11 Locate one of the circlips in the outer groove of the knuckle.

12 Press or drive the new bearing into the knuckle until it contacts the circlip, using a length of metal tube of diameter slightly less than the outer race. Do not apply any pressure to the inner race.

13 Locate the remaining circlip in the inner groove of the knuckle.

14 Support the inner race on a length of metal tube, then press or drive the hub fully into the bearing.

15 Refit the steering knuckle and hub assembly as described in Section 2.

4 Front suspension strut - removal and refitting

Removal

1 Apply the handbrake, then jack up the front of the vehicle and support it on axle stands. Remove the appropriate front wheel.

2 Unbolt the brake hose support bracket from the front of the suspension strut **(see illustration)**.

3 Remove the brake caliper as described in Chapter 9, but do not disconnect the flexible hydraulic hose from the caliper. Suspend the caliper from a suitable point under the wheel arch, taking care not to strain the hose.

4 Extract the split pin from the track rod end balljoint nut. Unscrew the nut, and detach the rod from the arm on the steering knuckle using a conventional balljoint removal tool. Take care not to damage the balljoint seal.

5 Remove the ABS sensor (when fitted) from the steering knuckle, as described in Chapter 9.

6 Remove the clip securing the driveshaft inner gaiter to the inner CV joint. Disconnect the gaiter from the CV joint housing.

7 Remove the nut and disconnect the anti-roll bar link from the strut. Note that, on models fitted with ABS, the ABS wheel sensor wiring support bracket is located beneath the nut **(see illustration)**.

8 Note which way round the lower arm balljoint clamp bolt is fitted, then unscrew and remove it from the knuckle assembly. Lever the balljoint down from the knuckle; if it is tight, prise the clamp open carefully using a large flat-bladed tool. Take care not to damage the balljoint seal during the separation procedure.

9 Support the strut and steering knuckle on an axle stand. Working inside the engine compartment, remove the strut cap (if fitted). Unscrew and remove the front suspension strut upper mounting nut, holding the piston rod stationary with an 8 mm Allen key **(see illustration)**.

10 Lower the suspension strut, together with the driveshaft and steering knuckle, from under the wheel arch, withdrawing the tripod

on the inner end of the driveshaft from the CV joint housing.

11 Unscrew and remove the pinch-bolt securing the steering knuckle assembly to the front suspension strut, noting which way round it is fitted. Prise open the clamp using a wedge-shaped tool, and release the knuckle from the strut **(see illustrations)**.

Refitting

12 With the clamp prised open, locate the front suspension strut on the steering knuckle, and refit the pinch-bolt with its head facing forwards. Tighten the bolt to the specified torque.

13 Locate the suspension strut (together with the driveshaft and steering knuckle) in its upper mounting, and loosely screw on the nut.

14 Locate the tripod on the inner end of the driveshaft in the CV joint housing, then manipulate the gaiter onto the housing, and fit a new clip.

15 Locate the lower arm balljoint fully in the bottom of the steering knuckle. Refit the clamp bolt and tighten it to the specified torque.

16 Reconnect the anti-roll bar link to the strut, and tighten the nut to the specified torque. On models fitted with ABS, do not forget to locate the sensor wiring support bracket beneath the nut.

17 Where fitted, refit the ABS sensor as described in Chapter 9.

18 Refit the track rod end balljoint to the steering knuckle, and tighten the nut to the specified torque. Check that the split pin holes are aligned; if necessary, turn the nut to the nearest alignment, making sure that the torque wrench setting is still within the specified range. Insert a new split pin, and bend it back to secure.

19 Refit the brake caliper as described in Chapter 9.

20 Refit the brake hose support bracket to the strut, and tighten the bolt.

21 Refit the wheel, and lower the vehicle to the ground. Tighten the wheel nuts to the specified torque.

22 Tighten the suspension strut upper mounting nut to the specified torque, while holding the piston rod with an 8 mm Allen key.

4.11a Steering knuckle-to-strut pinch-bolt

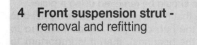

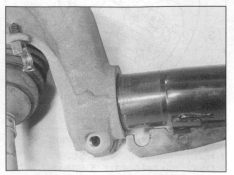

4.11b Releasing the knuckle from the strut

4.22 Final tightening of the front suspension strut upper mounting nut

5.3 Coil spring compressor tools fitted to the coil spring

5.4 Unscrewing the nut from the top of the strut

If the adaptor needed to do this is not available, the nut can be tightened initially with a ring spanner while the piston rod is held. Final tightening can then be carried out using a torque wrench and a conventional socket (see illustration).

2 With the strut removed from the vehicle, clean away all external dirt, then mount it in a vice.
3 Fit the coil spring compressor tools (ensuring that they are fully engaged), and compress the spring until all tension is relieved from the upper mounting (see illustration).

4 Hold the strut piston with an Allen key, and unscrew the thrust bearing retaining nut with a ring spanner (see illustration).
5 Withdraw the top mounting, thrust bearing, upper spring seat and spring, followed by the gaiter and the bump stop (see illustrations).
6 If a new spring is to be fitted, the original spring must now be carefully released from

5 Front suspension strut - overhaul

 Warning: Before attempting to dismantle the front suspension strut, a tool to hold the coil spring in compression must be obtained. Do not attempt to use makeshift methods. Uncontrolled release of the spring could cause damage and personal injury. Use a high-quality spring compressor, and carefully follow the tool manufacturer's instructions provided with it. After removing the coil spring with the compressor still fitted, place it in a safe, isolated area.

1 If the front suspension struts exhibit signs of wear (leaking fluid, loss of damping capability, sagging or cracked coil springs) then they should be dismantled and overhauled as necessary. The struts themselves cannot be serviced, and should be renewed if faulty, but the springs and related components can be renewed. To maintain balanced characteristics on both sides of the vehicle, the components on both sides should be renewed at the same time.

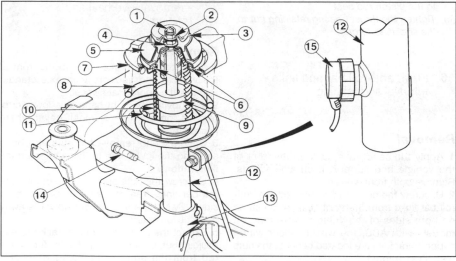

5.5a Front suspension strut components

1 Cap	7 Upper spring seat	12 Strut
2 Nut	8 Spring	13 Steering knuckle
3 Retainer	9 Bump stop	14 Clamp bolt
4 Nut	10 Gaiter	15 Solenoid valve for models
5 Top mounting	11 Lower spring seat	with adaptive damping
6 Thrust bearing		

5.5b Removing the top mounting from the strut

5.5c Removing the gaiter

5.5d Removing the bump stop

10

the compressor. If it is to be re-used, the spring can be left in compression.

7 With the strut assembly now completely dismantled, examine all the components for wear and damage, and check the bearing for smoothness of operation. Renew components as necessary.

8 Examine the strut for signs of fluid leakage. Check the strut piston for signs of pitting along its entire length, and check the strut body for signs of damage. Test the operation of the strut, while holding it in an upright position, by moving the piston through a full stroke, and then through short strokes of 50 to 100 mm. In both cases, the resistance felt should be smooth and continuous. If the resistance is jerky, uneven, or if there is any visible sign of wear or damage to the strut, renewal is necessary.

9 Reassembly is a reversal of dismantling, noting the following points:

(a) Make sure that the coil spring ends are correctly located in the upper and lower seats before releasing the compressor.

(b) Check that the bearing is correctly fitted to the piston rod seat.

(c) Tighten the thrust bearing retaining nut to the specified torque.

---

6 Front anti-roll bar and links - removal and refitting

Removal

1 Apply the handbrake, jack up the front of the vehicle and support it on axle stands. Remove both front wheels.

2 Unscrew the nuts, and disconnect the anti-roll bar links from the front suspension struts on both sides of the vehicle. Note that, on models with ABS, the wheel sensor wiring support brackets are located beneath the nuts **(see illustrations)**.

3 Unscrew and remove the anti-roll bar mounting bolts from the engine subframe on both sides of the vehicle.

4 Withdraw the anti-roll bar from one side of the vehicle, taking care not to damage the surrounding components.

6.2a Unscrew the nut . . .

5 If necessary, unscrew the nuts and remove the links from the anti-roll bar.

Refitting

6 Refitting is a reversal of the removal procedure.

---

7 Front suspension lower arm - removal, overhaul and refitting

Removal

1 Apply the handbrake, jack up the front of the vehicle and support it on axle stands. Remove the appropriate wheel.

2 If removing the right-hand side lower arm, remove the auxiliary drivebelt cover where necessary.

3 Unscrew and remove the nuts and bolts securing the lower arm to the subframe **(see illustration)**.

4 Unscrew the nuts and disconnect the anti-roll bar links from the anti-roll bar on both sides. Swivel the anti-roll bar upwards away from the lower arm.

5 Extract the split pin from the track rod end balljoint nut. Unscrew the nut, and detach the rod from the arm on the steering knuckle using a conventional balljoint removal tool. Take care not to damage the balljoint seal.

6 Remove the clip securing the driveshaft inner gaiter to the inner CV joint, and disconnect the gaiter from the CV joint housing. This is necessary to prevent damage

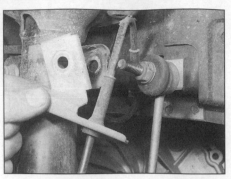

6.2b . . . and disconnect the anti-roll bar link and (on ABS models) the sensor wiring support bracket

to the gaiter when the steering knuckle is moved outwards to remove the lower arm.

7 Note which way round the front suspension lower arm balljoint clamp bolt is fitted, then unscrew and remove it from the knuckle assembly. Lever the balljoint down from the knuckle; if it is tight, prise the joint open carefully using a large flat-bladed tool. Take care not to damage the balljoint seal during the separation procedure. Support the inner end of the driveshaft on an axle stand **(see illustrations)**.

8 Remove the lower arm from the subframe, and withdraw it from the vehicle.

Overhaul

9 Examine the rubber bushes and the suspension lower balljoint for wear and damage. The balljoint may be renewed as described in Section 8. The rubber bushes may be removed using a press, or a length of metal tubing together with a long bolt, washers and nut.

10 Note that the front and rear bushes are different. The front one has a solid rubber bush with a cylindrical inner tube, whereas the rear one has a voided rubber bush with a barrel-shaped inner tube **(see illustration)**.

11 Press the new bushes into the lower arm, using the same method as used for removal. Note that, when fitting the rear bush, the voids must be in line with the front bush location. On later models, a pip on the rear bush must be aligned with a triangular alignment mark on the arm.

7.3 One of the nuts and bolts securing the lower arm to the subframe

7.7a Unscrew the lower arm balljoint clamp bolt . . .

7.7b . . . and disconnect the balljoint from the knuckle

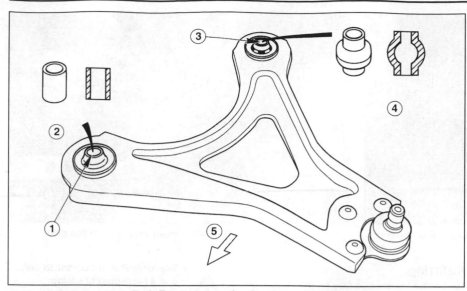

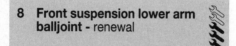

7.10 Front suspension lower arm bushes

1 *Front bush*
2 *Cylindrical inner tube*
3 *Rear bush*
4 *Barrel-shaped inner tube*
5 *Front of vehicle*

Refitting

12 Locate the lower arm on the subframe, and insert the mounting bolts. Fit the nuts and tighten them in stages, first to the specified torque and then through the angle specified.

13 If removed, locate the tripod on the inner end of the driveshaft in the CV joint housing, then refit the gaiter, together with a new clip.

14 Refit the front suspension lower arm balljoint to the knuckle assembly, and insert the clamp bolt with its head facing forwards. Refit the nut and tighten to the specified torque.

15 Refit the track rod end balljoint to the steering knuckle, and tighten the nut to the specified torque. Check that the split pin holes are aligned; if necessary, turn the nut to align the holes, making sure that the torque wrench setting is still within the specified range. Insert a new split pin, and bend it back to secure.

16 Swivel the anti-roll bar down, then reconnect the links to the bar and tighten the nuts to the specified torque.

17 If working on the right-hand side, refit the auxiliary drivebelt cover where necessary.

18 Refit the wheel, and lower the vehicle to the ground.

8 Front suspension lower arm balljoint - renewal

Note: *If the lower arm balljoint is worn, either the complete lower arm or the balljoint alone can be renewed. If the balljoint has already been renewed, it will be bolted in position; if the original balljoint is being renewed, then it will be riveted in position* (see illustration). *This Section describes the renewal of a riveted balljoint.*

1 Remove the front suspension lower arm as described in Section 7. It is not recommended that the balljoint be replaced with the lower arm in position on the vehicle; the accurate drilling necessary may not be possible, and the holes in the arm may be enlarged.

2 With the lower arm on the bench, use a 3 mm drill to make a pilot hole through each of the three rivets. Now use a 9 mm drill to drill the rivets to a depth of 12 mm, then use a 7 or 8 mm drift to drive the rivets out of the arm.

3 Clean any rust or dirt from the rivet holes.

4 The new balljoint is supplied with a protective plastic cover over the rubber boot and stub, and it is recommended that this remains in position until it is time to connect the balljoint to the steering knuckle.

5 Locate the new balljoint on the lower arm, and use three new bolts to secure it, inserting the bolts from the top of the arm. Tighten the nuts to the specified torque. Make sure that the location lug on the balljoint engages the hole in the lower arm **(see illustration)**.

6 Refit the front suspension lower arm as described in Section 7.

9 Rear hub and bearings (Saloon/Hatchback models) - inspection and renewal

Note: *Removal of the rear hub damages the bearings, and renders them unserviceable for future use. The hub and bearing assembly **must** always be renewed if it is removed.*

Inspection

1 The rear hub bearings are non-adjustable, and are supplied complete with the hub. It is not possible to renew the bearings separately from the hub.

2 To check the bearings for excessive wear, chock the front wheels, then jack up the rear of the vehicle and support it on axle stands. Fully release the handbrake.

3 Grip the rear wheel at the top and bottom, and attempt to rock it. If excessive movement is noted, or if there is any roughness or vibration felt when the wheel is spun, it is indicative that the hub bearings are worn.

Renewal

4 Remove the rear wheel.

5 Remove the rear brake drum as described in Chapter 9.

6 On all models, tap off the dust cap and unscrew the hub nut. Note that the nut is of special laminated design, and should only be re-used a maximum of 5 times. It is a good idea to mark the nut with a file every time it is removed. Obtain a new one if necessary.

7 Using a suitable puller, draw the hub and bearing assembly off the stub axle. Note that this procedure renders the bearings unserviceable for future use.

8 Locate the new rear hub and bearing assembly on the stub axle, then refit the hub nut and tighten it to the specified torque.

9 Tap the dust cap fully onto the hub.

10 Refit the rear brake drum, as described in Chapter 9.

11 Refit the rear wheel, and lower the vehicle to the ground.

8.0 Original riveted front suspension lower arm balljoint

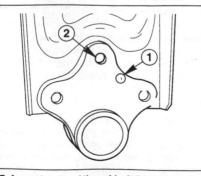

8.5 Location lug (1) and bolt hole (2) in the front suspension lower arm balljoint

10

10.5 Two of the bolts securing the brake backplate to the rear suspension knuckle

11.3 Unclipping the ABS sensor wiring from the strut

10 Rear suspension knuckle (Saloon/Hatchback models) - removal and refitting

Note: *Removal of the rear hub from the knuckle damages the bearings, and renders them unserviceable for future use. The hub and bearing assembly* **must** *always be renewed if it is removed.*

Removal

1 Chock the front wheels, then jack up the rear of the vehicle and support it on axle stands. Remove the appropriate rear wheel.
2 When applicable, remove the ABS sensor from the knuckle as described in Chapter 9.
3 Remove the rear hub and bearing assembly as described in Section 9.
4 Fit a brake hose clamp to the flexible brake hose, then release the clip and detach the flexible hose from the strut. Unscrew the union nut, and detach the rigid brake pipe from the wheel cylinder. If preferred (to eliminate any bleeding procedure during refitting) the rigid brake pipe may remain attached to the wheel cylinder, provided that care is taken to prevent damage to both the rigid and flexible brake pipes.
5 Unbolt the backplate from the rear suspension knuckle **(see illustration)**, and support it to one side on an axle stand. The brake shoes and handbrake cable can remain attached.
6 Unscrew and remove the bolt securing the tie-bar to the bottom of the knuckle, and move the tie-bar downwards.
7 Unscrew and remove the bolts securing the front and rear lower arms to the knuckle, and move the arms to one side.
8 Support the knuckle on an axle stand, then unscrew and remove the clamp bolt securing the knuckle to the strut.
9 Prise the top of the knuckle apart carefully using a large flat-bladed tool, and withdraw the knuckle downwards from the strut. Withdraw the knuckle from under the rear wheel arch.

Refitting

10 Locate the knuckle fully on the strut, then insert the clamp bolt and tighten to the specified torque.
11 Refit the front and rear lower arms to the knuckle, and insert the bolts finger-tight at this stage.
12 Refit the tie-bar to the bottom of the knuckle, and insert the bolt finger-tight at this stage.
13 Refit the backplate to the rear suspension knuckle, and tighten the bolts to the specified torque.
14 Reconnect the rigid brake pipe to the wheel cylinder (if disconnected), and tighten the union nut.
15 Attach the flexible hose to the strut, refit the clip, and remove the hose clamp.
16 Fit a new rear hub and bearing assembly as described in Section 9.
17 Where applicable, refit the ABS sensor as described in Chapter 9.
18 Refit the wheel, and lower the vehicle to the ground.
19 With the weight of the vehicle on the suspension, fully tighten the mounting bolts for the tie-bar and lower arms.
20 Where applicable, bleed the hydraulic brake circuit as described in Chapter 9.

11 Rear suspension strut (Saloon/Hatchback models) - removal and refitting

Note: *Before attempting to remove the rear suspension strut, a tool to hold the coil spring in compression must be obtained. Careful use of conventional coil spring compressors will prove satisfactory.*

Removal

1 In order to remove the rear suspension strut, the coil spring must be temporarily compressed. This will enable the piston rod to be retracted into the strut, and will provide additional room for releasing the strut from the bump stop on top of the rear suspension crossmember.

⚠️ **Warning:** *It is important to only use a high-quality spring compressor; carefully follow the tool manufacturer's instructions provided with it.*

2 Chock the front wheels, then jack up the rear of the vehicle and support it on axle stands. Remove the appropriate wheel.
3 Where fitted, unclip the ABS sensor wiring from the strut, and remove the sensor from the knuckle as described in Chapter 9 **(see illustration)**.
4 Fit a brake hose clamp to the rear flexible brake hose, then unscrew the union nut securing the rigid brake pipe to the flexible hose on the strut. Extract the clip, and disconnect the flexible hose from the strut.
5 Unscrew the nut securing the rear anti-roll bar link to the front lower arm on the appropriate side. Hold the actual link with an adjustable spanner or grips while unscrewing the nut, to prevent damage to the link joint.
6 Unscrew and remove the bolt securing the tie-bar to the bottom of the knuckle. Move the tie-bar downwards **(see illustrations)**.
7 Unscrew and remove the bolts securing the front and rear lower arms to the knuckle, and move the arms to one side **(see illustrations)**.
8 Support the knuckle on a trolley jack, then unscrew and remove the clamp bolt securing the knuckle to the strut **(see illustrations)**.

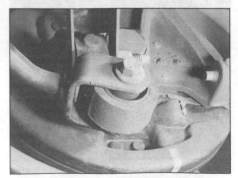

11.6a Tie-bar mounting bolt on knuckle

11.6b Remove the bolt . . .

11.6c . . . and move the tie-bar downwards

11.7a Unscrew the bolt . . .

9 Prise the clamp on the knuckle apart using a large flat-bladed tool. Disconnect the knuckle from the strut, and lower it on the trolley jack as far as possible, taking care not to damage the handbrake cable **(see illustration)**.

10 Fit the coil spring compressor tool (ensuring that it is fully engaged), and compress the coil spring until all tension is relieved from the upper and lower mountings **(see illustration)**. This will also release the bracket on the strut from the bump stop rubber on the top of the rear crossmember.

11 Support the strut, then reach up under the wheel arch, and unscrew the two bolts securing the upper mounting to the underbody **(see illustration)**.

12 Slightly lift the strut, to force the piston into the shock absorber and release the strut bracket from the bump stop on the crossmember. Lower the strut assembly and withdraw it from under the vehicle **(see illustration)**.

Refitting

13 Locate the strut assembly (together with the coil spring compressor tool) under the wheel arch, and locate the bracket on the bump stop on the rear suspension crossmember. Insert the two bolts securing the upper mounting to the underbody tower, and tighten them to the specified torque.

14 Carefully release the coil spring compressor tool, making sure that the spring

11.7b . . . and remove the rear lower arm from the knuckle

11.8a Support the knuckle on a trolley jack . . .

11.8b . . . and remove the knuckle-to-strut clamp bolt

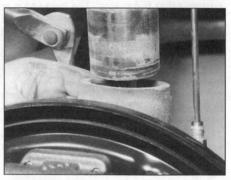

11.9 Separating the knuckle from the strut

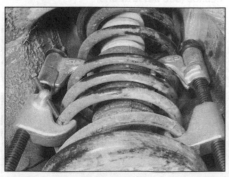

11.10 Compressor tools fitted to the rear coil spring

11.11 Bolts (arrowed) securing the strut upper mounting to the underbody

11.12 Removing the rear suspension strut

10

12.1a Rear strut dismantling - unscrew the upper mounting nut . . .

12.1b . . . remove the cup . . .

12.1c . . . upper mounting bracket and seat . . .

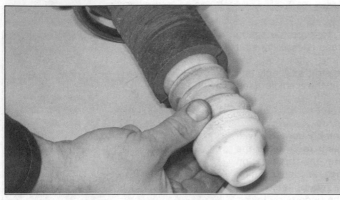

12.1d . . . gaiter and bump stop . . .

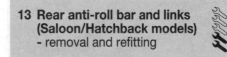
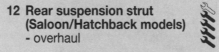

12.1e . . . and coil spring

locates correctly in the upper and lower seats, and that the strut bracket locates on the crossmember bump stop. The bump stop is tapered inwards, and the strut bracket should be fully engaged with it before releasing the coil spring.

15 Raise the knuckle and engage it with the strut, then insert the clamp bolt and tighten to the specified torque.

16 Reconnect the front and rear lower arms to the knuckle, and finger-tighten the bolts at this stage.

17 Reconnect the tie-bar to the bottom of the knuckle, and finger-tighten the bolt at this stage.

18 Refit the anti-roll bar link to the lower arm, and tighten the nut to the specified torque.

19 Connect the flexible hose to the strut, insert the clip, then insert the rigid brake line and tighten the union nut. Remove the brake hose clamp, then bleed the hydraulic brake circuit as described in Chapter 9.

20 Where applicable, refit the ABS sensor as described in Chapter 9, and clip the wiring to the strut.

21 Refit the wheel, and lower the vehicle to the ground.

22 With the weight of the vehicle on the rear suspension, fully tighten the lower arm and tie-bar mounting bolts.

12 Rear suspension strut (Saloon/Hatchback models) - overhaul

1 The procedure is similar to that for the front suspension strut, and reference should be made to Section 5. Note that the spring compressor tools will already be in position on the coil spring following the removal operation. Refer also to the accompanying illustrations for details of the separate components **(see illustrations)**.

13 Rear anti-roll bar and links (Saloon/Hatchback models) - removal and refitting

Removal

1 Chock the front wheels, then jack up the rear of the vehicle and support it on axle stands. Remove both rear wheels.

2 Unscrew the nuts securing the anti-roll bar links to the front lower arms on both sides. Hold the upper part of the links with a spanner while loosening the nuts. Recover the rubber bushes **(see illustrations)**.

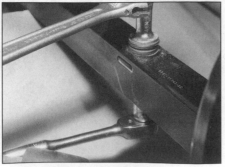

13.2a Loosen the nut . . .

13.2b . . . remove the nut and rubber bush . . .

13.2c . . . and remove the anti-roll bar link from the lower arm

13.3 Rear anti-roll bar mounting clamp

14.9 Bolt securing the rear lower arm to the crossmember

14.11 "TOP" marking on the rear lower arm

3 Unscrew the bolts securing the anti-roll bar mounting clamps to the rear suspension crossmember, then unhook the clamps and withdraw the anti-roll bar from under the vehicle **(see illustration)**.

4 Examine the rubber bushes for the mounting clamps and links, and if necessary renew them. The links are available individually.

Refitting

5 Locate the anti-roll bar on the rear crossmember, hook the mounting clamps in position, and insert the bolts. Tighten the bolts to the specified torque.

6 Locate the anti-roll bar links in the front lower arms on both sides, making sure that the rubber bushes are in position. Refit the nuts and tighten them to the specified torque.

7 Refit the rear wheels, and lower the vehicle to the ground.

14 Rear suspension lower arms (Saloon/Hatchback models) - removal and refitting

Removal

1 Chock the front wheels, then jack up the rear of the vehicle and support it on axle stands. Remove the appropriate rear wheel.

Front lower arm

2 To remove the front lower arm, it is necessary to remove the fuel tank first. Refer to Chapter 4 for details.

3 Unscrew the nut and disconnect the anti-roll bar link from the lower arm. Hold the actual link with an adjustable spanner or grips while unscrewing the nut, to prevent damage to the link joint. Recover the rubber bush.

4 Unscrew and remove the bolt securing the front lower arm to the knuckle.

5 Unscrew and remove the bolt securing the front lower arm to the crossmember.

6 Withdraw the front lower arm from under the vehicle.

Rear lower arm

7 Unscrew and remove the bolt securing the rear lower arm to the knuckle.

8 The bolt securing the rear lower arm to the crossmember has an eccentric head and spacer, which are used to adjust the rear toe setting. Before removing this bolt, mark its position, using a scriber or similar sharp instrument through the aperture in the crossmember.

9 Unscrew and remove the bolt securing the rear lower arm to the crossmember **(see illustration)**. The bolt may be removed through the aperture in the crossmember. Recover the eccentric spacer.

10 Withdraw the rear lower arm from under the vehicle.

Refitting

11 Refitting is a reversal of the removal procedure, but the arm mounting bolts should be finger-tightened initially, and only fully tightened after the vehicle is lowered to the ground, so that its weight is on the rear suspension. Note that the rear lower arm is marked "TOP" for correct refitting **(see illustration)**. The rear toe setting should be checked, and if necessary adjusted, at the earliest opportunity.

15 Rear suspension tie-bar (Saloon/Hatchback models) - removal and refitting

Removal

1 Chock the front wheels, then jack up the rear of the vehicle and support it on axle stands. Remove the appropriate rear wheel.

2 Disconnect the handbrake cable from the tie-bar bracket on the underbody.

3 Unscrew and remove the bolt securing the tie-bar bracket to the rear suspension knuckle.

4 Unscrew the bolts securing the tie-bar bracket to the underbody, and withdraw the bracket from the vehicle **(see illustration)**.

5 Mount the bracket in a vice, then unscrew and remove the bolt, and remove the tie-bar from the bracket.

6 It is not possible to renew the rubber bushes - if they are worn excessively, the tie-bar should be renewed complete.

Refitting

7 Refitting is a reversal of the removal procedure. The bracket-to-underbody bolts should be fully tightened to the specified torque before lowering the vehicle. The bolts securing the tie-bar to the bracket and knuckle should be finger-tightened initially, and only fully tightened after the vehicle is lowered to the ground, so that its weight is on the rear suspension.

16 Rear suspension crossmember (Saloon/Hatchback models) - removal and refitting

Note: *Before attempting to remove the rear suspension crossmember, tools to hold the coil springs in compression must be obtained. Careful use of conventional coil spring compressors will prove satisfactory.*

Removal

1 Chock the front wheels, then jack up the rear of the vehicle and support it on axle stands. Remove both rear wheels.

2 Remove the complete exhaust system as described in Chapter 4.

3 Unscrew and remove the bolts securing the tie-bars to the rear suspension knuckles, and disconnect the tie-bars.

15.4 Tie-bar bracket on the underbody

10

16.8 One of the rear suspension crossmember mounting bolts

4 Unscrew the nuts securing the rear anti-roll bar links to the front lower arms. Hold the actual links stationary while the nuts are being unscrewed, to prevent damage to the joints. Swivel the anti-roll bar upwards, and recover the rubber bushes.

5 Where applicable, remove the ABS wheel sensor from the rear suspension knuckle as described in Chapter 9.

6 Unscrew and remove the bolts, and disconnect both lower arms from the rear suspension knuckle.

7 To allow the rear suspension struts to be released from the rubber stops on the top of the crossmember, it is necessary to fit coil spring compressor tools to both of the rear coil springs, and compress them until all tension is removed from the upper and lower mountings.

⚠️ **Warning: It is important to only use high-quality spring compressors, and to carefully follow the tool manufacturer's instructions provided with them. With the compressor tools fitted, support the struts to one side.**

8 Support the rear suspension crossmember on a trolley jack, then unscrew the four mounting bolts from the underbody **(see illustration)**.

9 Lower the crossmember to the ground.

10 Unscrew the bolts securing the anti-roll bar clamps to the crossmember, then

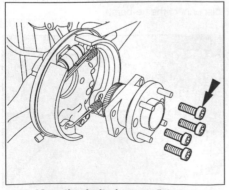

17.6 Mounting bolts (arrowed) for the rear hub on Estate models

remove the clamps and withdraw the anti-roll bar.

11 Remove the lower arms from the crossmember as described in Section 14.

Refitting

12 Refitting is a reversal of the removal procedure. Ford specify the use of a special tool (tool number 15-097) to accurately align the crossmember onto the underbody before tightening the mounting bolts. This tool should be obtained if possible, since inaccurate alignment would result in bad handling and excessive tyre wear. The tie-bar and arm mounting bolts should be finger-tightened initially, and only fully tightened after the vehicle is lowered to the ground, so that its weight is on the rear suspension. The rear toe setting should be checked, and if necessary adjusted, at the earliest opportunity.

17 Rear hub and bearings (Estate models) - inspection and renewal

Inspection

1 The rear hub bearings are non-adjustable, and are supplied complete with the hub. It is not possible to renew the bearings separately from the hub.

2 To check the bearings for excessive wear, chock the front wheels, then jack up the rear of the vehicle and support it on axle stands. Fully release the handbrake.

3 Grip the rear wheel at the top and bottom, and attempt to rock it. If excessive movement is noted, or if there is any roughness or vibration felt when the wheel is spun, it is indicative that the hub bearings are worn.

Renewal

4 Remove the rear wheel.

5 Remove the rear brake drum as described in Chapter 9.

6 Turning the hub as necessary, line up the hole in the flange with the each of the bolts securing the hub assembly to the rear suspension knuckle; unscrew and remove the bolts **(see illustration)**.

7 Withdraw the hub and bearing assembly. Refit two of the hub mounting bolts, to hold the backplate in place.

8 If necessary, the stub shaft may be removed from the hub for inspection of the bearing, by unscrewing the hub nut. Note that the hub nut is of special laminated design, and may only be re-used a maximum of five times. (It is a good idea to file a small notch on the nut every time it is removed; obtain a new nut if necessary.) Tighten the nut on reassembly.

9 Fit the new hub and bearing assembly using a reversal of the removal procedure. Tighten all nuts and bolts to the specified torque.

18 Rear suspension knuckle (Estate models) - removal and refitting

Removal

1 Chock the front wheels, then jack up the rear of the vehicle and support it on axle stands. Remove the appropriate rear wheel, and release the handbrake.

2 Position a trolley jack or axle stand beneath the rear suspension lower arm, to keep the coil spring in compression.

3 Where applicable, remove the ABS sensor as described in Chapter 9.

4 Remove the rear brake drum as described in Chapter 9.

5 Disconnect the flexible hydraulic brake hose at the bracket on the rear suspension crossmember as described in Chapter 9.

All models

6 Remove the rear hub as described in Section 17.

7 Remove the backplate, support the backplate assembly on an axle stand, to prevent damage to the handbrake cable.

8 Unscrew and remove the shock absorber lower mounting bolt.

9 Unscrew and remove the three bolts securing the tie-bar to the knuckle.

10 Unscrew and remove the bolt securing the front lower arm to the knuckle.

11 Unscrew and remove the bolt securing the upper arm to the knuckle.

12 Support the knuckle, then unscrew and remove the bolt securing the rear lower arm to the knuckle, and withdraw the knuckle.

Refitting

14 Refitting is a reversal of the removal procedure, but delay fully tightening the rubber bush mounting bolts until the weight of the vehicle is on the suspension. Tighten all bolts to the specified torque. Where the flexible rear brake hose was disconnected, bleed the hydraulic system as described in Chapter 9. Finally check, and if necessary adjust, the rear wheel toe setting as described in Section 36.

19 Rear shock absorber (Estate models) - removal, testing and refitting

Removal

1 Chock the front wheels, then jack up the rear of the vehicle and support it on axle stands. Remove the appropriate wheel.

2 Position a trolley jack under the coil spring area of the rear lower suspension arm, to keep the coil spring in compression.

3 Unscrew and remove the shock absorber lower mounting bolt **(see illustration)**.
4 Unscrew and remove the upper mounting bolt, and withdraw the shock absorber from under the vehicle.

Testing

5 Check the mounting rubbers for damage and deterioration. If they are worn, they may be renewed separately from the shock absorber body.
6 Mount the shock absorber in a vice, gripping it by the lower mounting. Examine the shock absorber for signs of fluid leakage. Test the operation of the shock absorber by moving it through a full stroke, and then through short strokes of 50 to 100 mm. In both cases, the resistance felt should be smooth and continuous. If the resistance is jerky or uneven, the shock absorber should be renewed.

Refitting

7 Refitting is a reversal of the removal procedure, but tighten the mounting bolts to the specified torque.

20 Rear anti-roll bar and links (Estate models) - removal and refitting

Removal

1 Chock the front wheels, then jack up the rear of the vehicle and support it on axle stands. Remove both rear wheels.
2 Unscrew the nuts, and remove the washers and bushes securing the anti-roll bar links to the rear lower arms **(see illustrations)**.
3 Using a Torx key, unscrew the bolts securing the anti-roll bar mounting clamps to the rear suspension crossmember; release the clamps, and withdraw the anti-roll bar from under the vehicle **(see illustration)**.
4 Examine the rubber bushes for the mounting clamps and links, and if necessary

19.3 Rear shock absorber lower mounting bolt (Estate)

renew them. The links are available individually.

Refitting

5 Locate the anti-roll bar on the rear crossmember, then refit the clamps and tighten the bolts to the specified torque.
6 Refit the anti-roll bar links to the rear lower arms, together with the bushes and washers. Tighten the nuts to the specified torque, while holding the actual links stationary in their central position.
7 Refit the rear wheels, and lower the vehicle to the ground.

21 Rear coil spring (Estate models) - removal and refitting

Note: *Before attempting to remove the rear suspension coil spring, a tool to hold the coil spring in compression must be obtained. Careful use of conventional coil spring compressors will prove satisfactory.*

Removal

1 Chock the front wheels, then jack up the rear of the vehicle and support it on axle stands. Remove the appropriate wheel.
2 Support the weight of the rear lower arm beneath the coil spring position with a trolley jack.

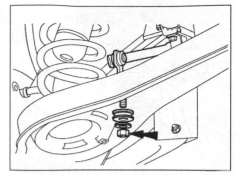

20.2a Mounting nut (arrowed) and rubber bush securing the rear anti-roll bar link to the rear lower arm

20.2b View of the anti-roll bar link nut through the rear lower arm

3 Fit the coil spring compressor tool (ensuring that it is fully engaged), and compress the coil spring until all tension is relieved from the upper mounting.
4 Unscrew the nut, and remove the washer and bush attaching the anti-roll bar link to the rear lower arm.
5 Unscrew and remove the bolt securing the rear lower arm to the knuckle **(see illustration)**.
6 Unscrew and remove the bolt securing the front lower arm to the knuckle **(see illustration)**.
7 Lower the rear lower arm, and withdraw the coil spring from under the vehicle. Take care to keep the compressor tool in full

20.3 Anti-roll bar mounting clamp on the rear suspension crossmember

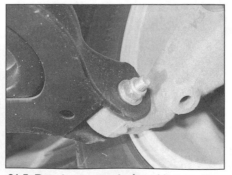

21.5 Rear lower arm-to-knuckle mounting bolt

21.6 Front lower arm-to-knuckle mounting bolt

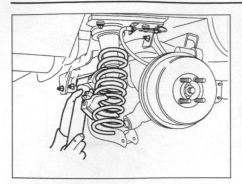

21.7 Removing the coil spring, with compressor tool attached, from under the vehicle

21.9 Correct location of the coil spring in the upper seat (arrowed)

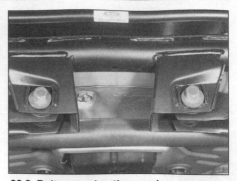

22.3 Bolts securing the rear lower arms to the crossmember - note the eccentric spacers

engagement with the coil spring **(see illustration)**.

8 If a new coil spring is to be fitted, the original coil spring must be released from the compressor. If it is to be re-used, the coil spring can be left in compression.

Refitting

9 Refitting is a reversal of the removal procedure, but make sure that the coil spring is located correctly in the upper and lower seats **(see illustration)**. Delay fully tightening the two lower arm mounting bolts until the weight of the vehicle is on the rear suspension. Finally check, and if necessary adjust, the rear wheel toe setting as described in Section 36.

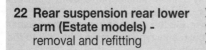

22 Rear suspension rear lower arm (Estate models) - removal and refitting

Removal

1 Remove the rear suspension coil spring as described in Section 21.

2 The bolt securing the rear lower arm to the crossmember has an eccentric head and spacer, which are used to adjust the rear toe setting. Before removing this bolt, mark its position, using a scriber or similar sharp

instrument through the aperture in the crossmember.

3 Unscrew and remove the bolt securing the rear lower arm to the crossmember. The bolt may be removed through the aperture in the crossmember. Recover the eccentric spacer **(see illustration)**.

4 Withdraw the rear lower arm from under the vehicle.

Refitting

5 Refitting is a reversal of the removal procedure, but delay fully tightening the lower arm mounting bolts until the weight of the vehicle is on the rear suspension. Finally check, and if necessary adjust, the rear wheel toe setting as described in Section 36.

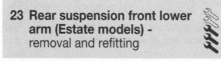

23 Rear suspension front lower arm (Estate models) - removal and refitting

Removal

1 Chock the front wheels, then jack up the rear of the vehicle and support it on axle stands. Remove the appropriate wheel.

2 Unscrew and remove the bolt securing the front lower arm to the crossmember **(see illustration)**.

3 Unscrew and remove the bolt securing the front lower arm to the knuckle, and withdraw

the arm from under the vehicle **(see illustration)**.

Refitting

4 Refitting is a reversal of the removal procedure, but delay fully tightening the mounting bolts until the weight of the vehicle is on the rear suspension.

24 Rear suspension upper arm (Estate models) - removal and refitting

Removal

1 Chock the front wheels, then jack up the rear of the vehicle and support it on axle stands. Remove the appropriate wheel.

2 Using a trolley jack, support the rear lower arm beneath the coil spring position.

3 Unscrew and remove the bolt securing the upper arm to the knuckle **(see illustration)**.

4 Unscrew and remove the bolt securing the upper arm to the crossmember, and withdraw the arm from under the vehicle.

Refitting

5 Refitting is a reversal of the removal procedure, but delay fully tightening the mounting bolts until the weight of the vehicle is on the rear suspension.

23.2 Front lower arm-to-crossmember securing bolt

23.3 Front lower arm (arrowed)

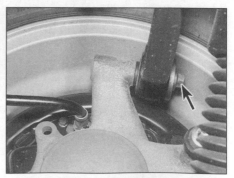

24.3 Bolt (arrowed) securing the upper arm to the knuckle

25.7 Bolts (arrowed) securing the rear suspension tie-bar to the knuckle

25.8a Tie-bar bracket front bolt (arrowed) on the underbody

25.8b Tie-bar bracket rear bolt (arrowed) on the underbody

25 Rear suspension tie-bar (Estate models) - removal and refitting

Removal

1 Chock the front wheels, then jack up the rear of the vehicle and support it on axle stands. Remove the appropriate wheel.
2 Using a trolley jack, support the rear lower arm beneath the coil spring position.
3 Unscrew and remove the bolt securing the rear shock absorber to the knuckle.
4 Where applicable, release the ABS wheel sensor lead from the tie-bar.
5 Detach the handbrake cable from the tie-bar bracket.
6 Refer to Chapter 9, and disconnect the handbrake cable from the rear brake shoes. Pass the cable through the hole in the tie-bar.
7 Unscrew and remove the three bolts securing the tie-bar to the knuckle **(see illustration)**.
8 Unbolt the tie-bar bracket from the underbody, and withdraw the assembly from under the vehicle **(see illustrations)**.
9 Mount the tie-bar in a vice, then unscrew the bolt, and separate the tie-bar from its bracket.
10 It is not possible to renew the rubber bush in the tie-bar, and if it is excessively worn, the complete tie-bar must be renewed.

Refitting

11 Refitting is a reversal of the removal procedure, but delay fully tightening the bolt which secures the arm to the bracket until the weight of the vehicle is on the rear suspension. On completion, check the operation of the handbrake.

26 Rear suspension crossmember (Estate models) - removal and refitting

Removal

1 Chock the front wheels, then jack up the rear of the vehicle and support on axles stands. Remove both rear wheels. Make sure that the vehicle is supported high enough for the crossmember to be removed.
2 Disconnect the handbrake rear cables from the front primary cable, as described in Chapter 9.
3 Where applicable, remove the ABS wheel sensors from the rear knuckles, and disconnect the wiring leads from the clips as described in Chapter 9.
4 Disconnect the flexible brake hoses from the brackets on both sides of the crossmember, as described in Chapter 9.
5 Working on each side of the vehicle, unbolt the tie-bar brackets from the underbody.
6 Support the rear suspension crossmember on a trolley jack.

7 Unscrew the mounting bolts, and lower the crossmember to the ground **(see illustrations)**.
8 If necessary, remove the suspension components from the crossmember as described in the appropriate Sections of this Chapter.

Refitting

9 Refitting is a reversal of the removal procedure, noting the following points:
(a) When raising the crossmember, note that guide pins are provided to ensure correct alignment **(see illustration)**.
(b) Delay fully tightening the suspension mounting bolts until the weight of the vehicle is on the rear suspension.
(c) Tighten all bolts to the specified torque.
(d) Bleed the brake hydraulic system as described in Chapter 9.
(e) Check, and if necessary adjust, the rear wheel toe setting as described in Section 36.

27 Steering wheel - removal and refitting

 Warning: All models are equipped with an air bag system. Make sure that the safety recommendations given in Chapter 12 are followed, to prevent personal injury.

26.7a Rear suspension crossmember rear mounting bolt

26.7b Rear suspension crossmember front mounting bolt

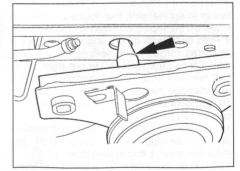

26.9 Guide pin (arrowed) for correct alignment of the rear crossmember

10

27.6 Removing the steering wheel retaining bolt

27.7 Feeding the horn and air bag wiring through the hole in the steering wheel hub

27.9 Tightening the steering wheel retaining bolt

Removal

1 Disconnect the battery negative (earth) lead (refer to Chapter 5, Section 1).

 Warning: Before proceeding, wait a minimum of 15 minutes, as a precaution against accidental firing of the air bag unit. This period ensures that any stored energy in the back-up capacitor is dissipated.

2 Turn the steering wheel so that the front wheels are in the straight-ahead position.
3 Unscrew the screws, and remove the steering column upper and lower shrouds.
4 From the rear of the steering wheel, unscrew the air bag module mounting screws.
5 Carefully lift the module from the steering wheel, and disconnect the air bag multi-plug and horn wiring connections.

 Warning: Position the air bag module in a safe place, with the mechanism facing downwards as a precaution against accidental operation.

6 Make sure that the steering lock is not engaged. Unscrew the retaining bolt from the centre of the steering wheel **(see illustration)**.
7 Remove the steering wheel from the top of the column, while feeding the horn and air bag wiring through the hole in the steering wheel hub **(see illustration)**.

Refitting

8 Make sure that the front wheels are still facing straight-ahead, then locate the steering wheel on the top of the steering column.
9 Refit the retaining bolt, and tighten it to the specified torque while holding the steering wheel **(see illustration)**. Do not tighten the bolt with the steering lock engaged, as this may damage the lock.
10 Reconnect the horn wiring connections and air bag multi-plug.
11 Locate the air bag module/horn contact on the steering wheel, then insert the mounting screws and tighten them.
12 Refit the steering column upper and lower shrouds. Insert and tighten the screws.
13 Reconnect the battery negative lead.

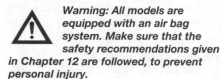

28 Steering column - removal, inspection and refitting

 Warning: All models are equipped with an air bag system. Make sure that the safety recommendations given in Chapter 12 are followed, to prevent personal injury.

Removal

1 Disconnect the battery negative (earth) lead (refer to Chapter 5, Section 1).

⚠ *Warning: Before proceeding, wait a minimum of 15 minutes, as a precaution against*

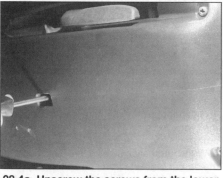

28.4a Unscrew the screws from the lower shroud . . .

28.4c . . . and remove the lower shroud

accidental firing of the air bag unit. This period ensures that any stored energy in the back-up capacitor is dissipated.

2 Turn the steering wheel so that the front wheels are in the straight-ahead position.
3 Remove the ignition key, then turn the steering wheel slightly as necessary until the steering lock engages.
4 Unscrew the screws, and remove the steering column lower and upper shrouds. As the lower shroud is being removed, it will be necessary to remove the rubber ring from the ignition switch/steering lock **(see illustrations)**.
5 Remove the driver's side lower facia panel (see Chapter 11).
6 Unscrew the clamp plate bolt securing the steering column shaft to the flexible coupling. Swivel the clamp plate around, and disengage

28.4b . . . remove the rubber ring . . .

28.4d Upper shroud retaining screws (arrowed)

28.4e Removing the upper shroud

28.6a Unscrew the clamp plate bolt . . .

28.6b . . . and swivel the clamp plate around

it from the flexible coupling stub **(see illustrations)**.

7 Release the cable tie from the wiring loom at the steering column, and disconnect the multi-plugs **(see illustrations)**.

8 Unscrew and remove the steering column mounting bolts, then slide the column upwards to disengage the retaining tab from the groove in the cross-beam bracket, and withdraw it from inside the vehicle **(see illustrations)**.

Inspection

9 With the steering column removed, check the universal joints for wear, and examine the column upper and lower shafts for any signs of damage or distortion **(see illustration)**.

Where evident, the column should be renewed complete.

10 Examine the height adjustment lever mechanism for wear and damage **(see illustration)**.

11 With the steering lock disengaged, turn the inner column, and check the upper and lower bearings for smooth operation. The bearings are obtainable separately, and should be renewed if necessary. Dismantling and reassembly of the column assembly is a relatively easy operation.

Refitting

12 Locate the steering column on its bracket, making sure that the tab slides down into the groove correctly.

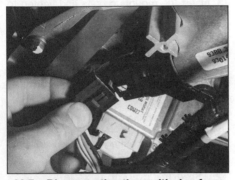

28.7a Disconnecting the multi-plug from the ignition switch

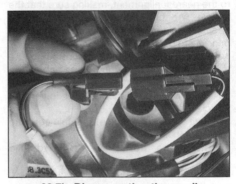

28.7b Disconnecting the small multi-plug . . .

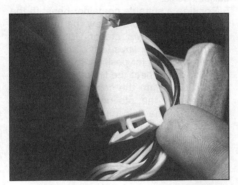

28.7c . . . and main multi-plug from the steering column

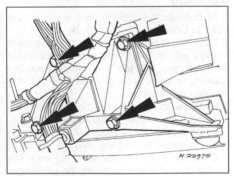

28.8a Steering column mounting bolt locations (arrowed)

28.8b Removing the steering column

28.9 Steering column and universal joint

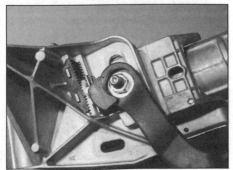

28.10 Height adjustment lever mechanism

10

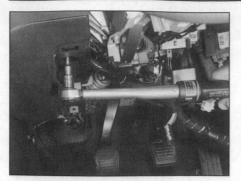

28.13 Tightening the steering column mounting bolts

13 Insert the mounting bolts and tighten to the specified torque **(see illustration)**.
14 Reconnect the multi-plugs, and secure the wiring loom with the cable tie.
15 Locate the steering column shaft on the flexible coupling, swivel the clamp plate round, then insert the bolt and tighten to the specified torque.
16 Refit the driver's side lower trim panel.
17 Refit the steering column upper and lower shrouds.
18 Reconnect the battery negative lead.

29 Steering column flexible coupling - removal and refitting

Removal

1 Disconnect the battery negative (earth) lead (refer to Chapter 5, Section 1).
2 Turn the steering wheel so that the front wheels are in the straight-ahead position. Remove the ignition key, then turn the steering wheel slightly as necessary until the steering lock engages.
3 Unscrew the clamp plate bolt securing the steering column shaft to the flexible coupling. Swivel the clamp plate around, and disengage it from the flexible coupling stub.
4 Carefully prise the rubber boot from the bulkhead, and withdraw it into the passenger compartment. Take care not to damage the sealing lip of the boot.

5 Using an Allen key, unscrew the clamp bolt securing the flexible coupling to the pinion shaft on the steering gear, and withdraw the coupling from inside the vehicle.

Refitting

6 Refitting is a reversal of the removal procedure, but tighten the clamp bolts to the specified torque. Make sure that the rubber boot engages correctly in the bulkhead and on the flexible coupling.

30 Power steering gear (all except left-hand-drive models with ABS) - removal and refitting

Removal

1 Remove the steering column flexible coupling as described in Section 29.
2 Apply the handbrake, then jack up the front of the vehicle and support it on axle stands. Remove both front wheels.
3 Working beneath the vehicle, unbolt the rear engine mounting from the transmission and underbody.
4 Extract the split pins from the track rod end balljoint nuts, then unscrew the nuts, and detach the rods from the arms on the steering knuckles using a conventional balljoint removal tool. Take care not to damage the balljoint seals.
5 Position a suitable container beneath the steering gear, then unscrew the union nuts securing the power steering fluid supply, return, and cooler lines to the steering gear. Identify the lines for position, then unbolt the clamps, disconnect the lines, and allow the fluid to drain into the container. Cover the apertures in the steering gear and also the ends of the fluid pipes, to prevent the ingress of dust and dirt into the hydraulic circuit.
6 Unscrew and remove the steering gear mounting bolts. The bolts are located on top of the steering gear, and are difficult to reach. Ideally, the special U-shaped Ford spanner should be used, but it is just possible to

reach them with a normal spanner **(see illustration)**.
7 Withdraw the steering gear through the wheel arch.

Refitting

8 If the steering gear is being replaced with a new one, the new unit will be supplied together with union nuts already fitted. The new nuts must only be used with new feed and return lines - otherwise, they must be removed and discarded. If the original lines and union nuts are being used, the Teflon rings on the union nuts must be renewed. To do this, the rings must be expanded individually onto a fitting adaptor **(see illustration)**, then located in the grooves of the union nuts.
9 Locate the steering gear on the subframe, and insert the two mounting bolts. Tighten the bolts to the specified torque **(see illustration)**. Note that, if the special Ford tool is being used, the bottom of the tool must be turned anti-clockwise in order to tighten the mounting bolts.
10 Remove the covers from the apertures on the steering gear, then reconnect the fluid lines and tighten the union nuts to the specified torque. Refit the clamps and tighten the bolts.
11 Refit the track rod end balljoints to the steering knuckles, and tighten the nuts to the specified torque. Check that the split pin holes are aligned; if necessary, turn the nuts to the nearest alignment, making sure that the torque wrench setting is still within the specified range. Insert new split pins, and bend them back to secure.
12 Refit the rear engine mounting to the transmission and underbody, and tighten the bolts to the specified torque.
13 Refit the front wheels, and lower the vehicle to the ground.
14 Refit the steering column flexible coupling with reference to Section 29.
15 Bleed the power steering hydraulic system as described in Section 33.
16 Have the front wheel alignment checked, and if necessary adjusted, at the earliest opportunity (refer to Section 36).

30.6 U-shaped Ford spanner for unscrewing the steering gear mounting bolts

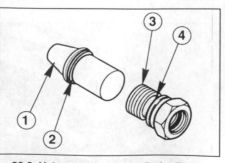

30.8 Using an adaptor to fit the Teflon rings to the union nuts

1 Adaptor   2 Teflon ring   3 Union nut
4 Groove location for the Teflon ring

30.9 Tightening the steering gear mounting bolts using the U-shaped spanner (arrowed)

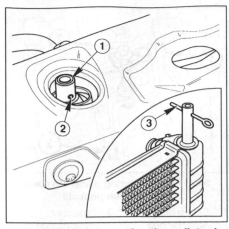

31.7 Method of supporting the radiator in its raised position

1 Radiator upper mounting extension
2 Small hole
3 Pin or split pin inserted through hole

31 Power steering gear (left-hand-drive models with ABS) - removal and refitting

Removal

1 Disconnect the battery negative (earth) lead (refer to Chapter 5, Section 1).
2 Working inside the vehicle, unscrew the clamp plate bolt securing the steering column shaft to the flexible coupling. Swivel the clamp plate around, and disengage it from the flexible coupling stub.
3 Apply the handbrake, then jack up the front of the vehicle and support it on axle stands. Remove both wheels.
4 Disconnect the gearchange linkage and support rods from the transmission, as described in Chapter 7.
5 Remove the exhaust downpipe complete, as described in Chapter 4.
6 Remove the cover from under the radiator by unscrewing the screws and releasing the clips.
7 Support the radiator in its raised position, by inserting split pins through the small holes in the radiator mounting extensions which protrude through the upper mountings **(see illustration)**.
8 Unbolt and remove the radiator lower mounting brackets.
9 Where applicable, unscrew the bolts securing the air conditioning accumulator to the subframe.
10 Working beneath the vehicle, unbolt the engine rear mounting from the transmission and underbody
11 Unscrew the front engine mounting-to-cylinder block bolts, and also the through-bolt.
12 Extract the split pins from the track rod end balljoint nuts, then unscrew the nuts, and detach the rods from the arms on the steering

knuckles using a conventional balljoint removal tool. Take care not to damage the balljoint seals.
13 Working on each side in turn, unscrew the mounting nuts, and remove the anti-roll bar links from the front suspension struts. Note that, on models fitted with ABS, the ABS sensor wiring support brackets are located beneath the nuts.
14 Working on each side in turn, note which way round the front suspension lower arm balljoint clamp bolt is fitted, then unscrew and remove it from the knuckle assembly. Lever the balljoint down from the knuckle - if it is tight, prise the joint open carefully using a large flat-bladed tool. Take care not to damage the balljoint seal during the separation procedure.
15 Support the weight of the front subframe assembly on two trolley jacks (or two scissor jacks).
16 Unscrew and remove the subframe mounting bolts, then lower the subframe sufficiently to gain access to the power steering fluid pipes on top of the steering gear. Note that the front subframe mounting bolts are gold in colour - the rear ones are silver.
17 Position a suitable container beneath the steering gear, then unscrew the union nuts securing the power steering fluid supply, return, and cooler lines to the steering gear. Identify the lines for position, then unbolt the clamps, disconnect the lines, and allow the fluid to drain into the container. Cover the apertures in the steering gear and also the ends of the fluid pipes, to prevent the ingress of dust and dirt into the hydraulic circuit.
18 Lower the subframe, together with the power steering gear, to the ground.
19 Unscrew the mounting bolts and remove the power steering gear from the subframe.
20 Using a suitable Allen key, unscrew the clamp bolt securing the flexible coupling to the pinion shaft on the steering gear, and withdraw the coupling.
21 Refer to Section 30, paragraph 8 for details of renewing the Teflon rings.

Refitting

22 Refit the flexible coupling to the pinion shaft on the steering gear, then insert and tighten the clamp bolt using an Allen key.
23 Locate the power steering gear on the subframe, then insert the mounting bolts and tighten to the specified torque.
24 Raise the subframe until it is possible to refit the fluid lines. Tighten the union nuts and clamps.
25 Raise the subframe, making sure that the alignment holes are in line with the holes in the underbody. At the same time, make sure that the flexible coupling locates correctly on the steering column. Ford technicians use a special tool to ensure that the subframe is correctly aligned - refer to Chapter 2, Section 10 for more details of the alignment

procedure. With the subframe aligned, insert and tighten the mounting bolts to the specified torque. Note that the front mounting bolts are gold in colour - the rear bolts are silver.
26 Working on each side in turn, refit the front suspension lower arm balljoint to the knuckle assembly, and insert the clamp bolt with its head facing forwards. Refit the nut and tighten to the specified torque.
27 Working on each side in turn, refit the anti-roll bar links and tighten the mounting nuts to the specified torque. On models fitted with ABS, don't forget to locate the wheel sensor wiring support brackets beneath the nuts.
28 Refit the track rod end balljoints to the steering knuckles, and tighten the nuts to the specified torque. Check if the split pin holes are aligned, and if necessary turn the nuts to the nearest alignment, making sure that the torque wrench setting is still within the specified range. Insert new split pins, and bend them back to secure.
29 Refit and tighten the engine front mounting bolts.
30 Refit the engine rear mounting and tighten the bolts.
31 Where applicable, insert and tighten the air conditioning accumulator bolts.
32 Refit the radiator lower mounting brackets and tighten the bolts.
33 Remove the split pins supporting the radiator in its raised position.
34 Refit the cover under the radiator.
35 Refit the exhaust downpipe as described in Chapter 4.
36 Reconnect the gearchange linkage and support rods.
37 Refit the front wheels, and lower the vehicle to the ground.
38 Working inside the vehicle, reconnect the steering column clamp plate, then insert the bolt and tighten to the specified torque.
39 Reconnect the battery negative lead.
40 Bleed the power steering hydraulic system as described in Section 33.
41 Have the front wheel alignment checked, and if necessary adjusted, at the earliest opportunity (refer to Section 36).

32 Power steering gear rubber gaiters - renewal

1 Remove the track rod end and its locknut from the track rod, as described in Section 35. Make sure that a note is made of the exact position of the track rod end on the track rod, in order to retain the front wheel alignment setting on refitting.
2 Release the outer retaining clip and inner plastic clamp band, and disconnect the gaiter from the steering gear housing.
3 Disconnect the breather from the gaiter, then slide the gaiter off the track rod.

10

34.1a Removing the power steering pump drivebelt cover

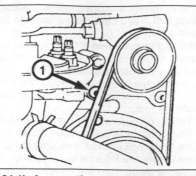

34.1b Loosen the power steering pump mounting bolt (arrowed)

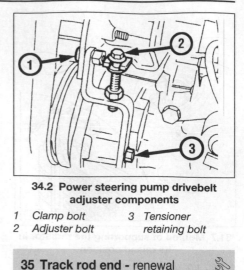

34.2 Power steering pump drivebelt adjuster components

1 Clamp bolt	3 Tensioner
2 Adjuster bolt	retaining bolt

4 Scrape off all grease from the old gaiter, and apply to the track rod inner joint. Wipe clean the seating areas on the steering gear housing and track rod.

5 Slide the new gaiter onto the track rod and steering gear housing, and reconnect the breather.

6 Fit a new inner plastic clamp band and outer retaining clip.

7 Refit the track rod end as described in Section 35.

8 Have the front wheel alignment checked, and if necessary adjusted, at the earliest opportunity (refer to Section 36).

33 Power steering hydraulic system - bleeding

1 Following any operation in which the power steering fluid lines have been disconnected, the power steering system must be bled, to remove any trapped air.

2 With the front wheels in the straight-ahead position, check the power steering fluid level in the reservoir and, if low, add fresh fluid until it reaches the "MAX" or "MAX COLD" mark. Pour the fluid slowly, to prevent air bubbles forming, and use only the specified fluid (refer to Chapter 1 Specifications).

3 Start the engine, and allow it to run at a fast idle. Check the hoses and connections for leaks.

4 Stop the engine, and recheck the fluid level. Add more if necessary, up to the "MAX" or "MAX COLD" mark.

5 Start the engine again, allow it to idle, then bleed the system by slowly turning the steering wheel from side to side several times. This should purge the system of all internal air. However, if air remains in the system (indicated by the steering operation being very noisy), leave the vehicle overnight, and repeat the procedure again the next day.

6 If air still remains in the system, it may be necessary to resort to the Ford method of bleeding, which uses a vacuum pump. Turn the steering to the right until it is near the stop, then fit the vacuum pump to the fluid reservoir, and apply 0.15 bar of vacuum.

Maintain the vacuum for a minimum of 5 minutes, then repeat the procedure with the steering turned to the left.

7 Keep the fluid level topped-up throughout the bleeding procedure; note that, as the fluid temperature increases, the level will rise.

8 On completion, switch off the engine, and return the front wheels to the straight-ahead position.

34 Power steering pump - removal and refitting

Removal

1 Remove the two bolts retaining the cover of the power steering pump drivebelt. Remove the cover and loosen the pump mounting bolt **(see illustrations)**.

2 Loosen the power steering pump clamp bolt. Rotate the adjuster screw to detension the drivebelt and remove the tensioner from the front cover **(see illustration)**.

3 Remove the pump drivebelt

4 Disconnect the fluid pressure and return hoses from the pump and allow the fluid to drain into a suitable container. Plug or cap hoses and unions to keep dirt out.

5 Remove the pump mounting bolt and lift the pump clear of the engine.

Refitting

6 Refitting is the reverse of the removal procedure, noting the following points:
a) Tighten all fasteners to the torque wrench settings specified
b) Remove the plugs when reconnecting the hoses, ensure no dirt is allowed to enter the system and check that both hoses are correctly routed, well clear of any adjacent components
c) Refit and adjust the alternator/pump drivebelt
d) Refill the system with the specified type of fluid, then bleed any air from it as described in the following sub Section

7 Bleeding the power steering hydraulic system as described in Section 33.

35 Track rod end - renewal

1 Apply the handbrake, then jack up the front of the vehicle and support it on axle stands. Remove the appropriate front roadwheel.

2 Using a suitable spanner, slacken the locknut on the track rod by a quarter-turn. Hold the track rod end stationary with another spanner engaged with the special flats while loosening the locknut.

3 Extract the split pin, then unscrew and remove the track rod end balljoint retaining nut.

4 To release the tapered shank of the balljoint from the steering knuckle arm, use a balljoint separator tool (if the balljoint is to be re-used, take care not to damage the dust cover when using the separator tool) **(see illustration)**.

5 Count the number of exposed threads visible on the inner section of the track rod, and record this figure.

6 Unscrew the track rod end from the track rod, counting the number of turns necessary to remove it. If necessary, hold the track rod stationary with grips.

Refitting

7 Screw the track rod end onto the track rod by the number of turns noted during removal, until it just contacts the locknut.

35.4 Using a balljoint separator tool to release the track rod end balljoint

8 Engage the shank of the balljoint with the steering knuckle arm, and refit the nut. Tighten the nut to the specified torque. If the balljoint shank turns while the nut is being tightened, press down on the balljoint. The tapered fit of the shank will lock it, and prevent rotation as the nut is tightened.

9 Check that the split pin holes in the nut and balljoint shank are aligned. If necessary turn the nut to the nearest alignment, making sure that the torque wrench setting is still within the specified range. Insert a new split pin, and bend it back to secure.

10 Now tighten the locknut, while holding the track rod end as before.

11 Refit the roadwheel, and lower the vehicle to the ground.

12 Finally check, and if necessary adjust, the front wheel alignment as described in Section 36.

36 Wheel alignment and steering angles - general information

1 Accurate front wheel alignment is essential to provide positive steering, and to prevent excessive tyre wear. Before considering the steering/suspension geometry, check that the tyres are correctly inflated, that the front wheels are not buckled, and that the steering linkage and suspension joints are in good order, without slackness or wear.

2 Wheel alignment consists of four factors **(see illustration)**:

Camber is the angle at which the front wheels are set from the vertical, when viewed from the front of the vehicle. "Positive camber" is the amount (in degrees) that the wheels are tilted outward at the top of the vertical. *Castor* is the angle between the steering axis and a vertical line, when viewed from each side of the car. "Positive castor" is when the steering axis is inclined rearward at the top.

Steering axis inclination is the angle (when viewed from the front of the vehicle) between the vertical and an imaginary line drawn through the suspension strut upper mounting and the lower suspension arm balljoint.

Toe setting is the amount by which the distance between the front inside edges of the roadwheels (measured at hub height) differs from the diametrically-opposite distance measured between the rear inside edges of the front roadwheels.

3 With the exception of the toe setting, all other steering angles are set during manufacture, and no adjustment is possible. It can be assumed, therefore, that unless the vehicle has suffered accident damage, all the preset steering angles will be correct. Should there be some doubt about their accuracy, it will be necessary to seek the help of a Ford dealer, as special gauges are needed to check the steering angles.

4 Two methods are available to the home mechanic for checking the toe setting. One method is to use a gauge to measure the distance between the front and rear inside edges of the roadwheels. The other method is to use a scuff plate, in which each front wheel is rolled across a movable plate which records any deviation, or scuff, of the tyre from the straight-ahead position as it moves across the plate. Relatively-inexpensive equipment of both types is available from accessory outlets.

5 If, after checking the toe setting using whichever method is preferable, it is found that adjustment is necessary, proceed as follows.

6 Turn the steering wheel onto full-left lock, and record the number of exposed threads on the right-hand track rod. Now turn the steering onto full-right lock, and record the number of threads on the left-hand track rod. If there are the same number of threads visible on both sides, then subsequent adjustment can be made equally on both sides. If there are more threads visible on one side than the other, it will be necessary to compensate for this during adjustment. *After adjustment, there must be the same number of threads visible on each track rod. This is most important.*

7 To alter the toe setting, slacken the locknut on the track rod, and turn the track rod using self-locking pliers to achieve the desired setting. When viewed from the side of the car, turning the rod clockwise will increase the toe-in, turning it anti-clockwise will increase the toe-out. Only turn the track rods by a quarter of a turn each time, and then recheck the setting.

8 After adjustment, tighten the locknuts. Reposition the steering gear rubber gaiters, to remove any twist caused by turning the track rods.

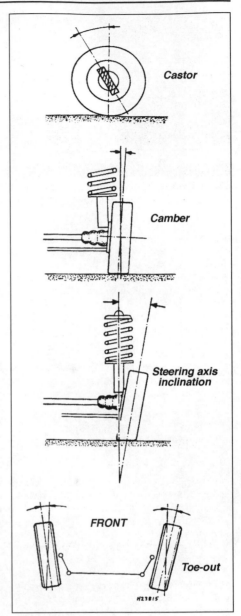

Castor

Camber

Steering axis inclination

FRONT

Toe-out

H21815

36.2 Wheel alignment and steering angles

9 The rear wheel toe-setting may also be checked and adjusted, but as this additionally requires alignment with the front wheels, it should be left to a Ford garage or specialist having the special equipment required.

10

Notes

Chapter 11 Bodywork and fittings

Contents

Degrees of difficulty

Easy, suitable for novice with little experience	**Fairly easy,** suitable for beginner with some experience	**Fairly difficult,** suitable for competent DIY mechanic	**Difficult,** suitable for experienced DIY mechanic	**Very difficult,** suitable for expert DIY or professional

Specifications

Torque wrench settings	Nm	lbf ft
Bonnet and tailgate hinges	24	18
Boot lid	10	7
Front seat mounting bolts	38	28
Seat belt mounting nuts and bolts	38	28
Bumper mounting nuts	10	7

1 General information

The bodyshell and underframe on all models is of all-steel welded construction, incorporating progressive crumple zones at the front and rear, and a rigid centre safety cell. The bulkhead behind the engine compartment incorporates crash grooves which determine its energy-absorption characteristics, and special beams to prevent the intrusion of the front wheels into the passenger compartment during a serious accident. All passenger doors incorporate side impact bars.

All sheet metal surfaces which are prone to corrosion are galvanized. The painting process includes a base colour which closely matches the final topcoat, so that any stone damage is not noticeable.

Hatchback, Saloon and Estate versions are available. The front section of the vehicle up to the "B" pillar is identical on all models.

Automatic seat belts are fitted to all models, and the front seat belt stalks are mounted on automatic tensioners (also known as "grabbers") (see illustration). In the event of a serious front impact, a spring mass sensor releases a coil spring which pulls the stalk buckle downwards and tensions the seat belt. It is not possible to reset the tensioner once fired, and it must therefore be renewed.

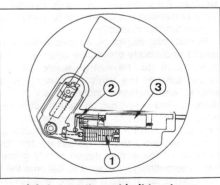

1.4 Automatic seat belt tensioner

1 Coil spring   *3 Spring mass sensor*
2 Lever system

11

In the UK, central locking is standard on all models **(see illustration)**. In other countries, it is available on certain models only. Where double-locking is fitted, the lock mechanism is disconnected (when the system is in use) from the interior door handles, making it impossible to open any of the doors or the tailgate/bootlid from inside the vehicle. This means that, even if a thief should break a side window, he will not be able to open the door using the interior handle. Models with the double-locking system are fitted with a control module located beneath the facia on the right-hand side. In the event of a serious accident, a crash sensor unlocks all doors if they were previously locked.

Many of the procedures in this Chapter require the battery to be disconnected. Refer to Chapter 5, Section 1 first.

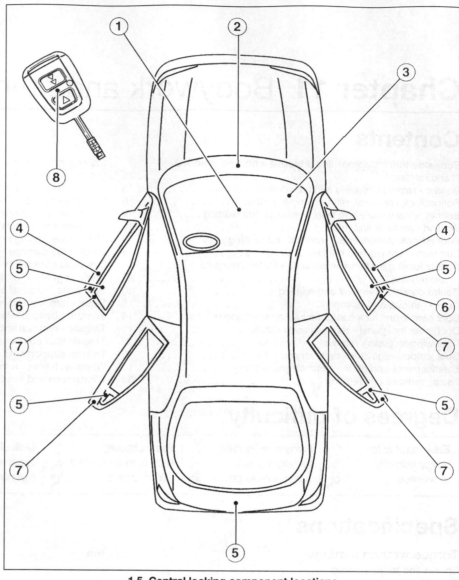

1.5 Central locking component locations

1 *Indicator light*	4 *Infra-red receiver*	7 *Ajar switch*
2 *Buzzer*	5 *Lock motor*	8 *Infra-red transmitter*
3 *Central locking module*	6 *Set/reset switch*	

2 Maintenance - bodywork and underframe

The general condition of a vehicle's bodywork is the one thing that significantly affects its value. Maintenance is easy, but needs to be regular. Neglect, particularly after minor damage, can lead quickly to further deterioration and costly repair bills. It is important also to keep watch on those parts of the vehicle not immediately visible, for instance the underside, inside all the wheel arches, and the lower part of the engine compartment.

The basic maintenance routine for the bodywork is washing - preferably with a lot of water, from a hose. This will remove all the loose solids which may have stuck to the vehicle. It is important to flush these off in such a way as to prevent grit from scratching the finish. The wheel arches and underframe need washing in the same way, to remove any accumulated mud, which will retain moisture and tend to encourage rust. Paradoxically enough, the best time to clean the underframe and wheel arches is in wet weather, when the mud is thoroughly wet and soft. In very wet weather, the underframe is usually cleaned of large accumulations automatically, and this is a good time for inspection.

Periodically, except on vehicles with a wax-based underbody protective coating, it is a good idea to have the whole of the underframe of the vehicle steam-cleaned, engine compartment included, so that a thorough inspection can be carried out to see what minor repairs and renovations are necessary. Steam-cleaning is available at many garages, and is necessary for the removal of the accumulation of oily grime, which sometimes is allowed to become thick in certain areas. If steam-cleaning facilities are not available, there are some excellent grease solvents available which can be brush-applied; the dirt can then be simply hosed off.

Note that these methods should not be used on vehicles with wax-based underbody protective coating, or the coating will be removed. Such vehicles should be inspected annually, preferably just prior to Winter, when the underbody should be washed down, and any damage to the wax coating repaired. Ideally, a completely fresh coat should be applied. It would also be worth considering the use of such wax-based protection for injection into door panels, sills, box sections, etc, as an additional safeguard against rust damage, where such protection is not provided by the vehicle manufacturer.

After washing paintwork, wipe off with a chamois leather to give an unspotted clear finish. A coat of clear protective wax polish will give added protection against chemical pollutants in the air. If the paintwork sheen has dulled or oxidised, use a cleaner/polisher combination to restore the brilliance of the shine. This requires a little effort, but such dulling is usually caused because regular washing has been neglected. Care needs to be taken with metallic paintwork, as special non-abrasive cleaner/polisher is required to avoid damage to the finish. Always check that the door and ventilator opening drain holes and pipes are completely clear, so that water can be drained out. Brightwork should be treated in the same way as paintwork. Windscreens and windows can be kept clear of the smeary film which often appears, by the use of proprietary glass cleaner. Never use any form of wax or other body or chromium polish on glass.

3 Maintenance - upholstery and carpets

Mats and carpets should be brushed or vacuum-cleaned regularly, to keep them free of grit. If they are badly stained, remove them from the vehicle for scrubbing or sponging, and make quite sure they are dry before refitting. Seats and interior trim panels can be kept clean by wiping with a damp cloth. If they do become stained (which can be more apparent on light-coloured upholstery), use a little liquid detergent and a soft nail brush to scour the grime out of the grain of the material. Do not forget to keep the headlining clean in the same way as the upholstery. When using liquid cleaners inside the vehicle, do not over-wet the surfaces being cleaned. Excessive damp could get into the seams and padded interior, causing stains, offensive odours or even rot.

HAYNES HiNT *If the inside of the vehicle gets wet accidentally, it is worthwhile taking some trouble to dry it out properly, particularly where carpets are involved.* **Do not leave oil or electric heaters inside the vehicle for this purpose.**

4 Minor body damage - repair

Note: *For more detailed information about bodywork repair, Haynes Publishing produce a book by Lindsay Porter called "The Car Bodywork Repair Manual". This incorporates information on such aspects as rust treatment, painting and glass-fibre repairs, as well as details on more ambitious repairs involving welding and panel beating.*

Repairs of minor scratches in bodywork

If the scratch is very superficial, and does not penetrate to the metal of the bodywork, repair is very simple. Lightly rub the area of the scratch with a paintwork renovator, or a very fine cutting paste, to remove loose paint from the scratch, and to clear the surrounding bodywork of wax polish. Rinse the area with clean water.

Apply touch-up paint to the scratch using a fine paint brush; continue to apply fine layers of paint until the surface of the paint in the scratch is level with the surrounding paintwork. Allow the new paint at least two weeks to harden, then blend it into the surrounding paintwork by rubbing the scratch area with a paintwork renovator or a very fine cutting paste. Finally, apply wax polish.

Where the scratch has penetrated right through to the metal of the bodywork, causing the metal to rust, a different repair technique is required. Remove any loose rust from the bottom of the scratch with a penknife, then apply rust-inhibiting paint to prevent the formation of rust in the future. Using a rubber or nylon applicator, fill the scratch with bodystopper paste. If required, this paste can be mixed with cellulose thinners to provide a very thin paste which is ideal for filling narrow scratches. Before the stopper-paste in the scratch hardens, wrap a piece of smooth cotton rag around the top of a finger. Dip the finger in cellulose thinners, and quickly sweep it across the surface of the stopper-paste in the scratch; this will ensure that the surface of the stopper-paste is slightly hollowed. The scratch can now be painted over as described earlier in this Section.

Repairs of dents in bodywork

When deep denting of the vehicle's bodywork has taken place, the first task is to pull the dent out, until the affected bodywork almost attains its original shape. There is little point in trying to restore the original shape completely, as the metal in the damaged area will have stretched on impact, and cannot be reshaped fully to its original contour. It is better to bring the level of the dent up to a point which is about 3 mm below the level of the surrounding bodywork. In cases where the dent is very shallow anyway, it is not worth trying to pull it out at all. If the underside of the dent is accessible, it can be hammered out gently from behind, using a mallet with a wooden or plastic head. Whilst doing this, hold a suitable block of wood firmly against the outside of the panel, to absorb the impact from the hammer blows and thus prevent a large area of the bodywork from being "belled-out".

Should the dent be in a section of the bodywork which has a double skin, or some other factor making it inaccessible from behind, a different technique is called for. Drill several small holes through the metal inside the area - particularly in the deeper section. Then screw long self-tapping screws into the holes, just sufficiently for them to gain a good purchase in the metal. Now the dent can be pulled out by pulling on the protruding heads of the screws with a pair of pliers.

The next stage of the repair is the removal of the paint from the damaged area, and from an inch or so of the surrounding "sound" bodywork. This is accomplished most easily by using a wire brush or abrasive pad on a power drill, although it can be done just as effectively by hand, using sheets of abrasive paper. To complete the preparation for filling, score the surface of the bare metal with a screwdriver or the tang of a file, or alternatively, drill small holes in the affected area. This will provide a really good "key" for the filler paste.

To complete the repair, see the Section on filling and respraying.

Repairs of rust holes or gashes in bodywork

Remove all paint from the affected area, and from an inch or so of the surrounding "sound" bodywork, using an abrasive pad or a wire brush on a power drill. If these are not available, a few sheets of abrasive paper will do the job most effectively. With the paint removed, you will be able to judge the severity of the corrosion, and therefore decide whether to renew the whole panel (if this is possible) or to repair the affected area. New body panels are not as expensive as most people think, and it is often quicker and more satisfactory to fit a new panel than to attempt to repair large areas of corrosion.

Remove all fittings from the affected area, except those which will act as a guide to the original shape of the damaged bodywork (eg headlight shells etc). Then, using tin snips or a hacksaw blade, remove all loose metal and any other metal badly affected by corrosion. Hammer the edges of the hole inwards, in order to create a slight depression for the filler paste.

Wire-brush the affected area to remove the powdery rust from the surface of the remaining metal. Paint the affected area with rust-inhibiting paint, if the back of the rusted area is accessible, treat this also.

Before filling can take place, it will be necessary to block the hole in some way. This can be achieved by the use of aluminium or plastic mesh, or aluminium tape.

Aluminium or plastic mesh, or glass-fibre matting, is probably the best material to use for a large hole. Cut a piece to the approximate size and shape of the hole to be filled, then position it in the hole so that its edges are below the level of the surrounding bodywork. It can be retained in position by several blobs of filler paste around its periphery.

Aluminium tape should be used for small or very narrow holes. Pull a piece off the roll, trim it to the approximate size and shape required, then pull off the backing paper (if used) and stick the tape over the hole; it can be overlapped if the thickness of one piece is insufficient. Burnish down the edges of the tape with the handle of a screwdriver or similar, to ensure that the tape is securely attached to the metal underneath.

Bodywork repairs - filling and respraying

Before using this Section, see the Sections on dent, deep scratch, rust holes and gash repairs.

Many types of bodyfiller are available, but generally speaking, those proprietary kits which contain a tin of filler paste and a tube of resin hardener are best for this type of repair. A wide, flexible plastic or nylon applicator will be found invaluable for imparting a smooth and well-contoured finish to the surface of the filler.

11

Mix up a little filler on a clean piece of card or board - measure the hardener carefully (follow the maker's instructions on the pack), otherwise the filler will set too rapidly or too slowly. Using the applicator, apply the filler paste to the prepared area; draw the applicator across the surface of the filler to achieve the correct contour and to level the surface. As soon as a contour that approximates to the correct one is achieved, stop working the paste - if you carry on too long, the paste will become sticky and begin to "pick-up" on the applicator. Continue to add thin layers of filler paste at 20-minute intervals, until the level of the filler is just proud of the surrounding bodywork.

Once the filler has hardened, the excess can be removed using a metal plane or file. From then on, progressively-finer grades of abrasive paper should be used, starting with a 40-grade production paper, and finishing with a 400-grade wet-and-dry paper. Always wrap the abrasive paper around a flat rubber, cork, or wooden block - otherwise the surface of the filler will not be completely flat. During the smoothing of the filler surface, the wet-and-dry paper should be periodically rinsed in water. This will ensure that a very smooth finish is imparted to the filler at the final stage.

At this stage, the "dent" should be surrounded by a ring of bare metal, which in turn should be encircled by the finely "feathered" edge of the good paintwork. Rinse the repair area with clean water, until all of the dust produced by the rubbing-down operation has gone.

Spray the whole area with a light coat of primer - this will show up any imperfections in the surface of the filler. Repair these imperfections with fresh filler paste or bodystopper, and once more smooth the surface with abrasive paper. Repeat this spray-and-repair procedure until you are satisfied that the surface of the filler, and the feathered edge of the paintwork, are perfect. Clean the repair area with clean water, and allow to dry fully.

> **HAYNES HINT**
>
> *If bodystopper is used, it can be mixed with cellulose thinners, to form a really thin paste which is ideal for filling small holes.*

The repair area is now ready for final spraying. Paint spraying must be carried out in a warm, dry, windless and dust-free atmosphere. This condition can be created artificially if you have access to a large indoor working area, but if you are forced to work in the open, you will have to pick your day very carefully. If you are working indoors, dousing the floor in the work area with water will help to settle the dust which would otherwise be in the atmosphere. If the repair area is confined to one body panel, mask off the surrounding panels; this will help to minimise the effects of a slight mis-match in paint colours. Bodywork fittings (eg chrome strips, door handles etc) will also need to be masked off. Use genuine masking tape, and several thicknesses of newspaper, for the masking operations.

Before commencing to spray, agitate the aerosol can thoroughly, then spray a test area (an old tin, or similar) until the technique is mastered. Cover the repair area with a thick coat of primer; the thickness should be built up using several thin layers of paint, rather than one thick one. Using 400-grade wet-and-dry paper, rub down the surface of the primer until it is really smooth. While doing this, the work area should be thoroughly doused with water, and the wet-and-dry paper periodically rinsed in water. Allow to dry before spraying on more paint.

Spray on the top coat, again building up the thickness by using several thin layers of paint. Start spraying at one edge of the repair area, and then, using a side-to-side motion, work until the whole repair area and about 2 inches of the surrounding original paintwork is covered. Remove all masking material 10 to 15 minutes after spraying on the final coat of paint.

Allow the new paint at least two weeks to harden, then, using a paintwork renovator, or a very fine cutting paste, blend the edges of the paint into the existing paintwork. Finally, apply wax polish.

Plastic components

With the use of more and more plastic body components by the vehicle manufacturers (eg bumpers. spoilers, and in some cases major body panels), rectification of more serious damage to such items has become a matter of either entrusting repair work to a specialist in this field, or renewing complete components. Repair of such damage by the DIY owner is not really feasible, owing to the cost of the equipment and materials required for effecting such repairs. The basic technique involves making a groove along the line of the crack in the plastic, using a rotary burr in a power drill. The damaged part is then welded back together, using a hot-air gun to heat up and fuse a plastic filler rod into the groove. Any excess plastic is then removed, and the area rubbed down to a smooth finish. It is important that a filler rod of the correct plastic is used, as body components can be made of a variety of different types (eg polycarbonate, ABS, polypropylene).

Damage of a less serious nature (abrasions, minor cracks etc) can be repaired by the DIY owner using a two-part epoxy filler repair material. Once mixed in equal proportions, this is used in similar fashion to the bodywork filler used on metal panels. The filler is usually cured in twenty to thirty minutes, ready for sanding and painting.

If the owner is renewing a complete component himself, or if he has repaired it with epoxy filler, he will be left with the problem of finding a suitable paint for finishing which is compatible with the type of plastic used. At one time, the use of a universal paint was not possible, owing to the complex range of plastics encountered in body component applications. Standard paints, generally speaking, will not bond to plastic or rubber satisfactorily. However, it is now possible to obtain a plastic body parts finishing kit which consists of a pre-primer treatment, a primer and coloured top coat. Full instructions are normally supplied with a kit, but basically, the method of use is to first apply the pre-primer to the component concerned, and allow it to dry for up to 30 minutes. Then the primer is applied, and left to dry for about an hour before finally applying the special-coloured top coat. The result is a correctly-coloured component, where the paint will flex with the plastic or rubber, a property that standard paint does not normally posses.

5 Major body damage - repair

Where serious damage has occurred, or large areas need renewal due to neglect, it means that complete new panels will need welding-in; this is best left to professionals. If the damage is due to impact, it will also be necessary to check completely the alignment of the bodyshell; this can only be carried out accurately by a Ford dealer, using special jigs. If the body is left misaligned, it is primarily dangerous, as the car will not handle properly, and secondly, uneven stresses will be imposed on the steering, suspension and possibly transmission, causing abnormal wear or complete failure, particularly to items such as the tyres.

6 Bumpers - removal and refitting

Removal

Front bumper

1 Apply the handbrake, jack up the front of the vehicle and support it on axle stands.
2 Where applicable, remove the foglights from the front bumper (Chapter 12).
3 Where applicable, disconnect the tubing from the headlight washer jets.
4 Unscrew the screws securing the wheel arch liners to the front bumper (see illustration).

6.4 Screw (arrowed) securing the wheel arch liner to the front bumper

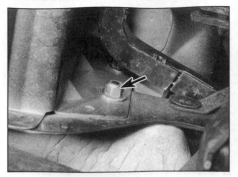

6.5a Front bumper mounting bolt
(arrowed)

6.5b Disconnecting the front bumper from
the side guides

6.9 Rear bumper mounting nuts

5 Unscrew the bumper mounting nuts, and withdraw the bumper forwards from the vehicle, at the same time disconnecting the guides from the side pins **(see illustrations)**.

Rear bumper

6 Chock the front wheels, jack up the rear of the vehicle and support it on axle stands.
7 Disconnect the rear exhaust mounting rubber, and support the exhaust system on an axle stand.
8 Remove the screws securing the wheel arch liners to the rear bumper.
9 Unscrew the bumper mounting nuts, and withdraw the bumper rearwards from the vehicle, at the same time disconnecting the guides from the side pins **(see illustration)**.

Refitting

Front and rear bumpers

10 Refitting is a reversal of the removal procedure. Make sure that the guides locate correctly on the side pins.

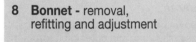
7 Radiator grille -
removal and refitting

Removal

1 Support the bonnet in the open position.
2 Using a Torx key, unscrew the radiator grille mounting screws **(see illustration)**.
3 Unclip the radiator grille from the front panel **(see illustration)**.

Refitting

4 Refitting is a reversal of the removal procedure.

8 Bonnet - removal,
refitting and adjustment

Removal

1 Open the bonnet, and support it in the open position using the stay.
2 Disconnect the battery negative (earth) lead (Chapter 5, Section 1).
3 Prise out the clips from the insulator on the underside of the bonnet, for access to the

7.2 Removing a radiator grille mounting
screw

7.3 Unclipping the radiator grille from the
front panel

windscreen washer hoses and engine compartment light. It is not necessary to completely remove the insulator.
4 Disconnect the wiring from the engine compartment light, and unclip the wiring from the bonnet.
5 Unbolt the earth lead from the bonnet **(see illustration)**.
6 Disconnect the windscreen washer hoses from the bottom of the jets, and unclip the hose from the bonnet.
7 To assist in correctly realigning the bonnet when refitting it, mark the outline of the hinges with a soft pencil. Loosen the two hinge retaining bolts on each side **(see illustration)**.
8 With the help of an assistant, unscrew the four bolts, release the stay, and lift the bonnet from the vehicle **(see illustration)**.

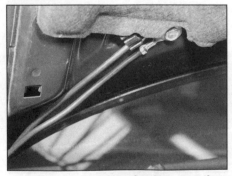

8.5 Earth lead and washer hoses on the
underside of the bonnet

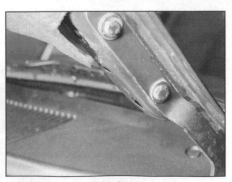

8.7 Mark around the bonnet hinges with a
soft pencil before removal

8.8 Removing the bonnet

11

Refitting

9 Refitting is a reversal of the removal procedure. Position the bonnet hinges within the outline marks made during removal, but if necessary alter its position to provide a uniform gap all round. Adjust the rear height of the bonnet by repositioning it on the hinges. Adjust the front height by repositioning the lock (see Section 10) and turning the rubber buffers on the engine compartment front cross panel up or down to support the bonnet **(see illustration)**.

8.9 Buffer for adjustment of the bonnet front height

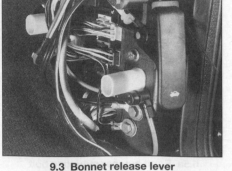

9.3 Bonnet release lever

9 Bonnet release cable and lever - removal and refitting

Removal

1 With the bonnet open, disconnect the battery negative (earth) lead (Chapter 5, Section 1).
2 Working inside the vehicle, remove the trim from the "B" pillar, and pull off the door weatherstrips from the bottom of the door apertures.
3 Remove the clips and screws, and withdraw the lower side trim, to give access to the bonnet release lever **(see illustration)**.
4 Release the outer cable from the lever bracket.
5 Unscrew and remove the lever mounting screws, and turn the lever clockwise through a quarter-turn to disconnect it from the cable.
6 Remove the radiator grille (Section 7). Also remove the backing panel from the engine compartment front crossmember.
7 Release the inner and outer cables from the lock.
8 Withdraw the cable from the engine compartment, feeding it through the front crossmember, and removing the grommet from the bulkhead.

Refitting

9 Refitting is a reversal of the removal procedure.

10 Bonnet lock - removal, refitting and adjustment

Removal

1 Remove the radiator grille (Section 7).
2 Release the inner and outer cables from the bonnet lock.
3 Mark the position of the lock on the crossmember, then unscrew the mounting nuts and withdraw the lock.

Refitting and adjustment

4 Refitting is a reversal of the removal procedure, starting by positioning the lock as noted before removal.
5 If the front of the bonnet is not level with the front wings, the lock may be moved up or

11.2a Prise out the plastic cover . . .

down within the mounting holes. After making an adjustment, raise or lower the rubber buffers to support the bonnet correctly.

11 Door inner trim panel - removal and refitting

Removal

1 Disconnect the battery negative (earth) lead (Chapter 5, Section 1).
2 Carefully prise out the plastic cover with a small screwdriver. Remove the screw, and ease the bezel off the inner door handle **(see illustrations)**.
3 Where applicable, remove the window operating switch and disconnect the multi-plug **(see illustrations)**.

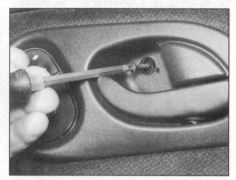

11.2b . . . remove the screw . . .

11.2c . . . and withdraw the bezel from the inner door handle

11.3a Remove the window operating switch . . .

11.3b . . . and disconnect the multi-plug

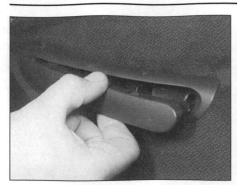

11.4a Remove the cover . . .

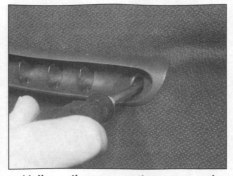

11.4b . . . then remove the screws and withdraw the door pull handle

11.5a Remove the plastic cap and the screw . . .

Front door

4 Carefully prise out the cover, remove the screws and withdraw the door pull handle **(see illustrations)**.

5 Prise off the plastic cap, remove the screw, and withdraw the quarter bezel from the front of the window opening **(see illustrations)**.

Rear door

6 Prise off the cap, then remove the screw and withdraw the door pull handle **(see illustrations)**.

Front and rear doors

7 On models fitted with manual (ie non-electric) windows, fully shut the window, and note the position of the regulator handle. Release the spring clip by inserting a clean cloth between the handle and the door trim. Pull the cloth against the open ends of the clip to release it, at the same time pulling the handle from the regulator shaft splines. Withdraw the handle (and where fitted, the spacer) and recover the clip **(see illustrations)**.

8 Prise the caps from the trim panel retaining screws, then remove the screws and lift off the panel. Where a speaker is attached to the trim panel, disconnect the multi-plug **(see illustrations)**.

9 If necessary, the foam insulation may be removed from the door. First remove the speaker as described in Chapter 12.

11.5b . . . then withdraw the quarter bezel

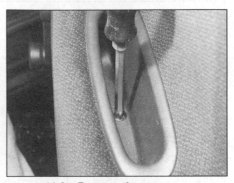

11.6a Remove the screw . . .

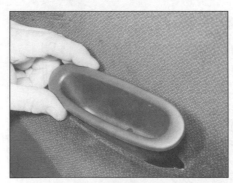

11.6b . . . and withdraw the rear door pull handle

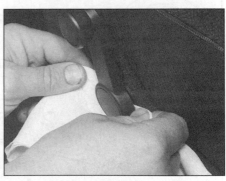

11.7a Using a clean cloth to release the spring clip from the window regulator handle

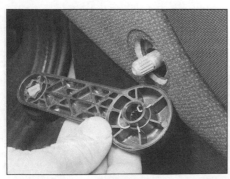

11.7b Withdrawing the window regulator handle

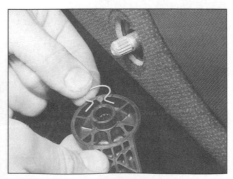

11.7c Recover the spring clip from the window regulator handle

11.8a Prise out the caps . . .

11

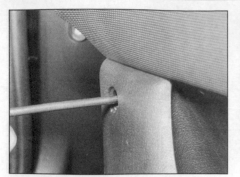

11.8b . . . remove the inner-facing screws . . .

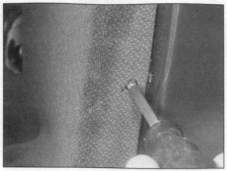

11.8c . . . and the side screws . . .

11.8d . . . then lift off the trim panel

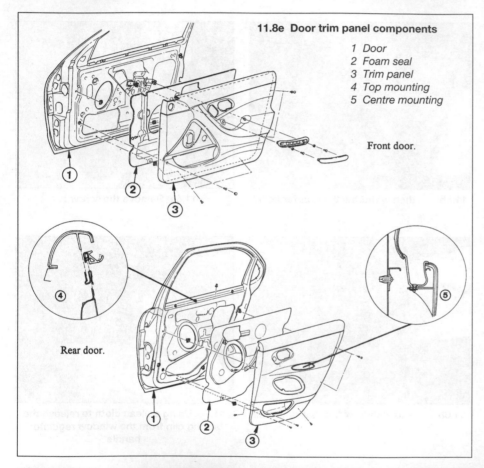

11.8e Door trim panel components

1 Door
2 Foam seal
3 Trim panel
4 Top mounting
5 Centre mounting

Front door.

Rear door.

10 On models with manual windows, remove the foam spacer from the regulator spindle **(see illustration)**.

11 On the rear door, unscrew the screws and remove the door pull bracket **(see illustration)**.

12 Carefully cut the adhesive with a knife, and remove the foam insulation **(see illustration)**.

Refitting

13 Refitting is a reversal of the removal procedure.

---

12 Door window glass -
removal and refitting

Removal

Front (manual/non-electric)

1 Disconnect the battery negative (earth) lead (Chapter 5, Section 1).

2 Remove the door inner trim panel (Section 11).

3 Remove the door exterior mirror (Section 16).

4 Temporarily refit the regulator handle on its splines.

5 Lower the window until the glass support bracket is visible through the holes in the door inner panel. Remove the regulator handle.

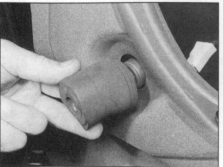

11.10 Removing the foam spacer

11.11 Removing the door pull bracket from a rear door

11.12 Removing the foam insulation

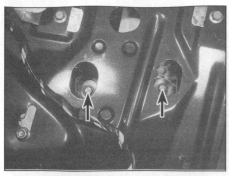

12.12 Window support bracket bolts (arrowed) viewed through the holes in the door inner panel

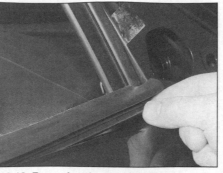

12.13 Removing the weatherstrip from the outside of the door

12.15 Lifting the glass from the front door

12.21a Unscrew the screws . . .

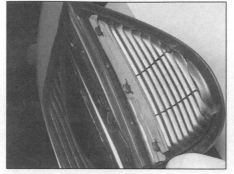

12.21b . . . and remove the air vent grilles from the rear door

12.26 Lifting the glass from the rear door

6 Carefully prise off the weatherstrip from the outside of the door.

7 Support the glass, then unscrew the bolts from the support bracket.

8 Lift the glass from the door while tilting it at the rear, and withdraw it from the outside.

Front (electric)

9 Disconnect the battery negative (earth) lead (Chapter 5, Section 1).

10 Remove the door inner trim panel (Section 11).

11 Remove the door exterior mirror (Section 16).

12 Temporarily reconnect the battery and the window operating switch. Lower the window until the support bracket and bolts are visible through the holes in the door inner panel **(see illustration)**. Disconnect the battery lead and the operating switch again.

13 Carefully prise off the weatherstrip from the outside of the door **(see illustration)**.

14 Support the glass, then unscrew the bolts from the support bracket.

15 Lift the glass from the door while tilting it at the rear, and withdraw it from the outside **(see illustration)**.

Rear (manual/non-electric)

16 Disconnect the battery negative (earth) lead (Chapter 5, Section 1).

17 Remove the door inner trim panel (Section 11).

18 Temporarily refit the regulator handle on its splines.

19 Lower the window until the glass support bracket and bolts are visible through the holes in the door inner panel. Remove the regulator handle.

20 Support the glass, then unscrew the bolts from the support bracket.

21 Unscrew the screws, and remove the air vent grilles from the rear of the rear door **(see illustrations)**.

22 Carefully prise off the weatherstrip from the outside of the door.

23 Have an assistant raise the glass from the outside, and hold it near its shut position.

24 Loosen (but do not remove) the three regulator mounting bolts, then slide the top bolts to the right, and push them out. Slide the bottom bolt upwards, and push it out. Lower the regulator assembly inside the door.

25 Working inside the door, lower the glass until it is below the regulator position, and move the glass to the outer side of its channels.

26 With the help of an assistant, lift the glass out of the door, and withdraw it from the outside **(see illustration)**.

Rear (electric)

27 The procedure is as just described for manual windows, making allowances for the difference in the regulator mechanism.

Refitting

All doors

28 Refitting is a reversal of the removal procedure, making sure that the glass is correctly located in the support bracket.

13 Door window regulator - removal and refitting

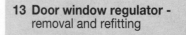

Removal

1 Remove the window glass (Section 12).

2 Loosen (but do not remove) the regulator and manual winder/electric motor mounting bolts **(see illustrations)**.

3 Twist the winder or motor (as applicable) in the bolt slots, and push it inwards.

4 Slide the top bolts to the right, and push them out. Slide the bottom bolt upwards, and push it out.

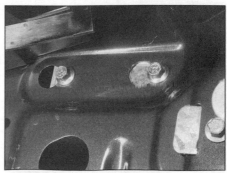

13.2a Window regulator upper mounting bolts (front door)

11

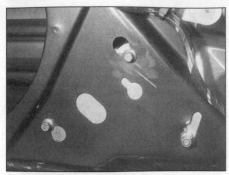

13.2b Electric window motor mounting bolts (front door)

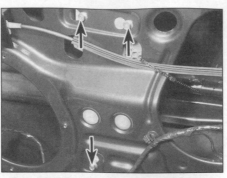

13.2c Window regulator mounting bolts - arrowed (rear door)

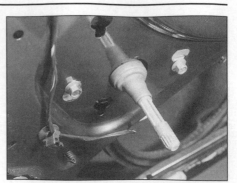

13.2d Manual winder mounting bolts (rear door)

5 On electric windows, disconnect the wiring multi-plug from the motor **(see illustration)**.
6 Withdraw the window regulator mechanism from inside the door, through the hole in the inner panel **(see illustrations)**.

Refitting

7 Refitting is a reversal of the removal procedure.

13.5 Disconnecting the wiring multi-plug from an electrically-operated window

13.6a Removing the window regulator mechanism from the front door

14 Door handle and lock components - removal and refitting

Removal

Front door exterior handle

1 Remove the door inner trim panel (Section 11).
2 Use a knife to cut through the adhesive strip, so that the foam insulator can be peeled back locally for access to the lock. *Do not* peel back the foam insulator without first cutting through the adhesive strip, otherwise the insulator will be damaged. To ensure a good seal when the insulator is pressed back, do not touch the adhesive strip.
3 Unscrew and remove the two bolts for the exterior handle outer bezel, and remove the bezel **(see illustrations)**.

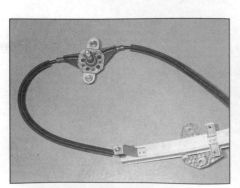

13.6b Front door window regulator removed from the vehicle

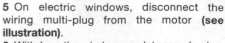

13.6c Removing the window regulator mechanism from the rear door

13.6d Rear door window regulator removed from the vehicle

14.3a Remove the two bolts (arrowed) . . .

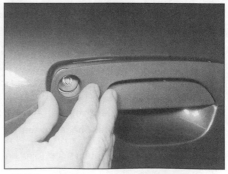

14.3b . . . followed by the exterior handle bezel

14.4a Unscrew the lock mounting bolts . . .

14.4b . . . and remove the plate

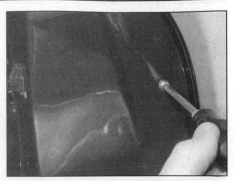

14.4c Removing the additional support screw

4 Unscrew and remove the lock mounting bolts on the inner rear edge of the door, and remove the plate. Also remove the additional support screw **(see illustrations)**.

5 Unclip and disconnect the wiring multi-plugs for the central locking and alarm systems **(see illustration)**.

6 Disconnect the wiring multi-plug from the door lock.

7 Disconnect the inner handle illumination light. Undo the screws and remove the inner handle. Disconnect the operating cable from the inner handle, as described later in this Section **(see illustrations)**.

8 Manipulate the lock and handle assembly as necessary, and disconnect the wiring multi-plugs for the alarm sensor and central locking. Withdraw the complete assembly from inside the door **(see illustrations)**.

9 To disconnect the handle assembly from the lock bracket, slide the rubber posts inwards, and push out the assembly **(see illustration)**.

10 To remove the handle itself, twist the door handle through a quarter-turn, and pull out the connecting rods **(see illustration)**.

11 Remove the alarm sensor and the central locking "Set-reset" sensor **(see illustration)**.

Rear door exterior handle

12 Remove the door inner trim panel (Section 11).

13 Use a knife to cut through the adhesive strip, so that the foam insulator can be peeled

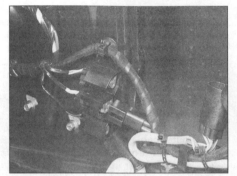

14.5 Disconnecting the central locking and alarm system wiring multi-plugs

14.7a Removing the inner handle

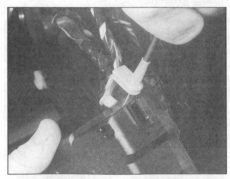

14.7b Disconnecting the operating cable from the inner handle

14.8a Removing the lock and exterior handle assembly from inside the door

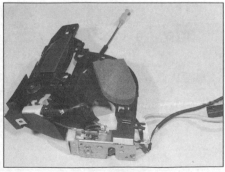

14.8b Front door lock and exterior handle assembly removed from the vehicle

14.9 Disconnecting the handle assembly from the lock bracket

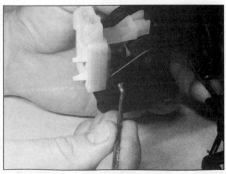

14.10 Pulling out the handle connecting rods

11

14.11 Removing the central locking "Set-reset" sensor

14.14a Prise out the plug . . .

14.14b . . . and unscrew the handle mounting nuts

back for access to the lock. *Do not* peel back the foam insulator without first cutting through the adhesive strip. To ensure a good seal when the insulator is pressed back, do not touch the adhesive strip.

14 Prise out the plug from the rear edge of the door, then unscrew the handle mounting nuts **(see illustrations)**.

15 Prise up the clip, and disconnect the operating rod from the lock **(see illustration)**.

16 Withdraw the handle from the outside of the door **(see illustration)**.

Interior handle

17 Remove the door inner trim panel (Section 11).

18 Use a knife to cut through the adhesive strip, so that the foam insulator can be peeled

back for access to the lock. *Do not* peel back the foam insulator without first cutting through the adhesive strip. To ensure a good seal when the insulator is pressed back, do not touch the adhesive strip.

19 Disconnect the interior handle illumination light.

20 Undo the screws and remove the interior handle.

21 To remove the cable, first pull back the plastic outer cable end and blanking piece. Apply light inward pressure to the control lever, with the lever in the locked position, until the inner cable is aligned with the release slot in the bottom of the cable holder.

22 Push down on the cable ferrule, and disconnect the inner cable. Remove the handle assembly.

Lock barrel

23 Remove the exterior handle as described earlier in this Section.

24 Prise out the barrel retaining tab from the handle body, using a small screwdriver **(see illustration)**.

25 Insert the key, turn it so that it engages the barrel, then pull out the barrel **(see illustration)**.

Lock motor - front door

26 Remove the exterior handle as described earlier in this Section.

27 Extract the clip, and pull out the operating rod.

28 Remove the operating rod from the plastic bush, by turning it through a quarter-turn.

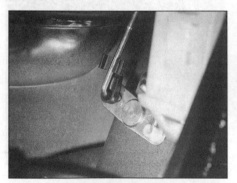

14.15 Disconnect the operating rod from the lock

14.16 Removing the rear door exterior handle

14.24 Prise out the barrel retaining tab . . .

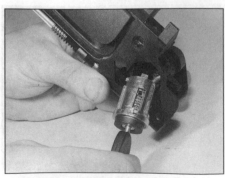

14.25 . . . and pull out the lock barrel

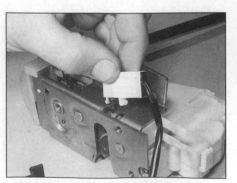

14.31 Unclipping the door-ajar sensor

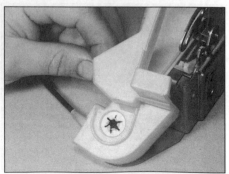

14.32 Removing the plastic shield from the locating post

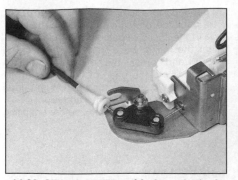

14.33 Slide the outer cable from the lock bracket

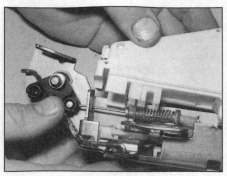

14.34 Removing a lock motor

15.2a Front door check strap mounting screw removal

29 Release the sensor wiring loom from the clip.

30 Detach the mounting plate from the lock.

31 Release the door-ajar sensor from the clip **(see illustration)**.

32 Prise the plastic shield from the locating post **(see illustration)**.

33 Slide the outer cable from the lock bracket **(see illustration)**, then turn the inner cable through a quarter-turn to remove it from the bell crank.

34 Unscrew the mounting screws and remove the lock motor **(see illustration)**.

Lock motor - rear door

35 Remove the exterior handle as described earlier in this Section.

36 Unscrew and remove the three lock mounting screws.

37 Release the sensor wiring loom from the clip on the door.

38 Disconnect the wiring multi-plug from the door lock.

39 Disconnect the interior handle illumination light.

40 Remove the screws, and remove the interior handle.

41 Remove the lock assembly.

42 Release the door-ajar sensor from the clip.

43 Prise the plastic shield from the locating post.

44 Slide the outer cable from the lock bracket, then turn the inner cable through a quarter-turn to remove it from the bell crank.

45 Unscrew the mounting screws and remove the lock motor.

Striker

46 Using a pencil, mark the position of the striker.

47 Undo the mounting screws using a Torx key, and remove the striker.

Check strap

48 Disconnect the battery negative (earth) lead (Chapter 5, Section 1).

49 Using a Torx key, unscrew and remove the check strap mounting screw(s). On the front door, there are two screws; on the rear door, there is only one.

50 Prise the rubber grommet from the door aperture, then unscrew the mounting nuts and withdraw the check strap from the door.

Refitting

Handles (exterior and interior)

51 Refitting is a reversal of the removal procedure.

Lock barrel

52 Check that the retaining clip is fitted correctly.

53 Align the grooves on the barrel with the grooves on the body and operating lever, then carefully push the barrel into the handle until it engages the clip.

54 The remaining refitting procedure is a reversal of removal.

Lock motor

55 Refitting is a reversal of the removal procedure.

Striker

56 Refitting is a reversal of the removal procedure, but check that the door lock passes over the striker centrally. If necessary, re-position the striker before fully tightening the mounting screws.

Check strap

59 Refitting is a reversal of the removal procedure.

15 Door - removal and refitting

Removal

1 Disconnect the battery negative (earth) lead (Chapter 5, Section 1).

2 Using a Torx key, unscrew and remove the check strap mounting screw(s). On the front door, there are two screws; on the rear door, there is only one **(see illustrations)**.

3 Disconnect the wiring connector(s) by twisting them anti-clockwise. On the front door, there are two connectors; on the rear door, there is only one **(see illustration)**.

4 Extract the small circlips from the top of the upper and lower hinge pins **(see illustration)**.

15.2b Front door check strap removed

15.3 Disconnecting a door wiring connector

15.4 Extract the small circlips . . .

15.5a ... then drive out the hinge pins ...

5 Have an assistant support the weight of the door, then drive the hinge pins down through the hinges using a small drift **(see illustrations).**
6 Carefully withdraw the door from the hinges.

Refitting

7 Refitting is a reversal of the removal procedure, but check that the door lock passes over the striker centrally. If necessary, re-position the striker.

16 Exterior mirror and glass - removal and refitting

Removal

1 Where electric mirrors are fitted, disconnect the battery negative (earth) lead (Chapter 5, Section 1).
2 Prise off the cap, unscrew the screw, and remove the quarter bezel from the front of the window opening.\
3 On manual mirrors, detach the adjustment lever.
4 On electric mirrors, disconnect the wiring multi-plug **(see illustration).**
5 On both types of mirror, use a Torx key to unscrew the mirror mounting screws, then withdraw the mirror from the outside of the door **(see illustrations).** Recover the gasket.

Refitting

6 Refitting is a reversal of the removal procedure.

15.5b ... and remove them

17 Interior mirror - removal and refitting

Removal

1 Using a length of strong thin cord or fishing line, break the adhesive bond between the base of the mirror and the glass. Have an assistant support and remove the mirror as it is released.
2 If the original mirror is to be refitted, thoroughly clean its base with methylated spirit and a lint-free cloth. Allow a period of one minute for the spirit to evaporate. Clean the windscreen black patch in a similar manner.

Refitting

3 During the installation of the mirror, it is important that the mirror base, windscreen black patch and the adhesive patch are not touched or contaminated in any way, otherwise poor adhesion will result.
4 Prior to fitting the mirror, the vehicle should have been at an ambient temperature of at least 20ºC.
5 With the contact surfaces thoroughly cleaned, remove the protective tape from one side of the adhesive patch, and press it firmly into contact with the mirror base.
6 If fitting the mirror to a new windscreen, the protective tape must also be removed from the windscreen black patch.
7 Using a hairdryer or a hot air gun, warm the mirror base and the adhesive patch for about

30 seconds to a temperature of 50 to 70ºC. Peel back the protective tape from the other side of the adhesive patch on the mirror base. Align the mirror base and the windscreen patch, and press the mirror firmly into position. Hold the base of the mirror firmly against the windscreen for a minimum period of two minutes, to ensure full adhesion.
8 Wait at least thirty minutes before adjusting the mirror position.

18 Boot lid - removal and refitting

Removal

1 Disconnect the battery negative (earth) lead (Chapter 5, Section 1), and open the boot lid.
2 Where applicable, pull off the trim covering, and release the wiring on the hinge arm.
3 Where fitted, remove the trim from inside the boot lid.
4 Disconnect the wiring at the connectors visible through the boot lid inner skin aperture.
5 Attach a length of strong cord to the end of the wires in the aperture, to act as an aid to guiding the wiring through the lid when it is refitted.
6 Release the cable guide rubber grommet, and withdraw the wiring loom through it. Untie the cord, and leave it in the boot lid.
7 Mark the position of the hinge arms with a pencil.
8 Place rags beneath each corner of the boot lid, to prevent damage to the paintwork.
9 With the help of an assistant, unscrew the mounting bolts and lift the boot lid from the car.

Refitting

10 Refitting is a reversal of the removal procedure. Check that the boot lid is correctly aligned with the surrounding bodywork, with an equal clearance around its edge. Adjustment is made by loosening the hinge bolts, and moving the boot lid within the elongated mounting holes. Check that the lock enters the striker centrally when the boot lid is closed.

16.4 Disconnecting the wiring multi-plug from an electric exterior mirror

16.5a Unscrew the screws ...

16.5b ... and withdraw the mirror

20.6a Unclipping the upper trim panel from the tailgate

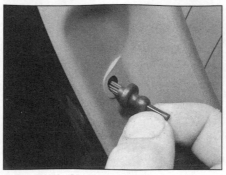

20.6b Shelf cord post removal

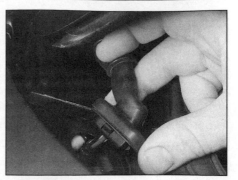

20.7 Removing the wiring loom rubber grommet

19 Boot lid lock components - removal and refitting

Removal

Lock barrel

1 Disconnect the battery negative (earth) lead (Chapter 5, Section 1).
2 With the boot lid open, remove the luggage space trim from the right-hand rear corner.
3 Remove the screws, and prise out the rear light trim cover from the guides.
4 Release the door-ajar sensor from the clip near the lock.
5 Slide the outer cable from the lock bracket. Raise the inner cable until it is aligned with the slot in the barrel lever, and disconnect it.
6 Pull out the lock locating spring clip.
7 Detach the cable mounting bracket from the barrel, and remove the barrel.

Lock

8 Disconnect the battery negative (earth) lead (Chapter 5, Section 1).
9 With the boot lid open, prise out the clips and remove the trim from inside the boot lid.
10 Release the door-ajar sensor from the clip near the lock.
11 Using a Torx key, unscrew the lock mounting screws, and withdraw the lock for access to the cables.
12 Disconnect both the inner and outer cables from the lock bracket.

13 Prise open the plastic lip, and remove the central locking control rod.
14 Withdraw the lock assembly.

Refitting

Lock barrel and lock

15 Refitting is a reversal of the removal procedure.

20 Tailgate - removal and refitting

Removal

Hatchback

1 Disconnect the battery negative (earth) lead (Chapter 5, Section 1). Open the tailgate.
2 The tailgate may be unbolted from the hinges and the hinges left in position, or the hinges may be detached from the roof panel by unscrewing the mounting nuts. In the latter case, carefully pull down the rear edge of the headlining for access to the nuts. Take care not to damage the headlining.
3 Remove the parcel shelf left-hand support bracket as follows. Fold the rear seat forwards, and disconnect the left-hand seat pull cable from the bracket and clips. Unscrew the screws and remove the bracket.
4 Pull up the rear seat side bolster, then carefully remove the side trim from the left-hand side of the luggage area. On low-

series models, the bolster is retained with a screw.
5 Separate the tailgate wiring loom multi-plugs, located on the left-hand side of the luggage compartment, on top of the wheel arch.
6 Unclip and remove the upper trim panel from the inside of the tailgate. Also remove the rear shelf cord plastic post **(see illustrations)**.
7 Prise out the rubber grommet from the top of the tailgate aperture, and pull the wiring loom out through the hole in the body **(see illustration)**.
8 Disconnect the rear window washer tube from the jet.
9 Prise out the rubber grommet from the right-hand side of the tailgate aperture, and pull out the washer tube.
10 Have an assistant support the tailgate in its open position.
11 Using a small screwdriver, prise off the clips securing the struts to the tailgate. Pull the sockets from the ball-studs, and move the struts downwards.
12 If the headlining has been pulled back, unscrew and remove the hinge nuts from the roof panel. Otherwise, unscrew the bolts securing the tailgate to the hinges **(see illustration)**.
13 Withdraw the tailgate from the body aperture, taking care not to damage the paintwork.

Estate

14 Disconnect the battery negative (earth) lead (Chapter 5, Section 1).
15 The tailgate may be unbolted from the hinges and the hinges left in position, or the hinges may be detached from the rear roof panel by unscrewing the mounting nuts. In the latter case, carefully pull down the rear edge of the headlining for access to the nuts. Take care not to damage the headlining.
16 Unscrew the retaining screws, then unclip the "D" pillar trim panels from both sides **(see illustration)**.
17 Unclip and remove the upper trim panel from inside the tailgate.
18 Carefully remove the side trim from the left-hand side of the luggage area, and

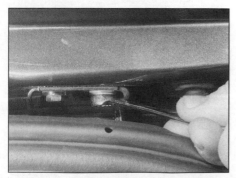

20.12 Unscrewing the bolts securing the tailgate to the hinges

20.16 "D" pillar trim panel retaining screws (arrowed) - Estate models

11

20.24 Tailgate hinge and bolts - Estate models

21.2 Prising the spring clip from the upper end of the strut

21.3 Prising the spring clip from the lower end of the strut

separate the tailgate wiring loom multi-plugs in the rear light cluster housing.

19 Attach a strong fine cord to the end of the wiring loom, to act as an aid to guiding the wiring through the tailgate when it is refitted.

20 Prise the rubber grommet from the top left-hand side of the tailgate aperture, and pull out the wiring loom. Untie the cord, leaving it in position in the "D" pillar.

21 Disconnect the rear window washer tube from the jet. Pull out the rubber grommet, and remove the tube.

22 Have an assistant support the tailgate in its open position.

23 Using a small screwdriver, prise off the clip securing the struts to the tailgate. Pull the sockets from the ball-studs, and move the struts downwards.

24 Unscrew and remove the hinge nuts from the roof panel, or the hinge bolts from the hinge, as desired **(see illustration)**. Withdraw the tailgate from the body aperture, taking care not to damage the paintwork.

Refitting

Hatchback and Estate

25 Refitting is a reversal of the removal procedure, but check that the tailgate is located centrally in the body aperture, and that the striker enters the lock centrally. If necessary, loosen the mounting nuts and re-position the tailgate as required.

21 Tailgate support strut - removal and refitting

Removal

1 Support the tailgate in its open position.
2 Prise off the upper spring clip securing the strut to the tailgate, then pull the socket from the ball-stud **(see illustration)**.
3 Similarly prise off the bottom clip **(see illustration)**, and pull the socket from the ball-stud. Withdraw the strut.

Refitting

4 Refitting is a reversal of the removal procedure, but make sure that the piston end of the strut is fitted on the body (ie downwards).

22 Tailgate lock components - removal and refitting

Removal

Lock barrel (Hatchback)

1 Disconnect the battery negative (earth) lead (Chapter 5, Section 1).
2 With the tailgate open, pull up the weatherstrip for access to the lock. Remove the screws and clips, and remove the trim

panel from the rear of the luggage compartment.
3 Unhook the parcel net, then remove the screws and clips, and remove the rear crossmember trim.
4 Remove the screws, and prise out the rear light trim cover from the guides.
5 Release the door-ajar sensor from the clip near the lock.
6 Slide the outer cable from the lock bracket. Raise the inner cable until it is aligned with the slot in the barrel lever, and disconnect it **(see illustration)**.
7 Pull out the lock barrel locating spring clip.
8 Detach the cable mounting bracket from the barrel, and remove the barrel and cylinder **(see illustrations)**.

Lock barrel (Estate)

9 Disconnect the battery negative (earth) lead (Chapter 5, Section 1).
10 Unclip and remove the tailgate trim panel. Undo the three screws and remove the lock shield, then unclip the door-ajar sensor.
11 Working through the aperture in the tailgate inner panel, pull out the lock barrel locating spring clip. Unhook the operating rod and withdraw the lock barrel.

Lock (Hatchback)

12 Disconnect the battery negative (earth) lead (Chapter 5, Section 1).
13 With the tailgate open, pull up the weatherstrip for access to the lock. Remove the screws and clips, and remove the trim

22.6 Tailgate lock barrel and bracket

22.8a Removing the lock barrel . . .

22.8b . . . and cylinder

22.14 Removing the door-ajar sensor from the lock

22.15 Removing a lock mounting screw

22.16 Disconnecting the cables from the lock

panel from the rear of the luggage compartment.

14 Release the door-ajar sensor from the clip near the lock **(see illustration)**.

15 Using a Torx key, unscrew the lock mounting screws, and withdraw the lock for access to the cables **(see illustration)**.

16 Disconnect both the inner and outer cables from the lock bracket **(see illustration)**.

17 Prise open the plastic clip, and remove the central locking control rod.

18 Withdraw the lock assembly.

Lock (Estate)

19 Disconnect the battery negative (earth) lead (Chapter 5, Section 1).

20 Open the tailgate. Undo the screws and remove the inner trim.

21 Using a Torx key, unscrew the lock mounting screws, and carefully withdraw the lock **(see illustration)**.

22 Release the door-ajar sensor from the clip near the lock.

23 Disconnect the barrel operating rod, and remove the lock.

24 If necessary, the lock striker assembly may be removed by disconnecting the release cable and unscrewing the mounting bolts **(see illustration)**.

Refitting

Lock barrel and lock - all models

25 Refitting is a reversal of the removal procedure.

---

23 Central locking system components - testing, removal and refitting

Testing

1 The central locking module incorporates a service-test mode, which is activated by operating one of the lock position switches 8 times within 10 seconds. A buzzer will sound, to indicate that the service-test mode is operating, and to indicate that no faults have been found in the system. If a fault has been found, the system should be checked by a Ford dealer or electrical specialist. The central locking module also incorporates the alarm system module.

Removal

Central locking/alarm module

2 To remove the module, first remove the lower right-hand facia panel (right-hand-drive models) or the glovebox (left-hand-drive models).

3 Disconnect the battery negative (earth) lead (Chapter 5, Section 1).

4 Unscrew the mounting bolts, and remove the module from the bracket beneath the facia.

5 Disconnect the wiring multi-plug, and withdraw the module from inside the vehicle.

6 Note that a different module is used for models without an anti-theft alarm.

Central locking set/reset switch

7 This procedure is covered in Section 14, under front door handle removal.

Central locking door-ajar switch

8 This procedure is covered in Section 14, under front door lock motor removal.

Refitting

Central locking/alarm module

9 Refitting is a reversal of the removal procedure.

Central locking set/reset switch

10 Refitting is a reversal of the removal procedure.

Central locking door-ajar switch

11 Refitting is a reversal of the removal procedure.

---

24 Windscreen and fixed windows - removal and refitting

1 The windscreen and rear window on all models are bonded in place with special mastic, as are the rear side windows on Estate models. Special tools are required to cut free the old units and fit replacements; special cleaning solutions and primer are also required. It is therefore recommended that this work is entrusted to a Ford dealer or windscreen replacement specialist.

2 Note that the windscreen contributes towards the structural strength of the vehicle as a whole, so it is important that it is fitted correctly.

---

25 Body side-trim mouldings and adhesive emblems - removal and refitting

Removal

1 Insert a length of strong cord (fishing line is ideal) behind the moulding or emblem concerned. With a sawing action, break the

22.21 Tailgate lock - Estate models

22.24 Lock striker assembly - Estate models

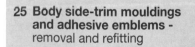

11

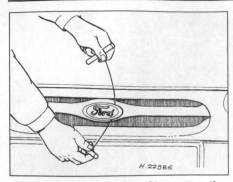

25.1 Using a length of cord to remove the emblem from the radiator grille

27.2a Unscrew the Torx-headed screws . . .

27.2b . . . and remove the mounting trims for access to the front seat rear mounting bolts

adhesive bond between the moulding or emblem and the panel **(see illustration)**.
2 Thoroughly clean all traces of adhesive from the panel using
methylated spirit, and allow the location to dry.

Refitting

3 Peel back the protective paper from the rear face of the new moulding or emblem. Carefully fit it into position on the panel concerned, but take care not to touch the adhesive. When in position, apply hand pressure to the moulding/emblem for a short period, to ensure maximum adhesion to the panel.

27.4 Disconnecting an electric seat multi-plug

26 Sunroof - general information and adjustment

1 The sunroof should operate freely, without sticking or binding, as it is opened and closed. When in the closed position, check that the panel is flush with the surrounding roof panel.
2 If adjustment is required, open the sun blind, but leave the glass panel shut. Unscrew and remove the three lower frame-to-glass panel retaining screws. Slide the lower frame back into the roof.
3 Loosen the central and front securing screws. Adjust the glass roof panel so that it is flush at its front edge with the roof panel, then retighten the securing screws.
4 Pull the lower frame forwards, and insert and tighten its retaining screws to complete.

27 Seats - removal and refitting

Removal

Front seat

1 Release the seat belt, and slide the seat fully forwards.
2 Using a Torx key, undo the screws and remove the rear mounting trims, then unscrew the rear mounting bolts **(see illustrations)**.

3 Slide the seat fully rearwards.
4 Where electric seats are fitted, disconnect the battery negative (earth) lead (Chapter 5, Section 1). Disconnect the seat wiring multi-plugs **(see illustration)**.
5 Unscrew the front mounting bolts, and remove the seat from the vehicle **(see illustration)**.

Rear seat cushion

6 Fold the rear seat cushion forwards. (Note that, on some models, the seat cushion is held in place by screws which must be removed first.) Using a Torx key, unscrew and remove the mounting bolts from the hinges on each side **(see illustration)**.
7 Withdraw the seat cushion from the vehicle.

Rear seat backrest

8 Fold the rear seat cushion and both backrests forwards.
9 Unclip the backrest rear trims, where fitted, and raise them.
10 Using a Torx key, unscrew the mounting bolts **(see illustration)**.
11 Withdraw the backrest from inside the vehicle.

Rear seat side bolster

12 Fold the rear seat backrest forwards.
13 On low-series models, remove the screw and pull the bolster forwards to disengage the clips. On high-series models, simply pull the bolster upwards to disengage the clips.

27.5 Front seat front mounting bolt

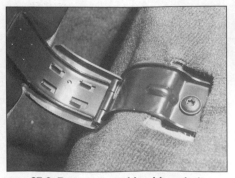

27.6 Rear seat cushion hinge bolt

27.10 Rear seat backrest mounting bolts

28.2 Front seat belt reel unit lower mounting bolt

28.3a Front seat belt guide and mounting bolt

28.3b Front seat belt shackle and mounting nut

Refitting

14 Refitting is a reversal of the removal procedure, but tighten the mounting bolts to the specified torque.

28 Seat belts - removal and refitting

> **Warning: Be careful when handling the seat belt tensioning device ("grabber"). It contains a powerful spring, which could cause injury if released in an uncontrolled fashion. Once fired, the grabber cannot be reset, and must be renewed. Note also that seat belts and**

associated components which have been subject to impact loads must be renewed.

Removal

Front seat belt

1 Remove the trim from the "B" pillar and the scuttle.
2 Unscrew the mounting bolts and remove the seat belt reel unit **(see illustration)**.
3 Unscrew the bolt securing the seat belt guide to the "B" pillar, then unscrew the nut securing the seat belt shackle **(see illustrations)**.
4 Detach the stalk cable, then undo the mounting nut, and remove the stalk and grabber assembly from the front seat **(see illustrations)**.

> **Warning: There is a potential risk of the grabber firing during removal, so it should be handled carefully. As an extra precaution, a spacer may be fitted on the cable before removal. Hold the adjustment lever in the "adjust" position while inserting the spacer.**

5 Remove the recline adjustment knob and trim from the outer side of the front seat, then unscrew the bolt and remove the seat belt end from the seat **(see illustrations)**.

Rear side seat belt

6 Unscrew the screws and remove the trim from the "C" pillar. It will be necessary to detach the rear seat release cable, and remove the plastic cover from the rear seat lock **(see illustrations)**.

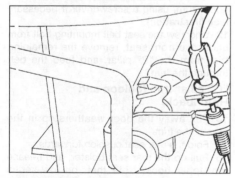

28.4a Front seat belt stalk cable

28.4b Front seat stalk mounting nut

28.5a Remove the recline adjustment knob . . .

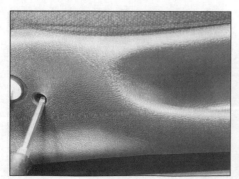

28.5b . . . unscrew the trim retaining screws . . .

28.5c . . . and unscrew the seat belt end retaining bolt

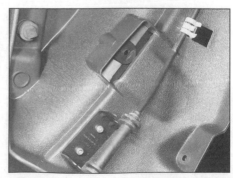

28.6a Detach the rear seat release cable

11

28.6b Removing the plastic cover from the rear seat lock

28.7a Rear seat belt shackle mounting bolt

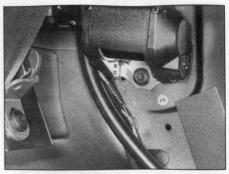

28.7b Rear seat belt reel mounting bolt

7 Fold the rear seat cushions forward. Unscrew the mounting bolts from the seat belt shackle and reel **(see illustrations)**.

8 Unscrew the mounting bolt securing the seat belt stalk, and withdraw the stalk. Also unscrew the mounting bolt from the lower anchorage, where applicable **(see illustration)**.

Rear centre seat belt

9 Unscrew the mounting bolts securing the seat belt and stalks to the floor. Note that the stalks are handed, and are marked Left or Right.

Refitting

10 Refitting is a reversal of the removal procedure. Tighten the mounting nuts and bolts to the specified torque.

28.8 Rear seat belt lower anchorage

29 Interior trim panels - removal and refitting

Removal

Sun visor

1 Disconnect the wiring for the vanity mirror light, where fitted.

2 Unscrew the mounting screws and remove the visor.

3 Prise up the cover, unscrew the inner bracket mounting screws, and remove the bracket.

Passenger grab handle

4 Prise up the covers, then unscrew the

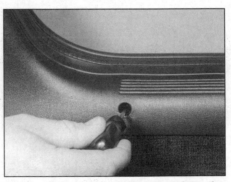

29.10a Removing a middle screw from the lower trim

mounting screws and remove the grab handle.

"A" pillar trim

5 Pull away the door weatherstrip in the area of the trim.

6 Release the alarm and aerial wiring from the upper and middle clips.

7 Carefully press the trim away from the upper and middle clips, and pull the trim upwards. Recover the lower sealing strip.

8 Remove the upper and middle clips from the pillar.

"B" pillar and cowl side trim

9 Pull away the door weatherstrip in the area of the trim.

10 Undo the screws, release the fasteners and remove the lower trim **(see illustrations)**.

11 Carefully separate the lower trim from the upper trim, using a screwdriver if necessary **(see illustration)**.

12 Unscrew the seat belt mounting bolt from under the front seat, remove the remaining trim from the "B" pillar, and feed the belt through the trim.

"C" pillar trim (Saloon and Hatchback)

13 Pull away the door weatherstrip in the area of the trim.

14 Fold the rear seat cushion forwards.

15 Pull up the rear seat bolster, and release the upper hook. Note that, on low-series models, the bolster is retained with a screw **(see illustrations)**.

29.10b Releasing the fasteners from the cowl side trim

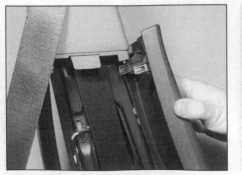

29.11 Separating the "B" pillar lower and upper trim

29.15a Pull up the rear seat bolster . . .

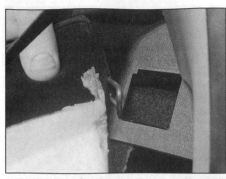

29.15b ... and release the upper hook

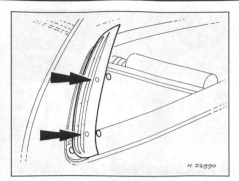

29.18 Screw locations (arrowed) for the "C" pillar upper trim - Estate models

29.23a Unscrew the mounting screws from the upper corners ...

29.23b ... and above the coin tray position ...

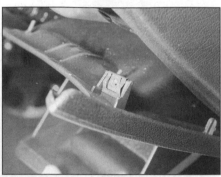

29.23c ... and withdraw the lower facia panel

position, and withdraw the lower facia panel from the facia (**see illustrations**).

Refitting

24 Refitting is a reversal of the removal procedure. Where seat belt fastenings have been disturbed, make sure that they are tightened to the specified torque.

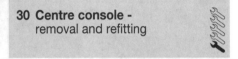

30 Centre console -
removal and refitting

Removal

1 Disconnect the battery negative (earth) lead (Chapter 5, Section 1).
2 Pull the ashtray from the facia.
3 Pull off the gear lever (or selector lever) knob (**see illustration**).
4 Using a screwdriver, carefully prise out the gear lever gaiter/switch panel or selector lever panel, as applicable. When necessary, disconnect the wiring multi-plugs (**see illustration**).
5 Prise off the plastic caps, then unscrew the centre console mounting screws. These are located on each side, on the front top, and inside the cassette storage box. The screws with the washers go on the side of the console; the front screws are smaller than the others, and black in colour (**see illustrations**).
6 Fully apply the handbrake lever. Withdraw

16 Undo the screw, release the clips, and detach the upper trim.
17 Remove the rear seat belt lower mounting

bolt, then remove the trim, and pass the seat belt through it.

"C" pillar trim (Estate)

18 Prise off the caps, unscrew the screws, and remove the upper trim from the "C" pillar (**see illustration**).
19 Unscrew the mounting bolt securing the rear seat belt upper shackle to the "C" pillar.
20 Unclip and remove the trim.

"D" pillar trim (Estate)

21 Remove the three mounting screws, then unclip the trim from the "D" pillar.

Lower facia panel

22 Remove the steering column top and bottom shrouds.
23 Unscrew the mounting screws from the upper corners and above the coin tray

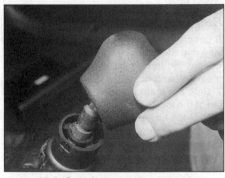

30.3 Gear lever knob removal

30.4 Prising out the gear lever gaiter

30.5a Prise off the plastic caps ...

30.5b ... and unscrew the mounting screws at the front top ...

11

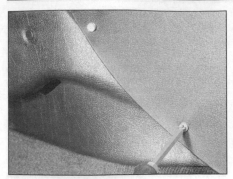

30.5c ...at the sides...

30.5d ...and inside the cassette storage box

30.6a Withdrawing the front of the console from the facia

30.6b Passing the gaiter over the handbrake lever

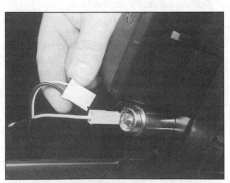

30.7 Disconnecting the cigar lighter wiring

the centre console, at the same time passing the gaiter over the handbrake lever (see illustrations).
7 Disconnect the cigar lighter wiring (see illustration).

Refitting

8 Refitting is a reversal of the removal procedure.

31 Overhead console - removal and refitting

Removal

1 Disconnect the battery negative (earth) lead (Chapter 5, Section 1).
2 When applicable, remove the sunroof switch (Chapter 12).
3 When applicable, remove the sunroof handle, after undoing the securing screw (see illustration).
4 Push the console towards the windscreen, to disengage it from the clips.

Refitting

5 Refitting is a reversal of the removal procedure.

32 Glovebox - removal and refitting

Removal

1 Open the glovebox. Using a screwdriver, carefully press in one side of the glovebox near the hinge, to release it from the plastic clip (see illustration).
2 Withdraw the glovebox and, where necessary, disconnect the wiring multi-plug for the light.
3 If necessary, the lock may be removed by unscrewing the mounting screws and removing the lock plate and spring (see illustration).
4 To remove the lock barrel, depress the spring tabs.

Refitting

5 Locate the barrel in the lock plate, making sure that the clips are fully engaged.
6 Hold the latch pins together, and engage the right-hand pin of the lock plate.
7 Refit the spring, and engage the left-hand pin of the lock plate.
8 Refit the lock plate, and tighten the screws.
9 Reconnect the wiring multi-plug and refit the glovebox, making sure that it is fully inserted in the plastic clips.

31.3 Removing the sunroof handle securing screw

32.1 Glovebox removal

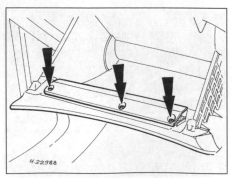

32.3 Glovebox lock mounting screws (arrowed)

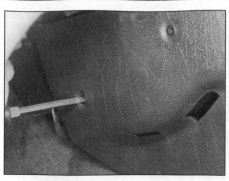

33.3a Unscrew the screws . . .

33.3b . . . and remove the heater side covers

33.18a Prise off the covers . . .

33 Facia -
removal and refitting

Removal

1 Disconnect the battery negative (earth) lead (Chapter 5, Section 1).

2 Remove the windscreen wiper arms (Chapter 12), then remove the cowl from just in front of the windscreen. The cowl is in two sections, with retaining screws located along its front edge. With the cowl removed, disconnect the speedometer cable by pulling it from the intermediate inner cable extension.

3 Remove the centre console (Section 30), then unscrew the screws and remove the heater side covers **(see illustrations)**.

4 Remove the steering column (Chapter 10).

5 Remove the instrument panel (Chapter 12).

6 Where fitted, unscrew the screws and remove the automatic warning system display.

7 Remove the radio and (if fitted) the CD player (Chapter 12).

8 Remove the heater control panel (Chapter 3).

9 Using a screwdriver, carefully prise out the headlight switch panel, and disconnect the wiring multi-plugs.

10 Remove the glovebox (Section 32).

11 Remove the small piece of carpet from under the passenger side of the facia.

12 Remove the side trim panels from the "A" and "B" pillars on each side of the vehicle (Section 29). The upper panels on the "B" pillars can be left in position.

13 At the base of the right-hand "A" pillar, disconnect the wiring multi-plugs, earth leads and aerial, noting their fitted positions.

14 Identify the position of the wiring multi-plugs on the fusebox, then disconnect them.

15 Disconnect the wiring from the footwell lights, where fitted.

16 Prise out the speedometer cable rubber grommet at the bulkhead near the pedal bracket, then release the cable from the clips.

17 Remove the screws and withdraw the glovebox side trim, for access to the side facia mounting screw.

18 Open the front doors. Prise off the trim covers, then pull away the door weatherstrip by the side mounting bolt positions on each side **(see illustrations)**.

19 Unscrew the facia side mounting bolts.

20 Unscrew the facia centre mounting bolts **(see illustrations)**.

21 Withdraw the facia from the bulkhead, far enough to be able to reach in behind it.

22 Disconnect the remaining multi-plugs and connections, noting their locations on the various components for correct refitting. It will also be necessary to release some wiring

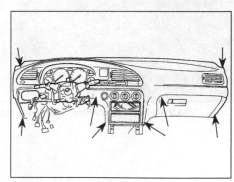

33.18b . . . and pull away the weatherstrip to reveal the facia mounting bolts

33.20a Facia mounting bolt positions (left-hand-drive shown, right-hand-drive similar)

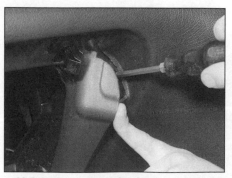

33.20b Facia mounting bolt next to the glovebox

33.20c Facia centre mounting bolt next to the heater panel

33.20d Facia mounting bolt near the heater

11

loom holders, clips and plastic ties, and the fresh air vent hoses **(see illustration)**.
23 Withdraw the facia from one side of the vehicle.

Refitting

24 Refitting is a reversal of the removal procedure. On completion, check the operation of all electrical components.

34 Wheel arch liner - removal and refitting

Removal

Front

1 Apply the handbrake, jack up the front of the vehicle and support it on axle stands. If wished, remove the wheel to improve access.

33.22 Disconnecting the fresh air hoses

2 Prise out the stud clip on the front lower edge of the liner.
3 Using a Torx key, unscrew the screws securing the liner to the inner wheel arch panel **(see illustration)**.
4 Remove the screws and clips securing the liner to the outer edge of the wheel arch and bumper. Withdraw the liner from under the vehicle **(see illustration)**.

Rear

5 Chock the front wheels, jack up the rear of the vehicle and support it on axle stands. If wished, remove the wheel to improve access.
6 Unscrew and remove the nuts, located on either side of the coil spring, securing the central section of the liner.
7 Using a Torx key, unscrew the screws securing the liner to the centre of the inner wheel arch panel.
8 Remove the clips securing the liner to the outer edge of the wheel arch, and withdraw the liner from under the vehicle.

Refitting

9 Refitting is a reversal of the removal procedure. If the wheels were removed, tighten the wheel nuts to the specified torque.

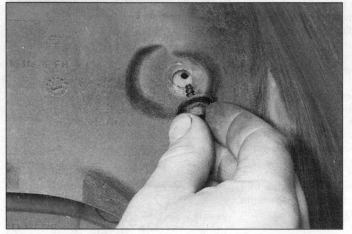

34.3 Removing a wheel arch liner retaining screw

34.4 Removing a front wheel arch liner

Chapter 12 Body electrical system

Contents

Degrees of difficulty

Easy, suitable for novice with little experience	Fairly easy, suitable for beginner with some experience	Fairly difficult, suitable for competent DIY mechanic	Difficult, suitable for experienced DIY mechanic	Very difficult, suitable for expert DIY or professional

Specifications

Fuses (auxiliary fusebox in engine compartment)

Note: *Fuse ratings and circuits are liable to change from year to year. Consult the handbook supplied with the vehicle, or consult a Ford dealer, for specific information.*

Fuse No	Rating	Colour	Circuit(s) protected
1	80	Black	Power supply to main fusebox
2	60	Yellow	Radiator electric cooling fans
3	60	Yellow	Diesel engine glow plugs and/or ABS braking system
4	20	Yellow	Ignition system, or ignition and daytime running lights
5	30	Light green	Heated windscreen (left-hand side)
6	30	Light green	Heated windscreen (right-hand side)
7	30	Light green	ABS braking system
8	30	Light green	Air conditioning compressor/heated seats or air conditioning compressor/daytime running lights
9	20	Light blue	ECU (petrol), Cold start solenoid (Diesel)
10	20	Light blue	Ignition switch
11	3	Violet	ECU memory
12	15	Light blue	Horn and hazard flasher warning system
13	15	Light blue	Oxygen sensor
14	15	Light blue	Fuel pump
15	10	Red	Dipped beam headlight (right-hand side)
16	10	Red	Dipped beam headlight (left-hand side)
17	10	Red	Main beam headlight (right-hand side)
18	10	Red	Main beam headlight (left-hand side)

12

Fuses (main fusebox in passenger compartment)

Note: *Fuse ratings and circuits are liable to change from year to year. Consult the handbook supplied with the vehicle, or consult a Ford dealer, for specific information.*

Fuse	Rating	Colour	Circuit(s) protected
19	7.5	Brown	Heated door mirrors
20	10	Black	Front/rear wiper motor (circuit breaker)
21	30	Light green	Front electric windows (only)
21	40	Orange	Front and rear electric windows
22	7.5	Brown	ABS module
23	15	Light blue	Reversing lights
24	15	Light blue	Stop-lights
25	20	Yellow	Central locking system/double-locking/anti-theft alarm
26	20	Yellow	Foglights
27	15	Light blue	Cigar lighter
28	30	Light green	Headlight washer system
29	30	Light green	Heated rear window
30	7.5	Brown	Interior lighting and auxiliary warning system
31	7.5	Brown	Instrument panel illumination
32	7.5	Brown	Radio
33	7.5	Brown	Front and rear sidelights (left-hand side)
34	7.5	Brown	Interior lighting and digital clock
35	7.5	Brown	Front and rear sidelights (right-hand side)
36	30	Light green	Air bag
37	30	Light green	Heater blower

Relays (auxiliary fusebox in engine compartment)

Relay	Colour	Circuit(s) protected
R1	Green	Daytime running lights (left-hand-drive, but not all countries) or dim-dip lights (UK)
R2	Black	Radiator electric cooling fan (high speed)
R3	Brown (Diesel)	Air conditioning in conjunction with Diesel engine
R4	Yellow	Windscreen heater time delay
R5	Black (Diesel)	Radiator electric cooling fan (low speed)
R6	Yellow	Starter solenoid
R7	Brown	Horns
R9	White	Dipped beam headlights
R10	White	Main beam headlights
R11	Brown	Cold start (Diesel)

Relays (main fusebox in passenger compartment)

Relay	Colour	Circuit(s) protected
R12	White	Interior, courtesy and footwell lights
R13	Yellow	Heated rear window
R14	Yellow	Heater blower
R15	Green	Windscreen wiper motor
R16	Black	Ignition

Auxiliary relays (not in the fuseboxes)

Relay	Colour	Circuit(s) protected	Location
R17	Black	Diesel glow plug	Battery tray
R18	Black	"One-touch down" driver's window relay	Driver's door
R19	Blue	Speed control cut-off	Central fuse box bracket below the instrument panel
R20	Blue	Headlight washer system	Bulb module bracket
R21	Orange	Rear screen wiper interval	Bulb module bracket
R22	White	Foglights (left-hand-drive only)	Interface module bracket
R23	Black	Direction indicators	Steering column
R24	White	Anti-theft alarm (left-hand side)	Door lock module bracket
R25	White	Anti-theft alarm (right-hand side)	Door lock module bracket
R26	Black	Heated seats	Door lock module bracket

Bulbs

	Wattage	Type
Headlight main beam	55	Halogen
Headlight dipped beam	55	Halogen
Foglights	55	Halogen
Sidelights	5	Wedge
Direction indicator lights	21	Bayonet
Side repeater lights	5	Wedge
Stop-lights	21	Bayonet
Reversing lights	21	Bayonet
Rear fog/tail lights (Saloon and Estate)	21/4	Bayonet
Rear tail light (Saloon and Hatchback)	5	Bayonet
Number plate lights	5	Festoon
Engine compartment	10	Wedge
Interior lights	10	Festoon
Reading light	5	Wedge

Torque wrench settings

	Nm	lbf ft
Windscreen wiper motor bolts:		
Into old motor (see text)	8	6
Into new motor (see text)	12	9

1 General information

![Warning triangle] **Warning: Before carrying out any work on the electrical system, read through the precautions given in "Safety first!" at the beginning of this manual.**

The electrical system is of 12-volt negative earth type. Power for the lights and all electrical accessories is supplied by a lead/acid battery which is charged by the alternator.

This Chapter covers repair and service procedures for the various electrical components not associated with the engine. Information on the battery, engine electrical system, alternator, and starter motor can be found in Chapter 5.

All models are fitted with a driver's air bag, which is designed to prevent serious chest and head injuries to the driver during an accident. A similar bag for the front seat passenger is also available **(see illustration)**. The sensor and electronic unit for the air bag is located next to the steering column inside the vehicle, and contains a back-up capacitor, crash sensor, decelerometer, safety sensor, integrated circuit and microprocessor **(see illustration)**. The air bag is inflated by a gas generator, which forces the bag out of the module cover in the centre of the steering wheel. A "clock spring" ensures that a good electrical connection is maintained with the air bag at all times - as the steering wheel is turned in each direction, the spring winds and unwinds.

All UK models are fitted with an alarm system incorporating a movement sensor and ignition immobiliser. On Saloon and Hatchback models, the alarm system horn is located on the left-hand side of the luggage compartment, but on Estate models, it is on the right-hand side.

Some models are fitted with a headlight levelling system, which is controlled by a knob

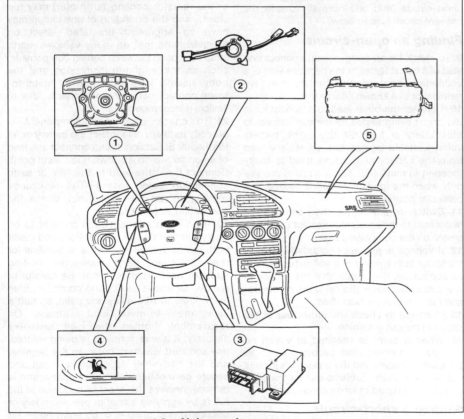

1.3a Air bag system components

1 Air bag module (driver's)
2 Clock spring
3 Diagnostic and sensor unit
4 Air bag indicator light
5 Air bag module (passenger's)

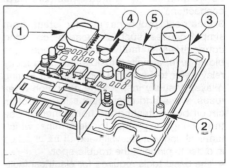

1.3b Air bag sensor and electronic unit

1 Crash sensor
2 Safety sensor
3 Voltage back-up
4 Application Specific Integrated Circuit
5 Microprocessor

12

on the facia. On position "0", the headlights are in their base position, and on position "5", the headlights are in their maximum inclined angle.

It should be noted that, when portions of the electrical system are serviced, the cable should be disconnected from the battery negative terminal, to prevent electrical shorts and fires.

Caution: When disconnecting the battery for work described in the following Sections, refer to Chapter 5, Section 1.

2 Electrical fault finding - general information

Note: *Refer to the precautions given in "Safety first!" and in Section 1 of this Chapter before starting work. The following tests relate to testing of the main electrical circuits, and should not be used to test delicate electronic circuits (such as engine management systems, anti-lock braking systems, etc), particularly where an electronic control module is used. Also refer to the precautions given in Chapter 5, Section 1.*

General

1 A typical electrical circuit consists of an electrical component, any switches, relays, motors, fuses, fusible links or circuit breakers related to that component, and the wiring and connectors which link the component to both the battery and the chassis. To help to pinpoint a problem in an electrical circuit, wiring diagrams are included at the end of this manual.

2 Before attempting to diagnose an electrical fault, first study the appropriate wiring diagram, to obtain a complete understanding of the components included in the particular circuit concerned. The possible sources of a fault can be narrowed down by noting if other components related to the circuit are operating properly. If several components or circuits fail at one time, the problem is likely to be related to a shared fuse or earth connection.

3 Electrical problems usually stem from simple causes, such as loose or corroded connections, a faulty earth connection, a blown fuse, a melted fusible link, or a faulty relay (refer to Section 3 for details of testing relays). Visually inspect the condition of all fuses, wires and connections in a problem circuit before testing the components. Use the wiring diagrams to determine which terminal connections will need to be checked in order to pinpoint the trouble-spot.

4 The basic tools required for electrical fault-finding include a circuit tester or voltmeter (a 12-volt bulb with a set of test leads can also be used for certain tests); an ohmmeter (to measure resistance and check for continuity); a battery and set of test leads; and a jumper wire, preferably with a circuit breaker or fuse

incorporated, which can be used to bypass suspect wires or electrical components. Before attempting to locate a problem with test instruments, use the wiring diagram to determine where to make the connections.

5 To find the source of an intermittent wiring fault (usually due to a poor or dirty connection, or damaged wiring insulation), a "wiggle" test can be performed on the wiring. This involves wiggling the wiring by hand to see if the fault occurs as the wiring is moved. It should be possible to narrow down the source of the fault to a particular section of wiring. This method of testing can be used in conjunction with any of the tests described in the following sub-Sections.

6 Apart from problems due to poor connections, two basic types of fault can occur in an electrical circuit - open-circuit, or short-circuit.

7 Open-circuit faults are caused by a break somewhere in the circuit, which prevents current from flowing. An open-circuit fault will prevent a component from working.

8 Short-circuit faults are caused by a "short" somewhere in the circuit, which allows the current flowing in the circuit to "escape" along an alternative route, usually to earth. Short-circuit faults are normally caused by a breakdown in wiring insulation, which allows a feed wire to touch either another wire, or an earthed component such as the bodyshell. A short-circuit fault will normally cause the relevant circuit fuse to blow.

Finding an open-circuit

9 To check for an open-circuit, connect one lead of a circuit tester or the negative lead of a voltmeter either to the battery negative terminal or to a known good earth.

10 Connect the other lead to a connector in the circuit being tested, preferably nearest to the battery or fuse. At this point, battery voltage should be present, unless the lead from the battery or the fuse itself is faulty (bearing in mind that some circuits are live only when the ignition switch is moved to a particular position).

11 Switch on the circuit, then connect the tester lead to the connector nearest the circuit switch on the component side.

12 If voltage is present (indicated either by the tester bulb lighting or a voltmeter reading, as applicable), this means that the section of the circuit between the relevant connector and the switch is problem-free.

13 Continue to check the remainder of the circuit in the same fashion.

14 When a point is reached at which no voltage is present, the problem must lie between that point and the previous test point with voltage. Most problems can be traced to a broken, corroded or loose connection.

Finding a short-circuit

15 To check for a short-circuit, first disconnect the load(s) from the circuit (loads are the components which draw current from

a circuit, such as bulbs, motors, heating elements, etc).

16 Remove the relevant fuse from the circuit, and connect a circuit tester or voltmeter to the fuse connections.

17 Switch on the circuit, bearing in mind that some circuits are live only when the ignition switch is moved to a particular position.

18 If voltage is present (indicated either by the tester bulb lighting or a voltmeter reading, as applicable), this means that there is a short-circuit.

19 If no voltage is present during this test, but the fuse still blows with the load(s) reconnected, this indicates an internal fault in the load(s).

Finding an earth fault

20 The battery negative terminal is connected to "earth" - the metal of the engine/transmission unit and the vehicle body - and many systems are wired so that they only receive a positive feed, the current returning via the metal of the car body. This means that the component mounting and the body form part of that circuit. Loose or corroded mountings can therefore cause a range of electrical faults, ranging from total failure of a circuit, to a puzzling partial failure. In particular, lights may shine dimly (especially when another circuit sharing the same earth point is in operation), motors (eg wiper motors or the radiator cooling fan motor) may run slowly, and the operation of one circuit may have an apparently-unrelated effect on another. Note that on many vehicles, earth straps are used between certain components, such as the engine/transmission and the body, usually where there is no metal-to-metal contact between components, due to flexible rubber mountings, etc.

21 To check whether a component is properly earthed, disconnect the battery (refer to Chapter 5, Section 1) and connect one lead of an ohmmeter to a known good earth point. Connect the other lead to the wire or earth connection being tested. The resistance reading should be zero; if not, check the connection as follows.

22 If an earth connection is thought to be faulty, dismantle the connection, and clean both the bodyshell and the wire terminal (or the component earth connection mating surface) back to bare metal. Be careful to remove all traces of dirt and corrosion, then use a knife to trim away any paint, so that a clean metal-to-metal joint is made. On reassembly, tighten the joint fasteners securely; if a wire terminal is being refitted, use serrated washers between the terminal and the bodyshell, to ensure a clean and secure connection. When the connection is remade, prevent the onset of corrosion in the future by applying a coat of petroleum jelly or silicone-based grease, or by spraying on (at regular intervals) a proprietary ignition sealer such as Holts Damp Start, or a water-dispersant lubricant such as Holts Wet Start.

3 Fuses, relays and timer module - testing and renewal

Note: *It is important to note that the ignition switch and the appropriate electrical circuit must always be switched off before any of the fuses (or relays) are removed and renewed. In the event of the fuse/relay unit having to be removed, the battery earth lead must be disconnected. When reconnecting the battery, reference should be made to Chapter 5.*

1 Fuses are designed to break a circuit when a predetermined current is reached, in order to protect components and wiring which could be damaged by excessive current flow. Any excessive current flow will be due to a fault in the circuit, usually a short-circuit (see Section 2). The main fusebox, which also carries some relays, is located inside the vehicle below the facia panel on the passenger's side, and is accessed by a lever behind the glovebox **(see illustration)**.

2 A central timer module is located on the bottom of the main fusebox. This module contains the time control elements for the heated rear window, interior lights and intermittent wiper operation. The module also activates a warning buzzer/chime when the vehicle is left with the lights switched on, or if a vehicle fitted with automatic transmission is not parked in position "P".

3 The auxiliary fusebox is located on the front left-hand side of the engine compartment, and is accessed by unclipping and removing the cover. The auxiliary fusebox also contains some relays **(see illustration)**. Each circuit is

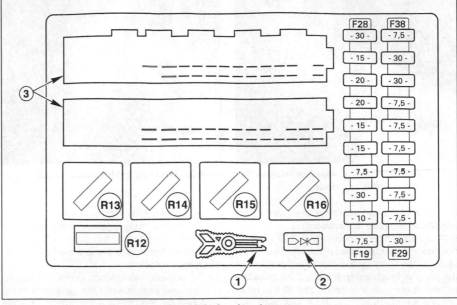

3.1 Main fusebox layout

1 Fuse/relay removal tweezers   2 Diode   3 Multi-plug connections

identified by numbers on the main fusebox and on the inside of the auxiliary fusebox cover. Reference to the fuse chart in the Specifications at the start of this Chapter will indicate the circuits protected by each fuse. Plastic tweezers are attached to the main fusebox and to the inside face of the auxiliary fuse and block cover, to remove and fit the fuses and relays.

4 To remove a fuse, use the tweezers provided to pull it out of the holder. Slide the fuse sideways from the tweezers. The

wire within the fuse is clearly visible, and it will be broken if the fuse is blown **(see illustration)**.

5 Always renew a fuse with one of an identical rating. Never substitute a fuse of a higher rating, or make temporary repairs using wire or metal foil; more serious damage, or even fire, could result. The fuse rating is stamped on top of the fuse. Never renew a fuse more than once without tracing the source of the trouble.

6 Spare fuses of various current ratings are provided in the cover of the auxiliary fusebox. Note that if the vehicle is to be laid up for a long period, fuse 34 in the main fusebox should be removed, to prevent the ancillary electrical components from discharging the battery.

7 Relays are electrically-operated switches, which are used in certain circuits. The various relays can be removed from their respective locations by carefully pulling them from the sockets. Each relay in the fuseboxes has a plastic bar on its upper surface to enable the use of the tweezers. The locations and

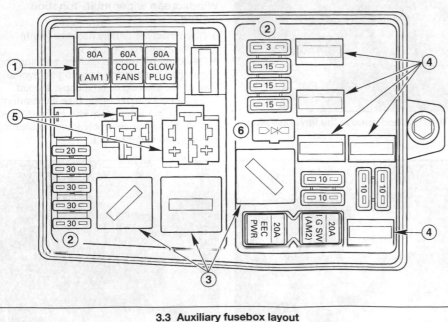

3.3 Auxiliary fusebox layout

1 Fuses 1 to 3
2 Fuses 4 to 8, 11 to 14
3 Relays R2, R5 and R6
4 Relays R7 to R11
5 Relay sockets for relays R1 and R4
6 Diode

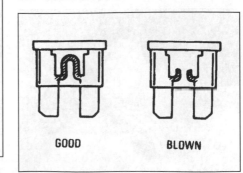

3.4 The fuses can be checked visually to determine if they are blown

12

3.7 "One-touch down" window relay in the driver's door

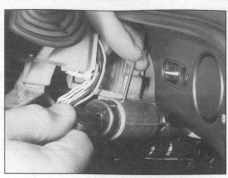

4.3a Depress the locking plunger . . .

4.3b . . . and withdraw the ignition lock barrel

functions of the various relays are given in the Specifications (see illustration).

8 If a component controlled by a relay becomes inoperative and the relay is suspect, listen to the relay as the circuit is operated. If the relay is functioning, it should be possible to hear it click as it is energized. If the relay proves satisfactory, the fault lies with the components or wiring of the system. If the relay is not being energized, then either the relay is not receiving a switching voltage, or the relay itself is faulty. (Do not overlook the relay socket terminals when tracing faults.) Testing is by the substitution of a known good unit, but be careful; while some relays are identical in appearance and in operation, others look similar, but perform different functions.

9 The central timer module located on the bottom of the main fusebox incorporates its own self-diagnosis function. Note that diagnosis cannot take place if the heated rear window is defective.

10 To activate the system, press the heated rear window button while the ignition is being switched on, then release the button. Operate the light switch, washer pump switch and all of the door switches one after the other, and check that the buzzer confirms that the input signals are correct.

11 Now move the wiper lever to the intermittent wipe position, and check the output signals by operating the same switches.

12 The self-diagnosis function is turned off by switching the ignition off and on again.

4 Switches - removal and refitting

Removal

Ignition switch and lock barrel

1 Disconnect the battery negative (earth) lead (refer to Chapter 5, Section 1).

2 Remove the rubber gaiters and locking rings, then remove the securing screws and take off the steering column upper and lower shrouds.

3 Insert the ignition key, and turn it to the accessory position. Using a small screwdriver or twist drill through the hole in the side of the lock housing, depress the locking plunger and withdraw the lock barrel (see illustrations).

4 The switch may be removed from the steering column assembly by disconnecting the multi-plug, then using a screwdriver to release the switch retaining tab (see illustrations).

Windscreen wiper multi-function switch

5 Disconnect the battery negative (earth) lead (refer to Chapter 5, Section 1).

6 Remove the rubber gaiters and locking rings, then remove the securing screws and take off the steering column upper shroud.

7 Disconnect the multi-plug (see illustration).

8 Depress the plastic tab with a screwdriver, and lift the switch assembly from the steering column (see illustrations).

4.4a Release the retaining tab . . .

4.4b . . . and remove the ignition switch

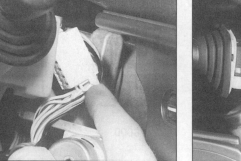

4.7 Disconnecting the multi-plug from the windscreen wiper multi-function switch

4.8a Depress the plastic tab with a screwdriver . . .

4.8b . . . and remove the windscreen wiper multi-function switch

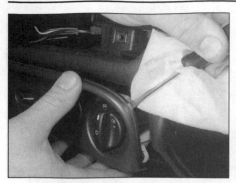

4.10 Prising out the light switch

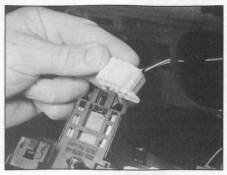

4.11 Disconnecting the multi-plugs from the light switch and rheostat

4.23 Removing the direction indicator, dipped beam and hazard flasher multi-function switch. Direction indicator relay (flasher unit) is attached

Main light, auxiliary foglight and rear foglight combination switch

Note: *From July 1994 a revised main light switch was introduced; this was fitted as standard in production. If the revised switch is to be fitted to a pre-July 1994 model, an adapter lead will also be required to prevent electrical damage ocurring. Refer to your Ford dealer for further information*

9 Disconnect the battery negative (earth) lead (refer to Chapter 5, Section 1).
10 Carefully prise the switch panel from the facia, using a screwdriver against a cloth pad to prevent damage to the facia **(see illustration)**.
11 Disconnect the multi-plugs and withdraw the switch panel **(see illustration)**.
12 Unscrew the four mounting screws, and remove the switch from the panel.
13 Pull off the switch control knob, and remove the blanking plug and retainer.
14 Depress the plastic tabs, and remove the front cover and switch.

Instrument light rheostat

15 Disconnect the battery negative (earth) lead (refer to Chapter 5, Section 1).
16 Carefully prise the light switch panel from the facia, using a screwdriver against a cloth pad to prevent damage to the facia.
17 Disconnect the multi-plugs from the rear of the switch, then remove the screws and withdraw the instrument light rheostat from the panel.

Door mirror control switch

18 Disconnect the battery negative (earth) lead (refer to Chapter 5, Section 1).
19 Carefully prise the switch from the facia, using a screwdriver against a cloth pad to prevent damage to the facia.
20 Disconnect the multi-plug and withdraw the switch.

Direction indicator, dipped beam and hazard flasher multi-function switch

21 Disconnect the battery negative (earth) lead (refer to Chapter 5, Section 1).
22 Remove the rubber gaiters and locking rings, then remove the screws and take off the steering column upper shroud.

23 Depress the retaining lug and withdraw the switch assembly, then disconnect the multi-plug **(see illustration)**.
24 With the switch assembly removed, pull out the direction indicator relay if required.

Horn switch (steering wheel without air bag)

Note: *When an air bag is fitted, the horn switch is removed with the air bag unit. Refer to Section 28.*

25 Disconnect the battery negative (earth) lead (refer to Chapter 5, Section 1).
26 Carefully pull off the padded centre of the steering wheel which incorporates the horn switch.
27 Disconnect the wiring and remove the switch assembly.

Luggage compartment switch

28 Disconnect the battery negative (earth) lead (refer to Chapter 5, Section 1).
29 With the tailgate/bootlid open, pull the weatherstrip from the centre of the rear cross panel.
30 Carefully prise out the trim fasteners from the bottom corners of the rear trim, then unscrew the retaining screws and remove the trim panel.
31 Disconnect the wiring multi-plug, and pull out the switch.

Electrically-operated window switch (single)

32 Disconnect the battery negative (earth) lead (refer to Chapter 5, Section 1).
33 Carefully prise out the switch from the door inner trim panel, using a cloth pad to prevent damage to the trim.
34 Disconnect the multi-plug and remove the switch.

Electrically-operated window switch (multiple) and isolator

35 Disconnect the battery negative (earth) lead (refer to Chapter 5, Section 1).
36 Prise the blanking cap from inside the inner door handle cavity, and remove the screw.

37 Hold the inner door handle in its open position, then remove the bezel and withdraw it over the handle.
38 Depress the retaining lug and remove the switch assembly, then disconnect the multi-plug.

Electrically-operated sunroof switch and traction control switch

39 Disconnect the battery negative (earth) lead (refer to Chapter 5, Section 1).
40 Carefully prise out the switch with a screwdriver, using a cloth pad to prevent damage to the trim.
41 Disconnect the multi-plug and remove the switch.

Handbrake-on warning switch

42 Disconnect the battery negative (earth) lead (refer to Chapter 5, Section 1).
43 Remove the centre console as described in Chapter 11.
44 Disconnect the multi-plug, then remove the screw and withdraw the switch from the handbrake lever mounting bracket **(see illustration)**.

Heated windscreen switch and heated rear window switch

45 Disconnect the battery negative (earth) lead (refer to Chapter 5, Section 1).

4.44 Disconnecting the multi-plug from the handbrake lever

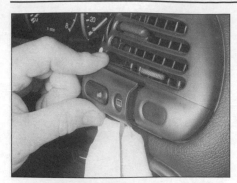

4.46 Prising out the heated rear window switch

4.47 Disconnecting the multi-plug from the heated rear window switch

4.51a Unscrew the cross-head screw . . .

4.51b . . . and pull out the courtesy light switch

46 Carefully prise out the switch, using a cloth pad to prevent damage to the trim (see illustration).
47 Disconnect the multi-plug and remove the switch (see illustration).

Electrically-operated seat switch and heated seat switch

48 Disconnect the battery negative (earth) lead (refer to Chapter 5, Section 1).
49 Carefully prise out the switch, using a cloth pad to prevent damage to the trim.
50 Disconnect the multi-plug and remove the switch.

5.1 Removing the cover from the rear of the headlight

Courtesy light door switch

51 Open the door, then unscrew the cross-head screw and carefully pull the switch from the pillar (see illustrations). Take care not to force the wire from the switch terminal, otherwise it will be difficult to retrieve it from the pillar.
52 Disconnect the wire, and tie it in a loose knot to prevent it dropping back into the pillar.

Refitting

53 Refitting of all switches is a reversal of the removal procedure.

5 Bulbs (exterior lights) - renewal

Note: *Ensure that all exterior lights are switched off before disconnecting the wiring connectors from any exterior light bulbs. Do not touch the glass of halogen-type bulbs (headlights, front foglights) with the fingers; if the glass is accidentally touched, clean it with methylated spirit.*

Headlight (dipped beam)

1 Working under the bonnet, depress the plastic clips and remove the cover from the rear of the headlight unit (see illustration).
2 Release the spring clip and withdraw the bulb, then disconnect the wiring lead (see illustrations).
3 Fit the new bulb using a reversal of the removal procedure. Have the headlight beam alignment checked as described later in this Chapter.

Headlight (main beam)

4 Working under the bonnet, depress the plastic clips and remove the cover from the rear of the headlight unit.
5 Turn the bulbholder anti-clockwise, and remove it from the rear of the headlight unit (see illustration).

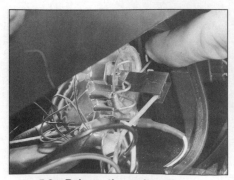

5.2a Release the spring clip . . .

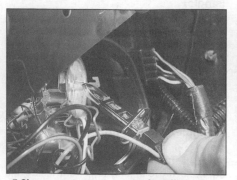

5.2b . . . and withdraw the headlight bulb

5.5 Removing the headlight (main beam) bulbholder

5.6 Removing the headlight (main beam) bulb from the bulbholder

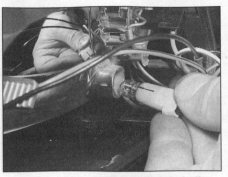

5.9 Removing the front sidelight bulb-holder from the rear of the headlight unit

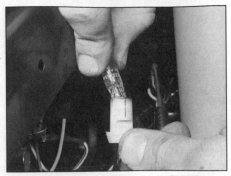

5.10 Pulling the wedge-type bulb from the bulbholder

6 Pull out the bulb and disconnect the wiring lead **(see illustration)**.
7 Fit the new bulb using a reversal of the removal procedure, making sure that the bulbholder is correctly located in the headlight unit. Have the headlight beam alignment checked as described later in this Chapter.

Front sidelight

8 Working under the bonnet, depress the plastic clips and remove the cover from the rear of the headlight unit.
9 Pull the bulbholder from the rear of the headlight unit **(see illustration)**.
10 Pull the wedge-type bulb from the bulbholder **(see illustration)**.
11 Fit the new bulb using a reversal of the removal procedure.

Front direction indicator

12 Open the bonnet. Loosen (but do not remove) the screw located above the front direction indicator (see illustration 7.10).
13 Withdraw the front direction indicator light unit.
14 Rotate the bulbholder anti-clockwise, and withdraw it from the light unit.
15 Twist the bulb anti-clockwise, and remove it from the bulbholder **(see illustration)**.
16 Fit the new bulb using a reversal of the

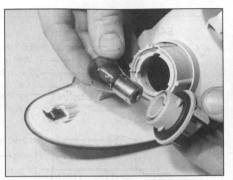

5.15 Removing the front direction indicator bulb

removal procedure, but before refitting the light unit, first insert the holding spring in its bore.

Side repeaters

17 The side repeater light is held in position by spring pressure.
18 Depending on how the light unit was previously fitted, press it either forwards or rearwards, and remove it from the front wing **(see illustration)**.
19 Turn the bulbholder anti-clockwise, and disconnect it from the housing **(see illustration)**.
20 Pull the wedge-type bulb from the holder **(see illustration)**.
21 Fit the new bulb using a reversal of the removal procedure.

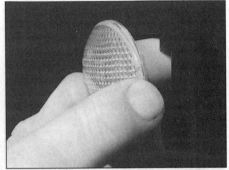

5.18 Removing the side repeater from the front wing

Front foglight

22 Unscrew the cross-head screws securing the front foglight unit to the valance, and withdraw the light unit.
23 Prise open the plastic clips and remove the rear cover from the light unit.
24 Release the spring clips and withdraw the bulb, then pull off the wiring connector.
25 Fit the new bulb using a reversal of the removal procedure.

Rear light cluster

26 With the tailgate or bootlid open, flip open the trim cover to reveal the bulbholder in the rear corner of the luggage compartment. On Estate models, pull back the weatherstrip and unclip the trim cover **(see illustrations)**.

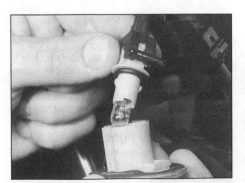

5.19 Removing the bulbholder from the side repeater lens/bulbholder

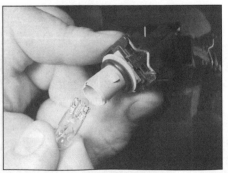

5.20 Removing the wedge-type bulb from the side repeater bulbholder

5.26a Pull back the weatherstrip . . .

12

5.26b ... and unclip the trim cover

5.27a Pressing the two plastic locking tabs together (Estate)

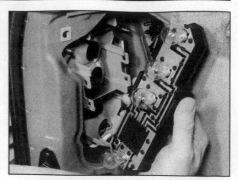

5.27b Removing the rear light cluster (Estate)

5.27c Removing the rear light cluster (Saloon)

5.28a Removing a bulb from the rear light cluster bulbholder

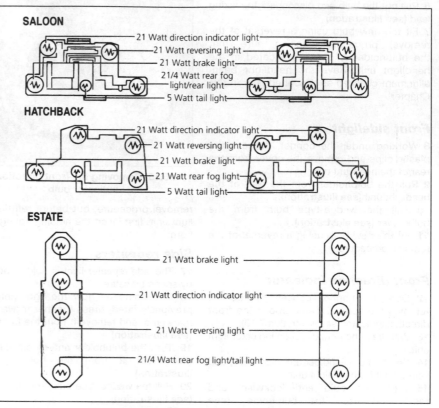

SALOON

- 21 Watt direction indicator light
- 21 Watt reversing light
- 21 Watt brake light
- 21/4 Watt rear fog light/rear light
- 5 Watt tail light

HATCHBACK

- 21 Watt direction indicator light
- 21 Watt reversing light
- 21 Watt brake light
- 21 Watt rear fog light
- 5 Watt tail light

ESTATE

- 21 Watt brake light
- 21 Watt direction indicator light
- 21 Watt reversing light
- 21/4 Watt rear fog light/tail light

5.28b Bulb positions in the rear light cluster

5.30 Remove the cross-head screws ...

5.31 ... for access to the festoon-type bulb

27 Press the two plastic locking tabs together, and withdraw the complete rear light cluster **(see illustrations)**.

28 Depress and twist the appropriate bulb to remove it from the bulbholder **(see illustrations)**.

29 Fit the new bulb using a reversal of the removal procedure. Make sure that the rear light cluster is fully inserted.

Number plate light

30 Remove the cross-head screws from the number plate light, and remove the light unit **(see illustration)**.

31 Release the festoon-type bulb from the contact springs **(see illustration)**.

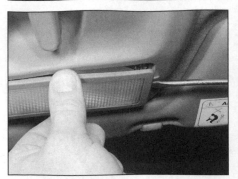

6.4 Prise out the interior light with a screwdriver

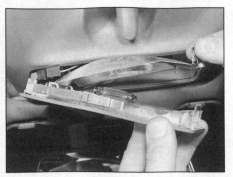

6.5 Lifting the reflector from the interior light

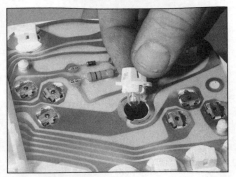

6.11 Removing a bulb from the rear of the instrument panel

32 Fit the new bulb using a reversal of the removal procedure. Make sure that the tension of the contact springs is sufficient to hold the bulb firmly.

6 Bulbs (interior lights) - renewal

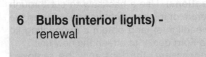

Engine compartment light

1 With the bonnet open, pull the wedge-type bulb from the bulbholder.
2 Fit the new bulb using a reversal of the removal procedure.

Interior lights

3 Switch off the interior light by locating the switch in its middle position.
4 Using a small screwdriver, carefully prise out the light or bulb cover, as applicable **(see illustration)**.
5 Lift up the reflector, then release the festoon-type bulb from the contact springs **(see illustration)**.
6 Fit the new bulb using a reversal of the

removal procedure. Make sure that the tension of the contact springs is sufficient to hold the bulb firmly.

Reading light

7 With the reading light switched off, prise out the light using a small screwdriver.
8 Hinge back the contact plate, and release the festoon-type bulb from the contact springs.
9 Fit the new bulb using a reversal of the removal procedure. Make sure that the tension of the contact springs is sufficient to hold the bulb firmly.

Instrument panel illumination and warning lights

10 Remove the instrument panel as described in Section 10.
11 Twist the bulbholder anti-clockwise to remove it **(see illustration)**.
12 Fit the new bulbholder using a reversal of the removal procedure.

Foglight warning indicator

13 Using a screwdriver, prise out the indicator from the facia, and disconnect the multi-plug.
14 Twist the bulbholder anti-clockwise with the screwdriver, and remove it **(see illustration)**.
15 Fit the new bulb using a reversal of the removal procedure.

Hazard warning light

16 Pull the cover directly up from the switch, then remove the bulb **(see illustrations)**.
17 Fit the new bulb using a reversal of the removal procedure.

Glovebox light

18 Open the glovebox, then pull out the wedge-type bulb from the light located under the upper edge.

Heater fan switch illumination

19 Pull off the switch knob, then depress and twist the bulb to remove it.

Interior door handle illumination

20 Disconnect the battery negative (earth) lead (refer to Chapter 5, Section 1).
21 Remove the door interior trim panel as described in Chapter 11.
22 Using a knife, cut free the foam watershield for access to the rear of the interior door handle.
23 Pull out the bulbholder and remove the bulb.

Clock illumination

24 Disconnect the battery negative (earth) lead (refer to Chapter 5, Section 1).
25 Remove the clock as described in Section 13.
26 Twist the bulbholder anti-clockwise using

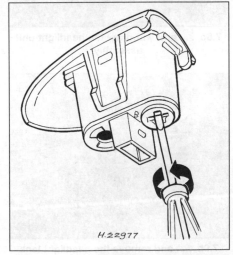

6.14 Removing the bulb from the foglight warning indicator

H.22977

6.16a Pull off the hazard warning light cover . . .

6.16b . . . and remove the bulb

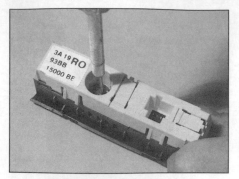

6.26a Twist the bulbholder anti-clockwise . . .

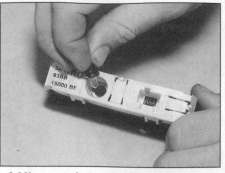

6.26b . . . and remove it from the rear of the clock

7.4 Disconnecting the headlight unit wiring multi-plug

a screwdriver, then remove the bulbholder from the rear of the clock **(see illustrations)**.

Heater control illumination

27 Remove the heater control panel (Chapter 3), then twist the bulbholder anti-clockwise and remove the bulb from the rear of the panel.

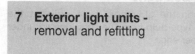

7 Exterior light units - removal and refitting

Removal

1 Disconnect the battery negative (earth) lead (refer to Chapter 5, Section 1).

Headlight unit

2 With the bonnet supported in its open position, loosen (but do not remove) the screw located above the front direction indicator.
3 Withdraw the front direction indicator unit forwards, and disconnect the wiring multi-plug. Place the unit to one side.
4 Disconnect the wiring multi-plug for the headlight unit **(see illustration)**.
5 Remove the radiator grille as described in Chapter 11.
6 Remove the front bumper as described in Chapter 11.
7 The headlights fitted from new are a single unit, joined by a plastic back-piece running across the front of the vehicle. However, if it is

required to renew a headlight unit on one side only, the back-piece must first be removed complete, then cut in half on the bench.
8 Unscrew the mounting bolts from each side of the headlight unit, and withdraw the unit from the front of the vehicle **(see illustrations)**. Use a hacksaw to cut through the centre of the headlight unit (ie between the two headlights), and obtain a connecting kit from a Ford dealer to attach the new unit.
9 If necessary, the lens may be removed separately by releasing the clips **(see illustrations)**. To remove the diffuser, release the clips, then remove the rubber seal.

Front direction indicator

10 With the bonnet supported in its open

7.8a Unscrew the outer mounting screws . . .

7.8b . . . and inner mounting screws . . .

7.8c . . . and withdraw the headlight unit assembly

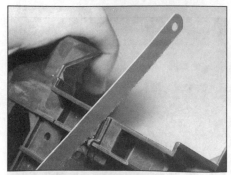

7.8d Using a hacksaw to cut through the middle of the headlight back-piece, in order to fit a new unit

7.9a Release the clips . . .

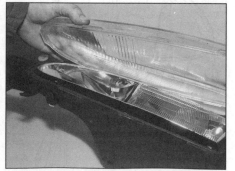

7.9b . . . and remove the headlight lens

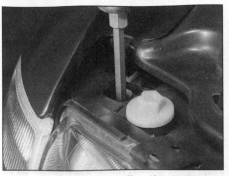

7.10 Loosen the front direction indicator retaining screw

7.12 Disconnecting the wiring plug from the indicator bulbholder

position, loosen (but do not remove) the screw located above the front direction indicator **(see illustration)**.

11 Withdraw the front direction indicator light unit.

12 Rotate the bulbholder anti-clockwise, and withdraw it from the light unit. Alternatively, the wiring plug can be disconnected from the bulbholder, leaving the bulb in position **(see illustration)**. Remove the light unit.

Foglight (front)

13 Unscrew the cross-head screws securing the front foglight unit to the valance, and withdraw the light unit from the valance.

14 Prise open the plastic clips, and remove the rear cover from the light unit.

15 Release the spring clips and withdraw the bulb, then pull off the wiring connector. Remove the foglight unit.

Rear light cluster

16 With the tailgate or bootlid open, unhook the parcel net (where fitted) from the rear of the luggage compartment.

17 On Saloon and Hatchback models, remove the screws, release the clips, and remove the trim panel from the rear cross panel. On Estate models, it is sufficient to open the flap.

18 Remove the screws, and press the rear light trim cover from the guides (where applicable).

19 Disconnect the wiring multi-plug.

20 Unscrew the four mounting nuts, and withdraw the light unit from the outside of the vehicle **(see illustrations)**.

Rear number plate light assembly

21 Remove both number plate light bulbs as described in Section 5.

22 With the tailgate or bootlid open, remove the screws and withdraw the inner trim panel.

23 Unscrew the nuts, and remove the outer cover and number plate base from the tailgate.

24 Disconnect the multi-plug and remove the light assembly.

Refitting

25 Refitting of all the external light units is a reversal of the removal procedure, noting the following points:

(a) When refitting the rubber seal on the headlight unit, note that it has a tapered seat.

(b) If one or both headlights have been disturbed, have the beam alignment checked as described in the next Section.

(c) When refitting the rear light cluster, check the condition of the sealer on the body panel, and if necessary renew it.

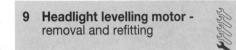

8 Headlight beam alignment - checking and adjustment

1 Accurate adjustment of the headlight beam is only possible using optical beam-setting equipment. This work should therefore be carried out by a Ford dealer, or other service station with the necessary facilities.

2 Temporary adjustment can be made after renewal of a headlight bulb or unit, or as an emergency measure if the alignment is incorrect following accident damage. Turn the adjustment screws on the top of the headlamp unit to make the adjustment **(see illustration)**.

3 Before making any adjustments to the settings, it is important that the tyre pressures are correct, and that the vehicle is standing on level ground. Bounce the front of the vehicle a few times to settle the suspension. Ideally, somebody of average size should sit in the driver's seat during the adjustment, and the vehicle should have a full tank of fuel. Where a vehicle is fitted with an electrical beam levelling system, set the switch to the "O" position before making any adjustments.

4 Whenever temporary adjustments are made, the settings must be checked and if necessary reset by a Ford dealer or other qualified person as soon as possible.

9 Headlight levelling motor - removal and refitting

Removal

1 Remove the headlight unit as described in Section 7, then remove the cover.

2 Disconnect the wiring multi-plug from the motor.

3 Rotate the motor upwards approximately 60°, then pull it forwards slightly.

4 Disconnect the adjustment spindle by pressing the ball coupling to one side, away from the socket on the reflector.

5 Withdraw the motor from the headlight unit.

Refitting

6 Refitting is a reversal of the removal procedure, but make sure that the motor is turned down until it engages the stop.

10 Instrument panel - removal and refitting

Removal

1 Disconnect the battery negative (earth) lead (refer to Chapter 5, Section 1).

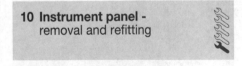

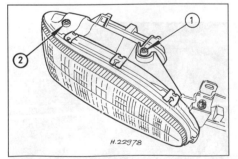

8.2 Headlight beam setting adjustment screws

1 Vertical alignment screw
2 Horizontal alignment screw

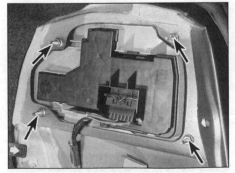

7.20a Rear light cluster mounting nuts (arrowed)

7.20b Removing the rear light cluster unit

10.6 Removing the foglight warning indicator

10.7 Removing a switch blanking cover

10.8a With the blanking covers removed, unscrew the concealed screws . . .

10.8b . . . and the remaining screws . . .

2 Where fitted, remove the clock as described in Section 13.

3 Where fitted, remove the trip computer module as described in Section 18.

4 Remove the heated rear window switch as described in Section 4.

5 Where fitted, remove the heated windscreen switch.

6 Where fitted, remove the display assembly warning indicator for the foglights **(see illustration)**.

7 Remove any blanking covers from the unused switch positions **(see illustration)**.

8 Prise out the blanking covers, then unscrew the retaining screws and remove the instrument panel surround **(see illustrations)**.

9 Unscrew the mounting screws, and withdraw the instrument panel a little way from the facia **(see illustration)**.

10 Disconnect the two multi-plugs from the rear of the instrument panel **(see illustration)**.

11 Withdraw the instrument panel from the facia, at the same time releasing the speedometer intermediate cable.

Refitting

12 Refitting is a reversal of the removal procedure.

11 Instrument panel components - removal and refitting

Removal

1 Remove the warning light and illumination bulbs by twisting them anti-clockwise **(see illustration)**.

2 Carefully prise off the glass and bezel from the front of the instrument panel, noting the positions of the retaining lugs **(see illustration)**.

3 Note the positions of the five diffusers, then remove them from the instrument panel.

4 To remove the speedometer head, unscrew the three mounting screws and withdraw the head from the housing.

5 To remove the tachometer, unscrew the

10.8c . . . and lift out the instrument panel surround

10.9 Three of the instrument panel mounting screws (arrowed)

10.10 Disconnecting the multi-plugs from the rear of the instrument panel

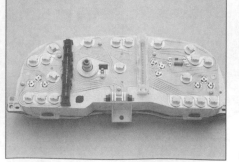

11.1 Rear view of the instrument panel, showing bulbholders

11.2 Bezel retaining lug on the instrument panel

12.7a Squeeze the collar . . .

12.7b . . . and disconnect the speedometer main cable from the intermediate cable

12.9a Unscrew the cable nut . . .

single screw and withdraw it from the housing.

6 Similarly remove the fuel gauge and temperature gauge by unscrewing the single screws.

7 Remove all the pin contacts.

8 Using a small punch, push in the multi-plug securing pins, and remove the multi-plugs.

9 Carefully lift the printed circuit from the location dowels on the housing, taking care not to damage it.

Refitting

10 Refitting is a reversal of the removal procedure.

12 Speedometer drive cable - removal and refitting

Removal

1 Remove the windscreen wiper arms as described in Section 15.

2 With the bonnet closed, release the grille panel upper edge from just in front of the windscreen, by prising off the caps and unscrewing the upper retaining screws.

3 Open the bonnet, and support with the stay.

4 Pull off the sealing strip from the cross panel at the rear of the engine compartment.

5 Unscrew the lower screws, and remove the grille panel halves from in front of the

windscreen, withdrawing first one side and then the other.

6 Disconnect the battery negative (earth) lead (refer to Chapter 5, Section 1).

7 Reach in behind the bulkhead. Squeeze the collar on the upper end of the speedometer cable, where it is attached to the intermediate cable from the rear of the speedometer head. Disconnect the cable, and withdraw it from the bulkhead inner panel, together with the rubber grommet **(see illustrations)**.

8 Apply the handbrake, jack up the front of the vehicle and support it on axle stands.

9 Unscrew the nut and disconnect the speedometer cable from the vehicle speed sensor on the transmission, then withdraw the cable from within the engine compartment. Use two spanners to loosen the nut - one to counterhold the sensor, and the other to unscrew the cable nut **(see illustrations)**.

Refitting

10 Refitting is a reversal of the removal procedure.

13 Clock - removal and refitting

Removal

1 Disconnect the battery negative (earth) lead (refer to Chapter 5, Section 1).

2 Using a small screwdriver, prise the clock out of the facia **(see illustration)**. To prevent damage to the facia, place a cloth pad beneath the screwdriver.

3 Disconnect the multi-plug from the rear of the clock, and withdraw the clock **(see illustration)**.

Refitting

4 Refitting is a reversal of the removal procedure. Reset the clock on completion.

14 Horn - removal and refitting

Removal

1 Apply the handbrake, jack up the front of the vehicle and support it on axle stands.

2 Unscrew the bolts, and release the clips securing the radiator lower cover to the front of the vehicle.

3 Disconnect the wiring from the horn terminal.

4 Unscrew the mounting bolt, and withdraw the horn with its mounting bracket from under the vehicle **(see illustration)**.

Refitting

5 Refitting is a reversal of the removal procedure.

12.9b . . . and disconnect the speedometer cable from the vehicle speed sensor

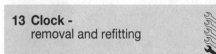

13.2 Prising the clock out of the facia

13.3 Disconnecting the multi-plug from the rear of the clock

14.4 Horn and mounting bracket (arrowed)

15.3 Loosening the wiper arm retaining nut

15.5 Removing the wiper arm from the spindle

15 Wiper arms - removal and refitting

Removal

1 Disconnect the battery negative (earth) lead (refer to Chapter 5, Section 1). If the windscreen wiper arms are to be removed, close the bonnet.
2 With the wiper(s) "parked" (ie in the normal at-rest position), mark the positions of the blade(s) on the screen, using a wax crayon or strips of masking tape.
3 Lift up the plastic cap from the bottom of the wiper arm, and loosen the nut one or two turns **(see illustration)**.
4 Lift the wiper arm, and release it from the taper on the spindle by moving it to one side.

5 Completely remove the nut, and withdraw the wiper arm from the spindle **(see illustration)**.

Refitting

6 Refitting is a reversal of the removal procedure. Make sure that the arm is fitted in the previously-noted position.

16 Windscreen wiper motor and linkage - removal and refitting

Removal

1 Disconnect the battery negative (earth) lead (refer to Chapter 5, Section 1).
2 Remove the wiper arms as described in Section 15.
3 With the bonnet closed, release the grille

panel upper edge from just in front of the windscreen, by prising off the caps and unscrewing the upper retaining screws **(see illustrations)**.
4 Open the bonnet, and support it with the stay.
5 Pull off the bonnet sealing strip from the cross panel at the rear of the engine compartment **(see illustration)**.
6 Unscrew the lower screws, and remove the grille panel halves from in front of the windscreen, withdrawing one side then the other side **(see illustrations)**.
7 Unscrew the mounting bolts securing the wiper motor and linkage to the bulkhead. On right-hand-drive models, the linkage is on the right-hand side of the bulkhead **(see illustration)**; on left-hand-drive models, it is on the left-hand side.

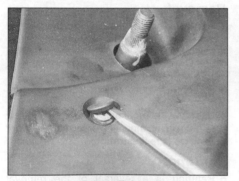

16.3a Prise off the cap . . .

16.3b . . . and remove the upper retaining screws

16.5 Removing the bonnet sealing strip

16.6a Unscrew the lower screws . . .

16.6b . . . and remove the grille panel from in front of the windscreen

16.7 Wiper motor mounting bolt locations (right-hand-drive)

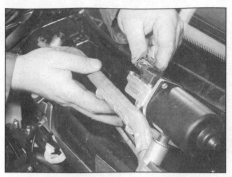

16.9 Removing the wiper motor and linkage

16.10 Wiper motor arm and mounting plate located on the motor

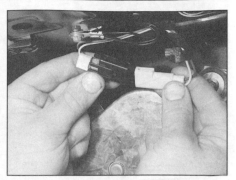

17.4 Disconnecting the tailgate wiper motor multi-plug

8 Disconnect the wiper motor multi-plug.
9 Withdraw the wiper motor, complete with the linkage, from the bulkhead **(see illustration)**.
10 Mark the position of the motor arm on the mounting plate, then unscrew the centre nut **(see illustration)**.
11 Unscrew the motor mounting bolts, and separate the motor from the linkage assembly.

Refitting

12 Refitting is a reversal of the removal procedure. There are two tightening torques for the motor mounting bolts - the lower one for bolts that are being re-inserted into an old motor, and the higher ones for bolts that are being inserted into a new motor. Make sure that the wiper motor is in its "parked" position before fitting the motor arm, and check that the wiper linkage is in line with the motor arm.

17 Tailgate wiper motor assembly - removal and refitting

Removal

1 Disconnect the battery negative (earth) lead (refer to Chapter 5, Section 1).
2 Remove the tailgate wiper arm as described in Section 15.
3 Remove the tailgate inner trim panel by unscrewing the retaining screws.
4 Release the multi-plug from the clip, then disconnect it **(see illustration)**.

5 Disconnect the wiper motor earth lead.
6 Unscrew the mounting bolts, and remove the wiper motor from inside the tailgate **(see illustrations)**.
7 Unbolt and remove the mounting plate. If necessary, remove the mounting rubbers for renewal **(see illustrations)**.

Refitting

8 Refitting is a reversal of the removal procedure. Make sure that the wiper motor is in its "parked" position before fitting the wiper arm.

18 Trip computer module - removal and refitting

Removal

1 Disconnect the battery negative (earth) lead (refer to Chapter 5, Section 1).
2 Using a small screwdriver, prise the trip computer module out of the facia. To prevent damage to the facia, place a cloth pad beneath the screwdriver.
3 Disconnect the multi-plug from the rear of the trip computer module, and withdraw the unit.
4 If necessary, the bulb can be removed by twisting it anti-clockwise.

Refitting

5 Refitting is a reversal of the removal procedure.

19 Auxiliary warning system - general information and component renewal

1 Some models are fitted with an auxiliary warning system, which monitors brake lights, sidelights, dipped beam and tail lights, external temperature, and door/tailgate/bootlid opening. An engine oil level warning light on the instrument panel is also part of the system.
2 The auxiliary warning system module and graphic warning display are combined into one unit.

Service interval reminder

3 The system also includes a service interval reminder warning light, which is illuminated if

17.6a Unscrew the mounting bolts . . .

17.6b . . . and remove the tailgate wiper motor assembly (Hatchback shown - Estate similar)

17.7a Tailgate wiper motor assembly and mounting plate

17.7b A mounting rubber removed from the mounting plate

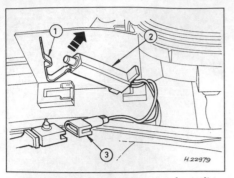

19.9 Low air temperature sender unit removal

1 Clip   2 Sender unit   3 Multi-plug

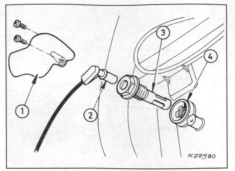

19.14 Engine oil level sensor removal

1 Cover   2 Multi-plug   3 Sensor   4 Seal

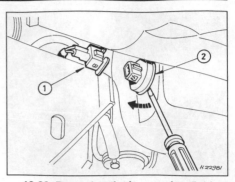

19.20 Removing the low washer fluid switch

1 Multi-plug   2 Switch

the specified mileage (or time) since the last service has been reached.

4 To reset the service interval system and turn off the light, a switch inside the glovebox must be depressed for a minimum of 4 seconds with the ignition switched on. This should be carried out by a Ford dealer if the vehicle is still in the warranty period.

Component renewal

5 The following paragraphs describe brief removal procedures for the auxiliary warning system components. Disconnect the battery negative (earth) lead before commencing work (refer to Chapter 5, Section 1). Refitting procedures are a reversal of removal.

Display warning bulb

6 Remove the control assembly.
7 Prise off the cover, and pull out the relevant bulb and bulbholder.

Low air temperature warning sender unit

8 Remove the front bumper.
9 Unclip the sender unit and disconnect the multi-plug **(see illustration)**.

Engine oil level sensor

10 Apply the handbrake, jack up the front of the vehicle and support it on axle stands.
11 Place a container beneath the oil level sensor, to catch any spilt oil.

12 Unscrew the screws and remove the cover from the sensor.
13 Disconnect the multi-plug.
14 Unscrew and remove the sensor, and remove the seal **(see illustration)**.

Door ajar sensor

15 Remove the door lock as described in Chapter 11, Section 14.
16 Unclip the sensor and disconnect the multi-plug.

Low coolant warning switch

17 Refer to Chapter 3, Section 6.

Low washer fluid switch

18 Disconnect the multi-plug from the washer fluid reservoir.
19 Drain or syphon out the fluid from the reservoir.
20 Using a screwdriver, lever out the switch from the reservoir **(see illustration)**.

Service indicator reset switch

21 Remove the glove compartment lid as described in Chapter 11, Section 32.
22 Carefully lever out the switch using a small screwdriver.
23 Remove the rear cover and disconnect the wiring **(see illustration)**.

Control assembly

24 Remove the instrument panel surround, referring to Section 10.
25 Unscrew the mounting screws,

disconnect the multi-plugs and remove the assembly.

Bulb failure module

26 Remove the lower facia panel from under the steering wheel.
27 Unclip the bulb failure module and disconnect the multi-plug.

20 Anti-theft alarm system - general information

Note: *From November 1993, for added security, a complex Bosch immobiliser system was fitted to some models. For further details, refer to your Ford dealer.*

1 All UK models are fitted with an anti-theft alarm system, incorporating movement sensors and an ignition immobiliser. The system is activated when the vehicle is locked.
2 The system includes a start inhibitor circuit, which makes it impossible to start the engine with the system armed.
3 The movement sensors consist of two ultrasonic units, located in the "B" pillars, incorporating transmitters and receivers **(see illustrations)**. The receivers check that the echo frequency matches the original frequency. If there is any significant difference, the system triggers the alarm.

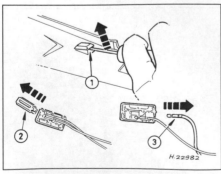

19.23 Service indicator switch removal

1 Lever out the switch   2 Cover   3 Wiring

20.3a Disconnecting a movement sensor multi-plug

20.3b Removing a movement sensor

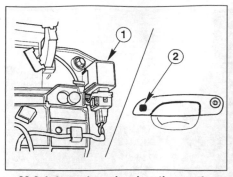

20.6 Infra-red receiver location on the door handle

1 Receiver 2 Infra-red eye on the door handle

20.7 Alarm system horn location on Hatchback and Saloon models

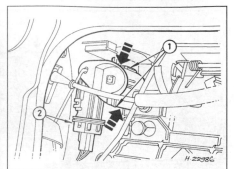

20.9 Alarm system door lock switch removal

1 Clips (arrowed)   2 Multi-plug

4 The system module is located on a bracket beneath the right-hand side of the facia. The set and reset switches are located in a housing by the lock barrel holder in the doors, tailgate or bootlid.

5 To allow temporary opening of the tailgate or bootlid, an inhibit switch is fitted to the lock barrel. This suppresses the alarm system until the tailgate or bootlid is closed again.

6 Where remote central locking is fitted, an infra-red receiver is located on the exterior door handle **(see illustration)**. Note that excessive heat can destroy this receiver; therefore, it should be covered with aluminium tape if (for instance) a paint-drying heat process is to be used.

7 The alarm system is fitted with its own horn. On Hatchback and Saloon models, it is located on the left-hand side of the luggage compartment; on Estate models, it is located on the right-hand side of the luggage compartment **(see illustration)**.

8 The alarm system incorporates a self-test function, which can be activated by operating the bonnet switch or one of the lock position switches eight times within 10 seconds. During the check, the horn or buzzer issues acoustic signals which should occur every time a door, bonnet or tailgate is opened. If

the doors are double-locked, the signal will occur when something is moved within the passenger compartment. A more comprehensive test can be made using the Ford FDS 2000 diagnostic tester.

9 The door lock switches associated with the alarm system are located behind the door trim panels **(see illustration)**.

21 Windscreen/tailgate washer system components - removal and refitting

Removal

Washer reservoir and pump

1 Unscrew the bolts, and release the clips to remove the radiator lower cover.

2 Unscrew the mounting bolts, and pull the reservoir forwards slightly **(see illustration)**. For better access, it may be necessary to remove the front bumper.

3 Disconnect the multi-plugs for the windscreen washer pump and fluid level sensor **(see illustration)**.

4 Disconnect the hoses from the windscreen washer pump and (where applicable) from the headlamp washer pump. Anticipate some loss

of fluid by placing a container beneath the reservoir.

5 Withdraw the reservoir from the vehicle.

6 Pull the level sensor, the windscreen washer pump, and (where applicable) the headlamp washer pump, from the reservoir **(see illustration)**.

7 Remove the rubber seals.

Washer nozzle (windscreen)

8 With the bonnet supported in its open position, carefully disconnect the washer tube from the bottom of the nozzle.

21.2 Washer reservoir mounting bolts (arrowed)

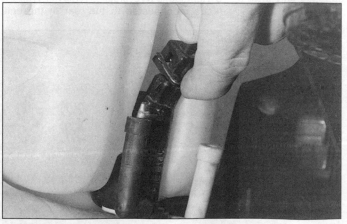

21.3 Disconnecting the washer pump and level sensor multi-plugs

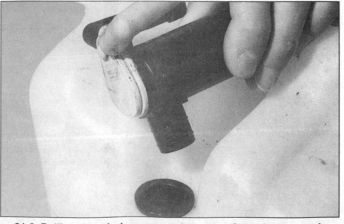

21.6 Pulling the windscreen washer pump from the reservoir

21.11 Pull the washer tube from the bottom of the nozzle

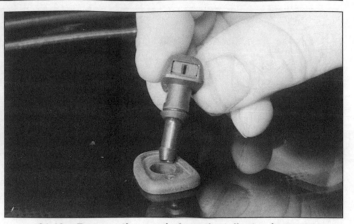

21.12a Remove the nozzle from the tailgate glass . . .

9 Using a screwdriver and working from under the bonnet, carefully prise out the nozzle. Where necessary, disconnect the wiring for the nozzle heater.

Washer nozzle (rear window)

10 With the tailgate open, carefully pull off the inner trim panel from the top of the tailgate.

11 Pull the washer tube from the bottom of the nozzle **(see illustration)**.

12 Carefully prise the nozzle out of the tailgate glass, then prise out the rubber grommet **(see illustrations)**. Where necessary, disconnect the wiring for the nozzle heater.

Refitting

13 Refitting is a reversal of the removal procedure. In the case of the washer nozzles, press them in until they are fully engaged. The rear window washer nozzle must rest against the rubber seal.

---

22 Radio/cassette player - coding, removal and refitting

Note: *Special tools are required to remove the radio.*

Coding

1 If a Ford "Keycode" unit is fitted, and the unit and/or the battery is disconnected, the unit will not function again on reconnection until the correct security code is entered. Details of this procedure are given in the "Ford Audio Systems Operating Guide" supplied with the vehicle when new, with the code itself being given in a "Radio Passport" and/or a "Keycode Label" at the same time.

2 For obvious security reasons, the re-coding procedure is not given in this manual - if you do not have the code or details of the correct procedure, but can supply proof of ownership and a legitimate reason for wanting this information, the vehicle's selling dealer may be able to help.

3 Note that these units will allow only ten attempts at entering the code - any further attempts will render the unit permanently inoperative until it has been reprogrammed by Ford themselves. At first, three consecutive attempts are allowed; if all three are incorrect, a 30-minute delay is required before another attempt can be made. Each of any subsequent attempts (up to the maximum of ten) can be made only after a similar delay.

Removal

4 Disconnect the battery negative (earth) lead.

5 Where fitted, prise the cover/surround from the front of the radio/cassette player. Note that the cover is not fitted to all models.

6 In order to release the radio retaining clips, two U-shaped rods must be inserted into the special holes on each side of the radio **(see illustration)**. If possible, it is preferable to obtain purpose-made rods from an audio specialist, as these have cut-outs which snap firmly into the clips so that the radio can be pulled out. Pull the unit squarely from its aperture, or it may jam. If the unit proves difficult to withdraw, remove the cassette tray (or where applicable, the CD player) from beneath the unit, then reach through the aperture and ease it out from behind.

7 With the radio partly withdrawn, disconnect the feed, earth, aerial and speaker leads. Where applicable, also detach and remove the plastic support bracket from the rear of the unit.

Refitting

8 Refitting is a reversal of removal. With the leads reconnected to the rear of the unit,

21.12b . . . and prise out the rubber grommet

22.6 Using the special U-shaped rods to remove the radio

press it into position until the retaining clips are felt to engage. Reactivate the unit by entering the correct code in accordance with the maker's instructions.

23 Radio/cassette player power amplifier - removal and refitting

Removal

1 Disconnect the battery negative (earth) lead. See Chapter 5, Section 1.
2 Unscrew the screws and remove the lower facia panel.
3 The radio/cassette player power amplifier is located beneath the facia.
4 Unscrew the cross-head screws, disconnect the wiring and remove the amplifier.

Refitting

5 Refitting is a reversal of the removal procedure.

24 Compact disc player - removal and refitting

1 A compact disc (CD) player is available as an optional extra on most models. On some models, an autochanger version is available, which can hold a number of discs at a time.

Removal

2 The battery negative (earth) lead should be disconnected before commencing work.

CD player, or autochanger control unit

3 The procedure is identical to that for the radio/cassette player described in Section 23.

CD player autochanger

4 The CD player autochanger unit is mounted on the right-hand side of the luggage

compartment. The wiring loom passes up the "C" pillar, across to the left-hand side "A" pillar, then to the centre console area.
5 Remove the trim cover from the autochanger unit.
6 Unscrew the mounting screws, and remove the autochanger unit from its mounting bracket.
7 Disconnect the multi-plug and remove the unit from inside the vehicle.

Refitting

8 Refitting is a reversal of the removal procedure.

25 Speakers - removal and refitting

Removal

1 Remove the door trim panel as described in Chapter 11.
2 Unscrew the cross-head screws, and withdraw the speaker from the door inner panel.
3 Disconnect the wiring and remove the speaker.

Refitting

4 Refitting is a reversal of the removal procedure.

26 Radio aerial - removal and refitting

Removal

1 Prise out the trim cover from the headlining immediately below the base of the aerial.
2 Unscrew the cross-head screw from the base of the aerial, and remove the aerial mast.

Refitting

3 Refitting is a reversal of the removal procedure.

27 Air bag unit (driver's side) - removal and refitting

⚠ **Warning: Handle the air bag unit with extreme care, as a precaution against personal injury, and always hold it with the cover facing away from the body. If in doubt concerning any proposed work involving the air bag unit or its control circuitry, consult a Ford dealer or other qualified speclalist.**

Removal

1 Disconnect the battery negative (earth) lead (refer to Chapter 5, Section 1).

⚠ **Warning: Before proceeding, wait a minimum of 15 minutes, as a precaution against accidental firing of the air bag unit. This period ensures that any stored energy in the back-up capacitor is dissipated.**

2 Rotate the steering wheel so that one of the mounting bolt holes is visible above the steering column upper shroud.
3 Unscrew and remove the first mounting bolt, then turn the steering wheel as necessary and remove the remaining mounting bolts **(see illustration)**.
4 Carefully withdraw the air bag unit from the steering wheel far enough to disconnect the wiring multi-plug, then remove it from inside the vehicle **(see illustration)**.

⚠ **Warning: Stand the unit with the cover uppermost, and do not expose it to heat sources in excess of 100°C.**

⚠ **Warning: Do not attempt to open or repair the air bag unit, or apply any electrical current to it. Do not use any air bag unit which is visibly damaged or which has been tampered with.**

Refitting

5 Refitting is a reversal of the removal procedure.

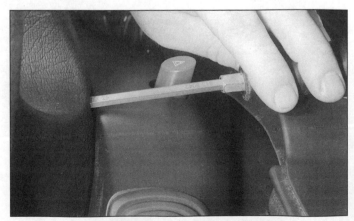

27.3 **Unscrewing an air bag mounting bolt**

27.4 **Disconnecting the air bag wiring multi-plug (arrowed)**

12

28 Air bag control module - removal and refitting

Removal

1 Disconnect the battery negative (earth) lead (refer to Chapter 5, Section 1).

 Warning: Before proceeding, wait a minimum of 15 minutes, as a precaution against accidental firing of the air bag unit. This period ensures that any stored energy in the back-up capacitor is dissipated.

2 Remove the facia panel as described in Chapter 11.

3 Disconnect the multi-plug from the module, by pressing the locking tab upwards and swivelling the retaining strap.

4 Unscrew the mounting bolts and remove the module from the vehicle.

Refitting

5 Refitting is a reversal of the removal procedure.

29 Air bag clock spring - removal and refitting

Removal

1 Remove the air bag unit as described in Section 28.

2 Disconnect the horn switch multi-plug.

3 If fitted, disconnect the multi-plugs for the cruise control.

4 Remove the steering wheel and shrouds.

5 Using a small screwdriver, release the retaining tabs, then remove the clock spring from the steering column.

Refitting

6 Refitting is a reversal of the removal procedure, but make sure that the steering wheel is centralised. The clock spring must be fitted in its central position, with the special alignment marks aligned and the TOP mark uppermost. To check for this position, turn the clock spring housing anti-clockwise until it is tight, then turn in the opposite direction by two-and-three-quarter turns.

30 Wiring diagrams - general information

The following wiring diagrams are designed to be used for Mondeo models fitted with either a petrol or Diesel engine, with specific information relating to the Diesel engine being provided in Diagram 35 at the end of this Chapter.

KEY TO SYMBOLS

PLUG-IN CONNECTOR		PRESSURE ACTUATED	----P	TRANSISTORISED CIRCUIT
PLUG		TEMPERATURE ACTUATED	----T	
SOCKET		LEVEL ACTUATED	----Q	BATTERY SUPPLY
EARTH	G20	MOTOR/PUMP	M	+ BUSBAR
BULB	⊗	HALL SENSOR		EARTH
DIODE		INDUCTOR/COIL		EARTH BUSBAR
ZENER DIODE		CAPACITOR		SWITCHED SUPPLY
LIGHT EMITTING DIODE		VARIABLE CAPACITOR		+ SWITCHED BUSBAR
SOLDERED JOINT	S96	CIRCUIT BREAKER		
FUSE/ FUSIBLE LINK	F8	HEATING ELEMENT		
RESISTOR		PIEZOELECTRIC SENSOR		
VARIABLE RESISTOR		SOLENOID VALVE		
CONNECTOR No. /PIN No.	C808a/9			

NOTES:

1. All diagrams are divided into numbered circuits depending on function e.g. Diagram 11 : Exterior lighting.
2. Items are arranged in relation to a plan view of the vehicle.
3. Wires may interconnect between diagrams and are located by using a grid reference e.g. 2/A1 denotes a position on diagram 2 grid location A1.
4. Complex items appear on the diagrams in sections and are shown in full on the internal connections page (see below).
5. Brackets show how the circuit may be connected in more than one way.
6. Items with a broken border have other connections shown elsewhere.
7. Not all items are fitted to all models.

INTERNAL CONNECTION DETAILS

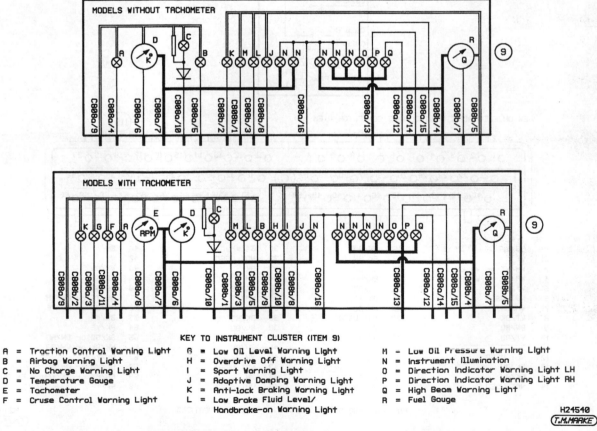

KEY TO INSTRUMENT CLUSTER (ITEM 9)

A = Traction Control Warning Light	G = Low Oil Level Warning Light	M = Low Oil Pressure Warning Light
B = Airbag Warning Light	H = Overdrive Off Warning Light	N = Instrument Illumination
C = No Charge Warning Light	I = Sport Warning Light	O = Direction Indicator Warning Light LH
D = Temperature Gauge	J = Adaptive Damping Warning Light	P = Direction Indicator Warning Light RH
E = Tachometer	K = Anti-lock Braking Warning Light	Q = High Beam Warning Light
F = Cruise Control Warning Light	L = Low Brake Fluid Level/ Handbrake-on Warning Light	R = Fuel Gauge

H24540

T.M.MARKE

Notes, internal connection details and key to symbols

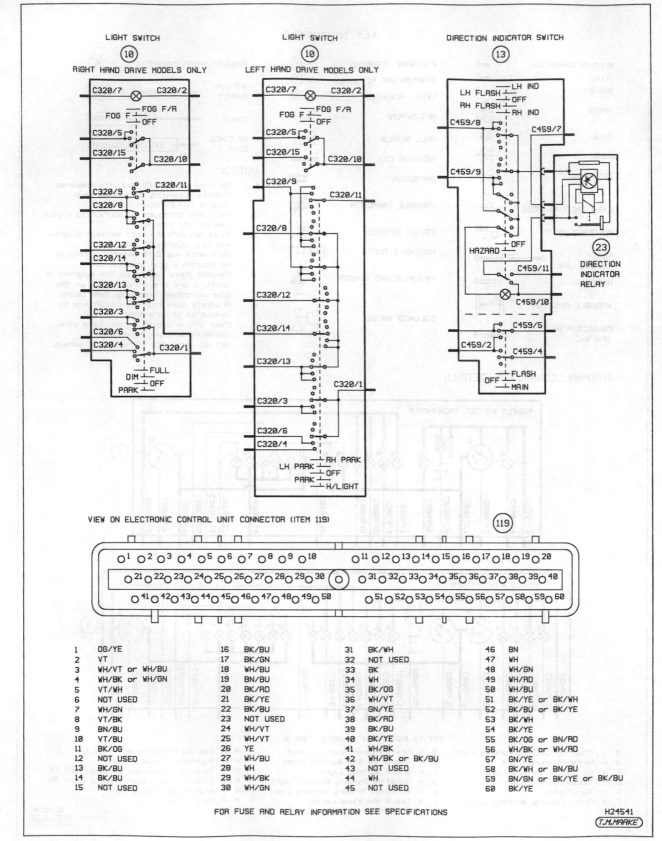

VIEW ON ELECTRONIC CONTROL UNIT CONNECTOR (ITEM 119)

1 OG/YE	16 BK/BU	31 BK/WH	46 BN
2 VT	17 BK/GN	32 NOT USED	47 WH
3 WH/VT or WH/BU	18 WH/BU	33 BK	48 WH/GN
4 WH/BK or WH/GN	19 BN/BU	34 WH	49 WH/RD
5 VT/WH	20 BK/RD	35 BK/OG	50 WH/BU
6 NOT USED	21 BK/YE	36 WH/VT	51 BK/YE or BK/WH
7 WH/GN	22 BK/BU	37 GN/YE	52 BK/BU or BK/YE
8 VT/BK	23 NOT USED	38 BK/RD	53 BK/WH
9 BN/BU	24 WH/VT	39 BK/BU	54 BK/YE
10 VT/BU	25 WH/VT	40 BK/YE	55 BK/OG or BN/RD
11 BK/OG	26 YE	41 WH/BK	56 WH/BK or WH/RD
12 NOT USED	27 WH/BU	42 WH/BK or BK/BU	57 GN/YE
13 BK/BU	28 WH	43 NOT USED	58 BK/WH or BN/BU
14 BK/BU	29 WH/BK	44 WH	59 BN/GN or BK/YE or BK/BU
15 NOT USED	30 WH/GN	45 NOT USED	60 BK/YE

FOR FUSE AND RELAY INFORMATION SEE SPECIFICATIONS

H24541

T.M.MARKE

Internal connection details continued

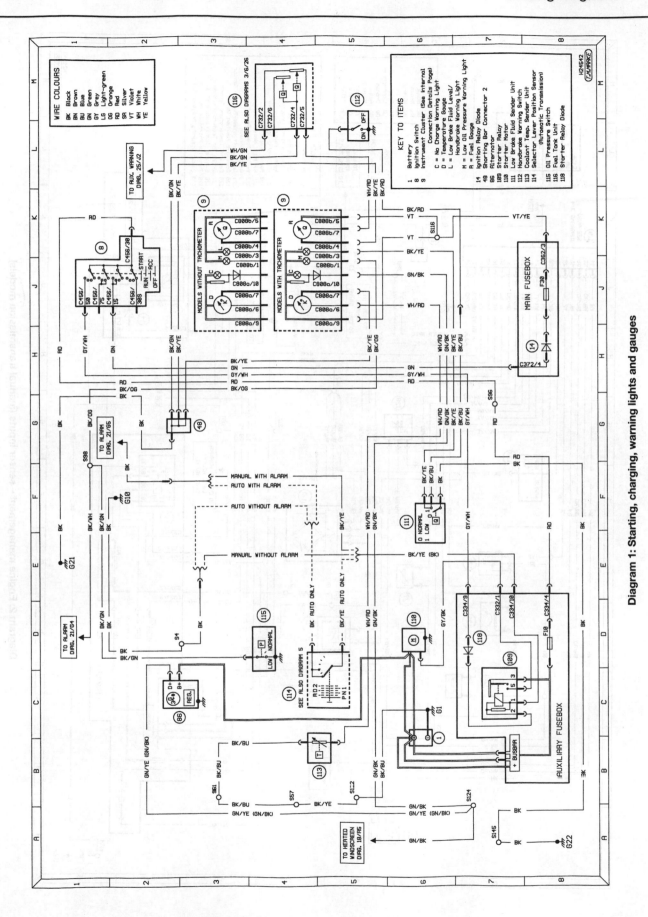

Diagram 1: Starting, charging, warning lights and gauges

WIRE COLOURS

BK	Black
BN	Brown
BU	Blue
GN	Green
GY	Grey
LG	Light-green
OG	Orange
RD	Red
SR	Silver
VT	Violet
WH	White
YE	Yellow

KEY TO ITEMS

1   Battery
8   Ignition Switch
9   Instrument Cluster (See Internal Connection Details page)
    C = No Charge Warning Light
    D = Temperature Gauge
    H = Low Brake Fluid Level/Handbrake Warning Light
    L = Low Oil Pressure Warning Light
    R = Fuel Gauge
14 Ignition Relay Diode
48 Starting Bar Connector 2
86 Alternator
108 Starter Relay
109 Starter Motor
111 Low Brake Fluid Sender Switch
112 Handbrake Warning Switch
113 Coolant Temp. Sender Unit
114 Selector Lever Position Sensor (Automatic Transmission)
115 Oil Pressure Switch
116 Fuel Tank Unit
118 Starter Relay Diode

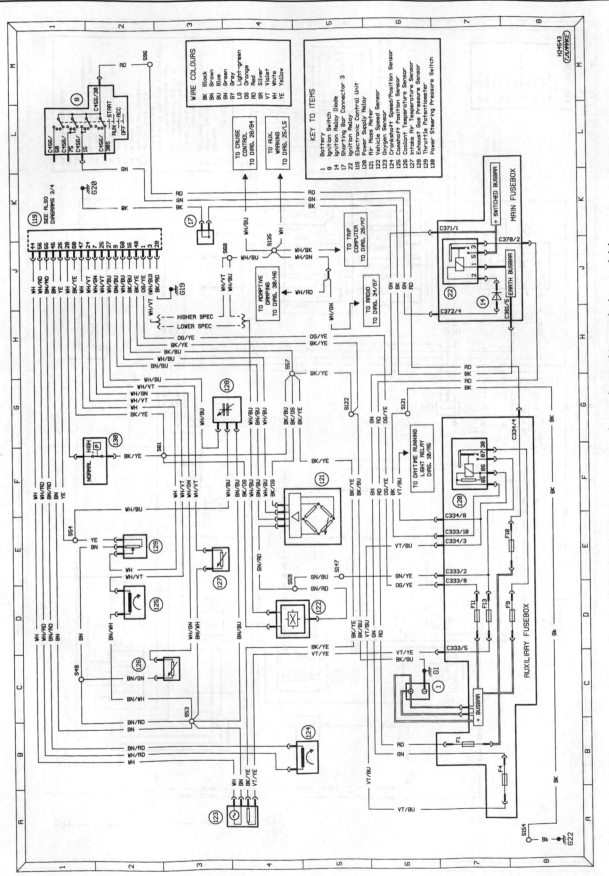

Diagram 2: Engine management – sensor inputs (manual transmission models)

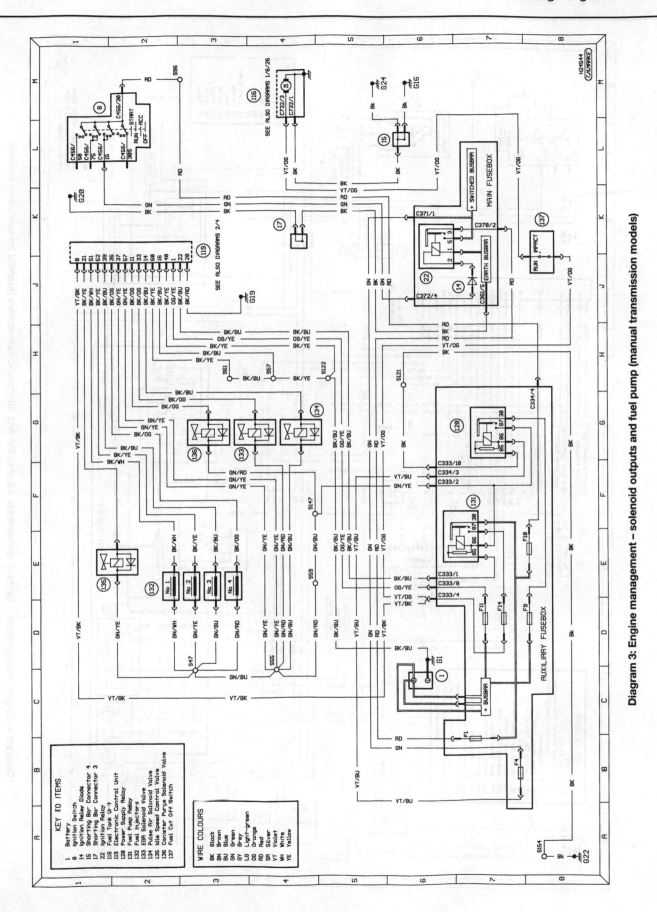

Diagram 3: Engine management – solenoid outputs and fuel pump (manual transmission models)

KEY TO ITEMS

1 Battery
8 Ignition Switch
14 Ignition Relay Diode
15 Shorting Bar Connector 1
17 Shorting Bar Connector 3
22 Ignition Relay
116 Fuel Tank Unit
119 Electronic Control Unit
128 Power Supply Relay
131 Fuel Pump Relay
132 Fuel Injectors
133 EGR Solenoid Valve
134 Pulse Air Solenoid Valve
135 Idle Speed Control Solenoid Valve
136 Canister Purge Solenoid Valve
137 Fuel Cut Off Switch

WIRE COLOURS

BK Black
BN Brown
BU Blue
GN Green
GY Grey
LG Light-green
OG Orange
RD Red
SR Silver
VT Violet
WH White
YE Yellow

12

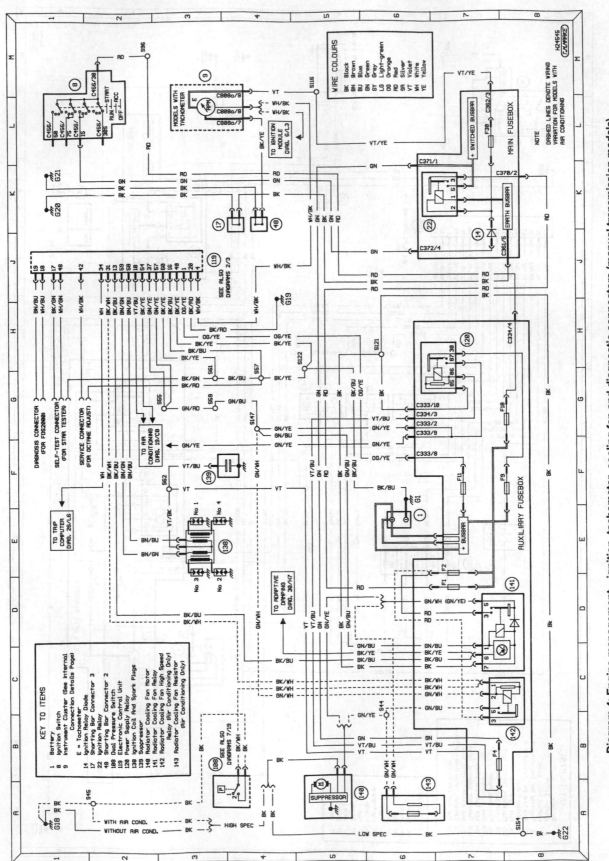

Diagram 4: Engine management – ignition, tachometer, cooling fan and diagnostic connectors (manual transmission models)

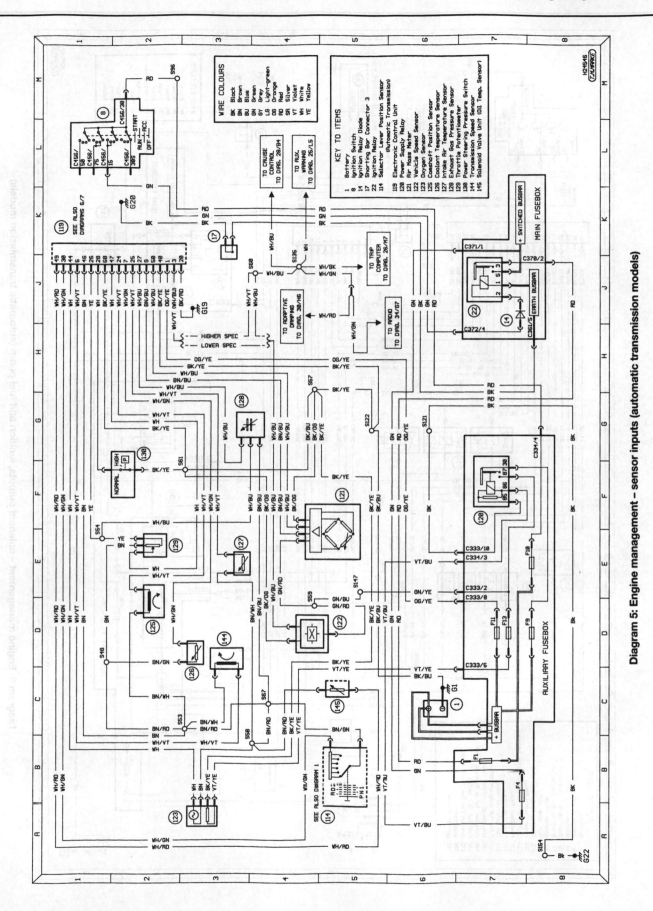

Diagram 5: Engine management – sensor inputs (automatic transmission models)

WIRE COLOURS

BK Black
BN Brown
BU Blue
GN Green
GY Grey
LG Light-green
OG Orange
RD Red
SR Silver
VT Violet
WH White
YE Yellow

KEY TO ITEMS

1 Battery
8 Ignition Switch
14 Ignition Relay Diode
17 Shorting Bar Connector 3
22 Ignition Relay
114 Selector Lever Position Sensor (Automatic Transmission)
119 Electronic Control Unit
120 Power Supply Relay
121 Air Mass Meter
122 Vehicle Speed Sensor
123 Camshaft Position Sensor
124 Oxygen Sensor
125 Coolant Temperature Sensor
126 Intake Air Temperature Sensor
127 Exhaust Gas Pressure Sensor
128 Throttle Potentiometer
129 Power Steering Pressure Switch
130 Transmission Speed Sensor
144 Solenoid Valve Unit (Oil Temp. Sensor)

12

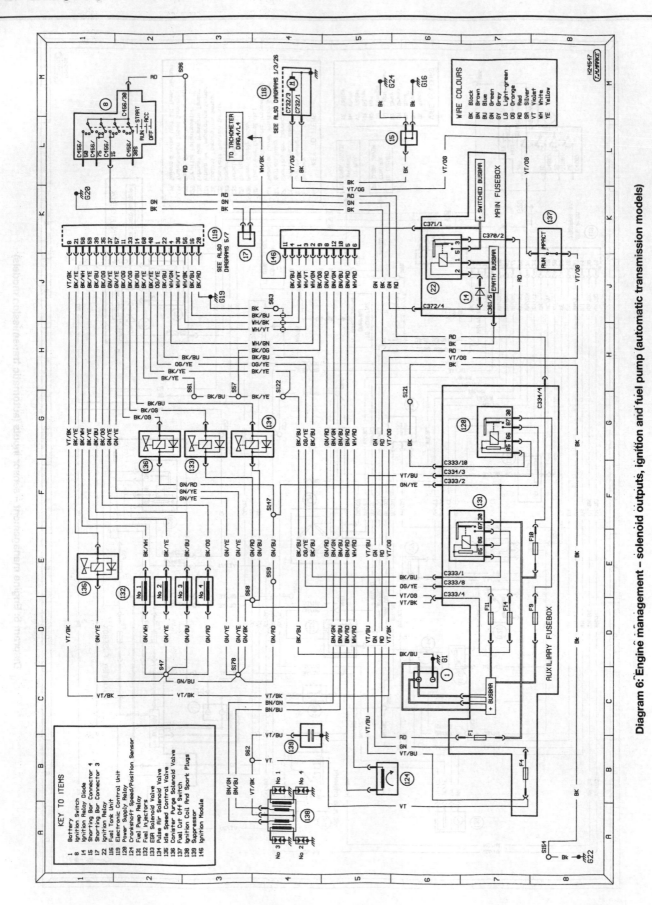

Diagram 6: Engine management – solenoid outputs, ignition and fuel pump (automatic transmission models)

KEY TO ITEMS

1 Battery
8 Ignition Switch
I4 Ignition Relay Diode
I5 Shorting Bar Connector 4
I7 Shorting Bar Connector 3
22 Ignition Relay
116 Fuel Tank Unit
119 Electronic Control Unit
128 Power Supply Relay
124 Crankshaft Speed/Position Sensor
131 Fuel Pump Relay
132 Fuel Injectors
133 EGR Solenoid Valve
134 Idle Speed Control Valve
135 Idle Air Solenoid Valve
136 Canister Purge Solenoid Valve
137 Fuel Cut Off Switch
138 Ignition Coil And Spark Plugs
139 Suppressor
146 Ignition Module

WIRE COLOURS

BK Black
BN Brown
BU Blue
GN Green
GY Grey
LG Light-green
OG Orange
RD Red
SR Silver
VT Violet
WH White
YE Yellow

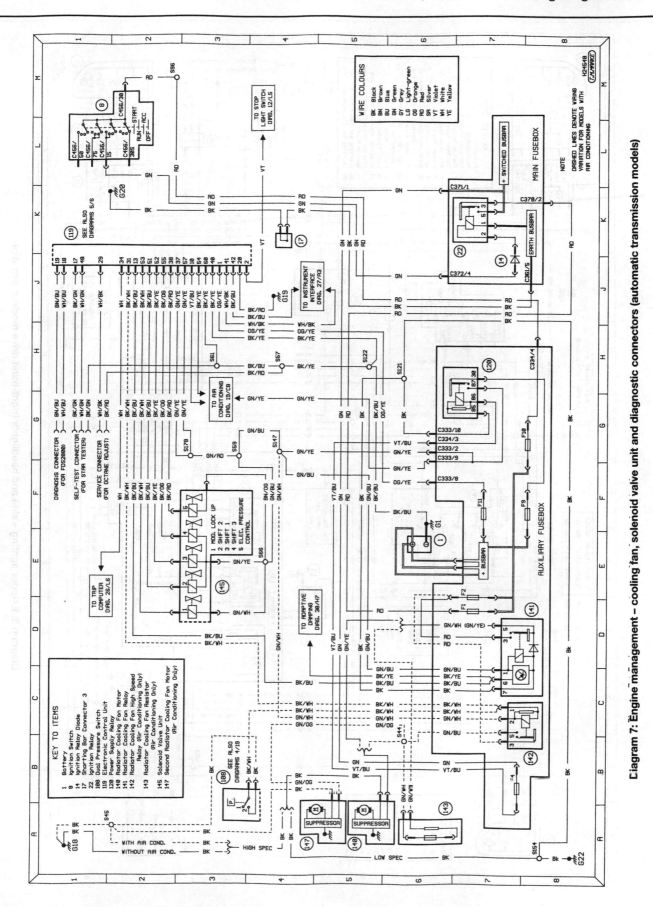

Diagram 7: Engine management – cooling fan, solenoid valve unit and diagnostic connectors (automatic transmission models)

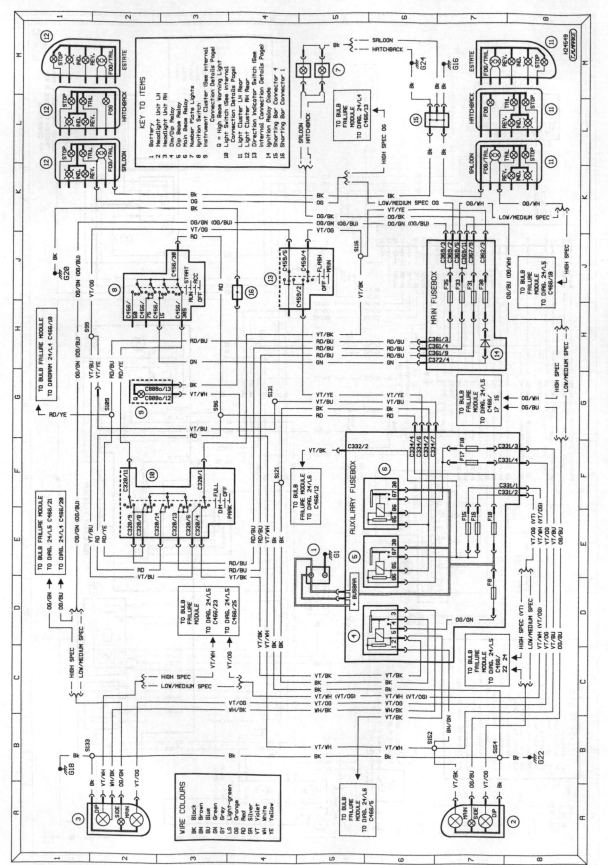

Diagram 8: Exterior lighting – side and headlights (right-hand drive models): dim-dip)

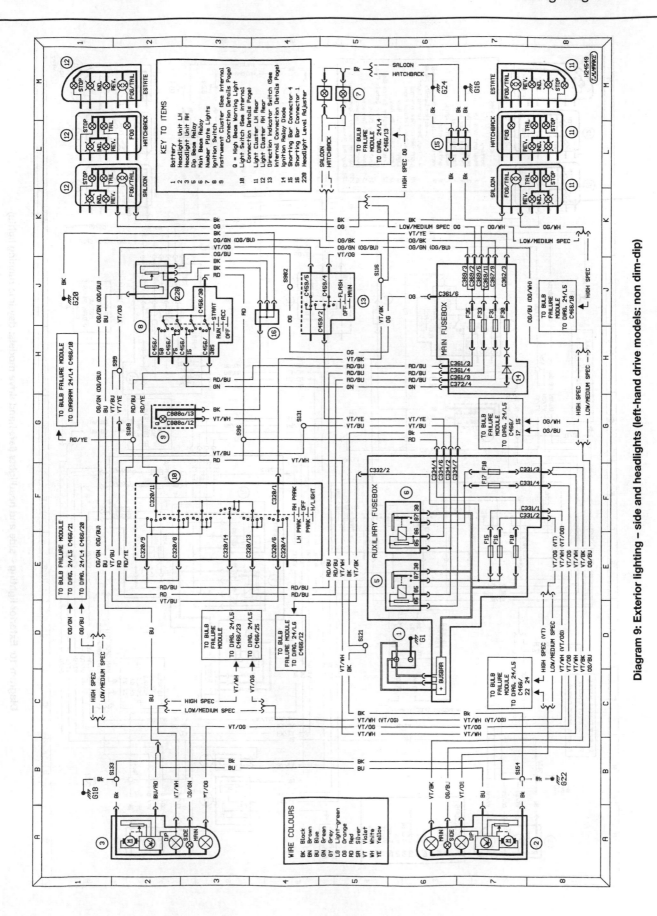

Diagram 9: Exterior lighting – side and headlights (left-hand drive models): non dim-dip)

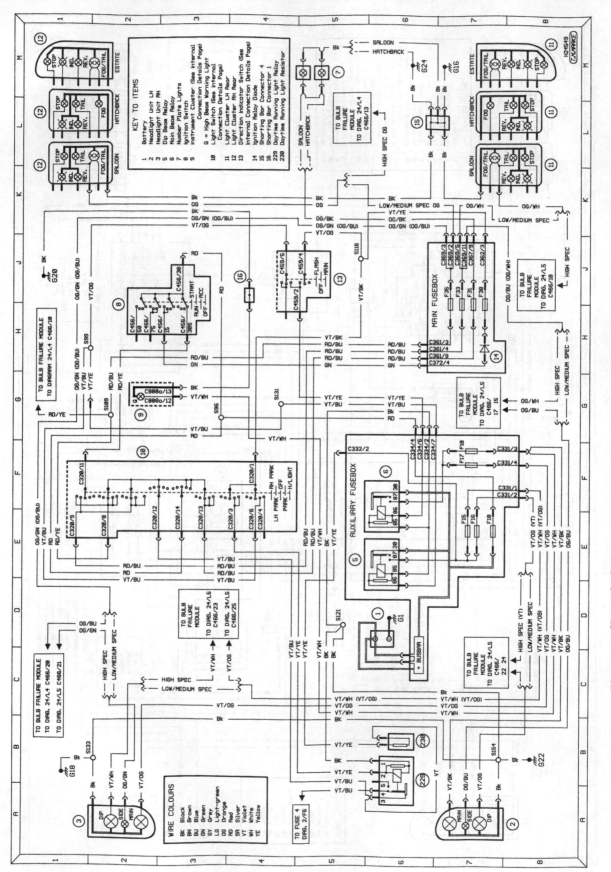

Diagram 10: Exterior lighting – side and headlights (left-hand drive models: daytime running lights)

KEY TO ITEMS

1 Battery
2 Headlight Unit LH
3 Headlight Unit RH
4 Dip Beam Relay
5 Main Beam Relay
6 Ignition Switch
7 Number Plate Lights
8 Light Switch (See Internal Connection Details Page)
9 Instrument Cluster (See Internal Connection Details Page)
   Q = High Beam Warning Light
10 Light Switch (See Internal Connection Details Page)
11 Light Cluster LH Rear
12 Light Cluster RH Rear
13 Direction Indicator Switch (See Internal Connection Details Page)
14 Ignition Relay Diode
16 Shorting Bar Connector 4
15 Shorting Bar Connector 1
229 Daytime Running Light Resistor
230 Daytime Running Light Relay

WIRE COLOURS

BK Black
BN Brown
BU Blue
GN Green
GY Grey
LG Light-green
OG Orange
RD Red
SR Silver
VT Violet
WH White
YE Yellow

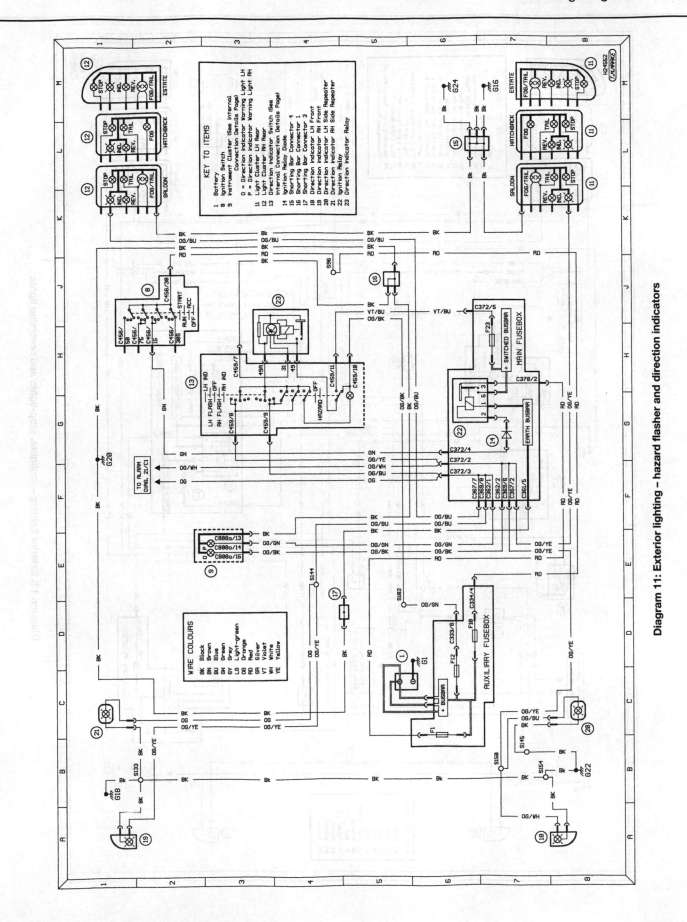

Diagram 11: Exterior lighting – hazard flasher and direction indicators

KEY TO ITEMS

1 Battery
8 Ignition Switch
9 Instrument Cluster (See Internal Connection Details Page)
   O = Direction Indicator Warning Light LH
   P = Direction Indicator Warning Light RH
11 Light Cluster LH Rear
12 Light Cluster RH Rear
13 Direction Indicator Switch (See Internal Connection Details page)
14 Ignition Relay Diode
15 Shorting Bar Connector 4
16 Shorting Bar Connector 1
17 Shorting Bar Connector 3
18 Direction Indicator LH Front
19 Direction Indicator RH Front
20 Direction Indicator LH Side Repeater
21 Direction Indicator RH Side Repeater
22 Ignition Relay
23 Direction Indicator Relay

WIRE COLOURS

BK Black
BN Brown
BU Blue
GN Green
GY Grey
LG Light-green
OG Orange
RD Red
SR Silver
VT Violet
WH White
YE Yellow

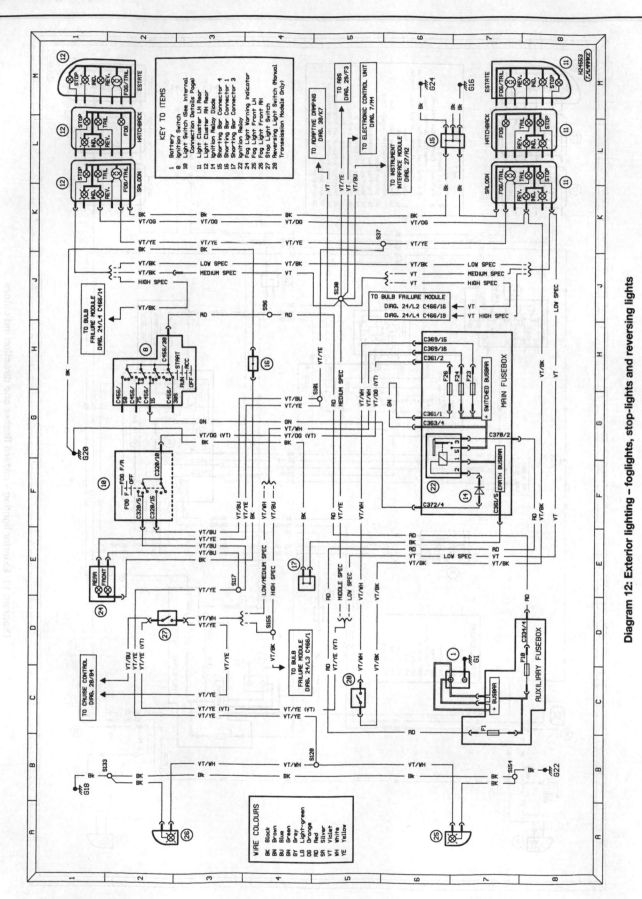

Diagram 12: Exterior lighting – foglights, stop-lights and reversing lights

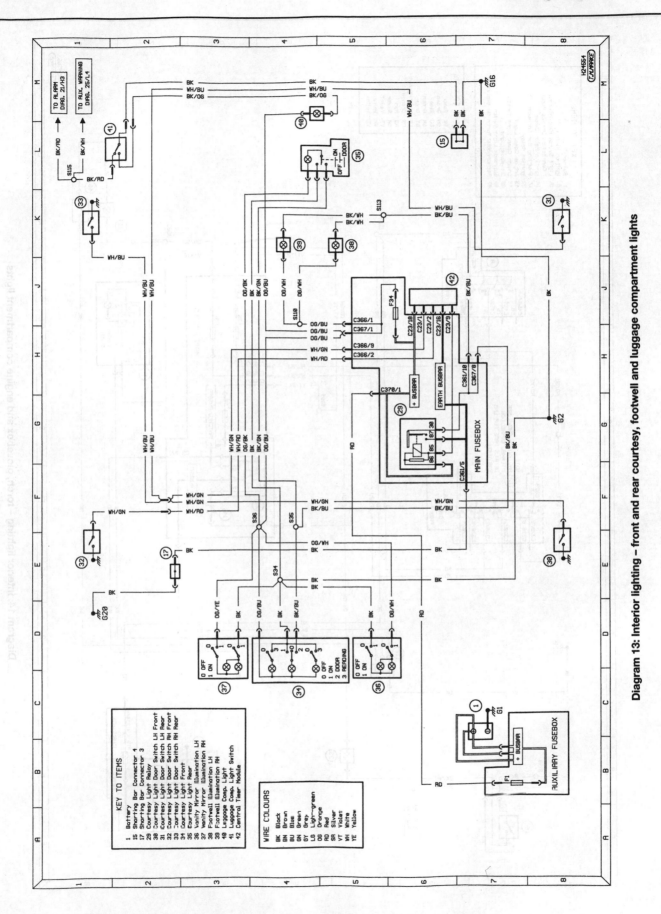

Diagram 13: Interior lighting – front and rear courtesy, footwell and luggage compartment lights

KEY TO ITEMS
1 Battery
15 Shorting Bar Connector 4
17 Shorting Bar Connector 3
29 Courtesy Light Relay
30 Courtesy Light Door Switch LH Front
31 Courtesy Light Door Switch LH Rear
32 Courtesy Light Door Switch RH Front
33 Courtesy Light Door Switch RH Rear
34 Courtesy Light Front
35 Courtesy Light Rear
36 Vanity Mirror Illumination LH
37 Vanity Mirror Illumination RH
38 Footwell Illumination LH
39 Footwell Illumination RH
40 Luggage Comp. Light
41 Luggage Comp. Light Switch
42 Central Timer Module

WIRE COLOURS
BK Black
BN Brown
BU Blue
GN Green
GY Grey
LG Light-green
OG Orange
RD Red
SR Silver
VT Violet
WH White
YE Yellow

12

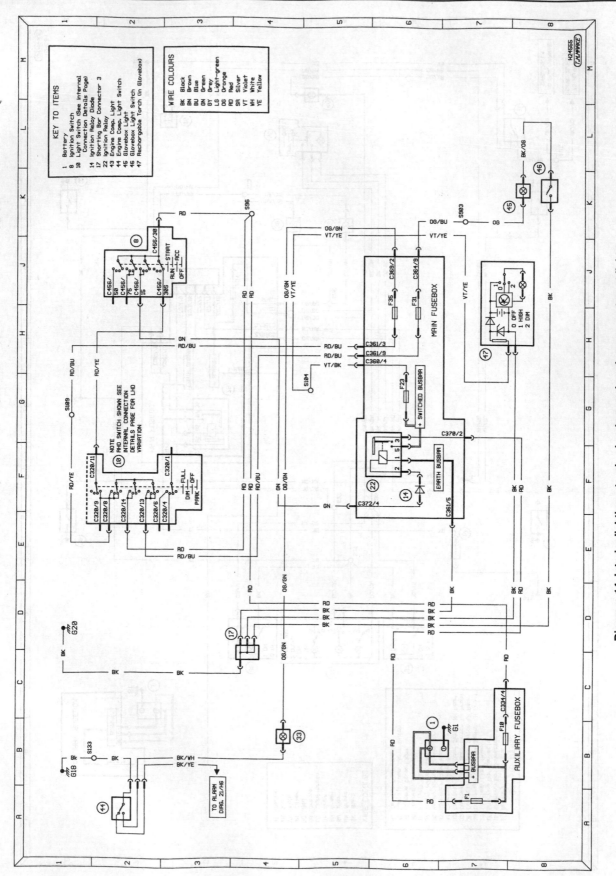

Diagram 14: Interior lighting – torch, glovebox and engine compartment lights

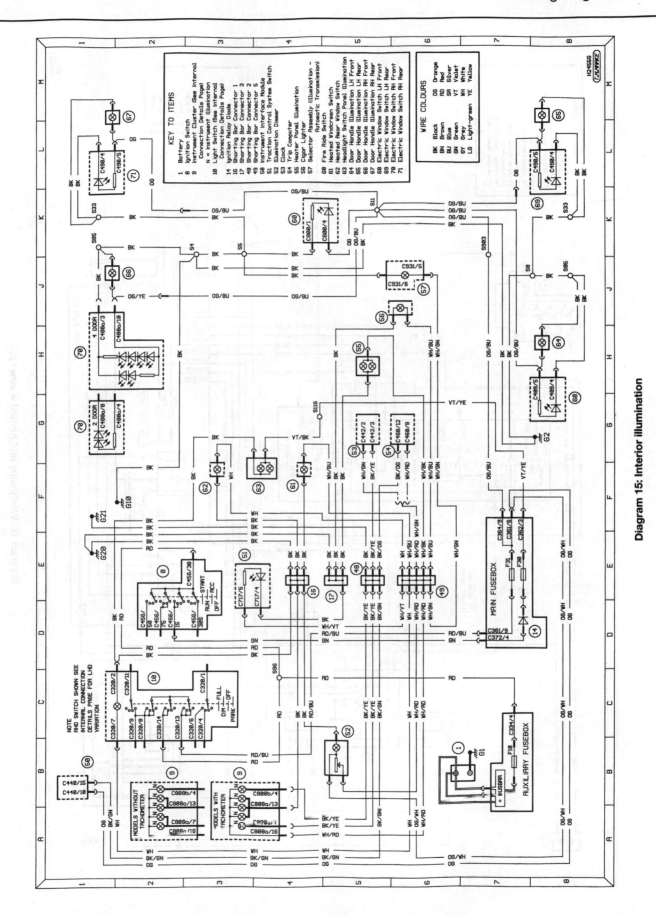

Diagram 15: Interior illumination

KEY TO ITEMS

1 Battery
8 Ignition Switch
9 Instrument Cluster (See Internal Connection Details page)
N = Instrument Illumination
10 Light Switch (See Internal Connection Details page)
14 Ignition Relay Diode
16 Shorting Bar Connector 1
17 Shorting Bar Connector 2
18 Shorting Bar Connector 3
48 Shorting Bar Connector 5
49 Shorting Bar Connector 5
50 Instrument Interface Module
51 Traction Control System Switch
52 Clock
53 Trip Computer
54 Heater Panel Illumination
55 Cigar Lighter
56 Illumination Dimmer
57 Selector Assembly Illumination – Automatic Transmission)
60 Firm Ride Switch
61 Heated Windscreen Switch
62 Heated Rear Window Switch
63 Headlight Switch Panel Illumination
64 Door Handle Illumination LH Front
65 Door Handle Illumination LH Rear
66 Door Handle Illumination RH Front
67 Door Handle Illumination RH Rear
68 Electric Window Switch LH Front
69 Electric Window Switch LH Rear
70 Electric Window Switch RH Front
71 Electric Window Switch RH Rear

WIRE COLOURS

BK	Black	OG	Orange
BN	Brown	RD	Red
BU	Blue	SR	Silver
GN	Green	VT	Violet
GY	Grey	WH	White
LG	Light-green	YE	Yellow

NOTE
RHD SWITCH SHOWN SEE INTERNAL CONNECTION DETAILS PAGE FOR LHD VARIATION

MAIN FUSEBOX

AUXILIARY FUSEBOX

MODELS WITHOUT TACHOMETER

MODELS WITH TACHOMETER

12

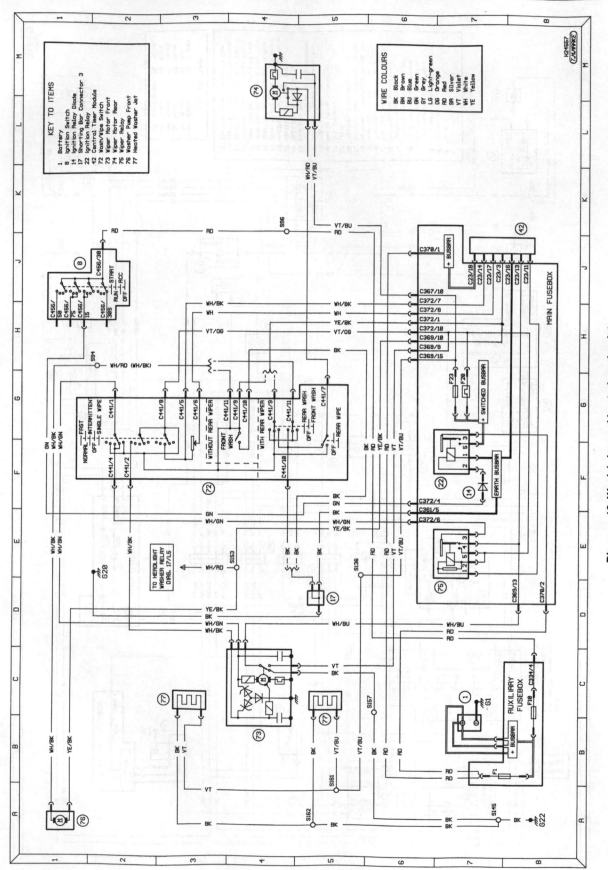

KEY TO ITEMS

1   Battery
8   Ignition Switch
14 Ignition Relay Diode
17 Shorting Bar Connector 3
22 Ignition Relay
42 Central Timer Module
72 Wash/Wipe Switch
73 Wiper Motor Front
74 Wiper Motor Rear
75 Wiper Relay
76 Washer Pump Front
77 Heated Washer Jet

WIRE COLOURS

BK Black
BN Brown
BU Blue
GN Green
GY Grey
LG Light-green
OG Orange
RD Red
SR Silver
VT Violet
WH White
YE Yellow

Diagram 16: Wash/wipe and heated washer jets

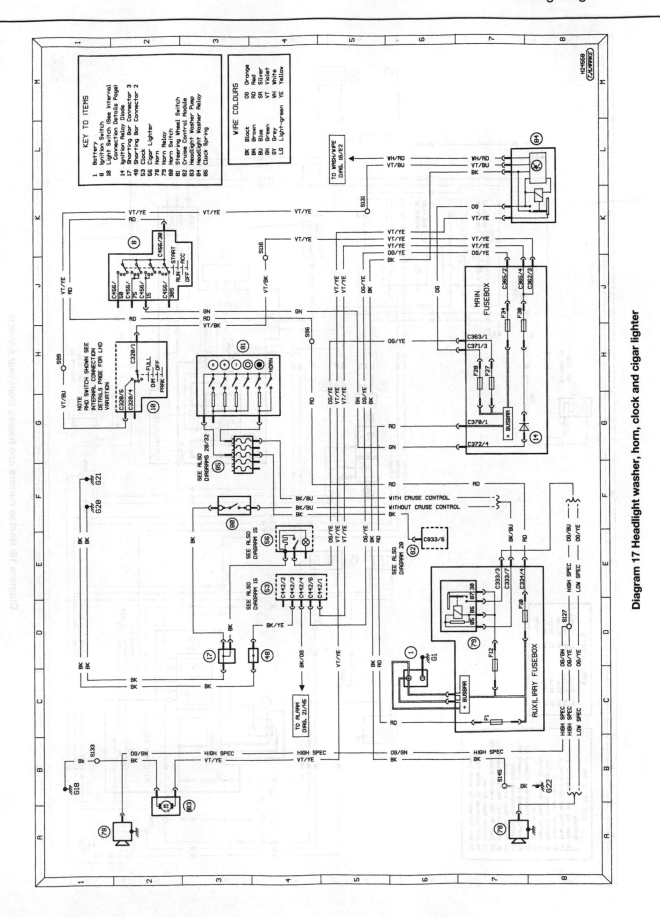

Diagram 17 Headlight washer, horn, clock and cigar lighter

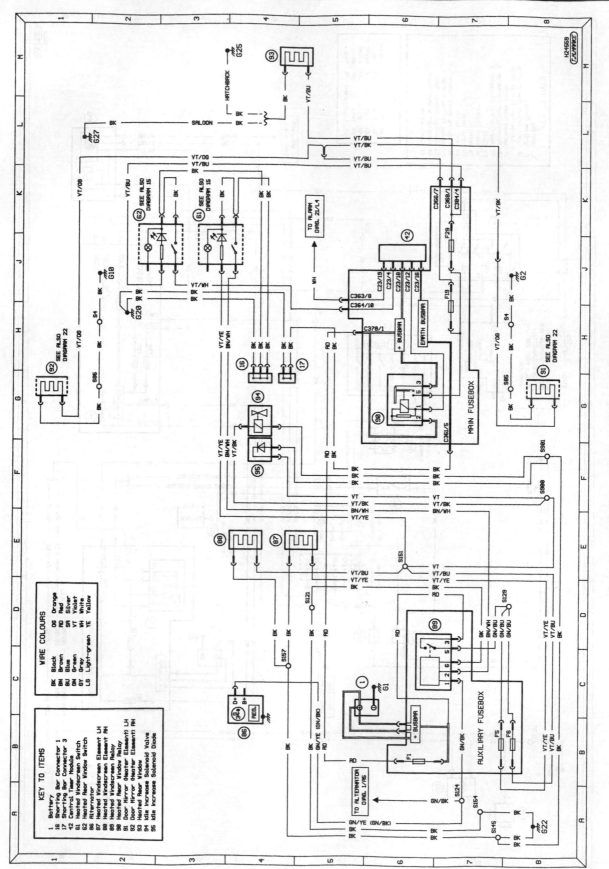

Diagram 18: Heated mirrors and heated front/rear screens

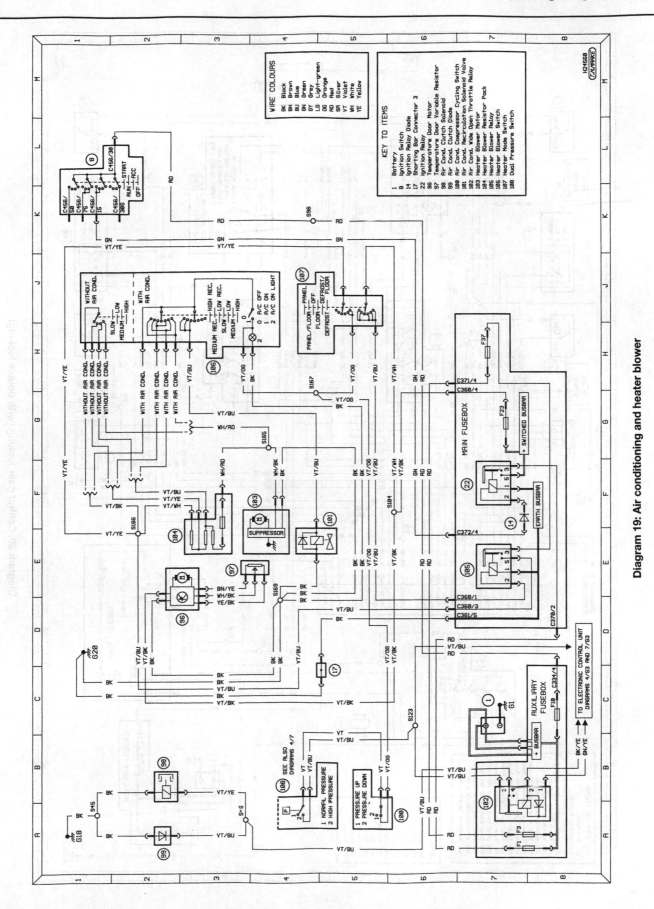

Diagram 19: Air conditioning and heater blower

WIRE COLOURS
BK Black
BN Brown
BU Blue
GN Green
GY Grey
LG Light-green
OG Orange
RD Red
SR Silver
VT Violet
WH White
YE Yellow

KEY TO ITEMS
1   Battery
8   Ignition Switch
14 Ignition Relay Diode
17 Shorting Bar Connector 3
22 Ignition Relay
96 Temperature Door Motor
97 Temperature Door Variable Resistor
98 Air Cond. Clutch Solenoid
99 Air Cond. Clutch Diode
100 Air Cond. Compressor Cycling Switch
101 Air Cond. Recirculation Solenoid Valve
102 Air Cond. Wide Open Throttle Relay
103 Heater Blower Motor
104 Heater Blower Resistor Pack
105 Heater Blower Relay
106 Heater Blower Switch
107 Heater Mode Switch
108 Dual Pressure Switch

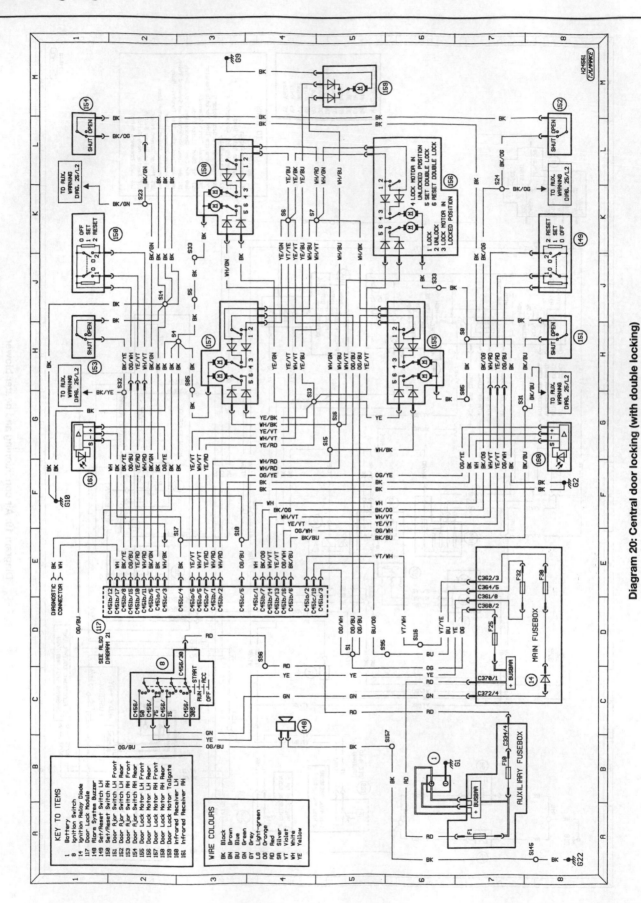

Diagram 20: Central door locking (with double locking)

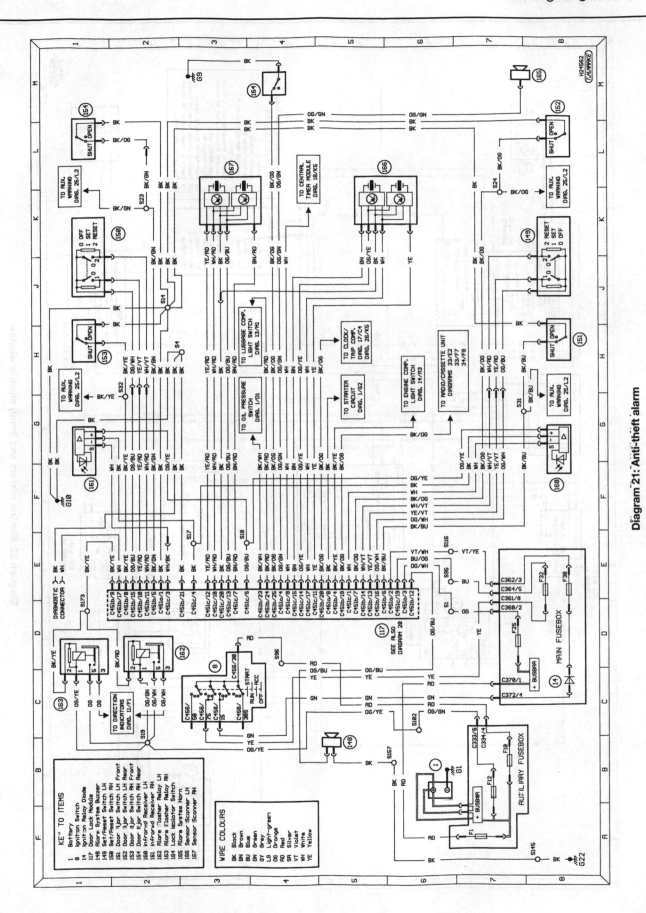

Diagram 21: Anti-theft alarm

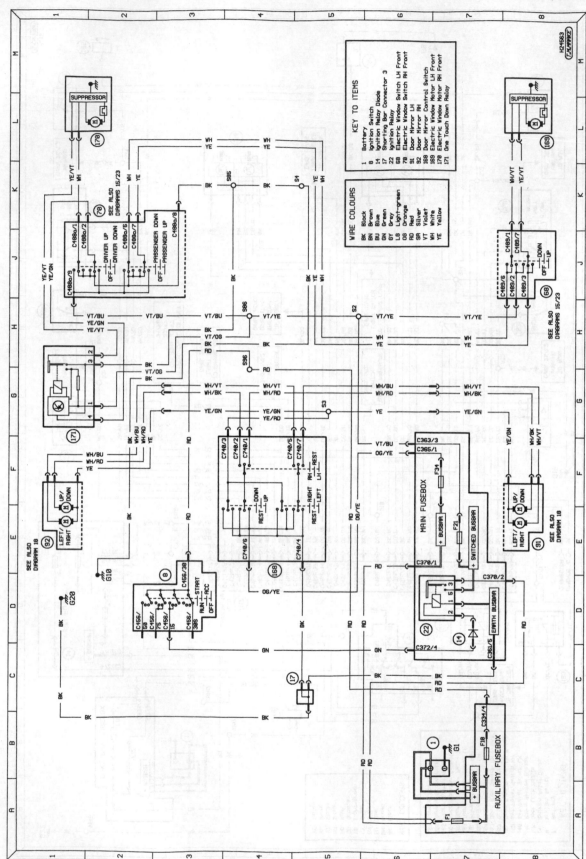

Diagram 22: Electric mirrors and (front) electric window

KEY TO ITEMS

1 Battery
8 Ignition Switch
14 Ignition Relay Diode
17 Shorting Bar Connector 3
22 Ignition Relay
68 Electric Window Switch LH Front
78 Electric Window Switch RH Front
91 Door Mirror LH
92 Door Mirror RH
168 Door Mirror Control Switch
169 Electric Window Motor LH Front
170 Electric Window Motor RH Front
171 One Touch Down Relay

WIRE COLOURS

BK Black
BN Brown
BU Blue
GN Green
GY Grey
LG Light-green
OG Orange
RD Red
SR Silver
VT Violet
WH White
YE Yellow

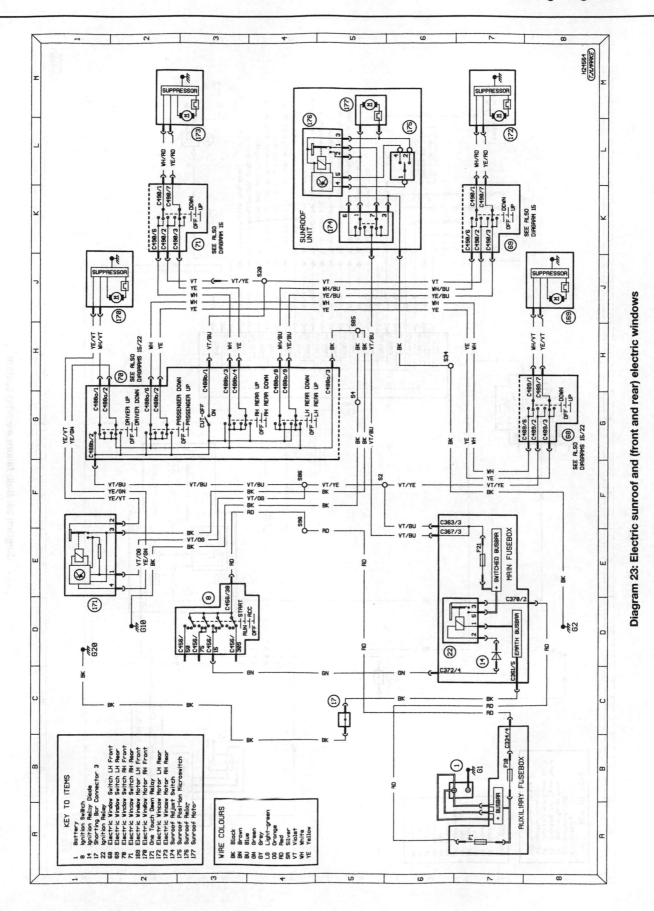

Diagram 23: Electric sunroof and (front and rear) electric windows

KEY TO ITEMS

1 Battery
8 Ignition switch
14 Ignition relay diode
17 Shorting bar connector 3
22 Ignition relay
68 Electric window switch LH front
69 Electric window switch LH rear
70 Electric window switch RH front
71 Electric window switch RH rear
169 Electric window motor LH front
170 Electric window motor LH rear
171 Electric window motor RH front
172 Electric window motor RH rear
173 One touch down relay
174 Sunroof adjust switch
175 Sunroof position microswitch
176 Sunroof relay
177 Sunroof motor

WIRE COLOURS

BK Black
BN Brown
BU Blue
GN Green
GY Grey
LG Light-green
OG Orange
RD Red
SR Silver
VT Violet
WH White
YE Yellow

12

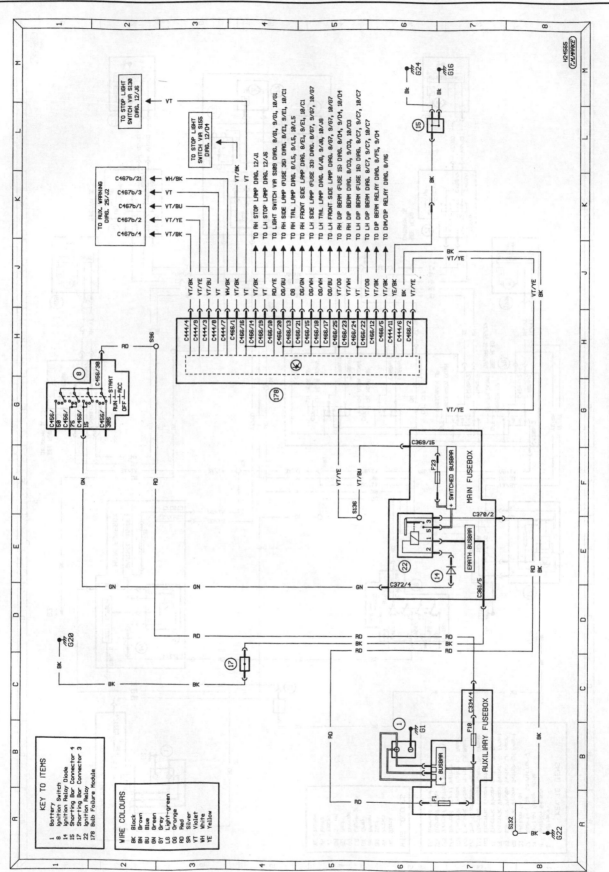

Diagram 24: Bulb failure warning system

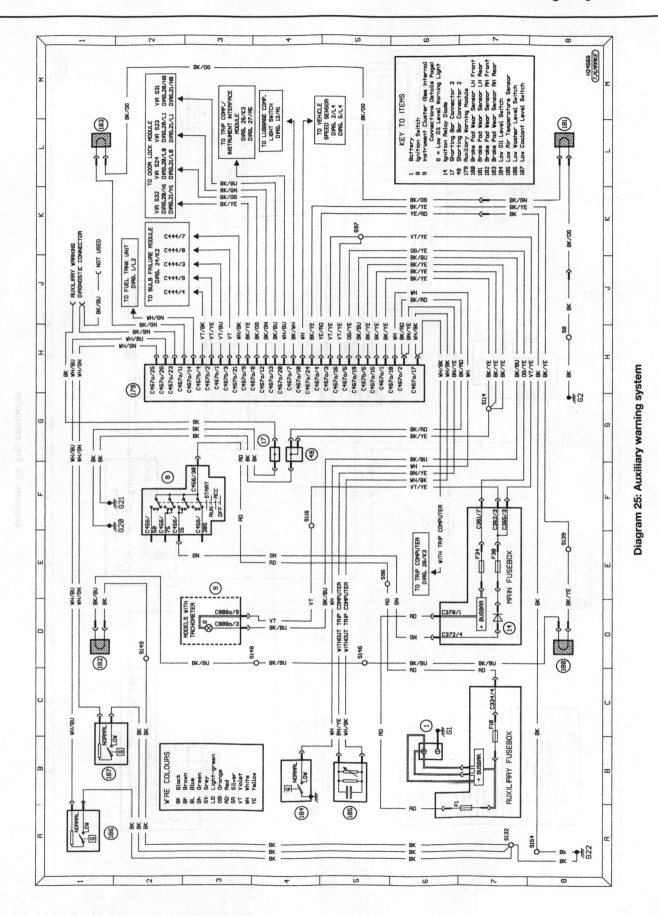

Diagram 25: Auxiliary warning system

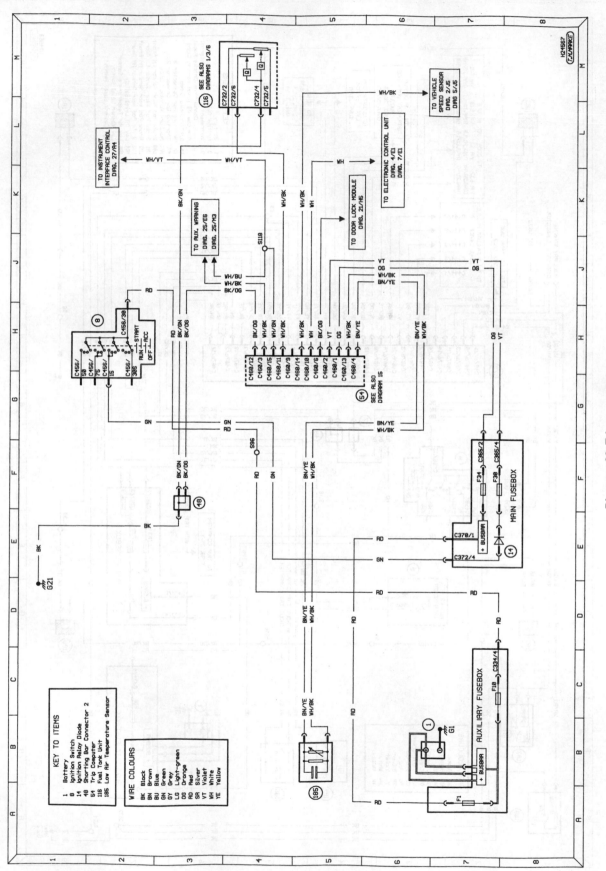

Diagram 26: Trip computer

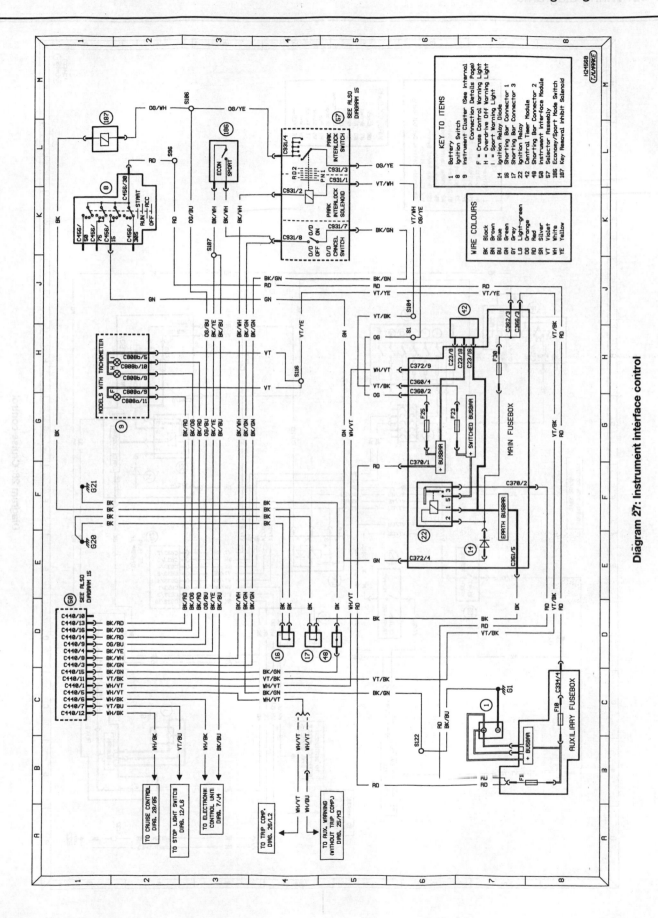

Diagram 27: Instrument interface control

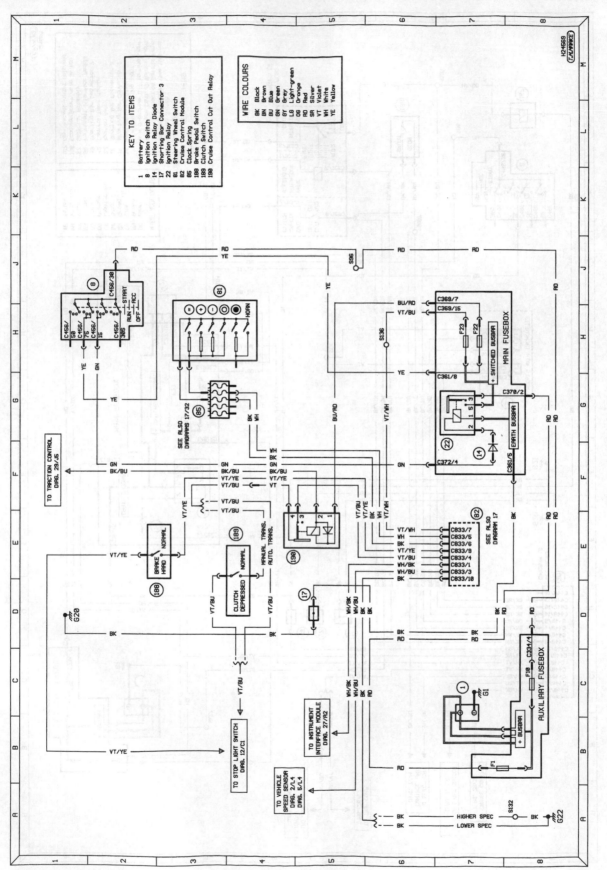

Diagram 28: Cruise control

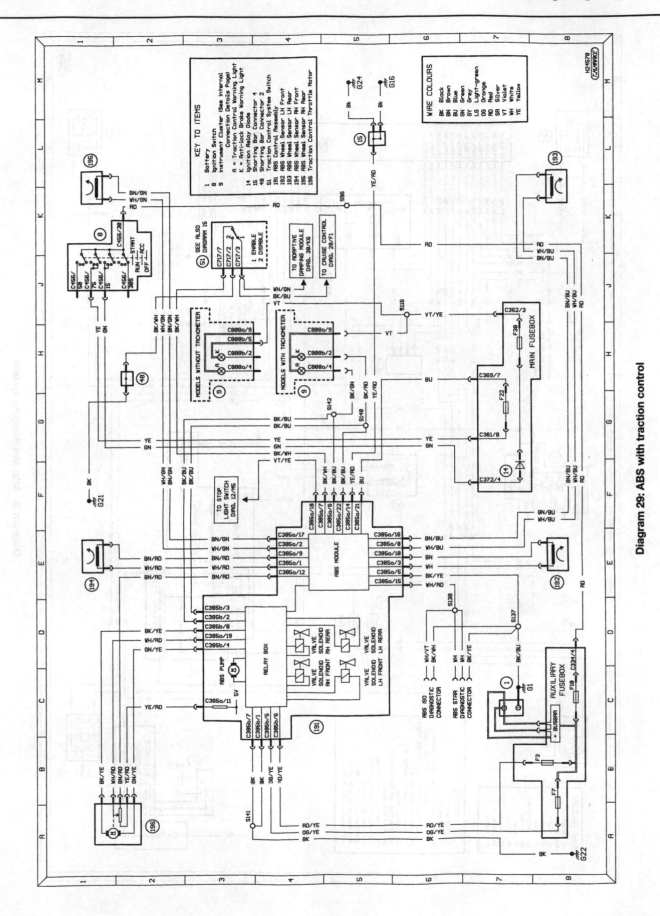

Diagram 29: ABS with traction control

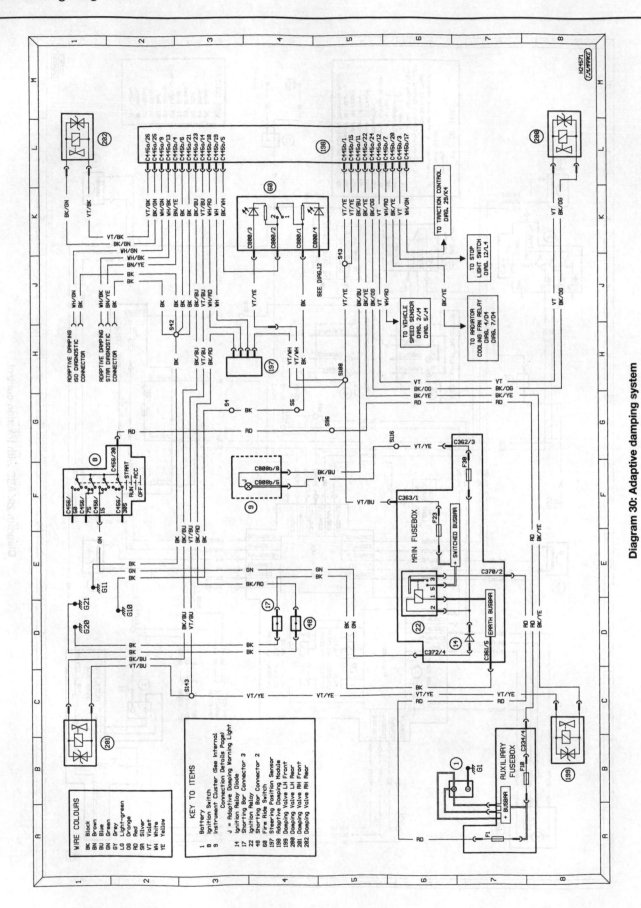

Diagram 30: Adaptive damping system

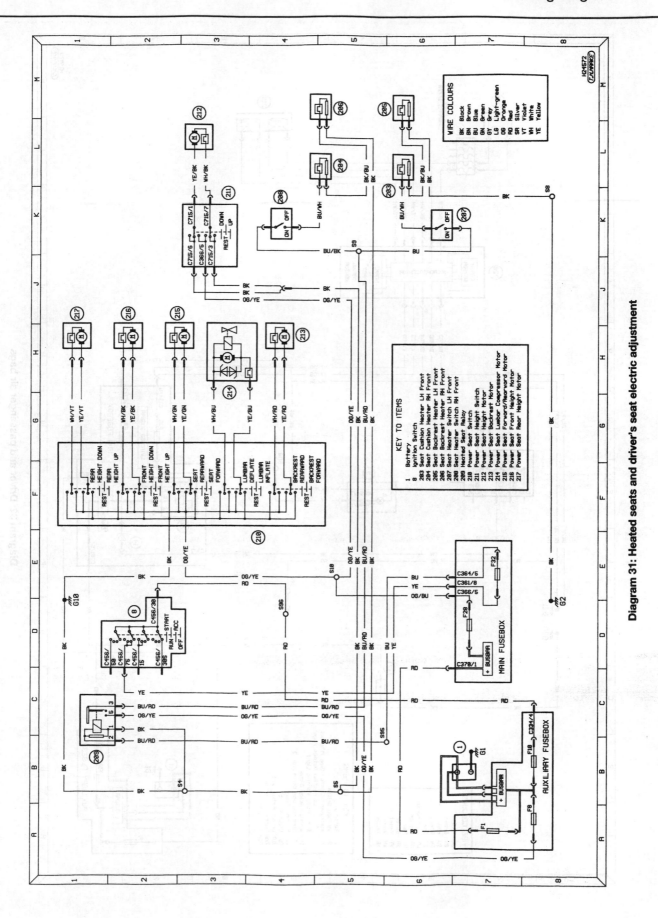

Diagram 31: Heated seats and driver's seat electric adjustment

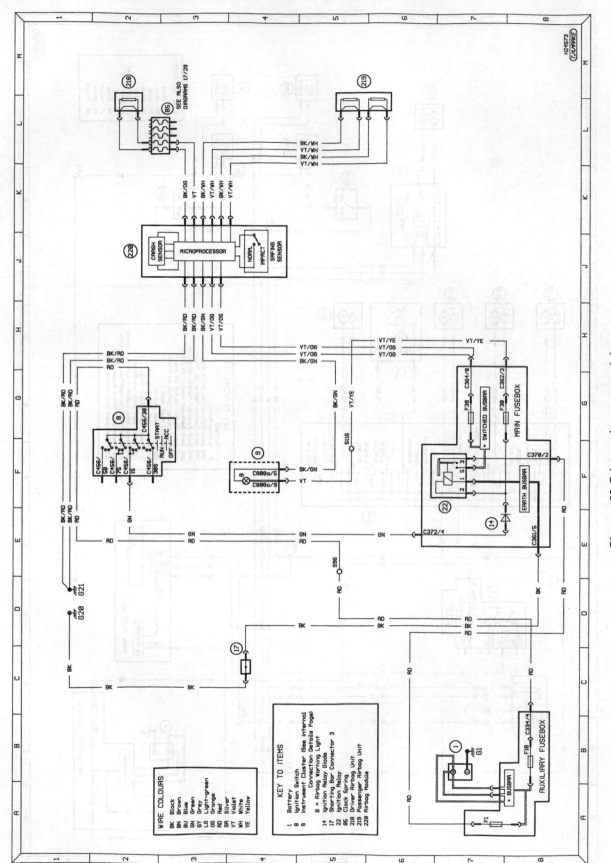

Diagram 32: Driver and passenger air bags

WIRE COLOURS

BK	Black
BN	Brown
BU	Blue
GN	Green
GY	Grey
LG	Light-green
OG	Orange
RD	Red
SR	Silver
VT	Violet
WH	White
YE	Yellow

KEY TO ITEMS

1	Battery
8	Ignition Switch
9	Instrument Cluster (See Internal Connection Details Page)
B	Airbag Warning Light
14	Ignition Relay Diode
17	Shorting Bar Connector 3
22	Ignition Relay
86	Clock Spring
218	Driver Airbag Unit
219	Passenger Airbag Unit
220	Airbag Module

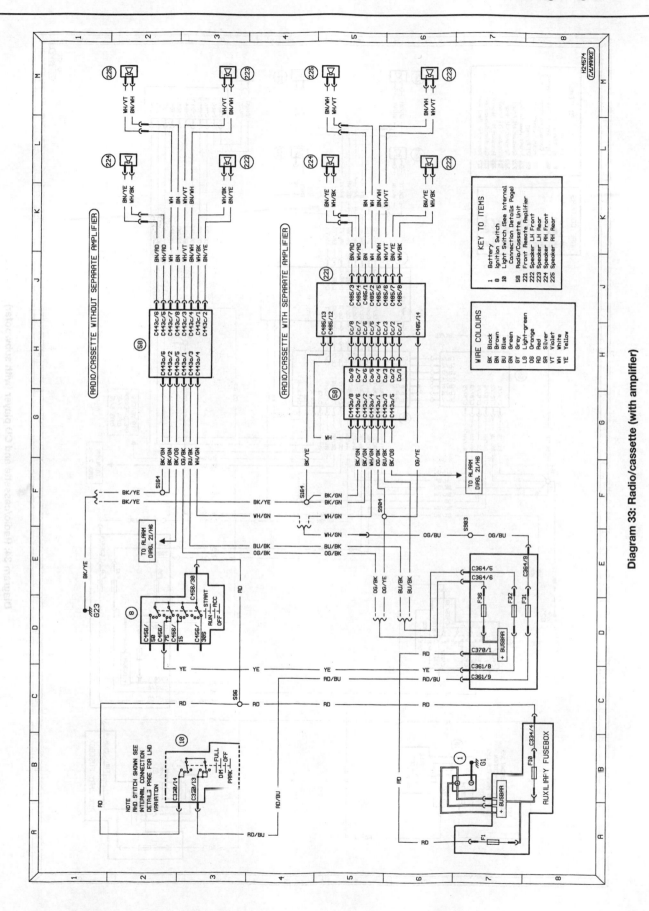

Diagram 33: Radio/cassette (with amplifier)

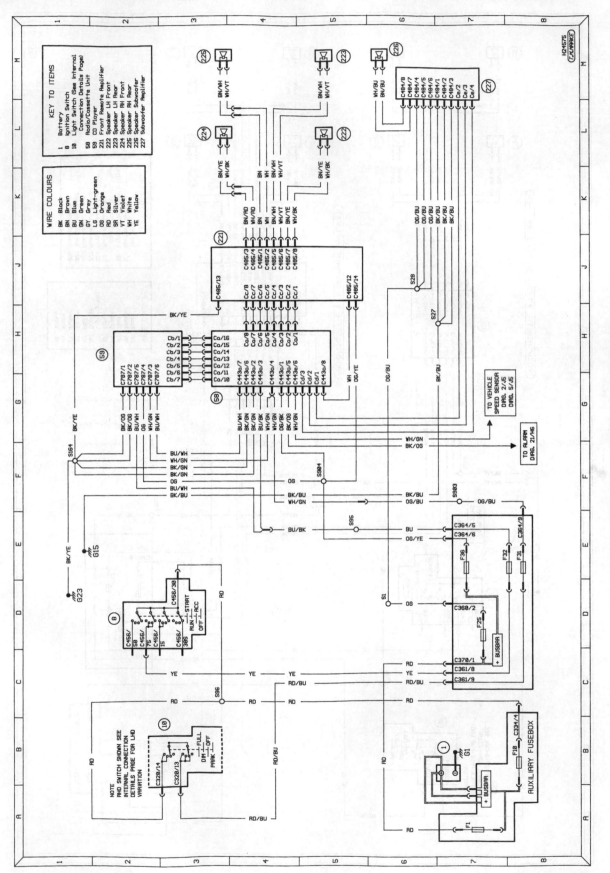

Diagram 34: Radio/cassette and CD player (with subwoofer)

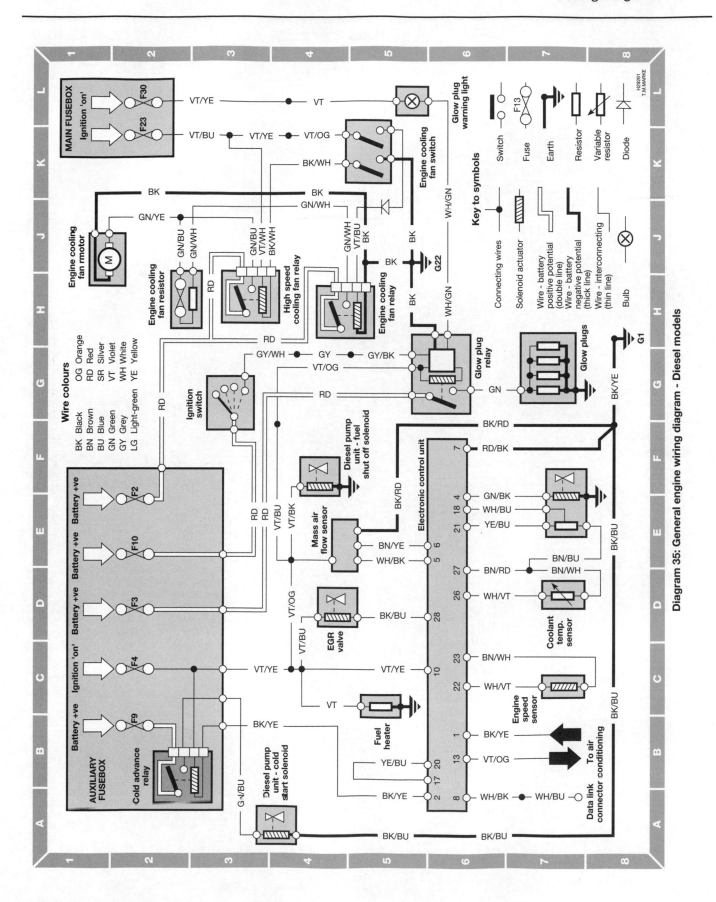

Diagram 35: General engine wiring diagram – Diesel models

Notes

Dimensions and weights

Dimensions

Overall length:
Saloon, Hatchback . . . . .4481 mm
Estate . . . . .4631 mm
Overall width - including mirrors .1925 mm
Overall height - at kerb weight:
Saloon, Hatchback .1403 to 1435 mm
Estate . . . . .1416 to 1501 mm
Wheelbase . . . . .2704 mm
Front track - all models . . . . .1503 mm
Rear track:
Saloon, Hatchback .1486 to 1487 mm
Estate . . . . .1504 mm
Turning circle . . . . .10.9 m

Weights

Kerb weight:
Saloon, Hatchback models . . . . .1305 to 1374 kg
Estate models . . . . .1360 to 1409 kg
Maximum gross vehicle weight . . . . .See VIN plate (under bonnet)
Maximum roof rack load.
Estate models with integral roof rack . . . . .100 kg
All others . . . . .75 kg
Maximum towing weight . . . . .1500 kg
Trailer nose weight limit . . . . .75 kg

Conversion factors

Length (distance)

Inches (in)	x 25.4	= Millimetres (mm)	x 0.0394	= Inches (in)
Feet (ft)	x 0.305	= Metres (m)	x 3.281	= Feet (ft)
Miles	x 1.609	= Kilometres (km)	x 0.621	= Miles

Volume (capacity)

Cubic inches (cu in; in³)	x 16.387	= Cubic centimetres (cc; cm³)	x 0.061	= Cubic inches (cu in; in³)
Imperial pints (Imp pt)	x 0.568	= Litres (l)	x 1.76	= Imperial pints (Imp pt)
Imperial quarts (Imp qt)	x 1.137	= Litres (l)	x 0.88	= Imperial quarts (Imp qt)
Imperial quarts (Imp qt)	x 1.201	= US quarts (US qt)	x 0.833	= Imperial quarts (Imp qt)
US quarts (US qt)	x 0.946	= Litres (l)	x 1.057	= US quarts (US qt)
Imperial gallons (Imp gal)	x 4.546	= Litres (l)	x 0.22	= Imperial gallons (Imp gal)
Imperial gallons (Imp gal)	x 1.201	= US gallons (US gal)	x 0.833	= Imperial gallons (Imp gal)
US gallons (US gal)	x 3.785	= Litres (l)	x 0.264	= US gallons (US gal)

Mass (weight)

Ounces (oz)	x 28.35	= Grams (g)	x 0.035	= Ounces (oz)
Pounds (lb)	x 0.454	= Kilograms (kg)	x 2.205	= Pounds (lb)

Force

Ounces-force (ozf; oz)	x 0.278	= Newtons (N)	x 3.6	= Ounces-force (ozf; oz)
Pounds-force (lbf; lb)	x 4.448	= Newtons (N)	x 0.225	= Pounds-force (lbf; lb)
Newtons (N)	x 0.1	= Kilograms-force (kgf; kg)	x 9.81	= Newtons (N)

Pressure

Pounds-force per square inch (psi; lbf/in²; lb/in²)	x 0.070	= Kilograms-force per square centimetre (kgf/cm²; kg/cm²)	x 14.223	= Pounds-force per square inch (psi; lbf/in²; lb/in²)
Pounds-force per square inch (psi; lbf/in²; lb/in²)	x 0.068	= Atmospheres (atm)	x 14.696	= Pounds-force per square inch (psi; lbf/in²; lb/in²)
Pounds-force per square inch (psi; lbf/in²; lb/in²)	x 0.069	= Bars	x 14.5	= Pounds-force per square inch (psi; lbf/in²; lb/in²)
Pounds-force per square inch (psi; lbf/in²; lb/in²)	x 6.895	= Kilopascals (kPa)	x 0.145	= Pounds-force per square inch (psi; lbf/in²; lb/in²)
Kilopascals (kPa)	x 0.01	= Kilograms-force per square centimetre (kgf/cm²; kg/cm²)	x 98.1	= Kilopascals (kPa)
Millibar (mbar)	x 100	= Pascals (Pa)	x 0.01	= Millibar (mbar)
Millibar (mbar)	x 0.0145	= Pounds-force per square inch (psi; lbf/in²; lb/in²)	x 68.947	= Millibar (mbar)
Millibar (mbar)	x 0.75	= Millimetres of mercury (mmHg)	x 1.333	= Millibar (mbar)
Millibar (mbar)	x 0.401	= Inches of water (inH₂O)	x 2.491	= Millibar (mbar)
Millimetres of mercury (mmHg)	x 0.535	= Inches of water (inH₂O)	x 1.868	= Millimetres of mercury (mmHg)
Inches of water (inH₂O)	x 0.036	= Pounds-force per square inch (psi; lbf/in²; lb/in²)	x 27.68	= Inches of water (inH₂O)

Torque (moment of force)

Pounds-force inches (lbf in; lb in)	x 1.152	= Kilograms-force centimetre (kgf cm; kg cm)	x 0.868	= Pounds-force inches (lbf in; lb in)
Pounds-force inches (lbf in; lb in)	x 0.113	= Newton metres (Nm)	x 8.85	= Pounds-force inches (lbf in; lb in)
Pounds-force inches (lbf in; lb in)	x 0.083	= Pounds-force feet (lbf ft; lb ft)	x 12	= Pounds-force inches (lbf in; lb in)
Pounds-force feet (lbf ft; lb ft)	x 0.138	= Kilograms-force metres (kgf m; kg m)	x 7.233	= Pounds-force feet (lbf ft; lb ft)
Pounds-force feet (lbf ft; lb ft)	x 1.356	= Newton metres (Nm)	x 0.738	= Pounds-force feet (lbf ft; lb ft)
Newton metres (Nm)	x 0.102	= Kilograms-force metres (kgf m; kg m)	x 9.804	= Newton metres (Nm)

Power

Horsepower (hp)	x 745.7	= Watts (W)	x 0.0013	= Horsepower (hp)

Velocity (speed)

Miles per hour (miles/hr; mph)	x 1.609	= Kilometres per hour (km/hr; kph)	x 0.621	= Miles per hour (miles/hr; mph)

Fuel consumption*

Miles per gallon (mpg)	x 0.354	= Kilometres per litre (km/l)	x 2.825	= Miles per gallon (mpg)

Temperature

Degrees Fahrenheit = (°C x 1.8) + 32   Degrees Celsius (Degrees Centigrade; °C) = (°F - 32) x 0.56

It is common practice to convert from miles per gallon (mpg) to litres/100 kilometres (l/100km), where mpg x l/100 km = 282

Spare parts are available from many sources, including vehicle manufacturer's appointed garages, accessory shops and motor factors. To be sure of obtaining the correct parts, it will sometimes be necessary to quote the vehicle identification number. If possible, it can also be useful to take the old parts along for positive identification. Items such as starter motors and alternators may be available under a service exchange scheme - any parts returned should always be clean.

Our advice regarding spare part sources is as follows.

Officially-appointed garages

This is the best source of parts which are peculiar to your vehicle and which are not otherwise generally available (eg. badges, interior trim, certain body panels, etc). It is also the only place at which you should buy parts if the vehicle is still under warranty.

Accessory shops

These are very good places to buy materials and components needed for the maintenance of your vehicle (oil, air and fuel filters, spark plugs, light bulbs, drivebelts, oils and greases, brake pads, touch-up paint, etc). Components of this nature sold by a reputable shop are of the same standard as those used by the vehicle manufacturer.

Besides components, these shops also sell tools and general accessories, usually have convenient opening hours, charge lower prices and can often be found not far from home. Some accessory shops have parts counters where the components needed for almost any repair job can be purchased or ordered.

Motor factors

Good factors will stock all the more important components which wear out comparatively quickly and can sometimes supply individual components needed for the overhaul of a larger assembly (eg. brake seals and hydraulic parts, bearing shells, pistons, valves, alternator brushes). They may also handle work such as cylinder block reboring, crankshaft regrinding and balancing, etc.

Tyre and exhaust specialists

These outlets may be independent or members of a local or national chain. They frequently offer competitive prices when compared with a main dealer or local garage but it will pay to obtain several quotes before making a decision. When researching prices, also ask what "extras" may be added - for instance, fitting a new valve and balancing the wheel are both commonly charged on top of the price of a new tyre.

Other sources

Beware of parts or materials obtained from market stalls, car boot sales or similar outlets. Such items are not invariably sub-standard but there is little chance of compensation if they do prove unsatisfactory. In the case of safety-critical components such as brake pads, there is the risk not only of financial loss but also of an accident causing injury or death.

Second-hand components or assemblies obtained from a car breaker can be a good buy in some circumstances but this sort of purchase is best made by the experienced DIY mechanic.

Vehicle identification

Modifications are a continuing and unpublicised process in vehicle manufacture, quite apart from major model changes. Spare parts manuals and lists are compiled upon a numerical basis, the appropriate identification number or code being essential to correct identification of the component concerned.

When ordering spare parts, always give as much information as possible. Quote the vehicle model, year of manufacture, Vehicle Identification Number and engine numbers, as appropriate.

The *vehicle identification plate* is located on the engine compartment front crossmember **(see illustration)**. In addition to many other details, it carries the Vehicle Identification Number, maximum vehicle weight information, and codes for interior trim and body colours.

The *Vehicle Identification Number* is given on the vehicle identification plate. It is also stamped on the engine compartment bulkhead, behind the air intake plenum chamber, and into the body, so that it can be seen through the bottom left-hand corner of the windscreen **(see illustrations)**.

The *engine number*, consisting of two letters and five digits, with the three-letter engine code nearby, is stamped into a flat-machined surface on the cylinder block/crankcase's forward-facing flange, between the pulse-air filter housing and the transmission. To read the number without removing the engine compartment air intake resonator - see Chapter 4 - it is easiest to raise and support the front of the vehicle on axle stands, so that the number can be seen from underneath **(see illustration)**. If the number cannot be seen in this location, possible alternative sites are on a lower flange on the cylinder block's forward face, immediately above the sump mating surface, or on the left-hand end of the cylinder head, between the oil filler cap and ignition coil.

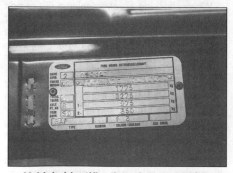

Vehicle identification plate on engine compartment front crossmember

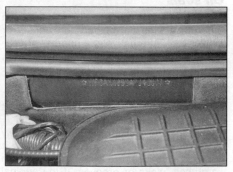

Vehicle identification number on engine compartment bulkhead

Vehicle identification number in body, visible through bottom left-hand corner of windscreen

Engine number (arrowed) on front of cylinder block/crankcase - seen from beneath vehicle

Whenever servicing, repair or overhaul work is carried out on the car or its components, it is necessary to observe the following procedures and instructions. This will assist in carrying out the operation efficiently and to a professional standard of workmanship.

Joint mating faces and gaskets

When separating components at their mating faces, never insert screwdrivers or similar implements into the joint between the faces in order to prise them apart. This can cause severe damage which results in oil leaks, coolant leaks, etc upon reassembly. Separation is usually achieved by tapping along the joint with a soft-faced hammer in order to break the seal. However, note that this method may not be suitable where dowels are used for component location.

Where a gasket is used between the mating faces of two components, ensure that it is renewed on reassembly, and fit it dry unless otherwise stated in the repair procedure. Make sure that the mating faces are clean and dry, with all traces of old gasket removed. When cleaning a joint face, use a tool which is not likely to score or damage the face, and remove any burrs or nicks with an oilstone or fine file.

Make sure that tapped holes are cleaned with a pipe cleaner, and keep them free of jointing compound, if this is being used, unless specifically instructed otherwise.

Ensure that all orifices, channels or pipes are clear, and blow through them, preferably using compressed air.

Oil seals

Oil seals can be removed by levering them out with a wide flat-bladed screwdriver or similar tool. Alternatively, a number of self-tapping screws may be screwed into the seal, and these used as a purchase for pliers or similar in order to pull the seal free.

Whenever an oil seal is removed from its working location, either individually or as part of an assembly, it should be renewed.

The very fine sealing lip of the seal is easily damaged, and will not seal if the surface it contacts is not completely clean and free from scratches, nicks or grooves. If the original sealing surface of the component cannot be restored, and the manufacturer has not made provision for slight relocation of the seal relative to the sealing surface, the component should be renewed.

Protect the lips of the seal from any surface which may damage them in the course of fitting. Use tape or a conical sleeve where possible. Lubricate the seal lips with oil before fitting and, on dual-lipped seals, fill the space between the lips with grease.

Unless otherwise stated, oil seals must be fitted with their sealing lips toward the lubricant to be sealed.

Use a tubular drift or block of wood of the appropriate size to install the seal and, if the seal housing is shouldered, drive the seal down to the shoulder. If the seal housing is unshouldered, the seal should be fitted with its face flush with the housing top face (unless otherwise instructed).

Screw threads and fastenings

Seized nuts, bolts and screws are quite a common occurrence where corrosion has set in, and the use of penetrating oil or releasing fluid will often overcome this problem if the offending item is soaked for a while before attempting to release it. The use of an impact driver may also provide a means of releasing such stubborn fastening devices, when used in conjunction with the appropriate screwdriver bit or socket. If none of these methods works, it may be necessary to resort to the careful application of heat, or the use of a hacksaw or nut splitter device.

Studs are usually removed by locking two nuts together on the threaded part, and then using a spanner on the lower nut to unscrew the stud. Studs or bolts which have broken off below the surface of the component in which they are mounted can sometimes be removed using a stud extractor. Always ensure that a blind tapped hole is completely free from oil, grease, water or other fluid before installing the bolt or stud. Failure to do this could cause the housing to crack due to the hydraulic action of the bolt or stud as it is screwed in.

When tightening a castellated nut to accept a split pin, tighten the nut to the specified torque, where applicable, and then tighten further to the next split pin hole. Never slacken the nut to align the split pin hole, unless stated in the repair procedure.

When checking or retightening a nut or bolt to a specified torque setting, slacken the nut or bolt by a quarter of a turn, and then retighten to the specified setting. However, this should not be attempted where angular tightening has been used.

For some screw fastenings, notably cylinder head bolts or nuts, torque wrench settings are no longer specified for the latter stages of tightening, "angle-tightening" being called up instead. Typically, a fairly low torque wrench setting will be applied to the bolts/nuts in the correct sequence, followed by one or more stages of tightening through specified angles.

Locknuts, locktabs and washers

Any fastening which will rotate against a component or housing during tightening should always have a washer between it and the relevant component or housing.

Spring or split washers should always be renewed when they are used to lock a critical component such as a big-end bearing retaining bolt or nut. Locktabs which are folded over to retain a nut or bolt should always be renewed.

Self-locking nuts can be re-used in non-critical areas, providing resistance can be felt when the locking portion passes over the bolt or stud thread. However, it should be noted that self-locking stiffnuts tend to lose their effectiveness after long periods of use, and should be renewed as a matter of course.

Split pins must always be replaced with new ones of the correct size for the hole.

When thread-locking compound is found on the threads of a fastener which is to be re-used, it should be cleaned off with a wire brush and solvent, and fresh compound applied on reassembly.

Special tools

Some repair procedures in this manual entail the use of special tools such as a press, two or three-legged pullers, spring compressors, etc. Wherever possible, suitable readily-available alternatives to the manufacturer's special tools are described, and are shown in use. In some instances, where no alternative is possible, it has been necessary to resort to the use of a manufacturer's tool, and this has been done for reasons of safety as well as the efficient completion of the repair operation. Unless you are highly-skilled and have a thorough understanding of the procedures described, never attempt to bypass the use of any special tool when the procedure described specifies its use. Not only is there a very great risk of personal injury, but expensive damage could be caused to the components involved.

Environmental considerations

When disposing of used engine oil, brake fluid, antifreeze, etc, give due consideration to any detrimental environmental effects. Do not, for instance, pour any of the above liquids down drains into the general sewage system, or onto the ground to soak away. Many local council refuse tips provide a facility for waste oil disposal, as do some garages. If none of these facilities are available, consult your local Environmental Health Department, or the National Rivers Authority, for further advice.

With the universal tightening-up of legislation regarding the emission of environmentally-harmful substances from motor vehicles, most current vehicles have tamperproof devices fitted to the main adjustment points of the fuel system. These devices are primarily designed to prevent unqualified persons from adjusting the fuel/air mixture, with the chance of a consequent increase in toxic emissions. If such devices are encountered during servicing or overhaul, they should, wherever possible, be renewed or refitted in accordance with the vehicle manufacturer's requirements or current legislation.

OIL CARE
FOLLOW THE CODE

OIL BANK LINE
0800 66 33 66

Note: It is antisocial and illegal to dump oil down the drain. To find the location of your local oil recycling bank, call this number free.

The jack supplied with the vehicle tool kit should only be used for changing the roadwheels - see *"Wheel changing"* at the front of this Manual.

Locate the jack head in the jacking point nearest to the wheel to be changed, ensuring that the channel in the jack head fits over the body flange **(see illustrations)** and turn its handle to raise the jack. When the wheel is clear of the ground, remove the nuts and lift off the wheel. Fit the spare wheel, and moderately tighten the nuts. Lower the vehicle, then tighten the nuts fully and refit the trim. With the spare wheel in position, remove the chock, and stow the jack and tools.

When jacking up the vehicle to carry out repair or maintenance tasks, position the jack as follows.

If the front of the vehicle is to be raised, place a jacking beam across the two front points "B" shown in the accompanying illustration, and lift the vehicle evenly.

To raise the rear of the vehicle, place a jacking beam across the two rear points "B" shown in the accompanying illustration, and lift the vehicle evenly.

To raise the side of the vehicle, place the jack head under the appropriate point indicated in the accompanying illustration - if a trolley jack or similar is used on the points

"A" provided for the vehicle's jack, make up a wooden spacer with a groove cut in it to accept the underbody flange, so that there is no risk of the jack slipping or buckling the flange. Never work under, around or near a raised vehicle unless it is adequately supported in at least two places with axle stands or suitable sturdy blocks.

The vehicle may be towed, for breakdown recovery purposes only, using the towing eyes positioned at the front and rear of the vehicle **(see illustrations)**. These eyes are intended for towing loads only, and must not be used for lifting the vehicle, either directly or indirectly.

A Jacking points (for vehicle jack in roadside use) - support points (for axle stands in servicing/overhaul work)
B Jacking points (for trolley jack or workshop hoist in servicing/overhaul work) - additional support points

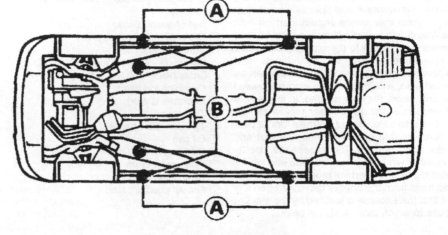

Jacking and supporting points

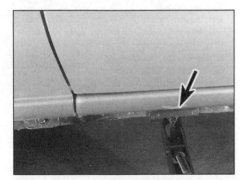

With jack base on firm ground, locate jack head in jacking point - indentations (arrowed) in sill identify jacking points

Front towing eye

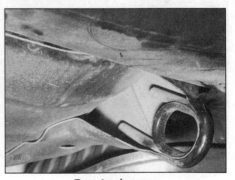

Rear towing eye

Radio/cassette unit anti-theft system - precaution

The radio/cassette unit fitted as standard equipment by Ford is equipped with a built-in security code, to deter thieves. If the power source to the unit is cut, the anti-theft system will activate. Even if the power source is immediately reconnected, the radio/cassette

unit will not function until the correct security code has been entered. Therefore, if you do not know the correct security code for the unit, do not disconnect the battery negative lead or remove the radio/cassette unit from the vehicle.

The procedure for reprogramming a unit that has been disconnected from its power supply varies from model to model. Consult the handbook supplied with the unit for specific details or refer to your Ford dealer.

Introduction

A selection of good tools is a fundamental requirement for anyone contemplating the maintenance and repair of a motor vehicle. For the owner who does not possess any, their purchase will prove a considerable expense, offsetting some of the savings made by doing-it-yourself. However, provided that the tools purchased meet the relevant national safety standards and are of good quality, they will last for many years and prove an extremely worthwhile investment.

To help the average owner to decide which tools are needed to carry out the various tasks detailed in this manual, we have compiled three lists of tools under the following headings: *Maintenance and minor repair, Repair and overhaul*, and *Special*. Newcomers to practical mechanics should start off with the *Maintenance and minor repair* tool kit, and confine themselves to the simpler jobs around the vehicle. Then, as confidence and experience grow, more difficult tasks can be undertaken, with extra tools being purchased as, and when, they are needed. In this way, a *Maintenance and minor repair* tool kit can be built up into a *Repair and overhaul* tool kit over a considerable period of time, without any major cash outlays. The experienced do-it-yourselfer will have a tool kit good enough for most repair and overhaul procedures, and will add tools from the *Special* category when it is felt that the expense is justified by the amount of use to which these tools will be put.

Maintenance and minor repair tool kit

The tools given in this list should be considered as a minimum requirement if routine maintenance, servicing and minor repair operations are to be undertaken. We recommend the purchase of combination spanners (ring one end, open-ended the other); although more expensive than open-ended ones, they do give the advantages of both types of spanner.

☐ *Combination spanners:*
 Metric - 8 to 19 mm inclusive
☐ *Adjustable spanner - 35 mm jaw (approx.)*
☐ *Spark plug spanner (with rubber insert) - petrol models*
☐ *Spark plug gap adjustment tool - petrol models*
☐ *Set of feeler blades*
☐ *Brake bleed nipple spanner*
☐ *Screwdrivers:*
 Flat blade - 100 mm long x 6 mm dia
 Cross blade - 100 mm long x 6 mm dia
☐ *Combination pliers*
☐ *Hacksaw (junior)*
☐ *Tyre pump*
☐ *Tyre pressure gauge*
☐ *Oil can*
☐ *Oil filter removal tool*
☐ *Fine emery cloth*
☐ *Wire brush (small)*
☐ *Funnel (medium size)*

Repair and overhaul tool kit

These tools are virtually essential for anyone undertaking any major repairs to a motor vehicle, and are additional to those given in the *Maintenance and minor repair* list. Included in this list is a comprehensive set of sockets. Although these are expensive, they will be found invaluable as they are so versatile - particularly if various drives are included in the set. We recommend the half-inch square-drive type, as this can be used with most proprietary torque wrenches.

The tools in this list will sometimes need to be supplemented by tools from the *Special* list:

☐ *Sockets (or box spanners) to cover range in previous list (including Torx sockets)*
☐ *Reversible ratchet drive (for use with sockets)*
☐ *Extension piece, 250 mm (for use with sockets)*
☐ *Universal joint (for use with sockets)*
☐ *Torque wrench (for use with sockets)*
☐ *Self-locking grips*
☐ *Ball pein hammer*
☐ *Soft-faced mallet (plastic/aluminium or rubber)*
☐ *Screwdrivers:*
 Flat blade - long & sturdy, short (chubby), and narrow (electrician's) types
 Cross blade – Long & sturdy, and short (chubby) types
☐ *Pliers:*
 Long-nosed
 Side cutters (electrician's)
 Circlip (internal and external)
☐ *Cold chisel - 25 mm*
☐ *Scriber*
☐ *Scraper*
☐ *Centre-punch*
☐ *Pin punch*
☐ *Hacksaw*
☐ *Brake hose clamp*
☐ *Brake/clutch bleeding kit*
☐ *Selection of twist drills*
☐ *Steel rule/straight-edge*
☐ *Allen keys (inc. splined/Torx type)*
☐ *Selection of files*
☐ *Wire brush*
☐ *Axle stands*
☐ *Jack (strong trolley or hydraulic type)*
☐ *Light with extension lead*

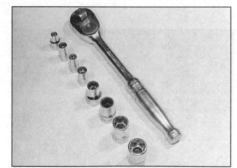
Sockets and reversible ratchet drive

Valve spring compressor

Spline bit set

Piston ring compressor

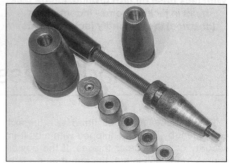
Clutch plate alignment set

Special tools

The tools in this list are those which are not used regularly, are expensive to buy, or which need to be used in accordance with their manufacturers' instructions. Unless relatively difficult mechanical jobs are undertaken frequently, it will not be economic to buy many of these tools. Where this is the case, you could consider clubbing together with friends (or joining a motorists' club) to make a joint purchase, or borrowing the tools against a deposit from a local garage or tool hire specialist. It is worth noting that many of the larger DIY superstores now carry a large range of special tools for hire at modest rates.

The following list contains only those tools and instruments freely available to the public, and not those special tools produced by the vehicle manufacturer specifically for its dealer network. You will find occasional references to these manufacturers' special tools in the text of this manual. Generally, an alternative method of doing the job without the vehicle manufacturers' special tool is given. However, sometimes there is no alternative to using them. Where this is the case and the relevant tool cannot be bought or borrowed, you will have to entrust the work to a dealer.

☐ Valve spring compressor
☐ Valve grinding tool
☐ Piston ring compressor
☐ Piston ring removal/installation tool
☐ Cylinder bore hone
☐ Balljoint separator
☐ Coil spring compressors (where applicable)
☐ Two/three-legged hub and bearing puller
☐ Impact screwdriver
☐ Micrometer and/or vernier calipers
☐ Dial gauge
☐ Stroboscopic timing light
☐ Dwell angle meter/tachometer
☐ Universal electrical multi-meter
☐ Cylinder compression gauge
☐ Hand-operated vacuum pump and gauge
☐ Clutch plate alignment set
☐ Brake shoe steady spring cup removal tool
☐ Bush and bearing removal/installation set
☐ Stud extractors
☐ Tap and die set
☐ Lifting tackle
☐ Trolley jack

Buying tools

Reputable motor accessory shops and superstores often offer excellent quality tools at discount prices, so it pays to shop around.

Remember, you don't have to buy the most expensive items on the shelf, but it is always advisable to steer clear of the very cheap tools. Beware of 'bargains' offered on market stalls or at car boot sales. There are plenty of good tools around at reasonable prices, but always aim to purchase items which meet the relevant national safety standards. If in doubt, ask the proprietor or manager of the shop for advice before making a purchase.

Care and maintenance of tools

Having purchased a reasonable tool kit, it is necessary to keep the tools in a clean and serviceable condition. After use, always wipe off any dirt, grease and metal particles using a clean, dry cloth, before putting the tools away. Never leave them lying around after they have been used. A simple tool rack on the garage or workshop wall for items such as screwdrivers and pliers is a good idea. Store all normal spanners and sockets in a metal box. Any measuring instruments, gauges, meters, etc, must be carefully stored where they cannot be damaged or become rusty.

Take a little care when tools are used. Hammer heads inevitably become marked, and screwdrivers lose the keen edge on their blades from time to time. A little timely attention with emery cloth or a file will soon restore items like this to a good finish.

Working facilities

Not to be forgotten when discussing tools is the workshop itself. If anything more than routine maintenance is to be carried out, a suitable working area becomes essential.

It is appreciated that many an owner-mechanic is forced by circumstances to remove an engine or similar item without the benefit of a garage or workshop. Having done this, any repairs should always be done under the cover of a roof.

Wherever possible, any dismantling should be done on a clean, flat workbench or table at a suitable working height.

Any workbench needs a vice; one with a jaw opening of 100 mm is suitable for most jobs. As mentioned previously, some clean dry storage space is also required for tools, as well as for any lubricants, cleaning fluids, touch-up paints etc, which become necessary.

Another item which may be required, and which has a much more general usage, is an electric drill with a chuck capacity of at least 8 mm. This, together with a good range of twist drills, is virtually essential for fitting accessories.

Last, but not least, always keep a supply of old newspapers and clean, lint-free rags available, and try to keep any working area as clean as possible.

Micrometer set

Dial test indicator ("dial gauge")

Stroboscopic timing light

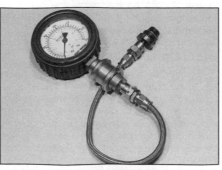
Compression tester

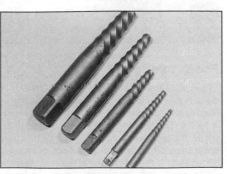
Stud extractor set

This is a guide to getting your vehicle through the MOT test. Obviously it will not be possible to examine the vehicle to the same standard as the professional MOT tester. However, working through the following checks will enable you to identify any problem areas before submitting the vehicle for the test.

Where a testable component is in borderline condition, the tester has discretion in deciding whether to pass or fail it. The basis of such discretion is whether the tester would be happy for a close relative or friend to use the vehicle with the component in that condition. If the vehicle presented is clean and evidently well cared for, the tester may be more inclined to pass a borderline component than if the vehicle is scruffy and apparently neglected.

It has only been possible to summarise the test requirements here, based on the regulations in force at the time of printing. Test standards are becoming increasingly stringent, although there are some exemptions for older vehicles. For full details obtain a copy of the Haynes publication Pass the MOT! (available from stockists of Haynes manuals).

An assistant will be needed to help carry out some of these checks.

The checks have been sub-divided into four categories, as follows:

1 Checks carried out **FROM THE DRIVER'S SEAT**

2 Checks carried out **WITH THE VEHICLE ON THE GROUND**

3 Checks carried out **WITH THE VEHICLE RAISED AND THE WHEELS FREE TO TURN**

4 Checks carried out on **YOUR VEHICLE'S EXHAUST EMISSION SYSTEM**

---

1 Checks carried out **FROM THE DRIVER'S SEAT**

Handbrake

☐ Test the operation of the handbrake. Excessive travel (too many clicks) indicates incorrect brake or cable adjustment.
☐ Check that the handbrake cannot be released by tapping the lever sideways. Check the security of the lever mountings.

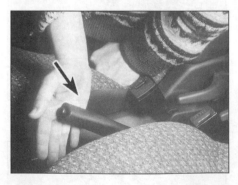

Footbrake

☐ Depress the brake pedal and check that it does not creep down to the floor, indicating a master cylinder fault. Release the pedal, wait a few seconds, then depress it again. If the pedal travels nearly to the floor before firm resistance is felt, brake adjustment or repair is necessary. If the pedal feels spongy, there is air in the hydraulic system which must be removed by bleeding.

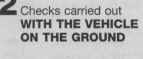

☐ Check that the brake pedal is secure and in good condition. Check also for signs of fluid leaks on the pedal, floor or carpets, which would indicate failed seals in the brake master cylinder.
☐ Check the servo unit (when applicable) by operating the brake pedal several times, then keeping the pedal depressed and starting the engine. As the engine starts, the pedal will move down slightly. If not, the vacuum hose or the servo itself may be faulty.

Steering wheel and column

☐ Examine the steering wheel for fractures or looseness of the hub, spokes or rim.
☐ Move the steering wheel from side to side and then up and down. Check that the steering wheel is not loose on the column, indicating wear or a loose retaining nut. Continue moving the steering wheel as before, but also turn it slightly from left to right.
☐ Check that the steering wheel is not loose on the column, and that there is no abnormal

movement of the steering wheel, indicating wear in the column support bearings or couplings.

Windscreen and mirrors

☐ The windscreen must be free of cracks or other significant damage within the driver's field of view. (Small stone chips are acceptable.) Rear view mirrors must be secure, intact, and capable of being adjusted.

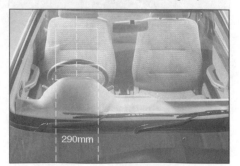

290mm

Seat belts and seats

Note: *The following checks are applicable to all seat belts, front and rear.*

☐ Examine the webbing of all the belts (including rear belts if fitted) for cuts, serious fraying or deterioration. Fasten and unfasten each belt to check the buckles. If applicable, check the retracting mechanism. Check the security of all seat belt mountings accessible from inside the vehicle.
☐ The front seats themselves must be securely attached and the backrests must lock in the upright position.

Doors

☐ Both front doors must be able to be opened and closed from outside and inside, and must latch securely when closed.

2 Checks carried out WITH THE VEHICLE ON THE GROUND

Vehicle identification

☐ Number plates must be in good condition, secure and legible, with letters and numbers correctly spaced – spacing at (A) should be twice that at (B).

☐ The VIN plate and/or homologation plate must be legible.

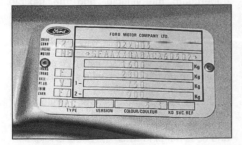

Electrical equipment

☐ Switch on the ignition and check the operation of the horn.
☐ Check the windscreen washers and wipers, examining the wiper blades; renew damaged or perished blades. Also check the operation of the stop-lights.

☐ Check the operation of the sidelights and number plate lights. The lenses and reflectors must be secure, clean and undamaged.
☐ Check the operation and alignment of the headlights. The headlight reflectors must not be tarnished and the lenses must be undamaged.
☐ Switch on the ignition and check the operation of the direction indicators (including the instrument panel tell-tale) and the hazard warning lights. Operation of the sidelights and stop-lights must not affect the indicators - if it does, the cause is usually a bad earth at the rear light cluster.
☐ Check the operation of the rear foglight(s), including the warning light on the instrument panel or in the switch.

Footbrake

☐ Examine the master cylinder, brake pipes and servo unit for leaks, loose mountings, corrosion or other damage.

☐ The fluid reservoir must be secure and the fluid level must be between the upper (A) and lower (B) markings.

☐ Inspect both front brake flexible hoses for cracks or deterioration of the rubber. Turn the steering from lock to lock, and ensure that the hoses do not contact the wheel, tyre, or any part of the steering or suspension mechanism. With the brake pedal firmly depressed, check the hoses for bulges or leaks under pressure.

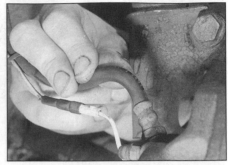

Steering and suspension

☐ Have your assistant turn the steering wheel from side to side slightly, up to the point where the steering gear just begins to transmit this movement to the roadwheels. Check for excessive free play between the steering wheel and the steering gear, indicating wear or insecurity of the steering column joints, the column-to-steering gear coupling, or the steering gear itself.
☐ Have your assistant turn the steering wheel more vigorously in each direction, so that the roadwheels just begin to turn. As this is done, examine all the steering joints, linkages, fittings and attachments. Renew any component that shows signs of wear or damage. On vehicles with power steering, check the security and condition of the steering pump, drivebelt and hoses.
☐ Check that the vehicle is standing level, and at approximately the correct ride height.

Shock absorbers

☐ Depress each corner of the vehicle in turn, then release it. The vehicle should rise and then settle in its normal position. If the vehicle continues to rise and fall, the shock absorber is defective. A shock absorber which has seized will also cause the vehicle to fail.

Exhaust system

☐ Start the engine. With your assistant holding a rag over the tailpipe, check the entire system for leaks. Repair or renew leaking sections.

3 Checks carried out **WITH THE VEHICLE RAISED AND THE WHEELS FREE TO TURN**

Jack up the front and rear of the vehicle, and securely support it on axle stands. Position the stands clear of the suspension assemblies. Ensure that the wheels are clear of the ground and that the steering can be turned from lock to lock.

Steering mechanism

☐ Have your assistant turn the steering from lock to lock. Check that the steering turns smoothly, and that no part of the steering mechanism, including a wheel or tyre, fouls any brake hose or pipe or any part of the body structure.
☐ Examine the steering rack rubber gaiters for damage or insecurity of the retaining clips. If power steering is fitted, check for signs of damage or leakage of the fluid hoses, pipes or connections. Also check for excessive stiffness or binding of the steering, a missing split pin or locking device, or severe corrosion of the body structure within 30 cm of any steering component attachment point.

Front and rear suspension and wheel bearings

☐ Starting at the front right-hand side, grasp the roadwheel at the 3 o'clock and 9 o'clock positions and shake it vigorously. Check for free play or insecurity at the wheel bearings, suspension balljoints, or suspension mountings, pivots and attachments.
☐ Now grasp the wheel at the 12 o'clock and 6 o'clock positions and repeat the previous inspection. Spin the wheel, and check for roughness or tightness of the front wheel bearing.

☐ If excess free play is suspected at a component pivot point, this can be confirmed by using a large screwdriver or similar tool and levering between the mounting and the component attachment. This will confirm whether the wear is in the pivot bush, its retaining bolt, or in the mounting itself (the bolt holes can often become elongated).

☐ Carry out all the above checks at the other front wheel, and then at both rear wheels.

Springs and shock absorbers

☐ Examine the suspension struts (when applicable) for serious fluid leakage, corrosion, or damage to the casing. Also check the security of the mounting points.
☐ If coil springs are fitted, check that the spring ends locate in their seats, and that the spring is not corroded, cracked or broken.
☐ If leaf springs are fitted, check that all leaves are intact, that the axle is securely attached to each spring, and that there is no deterioration of the spring eye mountings, bushes, and shackles.

☐ The same general checks apply to vehicles fitted with other suspension types, such as torsion bars, hydraulic displacer units, etc. Ensure that all mountings and attachments are secure, that there are no signs of excessive wear, corrosion or damage, and (on hydraulic types) that there are no fluid leaks or damaged pipes.
☐ Inspect the shock absorbers for signs of serious fluid leakage. Check for wear of the mounting bushes or attachments, or damage to the body of the unit.

Driveshafts (fwd vehicles only)

☐ Rotate each front wheel in turn and inspect the constant velocity joint gaiters for splits or damage. Also check that each driveshaft is straight and undamaged.

Braking system

☐ If possible without dismantling, check brake pad wear and disc condition. Ensure that the friction lining material has not worn excessively, (A) and that the discs are not fractured, pitted, scored or badly worn (B).

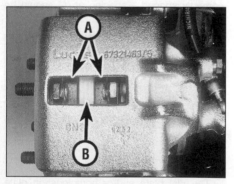

☐ Examine all the rigid brake pipes underneath the vehicle, and the flexible hose(s) at the rear. Look for corrosion, chafing or insecurity of the pipes, and for signs of bulging under pressure, chafing, splits or deterioration of the flexible hoses.
☐ Look for signs of fluid leaks at the brake calipers or on the brake backplates. Repair or renew leaking components.
☐ Slowly spin each wheel, while your assistant depresses and releases the footbrake. Ensure that each brake is operating and does not bind when the pedal is released.

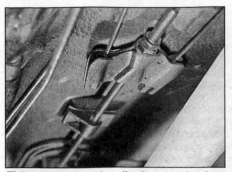

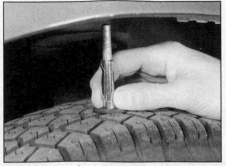

□ Examine the handbrake mechanism, checking for frayed or broken cables, excessive corrosion, or wear or insecurity of the linkage. Check that the mechanism works on each relevant wheel, and releases fully, without binding.

□ It is not possible to test brake efficiency without special equipment, but a road test can be carried out later to check that the vehicle pulls up in a straight line.

Fuel and exhaust systems

□ Inspect the fuel tank (including the filler cap), fuel pipes, hoses and unions. All components must be secure and free from leaks.

□ Examine the exhaust system over its entire length, checking for any damaged, broken or missing mountings, security of the retaining clamps and rust or corrosion.

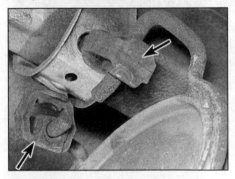

Wheels and tyres

□ Examine the sidewalls and tread area of each tyre in turn. Check for cuts, tears, lumps, bulges, separation of the tread, and exposure of the ply or cord due to wear or damage. Check that the tyre bead is correctly seated on the wheel rim, that the valve is sound and

properly seated, and that the wheel is not distorted or damaged.

□ Check that the tyres are of the correct size for the vehicle, that they are of the same size and type on each axle, and that the pressures are correct.

□ Check the tyre tread depth. The legal minimum at the time of writing is 1.6 mm over at least three-quarters of the tread width. Abnormal tread wear may indicate incorrect front wheel alignment.

Body corrosion

□ Check the condition of the entire vehicle structure for signs of corrosion in load-bearing areas. (These include chassis box sections, side sills, cross-members, pillars, and all suspension, steering, braking system and seat belt mountings and anchorages.) Any corrosion which has seriously reduced the thickness of a load-bearing area is likely to cause the vehicle to fail. In this case professional repairs are likely to be needed.

□ Damage or corrosion which causes sharp or otherwise dangerous edges to be exposed will also cause the vehicle to fail.

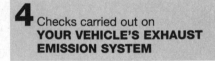

4 Checks carried out on **YOUR VEHICLE'S EXHAUST EMISSION SYSTEM**

Petrol models

□ Have the engine at normal operating temperature, and make sure that it is in good tune (ignition system in good order, air filter element clean, etc).

□ Before any measurements are carried out, raise the engine speed to around 2500 rpm, and hold it at this speed for 20 seconds. Allow

the engine speed to return to idle, and watch for smoke emissions from the exhaust tailpipe. If the idle speed is obviously much too high, or if dense blue or clearly-visible black smoke comes from the tailpipe for more than 5 seconds, the vehicle will fail. As a rule of thumb, blue smoke signifies oil being burnt (engine wear) while black smoke signifies unburnt fuel (dirty air cleaner element, or other carburettor or fuel system fault).

□ An exhaust gas analyser capable of measuring carbon monoxide (CO) and hydrocarbons (HC) is now needed. If such an instrument cannot be hired or borrowed, a local garage may agree to perform the check for a small fee.

CO emissions (mixture)

□ At the time of writing, the maximum CO level at idle is 3.5% for vehicles first used after August 1986 and 4.5% for older vehicles. From January 1996 a much tighter limit (around 0.5%) applies to catalyst-equipped vehicles first used from August 1992. If the CO level cannot be reduced far enough to pass the test (and the fuel and ignition systems are otherwise in good condition) then the carburettor is badly worn, or there is some problem in the fuel injection system or catalytic converter (as applicable).

HC emissions

□ With the CO emissions within limits, HC emissions must be no more than 1200 ppm (parts per million). If the vehicle fails this test at idle, it can be re-tested at around 2000 rpm; if the HC level is then 1200 ppm or less, this counts as a pass.

□ Excessive HC emissions can be caused by oil being burnt, but they are more likely to be due to unburnt fuel.

Diesel models

□ The only emission test applicable to Diesel engines is the measuring of exhaust smoke density. The test involves accelerating the engine several times to its maximum unloaded speed.

Note: *It is of the utmost importance that the engine timing belt is in good condition before the test is carried out.*

□ Excessive smoke can be caused by a dirty air cleaner element. Otherwise, professional advice may be needed to find the cause.

Engine   1

☐ Engine turns but will not start (cold)
☐ Engine turns but will not start (hot or cold)
☐ Low cranking speed
☐ Engine is difficult to start
☐ Engine starts but stops again
☐ Engine will not stop when switched off
☐ Misfiring/rough idle
☐ Lack of power
☐ Engine knocks
☐ Oil consumption excessive
☐ Overheating
☐ Crankcase pressure excessive (oil being blown out)
☐ Erratic running
☐ Vibration
☐ Low oil pressure
☐ High oil pressure
☐ Injector pipe(s) break or split repeatedly

Cooling system   2

☐ Corrosion
☐ External coolant leakage
☐ Internal coolant leakage
☐ Overcooling
☐ Overheating

Fuel and exhaust systems   3

☐ Fuel consumption excessive
☐ Black smoke in exhaust
☐ Blue or white smoke in exhaust
☐ Fuel leakage and/or fuel odour

Clutch   4

☐ Clutch fails to disengage (unable to select gears)
☐ Clutch slips (engine speed increases with no increase in vehicle speed)
☐ Judder as clutch is engaged
☐ Noise when depressing or releasing clutch pedal
☐ Pedal travels to floor - no pressure or very little resistance

Transmission   5

☐ Jumps out of gear
☐ Lubricant leaks
☐ Noisy in neutral with engine running
☐ Noisy in one particular gear
☐ Vibration

Driveshafts   6

☐ Clicking or knocking noise on turns (at slow speed on full-lock)
☐ Vibration when accelerating or decelerating

Braking system   7

☐ Brake pedal feels spongy when depressed
☐ Brakes binding
☐ Excessive brake pedal effort required to stop vehicle
☐ Excessive brake pedal travel
☐ Judder felt through brake pedal or steering wheel when braking
☐ Noise (grinding or high-pitched squeal) when brakes applied
☐ Rear wheels locking under normal braking
☐ Vehicle pulls to one side under braking

Suspension and steering systems   8

☐ Excessive pitching and/or rolling around corners, or during braking
☐ Excessive play in steering
☐ Excessively-stiff steering
☐ Lack of power assistance
☐ Tyre wear excessive
☐ Vehicle pulls to one side
☐ Wandering or general instability
☐ Wheel wobble and vibration

Electrical system   9

☐ Battery will not hold a charge for more than a few days
☐ Central locking system inoperative, or unsatisfactory in operation
☐ Electric windows inoperative, or unsatisfactory in operation
☐ Horn inoperative, or unsatisfactory in operation
☐ Ignition warning light fails to come on
☐ Ignition warning light remains illuminated with engine running
☐ Instrument readings inaccurate or erratic
☐ Lights inoperative
☐ Windscreen/tailgate washers inoperative, or unsatisfactory in operation
☐ Windscreen/tailgate wipers inoperative, or unsatisfactory in operation

Introduction

The vehicle owner who does his or her own maintenance according to the recommended service schedules should not have to use this section of the manual very often. Modern component reliability is such that, provided those items subject to wear or deterioration are inspected or renewed at the specified intervals, sudden failure is comparatively rare. Faults do not usually just happen as a result of sudden failure, but develop over a period of time. Major mechanical failures in particular are usually preceded by characteristic symptoms over hundreds or even thousands of miles. Those components which do occasionally fail without warning are often small and easily carried in the vehicle.

With any fault-finding, the first step is to decide where to begin investigations. Sometimes this is obvious, but on other occasions, a little detective work will be necessary. The owner who makes half a dozen haphazard adjustments or replacements may be successful in curing a fault (or its symptoms), but will be none the wiser if the fault recurs, and ultimately may have spent more time and money than was necessary. A calm and logical approach will be found to be more satisfactory in the long run. Always take into account any warning signs or abnormalities that may have been noticed in the period preceding the fault - power loss, high or low gauge readings, unusual smells, etc - and remember that failure of components such as fuses or glow plugs may only be pointers to some underlying fault.

The pages which follow provide an easy reference guide to the more common problems which may occur during the operation of the vehicle. These problems and their possible causes are grouped under headings denoting various components or systems, such as Engine,

Cooling system, etc. The Chapter and/or Section which deals with the problem is also shown in brackets. Whatever the fault, certain basic principles apply. These are as follows:

Verify the fault. This is simply a matter of being sure that you know what the symptoms are before starting work. This is particularly important if you are investigating a fault for someone else, who may not have described it very accurately.

Don't overlook the obvious. For example, if the vehicle won't start, is there fuel in the tank? (Don't take anyone else's word on this particular point, and don't trust the fuel gauge either!) If an electrical fault is indicated, look for loose or broken wires before digging out the test gear.

Cure the disease, not the symptom. Substituting a flat battery with a fully-charged one will get you off the hard shoulder, but if the underlying cause is not attended to, the new battery will go the same way. Similarly, changing oil-fouled spark plugs for a new set will get you moving again, but remember that the reason for the fouling (if it wasn't simply an incorrect grade of plug) will have to be established and corrected.

Don't take anything for granted. Particularly, don't forget that a "new" component may itself be defective (especially if it's been rattling around in the boot for months), and don't leave components out of a fault diagnosis sequence just because they are new or recently fitted. When you do finally diagnose a difficult fault, you'll probably realise that all the evidence was there from the start.

1 Engine

Engine turns but will not start (cold)

☐ Incorrect use of preheating system (Chapter 5)
☐ Preheating system fault (Chapter 5)
☐ Fuel waxing (in very cold weather) (Section 5)
☐ Overfuelling or cold start advance mechanism defective (Chapter 4)

Engine turns but will not start (hot or cold)

☐ Low cranking speed (see below)
☐ Poor compression (Chapter 3)
☐ No fuel in tank
☐ Air in fuel system (Chapter 4)
☐ Fuel feed restriction (Chapter 4)
☐ Fuel contaminated (Chapter 4)
☐ Stop solenoid defective (Chapter 4)
☐ Major mechanical failure (Chapter 2)
☐ Injection pump internal fault (Chapter 4)

Low cranking speed

☐ Inadequate battery capacity (Chapter 5)
☐ Incorrect grade of oil (*Lubricants, fluids and capacities*)
☐ High resistance in starter motor circuit (Chapter 5)
☐ Starter motor internal fault (Chapter 5)

Engine is difficult to start

☐ Incorrect starting procedure
☐ Battery or starter motor fault (Chapter 5)
☐ Preheating system fault (Chapter 5)
☐ Air in fuel system (Chapter 4)
☐ Fuel feed restriction (Chapter 4)
☐ Poor compression (Chapter 2)
☐ Valve clearances incorrect (Chapter 2)
☐ Valves sticking (Chapter 2)
☐ Blockage in exhaust system
☐ Valve timing incorrect (Chapter 2)
☐ Injector(s) faulty (Chapter 4)
☐ Injection pump timing incorrect (Chapter 4)
☐ Injection pump internal fault (Chapter 4)

Engine starts but stops again

☐ Fuel very low in tank
☐ Air in fuel system (Chapter 4)
☐ Idle adjustment incorrect (Chapter 2)
☐ Fuel feed restriction (Chapter 4)
☐ Fuel return restriction (Chapter 4)
☐ Air cleaner dirty (Chapter 2)
☐ Blockage in induction system (Chapter 4)
☐ Blockage in exhaust system
☐ Injector(s) faulty (Chapter 4)

Engine will not stop when switched off

☐ Stop solenoid defective (Chapter 4)

Misfiring/rough idle

☐ Air cleaner dirty (Chapter 4)
☐ Blockage in induction system (Chapter 4)
☐ Air in fuel system (Chapter 4)
☐ Fuel feed restriction (Chapter 4)
☐ Valve clearances incorrect (Chapter 2)
☐ Valve(s) sticking (Chapter 2)
☐ Valve spring(s) weak or broken (Chapter 2)
☐ Poor compression (Chapter 2)
☐ Overheating (Chapter 3)
☐ Injector pipe(s) wrongly connected or wrong type (Chapter 4)
☐ Valve timing incorrect (Chapter 2)
☐ Injector(s) faulty or wrong type (Chapter 4)
☐ Injection pump timing incorrect (Chapter 4)
☐ Injection pump faulty or wrong type (Chapter 4)

Lack of power

☐ Accelerator linkage not moving through full travel (cable slack or pedal obstructed) (Chapter 4)
☐ Injection pump control linkages sticking or maladjusted (Chapter 4)
☐ Air cleaner dirty (Chapter 2)
☐ Blockage in induction system (Chapter 4)
☐ Air in fuel system (Section 4)
☐ Fuel feed restriction (Section 5)
☐ Valve timing incorrect (Chapter 3)
☐ Injection pump timing incorrect (Chapter 4)
☐ Blockage in exhaust system
☐ Turbo boost pressure inadequate (Chapter 4)
☐ Valve clearances incorrect (Chapter 2)
☐ Poor compression (Chapter 2)
☐ Injector(s) faulty or wrong type (Chapter 4)
☐ Injection pump faulty (Chapter 4)

Engine knocks

☐ Air in fuel system (Chapter 4)
☐ Fuel grade incorrect or quality poor (*Lubricants, fluids and capacities*)
☐ Injector(s) faulty or wrong type (Chapter 4)
☐ Valve spring(s) weak or broken (Chapter 2)
☐ Valve(s) sticking (Chapter 2)
☐ Valve clearances incorrect (Chapter 2)
☐ Valve timing incorrect (Chapter 2)
☐ Injection pump timing incorrect (Chapter 4)
☐ Piston protrusion excessive/head gasket thickness inadequate (after repair) (Chapter 2)
☐ Valve recess incorrect (after repair) (Chapter 2)
☐ Piston rings broken or worn (Chapter 2)
☐ Pistons and/or bores worn (Chapter 2)
☐ Crankshaft bearings worn or damaged (Chapter 2)
☐ Small-end bearings worn (Chapter 2)
☐ Camshaft worn (Chapter 2)

1 Engine (continued)

Oil consumption excessive

- [ ] External leakage (standing or running)
- [ ] New engine not yet run-in
- [ ] Engine oil incorrect grade or poor quality (*Lubricants, fluids and capacities*)
- [ ] Oil level too high (Chapter 1)
- [ ] Crankcase ventilation system obstructed (Chapter 1)
- [ ] Oil leaking from oil feed pipe into fuel feed pipe (Chapter 4)
- [ ] Oil leakage from ancillary component (vacuum pump etc.) (Chapter 9)
- [ ] Oil leaking into coolant (Chapter 3)
- [ ] Oil leaking into injection pump (Chapter 4)
- [ ] Air cleaner dirty (Chapter 4)
- [ ] Blockage in induction system (Chapter 4)
- [ ] Cylinder bores glazed (Chapter 2)
- [ ] Piston rings broken or worn (Chapter 2)
- [ ] Pistons and/or bores worn (Chapter 2)
- [ ] Valve stems or guides worn (Chapter 2)
- [ ] Valve stem oil seals worn (Chapter 2)

Overheating (Section 15)

- [ ] Coolant leakage (Chapter 3)
- [ ] Engine oil level too high (Chapter 1)
- [ ] Electric cooling fan malfunctioning (Chapter 3)
- [ ] Coolant pump defective (Chapter 3)
- [ ] Radiator clogged externally
- [ ] Radiator clogged internally
- [ ] Coolant hoses blocked or collapsed
- [ ] Coolant reservoir pressure cap defective or incorrect
- [ ] Coolant thermostat defective or incorrect (Chapter 3)
- [ ] Thermostat missing (Chapter 3)
- [ ] Air cleaner dirty (Chapter 4)
- [ ] Blockage in induction system (Chapter 4)
- [ ] Blockage in exhaust system
- [ ] Head gasket blown (Chapter 2)
- [ ] Cylinder head cracked or warped (Chapter 2)
- [ ] Valve timing incorrect (Chapter 2)
- [ ] Injection pump timing incorrect (over-advanced) (Chapter 4)
- [ ] Injector(s) faulty or wrong type (Chapter 4)
- [ ] Injection pump faulty (Chapter 4)
- [ ] Imminent seizure (piston pick-up)

Crankcase pressure excessive (oil being blown out)

- [ ] Blockage in crankcase ventilation system (Chapter 2)
- [ ] Leakage in vacuum pump or exhauster (Chapter 9)
- [ ] Piston rings broken or sticking (Chapter 2)
- [ ] Pistons or bores worn (Chapter 2)
- [ ] Head gasket blown (Chapter 2)

Erratic running

- [ ] Operating temperature incorrect
- [ ] Accelerator linkage maladjusted or sticking (Chapter 4)
- [ ] Air cleaner dirty (Chapter 4)
- [ ] Blockage in induction system (Chapter 4)
- [ ] Air in fuel system (Chapter 4)
- [ ] Injector pipe(s) wrongly connected or wrong type (Chapter 4)
- [ ] Fuel feed restriction (Chapter 4)
- [ ] Fuel return restriction
- [ ] Valve clearances incorrect (Chapter 2)
- [ ] Valve(s) sticking (Chapter 2)
- [ ] Valve spring(s) broken or weak (Chapter 2)
- [ ] Valve timing incorrect (Chapter 2)
- [ ] Poor compression (Chapter 2)
- [ ] Injector(s) faulty or wrong type (Chapter 4)
- [ ] Injection pump mountings loose (Chapter 4)
- [ ] Injection pump timing incorrect (Chapter 4)
- [ ] Injection pump faulty (Chapter 4)

Vibration

- [ ] Accelerator linkage sticking (Chapter 4)
- [ ] Engine mountings loose or worn (Chapter 2)
- [ ] Cooling fan damaged or loose
- [ ] Crankshaft pulley/damper damaged or loose (Chapter 2)
- [ ] Injector pipe(s) wrongly connected or wrong type (Chapter 4)
- [ ] Valve(s) sticking (Chapter 2)
- [ ] Flywheel or (when applicable) flywheel housing loose (Chapter 2)
- [ ] Poor (uneven) compression (Section 2)

Low oil pressure

- [ ] Oil level low (Chapter 1)
- [ ] Oil grade or quality incorrect (*Lubricants, fluids and capacities*)
- [ ] Oil filter clogged (Chapter 1)
- [ ] Overheating (Chapter 3)
- [ ] Oil contaminated (Chapter 1)
- [ ] Gauge or warning light sender inaccurate (Chapter 5)
- [ ] Oil pump pick-up strainer clogged (Chapter 2)
- [ ] Oil pump suction pipe loose or cracked (Chapter 2)
- [ ] Oil pressure relief valve defective or stuck open (Chapter 2)
- [ ] Oil pump worn (Chapter 2)
- [ ] Crankshaft bearings worn (Chapter 2)

High oil pressure

- [ ] Oil grade or quality incorrect (*Lubricants, fluids and capacities*)
- [ ] Gauge inaccurate
- [ ] Oil pressure relief valve stuck shut (Chapter 2)

Injector pipe(s) break or split repeatedly

- [ ] Missing or wrongly located clamps (Chapter 4)
- [ ] Wrong type or length of pipe (Chapter 4)
- [ ] Faulty injector (Chapter 4)
- [ ] Faulty delivery valve (Chapter 4)

2 Cooling system

Overheating

- ☐ Insufficient coolant in system (Chapter 1).
- ☐ Thermostat faulty (Chapter 3).
- ☐ Radiator core blocked or grille restricted (Chapter 3).
- ☐ Radiator electric cooling fan(s) or coolant temperature sensor faulty (Chapter 3).
- ☐ Engine management system fault (Chapters 1, 4, 5 and 6).
- ☐ Pressure cap faulty (Chapter 3).
- ☐ Auxiliary drivebelt worn or slipping (Chapter 1).
- ☐ Inaccurate coolant temperature gauge sender (Chapter 3).
- ☐ Air-lock in cooling system (Chapter 3).

Overcooling

- ☐ Thermostat faulty (Chapter 3).
- ☐ Inaccurate coolant temperature gauge sender (Chapter 3).

External coolant leakage

- ☐ Deteriorated or damaged hoses or hose clips (Chapter 1).
- ☐ Radiator core or heater matrix leaking (Chapter 3).
- ☐ Pressure cap faulty (Chapter 3).
- ☐ Water pump seal leaking (Chapter 3).
- ☐ Boiling due to overheating (Chapter 3).
- ☐ Core plug leaking (Chapter 2).

Internal coolant leakage

- ☐ Leaking cylinder head gasket (Chapter 2).
- ☐ Cracked cylinder head or cylinder bore (Chapter 2).

Corrosion

- ☐ Infrequent draining and flushing (Chapter 1).
- ☐ Incorrect antifreeze mixture, or inappropriate antifreeze type (Chapter 1).

3 Fuel and exhaust system

Fuel consumption excessive

- ☐ External leakage
- ☐ Fuel passing into sump (Chapter 4)
- ☐ Air cleaner dirty (Chapter 4)
- ☐ Blockage in induction system (Chapter 4)
- ☐ Valve clearances incorrect (Chapter 2)
- ☐ Valve(s) sticking (Chapter 2)
- ☐ Valve spring(s) weak (Chapter 2)
- ☐ Poor compression (Section 2)
- ☐ Valve timing incorrect (Chapter 2)
- ☐ Injection pump timing incorrect (Chapter 4)
- ☐ Injector(s) faulty or wrong type (Chapter 4)
- ☐ Injection pump faulty (Chapter 4)

Fuel leakage and/or fuel odour

- ☐ Damaged or corroded fuel tank, pipes or connections (Chapter 4).

Black smoke in exhaust

- ☐ Air cleaner dirty (Chapter 4)
- ☐ Blockage in induction system (Chapter 4)
- ☐ Valve clearances incorrect (Chapter 2)
- ☐ Poor compression (Section 2)

- ☐ Turbo boost pressure inadequate, when applicable (Chapter 4)
- ☐ Blockage in exhaust system
- ☐ Valve timing incorrect (Chapter 2)
- ☐ Injector(s) faulty or wrong type (Chapter 4)
- ☐ Injection pump timing incorrect (Chapter 4)
- ☐ Injection pump faulty (Chapter 4)

Blue or white smoke in exhaust

- ☐ Engine oil incorrect grade or poor quality (Lubricants, fluids and capacities)
- ☐ Glow plug(s) defective, or controller faulty (smoke at start-up only) (Chapter 5)
- ☐ Air cleaner dirty(Chapter 4)
- ☐ Blockage in induction system (Chapter 4)
- ☐ Valve timing incorrect (Chapter 2)
- ☐ Injection pump timing incorrect (Chapter 4)
- ☐ Injector(s) defective, or heat shields damaged or missing (Chapter 4)
- ☐ Engine running too cool
- ☐ Oil entering via valve stems (Chapter 2)
- ☐ Poor compression (Chapter 2)
- ☐ Head gasket blown (Chapter 2)
- ☐ Piston rings broken or worn (Chapter 2)
- ☐ Pistons and/or bores worn (Chapter 2)

4 Clutch

Pedal travels to floor - no pressure or very little resistance

- ☐ Broken clutch cable (Chapter 8).
- ☐ Incorrect clutch adjustment (Chapter 8).
- ☐ Broken clutch release bearing or fork (Chapter 8).
- ☐ Broken diaphragm spring in clutch pressure plate (Chapter 8).

Clutch fails to disengage (unable to select gears)

- ☐ Incorrect clutch adjustment (Chapter 8).
- ☐ Clutch disc sticking on transmission input shaft splines (Chapter 8).
- ☐ Clutch disc sticking to flywheel or pressure plate (Chapter 8).
- ☐ Faulty pressure plate assembly (Chapter 8).
- ☐ Clutch release mechanism worn or incorrectly assembled (Chapter 8).

Clutch slips (engine speed increases with no increase in vehicle speed)

- ☐ Incorrect clutch adjustment (Chapter 8).
- ☐ Clutch disc linings excessively worn (Chapter 8).

- ☐ Clutch disc linings contaminated with oil or grease (Chapter 8).
- ☐ Faulty pressure plate or weak diaphragm spring (Chapter 8).

Judder as clutch is engaged

- ☐ Clutch disc linings contaminated with oil or grease (Chapter 8).
- ☐ Clutch disc linings excessively worn (Chapter 8).
- ☐ Clutch cable sticking or frayed (Chapter 8).
- ☐ Faulty or distorted pressure plate or diaphragm spring (Chapter 8).
- ☐ Worn or loose engine/transmission mountings (Chapter 2).
- ☐ Clutch disc hub or transmission input shaft splines worn (Chapter 8).

Noise when depressing or releasing clutch pedal

- ☐ Worn clutch release bearing (Chapter 8).
- ☐ Worn or dry clutch pedal bushes (Chapter 8).
- ☐ Faulty pressure plate assembly (Chapter 8).
- ☐ Pressure plate diaphragm spring broken (Chapter 8).
- ☐ Broken clutch disc cushioning springs (Chapter 8).

5 Transmission

Noisy in neutral with engine running

☐ Input shaft bearings worn (noise apparent with clutch pedal released, but not when depressed) (Chapter 7).*
☐ Clutch release bearing worn (noise apparent with clutch pedal depressed, possibly less when released) (Chapter 8).

Noisy in one particular gear

☐ Worn, damaged or chipped gear teeth (Chapter 7).*

Difficulty engaging gears

☐ Clutch fault (Chapter 8).
☐ Worn or damaged gear linkage (Chapter 7).
☐ Incorrectly-adjusted gear linkage (Chapter 7).
☐ Worn synchroniser assemblies (Chapter 7).*

Vibration

☐ Lack of oil (Chapter 1).
☐ Worn bearings (Chapter 7).*

Jumps out of gear

☐ Worn or damaged gear linkage (Chapter 7).
☐ Incorrectly-adjusted gear linkage (Chapter 7).
☐ Worn synchroniser assemblies (Chapter 7).*
☐ Worn selector forks (Chapter 7).*

Lubricant leaks

☐ Leaking differential side gear oil seal (Chapter 7).
☐ Leaking housing joint (Chapter 7).*
☐ Leaking input shaft oil seal (Chapter 7).*
☐ Leaking selector shaft oil seal (Chapter 7).
☐ Leaking speedometer drive pinion O-ring (Chapter 7).

* Although the corrective action necessary to remedy the symptoms described is beyond the scope of the home mechanic, the above information should be helpful in isolating the cause of the condition, so that the owner can communicate clearly with a professional mechanic.

6 Driveshafts

Clicking or knocking noise on turns (at slow speed on full-lock)

☐ Lack of constant velocity joint lubricant (Chapter 8).
☐ Worn outer constant velocity joint (Chapter 8).

Vibration when accelerating or decelerating

☐ Worn inner constant velocity joint (Chapter 8).
☐ Bent or distorted driveshaft (Chapter 8).

7 Braking system

Note: *Before assuming that a brake problem exists, make sure that the tyres are in good condition and correctly inflated, that the front wheel alignment is correct, and that the vehicle is not loaded with weight in an unequal manner. Apart from checking the condition of all pipe and hose connections, any faults occurring on the Anti-lock Braking System (ABS) should be referred to a Ford dealer for diagnosis - the same applies to the components of the Traction Control System (TCS).*

Vehicle pulls to one side under braking

☐ Worn, defective, damaged or contaminated front or rear brake pads/shoes on one side (Chapter 1).
☐ Seized or partially-seized front or rear brake caliper/wheel cylinder piston (Chapter 9).
☐ A mixture of brake pad/shoe lining materials fitted between sides (Chapter 1).
☐ Brake caliper mounting bolts loose (Chapter 9).
☐ Rear brake backplate mounting bolts loose (Chapter 9).
☐ Worn or damaged steering or suspension components (Chapter 10).

Noise (grinding or high-pitched squeal) when brakes applied

☐ Brake pad or shoe friction lining material worn down to metal backing (Chapter 1).
☐ Excessive corrosion of brake disc or drum (may be apparent after the vehicle has been standing for some time) (Chapter 1).
☐ Foreign object (stone chipping, etc) trapped between brake disc and splash shield (Chapter 1).

Excessive brake pedal travel

☐ Inoperative rear brake self-adjust mechanism (Chapter 9).
☐ Faulty master cylinder (Chapter 9).
☐ Air in hydraulic system (Chapter 9).

Brake pedal feels spongy when depressed

☐ Air in hydraulic system (Chapter 9).
☐ Deteriorated flexible rubber brake hoses (Chapter 9).
☐ Master cylinder mounting nuts loose (Chapter 9).
☐ Faulty master cylinder (Chapter 9).

Excessive brake pedal effort required to stop vehicle

☐ Faulty vacuum servo unit (Chapter 9).
☐ Disconnected, damaged or insecure brake servo vacuum hose (Chapter 9).
☐ Primary or secondary hydraulic circuit failure (Chapter 9).
☐ Seized brake caliper or wheel cylinder piston(s) (Chapter 9).
☐ Brake pads or brake shoes incorrectly fitted (Chapter 9).
☐ Incorrect grade of brake pads or brake shoes fitted (Chapter 1).
☐ Brake pads or brake shoe linings contaminated (Chapter 1).

Judder felt through brake pedal or steering wheel when braking

☐ Excessive run-out or distortion of front discs or rear drums (Chapter 9).
☐ Brake pad or brake shoe linings worn (Chapter 1).
☐ Brake caliper or rear brake backplate mounting bolts loose (Chapter 9).
☐ Wear in suspension or steering components or mountings (Chapter 10).

Brakes binding

☐ Seized brake caliper or wheel cylinder piston(s) (Chapter 9).
☐ Faulty handbrake mechanism (Chapter 9).
☐ Faulty master cylinder (Chapter 9).

Rear wheels locking under normal braking

☐ Rear brake shoe linings contaminated (Chapter 1).
☐ Faulty brake pressure regulator (Chapter 9).

8 Suspension and steering systems

Note: *Before diagnosing suspension or steering faults, be sure that the trouble is not due to incorrect tyre pressures, mixtures of tyre types, or binding brakes. Apart from checking the condition of all electrical connections, any faults occurring on the Adaptive Damping System should be referred to a Ford dealer for diagnosis.*

Vehicle pulls to one side

- [ ] Defective tyre (Chapter 1).
- [ ] Excessive wear in suspension or steering components (Chapter 10).
- [ ] Incorrect front wheel alignment (Chapter 10).
- [ ] Accident damage to steering or suspension components (Chapter 10).

Wheel wobble and vibration

- [ ] Front roadwheels out of balance (vibration felt mainly through the steering wheel) (Chapter 1).
- [ ] Rear roadwheels out of balance (vibration felt throughout the vehicle) (Chapter 1).
- [ ] Roadwheels damaged or distorted (Chapter 1).
- [ ] Faulty or damaged tyre (Chapter 1).
- [ ] Worn steering or suspension joints, bushes or components (Chapter 10).
- [ ] Roadwheel nuts loose (Chapter 1).

Excessive pitching and/or rolling around corners, or during braking

- [ ] Defective shock absorbers (Chapter 10).
- [ ] Broken or weak coil spring and/or suspension component (Chapter 10).
- [ ] Worn or damaged anti-roll bar or mountings (Chapter 10).

Wandering or general instability

- [ ] Incorrect front wheel alignment (Chapter 10).
- [ ] Worn steering or suspension joints, bushes or components (Chapter 10).
- [ ] Roadwheels out of balance (Chapter 1).
- [ ] Faulty or damaged tyre (Chapter 1).
- [ ] Roadwheel nuts loose (Chapter 1).
- [ ] Defective shock absorbers (Chapter 10).

Excessively-stiff steering

- [ ] Lack of steering gear lubricant (Chapter 10).
- [ ] Seized track-rod end balljoint or suspension balljoint (Chapter 10).

- [ ] Broken or slipping auxiliary drivebelt (Chapter 1).
- [ ] Incorrect front wheel alignment (Chapter 10).
- [ ] Steering rack or column bent or damaged (Chapter 10).

Excessive play in steering

- [ ] Worn steering column universal joint(s) or flexible coupling (Chapter 10).
- [ ] Worn steering track-rod end balljoints (Chapter 10).
- [ ] Worn rack-and-pinion steering gear (Chapter 10).
- [ ] Worn steering or suspension joints, bushes or components (Chapter 10).

Lack of power assistance

- [ ] Broken or slipping auxiliary drivebelt (Chapter 1).
- [ ] Incorrect power steering fluid level (Chapter 1).
- [ ] Restriction in power steering fluid hoses (Chapter 10).
- [ ] Faulty power steering pump (Chapter 10).
- [ ] Faulty rack-and-pinion steering gear (Chapter 10).

Tyre wear excessive

Tyres worn on inside or outside edges

- [ ] Tyres under-inflated (wear on both edges) (Chapter 1).
- [ ] Incorrect camber or castor angles (wear on one edge only) (Chapter 10).
- [ ] Worn steering or suspension joints, bushes or components (Chapter 10).
- [ ] Excessively-hard cornering.
- [ ] Accident damage.

Tyre treads exhibit feathered edges

- [ ] Incorrect toe setting (Chapter 10).

Tyres worn in centre of tread

- [ ] Tyres over-inflated (Chapter 1).

Tyres worn on inside and outside edges

- [ ] Tyres under-inflated (Chapter 1).

Tyres worn unevenly

- [ ] Tyres out of balance (Chapter 1).
- [ ] Excessive wheel or tyre run-out (Chapter 1).
- [ ] Worn shock absorbers (Chapter 10).
- [ ] Faulty tyre (Chapter 1).

9 Electrical system

Note: *For problems associated with the starting system, refer to the faults listed under "Engine" earlier in this Section.*

Battery will not hold a charge more than a few days

- [ ] Battery defective internally (Chapter 5).
- [ ] Battery electrolyte level low (Chapter 1).
- [ ] Battery terminal connections loose or corroded (Chapter 5).
- [ ] Auxiliary drivebelt worn or incorrectly-adjusted (Chapter 1).
- [ ] Alternator not charging at correct output (Chapter 5).
- [ ] Alternator or voltage regulator faulty (Chapter 5).
- [ ] Short-circuit causing continual battery drain (Chapters 5 and 12).

Ignition (no-charge) warning light remains illuminated with engine running

- [ ] Auxiliary drivebelt broken, worn, or incorrectly-adjusted (Chapter 1).
- [ ] Alternator brushes worn, sticking, or dirty (Chapter 5).
- [ ] Alternator brush springs weak or broken (Chapter 5).
- [ ] Internal fault in alternator or voltage regulator (Chapter 5).
- [ ] Broken, disconnected, or loose wiring in charging circuit (Chapter 5).

Ignition (no-charge) warning light fails to come on

- [ ] Warning light bulb blown (Chapter 12).
- [ ] Broken, disconnected, or loose wiring in warning light circuit (Chapters 5 and 12).
- [ ] Alternator faulty (Chapter 5).

9 Electrical system (continued)

Lights inoperative

- [ ] Bulb blown (Chapter 12).
- [ ] Corrosion of bulb or bulbholder contacts (Chapter 12).
- [ ] Blown fuse (Chapter 12).
- [ ] Faulty relay (Chapter 12).
- [ ] Broken, loose, or disconnected wiring (Chapter 12).
- [ ] Faulty switch (Chapter 12).

Instrument readings inaccurate or erratic

Instrument readings increase with engine speed

- [ ] Faulty voltage regulator (Chapter 12).

Fuel or temperature gauges give no reading

- [ ] Faulty gauge sender unit (Chapters 3 or 4).
- [ ] Wiring open-circuit (Chapter 12).
- [ ] Faulty gauge (Chapter 12).

Fuel or temperature gauges give continuous maximum reading

- [ ] Faulty gauge sender unit (Chapters 3 or 4).
- [ ] Wiring short-circuit (Chapter 12).
- [ ] Faulty gauge (Chapter 12).

Horn inoperative, or unsatisfactory in operation

Horn fails to operate

- [ ] Blown fuse (Chapter 12).
- [ ] Cable or cable connections loose, broken or disconnected (Chapter 12).
- [ ] Faulty horn (Chapter 12).

Horn emits intermittent or unsatisfactory sound

- [ ] Cable connections loose (Chapter 12).
- [ ] Horn mountings loose (Chapter 12).
- [ ] Faulty horn (Chapter 12).

Horn operates all the time

- [ ] Horn push either earthed or stuck down (Chapter 12).
- [ ] Horn cable to horn push earthed (Chapter 12).

Windscreen/tailgate wipers inoperative or unsatisfactory in operation

Wipers fail to operate, or operate very slowly

- [ ] Wiper blades stuck to screen, or linkage seized or binding (Chapter 12).
- [ ] Blown fuse (Chapter 12).
- [ ] Cable or cable connections loose, broken or disconnected (Chapter 12).
- [ ] Faulty relay (Chapter 12).
- [ ] Faulty wiper motor (Chapter 12).

Wiper blades sweep over too large or too small an area of the glass

- [ ] Wiper arms incorrectly-positioned on spindles (Chapter 1).
- [ ] Excessive wear of wiper linkage (Chapter 1).
- [ ] Wiper motor or linkage mountings loose or insecure (Chapter 12).

Wiper blades fail to clean the glass effectively

- [ ] Wiper blade rubbers worn or perished (Chapter 1).
- [ ] Wiper arm tension springs broken, or arm pivots seized (Chapter 1).
- [ ] Insufficient windscreen washer additive to adequately remove road film (Chapter 1).

Windscreen/tailgate washers inoperative, or unsatisfactory in operation

One or more washer jets inoperative

- [ ] Blocked washer jet (Chapter 1).
- [ ] Disconnected, kinked or restricted fluid hose (Chapter 1).
- [ ] Insufficient fluid in washer reservoir (Chapter 1).

Washer pump fails to operate

- [ ] Broken or disconnected wiring or connections (Chapter 12).
- [ ] Blown fuse (Chapter 12).
- [ ] Faulty washer switch (Chapter 12).
- [ ] Faulty washer pump (Chapter 12).

Washer pump runs for some time before fluid is emitted from jets

- [ ] Faulty one-way valve in fluid supply hose (Chapter 12).

Electric windows inoperative, or unsatisfactory in operation

Window glass will only move in one direction

- [ ] Faulty switch (Chapter 12).

Window glass slow to move

- [ ] Incorrectly-adjusted door glass guide channels (Chapter 11).
- [ ] Regulator seized or damaged, or in need of lubrication (Chapter 11).
- [ ] Door internal components or trim fouling regulator (Chapter 11).
- [ ] Faulty motor (Chapter 12).

Window glass fails to move

- [ ] Incorrectly-adjusted door glass guide channels (Chapter 11).
- [ ] Blown fuse (Chapter 12).
- [ ] Faulty relay (Chapter 12).
- [ ] Broken or disconnected wiring or connections (Chapter 12).
- [ ] Faulty motor (Chapter 12).

Central locking system inoperative, or unsatisfactory in operation

Complete system failure

- [ ] Blown fuse (Chapter 12).
- [ ] Faulty relay (Chapter 12).
- [ ] Broken or disconnected wiring or connections (Chapter 12).

Latch locks but will not unlock, or unlocks but will not lock

- [ ] Faulty master switch (Chapter 11).
- [ ] Broken or disconnected latch operating rods or levers (Chapter 11).
- [ ] Faulty relay (Chapter 12).

One lock motor fails to operate

- [ ] Broken or disconnected wiring or connections (Chapter 12).
- [ ] Faulty lock motor (Chapter 11).
- [ ] Broken, binding or disconnected latch operating rods or levers (Chapter 11).
- [ ] Fault in door latch (Chapter 11).

A

ABS (Anti-lock brake system) A system, usually electronically controlled, that senses incipient wheel lockup during braking and relieves hydraulic pressure at wheels that are about to skid.

Air bag An inflatable bag hidden in the steering wheel (driver's side) or the dash or glovebox (passenger side). In a head-on collision, the bags inflate, preventing the driver and front passenger from being thrown forward into the steering wheel or windscreen.

Air cleaner A metal or plastic housing, containing a filter element, which removes dust and dirt from the air being drawn into the engine.

Air filter element The actual filter in an air cleaner system, usually manufactured from pleated paper and requiring renewal at regular intervals.

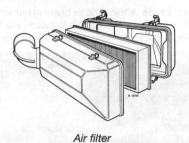
Air filter

Allen key A hexagonal wrench which fits into a recessed hexagonal hole.

Alligator clip A long-nosed spring-loaded metal clip with meshing teeth. Used to make temporary electrical connections.

Alternator A component in the electrical system which converts mechanical energy from a drivebelt into electrical energy to charge the battery and to operate the starting system, ignition system and electrical accessories.

Ampere (amp) A unit of measurement for the flow of electric current. One amp is the amount of current produced by one volt acting through a resistance of one ohm.

Anaerobic sealer A substance used to prevent bolts and screws from loosening. Anaerobic means that it does not require oxygen for activation. The Loctite brand is widely used.

Antifreeze A substance (usually ethylene glycol) mixed with water, and added to a vehicle's cooling system, to prevent freezing of the coolant in winter. Antifreeze also contains chemicals to inhibit corrosion and the formation of rust and other deposits that would tend to clog the radiator and coolant passages and reduce cooling efficiency.

Anti-seize compound A coating that reduces the risk of seizing on fasteners that are subjected to high temperatures, such as exhaust manifold bolts and nuts.

Asbestos A natural fibrous mineral with great heat resistance, commonly used in the composition of brake friction materials. Asbestos is a health hazard and the dust created by brake systems should never be inhaled or ingested.

Axle A shaft on which a wheel revolves, or which revolves with a wheel. Also, a solid beam that connects the two wheels at one end of the vehicle. An axle which also transmits power to the wheels is known as a live axle.

Axleshaft A single rotating shaft, on either side of the differential, which delivers power from the final drive assembly to the drive wheels. Also called a driveshaft or a halfshaft.

B

Ball bearing An anti-friction bearing consisting of a hardened inner and outer race with hardened steel balls between two races.

Bearing The curved surface on a shaft or in a bore, or the part assembled into either, that permits relative motion between them with minimum wear and friction.

Bearing

Big-end bearing The bearing in the end of the connecting rod that's attached to the crankshaft.

Bleed nipple A valve on a brake wheel cylinder, caliper or other hydraulic component that is opened to purge the hydraulic system of air. Also called a bleed screw.

Brake bleeding Procedure for removing air from lines of a hydraulic brake system.

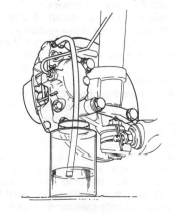
Brake bleeding

Brake disc The component of a disc brake that rotates with the wheels.

Brake drum The component of a drum brake that rotates with the wheels.

Brake linings The friction material which contacts the brake disc or drum to retard the vehicle's speed. The linings are bonded or riveted to the brake pads or shoes.

Brake pads The replaceable friction pads that pinch the brake disc when the brakes are applied. Brake pads consist of a friction material bonded or riveted to a rigid backing plate.

Brake shoe The crescent-shaped carrier to which the brake linings are mounted and which forces the lining against the rotating drum during braking.

Braking systems For more information on braking systems, consult the *Haynes Automotive Brake Manual*.

Breaker bar A long socket wrench handle providing greater leverage.

Bulkhead The insulated partition between the engine and the passenger compartment.

C

Caliper The non-rotating part of a disc-brake assembly that straddles the disc and carries the brake pads. The caliper also contains the hydraulic components that cause the pads to pinch the disc when the brakes are applied. A caliper is also a measuring tool that can be set to measure inside or outside dimensions of an object.

Camshaft A rotating shaft on which a series of cam lobes operate the valve mechanisms. The camshaft may be driven by gears, by sprockets and chain or by sprockets and a belt.

Canister A container in an evaporative emission control system; contains activated charcoal granules to trap vapours from the fuel system.

Canister

Carburettor A device which mixes fuel with air in the proper proportions to provide a desired power output from a spark ignition internal combustion engine.

Castellated Resembling the parapets along the top of a castle wall. For example, a castellated balljoint stud nut.

Castor In wheel alignment, the backward or forward tilt of the steering axis. Castor is positive when the steering axis is inclined rearward at the top.

Catalytic converter A silencer-like device in the exhaust system which converts certain pollutants in the exhaust gases into less harmful substances.

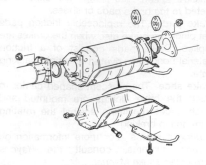

Catalytic converter

Circlip A ring-shaped clip used to prevent endwise movement of cylindrical parts and shafts. An internal circlip is installed in a groove in a housing; an external circlip fits into a groove on the outside of a cylindrical piece such as a shaft.

Clearance The amount of space between two parts. For example, between a piston and a cylinder, between a bearing and a journal, etc.

Coil spring A spiral of elastic steel found in various sizes throughout a vehicle, for example as a springing medium in the suspension and in the valve train.

Compression Reduction in volume, and increase in pressure and temperature, of a gas, caused by squeezing it into a smaller space.

Compression ratio The relationship between cylinder volume when the piston is at top dead centre and cylinder volume when the piston is at bottom dead centre.

Constant velocity (CV) joint A type of universal joint that cancels out vibrations caused by driving power being transmitted through an angle.

Core plug A disc or cup-shaped metal device inserted in a hole in a casting through which core was removed when the casting was formed. Also known as a freeze plug or expansion plug.

Crankcase The lower part of the engine block in which the crankshaft rotates.

Crankshaft The main rotating member, or shaft, running the length of the crankcase, with offset "throws" to which the connecting rods are attached.

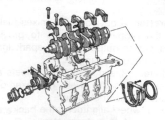

Crankshaft assembly

Crocodile clip See Alligator clip

D

Diagnostic code Code numbers obtained by accessing the diagnostic mode of an engine management computer. This code can be used to determine the area in the system where a malfunction may be located.

Disc brake A brake design incorporating a rotating disc onto which brake pads are squeezed. The resulting friction converts the energy of a moving vehicle into heat.

Double-overhead cam (DOHC) An engine that uses two overhead camshafts, usually one for the intake valves and one for the exhaust valves.

Drivebelt(s) The belt(s) used to drive accessories such as the alternator, water pump, power steering pump, air conditioning compressor, etc. off the crankshaft pulley.

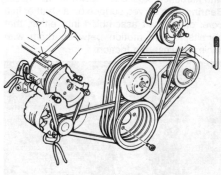

Accessory drivebelts

Driveshaft Any shaft used to transmit motion. Commonly used when referring to the axleshafts on a front wheel drive vehicle.

Drum brake A type of brake using a drum-shaped metal cylinder attached to the inner surface of the wheel. When the brake pedal is pressed, curved brake shoes with friction linings press against the inside of the drum to slow or stop the vehicle.

E

EGR valve A valve used to introduce exhaust gases into the intake air stream.

Electronic control unit (ECU) A computer which controls (for instance) ignition and fuel injection systems, or an anti-lock braking system. For more information refer to the *Haynes Automotive Electrical and Electronic Systems Manual.*

Electronic Fuel Injection (EFI) A computer controlled fuel system that distributes fuel through an injector located in each intake port of the engine.

Emergency brake A braking system, independent of the main hydraulic system, that can be used to slow or stop the vehicle if the primary brakes fail, or to hold the vehicle stationary even though the brake pedal isn't depressed. It usually consists of a hand lever that actuates either front or rear brakes mechanically through a series of cables and linkages. Also known as a handbrake or parking brake.

Endfloat The amount of lengthwise movement between two parts. As applied to a crankshaft, the distance that the crankshaft can move forward and back in the cylinder block.

Engine management system (EMS) A computer controlled system which manages the fuel injection and the ignition systems in an integrated fashion.

Exhaust manifold A part with several passages through which exhaust gases leave the engine combustion chambers and enter the exhaust pipe.

F

Fan clutch A viscous (fluid) drive coupling device which permits variable engine fan speeds in relation to engine speeds.

Feeler blade A thin strip or blade of hardened steel, ground to an exact thickness, used to check or measure clearances between parts.

Feeler blade

Firing order The order in which the engine cylinders fire, or deliver their power strokes, beginning with the number one cylinder.

Flywheel A heavy spinning wheel in which energy is absorbed and stored by means of momentum. On cars, the flywheel is attached to the crankshaft to smooth out firing impulses.

Free play The amount of travel before any action takes place. The "looseness" in a linkage, or an assembly of parts, between the initial application of force and actual movement. For example, the distance the brake pedal moves before the pistons in the master cylinder are actuated.

Fuse An electrical device which protects a circuit against accidental overload. The typical fuse contains a soft piece of metal which is calibrated to melt at a predetermined current flow (expressed as amps) and break the circuit.

Fusible link A circuit protection device consisting of a conductor surrounded by heat-resistant insulation. The conductor is smaller than the wire it protects, so it acts as the weakest link in the circuit. Unlike a blown fuse, a failed fusible link must frequently be cut from the wire for replacement.

G

Gap The distance the spark must travel in jumping from the centre electrode to the side electrode in a spark plug. Also refers to the spacing between the points in a contact breaker assembly in a conventional points-type ignition, or to the distance between the reluctor or rotor and the pickup coil in an electronic ignition.

Adjusting spark plug gap

Gasket Any thin, soft material - usually cork, cardboard, asbestos or soft metal - installed between two metal surfaces to ensure a good seal. For instance, the cylinder head gasket seals the joint between the block and the cylinder head.

Gasket

Gauge An instrument panel display used to monitor engine conditions. A gauge with a movable pointer on a dial or a fixed scale is an analogue gauge. A gauge with a numerical readout is called a digital gauge.

H

Halfshaft A rotating shaft that transmits power from the final drive unit to a drive wheel, usually when referring to a live rear axle.

Harmonic balancer A device designed to reduce torsion or twisting vibration in the crankshaft. May be incorporated in the crankshaft pulley. Also known as a vibration damper.

Hone An abrasive tool for correcting small irregularities or differences in diameter in an engine cylinder, brake cylinder, etc.

Hydraulic tappet A tappet that utilises hydraulic pressure from the engine's lubrication system to maintain zero clearance (constant contact with both camshaft and valve stem). Automatically adjusts to variation in valve stem length. Hydraulic tappets also reduce valve noise.

I

Ignition timing The moment at which the spark plug fires, usually expressed in the number of crankshaft degrees before the piston reaches the top of its stroke.

Inlet manifold A tube or housing with passages through which flows the air-fuel mixture (carburettor vehicles and vehicles with throttle body injection) or air only (port fuel-injected vehicles) to the port openings in the cylinder head.

J

Jump start Starting the engine of a vehicle with a discharged or weak battery by attaching jump leads from the weak battery to a charged or helper battery.

L

Load Sensing Proportioning Valve (LSPV) A brake hydraulic system control valve that works like a proportioning valve, but also takes into consideration the amount of weight carried by the rear axle.

Locknut A nut used to lock an adjustment nut, or other threaded component, in place. For example, a locknut is employed to keep the adjusting nut on the rocker arm in position.

Lockwasher A form of washer designed to prevent an attaching nut from working loose.

M

MacPherson strut A type of front suspension system devised by Earle MacPherson at Ford of England. In its original form, a simple lateral link with the anti-roll bar creates the lower control arm. A long strut - an integral coil spring and shock absorber - is mounted between the body and the steering knuckle. Many modern so-called MacPherson strut systems use a conventional lower A-arm and don't rely on the anti-roll bar for location.

Multimeter An electrical test instrument with the capability to measure voltage, current and resistance.

N

NOx Oxides of Nitrogen. A common toxic pollutant emitted by petrol and diesel engines at higher temperatures.

O

Ohm The unit of electrical resistance. One volt applied to a resistance of one ohm will produce a current of one amp.

Ohmmeter An instrument for measuring electrical resistance.

O-ring A type of sealing ring made of a special rubber-like material; in use, the O-ring is compressed into a groove to provide the sealing action.

Overhead cam (ohc) engine An engine with the camshaft(s) located on top of the cylinder head(s).

Overhead valve (ohv) engine An engine with the valves located in the cylinder head, but with the camshaft located in the engine block.

Oxygen sensor A device installed in the engine exhaust manifold, which senses the oxygen content in the exhaust and converts this information into an electric current. Also called a Lambda sensor.

P

Phillips screw A type of screw head having a cross instead of a slot for a corresponding type of screwdriver.

Plastigage A thin strip of plastic thread, available in different sizes, used for measuring clearances. For example, a strip of Plastigage is laid across a bearing journal. The parts are assembled and dismantled; the width of the crushed strip indicates the clearance between journal and bearing.

Plastigage

Propeller shaft The long hollow tube with universal joints at both ends that carries power from the transmission to the differential on front-engined rear wheel drive vehicles.

Proportioning valve A hydraulic control valve which limits the amount of pressure to the rear brakes during panic stops to prevent wheel lock-up.

R

Rack-and-pinion steering A steering system with a pinion gear on the end of the steering shaft that mates with a rack (think of a geared wheel opened up and laid flat). When the steering wheel is turned, the pinion turns, moving the rack to the left or right. This movement is transmitted through the track rods to the steering arms at the wheels.

Radiator A liquid-to-air heat transfer device designed to reduce the temperature of the coolant in an internal combustion engine cooling system.

Refrigerant Any substance used as a heat transfer agent in an air-conditioning system. R-12 has been the principle refrigerant for many years; recently, however, manufacturers have begun using R-134a, a non-CFC substance that is considered less harmful to the ozone in the upper atmosphere.

Rocker arm A lever arm that rocks on a shaft or pivots on a stud. In an overhead valve engine, the rocker arm converts the upward movement of the pushrod into a downward movement to open a valve.

Rotor In a distributor, the rotating device inside the cap that connects the centre electrode and the outer terminals as it turns, distributing the high voltage from the coil secondary winding to the proper spark plug. Also, that part of an alternator which rotates inside the stator. Also, the rotating assembly of a turbocharger, including the compressor wheel, shaft and turbine wheel.

Runout The amount of wobble (in-and-out movement) of a gear or wheel as it's rotated. The amount a shaft rotates "out-of-true." The out-of-round condition of a rotating part.

S

Sealant A liquid or paste used to prevent leakage at a joint. Sometimes used in conjunction with a gasket.

Sealed beam lamp An older headlight design which integrates the reflector, lens and filaments into a hermetically-sealed one-piece unit. When a filament burns out or the lens cracks, the entire unit is simply replaced.

Serpentine drivebelt A single, long, wide accessory drivebelt that's used on some newer vehicles to drive all the accessories, instead of a series of smaller, shorter belts. Serpentine drivebelts are usually tensioned by an automatic tensioner.

Serpentine drivebelt

Shim Thin spacer, commonly used to adjust the clearance or relative positions between two parts. For example, shims inserted into or under bucket tappets control valve clearances. Clearance is adjusted by changing the thickness of the shim.

Slide hammer A special puller that screws into or hooks onto a component such as a shaft or bearing; a heavy sliding handle on the shaft bottoms against the end of the shaft to knock the component free.

Sprocket A tooth or projection on the periphery of a wheel, shaped to engage with a chain or drivebelt. Commonly used to refer to the sprocket wheel itself.

Starter inhibitor switch On vehicles with an automatic transmission, a switch that prevents starting if the vehicle is not in Neutral or Park.

Strut See MacPherson strut.

T

Tappet A cylindrical component which transmits motion from the cam to the valve stem, either directly or via a pushrod and rocker arm. Also called a cam follower.

Thermostat A heat-controlled valve that regulates the flow of coolant between the cylinder block and the radiator, so maintaining optimum engine operating temperature. A thermostat is also used in some air cleaners in which the temperature is regulated.

Thrust bearing The bearing in the clutch assembly that is moved in to the release levers by clutch pedal action to disengage the clutch. Also referred to as a release bearing.

Timing belt A toothed belt which drives the camshaft. Serious engine damage may result if it breaks in service.

Timing chain A chain which drives the camshaft.

Toe-in The amount the front wheels are closer together at the front than at the rear. On rear wheel drive vehicles, a slight amount of toe-in is usually specified to keep the front wheels running parallel on the road by offsetting other forces that tend to spread the wheels apart.

Toe-out The amount the front wheels are closer together at the rear than at the front. On front wheel drive vehicles, a slight amount of toe-out is usually specified.

Tools For full information on choosing and using tools, refer to the *Haynes Automotive Tools Manual*.

Tracer A stripe of a second colour applied to a wire insulator to distinguish that wire from another one with the same colour insulator.

Tune-up A process of accurate and careful adjustments and parts replacement to obtain the best possible engine performance.

Turbocharger A centrifugal device, driven by exhaust gases, that pressurises the intake air. Normally used to increase the power output from a given engine displacement, but can also be used primarily to reduce exhaust emissions (as on VW's "Umwelt" Diesel engine).

U

Universal joint or U-joint A double-pivoted connection for transmitting power from a driving to a driven shaft through an angle. A U-joint consists of two Y-shaped yokes and a cross-shaped member called the spider.

V

Valve A device through which the flow of liquid, gas, vacuum, or loose material in bulk may be started, stopped, or regulated by a movable part that opens, shuts, or partially obstructs one or more ports or passageways. A valve is also the movable part of such a device.

Valve clearance The clearance between the valve tip (the end of the valve stem) and the rocker arm or tappet. The valve clearance is measured when the valve is closed.

Vernier caliper A precision measuring instrument that measures inside and outside dimensions. Not quite as accurate as a micrometer, but more convenient.

Viscosity The thickness of a liquid or its resistance to flow.

Volt A unit for expressing electrical "pressure" in a circuit. One volt that will produce a current of one ampere through a resistance of one ohm.

W

Welding Various processes used to join metal items by heating the areas to be joined to a molten state and fusing them together. For more information refer to the *Haynes Automotive Welding Manual*.

Wiring diagram A drawing portraying the components and wires in a vehicle's electrical system, using standardised symbols. For more information refer to the *Haynes Automotive Electrical and Electronic Systems Manual*.

Note: *References throughout this index are in the form - "Chapter number" • "page number"*

Haynes Manuals – The Complete List

Title	Book No.
ALFA ROMEO	
Alfa Romeo Alfasud/Sprint (74 - 88)	0292
Alfa Romeo Alfetta (73 - 87)	0531
AUDI	
Audi 80 (72 - Feb 79)	0207
Audi 80, 90 (79 - Oct 86) & Coupe (81 - Nov 88)	0605
Audi 80, 90 (Oct 86 - 90) & Coupe (Nov 88 - 90)	1491
Audi 100 (Oct 76 - Oct 82)	0428
Audi 100 (Oct 82 - 90) & 200 (Feb 84 - Oct 89)	0907
AUSTIN	
Austin Ambassador (82 - 84)	0871
Austin/MG Maestro 1.3 & 1.6 (83 - 95)	0922
Austin Maxi (69 - 81)	0052
Austin/MG Metro (80 - May 90)	0718
Austin Montego 1.3 & 1.6 (84 - 94)	1066
Austin/MG Montego 2.0 (84 - 95)	1067
Mini (59 - 69)	0527
Mini (69 - Oct 96)	0646
Austin/Rover 2.0 litre Diesel Engine (86 - 93)	1857
BEDFORD	
Bedford CF (69 - 87)	0163
Bedford Rascal (86 - 93)	3015
BL	
BL Princess & BLMC 18-22 (75 - 82)	0286
BMW	
BMW 316, 320 & 320i (4-cyl) (75 - Feb 83)	0276
BMW 320, 320i, 323i & 325i (6-cyl) (Oct 77 - Sept 87)	0815
BMW 3-Series (Apr 91 - 96)	3210
BMW 3-Series (sohc) (83 - 91)	1948
BMW 520i & 525e (Oct 81 - June 88)	1560
BMW 525, 528 & 528i (73 - Sept 81)	0632
BMW 5-Series (sohc) (81 - 91)	1948
BMW 1500, 1502, 1600, 1602, 2000 & 2002 (59 - 77)	0240
CITROEN	
Citroen 2CV, Ami & Dyane (67 - 90)	0196
Citroen AX Petrol & Diesel (87 - 94)	3014
Citroen BX (83 - 94)	0908
Citroen CX (75 - 88)	0528
Citroen Visa (79 - 88)	0620
Citroen Xantia Petrol & Diesel (93 - Oct 95)	3082
Citroen XM Petrol & Diesel (89 - 97)	3451
Citroen ZX Diesel (91 - 93)	1922
Citroen ZX Petrol (91 - 94)	1881
Citroen 1.7 & 1.9 litre Diesel Engine (84 - 96)	1379
COLT	
Colt 1200, 1250 & 1400 (79 - May 84)	0600
DAIMLER	
Daimler Sovereign (68 - Oct 86)	0242
Daimler Double Six (72 - 88)	0478
DATSUN (see also *Nissan*)	
Datsun 120Y (73 - Aug 78)	0228
Datsun 1300, 1400 & 1600 (69 - Aug 72)	0123
Datsun Cherry (71 - 76)	0195
Datsun Pick-up (75 - 78)	0277
Datsun Sunny (Aug 78 - May 82)	0525
Datsun Violet (78 - 82)	0430

Title	Book No.
FIAT	
Fiat 126 (73 - 87)	0305
Fiat 127 (71 - 83)	0193
Fiat 500 (57 - 73)	0090
Fiat 850 (64 - 81)	0038
Fiat Panda (81 - 95)	0793
Fiat Punto (94 - 96)	3251
Fiat Regata (84 - 88)	1167
Fiat Strada (79 - 88)	0479
Fiat Tipo (88 - 91)	1625
Fiat Uno (83 - 95)	0923
Fiat X1/9 (74 - 89)	0273
FORD	
Ford Capri II (& III) 1.6 & 2.0 (74 - 87)	0283
Ford Capri II (& III) 2.8 & 3.0 (74 - 87)	1309
Ford Cortina Mk IV (& V) 1.6 & 2.0 (76 - 83)	0343
Ford Cortina Mk IV (& V) 2.3 V6 (77 - 83)	0426
Ford Escort (75 - Aug 80)	0280
Ford Escort (Sept 80 - Sept 90)	0686
Ford Escort (Sept 90 - 97)	1737
Ford Escort Mk II Mexico, RS 1600 & RS 2000 (75 - 80)	0735
Ford Fiesta (inc. XR2) (76 - Aug 83)	0334
Ford Fiesta (inc. XR2) (Aug 83 - Feb 89)	1030
Ford Fiesta (Feb 89 - Oct 95)	1595
Ford Fiesta Petrol & Diesel (Oct 95 - 97)	3397
Ford Granada (Sept 77 - Feb 85)	0481
Ford Granada (Mar 85 - 94)	1245
Ford Mondeo 4-cyl (93 - 96)	1923
Ford Orion (83 - Sept 90)	1009
Ford Orion (Sept 90 - 93)	1737
Ford Sierra 1.3, 1.6, 1.8 & 2.0 (82 - 93)	0903
Ford Sierra 2.3, 2.8 & 2.9 (82 - 91)	0904
Ford Scorpio (Mar 85 - 94)	1245
Ford Transit Petrol (Mk 1) (65 - Feb 78)	0377
Ford Transit Petrol (Mk 2) (78 - Jan 86)	0719
Ford Transit Petrol (Mk 3) (Feb 86 - 89)	1468
Ford Transit Diesel (Feb 86 - 95)	3019
Ford 1.6 & 1.8 litre Diesel Engine (84 - 96)	1172
Ford 2.1, 2.3 & 2.5 litre Diesel Engine (77 - 90)	1606
FREIGHT ROVER	
Freight Rover Sherpa (74 - 87)	0463
HILLMAN	
Hillman Avenger (70 - 82)	0037
HONDA	
Honda Accord (76 - Feb 84)	0351
Honda Accord (Feb 84 - Oct 85)	1177
Honda Civic (Feb 84 - Oct 87)	1226
Honda Civic (Nov 91 - 96)	3199
HYUNDAI	
Hyundai Pony (85 - 94)	3398
JAGUAR	
Jaguar E Type (61 - 72)	0140
Jaguar MkI & II, 240 & 340 (55 - 69)	0098
Jaguar XJ6, XJ & Sovereign (68 - Oct 86)	0242
Jaguar XJ6 & Sovereign (Oct 86 - Sept 94)	3261
Jaguar XJ12, XJS & Sovereign (72 - 88)	0478

Title	Book No.
JEEP	
Jeep Cherokee Petrol (93 - 96)	1943
LADA	
Lada 1200, 1300, 1500 & 1600 (74 - 91)	0413
Lada Samara (87 - 91)	1610
LAND ROVER	
Land Rover 90, 110 & Defender Diesel (83 - 95)	3017
Land Rover Discovery Diesel (89 - 95)	3016
Land Rover Series IIA & III Diesel (58 - 85)	0529
Land Rover Series II, IIA & III Petrol (58 - 85)	0314
MAZDA	
Mazda 323 fwd (Mar 81 - Oct 89)	1608
Mazda 626 fwd (May 83 - Sept 87)	0929
Mazda B-1600, B-1800 & B-2000 Pick-up (72 - 88)	0267
MERCEDES-BENZ	
Mercedes-Benz 190, 190E & 190D Petrol & Diesel (83 - 93)	3450
Mercedes-Benz 200, 240, 300 Diesel (Oct 76 - 85)	1114
Mercedes-Benz 250 & 280 (68 - 72)	0346
Mercedes-Benz 250 & 280 (123 Series) (Oct 76 - 84)	0677
Mercedes-Benz 124 Series (85 - Aug 93)	3253
MG	
MGB (62 - 80)	0111
MG Maestro 1.3 & 1.6 (83 - 95)	0922
MG Metro (80 - May 90)	0718
MG Midget & AH Sprite (58 - 80)	0265
MG Montego 2.0 (84 - 95)	1067
MITSUBISHI	
Mitsubishi 1200, 1250 & 1400 (79 - May 84)	0600
Mitsubishi Shogun & L200 Pick-Ups (83 - 94)	1944
MORRIS	
Morris Ital 1.3 (80 - 84)	0705
Morris Marina 1700 (78 - 80)	0526
Morris Marina 1.8 (71 - 78)	0074
Morris Minor 1000 (56 - 71)	0024
NISSAN (See also *Datsun*)	
Nissan Bluebird 160B & 180B rwd (May 80 - May 84)	0957
Nissan Bluebird fwd (May 84 - Mar 86)	1223
Nissan Bluebird (T12 & T72) (Mar 86 - 90)	1473
Nissan Cherry (N12) (Sept 82 - 86)	1031
Nissan Micra (K10) (83 - Jan 93)	0931
Nissan Micra (93 - 96)	3254
Nissan Primera (90 - Oct 96)	1851
Nissan Stanza (82 - 86)	0824
Nissan Sunny (B11) (May 82 - Oct 86)	0895
Nissan Sunny (Oct 86 - Mar 91)	1378
Nissan Sunny (Apr 91 - 95)	3219
OPEL	
Opel Ascona & Manta (B Series) (Sept 75 - 88)	0316
Opel Ascona (81 - 88)	3215
Opel Astra (Oct 91 - 96)	3156
Opel Corsa (83 - Mar 93)	3160
Opel Corsa (Mar 93 - 94)	3159
Opel Kadett (Nov 79 - Oct 84)	0634

Title	Book No.
Opel Kadett (Oct 84 - Oct 91)	3196
Opel Omega & Senator (86 - 94)	3157
Opel Rekord (Feb 78 - Oct 86)	0543
Opel Vectra (88 - Oct 95)	3158
PEUGEOT	
Peugeot 106 Petrol & Diesel (91 - June 96)	1882
Peugeot 205 (83 - 95)	0932
Peugeot 305 (78 - 89)	0538
Peugeot 306 Petrol & Diesel (93 - 95)	3073
Peugeot 309 (86 - 93)	1266
Peugeot 405 Petrol (88 - 96)	1559
Peugeot 405 Diesel (88 - 96)	3198
Peugeot 406 Petrol & Diesel (96 - 97)	3394
Peugeot 505 (79 - 89)	0762
Peugeot 1.7 & 1.9 litre Diesel Engines (82 - 96)	0950
Peugeot 2.0, 2.1, 2.3 & 2.5 litre Diesel Engines (74 - 90)	1607
PORSCHE	
Porsche 911 (65 - 85)	0264
Porsche 924 & 924 Turbo (76 - 85)	0397
PROTON	
Proton (89 - 97)	3255
RANGE ROVER	
Range Rover V8 (70 - Oct 92)	0606
RELIANT	
Reliant Robin & Kitten (73 - 83)	0436
RENAULT	
Renault 5 (72 - Feb 85)	0141
Renault 5 (Feb 85 - 96)	1219
Renault 9 & 11 (82 - 89)	0822
Renault 12 (70 - 80)	0097
Renault 15 & 17 (72 - 79)	0763
Renault 18 (79 - 86)	0598
Renault 19 Petrol (89 - 94)	1646
Renault 19 Diesel (89 - 95)	1946
Renault 21 (86 - 94)	1397
Renault 25 (84 - 92)	1228
Renault Clio Petrol (91 - 93)	1853
Renault Clio Diesel (91 - June 96)	3031
Renault Espace (85 - 96)	3197
Renault Fuego (80 - 86)	0764
Renault Laguna (94 - 96)	3252
Renault Mégane Petrol & Diesel (96 - 97)	3395
ROVER	
Rover 111 & 114 (95 - 96)	1711
Rover 213 & 216 (84 - 89)	1116
Rover 214 & 414 (89 - 96)	1689
Rover 216 & 416 (89 - 96)	1830
Rover 618, 620 & 623 (93 - 97)	3257
Rover 820, 825 & 827 (86 - 95)	1380
Rover 2000, 2300 & 2600 (77 - 87)	0468
Rover 3500 (76 - 87)	0365
Rover Metro (May 90 - 94)	1711
SAAB	
Saab 90, 99 & 900 (79 - Oct 93)	0765
Saab 9000 (4-cyl) (85 - 95)	1686

Title	Book No.
SEAT	
Seat Ibiza & Malaga (85 - 92)	1609
SIMCA	
Simca 1100 & 1204 (67 - 79)	0088
Simca 1301 & 1501 (63 - 76)	0199
SKODA	
Skoda Estelle 105, 120, 130 & 136 (77 - 89)	0604
Skoda Favorit (89 - 92)	1801
SUBARU	
Subaru 1600 & 1800 (Nov 79 - 90)	0995
SUZUKI	
Suzuki SJ Series, Samurai & Vitara (82 - 97)	1942
Suzuki Supercarry (86 - Oct 94)	3015
TALBOT	
Talbot Alpine, Solara, Minx & Rapier (75 - 86)	0337
Talbot Horizon (78 - 86)	0473
Talbot Samba (82 - 86)	0823
TOYOTA	
Toyota Carina E (May 92 - 97)	3256
Toyota Celica (Feb 82 - Sept 85)	1135
Toyota Corolla (fwd) (Sept 83 - Sept 87)	1024
Toyota Corolla (rwd) (80 - 85)	0683
Toyota Corolla (Sept 87 - 92)	1683
Toyota Corolla (Aug 92 - 97)	3259
Toyota Hi-Ace & Hi-Lux (69 - Oct 83)	0304
Toyota Starlet (78 - Jan 85)	0462
TRIUMPH	
Triumph Acclaim (81 - 84)	0792
Triumph Herald (59 - 71)	0010
Triumph Spitfire (62 - 81)	0113
Triumph Stag (70 - 78)	0441
Triumph TR7 (75 - 82)	0322
VAUXHALL	
Vauxhall Astra (80 - Oct 84)	0635
Vauxhall Astra & Belmont (Oct 84 - Oct 91)	1136
Vauxhall Astra (Oct 91 - 96)	1832
Vauxhall Carlton (Oct 78 - Oct 86)	0480
Vauxhall Carlton (Nov 86 - 94)	1469
Vauxhall Cavalier 1300 (77 - July 81)	0461
Vauxhall Cavalier 1600, 1900 & 2000 (75 - July 81)	0315
Vauxhall Cavalier (81 - Oct 88)	0812
Vauxhall Cavalier (Oct 88 - Oct 95)	1570
Vauxhall Chevette (75 - 84)	0285
Vauxhall Corsa (93 - 97)	1985
Vauxhall Nova (83 - 93)	0909
Vauxhall Rascal (86 - 93)	3015
Vauxhall Senator (Sept 87 - 94)	1469
Vauxhall Vectra Petrol & Diesel (95 - 98)	3396
Vauxhall Viva HB Series (ohv) (66 - 70)	0026
Vauxhall Viva & Firenza (ohc) (68 - 73)	0093
Vauxhall/Opel 1.5, 1.6 & 1.7 litre Diesel Engines (82 - 96)	1222
VOLKSWAGEN	
VW Beetle 1200 (54 - 77)	0036
VW Beetle 1300 & 1500 (65 - 75)	0039
VW Beetle 1302 & 1302S (70 - 72)	0110

Title	Book No.
VW Beetle 1303, 1303S & GT (72 - 75)	0159
VW Golf Mk 1 1.1 & 1.3 (74 - Feb 84)	0716
VW Golf Mk 1 1.5, 1.6 & 1.8 (74 - 85)	0726
VW Golf Mk 1 Diesel (78 - Feb 84)	0451
VW Golf Mk 2 (Mar 84 - Feb 92)	1081
VW Golf Mk 3 Petrol & Diesel (Feb 92 - 96)	3097
VW Jetta Mk 1 1.1 & 1.3 (80 - June 84)	0716
VW Jetta Mk 1 1.5, 1.6 & 1.8 (80 - June 84)	0726
VW Jetta Mk 1 Diesel (81 - June 84)	0451
VW Jetta Mk 2 (July 84 - 92)	1081
VW LT vans & light trucks (76 - 87)	0637
VW Passat (Sept 81 - May 88)	0814
VW Passat (May 88 - 91)	1647
VW Polo & Derby (76 - Jan 82)	0335
VW Polo (82 - Oct 90)	0813
VW Polo (Nov 90 - Aug 94)	3245
VW Santana (Sept 82 - 85)	0814
VW Scirocco Mk 1 1.5, 1.6 & 1.8 (74 - 82)	0726
VW Scirocco (82 - 90)	1224
VW Transporter 1600 (68 - 79)	0082
VW Transporter 1700, 1800 & 2000 (72 - 79)	0226
VW Transporter with air-cooled engine (79 - 82)	0638
VW Transporter (82 - 90)	3452
VW Vento Petrol & Diesel (Feb 92 - 96)	3097
VOLVO	
Volvo 66 & 343, Daf 55 & 66 (68 - 79)	0293
Volvo 142, 144 & 145 (66 - 74)	0129
Volvo 240 Series (74 - 93)	0270
Volvo 262, 264 & 260/265 (75 - 85)	0400
Volvo 340, 343, 345 & 360 (76 - 91)	0715
Volvo 440, 460 & 480 (87 - 92)	1691
Volvo 740 & 760 (82 - 91)	1258
Volvo 850 (92 - 96)	3260
Volvo 940 (90 - 96)	3249
YUGO/ZASTAVA	
Yugo/Zastava (81 - 90)	1453
TECH BOOKS	
Automotive Brake Manual	3050
Automotive Carburettor Manual	3288
Automotive Diesel Engine Service Guide	3286
Automotive Electrical & Electronic Systems	3049
Automotive Engine Management and Fuel Injection Systems Manual	3344
Automotive Tools Manual	3052
Automotive Welding Manual	3053
In-Car Entertainment Manual (3rd Edition)	3363
CAR BOOKS	
Automotive Fuel Injection Systems	9755
Car Bodywork Repair Manual	9864
Caravan Manual (2nd Edition)	9894
Haynes Technical Data Book (89 - 98)	1998
How to Keep Your Car Alive	9868
Japanese Vehicle Carburettors	1786
Small Engine Repair Manual	1755
SU Carburettors	0299
Weber Carburettors (to 79)	0393

CL05.01/98

Preserving Our Motoring Heritage

<
The Model J Duesenberg Derham Tourster. Only eight of these magnificent cars were ever built – this is the only example to be found outside the United States of America

Almost every car you've ever loved, loathed or desired is gathered under one roof at the Haynes Motor Museum. Over 300 immaculately presented cars and motorbikes represent every aspect of our motoring heritage, from elegant reminders of bygone days, such as the superb Model J Duesenberg to curiosities like the bug-eyed BMW Isetta. There are also many old friends and flames. Perhaps you remember the 1959 Ford Popular that you did your courting in? The magnificent 'Red Collection' is a spectacle of classic sports cars including AC, Alfa Romeo, Austin Healey, Ferrari, Lamborghini, Maserati, MG, Riley, Porsche and Triumph.

A Perfect Day Out

Each and every vehicle at the Haynes Motor Museum has played its part in the history and culture of Motoring. Today, they make a wonderful spectacle and a great day out for all the family. Bring the kids, bring Mum and Dad, but above all bring your camera to capture those golden memories for ever. You will also find an impressive array of motoring memorabilia, a comfortable 70 seat video cinema and one of the most extensive transport book shops in Britain. The Pit Stop Cafe serves everything from a cup of tea to wholesome, home-made meals or, if you prefer, you can enjoy the large picnic area nestled in the beautiful rural surroundings of Somerset.

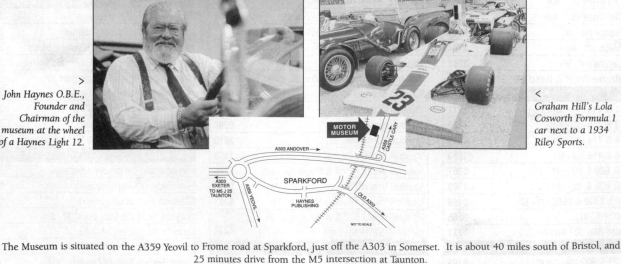

>
John Haynes O.B.E., Founder and Chairman of the museum at the wheel of a Haynes Light 12.

<
Graham Hill's Lola Cosworth Formula 1 car next to a 1934 Riley Sports.

The Museum is situated on the A359 Yeovil to Frome road at Sparkford, just off the A303 in Somerset. It is about 40 miles south of Bristol, and 25 minutes drive from the M5 intersection at Taunton.

Open 9.30am - 5.30pm (10.00am - 4.00pm Winter) 7 days a week, *except Christmas Day, Boxing Day and New Years Day*
Special rates available for schools, coach parties and outings Charitable Trust No. 292048